British
Columbia

Ryan Ver Berkmoes
Graham Neale

Contents

Yukon Territory
(pp336-65)

The North
(pp300-35)

Cariboo-Chilcotin
(pp288-99)

Whistler &
the Sunshine
Coast (pp100-19)

Fraser-Thompson
Region (pp186-200)

The Rockies
(pp257-87)

The Kootenays
(pp227-56)

Vancouver Island
(pp120-72)

Vancouver
& Around
(pp48-99)

Okanagan Valley
(pp201-26)

Southern Gulf
Islands (pp173-85)

Lonely Planet books provide independent advice. Lonely Planet does not accept advertising in guidebooks, nor do we accept payment in exchange for listing or endorsing any place or business. Lonely Planet writers do not accept discounts or payments in exchange for positive coverage of any sort.

Destination: British Columbia & the Yukon

Wow. In British Columbia and the Yukon you could start a collection of wows. There's the awed wow as you hike around a ridge and another jagged peak of the Rockies comes into the view for the first time – reality isn't supposed to look better than the postcard.

There's the soft sensual wow that gets caught in the back of the throat, as you bite into a perfect, luscious, Penticton peach. There's the breathless wow as you get your canoe through some gorgeous white water on the Yukon River.

There's the screamed 'look over here right this second!' wow as a pod of orcas swims past the Inland Passage ferry. And there's the mystified, entranced wow as you contemplate the Haida totem poles at Gwaii Haanas National Park.

You might say wow when the lid comes off some steaming shrimp dim sum at a world-class restaurant in Vancouver, but more likely you'll have better things to do with your mouth.

Sometimes you won't even say wow, but everyone will think you did. Like after you finish a run in a cloud of powder so perfect you might be dreaming, or you look around in Dawson City and try to imagine getting there during the gold rush.

Ultimately though, maybe you'll just want to think about your BC and Yukon wows and say, well, wow.

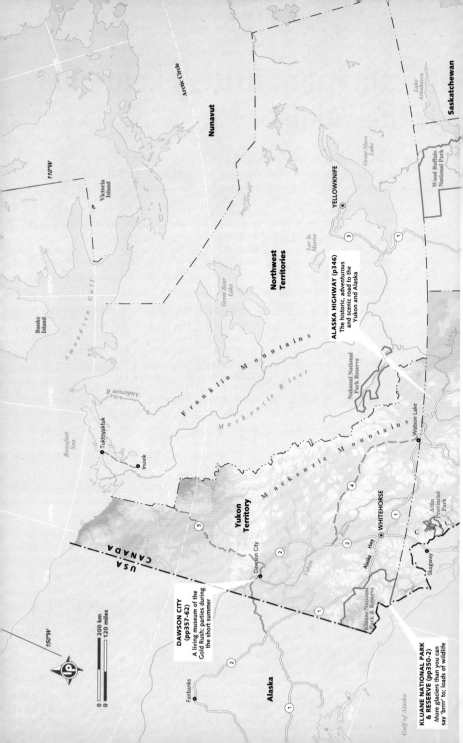

Nunavut

Arctic Circle

110°W

Victoria
Island

Amundsen Gulf

Banks
Island

**Northwest
Territories**

Great Bear
Lake

*Beaufort
Sea*

Tuktoyaktuk

Inuvik

Anderson R

Franklin Mountains

Mackenzie River

Lac la
Martre

Great Slave
Lake

YELLOWKNIFE

3

1

Wood Buffalo
National Park

Lake
Athabasca

Saskatchewan

Nahanni National
Park Reserve

ALASKA HIGHWAY (p346)
The historic, adventurous
and scenic road to the
Yukon and Alaska

Liard

Watson Lake

Mackenzie Mountains

150°W

USA
CANADA

5

**Yukon
Territory**

Dawson City

2

Yukon

4

2

WHITEHORSE

1

Alaska Hwy

Skagway

Atlin
Provincial
Park

**DAWSON CITY
(pp357–62)**
A living museum of the
Gold Rush; parties during
the short summer

Fairbanks

2

1

Alaska

1

Kluane National
Park & Reserve

**KLUANE NATIONAL PARK
& RESERVE (pp350–2)**
More glaciers than you can
say 'brrr' to; loads of wildlife

Gulf of Alaska

0   200 km
0   120 miles

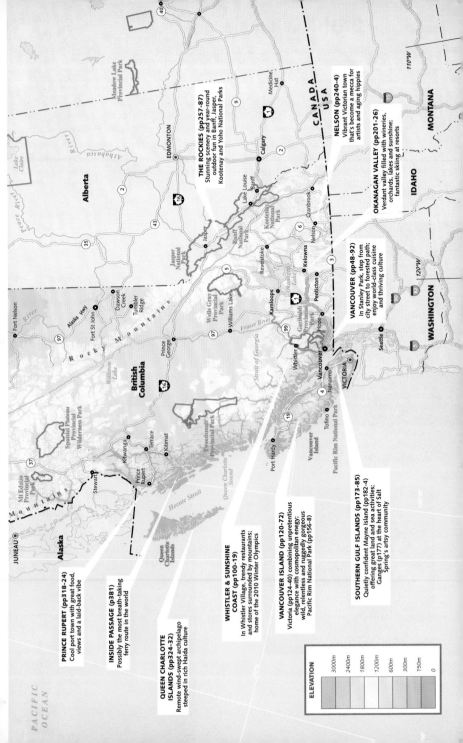

PRINCE RUPERT (pp318-24)
Cool port town with great food, views and a laid-back vibe

INSIDE PASSAGE (p381)
Possibly the most breath-taking ferry route in the world

QUEEN CHARLOTTE ISLANDS (pp324-32)
Remote wind-swept archipelago steeped in rich Haida culture

WHISTLER & SUNSHINE COAST (pp100-19)
In Whistler Village, trendy restaurants and stores surrounded by mountains; home of the 2010 Winter Olympics

VANCOUVER ISLAND (pp120-72)
Victoria (pp124-40) combining unpretentious elegance with cosmopolitan enegy; wild, relentless and ruggedly gorgeous Pacific Rim National Park (pp156-8)

SOUTHERN GULF ISLANDS (pp173-85)
Quietly confident Mayne Island (pp182-4) offering great land and sea activities; Ganges (p177) at the heart of Salt Spring's artsy community

THE ROCKIES (pp257-87)
Stunning scenery and year-round outdoor fun in Banff, Jasper, Kootenay and Yoho National Parks

NELSON (pp240-4)
Vibrant Victorian town that's become a mecca for artists and aging hippies

OKANAGAN VALLEY (pp201-26)
Verdant valley filled with wineries, orchards, lakes and sunshine; fantastic skiing at resorts

VANCOUVER (pp48-92)
In Stanley Park, step from city street to forested path; enjoy world-class cuisine and thriving culture

ELEVATION

3000m
2400m
1800m
1200m
600m
300m
150m
0

British Columbia is home to fantastic wilderness and unexpected beauty. **Banff** (p264), Canada's first national park, remains a star with its soaring peaks, hot springs and glaciers - take to the slopes or the water for a close-up. Hip **Vancouver** offers world-class cuisine (p78) and vibrant, eclectic nightlife (p87). Head to the lush Okanagan Valley to sample the vintages at famous **wineries** (p210). For a totally different trip, venture north to the Yukon's **Herschel Island** (p363) for pristine tundra or **Dawson City** (p357) for gold-rush charm.

GLENN VAN DER KNIJFF

Go skiing or snowboarding on **Whistler Mountain** (p108)

Hike one of the many trails in the **Yoho National Park** (p260)

LAWRENCE WORCESTE

FRANK CARTER

Dine alfresco near the public market on **Granville Island** (p83)

WITOLD SKRYPCZAK

Admire the beautiful, green **Emerald Lake** (p262), Yoho National Park

LEE FOSTER

View the totem poles in
Stanley Park (p61)

Rollerblade along the shoreline in **Vancouver** (p61)

ROSS BARNETT

Be entertained during Chinese New Year in **Chinatown** (p63)

Explore the wilderness in **Kluane National Park** (p350), the Yukon

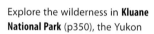

Take a ferry ride across **Kootenay Lake** (p237)

Soak away the bone-chilling cold in natural springs at **Gwaii Haanas National Park** (p331)

TRAVEL LITERATURE

Books can be a great way to get a feel for a place before you go. Reading about a location builds anticipation and adds meaningful context to your trip from the moment you arrive. British Columbia and the Yukon have inspired many books – including some classics – so you can delve right in.

The Forest Lover by Susan Vreeland is an engrossing historical novel about BC artist Emily Carr, one of the world's premier female artists in the first part of the 20th century. Vreeland, author of the wonderful *Girl in Hyacinth Blue*, weaves a delightful plot which follows Carr from illegal potlatches in BC to the salons of Paris.

If you can get your hands on the big and lavishly illustrated *Haida Monumental Art: Villages of the Queen Charlotte Islands*, by George F MacDonald and Richard J Huyda, before you arrive in Queen Charlotte

TOP TENS

TOP READS

Maybe it's just the basic charm and beauty of the place, but for whatever reason BC and the Yukon produce bumper crops of good authors and good books.

- *Notes from the Century Before: A Journal from British Columbia*, Edward Hoagland (p20)
- *Never Cry Wolf*, Farley Mowatt (p32)
- *Klondike Tales*, Jack London (p24)
- *British Columbia: An Illustrated History*, Geoff Molyneux (p18)
- *Mountains, Campfires & Memories*, Jack Boudreau (p24)
- *Cremation of Sam McGee*, Robert W Service (p24)
- *The Cure for Death by Lightning*, Gail Anderson-Dargatz (p25)
- *Raven's Cry*, Christie Harris (p29)
- *The Art of Emily Carr*, Doris Shadbolt (p29)
- *Rainforest: Ancient Realm of the Pacific Northwest*, Graham Osboe & Wade Davis (p28)

FESTIVALS & EVENTS

Except at the ski resorts, people make the most of every warm day – from summer fun in the north to festivals around the fall harvest in the temperate south.

- Big Mountain Experience (Whistler) January (p109)
- Victoria Day (Victoria) May (p132)
- Williams Lake Stampede (Williams Lake) An annual four-day party in July (p292)
- Merritt Mountain Music Festival (Merritt) Another four-day music fest in July (p198)
- Nelson International Street Performers & Arts Festival (Nelson) Third weekend in July (p242)
- Peach Festival (Penticton) Early August (p209)
- Discovery Day (Dawson City) The third Monday in August (p361)
- Pacific National Exposition (PNE; Vancouver) Massive state fair in August (p73)
- Vancouver International Film Festival (Vancouver) October (p73)
- Okanagan Fall Wine Fest (Okanagan Valley) October (p210)

Getting Started

WHEN TO GO

British Columbia is a good destination to visit year-round. The vibrancy of Vancouver can be enjoyed at any time. So too, cities and towns such as Victoria, Kelowna, Nelson and Fernie can be enjoyed at any time of the year. Be aware that during winter things may be very quiet, though this may be an advantage.

If you're headed outside, summer is the time for hiking, kayaking, canoeing and more. Parks and sights are all open and the days are long. Summer is also the prime time for festivals. Depending on the location, the months on either side of summer can be truly delightful as the air is crisp and the crowds are few. In winter you head straight to the hills and enjoy what is possibly the finest skiing and snowboarding on the planet.

Some places, like the Queen Charlotte Islands, are best visited in the summer, as at other times of the year the weather and conditions are so rugged that only the hardiest of folk can enjoy themselves. The same holds true of the Yukon. Most people enjoy this vast territory from June until early September.

COSTS

BC is really a place for all budgets. In Vancouver and the posh ski resorts at Whistler and the Rockies, costs can be $500 a day or more. But that's only if you want to enjoy a high level of luxury. A more realistic budget of $200 to $300 a day for two people will get you decent accommodation, nice meals, let you participate in various activities and enjoy the sights via a rented car.

Budget more if you are looking to ski (lift tickets average $50 a day) or go on guided adventures such as white-water rafting. Budget less if you are going to be camping (sites $15 to $35) or driving your own car. Families can save money with the family-group admissions available at many attractions. And look for places that allow kids to stay free in their parents' room – a common bonus.

It's also possible to travel easily through BC on a tight budget. You should be able to spend less than $100 per day by staying in hostels ($15 to $22 per night), cooking your own meals or eating at cheap cafés ($4 to $8) and riding the bus (usually $20 to $40 for a trip of several hours). If you pool your resources with other travelers, a cheap rental car gives you freedom and can cost less than the bus.

See clin (p369) f. informati

HOW M

One-day Whis pass $68

Ferry to Victoria driver and a car $

Night at a Yukon campground $12

Dip in Banff Hot Spri $7.50

Collecting beach treasu on a remote Vancouver Island beach $0

LONELY PLANET INDEX

Beer (bottle of Kokanee) $2

Liter of bottled water $1

Liter of petrol/gas 75¢

Souvenir T-shirt $15

Street snack (donut) 50¢

DON'T LEAVE HOME WITHOUT...

- Great shoes already broken in for a hike
- A corkscrew for sampling purchases in the Okanagan Valley (p201)
- Bug repellent so you don't have to try to find some if the mosquitoes attack (p387)
- A second form of ID like a birth certificate to go with your driver's license if you're from the USA and not bringing a passport
- Favorite CDs for long car rides
- Your best sunglasses to combat white-out from the beautiful winter powder

Islands, by all means do so. The richness and mysteries of the Haida culture are fully documented. It's a book that will concurrently impress and send a shiver of amazement down your spine.

The Call of the Wild by Jack London is prerequisite pre-departure reading for anyone going to the Yukon. The story of the dog Buck is timeless, and you will think of it often as you explore the territory – especially when you reach Dawson City.

In the satirical novel *Alice, I Think* by Susan Juby, little Alice must deal with the inconveniences foisted on her by her hippie mom, and otherwise make a place for herself in the community. BC has scores of little towns like Smithers where people feel they can escape from the rigors of modern life and live as they want.

The Yukon has been mined for gold, and it's also been mined for some very good fiction. *Treasures of the North* by Tracie Peterson, the first novel in a new series about the gold rush, follows the exploits of a woman from Chicago who gets caught up with thieving miners. However, its best parts deal with the Tlingit Indians who are on the sidelines watching their lives change forever.

The prosaic series *Backroads Mapbooks*, by Russell Mussio et al, takes you down the tiniest roads and most obscure paths in BC to find the wilderness' wilderness. If anything will get you charged up to get lost in BC, one of these books will.

In *Exile: A Novel* by Ann Ireland, a writer threatened in his Latin-American home escapes to Vancouver, where he tries to fit into the city's renowned melting pot. Unable to do so, what he learns in BC teaches him about what's he's left behind. This is a good novel for understanding that travel often teaches us more about ourselves than the places we've visited.

The historical novel *Salthill: A Novel*, by Judith Barnes, combines evocative prose detailing the BC wilderness with the struggles of an African-American in supposedly tolerant Canada. Fleeing racism in the southern USA, Garnet Harris heads north to BC in hopes of starting a new life in a place where he can put his ranching skills to use.

'BC has scores of little towns where people feel they can escape from the rigors of modern life'

INTERNET RESOURCES

BC Adventure Network (www.bcadventure.com) Vast and useful site about all things active in BC.

British Columbia.com (www.britishcolumbia.com) A large and detailed site about a huge range of topics, with good forums.

Parks Canada (www.parkscanada.ca) The government site for the national parks has information on all facets of the parks in BC and the Yukon.

Tour Yukon (www.touryukon.com) The official site for Yukon tourism is stuffed with information.

Tourism British Columbia (www.hellobc.com) The official site for Tourism BC, has lots of good trip-planning ideas.

Itineraries

CLASSIC ROUTES

THE GRAND TOUR
One month / Vancouver to Vancouver

From the **Okanagan Valley** (p201), head east through the pretty West Kootenays to **Nelson** (p240), a laid-back old town. From here it's north through **Kootenay** (p263), **Banff** (p264) and **Jasper** (p279) National Parks and the incredible Canadian **Rockies** (p257).

A drive through Alberta takes you to the start of the legendary **Alaska Highway** (p308). **Whitehorse** (p340) is the lively capital of the Yukon. Head north on the Klondike Highway to **Dawson City** (p357), the heart of the Klondike gold rush. Take the **Top of the World Highway** (p362) to a short Alaska detour before crossing back into the Yukon. **Kluane National Park** (p350) looms in all its magnificence as you head south to **Haines** (p348).

Take the **Alaska Marine Highway** (p380) for one of the world's great ferry voyages to lively **Prince Rupert** (p318). Consider a side trip out to the **Queen Charlotte Islands** (p324) – you've come this far! – and then take the BC Ferries **Inside Passage** (p381) cruise south to **Port Hardy** (p171) and **Vancouver Island** (p121). One more quick ferry ride returns you to **Vancouver** (p52).

This trip is for the pure adventurer who wants to see all the wonders of British Columbia and the Yukon. It features drives through some incredible scenery followed by two of the best ferry trips on earth.

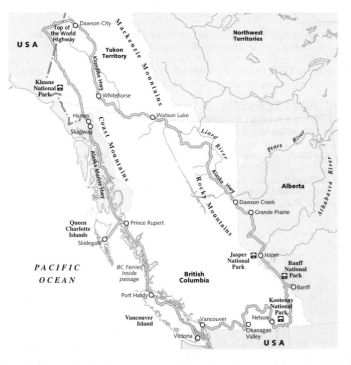

THE CIRCLE TOUR   Two–four days / Vancouver to Vancouver

Head north from Vancouver on Hwy 99 to **Horseshoe Bay** (p95) for the ferry to Langdale. The Sunshine Coast is noted for its rugged mountains and its dramatic shoreline and you'll be right in between both. Hang out in **Gibsons** (p114) for a bit and then head north through the forests and along the water to **Sechelt** (p116), the cultural center of the coast.

Continuing north, stop at **Skookumchuck Narrows Provincial Park** (p117) for a good hike to the rapids. Take the ferry across Jarvis Inlet to Saltery Bay and the Upper Sunshine Coast. Wander historic **Powell River** (p117) and decide if you might like to try a little kayaking in the area. Catch the Powell River ferry to **Comox** (p164) on Vancouver Island. Going south you can visit the interesting little beach towns of **Qualicum Beach** (p152) and **Parksville** (p152). At this point you may want to take a detour out to **Tofino** (172km; p158), with its spectacular setting and unique mix of people. Try the trails and enjoy the pounding surf at **Pacific Rim National Park Reserve** (p156).

Have a Nanaimo Bar in **Nanaimo** (p147). Onwards, **Victoria** (p124) and its sights and museums can occupy an afternoon or several days. If you have the luxury of time, stay as long as you want. Then take the short drive to Swartz Bay and the ferry to Tsawwassen. Vancouver is just 36km north. For details on the ferries for this trip and a special fare offered by BC Ferries, see p380.

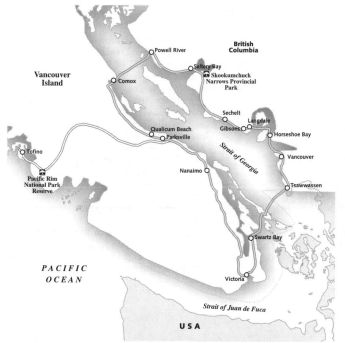

This classic trip includes the rugged and interesting Sunshine Coast, the charming towns of Southern Vancouver Island, a possible side trip to wild Tofino and a chance to partake of the traditional charms of Victoria.

TAILORED TRIPS

EXPEDITION TO THE ARCTIC

Begin at **Skagway** (p353) and climb the **Chilkoot Trail** (p354) into the Yukon. You'll gain 1110m and cover 53km. Catch the White Pass and Yukon Route train a short distance to Bennett, where you transfer to a bus to **Whitehorse** (p340). Here you get a canoe and spend the next 16 days

paddling downriver to **Dawson City** (p357), the preserved gold-rush town. About halfway there you join the chilly, surging waters of the Yukon River.

From Dawson it's the Dempster Hwy by vehicle to isolated **Inuvik** (p364) in the Northwest Territories. You'll pass the treeline and be driving through pure tundra for much of the trip on this rugged gravel road – one of the last great adventure drives. In Inuvik you transfer to a float plane for the flight over the Arctic Ocean to **Herschel Island** (p363) on the Yukon's coast. To return you can make a series of scheduled flights back to Whitehorse or further south.

MOUNTAINS, HISTORY & FUN

Begin in beautiful **Banff** (p264) which, in common with all the towns named on this tour, has skiing. Head north to **Lake Louise** (p276) and then take the **Icefields Parkway** (p278) to **Jasper** (p279). Return to Lake Louise and head west through **Yoho National Park** (p260) and **Golden** (p255) to **Glacier** (p234) and **Mt Revelstoke** (p234) National Parks.

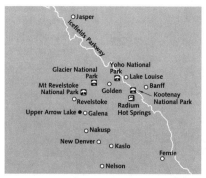

Revelstoke (p230) is a fun little town. Driving south you'll cross Upper Arrow Lake on the **ferry** (p237) from Galena Bay. **Nakusp** (p235), **New Denver** (p237) and **Kaslo** (p239) are historic little towns along the way. The prize is **Nelson** (p240) with its groovy, friendly vibe and good places to hang out. Follow Kootenay Lake south and then make your way east on the scenic Crows Nest Highway to **Fernie** (p249), another town with a beautiful downtown.

Take Hwy 93 north to **Radium Hot Springs** (p254), where you can soak the road pain out of your joints, and then to **Kootenay National Park** (p263) and back to Banff.

OKANAGAN VALLEY

Beginning in **Osoyoos** (p204), with its lovely lakeside setting and close proximity to Canada's only desert, and driving north, you'll pass dozens of orchards. In season you can stop and sample what's ripe, and at many you can just head out and pick your own while partaking of the heady scents. **Oliver** (p206) is one of the epicenters of the local wine industry.

For this trip you'll want to make a few decisions about which wineries to visit (see the boxed text, p210) in advance, otherwise the range of choices might leave you befuddled (and in need of a drink).

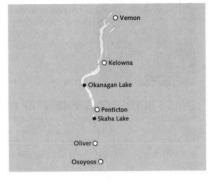

Penticton (p207) is a relaxed place and enjoys its location hemmed in by Skaha and Okanagan Lakes. This is the site of the annual **Peach Festival** (p209). The scenery gets less verdant and more rugged north to **Kelowna** (p214), the cultural capital of the valley. The museums and galleries here are a good counterpoint to the many outdoorsy attractions in the area. Orchards are back in force in **Vernon** (p222), where you can visit several.

CLASSIC BC

Take one of the ferries from Vancouver to Vancouver Island and check out **Victoria** (p124). Drive north the length of the island, and take the time to trek to **Della Falls** (p155), Canada's highest. At **Port Hardy** (p171), board the BC Ferries boat for the **Inside Passage** (p381) to Prince Rupert. During this fantastic, 16-hour, daytime voyage, you'll pass the **Great Bear Rainforest** (p298), a rare type of forest marked by granite cliffs and deepwater fjords.

In **Prince Rupert** (p318), consider the option of a **Queen Charlotte Islands** (p324) detour; plan it while in one of the city's wonderful restaurants. Otherwise head west up the spectacular Skeena River Valley and on to **Hazelton** (p317), with their many totem poles. The funky little town of **Smithers** (p314) is a good place to break the drive. Close to **Prince George** (p304), make the 68km-detour to the national historic site at **Fort St James** (p313). Heading south, it's ranch and old mining country to Hwy 99 which goes southwest to **Whistler** (p105), site of the 2010 Winter Olympics. From there you get the blue panorama of the **Sea to Sky Hwy** (p102) back to **Vancouver** (p52).

The Authors

RYAN VER BERKMOES

Coordinating Author,
Thompson Region, Okanagan, The Kootenays,
The Rockies, Cariboo-Chilcotin, The North, The Yukon

Ryan Ver Berkmoes has been entranced by all things BC since the mid-1980s, when he took a midnight walk all the way around Stanley Park in Vancouver and thought he'd never try that at his then-home in Chicago. Since covering the region for Lonely Planet's *Canada*, he's been itching to return in order to see what's changed, enjoy the new and the old, find some new roads to travel and do a quality check on a bottle of Okanagan Valley wine. During his research and writing for this edition, he accomplished all his goals.

RYAN'S BRITISH COLUMBIA & THE YUKON

What I like best about BC and the Yukon is that there's lots of places that don't remind you of anywhere else – they stand out for what they are. Take the tiny towns of **Nelson** (p240) and **Fernie** (p249) – funky mixtures of characters in perfectly preserved mountain towns. The **Queen Charlotte Islands** (p324) are also unlike any place anywhere – mystical and beautiful. The unheralded **Cottonwood House** (p294) on the road to the much-heralded **Barkerville** (p294) is a real step back in time. And there's the **Yukon** (p336), which is both a step back in time and a place with its own personality. Ferry rides on the **Inside Passage** (p381), perfectly grilled fresh seafood, there's too much to mention.

GRAHAM NEALE

Vancouver & Around, Whistler & the Sunshine Coast, Vancouver Island, Southern Gulf Islands, Fraser Region

Graham Neale grew up in North Delta, a suburb of Vancouver, where summertime or weekend camping, fishing and skiing trips, plus having 'the Big Smoke' only minutes away was a normal life. When he ventured out to explore other places, he realized the truth of the axiom 'There's no place like home'. The opportunity to write about BC southwest of Lillooet – his backyard for 25 years – was a chance not to pass up. He found comfort in places that hadn't changed in years and relished in discovering gems he'd never seen before – and may never get the backroad dust out of his car.

GRAHAM'S BRITISH COLUMBIA

When I try and sell the glory and gorgeousness of BC, people often say, 'Yeah, but you're biased'. I can't argue that truth; I am biased. But my answer is, 'I'm not biased because I'm from there, I'm biased because I've been there'. Another truth is that BC doesn't need to be pitched; it sells itself. It has enough to justify shameless self-promotion but, instead, BC simply shows you what it has. Since I've had 30 years to explore, I can say that **Big White** (p222) is my favorite place to ski and that on a roadtrip from **Vancouver** (p52) to **Fort St John** (p310) in early October I'll see skies of impossible purples and oranges.

CONTRIBUTING AUTHORS

David Goldberg, MD, completed his training in internal medicine and infectious diseases at Columbia-Presbyterian Medical Center in New York City. He is now an infectious diseases specialist in Scarsdale, NY, and the editor-in-chief of www.mdtravelhealth.com. Dr Goldberg is the author of the Health chapter.

Snapshot

Just as the outdoors and nature play a starring role in the plans of visitors to British Columbia and the Yukon, they also play an ongoing role in the everyday life in the region.

Recently much talk has been about the weather. But whereas this old staple of meaningless conversation can be heard worldwide, in BC and the Yukon the weather has become a major factor in a number of ongoing events. Fires made catastrophic by drought and high temperatures devastated large parts of central BC in 2003, including hundreds of homes near Kelowna, and rampaged through Kootenay and Jasper National Parks in the Rockies. The effects of these fires on tourism, the forest industry, the wine industry and more are being hotly discussed in an attempt at finding a way to prevent future conflagrations.

It wasn't fires but floods that have bedeviled the region near Whistler in recent times. Already an ongoing topic after the successful bid for the 2010 Winter Olympics, fears now focus on the road from Vancouver being at risk to wash-out (as it did spectacularly in 2003) during the games. Then there's the perennial worry that the rainy conditions which can mar an otherwise perfect ski experience at Whistler will mar the Olympics.

The games themselves will continue to be a hot (should we say cool?) topic until long after 2010 – especially if the doomsayers' predictions come true and the games cost BC taxpayers a bundle. You'll find a sizable minority who continue to decry the Olympic bid.

Another topic always in the news is First Nations settlements. The BC government is slowly coming to terms with First Nations groups who hold claim to most of the province, including central Vancouver. Settlements run into the hundreds of millions of dollars.

BC's beautiful countryside is always in the news as the rarely compatible forces of forestry and tourism square off over future logging in the region. Overall low prices and competition worldwide have depressed demand for BC lumber, but despite (or perhaps because of) lower profitability, threats to untouched areas like the astounding Great Bear Rainforest are continual.

In the Yukon, the health – or lack thereof – of the vast forests around Kluane National Park is both a concern and a tragedy. Causes are not definite, but a growing body of evidence points to a combination of factors brought on by global warming. Much local concern focuses on what will happen when all the dead trees catch fire.

Up in gold country, you'll see no end of 'Save Placer Mining' signs in the Yukon. This refers to the hundreds of small gold-mining operations that are usually family-run by direct descendents of the gold rush prospectors who came up here over 100 years ago. Environmental concerns are sparking regulations that the placer miners fear will cause them to be shut down.

A safe bet conversationally (if not monetarily) is the National Hockey League's Vancouver Canucks, which have a loyal and passionate following region-wide. People follow the team and its players with religious fervor, despite their less-than-holy performance in some years. If you don't catch a pro game, you'll probably see kids wherever you go playing stick hockey on the streets or frozen ponds. It's the national pastime, after all.

FAST FACTS

BC population: 4.2 million

BC area: 9.5 million sq km

Sq km per person: 2.3

BC grizzly bear population: 11,000

Yukon population: 31,000

Yukon area: 483,450 sq km

Sq km per person: 15.6

Yukon moose population: 60,000

History

BRITISH COLUMBIA

BC's growth and development since European arrival has centered on Vancouver Island's Fort Victoria. The history of the Yukon has really been a separate story (p21).

Early Inhabitants

The ancestors of BC's First Nations peoples showed up in North America at least 15,000 to 20,000 years ago. It's likely that, after the last Ice Age, they crossed to Alaska on a land bridge over what is now the Bering Strait. Some settled along the Pacific coast, while others found their way to the interior.

The Pacific coast Native Indians included the Nuxalk (Bella Coola), Cowichan, Gitksan, Haida, Kwakwaka'wakw, Nisga'a, Nuu-chah-nulth (Nootka), Salish, Sechelt and Tsimshian groups. With plenty of animal, marine and plant life available, they were able to evolve a sophisticated, structured culture and an intricate trade network. Coastal peoples dwelled as extended families in large, single-roofed cedar lodges. Living off the land and the sea, they staked out hunting and fishing grounds and good places to collect berries, bark and roots.

Inland, where climate extremes are greater than on the coast, the people led a more nomadic, subsistence-level life. In the north they followed the migratory herds of animals such as the caribou and the moose; in the south they pursued the bison. Most of these people were Athapaskans (now called Dene, pronounced 'de-nay'), which included such groups as Beaver, Chilcotin, Carrier, Sekani and Tahltan. Other important groups were the Interior Salish (divided into the Lillooet, Okanagan, Shuswap and Thompson) and the Kootenay.

BC's aboriginal peoples are known for a ceremony called a potlatch, held by Native communities to mark special occasions, and establish ranks and privileges. Often lasting many days, potlatches still take place today. They feature dancing, feasting and elaborate gift-giving from the chief to his people; the more he gives, the wealthier he shows himself to be.

European Settlement

During the 18th century, European explorers in search of new sources of wealth appeared off the West Coast. Alexsey Chirikov is thought to have been first, exploring for Russia in 1741, though his travels were mainly along what is now the Alaskan coast. Spaniards were next: Juan Pérez Hernández sailed from Mexico to the Queen Charlotte Islands and Nootka Sound in 1774, followed by Juan Francisco de la Bodega y Quadra in 1775.

Britain's Captain James Cook arrived in 1778, looking for a water route across North America from the Pacific to the Atlantic – the legendary Northwest Passage. He was unable to find it, but his account of the riches to be had from furs brought traders eager to cash in. The most famous of these were Alexander Mackenzie, Simon Fraser and David Thompson,

British Columbia: An Illustrated History by Geoff Molyneux
Great old photos from 100 years ago.

Historical Atlas of the Pacific Northwest Maps of Exploration and Discovery by Derek Hayes
A good look at the maps drawn by Captains Cook, Vancouver and Thompson of the BC they found and explored.

TIMELINE **1778**

Captain James Cook spreads word of BC's riches to Great Britain

1858

The discovery of gold leads to massive population growth. The mainland becomes home to many settlers who explored overland routes from the east. Fort St John, on the Peace River, became the first European settlement in 1794; and in its wake came many more trading posts which, by the 1820s, went under the control of the Hudson's Bay Company (HBC). For a good idea of how HBC settlements worked, visit the restored one at Fort St James (p313).

In the meantime, initially to counter the Spanish presence, Captain George Vancouver had circumnavigated and claimed Vancouver Island for Britain from 1792 to 1794. 'The serenity of the climate, the innumerable pleasing landscapes and the abundant fertility that unassisted nature puts forth requires only to be enriched by man to render it the most lovely country that can be imagined,' Vancouver observed in 1792. The comment has long been a source of ire to First Nations people, who resent Vancouver's implication that there was no one around when he arrived. Evidence shows the local population was about 80,000 at the time.

Indian-European Relations in British Columbia, 1774-1890 by Robin Fisher The definitive book on a subject which continues to affect BC life today.

Vancouver also explored far up BC's north coast. By the 1840s the Hudson's Bay Company was warily watching the USA make an increasingly indisputable claim to the Oregon country anchored by HBC's Fort Vancouver on the Columbia River near present-day Portland. In 1843, the HBC dispatched James Douglas to Vancouver Island, where he established Fort Victoria. Vancouver Island became a crown colony in 1849.

The discovery of gold along the Fraser River in 1858 brought a flood of people seeking their fortunes, and led to mainland BC also being declared a crown colony, with New Westminster its capital. A second wave of fortune hunters arrived when gold was discovered further north in the Cariboo region. Although the gold rush only lasted a few years, many of those who came remained behind to form more permanent settlements. A downside to the gold rush was soaring debt created by massive infrastructure projects like the Cariboo Rd (which cost about $300,000). You can relive the feeling of a gold rush town at Barkerville (p294).

victoria.tc.ca/Resources /bchistory.html A central resource that catalogues websites relating to BC history.

Mainland BC and Vancouver Island were united in 1866, with Victoria named capital in 1868. Meanwhile, in 1867, the British government passed the British North American Act, creating the Dominion of Canada, a confederation that maintained British ties but conferred many powers to a central Canadian government and individual provinces. The eastern provinces of Canada united under the confederation, and BC decided to join in 1871 on the condition that a transcontinental railroad be extended to the West Coast. This was finally achieved in 1885; the settlement of the prairies around this same time created demand for the BC's resources, particularly timber.

www.bcarchives.gov .bc.ca/index.htm This site is run by the Royal BC Museum in Victoria and features a vast and searchable library of images, sounds, movies and reference works on all aspects of BC history.

The late 19th century proved a difficult time for BC's First Nations people. The gold-rush era caused displacement from their traditional lands, leading to violence among both the Native Indians and the Whites. Moreover, the Canadian government, heeding complaints from missionaries and others about pagan Native practices, outlawed potlatches in the 1880s with legislation that was not repealed until 1951.

The Early 20th Century

The building of the Panama Canal, which was completed in 1914, meant easier access for BC to markets in Europe and along North America's east coast. The province's interior profited too, with the completion of

1866	1887
Mainland BC and Vancouver Island unite	The Canadian Pacific Railway arrives in Vancouver, linking Canada's west with the east

the Grand Trunk Railway from Edmonton, Alberta, to Prince Rupert. As big business grew, so did big unions. Workers in great numbers organized into labor unions in the 1910s, protesting about working conditions and pay rates. A number of strikes targeted key industries like lumber mills and shipping, and in several instances BC saw armed confrontations between union members and soldiers. However one issue where the unions, the government and business were in accord was with non-White workers – all three felt the growing Chinese and Japanese population was a problem that only punitive legislation and violence could solve.

Large numbers of Chinese had moved to the province, and were instrumental in building the Canadian Pacific Railway (see the boxed text, p236, for places in the Kootenays to learn more about this). Japanese settlers came slightly later, establishing truck farms and becoming the area's principal commercial fishermen. That these were hard working people seeking opportunity, like the Europeans who were also flooding the province, seemingly didn't matter to Whites. On several occasions in the province's early history, Vancouver's Chinatown and Little Tokyo were the scene of White mob violence.

Following WWI, Canada experienced an economic downturn that led to industrial unrest and unemployment. After a brief recovery, the Wall St crash of 1929 brought severe depression and hardship. Prosperity only returned with the advent of WWII and was sustained after the war with the discovery of new resources and the development of a manufacturing base.

The war years were hard times for immigrants. During WWI anti-German riots took hold of the streets of Vancouver, and many German-owned businesses were burned. In 1941, Japanese Canadians were removed from their land and their fishing boats, and were interned by the government on farms and work camps in inland BC and Alberta, Saskatchewan and Manitoba. You can see good exhibits about this in New Denver (p237).

First Nations people remained under siege too. In 1921 Kwakwaka'wakw chief Dan Cranmer defied the ban on potlatches by staging what may have been the largest gathering of that type ever. Chiefs gathered at Alert Bay to celebrate and exchange gifts, but local Whites called the authorities to report the then-illegal activity. Chiefs who agreed to surrender their potlatch possessions were freed, but those who refused – including Cranmer – were sent to jail. Many of the potlatch artifacts wound up at the National Museum of Canada in Ottawa, which finally agreed to return them to the Native Indians in the 1980s. They now can be seen at museums at Alert Bay (p170) and on Quadra Island (p166).

Post-War Prosperity

BC's natural resources-based economy enjoyed periods of great prosperity in the mid-20th century, following WWII, as transportation networks extended further into the resource-rich interior. Forestry led the way, as BC's mills worked to meet ever-growing demands for pulp, paper and plywood. At the time, small operations dominated logging, but this is no longer true; today, a handful of companies dominate the industry.

1896	1898
Gold found near today's Dawson City sets off legendary Klondike Gold Rush	The creation of the Yukon as a separate territory from the Northwest Territories

At the beginning of the 1990s, BC experienced another economic upsurge, led by Vancouver, which enjoyed its links to then-booming Asia. The area also experienced a large influx of moneyed immigrants fleeing Hong Kong ahead of its handover to China. Recently BC has been buoyed by an increasing number of Americans who are both investing and living in the province. Drawn by the comparatively low cost of living and the truly pleasant living conditions, Americans have begun a small but significant migration north.

THE YUKON

Until 60 years ago you traveled to the Yukon primarily through Alaskan ports because of the region's isolation, so the Yukon has a history distinct from British Columbia.

The first people to arrive in the region were part of the groups that crossed the land bridge linking Asia and the Americas. They followed the woolly mammoths, mastodons and steppe bison. Archeologists date their arrival to the Porcupine River area near Old Crow from between 15,000 and 20,000 years ago. They are considered the ancestors of today's Dene (also called Athabaskan) people.

In the 1840s Robert Campbell, a Hudson's Bay Company explorer, was the first European to travel extensively in the district. Fur traders, prospectors, whalers and missionaries followed him. Until that point there had been only limited contact between Native Indians and Europeans, and many First Nations populations were hit with measles, small pox and influenza.

In 1870 the region became part of the Northwest Territories. But it was in 1896 that the biggest changes began, when gold was found in a tributary of the Klondike River near what became Dawson City. The ensuing gold rush attracted hopefuls from around the world. The population expanded to around 38,000 and transport routes opened up. Towns grew overnight to support the wealth-seekers, who were not prepared for the harsh conditions. First Nations men worked as guides, hunters and freight packers. The women made and sold weather-appropriate clothing. Their traditional patterns of moving with the seasons changed dramatically.

In 1898 the Yukon became a separate territory, with Dawson City the capital, but the city declined as the gold ran out. The construction of the Alaska Hwy in 1942 opened up the territory to development and provided it with its first tangible link to British Columbia. In 1953 Whitehorse became the capital, for it had the railway and the Alaska Hwy.

There are 14 First Nations groups in the Yukon, speaking eight languages. Due to the relative isolation of the territory until WWII, First Nations groups have maintained their relationship to the land and their traditional culture, compared to other groups forced to assimilate in British Columbia and the rest of Canada.

GOVERNMENT & POLITICS

British Columbia has a parliamentary government, with a 75-member unicameral legislature that convenes in Victoria. The lieutenant governor is the formal head of state, but real power goes to the premier, who is

The Other Side of Eden: Hunters, Farmers and the Shaping of the World by Hugh Brody
An evocative work that looks at the cultures of the Dunne-za nation of the Peace River in Northern BC as well as other First Nations groups in the Yukon and North. It explores their vibrant yet vanishing cult

Martha Black by Flo Whyard
Tremendous biography of a woman who fought her way to Dawson City with the prospectors and then owned her own business, became *the* hostess of the territory and eventually was elected to the Canadian parliament.

Good Time Girls by Lael Morgan
More scholarly than you might think, this is a story of the prostitutes who were as much a part of the Gold Rush as the miners.

1921	1942
Chief Dan Cranmer defies the ban on holding potlatches. Scores are arrested	Opening of the Alaska Highway links the Yukon and much of Northern BC to the rest of Canada

usually the head of the majority party. The premier is Gordon Campbell of the Liberal Party, who was elected by a wide margin in 2001.

BC also sends representatives to the national House of Commons and Senate in Ottawa. But, since Canadian power is concentrated on the provincial level, most people in BC pay little heed to what's happening in the national capital. The Social Credit Party (Socreds), ostensibly the party of small business, came to power in BC in the 1950s and governed into the 1970s. During the 1960s the New Democratic Party (NDP) emerged, advocating a form of limited socialism. Beset by scandals, the Socreds fell out of favor by 1990. The NDP was in charge during much of the 1990s, but it also has had its share of scandal. The Liberals (who, despite their name, actually take mostly right-wing-to-moderate stands) swept to power in a 2001 landslide fueled by promises of tax cuts and the perennial conservative political promise of 'less government'.

The ongoing effort to resolve aboriginal land claims is a major issue in BC politics. In 1993 the provincial government established the BC Treaty Commission, intended to set up a framework by which land claims can be worked out. In 2000 the province and federal government reached the first modern-day treaty agreement, a pact which would give the Nisga'a Nation in northwestern BC's Nass River valley extensive self-rule rights and about $190 million in cash. Negotiating the implementation of that treaty and more than 60 others covering much of BC is proving predictably complex.

In the Yukon, the federal government appoints a commissioner who represents Ottawa; the actual governing of the territory is accomplished by the Executive Council, who are drawn from the legislative branch, the elected Yukon Council. Major political challenges tend to center on how much money the feds are going to send north (with its tiny population and myriad of needs for things like better roads, the Yukon takes in far more federal money than it pays out in taxes).

First Nations claims in the Yukon have proved easier to negotiate than in BC, as so much of the land is not part of competing claims.

ECONOMY

Perhaps more so than the rest of Canada, BC's economy is driven by factors outside its control. The province's fortunes are closely tied to Asian economies; when the East prospers, BC's timber and forestry exports boom. Also the Lower Mainland sits in the shadow of nearby Seattle, the headquarters of such thriving companies as Microsoft and Amazon.com and one of the principal areas driving the continuing US-based high-technology boom. The Okanagan Valley has become BC's own little high-tech Mecca, producing far more revenue from its 200 high-tech firms than from its more widely known wines and produce. Finally, due to its location on the main north–south transportation corridors of western North America, BC was strongly affected by implementation of the North American Free Trade Act (NAFTA), which liberalized trade among Canada, the USA and Mexico.

While service-sector jobs such as tourism are doing well, traditional jobs based on resource exploitation continue to have troubles. The vast mining operations around areas such as the Peace River have been

Pictorial History of the Mounted Police in the Yukon by Helene Dobrowolsky Long saddled with the *Dudley Do-Right* image, this book looks at the original Mounties in the Yukon, who would venture forth between towns with little of the gear or tools taken for granted now. The book looks at the role First Nations people and the Mounties' own families played in these exploits.

DID YOU KNOW?

Much of downtown Vancouver is the subject of claims of ownership by First Nations people.

1993

The Treaty Commission is established to negotiate land claims between First Nations groups, BC and the federal government severely hurt due to low worldwide prices for raw minerals, and fishing has been decimated by depleted stocks. Forestry has also suffered, especially after the largest customer for BC timber, the USA, imposed stiff anti-dumping penalties on BC wood products. The situation has not been helped by the many forest fires and the devastation caused by spruce-bark beetle infestations around Prince George. Meanwhile debate about hosting the 2010 Winter Olympics focuses on whether the cost of the games will drain the provincial treasury or spur economic growth.

In the Yukon most people work for the government in some way – either as teachers, administrators, bureaucrats or in jobs dependent on government funding. Many count on the short tourist season for their livelihoods – with some wise characters working in southern winter retreats in Mexico or the Caribbean before enjoying profitable summers in the Yukon. Placer mining is actually an economic factor as worthwhile quantities of gold and silver continue to be extracted from the land. However recent efforts to rein in practices that may be harmful to the environment have stirred debate.

DID YOU KNOW?

The population of Dawson City in 1898 (around 38,000) was greater than that of the entire Yukon today (31,000).

The Culture

It should come as no surprise that the predominantly laid-back attitude of British Columbia and the Yukon's inhabitants is due in large part to the natural land and seascapes. The words that come to mind when one thinks of this part of the world are 'mountainous' and 'coastal'. Throw the Yukon in there and you've got 'Klondike'; include Vancouver in the mix and you can add 'cosmopolitan'; put Fort Nelson in that group and you can include 'remote'. When you realize the mix of words you're a step closer to understanding the complexity of the area's culture.

Klondike Tales by Jack London London drew on his first-hand experiences for these 23 stories showing the hardships, triumphs and betrayals of the Yukon gold rush.

REGIONAL IDENTITY

BC and the Yukon cover such a huge area that it's impossible to succinctly describe their cultural identity. A man from Vancouver Island feels uncomfortable when he's off it; a boy from Nelson couldn't imagine less than six months of outdoor hockey; a woman in Williams Lake looks forward to her weekend hikes and a couple in Dawson City appreciates the area's history.

The region's different pockets have different qualities and different characteristics. But the people who live in these great lands know exactly what they have and are rarely at a loss for words when asked what they like most about their home. A visit to the region will reveal that, though a visitor, you're not really considered a stranger, and your reason for coming will never be questioned; it's obvious why you come – to enjoy what those lucky enough to live here never take for granted.

Cremation of Sam McGee by Robert W Service The renowned Bard of the Yukon was at his peak with this classic of regional prose about two gold miners, the cold and what men will sometimes do.

Friendliness rarely takes a back seat in this part of the world. From Osoyoos to Port Hardy to Fort St John to Cranbrook, the people of BC, at their root, are the same. So don't be afraid to talk to the stranger at the bar, ask the ferry-worker for her favorite hike, get fishing tips from your hotel owner or invite the couple in the campsite beside you over for marshmallows. They're more than happy to make new friends or just help out-of-towners with simple back-road shortcuts.

LIFESTYLE

Mountains, Campfires & Memories by Jack Boudreau People missing in the woods where wild beasts and critters lurk: sounds like a horror-movie screenplay but was real-life survival in post-WWII northern BC, as depicted in this colorfully written anthology.

The people of BC and the Yukon are real-world – fame and glory are not high on the priority list, instead they'd rather rely on teamwork combined with a live-and-let-live attitude. This seems to function beautifully.

BC lifestyle is about backyard barbecues, family reunions, week-long camping adventures, weekend fishing trips and nights at the pub. Family and community are a big part of life; families sit down together for dinner and the communities follow the local sports teams with fervor and attend the high school plays willingly. Community-sponsored events, from fringe festivals to pancake breakfasts, are well attended and are a fun way to meet locals.

Obviously, lifestyles vary as you spread out from the major centers. The price of an 800-sq-ft condo in Vancouver will buy a two-bedroom house in Kamloops or a four-acre ranch in Smithers. On the same note, $100,000 salaries are more common in Vancouver than in a place like Prince George. The great thing about BC and the Yukon is the absence of rivalry between the different areas – in fact, there's more of a symbiotic relationship. City folk love the fact that escape from the city is just a short drive away and small-town people appreciate that city life is within close reach.

POPULATION

It's well documented that 90% of the Canadian population live within 160km of the US border, but a lesser-known stat is that 75% of BC's four million people live within 60 km of the coast. These results are obviously skewed by the fact that the Lower Mainland's two million people satisfy both requirements and 650,000-resident Vancouver Island is only 100km wide; but they also show just how much BC's people identify with its coastal setting.

As you move away from the population centers into the interior of the region, you'll find plenty of small towns with their own unique flavor. Larger cities or towns (with populations over 50,000) are usually tied into an area of abundant recreation, like Kelowna; or major industries, typically forestry, like Powell River; or fishing, like Prince Rupert.

The Cure for Death by Lightening by Grail Anderson-Dargatz An image-filled fictional narration by 15-year-old Beth conveys the loneliness and difficulties of growing up on a farm in BC during WWII.

SPORT

Since BC and the Yukon are in Canada, we must first mention Canada's national sport, lacrosse. It's an odd game: like soccer without kicking, polo without horses, and field-hockey with different sticks. Despite its national claim, it's not a terribly popular sport, though the Vancouver Ravens play the National Lacrosse League (NLL) professionally. Most communities in the region will have a local league, or at least a team, that plays in the summer months.

Hockey

In wintertime, the northern parts of the region transform into a myriad of frozen lakes, ponds and sloughs presenting the opportunity for countless hours of Canada's favorite pastime. Hockey is a religion in Canada – akin to high school football in Texas – and BC and the Yukon are no exception. People will watch at least two shows on the Canadian Broadcasting Company (CBC), guaranteed: The *National* on weekday evenings, and *Hockey Night in Canada* every Saturday. Pick any random town and the majority of boys and girls will be on an organized team or play for fun on a regular basis. Iced-over ponds will be full of people playing out a complicated series of movements that cannot be confused with anything but the game of hockey. Pick a random residential street in places that don't have extended winters and street-hockey kids will yell, 'Car!' before moving the nets and gear aside, allowing you to pass. In your rearview mirror you'll then see them replace the equipment and resume play. You'll also find plenty of adult's and old-timer's casual leagues. BC has bred dozens of past and current players who've had success in the National Hockey League (NHL), including Steve Yzerman, Scott and Rob Niedermayer and Cam Neely; even unfrozen Vancouver has seen its children prosper in the NHL: Paul Kariya, Cliff Ronning and 'Burnaby Joe' Sakic, to name as few.

DID YOU KNOW?

Vancouver actually won a Stanley Cup in pre-NHL 1915, when the Vancouver Millionaires defeated the Ottawa Senators.

THE NHL: A REAL BARGAIN

September 2004 marks the end of the current Collective Bargaining Agreement (CBA) between the NHL Player's Association (NHLPA) and NHL owners. What this means for everyone involved, from casual fan to $10-million player, is no NHL without a new agreement. Quiet negotiations are underway and both sides are optimistic a new deal will be reached – the most likely scenario is an 11th-hour decision.

This could all be a moot point, since everything could be rosy by the time you're reading this and looking forward to attending a Canucks game, but check www.nhl.com for news and details.

The Kamloops Blazers, Kootenay Ice, Prince George Cougars, Kelowna Rockets and Vancouver Giants (p88), in the 20-and-under Western Hockey League (WHL), have served as the training grounds for players moving on to the NHL; the fans in these areas are just as excited about their teams as you'll find in any sporting market, and the games are incredibly exhilarating as these players are trying hard to make the big league.

Slap Shot directed by George Roy Hill This is a cult film for all Canadians and hockey fans. Profane humor and bloody violence blend as Paul Newman stars as a player/coach of a terrible minor-league team chronicling the on- and off-ice activities.

Though 'Vancouver' precedes the team's name, the Canucks (p88) represent the entire region in the NHL, and have fan support throughout. Team success has fluctuated between mediocrity, flukiness and greatness since its 1970 inception, with fans constantly lighting up the phone talkshow switchboards and waiting patiently for a Stanley Cup parade down Robson St. The current roster boasts All-Stars Todd Bertuzzi and Markus Naslund, as well as a true-blue Canuck in former team captain and current team leader Trevor Linden who, although he spent a few years away from the team, never sold his house and has called no place other than Vancouver home.

Football

The BC Lions (p88), the only professional team to be an officially labeled regional representative, play in Vancouver for the Canadian Football League (CFL), which has long been considered a minor league for America's National Football League (NFL). It's partly true, since the CFL has seen players like Warren Moon, Doug Flutie and Jeff Garcia do well and then sign for big bucks south of the border, but it's also misleading (and disrespectful), since there's no possible way the CFL can compete with the marketing and market sizes of the NFL. Besides, the CFL is a different, more exciting game; there's more passing, a longer and wider field, only three chances to move the ball 10 yards, and the rouge – the coolest way to score in all of sports. The Lions won the Grey Cup Championship in 1964, 1985, 1994 and 2000 and if you're looking for one player synonymous with the team, look no further than 25-year veteran kicker Lui Passaglia, who retired in 2000 but is still part of the team's management.

Oldtimers: On the Road with the Legendary Heroes of Hockey by Gary Mason Mason participates on a northwestern Canada old-timers tour with former NHL superstars. You'll laugh more than once as they relive the sport that was more about pranks, late nights and relationships than contracts and stats.

Soccer

BC is arguably the soccer capital of Canada. It's one of the more popular after-school and weekend sports played by kids and supported by soccer-moms and soccer-dads around the region; many a bookshelf proudly displays trophies and team photos. The Vancouver Whitecaps (p88) have both an A-League Men's and a W-League Women's team. Bob Lenarduzzi played for the team that brought a professional sports title to Vancouver when his 1979 Whitecaps won the NASL Championship. Bobby's now the General Manager of the Whitecaps and also directs a number of soccer camps for children around BC in the off season.

CURLING

Few sports allow the champion to hold a trophy in one hand, a beer in the other and have a cigarette dangling from his or her lips, but curling, one of Canada's favorite sports, is one of them. Loosely defined as shuffleboard on ice with 44lb stones, a 146-foot-long playing surface and brooms, it's a game of precision and every town in the region will have a curling rink close by; check www.curlbc.bc.ca if you want to watch.

MULTICULTURALISM & RELIGION

Canada west of the Rocky Mountains is the quintessential melting pot of cultures, ideals, rituals, creeds and ethnicities, making the region as varied culturally as it is ecologically. Canada aims to promote cultural diversity and the west coast in particular has been a portal for emigrants from Asia, India and Eastern Europe. Vancouver is a cultural hodgepodge with a bustling Chinatown, Commercial Drive's 'Little Italy', Asian-influenced Richmond and Indians taking up residence in suburban Burnaby, Delta and Surrey. Pretty much every town in BC and the Yukon has a good Chinese restaurant, and several have tributes to Japanese and Chinese settlers, who helped build the railroad. Some communities throughout the region started as Scandinavian settlements, and still retain a strong Nordic influence.

There has never been a dominant African community or cultural impact, but it shouldn't be a surprise that they have a history in this part of the world. It's believed that Governor General James Douglas had African ancestry, and encouraged the first documented wave of Black immigration to Salt Spring Island from California.

A constant front-burner topic on the multicultural hot stove is the issue concerning First Nations groups and their rights to cultural heritage and lands claimed by White people. An exception is the Inuit in the north, who don't face the problems on such a large scale. They've inhabited northern BC and the Yukon for centuries and their traditions are still practiced today. Reservations are found throughout the region; residents form self-sufficient communities and pass their heritage to the next generation. These communities vary, some are down-trodden villages but many others have cultural museums, bighouses, totem-pole carvers and other traditional aspects of their culture and are proud and ready to share their history with others.

As with any other place in the world, you'll find the odd racist jackass with predictable derogatory slurs referring to other cultures. And some cultures aren't exactly rushing to melt into the pot: some residential pockets feature a strong ethnic majority, but generally there's a high level of understanding and appreciation between cultures.

BC and the Yukon are predominantly Christian, with the major denominations being Catholic and Protestant, and no real territorial claim by either. Most Jewish people arriving in British Columbia move to the Vancouver region, which is now the third-largest Jewish community in Canada, although Victoria and Kelowna have had their own population booms. With the influx of various cultures over the years, so too comes their beliefs – Buddhist, Sikh and Hindu temples are found all over the Lower Mainland.

MEDIA

Barely a day goes by where the provincial or federal governments aren't in the news being criticized for one thing or another. Like any democratic society, there are people who have a list of things they would do differently if they were in charge, and they'll tell anyone who'll listen just what those things are. This has become a staple of the news, it seems.

Aside from beating up on the government, media coverage is excellent in this part of the world, with a focus on local and national topics. There is always a broad range of international news as well, which is somewhat unusual for a region that has so many rural residents. Most radio talkshow hosts and TV news anchors deliver the stories in a personable, professional way. BCTV's Tony Parsons and CBC's Peter Mansbridge

Blueprint: Black British Columbian Literature and Orature edited by Wayde Compton
A collection of stories of the rarely told migration of Blacks to British Columbia and the formation of their communities from 1858 to the present.

www.bctreaty.net
The website for the BC Treaty Commission with news and information on treaties between First Nations groups and the provincial government.

Wisdom of the Elders: Sacred Native Stories of Nature by David Suzuki & Peter Knudtson
A thought-provoking and insightful view into the relationship First Nations groups have with nature and the western world's need to learn the same.

are invited through the TV into living rooms around the province and CKNW's Bill Good is a daytime radio mainstay. The major US-based broadcast and cable networks are also carried on many cable systems in BC.

The *Vancouver Sun* and the *Province* are available throughout British Columbia each morning. Though if you're outside of the Lower Mainland, you'll have to wait until tomorrow's edition for last night's late news – a printer cutoff time needs to be met in order to deliver current issues to the far-reaching corners of the region. Most communities have a weekly newspaper, often free, dishing out the local stories. These are a good way to get a feel for what's happening locally.

ARTS

The art scene is huge in this corner of the world; British Columbians and Yukoners love to be culturally stimulated. Most art takes the obvious route and uses the natural beauty as its stage or protagonist, but almost every community will have some kind of arts or fringe festival at some point in the year celebrating local and international talent. There's enough inspiration oozing from the sights and people to help turn any work into a masterpiece.

Literature

Canadians are known for witty observations that make you think, then make you laugh. The dry humor and imaginativeness of Vancouver author Douglas Coupland has earned him a kind of cult-like following. His keen cultural observations are meaningful, humorous and accessible. His stories range from far-flung to close-to-home but are never unrealistic.

Canadian authors in general are a visual bunch. The tendency is to set the scene, introduce the characters, maybe add an elk or two and let the story unfold, where vivid scene descriptions are as important as the tale itself. Historical and hysterical anecdotes appear randomly throughout texts, and authors have a way of noticing the subtleties of life and bringing them to the forefront.

Cinema & Television

The BC Film Commission was established in 1978 and has turned the region's filmscape from a $12-million afterthought to a multi-billion-dollar industry. It has set up tax breaks and reduced costs for filming and production while creating thousands of jobs for local residents. The Canadian dollar being lower then the US dollar is also a big, juicy carrot dangling on front of producers, but once they get here, they realize the backdrop of the region is the real attraction. Vancouver is constantly acting as a stand-in for the intended 'real-life' location of movies, TV shows and advertisements, and other parts of the region are beginning to achieve film-worthy recognition as well – Jennifer Lopez and Robert Redford recently shot *An Unfinished Life* near Kamloops. Sadly, few features filmed in BC are actually about BC. The region is consistently portrayed as some other place, or obscurely left as the backdrop to no place in particular.

Music

Yes, Bryan Adams is from Vancouver but whether or not he really got his 'first, real six-string' at the 'Five & Dime' and 'played it 'til his fingers bled' is up for debate. Bryan emerged as the poster-boy for Canadian

---

Hey Nostradamus!: A novel by Douglas Coupland
An odd but captivating before and after account of a fictional North Vancouver high school massacre *à la* Columbine shootings. Coupland exploits a touchy subject but does so with imaginative skill – and sometimes sorrowful dignity.

DID YOU KNOW?
In 2002, 205 productions were filmed in BC, including 37 feature films; 38 movies-of-the-week, pilots, and mini-series; 19 TV series; 20 animation projects and 91 documentaries and shorts.

Rainforest: Ancient Realm of the Pacific Northwest by Graham Osboe (photographer) and Wade Davis
Eloquent and evocative text combine with some of the most beautiful photos of Pacific Northwest rainforests ever taken to depict these ancient and mythic ecosystems. If you can't get to a rainforest, this is the next best thing.

music with his 1980s album *Reckless*, putting him on the ambassador list along with Neil Young, The Guess Who, Joni Mitchell and Rush. The fact that he's from Vancouver was secondary to the fact that he's Canadian, but it did open the door for other BC musicians heard today, including Sarah McLachlan and Nickelback. Artists from other parts of the country have drawn on it for material, such as The Tea Party, who wrote the song 'Shadows on the Mountainside' while on a trip through the Rockies. The region has also become a destination for recording, and big-name bands like REM and Metallica have come here to record their albums in studios like Gastown's Warehouse Studio (owned by Bryan Adams).

BC couldn't be as cool as it is without paying homage to the music that defines 'cool' and Nanaimo's talented Diana Krall is jazz's latest commercial success. Most towns or regions will have at least one jazz festival during the year, and larger centers such as Vancouver and Victoria have nightclubs that are all that jazz.

The down-to-earth and campfire feel of the region goes hand in hand with the acoustic guitar, so check for folkfests when you're in the area. First Nations' music and dances are not only a delight to the visual and aural senses, they are a fundamental part of each tribe's heritage. Check with cultural centres or bighouses for information.

Visual Arts

The colors and textures of the Southern Gulf Islands' seascape, an Okanogan basin, a Peace River sunset or a Yukon arctic tundra are enough to inspire even the un-artistic. BC and the Yukon are like works of art themselves and leave most people awestruck. Not surprisingly, most art is of the landscape or wildlife variety. Take a look at any of the photos in the pages of *Beautiful British Columbia* magazine or roll into any art gallery to look at local paintings and you begin to get a sense of it.

First Nations' art is also huge, and it goes beyond totem poles. Masks, drums and paintings featuring the distinctive black and red sweeping brush strokes depict wolves, ravens and other animals from the spirit world. Bill Reid is one of the best-known names from the First Nations' art circle and the UBC Museum of Anthropology (p69) is a huge showcase for his work.

Born in Victoria in 1871, Emily Carr was inspired by the Native Indian villages and the landscape of Vancouver Island, but it wasn't until she met the acclaimed eastern-Canadian Group of Seven that she took off as an artist and found her inspiration. The Emily Carr House (p130), in Victoria, is open to the public, and her paintings are displayed at the Vancouver Art Gallery (p60) and the Art Gallery of Greater Victoria (p129).

Toronto-born Gulf Island resident Robert Bateman creates some incredibly realistic and beautiful paintings of BC's landscapes and wildlife that are displayed and sold in galleries and art stores all over the country.

Theatre

Vancouver shows the usual gambit of on- and off-Broadway shows and has its own selection of local groups and performers, but once you move out into the other areas, theater doesn't disappear. Local theaterhouses are found all over the region, providing entertaining performances with local talent. Chemanius Theatre (p146), a big theater in a little town, draws people from all over the southwest; while even towns as remote as Barkerville have theaters putting on productions. Fringe festivals are also popular; Prince Rupert has a great one (p322).

DID YOU KNOW?

In order to promote talent from within, 35% of music played on all Canadian radio stations must be Canadian content (endearingly known as 'CanCon').

The Art of Emily Carr by Doris Shadbolt
Often controversial and always inspired, BC's first lady of art has her spirit captured in this collection of paintings, sketches and writings.

Raven's Cry by Christie Harris
Until his death in 1998, Bill Reid was the greatest living Haida artist; his illustrations for this book about how contact changed the Haidas forever are remarkable.

Environment

THE LAND

British Columbia is Canada's most westerly province and, after Quebec and Ontario, the third-largest. Its 948,596 sq km make up about 9.5% of Canada's surface area. The Yukon adds another 483,450 sq km, which means the two combined account for over 14% of Canada. BC is bordered to the north by the Yukon and the Northwest Territories; to the east by Alberta; to the south by the three US states of Montana, Idaho and Washington; to the northwest by Alaska; and to the west by the Pacific Ocean. The Yukon's major borders are with Alaska to the west, BC to the south and Northwest Territories (NWT) to the east. The Arctic Ocean washes against the Yukon's narrow tip.

British Columbia: A Natural History by Sydney Cannings and Richard Cannings Offers a comprehensive look at the province's physical and natural environments, along with analyses of global warming, forestry practices and other environmental issues.

With its many inlets, BC's West Coast is more than 7000km long; alongside it are hundreds of islands ranging from large (Vancouver Island, the Queen Charlotte Islands) to tiny.

The bulk of BC lies within the Canadian Cordillera, a system of mountain ranges running roughly northwest to southeast. Within the cordillera are several major ranges – the Rocky Mountains to the east; the Cassiar Mountains in the north (including the Stikine, Kechia, Finlay and Ominica ranges); and the Columbia Mountains in the south (which include the Selkirk, Purcell, Monashee and Cariboo Ranges). The glaciated Coast Mountains loom over the Pacific almost to the water's edge from Vancouver north to the Alaskan panhandle. The province's high point is Mt Fairweather (4663m), part of the St Elias Range on the BC–Alaska border. The low point, of course, is sea level.

The province has scores of freshwater lakes and fast-flowing rivers. The Fraser River is BC's longest, stretching from the Rocky Mountains to the Pacific Ocean near Vancouver. Roughly 60% of BC is covered by forest, mainly coniferous trees. There's a small desert in the southern interior near Osoyoos, while the lush Pacific coastal area has countless inlets and islands. The Peace River region in northeast BC is the only really flat area. More than 90% of BC's landmass is 'Crown Land', and is therefore owned by the provincial government.

This high percentage of government-controlled land is even more the case in the Yukon, where the federal government holds more than 95% of the territory, although there are broad controls. The Rocky Mountains finally peter out at the Yukon border and much of the territory is characterized by the broad Yukon Plateau, which is drained through the width of Alaska by the Yukon River. In the south are the famous glaciers of Kluane Park, while the north above Dawson City features great expanses of treeless tundra and rugged mountain ranges such as the Mackenzies.

Geology

An Ice Age starting about a million years ago was the primary force shaping the geology of BC and the Yukon. Huge ice sheets repeatedly scraped over the lofty mountain ranges, wearing them down to bedrock and creating great valleys between the peaks. This continued until about 7000 years ago, when the last ice melted, giving rise to the province's lakes and rivers (which remain fed by annual snowmelt today). Since then, glacial, wind and water erosion have continued to alter the landscape in more subtle ways.

Mineral wealth spurred Europeans to settle in BC from the mid-19th century. The Yukon's one major boom stemmed from the fabled Klondike gold rush of 1897–98. The mineral industry remains important today. Major mineral deposits include coal on the coastal islands and the eastern slopes of the Rocky Mountains; gold in the Coast Mountains and the Yukon River and its tributaries; copper, lead, silver and zinc in the Kootenays; and natural-gas-containing sandstone and shale in the Peace River region. Jade is the official mineral of British Columbia and is widely used in jewelry and sculptures.

The Great Bear Rainforest: Canada's Forgotten Coast by Ian McAllister, Karen McAllister and Cameron Young A beautifully photographed, readable book that details grizzly bear ecology and forestry impacts along BC's north coast.

WILDLIFE

With all its geographical and climatic diversity, it's no surprise that BC has a wide range of plants and animals. There are 14 distinct ecological zones; nature flourishes everywhere, from the large urban parks of Vancouver and Victoria to the tops of the Rockies to tiny coastal tide pools. The Yukon shares many of these features and adds its vast expanse of Arctic territory.

The wildlife you see anywhere in the region is likely to be among the longest-lasting memories of your trip.

Animals

The Yukon and BC provide habitat for over 160 mammal species, 500 bird species, 500 fish species, 20 reptile species and 20 types of amphibians.

BEARS, OH MY

Bears are one of the top tourist draws to the north. Whether they be grizzly or black, these huge carnivores hold a definite attraction. However, you don't want it to be a fatal attraction, so here is some advice from Parks Canada for staying safe in bear country. Although some of it seems pretty basic, never underestimate a human's ability to behave like a dork.

- On foot, travel in groups
- Watch for signs of bear
- Keep pets on leash
- Avoid large dead animals
- Never approach a bear (!)
- Keep food and smells away from bears; use bear-resistant food containers

If the above doesn't work and the bear attacks, do the following:

- Don't drop your pack, it can provide protection
- Try to walk backward slowly
- Don't run, the bear will always outrun you
- Try to get somewhere safe like a car
- If the attack is imminent, use bear spray and/or play dead, but note that bear spray is not always effective (nor is playing dead)
- If the attack occurs after the bear has stalked you or happens in your tent, fight back

Finally two points:

- Seek out advice on bears and bear sightings from local park staff
- Be wary of 'bear whistles' as a way to make noise; some may sound like a marmot – a tasty bear snack; 'bear bells' are a better choice

Sounding the Blood by Amanda Hale A gripping historical novel about the British Columbia whaling industry during WWI that weaves the lives of the whalers with that of the whales.

Never Cry Wolf by Farley Mowatt Autobiographical tale of Mowatt who was sent north as an inexperienced biologist to study wolves. Slowly he realized that the wolves had something on him in the brains department and are not just the carnivorous beasts he suspected. Also a first-rate 1983 film.

Birds of Coastal British Columbia: A Field Guide to Common Birds of the Pacific Northwest Coast Covers the islands as well as coastal mainland BC.

About 100 species (including most of the whales, the burrowing owl and Vancouver Island marmot) are on the province's endangered species list; another 100 or so are considered at risk. Ecosystems are at their most diverse in southern BC, but that's also where threats from human pressures are at their strongest.

BC has more mountain goats than anywhere else in North America; in fact, 60% of all the world's mountain goats live here. Bears are another prominent mammal, with an estimated 160,000 black bears in BC and the Yukon and an unknown but much smaller number of grizzlies. Kermode bears, sometimes called spirit bears, are whitish in color. Unique to BC, they're found from Bella Bella north up the coast to Stewart, mostly along the lower Skeena River Valley near Prince Rupert and Terrace. The truly white polar bear is found in the Arctic reaches of the Yukon.

Another unusual species, the Columbia black-tailed deer, is a small subspecies native to Vancouver Island and BC's West Coast. Other large mammals include bighorn sheep, mountain lions (also called cougars), Roosevelt elk, Dall and Stone sheep, mule deer, white-tailed deer, coyotes and wolves. Moose are icons of the north and the sight of one raising its moss-covered antlers out of a swamp in the morning is not soon forgotten. In the far north the enormous herds of caribou travel ceaselessly about the tundra grazing.

Whales are among the best-known and most beloved of BC's mammal species. About 20,000 Pacific gray whales migrate along BC's coast twice each year: southbound to Mexico from October through December and northbound to the Bering and Chukchi seas in February through May. Less numerous and even more striking are the black-and-white orca (killer whales). Some groups (called pods) of orca live permanently off the coast of southern Vancouver Island; others range more widely in waters to the north, but they reliably spend late summer near the Robson Bight Ecological Reserve in Johnstone Strait near Port McNeill on northern Vancouver Island. Other commonly sighted sea mammals include porpoises, dolphins, sea lions, seals and otters.

Salmon rank among the most important fish in BC. Sacred to many First Nations bands, and a mainstay of the province's fishing industry, salmon come in five species: Chinook (also called king), Coho, chum, sockeye and pink. Salmon life cycles are among the most amazing in the animal world. At adulthood, they leave the ocean to swim upriver to the same spawning grounds where they were born. Once there, they take their turns at reproducing, and then they die. (See the boxed text, p199.) Other fascinating BC sea creatures include the world's largest species of octopus, playful wolf eels and colorful starfish, easily seen clinging to rocks and dock pilings all along the coast.

Of the 500-plus bird species, the black-and-blue Steller's jay is among the most famous; it was named the province's official bird after a government-sponsored contest. Prominent birds of prey include bald eagles, golden eagles, great horned owls and peregrine falcons. A variety of seabirds and waterfowl nest on the shores of BC's coastal areas; others migrate through the province, including snow geese, trumpeter swans, endangered harlequin ducks, sandhill cranes, brant and sandpipers. Blue herons are abundant in riparian areas. Look for ravens everywhere, coolly calculating their next endeavor to get a meal.

Plants

British Columbia has always been a lush place, with species varying widely depending on location, climate and human impact. The province's official symbol is the white flower of the Pacific dogwood, a tree known for springtime blossoms and red berries in autumn. BC's summertime wildflower displays are among the best in North America, with showy blooms of every hue scattered along trails and roadways. But BC is probably best known for its trees, which rank among the world's tallest and most majestic.

Western red cedar, Sitka spruce, hemlock and Douglas fir are prevalent trees in the moist coastal regions. Red cedar, the official provincial tree, was of special importance to indigenous coastal peoples, who used it to make everything from canoes and clothing to totem poles and medicines. The tallest tree in Canada, a Sitka spruce known as the Carmanah Giant, stands at 95m in the Carmanah Valley of western Vancouver Island. As evidence of the verdant growing conditions, this tree is less than 300 years old.

Coastal BC is well known for the arbutus (are-*byoo*-tus) tree, a distinctive species with twisted branches, reddish peeling bark and shiny dark green leaves. The only broad-leafed evergreen tree in Canada, it's similar to the madrona trees found elsewhere in North America. Southern Vancouver Island and the Gulf Islands are also home to Garry oak, though unfortunately, many of these once-prolific, low-growing trees have been wiped out by human development.

Ponderosa pine, Englemann and white spruce, Douglas fir, sub-alpine fir, birch, aspen, cottonwood and larch trees are among the species growing along the river valleys and mountains of the interior from Dawson City in the Yukon south. Closer to the Continental Divide, along the slopes of the Columbia and Rocky Mountains, rainforest species such as hemlock and red cedar once again predominate. Northern landscapes are characterized by such scrappy trees as white and black spruce, tamarack and the sub-alpine fir.

The tundra of the north largely consists of small shrubs, grasses and lichens that eke out life during an annual growing season measured in weeks.

Throughout the region you will see a large variety of wild berries growing profusely, and in the forests expect to see a myriad of mushrooms.

NATIONAL PARKS

British Columbia and the Yukon contain a number of world-famous parks and Unesco World Heritage sites:

Canadian Rocky Mountain Parks The place where Canadian tourism began. Comprises 2.3 million hectares consisting of Banff (p264), Jasper (p279), Kootenay (p263) and Yoho (p260) National Parks, Mt Robson (p286) and Mt Assiniboine (p264) Provincial Parks in BC and Hamber Provincial Park in Alberta.

Kluane/Wrangell-St Elias/Glacier Bay/Tatshenshini-Alsek This area teams with glaciers and raw landscape over two countries. Kluane National Park (p350) is solidly in the Yukon abutting against Tatshenshini-Alsek Provincial Wilderness Park (p335) in BC, while Glacier Bay and Wrangell-St Elias National Parks are found in adjoining Alaska.

SGaang Gwaii This is the island home to the abandoned town of Ninstints in Gwaii Haanas National Park Reserve (p331) in the Queen Charlotte Islands. Here some of the greatest totem poles and other aspects of the Haida culture can be found.

Other significant national parks include Glacier and Mount Revelstoke on the BC side of the Rockies and the Pacific Rim National Park on Vancouver Island. The Gulf Islands National Park Reserve, protecting the Southern Gulf Islands, was created in 2003.

In the far north of the Yukon, Ivvavik and Vuntut National Parks are wild and remote places.

Field Guide to Old-Growth Forests: Explore the Ancient Forests of California, Oregon, Washington and British Columbia by Larry Eifert
A good hands-on guide to the magical forests.

DID YOU KNOW?

Fireweed is the floral emblem of the Yukon. Growing two meters or more in height, its brilliant pinkish red color looks like a blaze across hillsides during the summer. However, its name stems from its quick appearance after a fire. Throughout Northern BC and the Yukon look for fireweed in images, café names, soap and especially nice honey.

DID YOU KNOW?

Marijuana may be the biggest cash crop in BC. For obvious reasons official statistics are hard to come by, but estimates put the cash value of the crop at $4 billion. Laws for possession are relatively lax, although penalties remain severe for people caught growing crops of the stuff in the large indoor hothouses common on the Lower Mainland.

A National Parks of Canada **annual pass** (www.parkscanada.ca; adult/child $45/22) is an excellent investment if you are going to spend any time in the national parks. Passes can be purchased at the parks, and options for visiting historic sites can be included as well.

BC has several hundred **provincial parks** (wlapwww.gov.bc.ca/bcparks/). There are more than 8.2 million hectares of protected land, which accounts for almost 10% of British Columbia's land base. The province has a goal of protecting 12% in the next few years. There is no annual pass for BC Parks, as there is a maze of fees and many parks charge nothing at all to visit.

The Yukon only has four **territorial parks** (www.environmentyukon.gov.yk.ca), but much of the territory is park-like and government campgrounds can be found in many places.

www.wilderness committee.org Site run by the Western Canada Wilderness Committee is an excellent clearinghouse for environmental news and issues.

ENVIRONMENTAL ISSUES

British Columbia is a schizophrenic place when it comes to the environment. Most Lower Mainlanders see the province's vast, wild lands and coastal environments as places to protect and enjoy, while people living in geographically far-flung, resource-dependent regions tend to view the environment as their meal ticket. Then there are areas like Tofino on

MAKING WAVES

The modern Canadian environmental movement can be traced to a Vancouver living room, where a group of concerned people met in 1969 to discuss a one-megaton nuclear bomb dropped as easily and quietly as a raindrop on Amchitka, an ecologically diverse island near the tip of Alaska's Aleutians. It was the first bomb in a series of US atmospheric nuclear tests, which were scheduled to continue intermittently over the following few years.

The meeting marked the birth of the Don't Make a Wave Committee, which came up with a plan to sail north and disrupt US atomic activity before the next bomb fell on Amchitka. Bad weather thwarted their efforts, but the group pressed on, soon taking the name Greenpeace and continuing to raise public awareness. The strategy worked. By 1972, all atomic testing on Amchitka ceased.

In the three decades since, Greenpeace has remained a leader in the international environmental movement. From confronting Russian whalers to convincing the *New York Times* to cancel all contracts with logging giant MacMillan Bloedel, Greenpeace has combined creative protest with dedication to attract high-profile media and focus public attention on environmental issues surrounding hydroelectric industries, forestry, commercial fishing and nuclear and chemical testing.

Greenpeace opponents have argued that the organization's renegade environmentalism and impromptu confrontations cause more harm than good. Like a pesky mosquito that just won't go away, Greenpeace has emitted an incessant, irritating buzz in the ear of many corporations, creating sleepless nights and public relations nightmares.

However annoying and aggressive, the buzz has made a difference: by forcing companies to wake up to global environmental problems and potential catastrophes, Greenpeace's eco-warfare has raised the standard for corporate accountability, or at least brought environmental concerns out of the cold and into the boardroom. Greenpeace's success has inspired a generation of activists.

In 1979, national Greenpeace organizations in Australia, Canada, France, the Netherlands, New Zealand, the UK and the US formed Greenpeace International, now headquartered in Amsterdam. There are organizations in more than 30 countries worldwide.

From its humble beginning in a Vancouver home, Greenpeace has gone on to protect rainforests, whales and drinking water, among many other things. As for Amchitka, the island is now a flourishing bird sanctuary.

Vancouver Island's West Coast, where a sometimes uneasy truce holds between people employed by extractive industries and those sworn to defend the planet from plunder.

In any case, BC has a long history of environmental activism, and even casual visitors are likely to encounter debates and perhaps protests over such issues as forestry practices and large-scale fish farming. Key groups include the following:

Friends of Clayoquot Sound (www.focs.ca) A Tofino-based group interested in the Sound and beyond.

Greenpeace (www.greenpeace.org) Founded in Vancouver more than 30 years ago (see the boxed text, p34).

Raincoast Conservation Society (www.raincoast.org) Spearheaded recognition of the Great Bear Rainforest on BC's central coast as the largest contiguous tract of coastal temperate rainforest left on Earth.

Valhalla Wilderness Society (www.savespiritbear.org) New Denver-based group whose efforts to protect wildlife habitat have moved far beyond its Kootenays base.

Western Canada Wilderness Committee (www.wildernesscommittee.org) A good omnibus group.

www.davidsuzuki.org The site for the foundation of the famed Canadian naturalist teams with information about Western Canada's environments and the threats to same.

Environmental debate is an ongoing and major part of the province's political focus. Besides the inevitable battle between those who wish to profit from natural resources and those that wish to save them, BC also has urgent environmental threats from forest fires brought on by climate change, infestations of beetles that are killing forests and new practices such as fish-farming that could pose grave environmental risks.

Spruce beetles and their relationship to global warming are at the heart of Yukon environmental debate, given that whole forests have been wiped out (p351). Another major issue involves placer mining, which is the extraction of gold and other valuable minerals that are near the surface. New regulations are designed to reduce some of the environmental effects of the mining, while the largely family-run industry claims it will hurt scores of small mining operations.

British Columbia Outdoors

When it comes to outdoor adventure, BC is hard to beat. There are few, if any, recreational activities that BC doesn't offer in one locale or another, usually in some of the loveliest surroundings you'll ever see. You'll find all the obvious pursuits here, including some of the planet's best hiking, skiing, canoeing and sea kayaking.

Listed below are a few of the best places to pursue each activity in BC. Turn to the appropriate regional chapters for lots more information. Contact the local Visitor Info Centre (VIC) for any area you are interested in visiting as the offices will have comprehensive details on tour operators, guides, conditions, equipment rental and more.

In the Yukon, canoeing and kayaking the rivers is justifiably popular. Hiking the Kluane region is also a major draw for visitors. For full details on activities in the Yukon, see p339.

EXPLORING BC'S POWDERY BLISS

Cypress Bowl Ski Area

Close to Vancouver, the wide, snow-filled Cypress Bowl sits in the heart of Cypress Provincial Park between Strachan and Black Mountains. Popular with intermediate downhill skiers, the mountain features 36 runs and 19km of groomed cross-country runs as well as a snowboard park. In the evening, the lights come on for great night skiing and excellent views of Howe Sound.

- Nearest town: West Vancouver (p95)
- One-day lift ticket: $42
- Information: ☎ 604-926-5612, 604-419-7669
- www.cypressbowl.com

Mt Seymour

This North Shore mountain is a haven for snowboarders, who come to rip it up in Seymour's three snowboard parks – Brockton, Mystery Peak and Mushroom Junior Park. Beginner skiers and boarders find Seymour a good place to learn, and the excellent ski/board school offers good deals on lessons, including equipment. Families are catered for with toboggan and inner-tube runs.

- Nearest town: North Vancouver (p92)
- One-day lift ticket: $34
- Information: ☎ 604-986-2261
- www.mountseymour.com

Grouse Mountain Resort

A short drive or bus ride from Vancouver, Grouse Mountain is a favorite for its easy access and night skiing (13 runs). An aerial tram whisks you to the mountaintop, offering incredible views along the way. Mogul dancers head to The Peak, or explore the mountain's backside on Blueberry or Purgatory. Anyone can enjoy the views skiing or boarding down The Cut, which is visible from all over Vancouver. The drop is 384m and there are 25 daytime runs.

- Nearest town: North Vancouver (p92)
- One-day lift ticket: $42
- Information: ☎ 604-984-0661
- www.grousemountain.com

Sun Peaks Resort

When there's no snow on Vancouver's mountains, head four hours northeast to Sun Peaks, where early snow falls on Tod Mountain. The resort boasts 117 runs, 10 lifts, a snowboard park and 881m of vertical rise. BC Olympian Nancy Greene is director of skiing. More than 70% of the runs are novice or intermediate, making the resort more family-oriented.

- Nearest town: Kamloops (p194)
- One-day lift ticket: $55
- Information: ☎ 250-578-5474, 800-807-3257
- www.sunpeakresort.com

SKIING

BC's mountains, which range from rugged alpine peaks to gradual valleys and gullies, combine with almost guaranteed snowfall to make the province ideal for winter sports. Backcountry touring and heli-skiing get you deep into unexplored territory, but most people head to the many resorts. Whether you're a seasoned skier, veteran snowboard rider or an utter novice standing in snow for the first time there are options galore.

With the Winter Olympics coming to Whistler in 2010, expect skiing in British Columbia to become even more fashionable than it is now. Prices will rise and crowds will grow. Happily – especially towards the Rockies – BC has relatively uncrowded resorts waiting to pick up the slack. The eastern resorts also feature weather that is sunnier more often than near the coast.

If you're interested in snowshoeing, you can generally snowshoe anywhere you can cross-country ski. It's an easy sport to learn, too, with guided treks and rentals widely available.

Big White Ski Resort

Known for its incredible powder, Big White is one of BC's best ski resorts. Its popularity grows every year. The highest ski resort in the province features 840 hectares of runs, which are covered in the noted deep dry powder for excellent downhill and backcountry skiing, and deep gullies that make for excellent snowboarding. The drop is 777m. There is also night skiing.

- Nearest town: Kelowna (p214)
- One-day lift ticket: $56
- Information: ☎ 250-765-8888, 800-663-2772
- www.bigwhite.com

Silver Star Mountain Resort

A recreated Klondike boomtown, Silver Star attracts every level of skier and snowboarder from late October to early April. The mountain's sunny south face, Vance Creek, features predominantly novice and intermediate runs, while Putnam Creek, the north face, mainly offers black-diamond runs boasting moguls, trees and powder. The vertical drop is 760m and there are 11 lifts. The powder is vaunted by locals in the know. A special machine carves wicked halfpipes for snowboarders. Cross-country skiers can enjoy 37km of groomed trails.

- Nearest town: Vernon (p222)
- One-day lift ticket: $56
- Information: ☎ 250-542-0224, 800-663-4431
- www.silverstarmtn.com

Whistler-Blackcomb

This world-famous, dual-mountain paradise can accommodate up to 59,000 skiers and snowboarders an hour on its 33 lifts. Among other stats, its drop is 1609 vertical meters and there are 29 sq km of bowls, glades and steeps. Separated by the steep Fitzsimmons Creek Valley, Whistler and Blackcomb are two distinct mountains, but the high-speed lift system allows you access to both. Four snowboard parks, more than 200 runs and university-caliber ski schools offer boundless options for all levels.

- Nearest town: Whistler (p105)
- One-day lift ticket: $68
- Information: ☎ 604-932-3434, 800-766-0449
- www.whistler-blackcomb.com

Fernie Alpine Resort

Vast investment dollars transformed Fernie from a well-kept local secret to a fast-growing resort that could be BC's next Whistler. Surrounded by spectacular alpine peaks, the mountain features 107 runs, five bowls and almost endless dumps of powder that draw droves of skiers and snowboarders looking for unspoiled terrain. Fully 30% of the runs are rated expert.

- Nearest town: Fernie (p249)
- One-day lift ticket: $58
- Information: ☎ 250-423-4655, 877-333-2339
- www.skifernie.com

(Continued on page 40)

SKIING

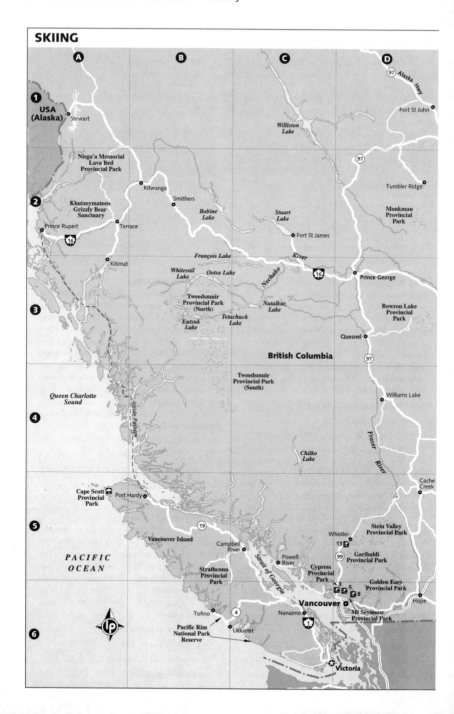

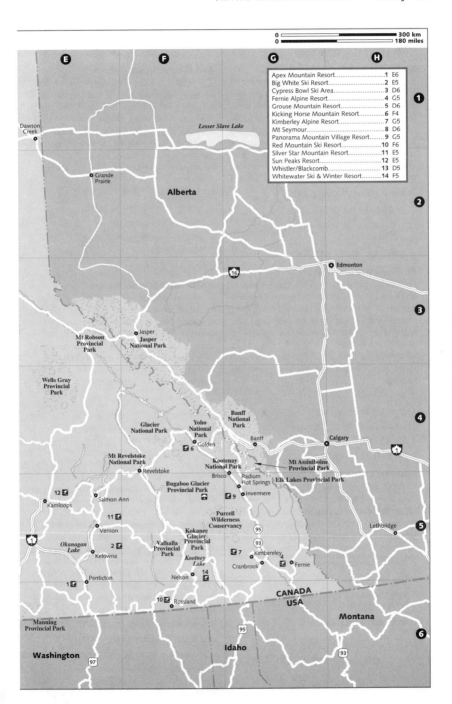

Apex Mountain Resort...........................1 E6
Big White Ski Resort............................2 E5
Cypress Bowl Ski Area.........................3 D6
Fernie Alpine Resort............................4 G5
Grouse Mountain Resort.......................5 D6
Kicking Horse Mountain Resort............6 F4
Kimberley Alpine Resort.......................7 G5
Mt Seymour...8 D6
Panorama Mountain Village Resort.......9 G5
Red Mountain Ski Resort....................10 F6
Silver Star Mountain Resort................11 E5
Sun Peaks Resort................................12 E5
Whistler/Blackcomb............................13 D5
Whitewater Ski & Winter Resort..........14 F5

(Continued from page 37)

Kicking Horse Mountain Resort

Big plans are underway for Golden's Whitetooth Mountain. This newish resort boasts a gondola and three lifts; a lodge near the gondola is set to open in 2004. A challenging 60% of its 96 runs are rated advanced or expert. With 1260 vertical meters and a relatively snow-heavy, wind-free position between the Rockies and Purcells, the resort is a future contender in the race for ski-resort tourist dollars.

- Nearest town: Golden (p255)
- One-day lift ticket: $53
- Information: ☎ 250-439-5400, 866-754-5425
- www.kickinghorseresort.com

Kimberley Alpine Resort

Millions of dollars have been spent building up this resort. The results show the effort and it boasts 728 hectares of skiable terrain, mild weather and 67 runs. There are 10 lifts and 45% of the runs are intermediate. A new high-speed quad lift serves the 8200m Main Run which has a 609m drop and which is fully lighted for night skiing. A snowboard park features an exciting half-pipe.

- Nearest town: Kimberley (p251)
- One-day lift ticket: $48
- Information: ☎ 250-427-4881, 877-754-5462
- www.skikimberley.com

Panorama Mountain Village Resort

A rather isolated resort 18km from the town of Invermere, built-up Panorama features a 1220m vertical drop, one of Canada's highest. The excellent ski school augments plenty of runs – over 100 – for all levels. Panorama is fast becoming a built-up and exclusive resort.

- Nearest town: Invermere (p254)
- One-day lift ticket: $59
- Information: ☎ 250-342-6941, 800-663-2929
- www.panoramaresort.com

Red Mountain Ski Resort

A breeding ground for Olympic skiers, 'Red' accesses two mountains – Red and Granite – and offers some of the province's best black-diamond runs. Many people come for a day and stay for a season, drawn by Rossland's low-key charm. Intermediate skiers and boarders will find lots to explore, but this is no place for novices, since the resort is known for its steep, tree-filled runs (83 at last count). There are five lifts and a drop of 880m.

- Nearest town: Rossland (p245)
- One-day lift ticket: $48
- Information: ☎ 250-362-7384, 800-663-0105
- www.ski-red.com

Whitewater Winter Resort

Filled with powdery charm, this small local mountain tends to attract skiers and boarders venturing into the backcountry. And in fact there are several local snowcat operators. The steep terrain boasts a 400m vertical drop, and snow seems to glue itself to sheer fingers such as Ymir Peak. It's known for its heavy powdery snowfall, which averages 10.5m per year.

- Nearest town: Nelson (p240)
- One-day lift ticket: $42
- Information: ☎ 250-354-4944, 800-666-9420
- www.skiwhitewater.com

Apex Mountain Resort

Apex features 67 downhill runs catering to all levels of ability, though the mountain is known for its plethora of double-black-diamond and technical runs (the drop is over 600m) as well as gladed chutes and vast powdery bowls. The crowds are smaller than at nearby Big White Mountain in Kelowna, and the high-speed quad chair hauls skiers and boarders up quickly, keeping the lines short. Close to the village you'll find 30km of accessible cross-country trails.

- Nearest town: Penticton (p207)
- One-day lift ticket: $48
- Information: ☎ 877-777-2739, 250-487-4848
- www.apexresort.com

SEA KAYAKING

If there is one activity you have to try in coastal BC, this is it. Sea kayaks are easy to paddle, amazingly stable and lots of fun. Unlike larger boats, kayaks can hug the shoreline, offering the perfect perch for watching shore birds and other marine life. Nearly every coastal and island town has at least one outfitter ready to take you on a guided trek lasting from a few hours (for about $50) to a week. These trips are by far the best way to learn the sport; once you know the ropes, you can rent or buy gear and go paddling on your own, though you'll always want to check local weather and traffic conditions.

You can kayak just about everywhere along BC's coast, but you'll find the greatest concentration of outfitters on Vancouver Island. For multi-day trips, the best-known destination is the Broken Group Islands, part of Pacific Rim National Park Reserve, on the west coast of Vancouver Island. If you don't have much time, you can always rent a kayak for a few hours or take an introductory lesson in nearly any coastal town. For more information, look up these towns in the Vancouver Island chapter: Victoria, Sooke, Port Renfrew, Nanaimo, Parksville, Qualicum Beach, Bamfield, Telegraph Cove, Port Hardy and Denman, Hornby and Quadra Islands.

In the Gulf Islands, you'll find outfitters and rental shops on each major island: Salt Spring, Galiano, Mayne and North Pender. Near Vancouver, try Bowen Island (p95). Further north, popular spots include Prince Rupert's Cow Bay (p318) and the legendary Gwaii Haanas National Park Reserve (p331) in the Queen Charlotte Islands.

Despite the name 'sea kayak', you can take one of these boats out on a lake too. For some prime paddling, try Lightning Lake at EC Manning Provincial Park (p191), east of Hope; Kootenay Lake, east of Nelson (p240); and Babine Lake (p313), north of Burns Lake.

It's always best to kayak with other people for safety. Someone in the group should know how to plot a course by navigational chart and compass, pilot in fog, read weather patterns, assess water hazards, interpret tide tables, handle boats in adverse conditions and perform group- and self-rescue techniques.

Campsites abound on BC's many islands, but more and more people are choosing 'mothership' sea kayaking over camping. The 'mothership', a larger boat, takes kayakers and their gear out to sea; the kayakers then spend their days paddling and nights bunked down in the big boat.

You might want to time your BC visit to coincide with the annual Vancouver Island **Paddlefest** (www.paddlefest.bc.ca), a major kayaking event held each June at Ladysmith.

'You can kayak just about everywhere along BC's coast'

DIVING

Justly famous for its superb diving conditions, BC features two of the top-ranked dive spots in the world: Vancouver Island and the Gulf Islands. It's best to go in winter, when the plankton has decreased and visibility often exceeds 20m. The water temperature drops to about 7°C to 10°C in winter; in summer, it reaches 15°C. At depths of more than 15m, though, visibility remains good throughout the year and temperatures rarely rise above 10°C. Expect to see a full range of marine life including oodles of crabs from tiny hermits to intimidating kings. If you're lucky you may also encounter mammals such as seals and sea lions.

The prime diving spots lie in Georgia Strait between Vancouver Island's east coast and the mainland. Dive shops abound in this region, and they are your best sources for air and gear as well as lessons, charters and tours (p131). The Queen Charlotte Islands (p324) also offer excellent diving but have no dive shops, so you have to bring everything, including air.

The province contains quite a few artificial reefs, created by the sinking of old ships to provide habitat for marine life. Artifical reefs include the *Chaudiere* at Sechelt on the Sunshine Coast; the *GB Church* and *Mackenzie* at Sidney; the *Columbia* at Campbell River; and the *Saskatchewan* and *Cape Breton* near Nanaimo. For more information on these and other sites, contact the Artificial Reef Society of British Columbia at the **Vancouver Maritime Museum** (☎ 604-220-8061; www.artificialreef.bc.ca).

Diver magazine covers scuba diving activities throughout Canada; read it online at www.divermag.com. **Aquatic Realm Illustrations** (☎ 604-980-5203, 877-384-3627; www.aquatic-realm.com), based in North Vancouver, creates maps to sites like Whytecliff Marine Park near Vancouver, the HMCS *Mackenzie* artificial reef and the Gabriola Passage near Nanaimo. For help in finding lessons, dive sites and resorts, visit the Professional Association of Diving Instructors' website (www.padi.com).

CANOEING

The 116km **Bowron Lake** canoe circuit in Bowron Lake Provincial Park (p295) is one of the world's great canoe trips, covering 10 lakes with easy portages between each. The lesser-known – but increasingly popular – 57km Powell Forest Canoe Route connects a dozen lakes on the upper reaches of BC's Sunshine Coast near Powell River (p118). Other good spots to paddle include Wells Gray Provincial Park (p291); Slocan Lake, just west of New Denver (p237) and Okanagan Lake, easily accessed from Kelowna (p214), Penticton (p207) or Vernon (p222). Ocean canoeing is possible around Vancouver, the Gulf Islands and the Queen Charlotte Islands.

'Rugged topography and an abundance of snow-melt make BC's rivers great for whitewater action'

WHITEWATER RAFTING

Rugged topography and an abundance of snowmelt make BC's rivers great for whitewater action. You don't need to be experienced to go out rafting. The provincial government regulates commercial rafting, and operators are allowed only on rivers that have been checked by experts. Guides must meet certain qualifications, and companies must provide equipment that meets government requirements. Trips can last from three hours up to a couple of weeks. Wilderness rafting averages about $200 per day for everything, while half-day trips start at about $50.

Wherever you are in BC, you're probably close to a good whitewater river. The Fraser, Thompson, Chilliwack and Nahatlatch Rivers all lie within day-trip distance of Vancouver, so they're the best bets for adding adventure to your city-based holiday. Many consider the Kicking Horse River (p255) to be one of the province's best raft trips. Visitors to Jasper National Park (p286) can book trips on the Sunwwapta and Athabasca Rivers. Other prime spots include the Clearwater River near Wells Gray Provincial Park (p291); the Adams River in the Shuswap region (p200); the Bulkley and Babine Rivers near Smithers (p315); and the remote Tatshenshini and Alsek Rivers in northern BC.

HIKING

BC is a hiker's paradise. Virtually every park has trails of lengths from simple to strenuous. If you want rugged and wet, you can hike in the Queen Charlotte Islands (p324) where you will have long storm-tossed beaches and vast stands of virgin spruce and cedar trees to yourself.

Lake O'Hara (p260) in Yoho National Park attracts hikers who reserve their spots months in advance. Its pretty Alpine setting and clear waters make it a memorable experience. But if you want to avoid crowds entirely, there are literally hundreds of other hikes in the Rockies.

The same can be said for the rest of BC as well. The eight-day West Coast Trail (p158) was originally constructed as an escape route for shipwreck survivors. Its 75km route features rock-face ladders, stream crossings and other challenges that may leave you thinking the shipwreck wasn't such a bad thing.

The Juan de Fuca Marine Trail (p144) is another good coastal hike which usually takes about four days. You can do day-trips as there are several access points.

The best approach to determining where to hike – unless you want to see what comes along in your travels – is through the following:

Alpine Club of Canada (www.alpineclubofcanada.ca) Great resources for serious hikers in the Rockies.

Don't Waste Your Time in the BC Coast Mountains (www.wildernesspress.com) This book and a companion volume covering the Rockies by Kathy and Craig Copeland win praise for their direct approach to rating hikes from excellent to not being worth the bother.

Trail Database (www.traildatabase.org/countries/canada.html) Contains a wealth of links to groups, organizations and individuals dedicated to hiking in western Canada.

YourAdventureZone (www.youradventurezone.com) A site and e-zine dedicated to hiking in BC and the Rockies.

SAILING & BOATING

The sheltered waters of BC's Pacific coast make sailing a popular form of recreation that's possible almost year-round, though it's best to take out a boat from mid-April to mid-October. Coastal marine parks provide safe, all-weather anchorage and offer boats for hire (powerboats as well as sailboats). Some of the great places to sail include the Strait of Georgia and the Gulf Islands. Inland, sailors tend to prefer Harrison Lake (p191); Okanagan and Skaha Lakes in the Okanagan Valley region; Arrow and Kootenay Lakes in the Kootenays; and Williston Lake (p307) north of Prince George.

Houseboating is another popular pastime on BC's biggest lakes, including Shuswap Lake (p198) north of the Okanagan and Powell Lake on the Sunshine Coast. It costs from $2000 a week, depending on location and time of year, to rent a self-contained boat that sleeps about 10 people.

SURFING

The Tofino area on Vancouver Island's west coast is ground zero for BC's best surfing. Weather conditions may be far from ideal – buckets of rain and chilly temperatures – but the waves are awesome, rolling directly off the North Pacific. Be sure to wear a wetsuit. See p160 for details on renting gear and taking lessons. Check out www.coastalbc.com for lots of information on surf sports and other outdoor activities.

FISHING

Fishing, both the saltwater and freshwater variety, is one of BC's major tourist attractions. Saltwater anglers particularly like to cast their nets and lines in the waters around Vancouver Island, where several places (Campbell River chief among them) claim the title 'salmon capital of the world', as well as at Prince Rupert, known for its halibut, and in the Queen Charlotte Islands. You'll find good river and lake fishing in every region. Near Vancouver, anglers enjoy casting at Steveston, where the Fraser River meets the ocean, and even right off the Stanley Park seawall. For some particularly good lake fishing further inland, try Birkenhead

'You'll find good river and lake fishing in every region'

Lake Provincial Park (p113) and Golden Ears Provincial Park (p98). The East Kootenays see some outstanding fly-fishing, especially on creek-size tributaries of the Columbia, Kicking Horse and Kootenay Rivers along and near Hwy 95.

The best destination of all may be northern BC, where hundreds of lakes – many reachable only by boat or plane – give anglers endless options. For good river fishing up north, head to the Fraser, Nass, Skeena, Kettle, Peace and Liard Rivers.

You must obtain separate licenses for saltwater/tidal fishing and freshwater fishing. The provincial **Ministry of Water, Land and Air Protection** (wlapwww.gov.bc.ca/fw/fish/recreational.html) controls freshwater licenses. Annual licenses cost $36 for BC residents, $55 for other Canadians and $80 for nonresidents. Eight-day licenses cost $20/36/50; one-day licenses cost $10/20/20. On top of this, you may need to buy a conservation surcharge stamp for some locations or species.

The federal **Department of Fisheries & Oceans** (www.pac.dfo-mpo.gc.ca/recfish /default_e.htm) issues licenses for saltwater/tidal fishing. An annual license costs $22.47/108.07 for Canadian residents/nonresidents. For five days, you'll pay $17.12/34.17; for three days, $11.17/20.33; and one day $5.62/ 7.49. An annual salmon conservation stamp costs $6.42.

Local sporting goods stores are good sources of licenses and help in navigating the thicket of regulations.

'There is world-class climbing around Banff in the Rockies'

CYCLING & MOUNTAIN BIKING

Mountain biking is huge in BC, and road cycling is popular, too. Home to some of BC's best technical trails, Rossland (p246) is often considered to be the mountain-biking capital of BC (and possibly Canada). Whistler (p108) also attracts lots of fat-tire riders, while Squamish (p104) to the south offers some good rides, too. Check out the Whistler Interpretive Forest (p105), just south of town, and the Four Lakes Trail at Alice Lake Provincial Park (p103)near Squamish.

Your best sources of information include local bike shops which we list for important towns and VICs. The **British Columbia Mountain Bike Directory** (www.mtb.bc.ca) features over 370 trail reports, message boards, bike-shop and bike-club links and a lot more. Another good source of information is **Cycling BC** (☎ 604-737-3034; www.cycling.bc.ca), BC's governing body for mountain-bike racing, road racing and track racing, Cycling BC also offers plenty of resources for recreational and touring cyclists.

ROCK CLIMBING & MOUNTAINEERING

BC is full of great venues for rock climbing and mountaineering. Squamish (p103) is home to the Stawamus Chief, a world-class granite monolith with about 200 climbing routes. But other climbers swear by the better weather at the compact gneiss rock of Skaha Bluffs near Penticton (p209), which boast a long climbing season on more than 400 bolted routes. There's world-class climbing around Banff in the Rockies (p271).

HORSEBACK RIDING

If you're a big fan of horseback riding, head to BC's Cariboo country, where dude ranches offer a range of activities from trail rides to cattle drives (see the boxed text, p292). You can also saddle up in Banff (p271) and Jasper (p279) National Parks; at Whistler and Pemberton on the Sea to Sky Hwy; on Salt Spring and Galiano Islands in the Southern Gulf Islands; and at Mt Washington, near Comox and Courtenay on Vancouver Island.

Food & Drink

British Columbia is a glorious place to eat. The province's fortuitous location, with sea bounty on the coast and long growing seasons on the islands and southern interior, means a constant supply of fresh, delicious food. That said, there aren't many signature foods that are unique to BC. One of the few is the Nanaimo bar, a rich treat that has spawned many spin-offs across the province. But other favorite foods are popular throughout the Pacific Northwest: salmon and sushi, all kinds of berries, inventive pasta and Asian dishes and some of the best vegetables you'll ever taste.

The Yukon, with barely 30,000 people, doesn't really have a local market for cutting-edge cuisine. Rather, what's good is anything made with fresh ingredients – look for fish and local vegetables during the summer.

DID YOU KNOW?

It's not uncommon for halibut caught near QCI to measure over 2m in length and weigh over 120kg.

STAPLES & SPECIALTIES

If you like seafood you are going to do very well, especially close to the coast. Salmon in its many forms, halibut, crabs and mussels are just some of the treats. Generally speaking, the fresher it is the simpler you want it. Look for grilled seafood: if it's fresh it is hard to go wrong. Seasonal produce is also excellent. The real specialties are mushrooms – there's an entire industry of pickers who scour the wet forests daily – and berries in their many varieties. Fruit from southern BC is excellent, led by Okanagan Valley peaches, apples, cherries and more.

Somewhat more exotic is game, which you'll see on some menus but which is primarily prepared and served in homes by the people who have bagged it. If you have a chance to order venison or a caribou steak, be prepared for a real taste of the outdoors. Flavors can be intense.

The girls who dish: Inspirations by Karen Barnaby, Caren McSherry-Valagao and Lesly Stowe
Part of a series of cookbooks by a well-known group of Vancouver female chefs who know their local markets.

EATING OUT

The restaurants of Vancouver have taken the best of Asian and European cooking and fused it with the wealth of local ingredients. You can find almost any kind of ethnic or international cuisine. Indian, Greek, regional Chinese, Japanese and much more are good and widely available. Outside of Vancouver, the urban parts of Vancouver Island, the lower mainland and the Okanagan Valley all offer excellent and varied choices.

In more rural places and much of the North, including the Yukon, you can expect simpler and more predictable fare. However, don't fret; while the cook in the kitchen may not be due for their own TV show next season, they may very well be able to whip up a fine cheeseburger or an inspired plate of pasta.

Typical menus feature burgers, pasta, sandwiches, the ubiquitous Cesar salad and fish and chips. But read carefully and keep a sharp look-out for the daily special of grilled wild salmon. Many pubs feature good food as well, in fact, in most towns you can get a decent meal; we've listed many places in this book which rise above the norm. What you shouldn't settle for is one of the all-too-common places advertising its 'Chinese and Canadian food'. All this usually means is that you can get a fried cheeseburger to go with your gelatinous safety-orange-colored sweet and sour pork.

Out on the Queen Charlotte Islands, ask at the Visitor Info Centre (VIC) and look for the frequent First Nations' feasts where you can

The Copper Bay Cookbook: Recipes from the Queen Charlotte Islands by Maria Ernst
A veteran chef and owner of a remote hunting lodge on QCI, Ernst knows what to do with venison, apples, berries, salmon and other local foodstuffs. And she knows what to do when the power fails and you're serving crab to the US president.

enjoy a range of local foods including grilled salmon and delectable berry treats.

It's very easy to eat healthy in most of BC, except in the northern reaches, where fresh fruits and vegetables are hard to come by. You're never far from a vegetarian restaurant in the populous areas, and almost all restaurants have not one or two but a whole range of health-conscious choices. Be on the lookout for the many farmers' markets around the province. They're great places to get fresh, tasty produce straight from the growers. Even the smallest towns will usually have some sort of natural foods store where you can get locally grown produce.

EATING HABITS

You can easily get anything you want at almost any time you want in Vancouver. But be aware that outside of the metropolis, restaurants can shut down early, even in seemingly hip places like Nelson. Be at the restaurant by 8pm outside of peak summer weekends or you may be wolfing down a glazed special from a donut shop.

Breakfast is usually eaten between 6am and 9am. Many accommodations offer a continental breakfast of some sort during these hours; it might include anything from coffee and toast to yogurt, cereal and fruit. Most BC residents eat breakfast at home on weekdays or grab a quick bite on the run with their morning coffee. But on weekends, a much more leisurely breakfast or brunch is often enjoyed at a restaurant. Look for tasty thick pancakes and omelets made with local mushrooms.

The midday meal is typically taken between 11am and 1pm. It can be as simple as a snack bought from a farmers' market or food cart, or a picnic taken on your hike. Or it can be a leisurely affair at a fine restaurant.

Dinner is served anytime from about 5pm to 8pm, sometimes later on weekends and in larger cities and resort areas such as Banff. It's a good idea to make reservations for dinner in resort areas.

Restaurants are all nonsmoking by provincial law. Pubs and bars have the option of allowing smoking on a patio or in an enclosed smoking room.

Dress is casual compared to Eastern Canadian cities; you'll be fine no matter what you're wearing in most restaurants. For more formal places, a nice shirt or sweater (jumper) and pants or a skirt are appropriate. Few restaurants require men to wear a jacket and tie.

The food section wouldn't be complete without any mention of White Spot, BC's most prominent regional sit-down restaurant chain, with more than 50 locations. Started by Nat Bailey in 1928, White Spot specializes in hamburgers (with Bailey's secret 'Triple-O' sauce) and creamy thick milk shakes, though its menu has plenty of other reasonably priced choices for breakfast, lunch and dinner.

DRINKS

Canadians drink much like the rest of North America, for fun, pleasure or to celebrate. In rural areas (much of both BC and the Yukon) the local bar or saloon is the major social gathering place. That said, people are less likely to have a beer with lunch as the priority is to get something to eat and get back to work.

Coffee

BC wouldn't be part of the Pacific Northwest if you couldn't get a good coffee almost anywhere. There's a coffee shop on just about every block in commercial areas, and many drive-up kiosks in suburban zones. Most

Lumiere by Rob Feenie
A TV chef for cable's The Food Network, Feenie was born in BC and has worked with famous chefs around the world. At his restaurant (p84), for which the book is named, he uses international techniques on BC seafood and produce.

DID YOU KNOW?

Soapberries, from a native BC plant that grows like a weed and features in First Nations cooking, live up to their name when made into a sort of froth, but what's wilder is that they taste quite good.

www.ffcf.bc.ca
A website that's a link between BC's many small, family-run farms specializing in organic produce and the markets and restaurants in the city where you can buy the goods. Excellent lists of outlets and great information on sustainable farming.

towns will have at least one place – often more – that specializes in good coffee and is in fact the de facto meeting spot for locals who can exchange news and gossip while awaiting their java. Tea is widely available, too; many coffee shops stock exotic and herbal blends.

Wine

British Columbia is becoming increasingly known for its high-quality wines, most produced in the Okanagan. See the boxed text, p210 for more information. However good wine is also coming from other sunny parts of southern BC as well. The Lower Mainland and Vancouver Island are home to numerous wineries. Overall BC wine is gaining a solid reputation for quality and value.

Beer

There are a number of good small brewers around BC that produce a variety of beers, including ales, bitters, lagers, pilsners, bocks, porters, stouts, fruit beer and even hemp ales. Names to look for, either in pubs or in cold beer stores, include Bear Brewing Co (Kamloops), Okanagan Spring Brewery (Vernon), Whistler Brewing Co (Whistler), Tin Whistle Brewing Co (Penticton), the Nelson Brewing Co (Nelson) and Pacific Coast Brewing (Prince George).

It's not a microbrew, but Kokanee is the closest thing BC has to an official provincial beer, and it's pretty good. It's made in Creston by the Columbia Brewing Co. The excellent beers by Whitehorse's Yukon Brewing are found throughout the territory.

Columbia Wine Country by John Schreiner and Kevin Miller A photographic journey through BC's wine areas from the Okanagan Valley to Vancouver Island. There are good profiles of the winemakers.

Alcohol Legalities

The legal drinking age in BC and the Yukon is 19, and the legal blood-alcohol limit is 0.08%, or the equivalent of two drinks for an 'average-sized' person. British Columbia is very serious about curbing drunk driving, and you may encounter a mandatory roadside checkpoint, especially on summer evenings or around winter holidays. At a checkpoint, an officer will ask whether you've had anything to drink. Answer honestly. Most times you just drive through and they say, 'have a good night'. But if the officer smells booze on your breath, or if you look suspicious, drunk or stoned, you will be told to pull over. You will either do a coordination test, and/or take a breathalyzer, which immediately determines your blood-alcohol level.

British Columbia has eased its liquor regulations over the past few decades, but some unusual laws remain on the books. One is the 'intent-to-eat' law. In any establishment with a 'restaurant license' you must order food if you're going to drink alcohol. Places with a 'liquor license' (pubs and the like) allow you to drink without ordering food. Liquor licenses are expensive, hard to come by and heavily regulated, which is why most restaurants don't have them.

The provincial government operates BC Liquor Stores, where you can buy beer, wine and spirits. If you want cold beverages in BC, head to the nearest 'cold beer and wine store' – often found attached to pubs, restaurants or hotels. In the Yukon, you must make all your purchases from government liquor stores.

Vancouver & Around

Vancouver is unlike any other city in the world. It really had no say in the matter – a simple case of geography would show that any city sandwiched between ocean and mountain is destined for greatness. Take the tall buildings and trend-setters away from this town and you'd still have people flocking here.

It's not something you can really understand unless you've seen it in person. Everything is here, and it's all so naturally beautiful. George Vancouver must have seen it when he arrived in 1792, and the Salish Indians definitely saw it for the centuries they lived here or they wouldn't have stayed so long.

The fact that the city has been able to remain so beautiful and unspoiled is a testament to the people who've taken up residence here. Vancouver and its people don't flaunt or show off what they have. Everything is simply shown the way it is, and the place sells itself. It dresses itself up a little with cafés, shops, restaurants and a vibrant social scene, but fortunately it didn't end up a major port overrun by the urban advance of the last century-and-a-half. Instead, Vancouver's growth has been gradual and sensitive of its surroundings, trying to find a balance between convenience, comfort and rugged beauty.

Vancouver has graciously accepted its destiny and is, in a word, matchless.

HIGHLIGHTS

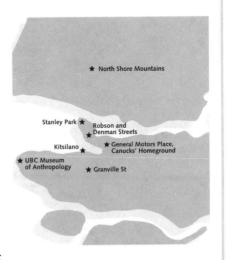

- Taking in the ocean, the mountains and the city while sitting on the shores of **Kitsilano** (p67)

- Shouting 'Go Canucks Go!' in a crowd of 18,000 at a **hockey game** (p88)

- Heading out to the **Granville St clubs** (p86)

- Hitting the slopes on the local mountains for some **skiing** (p93)

- Appreciating nature within city limits in **Stanley Park** (p61)

- Shopping for touristy trinkets or high fashion on **Robson Street** (p89)

- Enjoying a meal of any cuisine on **Denman Street** (p81)

- Drinking micro-brews on a macro scale at a **Brewpub** (p86)

- Marveling at First Nations art in the **UBC Museum of Anthropology** (p69)

- Being in Vancouver

★ North Shore Mountains

Stanley Park ★ ★ Robson and Denman Streets

Kitsilano ★ ★ General Motors Place, Canucks' Homeground

★ UBC Museum of Anthropology ★ Granville St

To Squamish (25km);
Whistler (90km);
Pemberton (120km);

Porteau Cove
Provincial Park

*Gambier
Island*

*Howe
Sound*

99

**Lions
Bay**

*Bowyer
Island*

Ferry to Langdale & Sunshine Coast

*Keats
Island*

*Horseshoe
Bay*

*Bowen
Island*

**Horseshoe
Bay**

99

Mt Seymour
Provincial
Park

Black
Mountain
(1220m)

Cypress
Provincial
Park

*Capilano
Lake*

Grouse Mtn
(1221m)

Lynn Headwaters
Regional
Park

Mt Seymour
Provincial
Recreation Area

**West
Vancouver**

Lynn Creek

Seymour River

Indian

Upper Levels Hwy

1

Marine Dr

1A

Lighthouse
Park

Pt Atkinson

Burrard Inlet

1A

**North
Vancouver**

Lynn Canyon
Park

Belcarra

Stanley Park

1A

Burrard Inlet

Ferry to Nainamo

*English
Bay*

Hastings St

7A

Barnet Hwy

Point Grey

E Broadway

7

Rupert St

1

Burnaby

Lougheed Hwy

99

Kingsway

99A

1A

Trans-Canada Hwy

10th Ave

**New
Westminster**

Granville St

*S t r a i t
o f
G e o r g i a*

*Iona
Island*

*Sea
Island*

Vancouver
International
Airport

*North Arm
Fraser River*

91

Richmond Fwy

Richmond

Westminster

*Annacis
Island*

Fraser River

Burns Bog

91

Steveston

Steveston Hwy

South Arm Fraser River

**North
Delta**

Reifel Migratory
Bird Sanctuary

99

Ladner Trunk Rd

10

*Westham
Island*

17

Delta

Ladner

28th Ave

Ferry to Nainamo

*Boundary
Bay*

Splashdown
Waterpark

56th St

**Boundary
Bay Park**

*Boundary
Bay Park*

Tsawwassen

Centennial
Beach Park

Ferry to Victoria
& Gulf Islands

Point Roberts
Border Crossing

Point Roberts

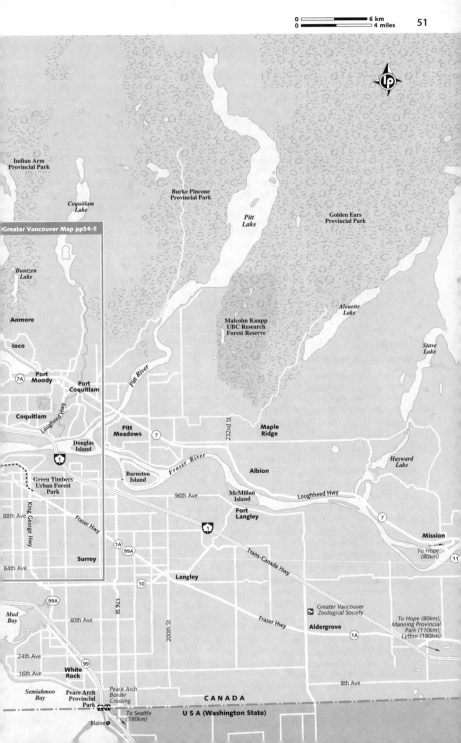

0   6 km
0   4 miles

Indian Arm
Provincial Park

*Coquitlam
Lake*

Burke Pincone
Provincial Park

*Pitt
Lake*

Golden Ears
Provincial Park

Greater Vancouver Map pp54-5

*Buntzen
Lake*

*Alouette
Lake*

Anmore

Malcolm Knapp
UBC Research
Forest Reserve

*Stave
Lake*

Ioco

(7A) **Port
Moody**

**Port
Coquitlam**

Pitt River

Coquitlam

Loughheed Hwy

**Pitt
Meadows**

(7)

**Maple
Ridge**

232nd St

*Hayward
Lake*

**Douglas
Island**

(1)

Fraser River

Albion

Loughheed Hwy

(7)

Green Timbers
Urban Forest
Park

**Barnston
Island**

96th Ave

**McMillan
Island**

**Fort
Langley**

Mission

88th Ave

Fraser Hwy

(1)

*To Hope
(80km)*

(11)

King George Hwy

Trans-Canada Hwy

64th Ave

(1A)
(99A)

Surrey

Langley

(10)

176 St

200th St

*Greater Vancouver
Zoological Society*

*To Hope (80km);
Manning Provincial
Park (110km);
Lytton (180km)*

*Mud
Bay*

(99A)

40th Ave

Fraser Hwy

Aldergrove

(1A)

24th Ave

16th Ave

**White
Rock**

(99)

*Peace Arch
Border
Crossing*

8th Ave

*Semiahmoo
Bay*

Peace Arch
Provincial Park

CANADA

*To Seattle
(180km)*

Blaine

U S A (Washington State)

VANCOUVER

ORIENTATION

Greater Vancouver is a series of peninsulas, islands, deltas, rivers and inlets. It's part of the 'Cool Cities Surrounded by Water on Three Sides Club' (like San Francisco and New York), bounded by Burrard Inlet on the north, Boundary Bay to the south, Georgia Strait to the west, and for good measure it's bisected east–west by the Fraser River. The North Shore Mountains rise up from the northern shore of Burrard Inlet; residential developments climb their slopes. With all that water in the way to the west, the only way for urban sprawl to grow has been east up the Fraser Valley.

Downtown Vancouver lies just 40km northwest of the Canada–US border, where Washington State's I-5 continues as BC's Hwy 99 and enters the city as Oak St. But Oak doesn't lead downtown; you have to divert west to Granville or Burrard Sts or east to Cambie St, and follow the 'City Centre' signs across their bridges. The Trans-Canada Hwy (Hwy 1) makes an eastern bypass of the city, where Hastings St connects it with downtown.

Downtown is one of those aforementioned peninsulas; False Creek to the south, English Bay to the west and Burrard Inlet to the north. Stanley Park occupies the northwestern tip and the intersection of Robson and Burrard Sts pretty much marks the center. Downtown streets run on diagonals (northwest–southeast and southwest–northeast); Robson and Georgia Sts are the two main northwest-southeast arteries and Burrard, Howe and Seymour Sts are the southwest–northeast routes. Only Georgia St continues through Stanley Park, as Stanley Park Causeway, to the Lions Gate Bridge.

Going out of town, Hwy 99 runs north over the Lions Gate Bridge to West Vancouver and North Vancouver in the North Shore – upper middle-class residential areas – and the Trans-Canada Hwy (Hwy 1). Further northwest along Hwy 1 you'll reach Horseshoe Bay and its BC ferries terminal, with sailings to Bowen Island, the Sunshine Coast and Vancouver Island. North of Horseshoe Bay Hwy 99 runs as the Sea to Sky Hwy to Whistler.

Put everything together and you have 2930 sq km covered by 22 communities known as the Lower Mainland.

Maps

Lonely Planet produces a good, laminated gatefold map for Vancouver. Tourism Vancouver distributes a nifty free map with a detailed downtown section on one side and a good metropolitan overview on the other. **International Travel Maps & Books** (Map p66; ☎ 604-879-3621; 345 W Broadway) not only sells guidebooks and maps, they also produce some good maps of their own for Vancouver and other parts of the world; check out their new store **downtown** (Map pp58-9; ☎ 687-3320; 539 West Pender).

INFORMATION
Bookstores

Duthie Books (Map p68; ☎ 604-732-5344; 2239 W 4th Ave) Vancouver's classic independent bookstore .

Banyen Books & Sound (Map p68; ☎ 604-732-7912;

SPANNING THE DECADES

The **Lions Gate Bridge** is as much a landmark as any in Vancouver. The Guinness family built the 842m span so people could drive to their 'British Properties' on the north shore. It rises 60m above the First Narrows and was named for the twin mountain peaks north of Vancouver. It opened in 1938 as the longest suspension bridge in the British Empire. Some 5600 vehicles drove across that first day.

It originally had a toll, but has been a freebie for decades; Vancouverites would be in an uproar to have to pay to use an out-of-date bridge. It only has three lanes, with two lanes supposedly traveling in the direction of highest volume. There were discussions on expanding the deck or building a new bridge or tunnel to ease the traffic burdens downtown, but several years and millions of dollars later, it's the same bridge with a new surface.

It's a good-looking bridge from afar (especially since the lights were added in 1986), and views from its crest are excellent, but you'll likely be singing a different tune if you're in the single lane going against the flow, which Murphy's Law dictates will be every time you cross it.

VANCOUVER IN TWO DAYS

Begin your day with a cinnamon bun and coffee, or bagel and tea, from **Hillary's** (p80) on the beach at **English Bay** (p57). Walk around, or through, **Stanley Park** (p61) to the concrete and glass neighborhood of Coal Harbour. From there, head south down **Denman St** (p57), stopping at any of the locally owned international restaurants for lunch. Spend an hour or two wandering aimlessly through the **West End** (p57) soaking up Vancouver's feel, but make it back to Davie St for sushi at **Kisha Poppo's** (p81), or Greek at **Stepho's** (p81). After dinner walk south to Sunset Beach to watch...the sunset; then head down Hamilton St in **Yaletown** (p80) for some martinis and serious lounge inactivity.

Start day two in a coffeehouse on Robson St and spend the morning **shopping** (p89), or watching shoppers, before lunch on the same street. Visit the **Art Gallery** (p60) and stroll through the **Provincial Law Courts** (p60) before heading south to walk around the promenade at **Canada Place** (p60), admiring the views. Go east to the cobblestone streets of **Gastown** (p82) for dinner, and stay for some latenight drinks. If there isn't much of a scene that night, try Vancouver's clubbing strip of **Granville St** (p87).

2671 W Broadway) New Age and metaphysical books and music.

Blackberry Books (Map p66; ☎ 604-685-6188; 1663 Duranleau St) Good independent shop.

Book Warehouse (Map p68; ☎ 604-872-5711; 632 W Broadway) Lots of bargain-priced books.

Chapters (Map pp58-9; ☎ 604-682-4066; 788 Robson St)

Granville Book Company (Map pp58-9; ☎ 604-687-2213; 850 Granville St) Fiction, sci-fi and computer books.

MacLeod's Books (Map pp58-9; ☎ 604-681-7654; 455 W Pender St) Stacks and stacks of books look chaotic; if you know what you want and they have it, they'll find it.

Magpie Magazine Gallery (Map pp64-5; ☎ 604-253-6666; 1319 Commercial Dr) One of the best newsstands in town.

Tanglewood Books (Map p66; ☎ 604-736-8876; 1553 W Broadway) Good used books and knowledgeable staff.

The Travel Bug (Map p68; ☎ 604-737-1122; 2667 W Broadway) Good bet for language tapes and travel accessories.

Wanderlust (Map p68; ☎ 604-739-2182; 1929 W 4th Ave)

Western Canada Wilderness Committee Outreach (Map pp64-5; ☎ 604-687-2567; 227 Abbott St) Hiking guidebooks and maps.

Women in Print (Map p68; ☎ 604-732-4128; 3566 W 4th Ave) Books by women, about women and for women.

Internet Access

Internet terminals are everywhere in the city and they come and go rapidly. Prices varied wildly at those we visited:

Digital Alliance (Map pp58-9; ☎ 604-668-8801; 1108 Homer St; $1.50per hr)

Kinko's (Map pp58-9; ☎ 604-685-3338; 789 W Pender St; $5 per hr)

Kitsilano's Cyber Café (Map p68; ☎ 604-737-0595; 3514 W 4th Ave; $3.50 per hr)

Mail Room (Map pp58-9; ☎ 604-681-6562; 1755 Robson St; 10¢ per min)

Royal Gastown Express Service (Map pp64-5; ☎ 604-688-9862; 104-12 Water St; $3.50 per hr)

The Virtual Coffee Bean (Map p66; ☎ 604-731-1011; 101-1595 W Broadway; $10 per hr) A neat café.

Vancouver Public Library (Map pp58-9; ☎ 604-331-3603; 350 W Georgia St) Free half-hour at the green-tagged computers.

Media
NEWSPAPERS

The *Vancouver Sun* (www.canada.com/vancouver/vancouversun) is Vancouver's straight-laced newspaper that strives to bring the whole story to light. The *Province* (www.canada.com/vancouver/theprovince) is Vancouver's sports and entertainment newspaper laced with news. *Georgia Straight* (www.straight.com) is the weekly freebie which is widely available and the best source for entertainment. There is also the *WestEnder* (www.westender.com), another entertainment-oriented weekly freebie.

RADIO
CBC (690 AM) National news.
CBUF-CBC (102.3 FM) French.
CKNW (980 AM) Local talk radio.
CKWX (1130 AM) 24-hour news.
The Fox (99.3 FM) Contemporary and alternative rock.
97KISS FM (97.9 FM) Adult contemporary.
Rock 101 (101.1 FM) Classic rock.
The Team (1040 AM) 24 hour sports talk and news.

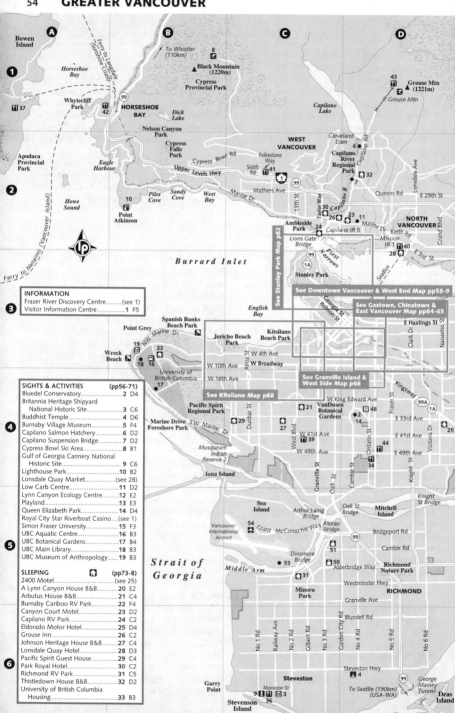

INFORMATION
Fraser River Discovery Centre..........(see 1)
Visitor Information Centre..............1 F5

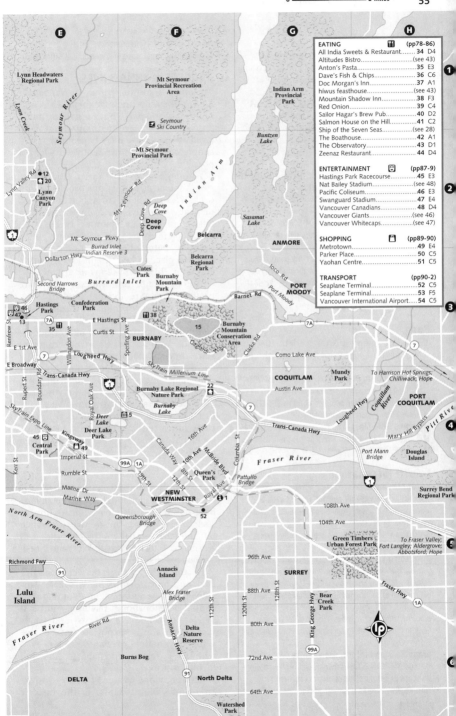

0   4 km
0   2 miles

EATING (pp78–86)
All India Sweets & Restaurant.......**34** D4
Altitudes Bistro............................(see 43)
Anton's Pasta.............................**35** E3
Dave's Fish & Chips.....................**36** C6
Doc Morgan's Inn.........................**37** A1
hiwus feasthouse........................(see 43)
Mountain Shadow Inn....................**38** F3
Red Onion..................................**39** C4
Sailor Hagar's Brew Pub................**40** D2
Salmon House on the Hill...............**41** C2
Ship of the Seven Seas.................(see 28)
The Boathouse...........................**42** A1
The Observatory..........................**43** D1
Zeenaz Restaurant.......................**44** D4

ENTERTAINMENT (pp87–9)
Hastings Park Racecourse..............**45** E3
Nat Bailey Stadium......................(see 48)
Pacific Coliseum..........................**46** E3
Swanguard Stadium......................**47** E4
Vancouver Canadians....................**48** D4
Vancouver Giants........................(see 46)
Vancouver Whitecaps....................(see 47)

SHOPPING (pp89–90)
Metrotown.................................**49** E4
Parker Place..............................**50** C5
Yaohan Centre............................**51** C5

TRANSPORT (pp90–2)
Seaplane Terminal.......................**52** C5
Seaplane Terminal.......................**53** F5
Vancouver International Airport.....**54** C5

Medical Services

Care Point Medical Centre (☀ 9am-9pm) West End (Map pp58-9; ☎ 604-681-5338; 1175 Denman St) East Vancouver (Map pp64-5; ☎ 604-254-5554; 1623 Commercial Dr)

St Paul's Hospital (Map pp58-9; ☎ 604-682-2344; 1081 Burrard St) 24-hour emergency service

Vancouver General Hospital (Map p66; ☎ 604-875-4111; 855 W 12th Ave)

Money

ATMs are widely available throughout the city. Exchange currency at:

Benny Lee Co (Map pp58-9; ☎ 604-683-4241; 619 W Hastings St)

Money Mart (Map pp58-9; ☎ 604-606-9555; 1195 Davie St) 24-hour currency exchange, check-cashing and telegraph services.

QuickEx (☎ 604-683-6789; www.quickex.ca) 24-hour currency exchange machines located about the city

Thomas Cook Pan Pacific Hotel (Map pp58-9; ☎ 604-641-1229; Canada Pl); Pacific Centre (Map pp58-9; ☎ 604-684-3291; 777 Dunsmuir St)

Post

There are many postal outlets in drugstores around town; look for the blue and red signs.

Commercial Drug Mart (Map pp64-5; ☎ 604-253-3266; 1850 Commercial Dr; ☀ 9am-6pm Mon-Fri)

Main Post Office (Map pp58-9; ☎ 604-662-5725; 349 W Georgia St; ☀ 8am-5:30pm Mon-Fri)

Shoppers Drug Mart (Map pp58-9; ☎ 604-685-0246; 1125 Davie St; 9am-9:30pm Mon-Fri; 9:30am-5:30pm Sat, 11:30am-5:30pm Sun)

Tourist Information

Britannia Centre (Map pp64-5; ☎ 604-718-5800; 1661 Napier St; ☀ 9am-5pm Mon-Fri) Not a tourist office per se, but has information on the multicultural Commercial Drive area.

Brockton Visitor Centre (Map p62; Stanley Park; ☀ 9am-5:30pm)

Downtown Visitor Info Centre (Map pp58-9; ☎ 604-683-2000; www.tourismvancouver.com; 200 Burrard St; 8am-6pm, 8:30am-5pm Mon-Sat Oct-May) Friendly and patient staff in an incredibly busy environment; they can help with bookings and information for accommodation, tours, transport and activities. Pick up *Official Visitors' Guide* and monthly mini-magazines *Where Vancouver* and *Visitor's Choice*.

Granville Island Information Centre (Map p66; ☎ 604-666-5784; 1398 Cartwright St; ☀ 9am-6pm)

Vancouver international airport information desks Domestic terminal (baggage carousel); International terminal (after Canadian Customs) Can arrange accommodation bookings and offer info on BC attractions.

DANGERS & ANNOYANCES

The most common crimes in Vancouver are car break-ins and bike thefts. Use common sense and park your car in high-traffic areas and don't leave anything within sight. Cyclists should use a U-shaped lock (not a simple chain lock) and remove a wheel if possible.

Although safer than many cities of its size, Vancouver has serious problems with drugs. Hastings St east of Abbott St is seedy, dirty and unless you're really interested in talking to the guy claiming there aren't enough jars of pickles, there's not much point in being there. It's not a recommended place to be at night and if you do end up in this area, keep your distance.

Among major annoyances, which are pretty minor, are the panhandlers, who have no set territory. Ignore them, or say, 'Sorry' if you want to be polite, and you'll be fine. Also keep your eyes out for 'squeegee kids' who are a little harder to ignore since they approach your car at red lights and wash your windshield, then hold out their hand like a bellhop. Tell them 'Hey, no thanks' before they get to your car, unless of course your window is actually dirty, in which case feel free to give them some lunch money. They tend to operate on Richards St between Pender and Robson but don't have a set territory.

SIGHTS

Vancouver's compact city center has enough of the major sights to keep anyone happy, but you also have the option of spending an extra day or two to branch out into the south-lying neighborhood of Kitsilano or northwards to West and North Vancouver (p92).

In the city center, between Stanley Park and downtown is the **West End**, Vancouver's oldest and most unassuming residential neighborhood. **Yaletown**, southeast of Hamilton and Nelson Sts, and partly the former site of Expo '86, has become a hip destination of warehouses packed with bars, restaurants, apartments and furniture stores.

Gastown, along Water St between Richards and Columbia Sts, is the historic center of old Vancouver, a neighborhood full of restored Victorian buildings. **Chinatown** is just to the southeast, in the area around Pender St between Carrall St and Gore Ave. East of Chinatown, Commercial Dr south of Hastings St is an eclectic, alternative and cultural strip centering on East Vancouver.

The rest of Vancouver is south of downtown. **Granville Island**, immediately south across False Creek, is a lively area full of shops and entertainment. Head west after crossing Burrard or Granville St Bridge and you'll enter **Kitsilano**, filled with students, young professionals and ex-granola-munching 40-to-60-somethings.

Downtown   Map pp58-9

Downtown Vancouver is small enough to get around on foot, and attractive enough that you'll want to. The only really steep streets are those that spill down to False Creek and English Bay on downtown's southwest end. A lot of people live downtown, so it's a vibrant community with activity at all times and plenty of good, established neighborhood groceries, eateries and shops.

Robson St is the main pedestrian artery of the city, full of coffeehouses, restaurants, tourist shops and fashion stores. Day or night it'll be packed with locals and visitors, and most places stay open late, often until midnight in summer. **Denman St** is another good walking street and has zero pretenses.

While Robson tries to flaunt, Denman just is. It has an excellent collection of locally owned, non-chain restaurants along its course from Coal Harbour to English Bay, and is where West End residents congregate.

ENGLISH BAY

Whether it's a hot, still day in August with families and sunbathers sharing the beach, or a cold, blustery day in November with just you and a dog-walker watching waves pound against the shore, **English Bay** is magnificent. The beach is just 30 seconds from city activity and a 10-minute walk from the center of downtown. Spend five minutes or spend the day, but when you see the ocean, the mountain and the city all at the same time you get a snapshot of why Vancouver is so great.

THE LOOKOUT!

An excellent way for cheaters to see all the sights in one shot is at **The Lookout!** (☎ 604-689-0421; 555 W Hastings St; Harbour Centre; adult/student $10/7; ⏲ 8:30am-10:30pm May-Oct, 9am-9pm Nov-Apr), a 169m outdoor elevator ride at Harbour Centre. Since information plaques point to the major sights across the magnificent 360° view of Vancouver and beyond, it's best on a clear day. Get your bearings before heading out to see the sights, or reflect on what you've already seen. Tickets are good all day, and coming back at night is a good wrap-up.

YOU'VE SEEN MORE OF VANCOUVER THAN YOU KNOW

It's not really a secret that Vancouver has become 'Hollywood North' over the last few decades, but what people don't realize is just how many productions are filmed here.

Well known as the *X-files* stage for its first five seasons, Vancouver has also broken Jackie Chan's ankle in *Rumble in the Bronx*, seen mutants battle it out in *X-Men* and *X-Men 2*, and turned Robin Williams into a jungleman in *Jumanji*. It's hard to say where Johnny Depp's career would be without his role as an undercover high-school cop in Vancouver-filmed *21 Jumpstreet*. Richard Dean Anderson's *MacGyver* had Vancouver's natural resources to inspire him to build cool things.

When the **BC Film Commission** (☎ 604-660-2732; www.bcfilmcommission.com; 201-865 Hornby St) was established in the 1970s to lure filmmakers to the great backdrop of Vancouver, and the rest of BC, industry spending was a paltry $12 million. In 2002, 205 productions were filmed here with an estimated spending of $994 million, and Vancouver has recently been the stage for *Stargate SG-1*, still serves as the setting for *Smallville*, and will be seen in the feature films *Catwoman* and *Blade 3*.

So you might be mistaken when you say, 'I can't wait to see Vancouver', because chances are you already have.

Ⓐ   Ⓑ   Ⓒ   Ⓓ

INFORMATION
BC Marijuana Party............(see 140)
Benny Lee Co.................................. 1 F3
Care Point Medical Centre........ 2 B2
Digital Alliance............................. 3 E5
Downtown Visitor Information
  Centre....................................... 4 F2
Kinko's.. 5 F3
Main Post Office......................... 6 F4
Money Mart.................................. 7 C3
Shoppers Drug Mart.................... 8 D4
St Paul's Hospital......................... 9 D4
The Mail Room............................ 10 C2
Thomas Cook..........................(see 50)
Tickets Tonight.........................(see 4)
Vancouver Public Library............ 11 F4
YMCA Child Care........................ 12 D3

SIGHTS & ACTIVITIES (pp57–71)
Alley Cat Rentals........................ 13 C2
Barbara-Jo's Books to Cooks...... 14 F3
Bikes 'n' Blades........................... 15 C2
Chapters....................................... 16 E4
Gay & Lesbian Centre.................. 17 C3
International Travel Maps &
  Books.. 18 F3
Little Sister's Book & Art
  Emporium.................................. 19 C3
MacLeod's Books.......................... 20 F3
Reckless Bike Store...................... 21 E5
Roundhouse Community
  Centre.. 22 E5
Science World............................... 23 G5
Seaplane Terminal........................ 24 F2
Spokes Bicycle Rental................... 25 C1
The Granville Book Company....... 26 E4
The Lookout!................................. 27 E4
Vancouver Aquatic Centre........... 28 C5
Vancouver Art Gallery.................. 29 E3

SLEEPING (pp74–7)
Barclay Hotel................................ 30 D2
Blue Horizon Hotel....................... 31 D3
Bosman's Motor Hotel.................. 32 D4
Cambie Hostel - Seymour............ 33 F3
Cambie International Hostel........ 34 F3
Century Plaza................................ 35 D4
Colibri Bed & Breakfast................ 36 D4
Crowne Plaza Hotel Georgia........ 37 E3
English Bay Inn............................. 38 B2
Fairmont Hotel Vancouver........... 39 E4
Global Village Backpackers.......... 40 E4
HI-Vancouver Central................... 41 E4
HI-Vancouver Downtown............. 42 C4
Kingston Hotel.............................. 43 E4
Le Soleil.. 44 E3
Listel Vancouver........................... 45 D2
Lord Stanley Suites on the
  Park.. 46 C1
Metropolitan Hotel...................... 47 E3
Opus Hotel.................................... 48 E5
Pacific Palisades Hotel.................. 49 D2
Pan Pacific Hotel.......................... 50 F2
Riviera Motor Inn......................... 51 D2
Rosedale on Robson..................... 52 F4
Rosellen Suites at Stanley Park... 53 B1
St Regis Hotel............................... 54 F3
Sunset Inn Travel Apartments...... 55 C4
Sylvia Hotel.................................. 56 B2
The Georgian Court...................... 57 F4
The Landis..................................... 58 D4
Tropicana Motor Inn..................... 59 D2
Victorian Hotel............................. 60 F3
West End Guest House.................. 61 D3
YMCA.. 62 D3
YWCA.. 63 F4

EATING (pp78–82)
a kettle of fish.............................. 64 D5
Akira Sushi................................... 65 B2
Brass Monkey................................ 66 B2
Bread Garden Bakery & Café....... 67 D3

Brix... 68 E5
C... 69 C5
Canadian Maple Delights............. 70 E3
Capers.. 71 C2
Centro Grill................................... 72 E4
cupcakes....................................... 73 B2
da Pasta Bar.................................. 74 D3
Death by Chocolate...................... 75 C2
Diva at the Met......................(see 47)
Doolin's Irish Pub......................... 76 E4
Elbow Room.................................. 77 D5
Glowbal/AFTERglow.................... 78 E5
Gotham... 79 F3
Hamburger Mary's........................ 80 C4
Hilary's Caffé................................ 81 B2
Il Giardino di Umberto.................. 82 D5
Joe Fortes..................................... 83 D3
Kisha Poppo.................................. 84 D4
Kitto Japanese House.................... 85 E4
Krishna Pure Vegetarian
  Restaurant................................. 86 B3
Liliget Feast House........................ 87 B3
Marquee Grill............................... 88 C4
Melriches Coffee House................ 89 E5
Mondo Gelato.......................(see 73)
Mum's Gelato............................... 90 C2
Musashi Japanese Restaurant...... 91 C2
Noodle King Café......................... 92 D2
Original Souvlaki Place................. 93 B2
O'Doul's..................................(see 45)
Pezzo.. 94 D3
Raincity Grill................................. 95 B2
Robson Public Market................... 96 C2
Rooster's Quarters....................... 97 C2
soupspoons................................... 98 C2
Stepho's Souvlaki.......................... 99 C4
Thai House Restaurant................. 100 D3
The Boathouse............................. 101 B3
The Riley...................................... 102 C5
Top of Vancouver...................(see 27)
Urban Fare.................................. 103 E5
Urban Thai Bistro....................... 104 E5
Waterfront Centre....................... 105 F2
White Spot.................................. 106 E4
Wild Garlic Bistro....................... 107 C2
Zin.. 108 D3

0 — 400 m
0 — 0.2 miles

DRINKING (pp86-7)
Balthazar.....................109 B3
Blunt Brothers.............(see 140)
Cellar............................(see 76)
Crush Champagne Lounge..110 D4
Dix.............................111 F4
Dufferin Hotel................112 E4
Ginger 62....................113 D4
Granville Room..............114 E4
Numbers.....................115 D4
Oasis.........................116 D4
Odyssey......................117 D4
Piccadilly Pub................118 F3
Pumpjack Pub...............119 C4
Richard's on Richards.....120 E4
The Drink....................121 F3
The Roxy.....................122 E4

The Yale.....................123 D5
Voda.........................124 E4
Vogue Theatre..............125 E4
Yaletown Brewing Co.......126 E5

ENTERTAINMENT (pp87-9)
Ballet British Columbia......127 F4
BC Lions.....................128 F4
BC Place Stadium..........(see 128)
Capitol Six Theatre..........129 E4
CN IMAX Theatre............130 F2
Commodore Ballroom.......131 E4
Denman Place Discount
  Cinema.....................132 C2
GM Place.....................133 G4
Granville Cineplex Odeon..(see 138)
Orpheum Theatre............134 E4
Pacific Cinémathèque.......135 D4
Queen Elizabeth Theatre..(see 127)
The Centre...................136 F4
The Rage.....................137 F5
Vancouver Canucks.........(see 133)
Vancouver Playhouse......(see 127)
Vancouver Symphony
  Orchestra..................138 E4
Yuk Yuk's....................(see 35)

SHOPPING (pp89-90)
a&b Sound...................139 F3
Altar8........................140 F3
Charlie's Music City.........141 E4
Pacific Centre................142 E3
Sinclair Centre...............143 F3
The Bay......................144 F3
Vancouver Antique Centre..145 F3
Vinyl Records................146 F3
Virgin Megastore............147 E3

TRANSPORT (pp90-2)
Aquabus......................148 C5
False Creek Ferries..........149 C5
Harbour Cruises.............150 C1
Pacific Central Station.......151 H5
Seabus.......................152 F2

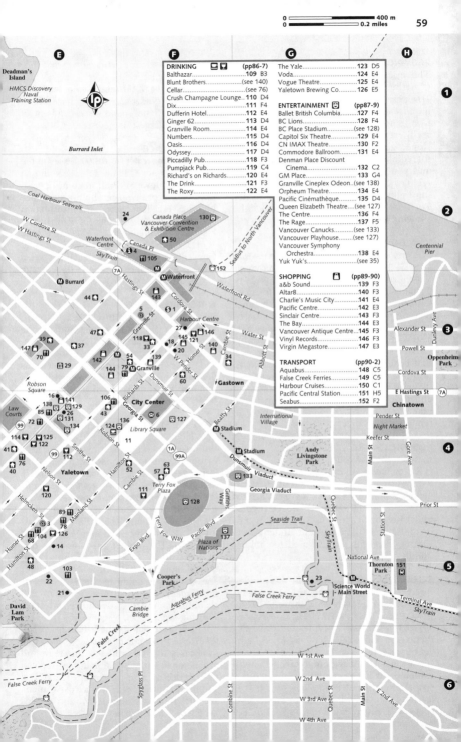

PROVINCIAL LAW COURTS

The series of waterfalls on the outside wall of Arthur Erickson's **law courts** (☎ 660-2910; 219 Smithe St; ☺ 8:30am-4:30pm) is only a glimpse of the tranquility that lies within. Maybe not your usual major sight but the architecture that went into creating this sloped-glass-roofed work of art is truly incredible. You don't have to stay long, and you should be quiet since these are real law courts, but it's remarkably relaxing walking through the atrium up to the 7th floor with nothing but natural light showing the way.

VANCOUVER ART GALLERY

The city's principal **art museum** (☎ 604-662-4719; 750 Hornby St; adult/child $12.50/8, $5 donation 5-9pm Thu; ☺ 10am-5:30pm, 10am-9pm Thu) is a handsome late 19th-century former-courthouse stone building. The 4th floor features works by Emily Carr, BC's best-known painter. The permanent collection also features a good selection of art by Canada's famed Group of Seven. It's true that beauty is in the eye of the beholder, but this gallery displays and organizes its exhibits in a way that is inspirational and thought-provoking. Exhibition tours take place hourly, though times have a tendency to change.

ROBSON SQUARE

Between the law courts and the art gallery is **Robson Square**, an outdoor concrete plaza with waterfalls, fountains and steps staggered in all directions; it's a great place to just sit, think and watch Vancouver. It goes under Robson St and houses a few cafés and institutions; in the winter the under-street rink is filled with ice and used for public skating.

SCIENCE WORLD

A great place to take the kids, especially on a rainy day, **Science World** (☎ 604-443-7440; 1455 Quebec St; adult/child $12.75/8.50; ☺ 10am-6pm summer, varies seasonally) occupies the geodesic dome, the 'Golf Ball', built as Expo '86's centerpiece at the east end of False Creek. It's a high-tech playground of interactive exhibits and live presentations on nature, space, physics and technology that make learning fun. Kids love it here and could spend the entire day, but you'll also see some of the adults fascinated by what they can do and discover.

The **Alcan OMNIMAX Theatre** (movie only $11.25/9, with Science World admission $17.75/13) features a 28-speaker digital sound system and one of the world's largest domed screens.

CANADA PLACE

The **convention center** (☎ 604-647-7390) with the distinctive white 'sails' juts into the harbor at the foot of Howe St. Built to coincide with Expo '86, a promenade circling the complex has excellent views and information plaques pointing out some of Vancouver's historical moments. It also contains the World Trade Centre, Vancouver Trade and Convention Centre, the Pan Pacific Hotel, a cruise-ship terminal and the **CN IMAX Theatre** (☎ 604-682-4629; adult/child $11/9).

WATERFRONT STATION

Just a block away from Canada Place on Waterfront Rd is **Waterfront Station**, the grand old Canadian Pacific Railway station. Once deteriorating, it has been resurrected and restored to grandeur and now serves as the terminus for the SeaBus, which travels to North Vancouver, and Skytrain's Waterfront Station.

BC PLACE STADIUM & GENERAL MOTORS PLACE

Both sports arenas at the eastern edge of downtown are impossible to miss. **BC Place** (☎ 604-669-2300; 777 Pacific Blvd; tours Gate H; adult/child $6/5; ☺ 11am-1pm Fri summer) was once the toast of the town, and now some want to tear it down. Personal opinion aside, there's no denying that the marshmallow of its translucent dome-shaped roof is unique. The quilted appearance is due to crisscrossing steel wires holding down the air-supported Teflon roof. The 60,000-seat stadium is home to the BC Lions of the Canadian Football League (CFL) and also hosts concerts, trade shows and other sporting events.

The **BC Sports Hall of Fame & Museum** (☎ 604-687-5520; Gate A; adult/child $6/4; ☺ 10am-5pm) showcases top BC athletes, amateur and professional, with special galleries devoted to each decade in sports, and to Terry Fox and his 'Marathon of Hope' across Canada and Rick Hanson's 'Man-in-Motion' worldwide wheelchair journey.

Adjacent **GM Place** (☎ 604-899-7889, tours 604-899-7440; 800 Griffiths Way; adult/child $9/4; ☻ 10:30am, noon & 1:30pm Wed & Fri), aka 'The Garage', also hosts concerts, with better sound than BC Place, and is where the Vancouver Canucks of the National Hockey League (NHL) play home games. Behind-the-scenes tours of both arenas take you into the locker rooms and other neat places.

Stanley Park   Map p62

This is Vancouver's much-beloved green space, so much so that some residents boldly declare they would move if they woke up and it was gone. **Stanley Park** (☎ 604-257-8400) is a 404-hectare evergreen forest northwest of downtown flanked by beaches. Governor General Lord Stanley, of Stanley Cup fame, opened the park in 1889 with these words: 'To the use and enjoyment of people of all colours, creeds and customs for all time.'

More than just a park, it's an oasis improbably close to a major urban center with hiking, cycling and jogging trails through the woods, though most people stay close to the edge on the 9.5km **seawall** winding along the park's shoreline. **Second Beach** and **Third Beach** are more secluded than English Bay (p57) and attract lots of sunbathers in summer.

Stop at **Brockton Point** for the outstanding views of downtown and to visit the Brockton Point Info Centre. A collection of **totem poles** is nearby and the **Nine O'clock Gun** (see boxed text, above) is a short walk away.

Lions Gate Bridge extends from the northern tip of the park. Just to its west sits **Prospect Point**, a popular spot for views of the First Narrows and passing ships. On the park's west side, the **National Geographic Tree**, a red cedar almost 30 meters around, is among the largest of its kind in the world – though it's not as well known as the nearby **Hollow Tree**.

A brief stroll from bustling Robson St, the Stanley Park Ecology Society's **Lost Lagoon Nature House** (☎ 257-6908; ☻ 10am-7pm Tue-Sun summer) has informative staff and a research library with information on the ecologies of Stanley Park and park history.

The park is an easy walk from downtown and has a free **Stanley Park Shuttle** (☻ 9:30am-6pm mid-Jun–Oct), which stops near major sights.

> ### THINGS THAT GO 'BOOM' BEFORE THE NIGHT
>
> Originally brought to Stanley Park in the 1890s to warn fishermen of the 6pm closing time of Sunday-fishing, the **Nine O'clock Gun** has been firing precisely at 9pm for over 100 years. Some residents still set their watch by it.
>
> The cannon used to be unprotected until pranksters started messing with it, so it now sits in a cage but can still be the punchline of an amusing practical joke: simply; take your victim to Brockton Point to 'look at the views of downtown' before 8:59pm. 'Ooh' and 'ah' at the pretty city lights (and subtly brace yourself). When the cannon fires, the person beside you may suffer a mild coronary but feel free to laugh at their expense. Not recommended for those with heart problems.

VANCOUVER AQUARIUM

This **aquarium** (☎ 604-659-3474; www.vanaqua.org; adult/child $15.95/8.95; ☻ 9:30am-7pm, 10am-5:30pm Sep-Jun) is well done and impressively and informatively displays more than 8000 marine creatures. Indoor tanks, outdoor boardwalks along outdoor exhibits, interactive play-rooms for kids and live beluga shows are just some of the attractions. It's an aesthetically pleasing aquarium, with displays covering the whole gamut of marine ecosystems. Plan on spending at least half a day without even noticing the time passing.

Gastown   Map pp64-5

Gastown's major attraction is **Gastown** itself; cobblestone streets, old-fashioned lampposts and Victorian houses and lodges are some of its exhibits. Why the name? The most-believed theory is that the area takes its name from 'Gassy' Jack Deighton, a character and windbag of a storyteller who built a saloon for the sawmill workers in 1876; the surrounding area was referred to as 'Gassy's Town'. Gastown was Vancouver's first official name, and a statue of **Gassy Jack** (cnr Cordova & Maple Sts) stands at Maple Tree Square.

Gastown hit hard times when the center of Vancouver moved elsewhere, and it went back to the dirty, muddy place it started as. In the 1970s the district's restoration

0 _____ 600 m
0 _____ 0.4 miles

Shuttle Stop

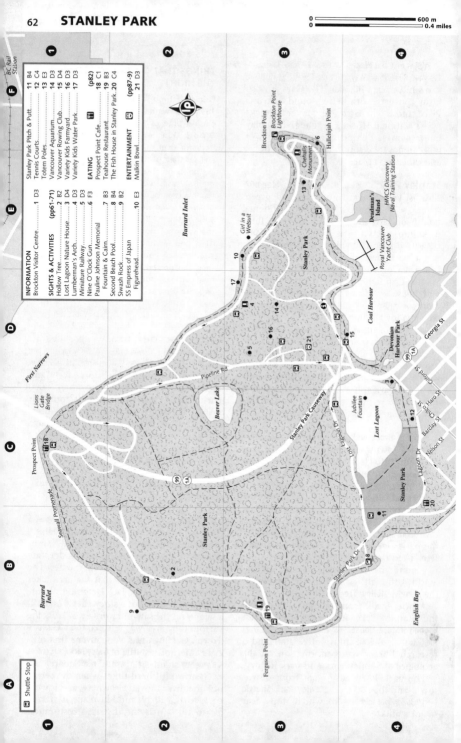

pushed Vancouver's seedier characters a little farther east and the old Victorians now house restaurants, boutiques, galleries and nightclubs.

GASTOWN STEAM CLOCK

The **steam clock** (cnr Cambie & Water Sts) is kind of a silly little landmark, though its charm is that it's the only one in the world. Misleadingly historic looking, it was only built and installed in 1977; it's been sounding and belching steam – the same steam used to heat many nearby buildings – every 15 minutes ever since.

VANCOUVER POLICE CENTENNIAL MUSEUM

Suitably housed in the city's former morgue and coroner's court, this **museum** (☎ 604-665-3346; 240 E Cordova St; adult/child $6/4; ☒ 9am-3pm Mon-Fri, 10am-3pm Sat Apr-Aug) has often-macabre displays, like a murder scene recreation, of police in Vancouver since 1886, which can get a little creepy. Depictions of infamous crimes and criminals are on display along with weapons, counterfeit money, forensic autopsy tools and drug paraphernalia. On the lighter side, you can sit in a c 1986 police cruiser and view the accomplishments of Vancouver's finest over more than a century.

Chinatown   Map pp64-5

The third-largest Chinatown in North America (between Gore, Abott, Powell and Union Sts) is right here and it's the real deal. Hanging ducks in the windows, fish guts in the gutters, buckets of strange dried items and jars of Asian remedies, it's got it all. The colors and smells; the street signs and red everywhere you look make this Chinatown as authentic as possible. The **entrance gate**, in all its dragon-displaying splendor is on Pender, just east of Abott.

As authentic as Vancouver's Chinatown is, there's a new kid on the block and recent Hong Kong arrivals have colonized Richmond (p96), now the center of Chinese Canadian business and a modernized spin on Chinatown. But if you're into the stimuli of the senses that traditional Chinatown evokes, Vancouver is the place.

Street parking can be had, but you may have to search for a while. Chinatown is an easy walk from downtown.

DR SUN YAT-SEN CLASSICAL CHINESE GARDEN

The harmoniously peaceful, classical **garden** (☎ 604-662-3207; 578 Carrall St; adult/child $8.25/5.75; ☒ 9:30am-7pm summer, varies seasonally) is the only full-scale Ming Dynasty-style garden outside China. Its tranquil pools, stone-laid paths, and bonsai trees take you into a Zen-like state, or very close to it. Guided tours of 45 minutes every hour give a better understanding and appreciation of its subtle design incorporating the Taoist principles of yin and yang.

Concerts take place on Friday evening in summer, and in the winter the garden hosts Twenty-Four Days of Winter Peace, and Chinese New Year celebrations. Adjacent to the formal garden, the city's free **Dr Sun Yat-Sen Park** features a similar design.

SAM KEE BUILDING

The **World's Narrowest Office Building** (cnr Pender & Carrall Sts), 'Slender on Pender', looks like the front of the larger building behind it and you may walk right by the first time or three looking for it. Built in 1913 by the Kee Co after the city widened Pender St and didn't compensate for the pilfered land, it's only 1.8m wide. It's currently home to an insurance company and nothing to see inside, but it's still neat.

East Vancouver   Map pp64-5

'East Van', the area east of Main St, has traditionally been the working class, non-British section of Vancouver. Long the center of Vancouver's 'Little Italy', **Commercial Dr** (The Drive), remains one of the city's liveliest melting pots. Counterculture also thrives here, with earnest political conversations overheard among the many vegetarian cafés, bookstores, hemp shops and coffeehouses. Don't leave Vancouver without spending some time here.

Granville Island   Map p66

The former site of major industrial activity is now a colorful, artsy, busy mix of restaurants, galleries and theaters on the southern side of False Creek under the Granville Bridge. The center of activity is the **Granville Island Public Market** (☎ 604-666-5784), a market-goers' dream made manifest with butchers, bakers and candlestick-makers among the green-grocers, fishmongers and other merchants.

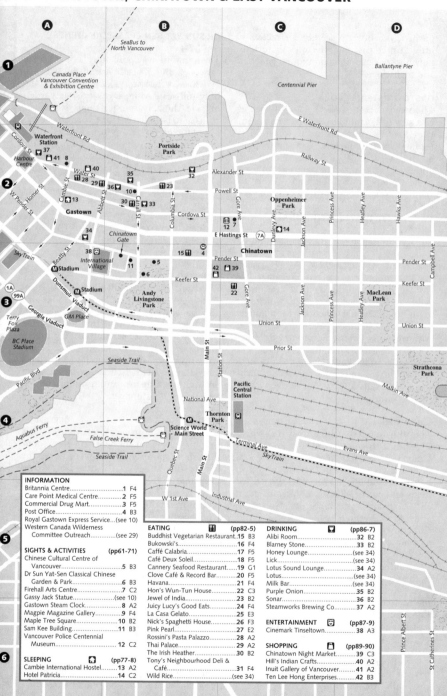

0 ————— 400 m
0 ————— 0.2 miles

E **F** **G** **H**

McGill St

McGill St

1

Eton St

Cambridge St

Oxford St

Dundas St

Triumph St

Pandora St

Pandora Park

Franklin St

2

Rogers St

Stewart St

Wall St

Powell St

Franklin St

Hastings St

Hastings St

To Hastings Park (1km);
Playland (1km); Hwy 1 (1.5km);
Second Narrows Bridge (2km);
Simon Fraser University (8km)

27 🍴

Pender St

Pender St

Ferndale St

Frances St

26 🍴

Turner St

Georgia St

Woodland Park

East Vancouver

Templeton Park

Georgia St

Adanac St

Adanac St

25 🍴

Venables St

Venables St

Parker St

Parker St

Napier St

Napier St

ℹ 1

31 🍴

William St

Lily St

Rosie St

William St

Grandview Park

21 🍴

Charles St

9 ●

Kitchener St

16 🍴 24

Victoria Park

Grant St

Graveley St

Il Mercato Mall ➕ 2

1st Av

E 1st Ave

Grandview Viaduct

17 🍴

E 2nd Ave

E 2nd Ave

E 3rd Ave

3 ●

E 3rd Ave

5

E 4th Ave

20 🍴

E 4th Ave

McSpadden Park

18 🍴

E 5th Ave

E 5th Ave

China Creek Park

Grandview Hwy N

E 6th Ave

SkyTrain

E 7th Ave

Windsor St

Glen Dr

Keith Dr

Vancouver Community College

E 8th Ave

Ⓜ Commercial

6

Rogers St

Glen Dr

Vernon Dr

Clarke Dr

McLean Dr

Woodland Dr

Commercial Dr

Salsbury Dr

Victoria Dr

Semlin Dr

Lakewood Dr

Templeton Dr

Garden Dr

Nanaimo St

Kamloops St

Raymur Ave

Cotton Dr

Odlum Dr

Clark Dr

Parking can be tight on Granville Island. Consider taking the Aquabus or False Creek Ferries (p92), catching a bus or taking the historic railway (below).

EMILY CARR INSTITUTE OF ART & DESIGN
This institute dedicates itself to art instruction and holds frequent exhibits in the **Charles H Scott Gallery** (☎ 604-844-3809; 1399 Johnston St; ☾ noon-5pm Mon-Fri, 10am-5pm Sat & Sun). This concrete-floored, white-walled gallery allows its students to immerse themselves in the field and produce some truly incredible pieces.

GRANVILLE ISLAND MUSEUMS
This **museum complex** (☎ 604-683-1939; 1502 Duranleau St; adult/child $6.50/3.50; ☾ 10am-5:30pm) houses three collections under one roof:
Model Ships Museum No ships in a bottle, but scaled-down models of historic gunships and tugboats show incredible levels of patience and craftsmanship.
Model Trains Museum Displays old model boxcars and engines; the huge room housing the mountains-and-villages display with running trains will send you home to clean out the basement and retire early.
Sport Fishing Museum An impossibly large collection of fishing reels and lures.

DOWNTOWN HISTORIC RAILWAY
Take a step into the past on this **old rail system** (☎ 604-665-3903; www.trams.bc.ca; adult/child $2/1; ☾ 1-5pm weekends & holidays mid-May–mid-Oct) that travels between 1st Ave and Ontario St and Granville Island. Park for free at Ontario St Station and save the hassle of trying to find a spot on Granville Island.

Kitsilano   Map p68
The neighborhood of Kitsilano (Kits) spreads across the southern shore of English Bay from Burrard St to the University of British Columbia (UBC). During the 1960s and 1970s, Kits pulled a Haight-Ashbury and became Vancouver's hippie enclave. Even though the hippies have grown up, Kits is still a fun, trendy neighborhood with an everlasting granola vibe.

W 4th Ave and **W Broadway** are the primary commercial streets, with lots of shops and cafés to explore. **Kits** and **Jericho Beaches** are popular, and with all they have to offer have good reason to be, but if you want a bit more breathing room with the same awesome view of the city, **Spanish Banks** a little further west along NW Marine Drive is a good idea.

VANIER PARK
On the south shore of English Bay below the Burrard Bridge, **Vanier Park** is well maintained and has an excellent vantage point of downtown with the mountains behind it. There is always activity going on, from beach volleyball and kite-flying to swimming. It's also the perfect place to just sit, enjoy the view and watch the ships moving between English Bay and False Creek.

The funny thing about the **Vancouver Museum** (☎ 604-736-4431; www.vanmuseum.bc.ca; 1100 Chestnut St; adult/child $8/5.50; ☾ 10am-5pm Tue-Sun, 10am-9pm Thu) is that many Vancouverites don't even know it exists, which is a shame because it's excellent. It vividly recounts both distant and recent Vancouver history. 'Go forward, look back' is the theme of the excellent orientation gallery, where exhibits include a look at the everyday life of First Nations people, plus artifacts of Vancouver at work and play. The 'Vancouver Story' galleries examine the city's early settlement in greater depth. The changing exhibits are also excellent, with a scope beyond Vancouver.

In the same complex as the museum, the main draw of the **HR MacMillan Space Centre** (☎ 604-738-7827; www.hrmacmillanspacecentre.com; 1100 Chestnut St; adult/child $13.50/9.50; ☾ 10am-5pm Tue-Sun Sep-Jun 30) is its planetarium; educational star shows and entertaining laser shows (choreographed to music like 'Laser Led Zeppelin') are projected onto a 20m-wide dome. Other exhibits delve into humankind's knowledge of our cosmic backyard where you can learn about astronauts, morph into an alien or take a virtual voyage to save human-inhabited Mars. The **Gordon Southam MacMillan Observatory** (☎ 604-738-2855; admission free; ☾ 7-11pm Fri-Sun), on the grounds here, is open to the public for telescope viewings and info; call ahead to double-check.

For a glimpse of the city's rich seafaring heritage, check out the **Vancouver Maritime Museum** (☎ 604-257-8300; 1905 Ogden Ave; adult/child $8/5; ☾ 10am-5pm Mon-Sat, noon-5pm Sun, closed Mon Sep-Jun) and stop to see the St Roch, a 1928 Royal Canadian Mounted Police (RCMP) Arctic patrol ship that was the first vessel to navigate the legendary Northwest Passage

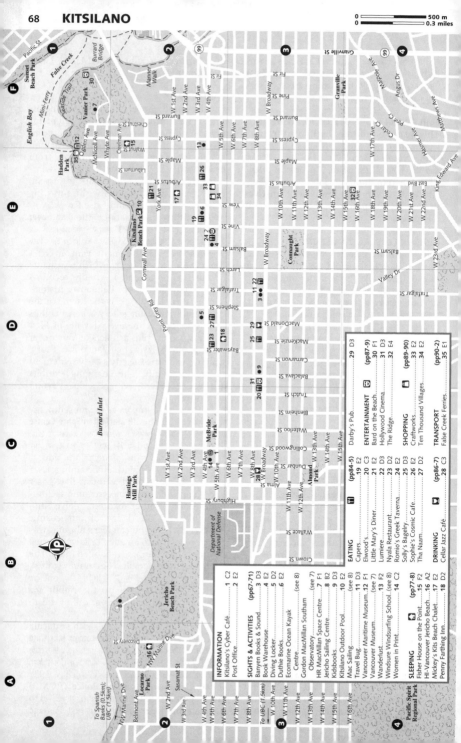

0 ⊢⊣ 500 m
0 ⊢⊣ 0.3 miles

INFORMATION
Kitsilano's Cyber Cafe.................1 C2
Post Office.................................2 E2

SIGHTS & ACTIVITIES (pp67-71)
Banyen Books & Sound..............3 D3
Book Warehouse.........................4 E2
Diving Locker.............................5 D2
Duthie Books.............................6 E2
Ecomarine Ocean Kayak
  Centre.................................(see 8)
Gordon MacMillan Southam
  Observatory...........................(see 7)
HR MacMillan Space Centre........7 F1
Jericho Sailing Centre..................8 B2
Kidsbooks.................................9 D3
Kitsilano Outdoor Pool..............10 E2
Mac Sailing..........................(see 8)
Travel Bug...............................11 D3
Vancouver Maritime Museum......12 F1
Vancouver Museum.............(see 7)
Wanderlust...............................13 F2
Windsure Windsurfing School...(see 8)
Women in Print.........................14 C2

SLEEPING 🏠 (pp77-8)
Fisher House on the Point.........15 F2
HI-Vancouver Jericho Beach......16 A2
Mickey's Kits Beach Chalet.......17 E2
Penny Farthing Inn...................18 D2

EATING 🍴 (pp84-5)
Capers....................................19 E2
Elwood's.................................20 C3
Little Mary's Diner....................21 E2
Lumiere..................................22 D3
Nyala Restaurant......................23 D2
Romio's Greek Taverna.............24 E2
Solly's Bagelry.........................25 D3
Sophie's Cosmic Cafe...............26 E2
Tha Naam..............................27 D2

DRINKING 🍷 (pp86-7)
Cellar Jazz Cafe......................28 C3
Darby's Pub............................29 D3

ENTERTAINMENT 🎭 (pp87-9)
Bard on the Beach...................30 F1
Hollywood Cinema...................31 D3
The Ridge...............................32 E4

SHOPPING 🛍 (pp89-90)
Craftworks..............................33 E2
Ten Thousand Villages.............34 D2

TRANSPORT (pp90-2)
False Creek Ferries..................35 E1

in both directions. Other displays tell of lighthouses, pirates, shipwrecks and more. Classic wooden boats often anchor outside in Heritage Harbour.

Elsewhere in Vancouver   Map pp54–5
UNIVERSITY OF BRITISH COLUMBIA
This 400-hectare college campus (UBC; ☎ 604-822-2211), made up of forested areas of the University Endowment Lands and Pacific Spirit Regional Park, has 32,000 students and a mini-city of cafés, residences and theatres. It's at the most westerly point of Vancouver.

UBC Museum of Anthropology
This well-done **museum** (☎ 604-822-5087; 6393 NW Marine Dr; adult/child $9/7; ☼ 10am-5pm, 10am-9pm Tue) contains outstanding art and artifacts following BC's First Nations peoples. Highlights include works by Haida artist Bill Reid, especially his monumental yellow cedar carving of *The Raven and the First Men*. Mungo Martin, who was born just before the Canadian government outlawed native practices in 1884, is also detailed. He struggled to preserve the traditions of his Kwakwaka'wakw people, eventually coming to UBC in 1949 to restore totem poles now on view at the museum.

The museum building itself is a work of art, designed by Arthur Erickson to mirror the post-and-beam structures of coastal First Nations people. The Great Hall's 15m walls of glass look out on still more totem poles and outdoor sculptures. Several guided walks take place each day.

UBC Botanical Gardens
Plants and flowers tell the year-long story of the seasons and these lovely **gardens** (☎ 604-822-3928; 6804 SW Marine Dr; adult/child $5/3, free in winter; ☼ 10am-6pm) are no exception. Over a dozen different types of gardens are found here, including a food garden and a winter garden of crazy plants that bloom in cooler months.

Nitobe Memorial Gardens
Near the museum, these authentic **Japanese tea gardens** (☎ 604-822-9666; adult/child $2.50/1.50, free in winter; ☼ 10am-6pm, 10am-2:30pm mid-Oct– mid-Mar), with their subtle harmonies, are immediately relaxing and mind clearing.

IT'S ONLY NATURAL

Wreck Beach is Vancouver's only nude sunbathing spot and attracts 100,000 people each year. Those mistaking this for the Riviera and expecting playmates and chiselled Adonises will be mildly disappointed; it's about Vancouver's live-and-let-live attitude and being natural, not sexual. What you'll find is people with zero inhibitions having a good time and trying to get as much as they can out of Vancouver's roughly 63 minutes of good sunbathing. The beach is socially and unspokenly divided into the north end for gay men; the central section for food venders and peddlers of other substances; and the southern stretch for everyone just letting it all hang out – and they do.

Wreck Beach lies on the west side of the UBC campus off NW Marine Dr south past the Museum of Anthropology. Look for trail No 6.

QUEEN ELIZABETH PARK
The highest point in Vancouver, Queen Elizabeth Park (Map pp54–5) carpets 150m-high Little Mountain in impeccable lawns and colorful, sunken gardens. It's a peaceful place to sit and gaze at the views of Vancouver, or to take a walk among flowers and under trees. The park also offers various other recreation facilities.

They pack a lot into the small dome of **Bloedel Conservatory** (☎ 604-257-8570; 30 E 30th Ave; adult/child $4/2; ☼ 9am-8pm Mon-Fri, 10am-9pm Sat & Sun) as it takes in three climate zones and houses 500 species of gorgeous plants, though the 50 species of free-flying tropical birds often steal the show – especially 'Charlie', an Amazon parrot who's quite a talker.

PLAYLAND
Vancouver's **amusement park** (☎ 604-253-2311; cnr Cassiar & Hastings Sts; $22.95; ☼ 11am-9pm summer, closed Oct-Apr), is located in the grounds of the Pacific National Exhibition (PNE; p73). The park offers such thrills and chills as a classic wooden roller coaster, rapidly gyrating machines, swings and other fun rides and things. Some rides have height restrictions, but lots cater to little tykes.

VANDUSEN BOTANICAL GARDEN

Get lost in a maze, gaze at rare ornamental plants and enjoy scenic views of Vancouver in these 22 hectares of **garden** (☎ 604-878-9274; www.vandusengarden.org; 5251 Oak St; adult/child $7.25/3.75; ☼ 10am-9pm Jun–mid-Aug, varies seasonally). There are three color-coded walks (20 minutes, two hours) or you can wander on your own following the well-drawn map. The gardens themselves are a visual flood of colors and texture, with the various themed gardens packed tightly together and separated by open spaces of lawn and tall trees.

ACTIVITIES

As cultural, funky, cool and sophisticated as the city is, a plethora of activities is also right there. The best of both worlds can be had as you can start the day untying bowlines, and end it with a martini in hand. See North Vancouver (p92) and West Vancouver (p95) for information on skiing and other activities on the local North Shore Mountains.

Canada's favorite outdoor mega-mart, **Mountain Equipment Co-op** (Map p66; ☎ 604-872-7858; 130 W Broadway; camping $9-21, climbing $22, snow sports $12-35; lifetime membership $5; ☼ 10am-7pm Mon-Wed, 10am-9pm Thu-Fri, 9am-6pm Sat, 11am-5pm Sun) rents outdoor equipment and has weekend specials where you take the gear Thursday, bring it back Monday and only pay for Saturday and Sunday.

Cycling & Blading

Stanley Park's seawall is a popular cycling and roller-blading route, but there's a network of bike paths to be found elsewhere. The old site of Expo '86 has been getting some much-needed attention over the last few years and False Creek is now lined with lovely parks and paths. The info center has a *Cycling in Vancouver* brochure and rental shops are scattered about the city. Most bike shops also rent roller-blades (same price).

Alleycat Rentals (Map pp58-9; ☎ 604-684-5117; 1779 Robson St; $10 per day; ☼ 9am-7pm summer)

Bikes 'n' Blades (Map pp58-9; ☎ 604-602-9899; 718 Denman St; $12 per day; ☼ 9am-6pm summer)

Reckless Bike Store (www.reckless.ca; $25 per day) Kitsilano (Map p68; ☎ 604-731-2420; 1810 Fir St; ☼ 9am-7pm Mon-Sat, 10-6pm Sun); Yaletown (Map pp58-9; ☎ 604-648-2600; 110 Davie St; ☼ 9am-7pm)

Spokes Bicycle Rental (Map pp58-9; ☎ 604-688-5141; 1798 W Georgia St; $27 per day; ☼ 9am-7pm summer)

Swimming

People do swim at English Bay beach, but the water's much cleaner at **Kitsilano** and **Jericho Beaches** or the shores off **UBC**. Kits Beach is the largest and most popular; as many as 10,000 people may hit the sand here on a hot summer day, and it has the **Kitsilano Outdoor Pool** (☎ 604-731-0011; 2305 Cornwall St; adult/child $4.15/2.10; ☼ 7am-8:45pm summer, closed Sep-May).

For serious swimmers, the **Vancouver Aquatic Centre** (Map pp58-9; ☎ 604-665-3424; 1050 Beach Ave; adult/child $4.25/2.25; ☼ 6:30am-9:45pm Mon-Fri, 8am-8:45pm Sat, 10am-8:45pm Sun) looks like a big sand pile under Burrard St Bridge.

Kayaking

The protection of Vancouver Island makes the waters of False Creek and Burrard Inlet relatively calm and perfect for a paddle.

Ecomarine Ocean Kayak Centre Jericho Beach (Map p68; ☎ 604-222-3565; 1300 Discovery St; www.ecomarine.com; lessons from $65, rentals $52-74 per day; ☼ 11am-dusk Mon-Fri, 9am-9pm Sat & Sun, closed Oct-Apr); Granville Island (Map p66; ☎ 604-689-7575; 1668 Duranleau; 2hr $32, 2-for-1 rentals Tue; ☼ 9am-6pm Sun-Wed, 9am-9pm Tue & Thu-Sat, varies seasonally)

Mountain Equipment Co-op (Map p66; ☎ 604-872-7858; 130 W Broadway; full-day kayak/canoe $30/45; ☼ 10am-7pm Mon-Wed, 10am-9pm Thu-Fri, 9am-6pm Sat, 11am-5pm Sun)

Windsurfing & Sailing

English Bay gets some huge winds whipping through, evidenced by the frequent whitecaps.

Jericho Sailing Centre (Map p68; 1300 Discovery St) Houses the outfitters, as well as a café and bar with a patio so you can look out at what you conquered.

Mac Sailing (Map p68; ☎ 604-224-7245; www.macsailing.com; adult/child courses $225/145, rental $18-30 per hr; ☼ 9am-7pm Mon-Fri, noon-6pm Sat & Sun summer, closed Oct–mid-Apr)

Windsure Windsurfing School (Map p68; ☎ 604-24-0615; full-day rental/2hr lesson $100/39; ☼ 9am-8pm Apr 1-Oct 1)

Scuba Diving

Despite extremely cold temperatures, the North Shore waters have a lot to offer divers, though the general consensus is

WE CAN PROVE IT

Sailing, swimming, golfing, biking, skating, hiking and skiing in the same day is something that Vancouverites do, not just say they do.

- **Sail** Jericho Beach (p70)
- **Swim** Spanish Banks (p67)
- **Golf** University Golf Course (below)
- **Bike** UBC Endowment lands (p69)
- **Skate** Summer: Roller-blade False Creek (p70); Winter: Ice-skate Robson Square (p60)
- **Walk** The Seawall (p61)
- **Ski** Night-ski Grouse (p93)
- **Drink** Steamworks Brewing Co (p86)
- **Dine** Joe Fortes (p79)
- **Club** Granville St (p86)

you can find much more comfortable diving elsewhere in the province. If your trip includes other coastal locations, you might want to wait for your diving and enjoy Vancouver above sea level instead.

North Shore dive spots include **Lighthouse Park** near West Vancouver and **Porteau Cove**, 26km north of Horseshoe Bay. For equipment, training and trips:

BC Dive and Kayak Adventures (Map p68; ☎ 604-732-1344; www.bcdive.com;1695 W 4th St; wetsuit/drysuit package $50/80; ☼ 10am-6pm)

Diving Locker (Map p68; ☎ 604-736-2681; www.kochersdiving.com; 2745 W 4th Ave; package $50; ☼ 10am-6pm Mon-Fri, 9:30am-5:30pm Sat, 9:30am-4pm Sun)

Golf

Vancouverites love to swing the sticks. There are little pitch-and-putt courses at **Stanley Park** (Map p62; ☎ 604-257-8400; $9.50) and **Queen Elizabeth Park** (Map pp54-5; ☎ 604-874-8336; $9.50), but to let the big dog eat, **University Golf Course** (Map pp54-5; ☎ 604-224-1818; 5185 University Blvd; $50) is open to the public. Also ask around or visit www.golfbc.com.

Tennis

With more than 180 free public courts (including some at Stanley Park, Queen Elizabeth Park and Kits Beach Park), Vancouver offers plenty of places to play tennis. City courts are available on a first-come, first-served basis; you can only occupy a court for 30 minutes if someone's waiting.

TOURS

Vancouver is a great city to get lost in – you'll end up seeing something you didn't expect, and it's small enough you won't be lost for long. If you prefer to let someone else lead the way:

Harbour Air Seaplanes (☎ 604-688-1277; www.harbour-air.com; from $89) Scenic tours aboard seaplanes.

Harbour Cruises (☎ 604-688-7246; 1 Denman St; tour adult/child $19/7, dinner adult/child $65/55) Offers 75-minute harbor tours and three-hour sunset dinner cruises around False Creek, English Bay and Burrard Inlet.

The X-Tour (☎ 604-609-2770, 888-250-7211; www.x-tour.com; from $145; ☼ varies) Focuses on Vancouver's film-and-TV industry; looks at past and current filming locations.

Bus Tours

Gray Line (☎ 604-879-3363; www.grayline.ca/vancouver; adult/child $29/16; ☼ 8:30am-4:30pm) Traditional bus sightseeing tours; the 'Hop-on and Hop-off' tour allows riders to spend as much time as they like at 22 designated stops over two consecutive days.

Stanley Park Horse-Drawn Tours (☎ 604-681-5115; adult/child $20.55/13.05; ☼ 9:40am-5:30pm) Narrated one-hour tours depart from the info center; free shuttle from select hotels to Stanley Park for riders of this tour.

The Vancouver Trolley Company (☎ 604-801-5515; adult/child $26/13; ☼ 9am-6pm) Bus tour with 16 stops.

West Coast Sightseeing (☎ 604-451-1600; www.vancouversightseeing.com; adult/child from $49/31; ☼ 6am-10:30pm May-Oct, 7am-10pm Nov-Apr)

Walking Tours

Discovery Walks 'n' Talks ($5; ☼ 1pm Sun) Naturalist-led walks teach about Stanley Park's species.

Erik's City & Canyon Tour (HI-Vancouver Downtown, ☎ 604-684-4565, van-downtown@hihostels.ca; adult/child $10/8; ☼ 9am Tue & Fri) Available to HI-Vancouver guests, freewheeling day-long tour covers city highlights and Lynn Canyon Park.

Historic Gastown Tours (☎ 604-683-5650; meet at Maple Tree Square; tours free; ☼ 2pm mid-Jun–Aug) Run by Gastown Business Improvement Society.

The Chinese Cultural Centre of Vancouver (Map pp64-5; ☎ 604-687-0729; 50 E Pender St; adult/child $6/4; ☼ Jun-Sep 11am & 2:30pm) Tours of Chinatown.

Walkabout Historic Vancouver (☎ 604-720-0006; www.walkabouthistoricvancouver.com; tours $25; ☼ 10am & 2pm) Informative and lively guides in period clothing lead various tours. Call for further information and departure locations.

COURSES

If you want to hone current skills, brush up on an old hobby or learn something entirely new, there are places to do such things.
Roundhouse Community Centre (Map pp58-9; ☎ 604-713-1800; www.roundhouse.ca; 181 Round-house Mews, Yaletown; from $15) Offers courses ranging from arts and crafts drop-ins to month-long drama classes.

Cooking

Barbara-Jo's Books to Cooks (Map pp58-9; ☎ 604-688-6755; www.bookstocooks.com; 1128 Mainland St; from $49) Literally covers the whole culinary gamut, from Scotches to street food.
Cookshop & Cookschool (Map p66; ☎ 604-873-5683; www.cookshop.ca; 3-555 W 12th Ave; from $49) Covers everything from sushi to turkey dinners and does 'Pacific Northwest' courses.
Low Carb Centre (Map pp54-5; ☎ 604-980-3394; www.lowcarbcentre.com; 1270 Marine Dr; $85-95) Courses to help you follow your Atkins diet.

VANCOUVER FOR CHILDREN

Little kids will have just as much fun in Vancouver as big kids. The visitor info centre has a *Kids in Vancouver* brochure and www.findfamilyfun.com and www.kidsvancouver.com are good resources.
Stanley Park's (p62) hits are **Variety Kids Farmyard** (adult/child $4.50/2.25) and the rainforest-themed **miniature railway** (adult/child $4.50/2.25). Kids and families frolic at Second Beach's **outdoor swimming pool** (adult/child $4.25/2.25; ☯ May-Sep) or the **Variety Kids Water Park** at Lumbermen's Arch. If you've had enough, send the kids to sleep with the fishes at the **Vancouver Aquarium** (☎ 604-659-3474; www.vanaqua.org; per person $83; ☯ 9:30am-7pm, 10am-5:30pm Sep-Jun). The aquarium hosts fun and informative sleepovers at the beluga viewing tanks.

Granville Island (p66) has a free **Water Park** (☯ dawn-dusk May-Sep) on the island's south side. The indoor **Kids Only Market** (1496 Cartwright St) lures young visitors with clowns, magicians, face-painters and stores featuring everything from fun wet-weather gear to toys and puppets.

If your children don't lose themselves at **Kidsbooks** (Map p68; ☎ 604-738-5335; 3083 W Broadway) you just might. Besides its fabulous collection of every kind of book imaginable for children, the store carries creative toys and games. **Vandusen Botanical Garden** (p70)

hands out a map and informative leaflet for a two-hour pond tour for little ones.
Vancouver International Children's Festival (☎ 604-708-5655; www.vancouverchildrensfestival.com) is a family-oriented performing-arts festival held in late May that takes place in Vanier Park. The **PNE** (p73) and **Playland** (p69) are summertime favorites.

The **Children's Maritime Discovery Centre** at the Maritime Museum (p67) features hands-on activities.

In Tsawwassen by the ferry terminal, **Splashdown Water Park** (Map pp50-1; ☎ 604-943-2251; 4799 Nulelum Way; adult/child $19.59/13.75; ☯ 10am-8pm Sat-Thu, 10am-6pm Fri summer, closed Sep-May) and its dozen-plus water slides is hugely popular with the kids on hot summer days.

Aldergrove, east of Vancouver, has plenty of wide-open farmland; a perfect spot for the expansive **Greater Vancouver Zoological Centre** (Map pp50-1; ☎ 604-857-9005; www.greatervancouverzoo.com; 5048 264 St; adult/child $13/10; ☯ 9:30am-dusk) which houses over 90 species of animals. The usual line-up of lions, tigers, bears, rhinos, giraffes, elephants, apes and hippos can all be seen.

A lot of accommodations offer childcare services if the kids need a night away from you; ask when you're making reservations. **YMCA Child Care** (Map pp58-9 ☎ 604-294-9622; childcare@vanymca.org; 500-1188 W Georgia St) has a network of childcare centers and affiliations around the Lower Mainland.

QUIRKY VANCOUVER

Vancouver's 'Little Amsterdam' is packed into the north side of **W Hastings St** between Richards and Cambie Sts and into the bowls of the people who frequent here. It's home to paraphernalia stores and the only cafés in town where you can smoke, yet you still can't light up a cigarette.

Years ago it was the place of frequent police raids and drug busts. Now the cafés and stores are 'marginally' profitable and the **BC Marijuana Party** (Map pp58-9; ☎ 604-684-7076; www.bcmarijuanaparty.ca; 307 W Hastings St), a legitimate provincial governmental party that got 3.5% of last election's votes, is headquartered here.

Blunt Brothers (Map pp58-9; ☎ 604-682-5868; 317 W Hastings St; munchies $5-7) is 'a respectable joint' with sandwiches such as 'The Cheech' with THC (Turkey, Ham and Cheddar). They

---

BEACH BLANKET BARD

On fine Vancouver summer evenings the annual **Bard on the Beach** (Map p68; ☎ 604-739-0559; www.bardonthebeach.com; Vanier Park; ☽ Jun–Sep) presents Shakespeare the way it should be seen – outdoors. Open tents at Vanier Park provide the stage for the entertaining productions and it's a real summertime treat to be able to enjoy a performance as the sun sets on English Bay.

Theatre Under the Stars (Map p62; ☎ 604-687-0174; www.tuts.bc.ca; ☽ mid-Jul–mid-Aug) also stages several Broadway musicals at Stanley Park's Malkin Bowl each year.

---

also have video games for playing, or big wooden tables for mellowing. **Altar8** (Map pp58-9; ☎ 604-669-4238; 315 W Hastings St) sells custom leatherware and fetish clothing in case you get in the mood. If there's a glass pipe you thought up at some point that was soooo cool, chances are someone else thought of it too, and it's here for sale.

Before you get too excited and buy a ticket to Van because you're going to 'score', you need to know that these are not places where you can buy drugs – the 'Smoke 'em if you got 'em' rule applies here. Despite public rumor, it's still illegal to sell pot in Canada, and it's also illegal to have it; but the laws are slowly being bent and twisted. It's also more than just a bunch of stoners here, the cafés are places where you can come, enjoy a coffee and a sandwich with some like-minded individuals and get absolutely baked.

FESTIVALS & EVENTS
Vancouver needs very little reason to throw a party or stage an event. Some of the bigger ones:

Participatory
Polar Bear Swim (☎ 604-605-2304) Traditional New Year's hangover cure in the chilly waters of English Bay (January 1).

Vancouver Sun Run (☎ 604-689-9441) One of the world's largest 10km races winds through downtown, finishing with a big party at BC Place (late April).

Arts
New Music West Festival (☎ 604-684-9338) International event with club crawls, band showcases, seminars and industry forums (May).

Vancouver International Jazz Festival (☎ 604-872-5200) (late June)

Vancouver Fringe Festival (☎ 604-257-0350) Drama, musical theatre, comedy and dance from around the world (mid-September).

Vancouver International Film Festival (☎ 604-685-0260; www.viff.org) Showcases 300 films from 50 nations (late September to early October).

Just for Fun
Abbotsford International Air Show (☎ 604-852-8511; Abbotsford, 40km east (early August)

Alcan Dragon Boat Festival (☎ 604-688-2382) Nearly 2000 competitors from around the world show off on False Creek (mid-June).

Pacific National Exposition (PNE; ☎ 604-253-2311) Second-largest fair in Canada (late August to early September).

Symphony of Fire (☎ 604-738-4304) International fireworks extravaganza at English Bay choreographed to music to determine which country has the biggest bang (early August).

Culture
Chinese New Year (☎ 604-687-6021) 15 days of dancing, music, fireworks and food in Chinatown (late January).

Canada Day Canada Place (☎ 604-666-8477); Granville Island (☎ 604-666-5784) Canada's birthday is celebrated with festivals, frenzy and fireworks (July 1).

Pride (☎ 604-687-0955) Celebrates Vancouver's gay and lesbian communities; culminates in a Sunday parade along Denman and Beach Sts, followed by a fair and entertainment at Sunset Beach (early August).

Christmas at Canada Place (☎ 604-666-8477) December holiday season features ornate trees, wreaths and holiday window displays.

SLEEPING
It should come as no surprise that Vancouver gets extremely busy in the summer. It's not impossible to find a place last-minute, but if you have your heart set on a specific place to stay, book it as soon as you know your travel plans. The **Super, Natural British Columbia reservations service** (☎ 604-663-6000, 800-663-6000, 250-387-1642; www.snbc-res.com) can be a great help in finding something to your liking, as can www.tourismvancouver.com.

Prices do drop outside of the high season; see if a spring, autumn or even winter visit works for you. Individual accommodations' websites often have specials and lower prices than the front desk, summertime rack-rates given here. Relative to

VANCOUVER & AROUND

GAY & LESBIAN VANCOUVER

Vancouver's gay and lesbian scene is part of Vancouver's culture, rather than a subsection of it. The legalization of same-sex marriages in BC has resulted in a huge number of couples suddenly loving Canada and using Vancouver as a gay Vegas. For more information on the laws, visit www.vs.gov.bc.ca/marriage/howto.html.

Xtra West, a weekly freebie, will tell you the current happenings, and you can check www .gayvan.com or www.superdyke.com before you go. The **Gay & Lesbian Centre** (Map pp58-9; ☎ 604-684-5307, help line 604-684-6869; 1170 Bute St) provides useful local and visitor information. **Little Sister's Bookstore** (Map pp58-9; ☎ 604-669-1753; 1238 Davie St) specializes in gay literature specifically geared for lesbians.

While gays and lesbians live all over the city, the biggest concentration of bars, hangouts and residents is on **Davie St** between Jervis and Burrard. **Numbers** (Map pp58-9; ☎ 604-685-4077; 1042 Davie St) is a multi-level men's cruise bar and the **Pumpjack Pub** (Map pp58-9; ☎ 604-685-3417; 1167 Davie St) is a place to hang out with the after-work crowd and go nuts in the late-night scene.

Dufferin Hotel (Map pp58-9; ☎ 604-683-4251; 900 Seymour St), 'The Duff,' has drag-karaoke nights and frequent strippers. **Odyssey** (Map pp58-9; ☎ 604-689-5256; 1251 Howe St) has the youngest crowd and a reputation as the wildest club, with go-go boys and shower-room viewing. **Oasis** (Map pp58-9; ☎ 604-685-1724; 1240 Thurlow St) is another popular spot. Ladies, **Lick** (Map pp58-9; ☎ 604-685-7777; 455 Abbott St), in the Lotus hotel, is a club just for you.

---

other North American cities, Vancouver is considered a bargain as you can stay in a budget room for less than $100, or a top-end room for $200 or more; mid-range is generally everything in between.

Downtown
Map pp58-9

BUDGET
Vancouver couldn't be funky if it didn't have places for the funky people to stay. Most hostels in town are excellent, but some are unsafe dumps. Do your research and trust your gut.

Cambie Hostel – Seymour (☎ 604-684-7757; www.cambiehostels.com; 515 Seymour St; d/r $22.50/55; ✗) A spin-off of the original Cambie hostel near Gastown, this one has just as much cool, but at a little lower decibel-level in a smaller building. It's a colorful hostel with narrow hallways, comfy beds and a definite hostel vibe.

Global Village Backpackers (☎ 604-682-8226, 888-844-7875; gvbp@interlog.com; 1018 Granville St; dm/r with bathroom $21/56; ✗) A colorfully funky hostel in the heart of the city's action. Loud music and loud conversations are the norm here, but it's the kind of place where it fits and you don't really take notice. They do cool hostel things like nightly pub runs with no-line-up access to some of downtown's hottest clubs.

HI-Vancouver Central (☎ 604-685-5335, 888-203-833; vancouver.central@hihostels.ca; 1025 Granville St; dm/r $28/66; ✗) Formerly the Royal Hotel, this place is right in the middle of downtown's action and soaks up all its energy. It is a fun place to stay, with above-hostel amenities – some of the private rooms have TVs.

HI-Vancouver Downtown (☎ 604-684-4565, 888-203-4302; van-downtown@hihostels.ca; 1114 Burnaby St; dm/r $28/66; ✗) The low-key, hospitable hostel enjoys an excellent location, quiet but close to the action; it's a block from Davie St and a short walk from central downtown. The dorm rooms have no more than four beds and they offer a free shuttle service to the train station and Jericho Beach HI hostel (p78).

Cambie International Hostel (☎ 604-684-6466, 877-395-5335; www.cambiehostels.com; 300 Cambie St; d/r $22.50/55; ✗) It shares a building with one of the most fun, down-to-earth, working-person pubs Downtown, so expect the same from this bunkhouse – it's like staying over after a house party. The sleeping rooms are nice, with four to six oversized beds and some en suite bathrooms and showers. No cooking facilities are available, but cheap eats are easy to come by in the bakery and café – guests' first breakfast is on the house.

YWCA (☎ 604-895-5830, 800-663-1424; www.ywca hotel.com; 733 Beatty St; s/d $73/113; ✗) Everyone is welcome at the 'Y' and people from all walks of life stay here. It's got the look of a 'real' hotel with the feel of everyday people. It's a bustling place with a kitchen on every other floor and 155 rooms in various configurations ranging from singles to rooms with five single beds.

YMCA (☎ 604-681-0221; www.vanymca.org; 955 Burrard St; s/d with TV $50/59; ⊗) The faded brown carpets aren't flattering but once you find yours through the labyrinth of hallways the rooms are clean and useful.

MID-RANGE

Victorian Hotel (☎ 604-681-6369, 877-681-6369; www.victorian-hotel.com; 514 Homer St; s/d $109/119; ⊗) This is a hidden gem in Vancouver. It's a beautifully renovated Victorian with European-style hospitality – muffins and tea are served in the morning. The 27 rooms vary in layout and color but rest assured, they are all comfortable and inviting.

Crowne Plaza Hotel Georgia (☎ 604-682-5566, 800-663-1111; www.hotelgeorgia.bc.ca; 801 W Georgia St; s/d $199/219; ⊗ ⊠) This landmark has the marble and mahogany you expect from early-19th century architecture with contemporary furniture and coverings to the rooms. The lobby on its own is a cavernous wonder full of 1920s ambience and activity, and the hallways up the stone steps ooze ageless charm.

The Georgian Court (☎ 604-682-5555, 800-663-1155; www.georgiancourt.com; 773 Beatty St; r/ste $165/190; ⊗ ⊠ ▯) With a certain European charm, this hotel is away from central downtown and easily overlooked. Yet it is an extremely attentive place that doesn't overlook any detail. The blue and taupe sun-filled rooms, and the friendly staff will make your Vancouver stay very relaxing.

Bosman's Motor Hotel (☎ 604-682-3171, 888-267-6267; bosmans@bc.sympatico.ca; 1060 Howe St; s/d $119/129; ℗ ⊗ ⊠ ▯) It isn't hip but it is clean, hospitable, well located and underrated. The basic rooms won't spoil or improve your Vancouver stay, as long as you get a room off the ground floor.

Kingston Hotel (☎ 604-684-9024, 888-713-3304; www.kingstonhotelvancouver.com; 757 Richards St; s/d $118/128; ⊗) As Vancouver's first B&B hotel, this old building still has some character. The rooms are small and basic and the beds have Hawaiian-print bedcovers.

St Regis Hotel (☎ 604-681-1135; www.stregishotel;.com; 602 Dunsmuir St; from $129; ⊗ ⊠) It's been a low-key landmark since it was built in 1916 and today it still provides comfortable accommodations without fanfare. The St Reeg 'just is', and it's definite value considering its central location.

Century Plaza (☎ 604-687-0575, 800-663-1818; www.century-plaza.com; 1015 Burrard St; $169-209; ⊗ ⊠ ▯) Floral print everything and slightly dated color schemes in some of the rooms here offset the ultra-comfortable and exquisite décor in others.

TOP END

Opus Hotel (☎ 604-642-6787, 866-642-6787; www.opushotel.com; 322 Davie St; from $229; ⊗ ⊠ ▯) Vancouver's newest entry in Yaletown has taken on the principle of 'less is more…but more is more as well' – less clutter, more color; fewer barriers, more windows; less forced character, more simple, natural style. Not to be confused with post-modernistic nonsense, the oddly shaped furniture is comfortable and the bright colors and open spaces are refreshing.

Fairmont Hotel Vancouver (☎ 604-684-3131, 800-441-1414; www.fairmont.com; 900 W Georgia St; s/d $267/287; ⊗ ⊠ ▯) This decades-old Vancouver landmark has learned a thing or two along the way. Smooth, refined, elegant and confident, the rooms, hallways and lobby mix classic architecture with contemporary style. The oxidized copper roof – turned green long ago – gives away its age, but it can't be called over the hill or has-been.

Metropolitan Hotel (☎ 604-687-1122, 800-667-2300; www.metropolitan.com; 645 Howe St; $189-229; ⊗ ▯ ⊠ ▯) While some hotels seek elegance through stone-built character, this hotel defines it on modern terms. Not avant-garde, but subtle reminders – like Italian linens, earth tones and soaker-tubs – show that luxury doesn't have to follow a time-tested formula.

Le Soleil (☎ 604-632-3000, 877-632-3030; www.lesoleilhotel.com; 567 Hornby St; r/ste $200/220; ⊗ ⊠ ▯) Royal red and regal gold are the primary colors at the hotel where detail and service are the primary focus. Where some hotels go for elegance or luxury, Le Soleil can be described as 'plush'.

The Landis (☎ 604-681-3555, 877-291-6111; www.lanissuitesvancouver.com; 1200 Hornby St; r $199-339; ⊗ ⊠ ▯) This high-rise features four suites per floor in two different floor plans. The spacious and unique design highlights incredible views and the furnishings are tasteful and comfortable.

Rosedale on Robson (☎ 604-689-8033, 800-661-8870; www.rosedaleonrobson.com; 838 Hamilton St; 1-/2-bedroom $195/235; ☒ ☒ ☐ ☒) This suite-only hotel in Yaletown combines comfort and convenience with affordability. It's an impressive glass tower with amazing views of the city and spacious, bright rooms.

Pan Pacific Hotel (☎ 604-662-8111, Canada 800-663-1515, USA 800-937-1515; www.panpac.com; 300-999 Canada Pl; views of harbor/city $449/399; ☒ ☒ ☐) The planners made use of their seemingly unlimited space in Canada Place by keeping it as open as possible. The rooms are huge and aren't filled with furniture, giving the impression that you're actually outdoors as you look out the floor-to-ceiling windows.

West End
Map pp58-9
B&BS
English Bay Inn (☎ 604-683-8002, 866-683-8002; 1968 Comox St; www.englishbayinn.com; r $190-225; ste $330; ☐ ☒) Among the high-rises of the West End sits an unassuming old Victorian with a quiet and pretty garden. Not quite an oasis, but it's a nice escape from the modern world. The rooms are all bright and refreshing but room No 4 has a quality about it that seems particularly inviting; it could be the four-poster bed.

West End Guest House (☎ 604-681-2889, 888-546-3327; www.westendguesthouse.com; 1362 Haro St; $135-250; ☐ ☒) This is another Victorian between the high rises, with bright rooms and fluffy, inviting, large beds. The paisley wallpaper, dark trim and old wooden furniture exude that old-fashioned feel and to keep up, you'll need to turn your internal speed down.

Colibri Bed & Breakfast (☎ 604-689-5100; colibri@home.com; 1101 Thurlow St; $65-90; ☒) This stuccoed and super friendly B&B is a favorite among gay and lesbian travelers. It's got a homey feel, and though the pastel-colored rooms aren't huge, they aren't cramped either.

MID-RANGE
Sylvia Hotel (☎ 604-681-9321; www.sylviahotel.com; 1154 Gilford St; r $85-145, ste $155-165; ☒) Well loved and ivy-covered, Sylvia enjoys a prime location on English Bay close to Stanley Park. The hallways are a little creaky, that happens with age, but the

granite steps and spacious rooms haven't changed. Families love it here and there are many return visitors, so book a year ahead for a bayside view in summer.

Barclay Hotel (☎ 604-688-8850; www.barclayhotel.com; 1348 Robson St; s/d $75/95; ☒) With its own sense of style and charm, this is right in the thick of the Robson St action. Stay off the 1st floor in a small but comfortable room.

Sunset Inn Travel Apartments (☎ 604-688-2474, 800-786-1997; www.sunsetinn.com; 1111 Burnaby St; ste $188; ☒ ☒) In a quiet-but-accessible neighborhood south of Davie St and near Sunset Beach and English Bay, these apartment-suites are a welcome respite.

Like Rosellen and Sunset Inn, many former West End apartment buildings have become suite-style properties, with kitchens and a bit of room to spread out. You'll find quite a few along Robson St between Jervis and Nicola Sts:

Blue Horizon Hotel (☎ 604-688-4461, 800-663-1333; www.bluehorizonhotel.com; 1225 Robson St; r $149-179; ☒ ☒)

Riviera Motor Inn (☎ 604-685-1301, 888-699-5222; www.rivieraonrobson.com; 1431 Robson St; r $148; ☒ ☒)

Tropicana Motor Inn (☎ 604-687-5724; 1361 Robson St; s/d $139/159; ☐ ☒ ☒)

TOP END
Pacific Palisades Hotel (☎ 604-688-0461, 800-663-1815; www.pacificpalisadeshotel.com; 1277 Robson St; $290-390; ☒ ☒) Recently refurbished, this

funky little place has a color scheme that would rival that of a smurf's. The offbeat attitude and 'How's it going?' disposition can be a relief from the 'Welcome, how may I help you' found in other places.

Listel Vancouver (☎ 604-684-8461, 800-663-5491; www.listel-vancouver.com; 1300 Robson St; r $199-239; ☒ ☒) Standard hotel rooms in very unstandard surroundings. Funky furniture and colors, art and sculptures all mingle with discreet lighting, wood and granite throughout the building. The rooms are warm and soothing and the 4th and 5th 'gallery floors' display original works.

Lord Stanley Suites on the Park (☎ 604-688-9299, 888-767-7829; fax 604-688-9297; info@lordstanley.com; 1889 Alberni St; $199-269; ☒ ☒) This beautiful, stylish building just south of Lost Lagoon and Coal Harbour enjoys spectacular views. The earth-tone suites are large, comfortable and well appointed. Only open since 1998, this place has that fresh feeling of newness, but also that calm feeling of maturity

Elsewhere in Vancouver

Outside the central core, Vancouver's neighborhoods offer plenty of sleeping options.

B&BS

Since Vancouver's neighborhoods are peppered with residential pockets, B&Bs exist throughout the city. For help in finding something that meets your needs, **Old English B&B Registry** (☎ 604-986-5069; www.bandbinn .com) and **Town & Country B&B** (☎ 604-731-5942; www .townandcountrybedandbreakfast.com) are your best bets; or contact the info center, www.bb canada.com or www.bedsandbreakfasts.ca.

Johnson Heritage House B&B (Map pp54-5; ☎ 604-266-4175; www.johnsons-inn-vancouver.com; 2278 W 34th Ave; r $135-185; ☒ ☒) The proprietors take owning a four-room B&B and have fun with it. Each of the rooms has a themed bathroom, and the 10-foot antique gas-pump in the Carousel room adds a certain charm. The whole place is antique and knick-knack filled and the hosts want you to get the most out of Vancouver with guest guides to local restaurants and step-by-step directions for day trips to Victoria and Whistler.

Arbutus House B&B (Map pp54-5; ☎ 604-738-6432; www.arbutushouse.com; 4470 Maple Crescent; 1-2 people $125, 3-4 people $165; ☒ ☒ ☒) In Shaughnessy Heights, this one has an upscale and modern

feel. There's a private computer station along with the more expected bathrobes, slippers, afternoon tea and bedtime sherry. It's close to an array of parks, gardens and historic homes.

Pacific Spirit Guest House (Map pp54-5; ☎ 604-261-6837; pspirit@vancouver.quik.com; 4080 W 35th Ave; 1/ 2 r $85/105; ☒ ☒) On the edge of the forest at Pacific Spirit Regional Park near UBC, this is a great spot for families. There are two rooms for rent that share a bath, and most families rent both. A scrumptious five-course breakfast is served in the sunroom and there's a hot tub, play area and access to a guest laundry, microwave and small fridge (often stocked with beverages).

Penny Farthing Inn (Map p68; ☎ 604-739-9002; www.pennyfarthinginn.com; 2855 W 6th Ave; s $110-145, d $120-180; ☒ ☒) Rooms here range from the very tiny Lucinda's to the ultra elegant Bettina's with hardwood floors, high-back chairs and a wood-burning fireplace. Sophie's is a good choice; with a four-poster wooden bed and small balcony overlooking the garden. The breakfast starts with pastries and home-made jams and continues onto huge portions from the seasonally changing menu.

Mickey's Kits Beach Chalet (Map p68; ☎ 604-739-3342, 888-739-3342; www.mickeysbandb.com; 2146 W 1st Ave; $85-105) The chalet has three rooms and it is right by Kits Beach. The Yew Room includes a fireplace.

Fisher House on the Point (Map p68; ☎ 604-731-6258; www.fisherhousevancouver.com; 1304 Walnut St; $85-125; ☒ ☒) This good-looking house is in a great neighborhood in Kits; it's only a short walk over the Burrard St Bridge to downtown. The rooms are bright, but the bathroom is shared.

Cambie Lodge (Map p66; ☎ 604-872-4753, 888-872-3060; 446 W 13th Ave; $95-105), **Windsor Guest House** (Map p66; ☎ 604-872-3060, 888-872-3060; ww.dougwin.com; 325 W 11th Ave; $75-105; ☒ ☒) and **Douglas Guest House** (Map p66; 456 W 13th Ave; $75-125; ☒ ☒) are all beautifully restored Victorians owned and run by the same proprietor. They all have big front porches, nice front yards and rooms lavished with period furniture and décor.

BUDGET

Hotel Patricia (Map pp64-5; ☎ 604-255-4301; www .budgetpathotel.bc.ca; 403 E Hastings St; s/d $89/99; ☒ ☒) Though East Hastings St is not what you'd call an accurate representative of Vancouver, 'The Pat' attempts to be the antithesis of the ugly duckling and succeeds. The rooms are neither luxurious nor spacious, but the lobby reflects on times when appearance mattered and the entire place is well looked-after. The west-facing rooms on the 5th floor have knockout views of downtown.

HI-Vancouver Jericho Beach (Map p68; ☎ 604-224-3208, 888-203-4303; van-jericho@hihostels.ca; 1515 Discovery St; dm/r $24/61; ☒) For the activity-minded this is the place. Seconds from Jericho Beach and minutes from downtown, there are 10 private rooms – some plain, others nice – dorms, an industrial-sized kitchen and a fun café (breakfast/dinner $5/7).

University of British Columbia Housing (Map pp64-5; ☎ 604-822-1000; www.ubcconferences.com; 5961 Student Union Blvd; s/d with bathroom & kitchenette $99/109; ℗ ☒) When the university kids pack up their video games and clean up their pizza boxes, you can move in. Rooms range from six-bed rooms to studios, and most of the housing is only available in the summer, though Westcoast Suites are available year-round. It's not a bad alternative, since UBC is a city in itself with plenty of greenspace, restaurants, cafeterias and pubs.

City Centre Motor Hotel (Map p66; ☎ 604-876-7166, 800-707-2489; www.citycentermotorhotel.com; 2111 Main St; $55-75; ℗ ☒ ☒) Clean, basic, green and burgundy sums up this motel near the east end of False Creek. It's about as close as you'll get to downtown in a motel that's a reminder of the days when the draw was the city, and your room was a place to sleep.

Shaughnessy Village (Map p66; ☎ 604-736-5511; www.shaughnessyvillage.com; 1125 W 12th Ave; studio s/d $70/80, ste s/d $89/99; ℗ ☒ ☒ ☒) This is actually an apartment building that rents short-term to travelers, but it's much nicer, safer and a lot more fun than other budget hotels. Imagine a mix of frumpy and nautical décor, if you can. Free breakfast in the onsite restaurant.

MID-RANGE

Pillow Suites (Map p66; ☎ 604-879-8977; www.pillow.net; 2859 Manitoba St; ste $115-255; ℗ ☒) Three heritage houses contain the seven fully furnished suites that make your stay seem more like house-sitting than staying at a hotel. 'Maya', in the purple building that used to be an old grocery store, is a steal considering the size of the suite and the location of the properties. A great place for families; big discounts are offered for extended stays.

Plaza 500 Hotel (Map p66; ☎ 604-873-1811, 800-473-1811; www.plaza500.com; 500 W 12th St; s/d $136/145; ℗ ☒ ☒) The views from 12th and Cambie Sts are among the best of the city; several floors above the power-lines are exponentially better. With tastefully furnished rooms, this hotel makes for excellent value.

TOP END

Granville Island Hotel (Map p66; ☎ 604-683-7373, 800-663-1840; www.granvilleislandhotel.com; 1253 Johnston St; r/ste/penthouse $220/250/499; ℗ ☒ ☒) All rooms are different here, with different luxuries and advantages. The plentiful bay windows let natural light in and allow for views of False Creek and the city that are unmatched.

Greater Vancouver   Map pp54-5

Kingsway Blvd is a major road that branches off Main St southeast of E 7th Ave and continues to Burnaby as a motel strip. It's not a bad part of the city if you don't mind being a few minutes away from downtown. They'll also have free parking and SkyTrain is only three blocks away. Recommended:

2400 Motel (☎ 604-434-2464, 888-833-2400; 2400motel@telus.net; 2400 Kingsway; r from $75/91) Collection of individual cottages.
Eldorado Motor Hotel (☎ 604-434-1341; 2330 Kingsway; s/d $65/80)

EATING

Vancouver has something for every palate, from street dogs to poached salmon. The beauty of Vancouver's location that's often overlooked by diners is the fact that not only is it close to the ocean, allowing for fresh seafood, but the fertile farms up Fraser Valley allow for fresh land-food. Local wine from the Okanagan Valley adds to the experience.

Downtown   Map pp58-9
BUDGET

In keeping up with other haute cuisines of the world, some amazingly good street food can be found on Vancouver's sidewalks. Before picking up that discarded candy bar, try one of the street vendors found throughout the city. Most offer a buffet of condiment jars filled with various relishes and peppers from the carts serving hotdogs, polish sausages and veggie-dogs. The one on the southeast corner of Robson and Burrard Sts is one of the best.

Shopping center food courts often offer low prices and some variety. At the large food court in **Waterfront Centre** (☎ 604-630-5306; 200 Burrard St), more than a dozen vendors serve meals you can eat at indoor or outdoor tables.

Canadian Maple Delights (☎ 604-682-6175; 769 Hornby St; mains $6-10) specializes in all sorts of untypical maple delights including soups, sandwiches, potatoes and such. **Pezzo** (☎ 604-669-9300; 1100 Robson St; $3-7) is a lively place for gourmet pizza by the slice, or lasagne. The stairs leading to one of the cheapest lunches on Robson front the **Thai House Restaurant** (☎ 604-683-3383; 1116 Robson St; lunch $7, dinner $10-20). Part of a popular local chain, **Bread Garden Bakery & Café** (☎ 604-688-3213, 812 Bute St; snacks $5), makes good soups and sandwiches.

MID-RANGE

a kettle of fish (☎ 604-682-6661; 900 Pacific St; mains $13-18; ☽ dinner, lunch Mon-Fri) 'eat lotsa fish' is their motto, and they do what they can to help you fulfill it. Oddly and overly decorated with land-based vegetation, this restaurant makes phenomenal dishes from ingredients under the sea.

Doolin's Irish Pub (☎ 604-605-4343; 654 Nelson St; mains $8-12; ☽ lunch-late) The central bar and wooden tables and chairs look well used, but Doolin's is a relative newcomer to Vancouver's pints-and-plates crowd. There's an Irish spin on pub favorites, but there are old-country standards like Irish coddle and ploughman's lunch as well. Gaelic, folksy songs are played in the afternoon and U2, Peter Gabriel and The Pogues are cranked up for the late-night crowd.

Zin (☎ 604-408-1700; 1277 Robson St; mains $10-25) Orange and purple funk meet urban retro décor in this semi-artsy, semi-trendy eatery where half-circular geometry makes subtle appearances. While the vibe is hip and fresh, the menu stays away from the 'fusion' route and serves traditional and original land-and-sea dishes.

Kitto Japanese House (☎ 604-687-6622; 833 Granville St; mains $7-11; ☽ lunch & dinner) The smell of grilled steak fills your nostrils the

TOP 5 SUNDAY MORNINGS

It's Sunday, probably not much before noon, and you're starving. Ah, yes, the long-favorite North American tradition of combining the best of two meals into one – brunch. Some Sunday brunch staples are:

- **Sophie's Cosmic Café** (p84)
- **Glowbal/AFTERglow** (p80)
- **The Fish House in Stanley Park** (p82)
- **Hamburger Mary's** (p81)
- **Raincity Grill** (p82)

minute you walk in the door. The booths and counter seats are always full at peak meal times and the sushi chefs behind the counter are constantly yelling, slicing and serving good sushi.

da Pasta Bar (☎ 604-688-1288; 1232 Robson St; mains $10-16; ☽ lunch & dinner) Under the rusted metal sign you'll find a casual, fun atmosphere and a selection of pastas and sauces that melt in your mouth.

Centro Grill (☎ 604-694-0202; 901 Granville St; mains $10-15; ☽ lunch & dinner) The smells from the open kitchen and the noise in the dining room let you know this is a Mediterranean restaurant. The cavernous wood-and-tile eating area can get loud, but it's hit or miss on whether it's going to be busy or not. Mixed antipasto plates for two and classic pasta dishes are a good bet. Open late.

TOP END

Diva at the Met (☎ 604-602-7788; 645 Howe St; mains $15-30) Famous for excellent desserts (including home-made ice creams), the Diva offers dinners of local fish, game with wonderful sauces and refined vegetarian terrines. The restaurant of the Metropolitan Hotel has an airy feel in a multi-tiered setting. It's a good place to escape the streets for a meal, or even just a drink after a performance.

Joe Fortes (☎ 604-669-1940; 777 Thurlow St; mains $15-25; ☽ lunch & dinner) Named after Vancouver's first official lifeguard, the gold-rush era dark wood and brass grand room, or the rooftop patio, are excellent places to go for seafood in the city. As-local-as-possible oysters, fish and crustaceans are used in their staples of Pacific Northwest cooking. They've been shucking oysters and preparing salmon and trout for almost 20 years and have gotten pretty good at it.

Il Giardino di Umberto (☎ 604-669-2422; 1382 Hornby St; mains $11-30; ◯ lunch & dinner) The original restaurant of the Umberto's chain has retained its Tuscan character in the old downtown house. Hidden behind the vines and plants are yellow stucco walls, dark wood and terracotta tiles. They also offer outstanding Tuscan cooking, updated with Canadian delicacies such as berries and wild game.

C (☎ 604-681-1164; 1600 Howe St; mains $18-32; ◯ lunch & dinner) This crisp, recommended seafood restaurant with white linens and high-back chairs enjoys a quiet location overlooking False Creek. Its West Coast dim sum business lunch and Dungeness crab and lemon myrtle cakes are popular midday selections. There's an elegant and innovative eight-course tasting menu and an excellent wine list.

Top of Vancouver (☎ 604-669-2220; 555 W Hastings St; mains $20-30; ◯ lunch & dinner) One floor below The Lookout! (p57), they could serve sawdust and you might not notice as you'd be captivated by the views in this revolving restaurant. Fortunately, they serve excellent meals and prepare seafood dishes to perfection.

Gotham (☎ 604-605-8282; 615 Seymour; mains $25-50; ◯ dinner) Gotham is for carnivores and people who believe vegetables and side dishes should be ordered separately. It is dark, sultry, intimate and substantial. Rooms on various levels provide different dining experiences, and in any of them you can order the steaks or seafood that have made this place rapidly famous, particularly in the Hollywood crowd.

Yaletown   Map pp58-9
As Vancouver's newest neighborhood gains popularity and residents, so does it again eateries. Trying to mirror the personalities of the people who live here, restaurants in Yaletown focus on style, presentation, coolness, and taste. **Urban Fare** (☎ 604-975-7550; 177 Davie St) is an industrially decorated and organically exhaustive grocery store that also has a deli serving sandwiches and such.

Melriches Coffee House (☎ 604-681-2120; 1043 Mainland St; mains $7-8; ◯ lunch & dinner) Light

wood colors mix with burgundy and brick in this popular Yaletown fuel-up spot.

Elbow Room (☎ 604-685-3628; 560 Davie St; mains $6-8; ◯ breakfast & lunch) A Vancouver mainstay for breakfast and lunch. The servers are abusive by design, so have fun with it and return the favor. When they ask 'Are you ready to order or what?' answer that you'll be ready when you're bloody ready. Breakfast runs until closing, and the menu highlights the mood of the joint, evidenced by the 'You've Got to be F-ing Kidding' burger (two 8oz beef patties plus mushrooms and bacon).

Urban Thai Bistro (☎ 604-408-7788; 1119 Hamilton St; mains $10-13; ◯ lunch & dinner) Lots of pork, beef, seafood and veggie options in this place where people are discovering 'Thai fusion' – local ingredients spiced to your liking. The open booths inside are cozy but not cramped, or you can opt for the concrete and metal patio out front.

Brix (☎ 604-915-9463; 1138 Homer St; mains $10-18; ◯ lunch & dinner) An eclectic, hip, definitely Yaletown joint decorated in violet and burgundy to complement the hardwood floors and polished aluminum trim. Lunch includes a chicken spring roll with sour cherry compote and dinner features tapas and entrées like seared Chilean sea bass.

Glowbal/AFTERglow (☎ 604-602-0835; 1079 Mainland St; mains $10-15; ◯ lunch-late) This place has cast a wide net and successfully caught the power-lunch, after-work, dinnertime, late-night and weekend-brunch crowds. The inventive menu features a daily-revolving lunch special and weekend brunches of seafood omelets and eggs Benedict. The place turns lounge in the evening, serving tapas and martinis on the granite bar or out on the patio.

The Riley (☎ 604-684-3666; 1661 Granville St; mains $8-20; ◯ lunch & dinner) This café has a perfect waterfront location on False Creek and takes advantage of it with a heated patio. Extremely friendly servers are always on hand, even after they bring your Rocky Mountain halibut with orange marmalade glaze or Chinese maple salmon. Other perks: lots of tapas for sharing, and brunch on weekends.

West End   Map pp58-9
BUDGET
Hillary's Caffé (☎ 604-608-6808; Suite 102, 1184 Denman St; mains $3-6; ◯ breakfast) This cosy little

coffeehouse tucked away off the sidewalk makes the best cinnamon buns in Vancouver – so much so that they frequently sell out. They also have bagels and breakfast sandwiches and it's a gem of a little spot, perfect for mornings at English Bay.

soupspoons (☎ 604-328-7687; 990 Denman St; mains $5-7) They're a lot nicer than Seinfeld's soup Nazi and the soups they make are the ultimate comfort food. They have 10 different soups on the menu. Happy hour is from 3pm to 5pm, when everything is 20% off.

Original Souvlaki Place (☎ 604-689-3064; 1181 Denman St; $5-6; ◷ lunch & dinner) This simple Greek grill is always cooking meat for gyros and souvlakis. The focus is on the taste rather than the presentation and you end up with honestly cooked and tangy food.

Akira Sushi (☎ 604-806-6321; 1069 Denman St; mains $7-12; ◷ lunch & dinner) A local favorite is this little sushi house with friendly service.

Because so many people live in the West End, there are plenty of grocery stores. There's the **Robson Public Market** (☎ 604-682-2733; 610 Robson St). **Capers** (☎ 604-687-5299; 1675 Robson St) features fresh and organic foods. Cakes of the cup and regular variety, with names like lemon drop and mint condition, are all at **cupcakes** (☎ 604-974-1300; 1116 Denman St; $2). Not exactly healthy, but since they are specialists, they're really, really good.

MID-RANGE

Stepho's Souvlaki (☎ 604-683-2555; 1124 Davie St; ◷ lunch & dinner) This mini Greek village has stucco walls, dim lighting, terracotta floors, busy ambience and mouthwatering smells. The food is delicious and it's a Vancouver standard, made evident by the nightly lines outside.

Death by Chocolate (☎ 604-899-2462; 1001 Denman St; dessert $5-15) Forget the diet and get a chocolate burger. They have new locations popping up around town but this location of the dessert-only place is the neighborhood favorite.

Hamburger Mary's (☎ 604-687-1293; 1202 Davie St; mains $7-10; ◷ lunch-late) Mary's is a throwback to the days of black and white checkered floors, chrome trim and juke-box playing diners. Burgers are the specialty and the all-day breakfasts and weekend brunches are as gluttonous as you'd expect from a greasy spoon. Sitting out on the

---

SOMETHING FISHY

At some point during your stay, you're going to have to try the sushi, it's simply too good not to sample. And at times of overindulgence we may ask ourselves, 'Why eat from an aquarium when you can have the ocean? Several of Vancouver's sushi restaurants have all-you-can-eat specials, and they don't cheap out on the quality; you still get the same rolls and sashimi you'd normally get.

Kisha Poppo (Map pp58-9; ☎ 604-681-0488; 1143 Davie St; lunch/dinner $11/19) There's an instant gratification in being here that's hard to properly explain. It's not the best sushi; but it is good, really good, almost melt-in-your-mouth good. It's not the best restaurant, either; the bamboo and light wood décor try for authenticity, and about half a dozen people will serve you throughout your meal. It must be that this place is the whole package; the food, the look and the ambience.

Other recommended eat-til-you-drop places:

- **Granville Sushi** (Map p66; ☎ 604-738-0388; 2526 Granville St; lunch/dinner $10/19)

- **Sui Sha Ya** (Map p66; ☎ 604-733-8886; 101-1401 W Broadway; lunch/dinner $10/19)

---

patio and watching Davie St life is a West End pleasure.

Rooster's Quarters (☎ 604-689-8023; 836 Denman St; mains $10-13; ◷ lunch & dinner) Whatever 'Montreal-style chicken and ribs' means, it's super good. It's a casual place where table manners are left at the door and 'Pardon my French' follows the frequent belching. Nobody seems to mind eating with their hands. Great spicy wings.

Brass Monkey (☎ 604-685-7626; 1072 Denman St; mains $7-13; ◷ lunch-late) This neighborhood favorite took spare parts to make tables and chairs and opened a retro-bistro for hipsters, nine-to-fivers and everyone in between. The menu's deceptively simple descriptions don't hint at the complex plates that come out. Try the ahi tuna or any martini.

The Boathouse (☎ 604-669-7375; 1795 Beach Ave; mains $12-20; ◷ lunch & dinner) A seafood restaurant popular among visitors for its super-chill lounge and rooftop patio.

TOP END

O'Doul's (☎ 604-661-1400; 1300 Robson St; mains $10-25) The hotel lounge of the Listel is a smooth bar/restaurant where manhattans fit in just as well as bottled beer. The menu fuses the cuisine of the Pacific Northwest and the American Deep South in such dishes as jambalaya with saffron risotto. Live jazz accompanies meals on Friday and Saturday night.

Wild Garlic Bistro (☎ 604-687-1663; 792 Denman St; lunch $8-12, dinner $17-21; ☯ dinner daily, lunch Sat & Sun) The flavorful menu is a stark contrast to the industrial metallic-and-black décor. Garlic is blended so well into the dishes you don't notice that it's there, but you'd notice if it wasn't.

Raincity Grill (☎ 604-685-7337; 1193 Denman St; mains $10-25) This well-known and popular restaurant on English Bay employs a semi-formal ambience for serving seafood and pasta. You can also get a gourmet lunch box ($10) to go and take to the beach. Weekend brunches are a real treat; you can watch the sun glitter on the water and enjoy Dungeness crab Benedict.

Liliget Feast House (☎ 604-681-7044; 1724 Davie St; mains $20-30; ☯ dinner) Pacific Northwest dining at its finest. The unique lodge-like setting features huge poles and lots of wood. Dishes involving salmon, venison and caribou make this a real cultural experience.

Stanley Park
Map p62

Stanley Park's restaurant choices are ensconced in premier settings and scenery.

Prospect Point Cafe (☎ 604-669-2737; 2099 Beach Ave; mains $17-25) This semi-casual seafood restaurant surrounded by totem poles and perched on a cliff beneath the Lions Gate Bridge serves excellent salmon dishes.

Teahouse Restaurant (☎ 604-669-3281; 7501 Stanley Park Dr; mains $12-28; ☯ lunch & dinner) This old house at Ferguson Point has great views and is one of the few places in town that still serves traditional tea in a traditional setting.

The Fish House in Stanley Park (☎ 604-681-7275; 8901 Stanley Park Dr; mains $10-26; ☯ lunch & dinner) Fresh and artistically arranged seafood is enjoyed in this semi-formal and autumnal-colored dining room. If the previous night was especially rough, a brunch with tranquil views and a delicious shrimp and brie omelet will make the day smoother.

Gastown
Map pp64-5

Italian food is really big in Gastown, but the neighborhood's been showing it can roll with times and has had a recent influx of other cuisines.

The Irish Heather (☎ 604-688-9779; 217 Carrall St; mains $10-15; ☯ lunch & dinner) This 'Gastropub' combines an old-country pub menu with fine-dining presentation. Classics such as bangers 'n' mash are on the menu, but artistically arranged. Several dining rooms create an air of privacy and you can still order pints or whiskeys – if you can choose from the selection of over 100.

Wild Rice (☎ 604-642-2882; 117 W Pender St; mains $10-15; ☯ lunch-late) The concept here is mixing East with West in an ultra-modern restaurant with open spaces and an illuminated bar. Chinese cuisine with local ingredients delight your senses. Small, tapas-size appetizers are perfect for sharing; try the tuna tataki lettuce wraps. This is also the perfect spot to relax and enjoy a couple of martinis.

Thai Palace (☎ 604-331-1660; 100 Water St; mains $10-12; ☯ lunch & dinner) Locals swear by this place for Thai. The food can be ordered spicy, or not at all, to please Western palates. The décor is purely Thai with close seating and a laid-back atmosphere.

Raintree at the Landing (☎ 604-688-5570; 375 Water St; mains $10-25) A true Gastown setting. The brick wall, wrought iron and wood-beam construction remind you what neighborhood you're in, while the amazing views of the sea and mountains and seafood dishes prepared with flair remind you what city you're in.

Rossini's Pasta Palazzo (☎ 604-408-1300; 162 Water St; mains $10-30; ☯ lunch & dinner) It's got the look, feel and sound of a speakeasy with its brick walls and dark woods and jazz music. The fantastic garlic mashed potatoes go for $27, but they'll throw in a steak dinner too.

Chinatown
Map pp64-5

The authenticity of Chinatown means that it's teaming with markets and places to grab a quick bite.

Hon's Wun-tun House (☎ 604-688-0871; 108-268 Keefer St; mains $5-7) There are several locations around town, but this is the hands-down flagship. The predictable tiled floors, black vinyl and chrome chairs, constant din and mouthwatering smells only set the table for the actual meal. Huge bowls of soup and pie plates full of noodles are served still steaming and are as delicious as you'd expect from the heart of Chinatown.

Buddhist Vegetarian Restaurant (☎ 604-683-8816; 137 E Pender St; mains $8-13) You first think you've walked into a grocer, but the restaurant is in the back. Black bean sauce makes several appearances on the menu and vegetables star in the chow meins and hot pots.

Pink Pearl (☎ 604-253-4316; 1132 E Hastings St; mains $6-13) It's east of Chinatown, but many locals swear it's the place for dim sum and consider it a Vancouver staple.

Granville Island   Map p66

The SandBar (☎ 604-669-9030; 1535 Johnston St; mains $8-13; ☻ lunch & dinner) In an unusual setting underneath a bridge sandwiched between a cement factory and a theater, the rooftop patio here works. There's also the welcoming interior and busy open kitchen serving wood-cooked, tender seafood.

Bridges (☎ 604-687-4400; 1696 Duranleau St; mains $7-12) There's a setting for everyone here in the formal dining-room, the pub, or the bistro, all with spectacular views of False Creek and the city. The outdoor dock is a long-time favorite with a good-time feel. It's a good place to spend an afternoon enjoying some baked halibut or a salmon burger.

Dockside (☎ 604-685-7070; 1253 Johnston St; mains $15-20; ☻ lunch & dinner) Its open kitchen and fish tanks under the bar are a sight, but the real views are from it's vantage point on the west side of Granville Island. There's lots of seafood on the menu, and it's cooked to perfection. They also make their own beer and have a kid's menu.

For the best selection of only-in-Vancouver picnic provisions, head to **Granville Island Public Market** (p63), where you can buy all the fixin's appropriate for any meal. There's also the fine-dining prepared by those learning to be pros and served at un-fine-dining prices at the **Pacific Institute of Culinary Arts** (☎ 604-734-4488; 1505 W 2nd St; mains $18-36; ☻ lunch & dinner).

West Side   Map p66

The Broadway and South Granville neighborhood includes creative upstarts and proven favorites. South Main St has also

been emerging as an up-and-comer for funky and unique dining options.

Ouisi (☎ 604-732-7550; 3014 S Granville St; mains $10-15; ☻ lunch & dinner) This New Orleans-style bistro is a down-to-earth and with-the-times place with jazz – live acts play during the week – flowing out of the speakers. Choose from mains like spicy pecan catfish crusted with orange chipotle cream.

Bin 942 (☎ 604-734-9421; 1521 W Broadway; tapas $9-11; ☻ dinner-late) The small, metallic lounge is the right kind of after-work drinks place. 'Tapatisers' – sashimi-style ahi tuna and portobello mushroom cutlets – could be paired with something from the 'hip hops' beer menu, or the 'who, what, where and damage' of the wine list.

Banana Leaf (☎ 604-731-6333; 820 W Broadway; mains $8-15; ☻ dinner) Vividly colored in yellow and blue, this Malaysian and Singaporean restaurant serves Indian-curried seafood in a lively, yet private, setting.

Vij's (☎ 604-736-6664; 1480 W 11th Ave; mains $10-25; ☻ dinner) Considered the high-water mark of Indian cuisine in Vancouver, the chefs are into making 'curry art'. Local ingredients are used in traditional Indian cooking and presented with care.

Seoul House (☎ 604-739-9001; 1215 W Broadway; mains $9-16; ☻ lunch & dinner) The smell of meat on the barbecue mingles with the aroma of spices providing olfactory delight before you taste your food. The tall ceilings and wooden floors characterize a welcoming hominess and the private booths allow privacy.

Monsoon (☎ 604-879-4001; 2526 Main St; mains $9-15; ☻ dinner) Carved wooden statues greet you before you take your seat at the long, green vinyl bench or your wire-mesh chair. The restaurant is small, it's also a bit loud, and it's definitely hip and lively. The menu is an Asian-Thai-Indian fusion with seafood, spices and fruits terrifyingly mixed together to make delicious meals.

Tojo's (☎ 604-872-8050; 777 W Broadway; mains $10-18) This is the birthplace of the BC roll, and some claim it's the best sushi in Vancouver. It's melt-in-your-mouth good and a few tables enjoy great city views.

West Restaurant & Bar (☎ 604-738-8938; 2881 Granville St; mains $9-15; ☻ dinner) Formerly called Ouest, star chef David Hawksworth's award-winning restaurant was revamped in early 2003 to become more casual and less

AUTHOR'S CHOICE

Sophie's Cosmic Cafe (☎ 604-732-6810; 2095 W 4th Ave; mains $7-12) This is the weekend breakfast choice of hangover sufferers, honest food seekers and anyone who knows a thing or two about eggs Benedict. If there were a 'Kits' Greatest Hits' collection of restaurants, this would be the opening track. There are line-ups every weekend for tables inside the garage-sale-item-walled café or out on the glassed-in, heated patio; folks crave BC salmon and BC eggs. Broken bits of crayons are scattered about the floor and small children run wild, but that's the organized chaos of Sophie's. Breakfast is the trademark but lunch and dinners are just as tasty. Sophie also makes her own hot sauce, and it tastes good on everything on the menu – except the desserts, they're delicious on their own.

Francophile. The specialty is small plates for multi-tasting. The menu changes seasonally and always features fresh, local ingredients. Order just 'foie gras' and you'll get a terrific pan-seared version with *confit* and endive. There are great views of the kitchen action behind the glass back wall.

The Budapest (☎ 604-877-1949; 3250 Main St; mains $10-15; ☽ lunch & dinner Wed-Sun) Schnitzels and cabbage rolls star in this small restaurant, and the goulash is simple, delicious and hearty.

Afghan Horsemen (☎ 604-873-5923; 445 W Broadway; mains $11-15; ☽ dinner) You can perch at either a standard table or join the communal seating on an Afghan cushion on the floor. This was Canada's first Afghan restaurant, opened in 1974. Try one of the huge platters for two to get a wide sampling of the cuisine.

Kitsilano   Map p68

Kits is the place to go to have a good meal with good times. There's a cornucopia of restaurant types, where most feed off Kits' vibe and are laid-back and fun. To purchase picnic fixings or other grocery items, stop in at **Capers** (☎ 604-739-6676; 2285 W 4th Ave).

The Naam (☎ 604-738-7151; 2724 W 4th Ave; mains $6-10) You can't spell 'hippie' without 'hip' and that's exactly what this small pocket of

continued Kitsilano tradition is – in the form of an always busy, 24-hour vegetarian restaurant. Well-used wooden chairs and floors have seen many plates of sesame fries with miso gravy and countless bowls of salad come and go. They've got a fireplace burning in the winter, a garden patio for the summer, and live music playing every evening all year long.

Romio's Greek Taverna (☎ 604-736-2118; 2272 W 4th Ave; mains $10-13; ☽ lunch & dinner) With blue and white checkered tablecloths, wooden banisters and stucco walls, this taverna is only missing an old man in shorts and black socks. If this place didn't serve delicious, zesty and tangy Greek food, it would be a major fraud and wouldn't have lasted the years that it has.

Nyala Restaurant (☎ 604-731-7899; 2930 W 4th Ave; mains $9-13; ☽ dinner) This place is every big kid's dream, as there are no utensils used. The richly spiced Ethiopian food is wrapped in injers (flatbread) and eaten. There's a vegetarian buffet ($10.95; ☽ 5-9pm Sun Mon & Wed) that includes delicious stews and dips.

Elwood's (☎ 604-736-4301; 3145 W Broadway; mains $7-12; ☽ lunch & dinner) It's skinny and narrow so you'll have to shimmy past people to get to the back, or you can just stay out front on the well-worn wooden patio, if you can find a spot. 'The Wood' is where Kits-folk hang out and enjoy a couple beers with some 'appies' (appetizers – true BC slang!) or a pizza.

Solly's Bagelry (☎ 604-738-2121; 2873 W Broadway; $3-5; ☽ breakfast & lunch) They're simply the best bagels in town and that's why people keep coming back. Must be the complicated marketing scam of making bagels fresh daily from fresh ingredients. They've also got good coffee, good soups and good times.

Little Mary's Diner (☎ 604-677-6767; 2184 Cornwall Ave; mains $6-8; ☽ lunch & dinner) When you get that craving for a great burger, and who doesn't, go to Mary's. It's got a classic diner appearance and classic diner formula. Simple pleasures don't get much simpler than a burger, onion rings and root-beer float on the beach.

Lumiere (☎ 604-739-8185; 2551 W Broadway; meals $90-130, with wine $140-180) Being voted best restaurant in Vancouver six years in a row, this trendsetter must be doing something right – and it is. The French-traditional cooking combines elegance with earthy, impeccable fresh local BC ingredients and a minimalist Asian sensibility. Like anyone who takes their job extremely seriously, chef Robert Feenie delivers the very best. The menus vary seasonally and are normally offered as *prix-fixe* tasting menus featuring vegetarian, seafood or chef's choice. If you can, order the braised halibut casserole with truffle butter.

East Vancouver   Map pp64-5

As Vancouver's most culturally diverse neighborhood, Commercial Drive has no shortage of different places to eat.

Nick's Spaghetti House (☎ 604-254-5633; 631 Commercial Dr; mains $9-13) This is an Italian restaurant with ambience. It's away from the bustle but makes a bustle of its own serving classic favorites like spaghetti and meatballs and traditional lasagne. The place for first dates, 25th anniversaries or just getting together with friends, Nick's is a Vancouver tradition.

Café Deux Soleil (☎ 604-254-1195; 2096 Commercial Dr; mains $4-7) A hip, open and fun place with a kid's menu and play area (on the small stage where acoustic musicians and poets often entertain). Breakfasts feature the usual egg dishes and croissants; the night menu features delights like black bean roll-ups and pesto burgers.

Caffé Calabria (☎ 604-253-7017; 1745 Commercial Dr; mains $4-8) If you hadn't soaked up enough culture on the street, step into this café for a cappuccino or panini. The black and white marble floor, big brick fireplace, marble statues and guys yelling at each other in Italian behind the counter will take you to the Mediterranean.

Havana (☎ 604-253-9119; 1212 Commercial Dr; mains $9-13) There's an art gallery in the back and the menu invents Cuban fusion like coconut tuna and eggs with grilled veggies. The atmosphere is uber-casual and breakfast is served into the afternoon.

Clove Café & Record Bar (☎ 604-255-5550; 2054 Commercial Dr; ✆ closed Mon) This is definitely one of Vancouver's most interesting Indian restaurants. The chairs are an ode to grade school and you can peruse, or buy, vintage vinyl while awaiting your meal. There are plenty of vegetarian options on the menu and a phenomenal calamari salad.

Bukowski's (☎ 604-253-4770; 1447 Commercial Dr; mains $8-15) This 21st-century hangout for beatniks features a varied menu ranging

from crêpes to udon. The shady willow tree makes the patio a perfect place to spend a hot afternoon, or chill with the lounge crowd in the evenings.

If you're just looking for quick eats **Juicy Lucy's Good Eats** (☎ 604-254-6101; 1420 Commercial Dr; mains $4) is a juice bar offering veggie and fruit concoctions, and **Tony's Neighbourhood Deli & Café** (☎ 604-253-7422; 1046 Commercial Dr; mains $4-6; ✆ breakfast & lunch) has awesome paninis.

Elsewhere in Vancouver

Red Onion (Map pp54-5; ☎ 604-263-0833; 2028 W 41st St; mains $5-7) The menu is simple and the service friendly, a combo that's worked for almost 20 years. Burgers are cooked over a grill, the way they should be, and the ingredients are always fresh.

Spread out along Main St from E 48th to E 51st Aves, the Punjabi Market area is

---

FLAVORS OF THE MONTH

First it was Pacific Northwest cuisine, then it was tapas, then 'fusion'; and while those cuisines are still enormously popular, Vancouver's latest culinary fad is simply ice cream. But not just any old dairy concoction – what reaches into Vancouver's heart and tempts its taste buds is a departure from tradition that combines normal and not so normal fresh ingredients to end up with a much smoother and lighter product. Italian gelato, also referred to as gelati, is all the rave and shops are popping up around town.

La Casa Gelato (Map pp64-5; ☎ 604-251-3211; 1033 Venables St) This bubblegum-pink and green building with the soda-fountain interior is a must-visit. Some of the 198 flavors are so ridiculous, you have to try them: Wasabi, garlic, pumpkin, blackbean and white chocolate, and wild asparagus are just some of the options waiting for you. Other places to get gelato:

- **Mondo Gelato** (Map pp58-9; ☎ 604-647-6638; 1094 Denman St) Enticing displays and chunks of real fruit in the gelato.

- **Mum's Gelato** (Map pp58-9; ☎ 604-681-1500; 849 Denman)

- **Amato Gelato** (Map p66 ☎ 604-879-9011; 78 East 1st Avenue) Old soda-fountain setting.

a great place to go for Indian food. **Zeenaz Restaurant** (Map pp54-5; ☎ 604-324-9344; 6460 Main St; buffet $9; 🕙 closed Tue) offers an all-you-can-eat buffet. Not to be outdone, the **All India Sweets & Restaurant** (Map pp54-5; ☎ 604-327-0891; 6505 Main St; buffet $7) sets out a 45-item vegetarian buffet.

DRINKING

In the best possible context of the phrase, Vancouver likes to drink. As with all Canadian cities, they love their beer, but with cosmopolitan status comes drinks ending in the letters 'ini' and most bars use their marketing tactics to invent their own specialties. Appletinis, Bellinis and Crantinis have replaced the standard vodka martini in all the colors of the rainbow and flavors of the orchard.

Bars & Nightclubs

As with most big cities, the club scene is an ever-revolving door. Granville St downtown and Gastown's Water St are your best bets for following the crowds. Cover charges range from zero to $20, depending on the day and what's going on inside.

DOWNTOWN   **Map pp58-9**
The Roxy (☎ 604-684-7699; 932 Granville St) While other clubs on Granville have come and gone, The Roxy has withstood the tests of time and fickle tastes of clubbers. It just wants to have a good time and bring you with it.

Some clubs serve as live music venues (p87), but when there isn't a concert that night, it's all about the club scene. Other bars and clubs:

The Drink (☎ 604-687-1307; 398 Richards St)
Granville Room (☎ 604-633-0056; 957 Granville St) Blue, silver and black, it's cool because it doesn't try to be; if you want to be cool, it's cobalt, metallic and dark.
Cellar (☎ 604-605-4350; 1006 Granville St) New club in medieval cellar setting.

GASTOWN   **Map pp64-5**
Purple Onion (☎ 604-602-9442; 15 Water St) Chill in the live jazz and blues room or gyrate in the DJ dance music room.
Blarney Stone (☎ 604-687-4322; 216 Carrall St) Good, honest fun.
Lotus (☎ 604-685-7777; 455 Abbott St) It's about dancing.
Sonar (☎ 604-683-6695; 66 Water St) Progressive

house, soul, R&B, reggae and electronica; grande hip-hop party Wednesdays attracts a younger crowd.
Alibi Room (☎ 604-623-3383; 157 Alexander St) Tucked away and discreet but well known among pretty people, famous people, and pretty-famous people; tapas upstairs and techno downstairs.

Lounges

When it's more of a night to sit back and admire the scene, Vancouver has you covered:
Backstage Lounge (Map p66; ☎ 604-687-1354; 1585 Johnston St) Live music and a great selection of single-malt Scotches.
Balthazar (Map pp58-9; ☎ 604-689-8822, 1215 Bidwell St; mains $10-25; 🕙 dinner-late) Trend-setting place contains hidden corners and alcoves for conversation and intimacy.
Crush Champagne Lounge (Map pp58-9; ☎ 604-684-0355; 1180 Granville St)
Ginger 62 (Map pp58-9; ☎ 604-688-5494; 1219 Gran-ville St)
Voda (Map pp58-9; ☎ 604-684-3003; 433 Robson St) Chic nightclub where the street-side patio swarms with beautiful people on warm evenings.

Brewpubs

Sure, you could go to another bar and order a draught instead of one of the many personally brewed and cared-for micro-brews in town; you could also eat frozen fish sticks instead of the available fresh seafood – it just makes a little less sense.

Steamworks Brewing Co (Map pp64-5; ☎ 604-689-2739; 375 Water St) This multi-purpose brewery in Gastown is a soda fountain, sitting-room, pub and oyster bar all in one converted brick warehouse. They have outstanding views of the North Shore and it's a favorite place of the downtown after-work crowd. The library style upstairs is perfect for sitting by the window or in one of the leather chairs by the fireplace.

Granville Island Brewery (Map p66; ☎ 604-687-2739; 1441 Cartwright St; $8; 🕙 10am-4pm) This brewery makes the most widely-available beer in stores and on taps around the city; the brewers really care about their beer and it shows in the final product. You'll learn a thing or two on the tour and tasting and may never go back to 'other' beer again.

Yaletown Brewing Co (Map pp58-9; ☎ 604-681-2739; 1111 Mainland St) The wooden beams, denim-covered seats and widely used rebar give the impression of a construction site, but it's definitely beer they're crafting. It's rustic and trendy at the same time and an afternoon on the patio can turn into a late night at the huge central bar without warning.

Dix (Map pp58-9; ☎ 604-682-2739; 871 Beatty St) They've got big-ass burgers and sandwiches and you can smell the burning applewood under the grill from the street. But the best part is that pitchers of their very own beer are only $12.

ENTERTAINMENT

Vancouverites can take off the bike shorts, throw on some khakis or a tux, and go out on the town anytime. It's a city that loves to entertain. Sports and live music take precedence, with theater very close behind.

Tickets for most events are available from **Ticketmaster** (performing arts ☎ 604-280-3311, concerts ☎ 604-280-4444, sports ☎ 604-280-4400; www .ticketmaster.ca). In the info center **Tickets Tonight** (Map pp58-9, ☎ 604-684-2787; www.ticketstonight.ca) sells half-price tickets when available for day-of events, and also sells advance tickets on its website.

Both the *Vancouver Sun* and the *Province* publish entertainment sections on Thursday. For details on upcoming performances and exhibitions, contact the **Arts Hotline** (☎ 604-684-2787) or **Alliance for Arts & Culture** (☎ 604-681-3535; www.allianceforarts.com).

The *Georgia Straight* is the best source of information on the arts and nightlife. The *West Ender* is a good backup while *Xtra West* focuses on the gay scene. For other information, check out www.clubvibes.com.

Cinema

Fifth Avenue Cinemas (Map p66; ☎ 604-734-7469; 2110 Burrard St; adult/child $12/9) First-run movies are shown at this moviehouse in Kits, but not the kind with car chases or explosions; more about character development and meaningful relationships.

There are plenty of uber-plexes popping up around the Lower Mainland but major first-run theaters downtown are the more traditional kind like **Granville Cineplex Odeon** (Map pp58-9; ☎ 604-684-4000; 855 Granville St) and **Capitol Six Theatre** (Map pp58-9; ☎ 604-669-6000; 820 Granville St). **Cinemark Tinseltown** (Map pp64-5; ☎ 604-806-0799; 88 W Pender St) is a newer complex. Discounts are available for Tuesday and matinee shows.

Hollywood Cinema (Map p68; ☎ 604-515-5864; 3123 W Broadway; adult/child $5/3) and **The Ridge**

(Map p68; ☎ 604-738-6311; 3131 Arbutus St; adult/ child $5/3) show between-theatre-and-DVD movies.

The **Denman Place Discount Cinema** (Map pp58-9; ☎ 604-663-2201; 1779 Comox St) shows three films for $4 on Tuesday and has $6 double-bills the rest of the week.

The schedule at **Pacific Cinémathéque** (Map pp58-9; ☎ 604-688-3456; 1131 Howe St) is so varied that it's best to think of it as an ongoing film festival.

Classical Music & Dance

Vancouver Symphony Orchestra (Map pp58-9; ☎ 604-876-3434; www.vancouversymphony.ca; Orpheum) 100 concerts annually.
Ballet British Columbia (Map pp58-9; ☎ 604-732-5003; www.balletbc.com; Queen Elizabeth Theatre; ☼ Sep-May) Vancouver's top dance troupe.
Vancouver Opera (☎ 604-683-0222; www.vancouver opera.ca; Queen Elizabeth Theatre; ☼ Oct-May)

Comedy

The ultimate in improvisation is **Theatre-Sports League** (Map p66; ☎ 604-738-7013; www.vtsl .com; New Revue Stage, 1601 Johnston St) as these actors compete against each other and use audience participation to do it. Stand-up comics from around the city and North America appear at **Yuk Yuk's** (Map pp58-9; ☎ 604-696-9857; 1015 Burrard St).

Live Music

Most of the live music venues double as nightclubs when there's nothing going on; call ahead to make sure there's a band if you're set on grooving to live music.

DOWNTOWN

GM Place and **BC Place Stadium** host big-name bands while outdoor concerts at **Plaza of Nations** (Map pp58-9; ☎ 604-682-0777; B100-750 Pacific Blvd) are a great way to spend a summertime evening. Lesser-known acts often perform in the more intimate settings of downtown nightclubs:
Commodore Ballroom (Map pp58-9; ☎ 604-739-4550; 868 Granville St) Cavernous place with great sound, classic architecture and a big bouncy dance floor.
The Rage (Map pp58-9; ☎ 604-685-5585; 750 Pacific Blvd S) Near BC Place; cutting-edge, top 40 and occasional live bands.
Richard's on Richards (Map pp58-9; ☎ 604-687-6794; 1036 Richards St) 'Dick's on Dicks' has been a top dance and live-music club for years.

Piccadilly Pub (Map pp58-9; ☎ 604-682-3221; 620 W Pender St) Local rock and blues bands; house or acid jazz midweek.

Vogue Theatre (Map pp58-9; ☎ 604-331-7900; 918 Granville St) Old-fashioned cinema-cum-music stage.

The Yale (Map pp58-9; ☎ 604-681-9253; 1300 Granville St) Excellent, smoky blues bar.

ELSEWHERE IN VANCOUVER

Darby's Pub (Map p68; ☎ 604-731-0617; 2001 MacDonald St) Pints, darts and live music on weekends.

Cellar Jazz Café (Map p68; ☎ 604-738-1959; 3611 W Broadway) Good local jazz.

Mainstream (Map p66; ☎ 604-873-4131; 2120 Main St) Jazz club where dancing is both expected and encouraged.

Sports

As active as Vancouverites are, they love to watch others play as well and the sports scene is tightly intertwined with the city's culture.

HOCKEY

Take the drama of baseball, the speed of basketball and the contact of football, throw it all onto a 17,000 sq-foot piece of ice with large men armed with sticks determined to put a black disc into a 4-foot-by-6-foot target at any cost and you have yourself the game of ice hockey.

Vancouver is a hockey-mad city; though that's an easy thing to be when your teams are playing well. It's much better seen live than on TV, particularly for those not accustomed to the action.

Vancouver Canucks (☎ 604-899-4625; www .canucks.com; GM Place; from $29.50; ☽ Oct-Apr) The city's National Hockey League (NHL) team toyed with fans in 1994's thrilling Stanley Cup finals before losing Game 7 to the New York Rangers and sinking to depressingly low levels in the late 1990s. However, 'Go Canucks Go!' is once again chanted with pride as good management, drafting and building from within has the team at the top of the standings now and produced a roster that boasts superstars such as Todd Bertuzzi, Trevor Linden and Markus Naslund.

Of course, with success comes popularity and the number of season tickets has risen – most home games sell out so get your tickets before you arrive in Vancouver, if possible.

Vancouver Giants (Map pp54-5; ☎ 604-444-2687; www.vancouvergiants.com; Pacific Coliseum, 100 North Renfrew St; from $15; ☽ Oct-Mar) If you can't find tickets to the Canucks, try to get to a Giants game – these are the future superstars. This team plays in the 20-and-under Western Hockey League (WHL) and has been able to put together a decent team in its short existence. Tickets cost a lot less, are more available and sometimes these guys play with a little more desire since they're working to get to the show.

FOOTBALL

BC Lions (Map pp58-9; ☎ 604-661-3626; www.bclions .com; BC Place; from $20; ☽ Jun-Oct) The Lions are Vancouver's team in the Canadian Football League (CFL), a game that features more passing and more excitement than its US counterpart. The Lions have had some decent showings in the last few years, winning the Grey Cup championship most recently in 2000. This is a team that relies on its make-you-jump-out-of-your-seat offense.

SOCCER

Vancouver Whitecaps (Map pp54-5; ☎ 604-669-9283; www.whitecapsfc.com; Swanguard Stadium, cnr Boundary Rd & Kingsway; from $12; ☽ May-Aug) Vancouver's women's and men's soccer teams share the same name and stadium and are both very competitive within their leagues – men play in the A-League and women play in the W-League. Vancouver is arguably the soccer capital of Canada as its history with the sport professionally goes back almost 30 years. Bob Lenarduzzi and his brothers have been mainstays in the organization since their playing days, when they brought a North American Soccer League (NASL) Championship to Vancouver in 1979.

BASEBALL

Vancouver Canadians (☎ 604-872-5232; www .canadiansbaseball.com; Nat Bailey Stadium, 4601 Ontario St; from $6.50; ☽ Jun-Aug) The single-A farm team (minor league) to US Major League Baseball's Oakland As plays near Queen Elizabeth Park (p69) at Nat Bailey Stadium, 'The Nat – The prettiest little ballpark in the world'. It's a short season but coincides perfectly with the dog days of summer for afternoons of foot-longs (hot dogs) and cups of beer.

MOTOR RACING

Molson Indy (☎ 866-670-4639; www.molsonindy.com; False Creek; Fri/Sat/Sun/3-day $19/35/50/60; ☼ late July) When the Indy comes to town, it's more than just about the race, it's a week-long party. The days before the actual event are full of festivities, signings, appearances and exhibitions, finishing with the race around False Creek's east shores on Sunday.

HORSE RACING

Hastings Park Racecourse (Map pp54-5; ☎ 604-254-1631, 800-677-7702; www.hastingspark.com; PNE grounds; ☼ Sat, Sun & holidays Apr-Nov) The races at this park in East Van will never equal the Triple Crown races, but there's still that feeling of freedom and 'Pow!' when the bell sounds and the gates open and thoroughbreds speed around the dirt track.

Theater

Vancouver has long been a stop for mainstream shows, but also produces some good fringe talent of its own. Get a copy of the brochure *Vancouver Theatre Guide* from the info center or theatres in town.

MAJOR VENUES

Most venues are multi-functional and can accommodate everything from ballet to rock concerts.

The Centre (Map pp58-9; ☎ 604-602-0616; www.centreinvancouver.com; 777 Homer St) Formerly The Ford Centre, it sat vacant for a while and is now a sponsor-less venue for Broadway and other major shows.

The Queen Elizabeth Theatre (Map pp58-9; ☎ 604-665-3050; 600 Hamilton St) A major venue for touring Broadway and off-Broadway shows.

The Orpheum Theatre (Map pp58-9; ☎ 604-665-3050; 884 Granville St) A classic theatre with columns, velvet, red carpets and gold trim recalling times when the word theatre carried a little more weight than it does these days.

Firehall Arts Centre (Map pp64-5; ☎ 604-689-0926; 280 E Cordova St) Guess what it used to be. Now it puts on dance presentations and plays by Canadian and foreign playwrights.

COMPANIES

Vancouver Playhouse Theatre Company (Map pp58-9; ☎ 604-873-3311; ☼ Sep-May) Presents a six-play season in Queen Elizabeth Theatre.

Arts Club Theatre Company Granville Island (Map p66; ☎ 604-687-1644; 1585 Johnston St); Stanley Theatre (Map p66; 2750 Granville St) Michael J Fox and many other Canadian actors got their starts on an Arts Club stage.

SHOPPING

Vancouver's central district contains some of the city's most dynamic shopping areas. On Robson St is Vancouver's answer to Rodeo Drive and the busiest shopping street in Vancouver. Tasteful fashion stores and tacky tourist shops share the same street and there isn't much you can't buy. Or you can buy nothing at all and simply enjoy the lively street scene.

The other major downtown shopping destination is **Pacific Centre** (Map pp58-9; ☎ 604-688-7236; 700 W Georgia St), a three-block-long underground shopping mall running from Robson to Pender Sts between Granville and Howe Sts. Most of the stores are national and international chains, including **The Bay** (Map pp58-9; ☎ 604-681-6211), a department store selling everything from armchairs to zippers since it was first built as a Hudson's Bay Company supply shop in 1898. **Sinclair Centre** (Map pp58-9; 757 W Hastings St) is a marble and brass pocket of specialty and fashion shops.

Before the digital age of MP3s and Ipods, Vancouver was the cheapest place in the world to buy music. Dinosaurs who still listen to CDs and conventional music fans should head to **a&b Sound** (Map pp58-9; ☎ 604-687-5837; 556 Seymour St) or **Virgin Megastore** (Map pp58-9; ☎ 604-669-2289; 788 Burrard St) for new, or get used CDs and videos at **Charlie's Music City** (Map pp58-9; ☎ 604-688-2516; 819 Granville St). **Vinyl Records** (Map pp58-9; ☎ 604-488-1234; 466 W Cordova St) has an awesome collection.

Yaletown is the place to head for unique home furnishings and interior décorating. The old warehouse-district-gone-lofts is loaded with stylish design shops. Main St south of Broadway is lined with antique shops where storeowners have established their own niches rather than compete for the same customers. **Vancouver Antique Centre** (Map pp58-9; ☎ 604-669-7444; 422 Richards St) has 15 antiques dealers under one roof.

Should you be looking for vintage clothing, hemp products or cigars, you'll find them in Gastown, which is also a good place to look for First Nations art. **Hill's Indian Crafts** (Map pp64-5; ☎ 604-685-4249; 165 Water St) features a selection of carvings, prints, masks and cozy Cowichan sweaters. The **Inuit Gallery of Vancouver** (Map pp64-5; ☎ 604-688-7323; 345 Water St) sells Inuit sculptures, drawings and tapestries and Northwest Coast Native Indian masks, carvings and jewelry.

While in the Gastown-Chinatown area, check out the **Chinatown Night Market** (Map pp64-5; ☎ 604-682-8998; 100-200 Keefer St; ☼ 6:30-11pm Fri-Sun Jun–mid-Sep). **Ten Lee Hong Enterprises** (Map pp64-5; ☎ 604-689-7598; 500 Main St) is an excellent tea and ginseng store in Chinatown that will teach you the art.

After Robson St, Granville Island is next on the 'Fun places to shop' list. The stalls at the warehouse-like public market overflow with more than just foodstuffs; merchants also sell fancy jams, syrups and other preserved foods that make good gifts; this is the place for Vancouver smoked salmon and it can be packed for air shipment. Granville Island also is a good spot to shop for books, and arts and crafts; **Circle Craft** (Map p66; ☎ 604-669-8021; 1666 Johnston St) sells lovely wearable art, pottery, and jewelry. **Forge and Form** (Map p66; ☎ 604-684-6298; 1334 Cartwright St) is a gold and silversmith where the jewelry is made on the premises.

Granville on the Rise heads up the hill along Granville St for 10 blocks from 6th to 16th, south of Granville Island. It's a collection of antique and fashion stores that has quietly become a trendy and established strip.

Broadway east of Cambie St is an excellent place for outdoor equipment and clothing. Buy something bearing the Mountain Equipment Co-op (p70) label and you'll be asked around the world if you're Canadian. It's a warehouse-sized store that's hip and ecologically sensitive and worth a visit if you're in the market for outdoor gear.

True to its counterculture past, Kitsilano is Vancouver's best neighborhood for anti-commercialism. W 4th Ave between Burrard and Arbutus is the place for unique gifts, hand made crafts and funky things. **Craftworks** (Map p68; ☎ 604-736-2113; 2112 W 4th Ave) sells handmade items created by people with disabilities. **Ten Thousand Villages** (Map p68; ☎ 604-730-6831; 2150 W 4th Ave) offers 'fairly traded' handicrafts from around the world; you'll find hammocks, drums, clothing and more.

GETTING THERE & AWAY

Vancouver is the main point of entry for travelers to BC; see p380 for more on transportation throughout the province.

Air

Vancouver international airport (YVR; Map pp54-5; ☎ 604-207-7077) is 10km south of the city on Sea Island, in Richmond. You'll have to pay an airport improvement fee ($5 to $15) at the airport before your flight departs.

The Vancouver area has seaplane terminals servicing regional flights at YVR's south terminal and the harbor near Canada Place. There's also a helicopter terminal on the harbor near Waterfront Station.

Bus

Pacific Central Station (Map pp58-9; 1150 Station St) is both a bus and train station. **Greyhound** (☎ 800-661-8747; www.greyhound.ca) buses link Vancouver with Seattle and other North American cities, but do not have a service on Vancouver Island.

TO/FROM VICTORIA

Pacific Coach Lines (☎ 604-662-7575, 800-661-1725; www.pacificcoach.com; adult/child $30.50/15.25) runs buses to Victoria from 5:45am to 7:45pm.

TO/FROM SEATTLE

Quick Coach Lines (☎ 604-940-4428; www.quickcoach.com; adult/child $33/18) runs four daily buses from Vancouver hotels to downtown Seattle with stops at Seattle's Sea-Tac Airport and Bellingham Airport. **Bigfoot Adventure Shuttle** (☎ 604-278-8224, 888-244-6673; www.bigfoottours.com) runs buses to Victoria from Pacific Central Station.

Car

If you're coming in on Washington State's I-5, you'll cross the border near the town of Blaine at the Peace Arch Provincial State Park. BC's Hwy 99 veers west then north to Vancouver. Along the way you'll pass under, then over, arms of the Fraser River; look for the 'City Centre' signs once you're on the Oak St Bridge.

For travelers from the eastern part of the province, the Trans-Canada Hwy (Hwy 1) crosses the Fraser River as the Port Mann Bridge, meets Lougheed Hwy (Hwy 7) and snakes through the eastern end of the city. Downtown-bound travelers take the Hastings St exit and turn left, those going to the North Shore stay on the freeway over the Second Narrows Bridge.

If you're coming from the north, the Trans-Canada Hwy heads through West Vancouver and North Vancouver before going over the Second Narrows Bridge. In West Vancouver, take the 'Taylor Way' exit for Hwy 99; which takes you over Lions Gate Bridge into Stanley Park.

Ferry

BC Ferries (☎ 888-223-3779; www.bcferries.com; adult/ child $10/5, car $34.75, reservation $15) has two terminals in the Vancouver area; both make trips to Vancouver Island. It's a 95-minute sailing from **Tsawwassen** (☎ 604-943-9331; ☯ 7am-10pm hourly Jun-Sep, varies seasonally) to Swartz Bay near Victoria – an absolutely beautiful trip through the Gulf Islands. Ferries also go to Nanaimo from Tsawwassen (5:45am to 10:45pm July to September) and from **Horseshoe Bay** (☎ 604-921-7414; ☯ 6:30am-10pm Jul-Sep).

Horseshoe Bay also runs ferries to Bowen Island (p96) and Langdale (adult/child $8.25/ 4.25, car $28.75; 7:20am to 11pm July to September) on the Sunshine Coast. A service also runs from Tsawwassen to the Gulf Islands, see p176 for more on these routes.

Reservations on island trips are highly recommended, especially on Friday and Sunday afternoons in the summer. It's not uncommon to arrive for the 4pm ferry and not get on a boat until 7pm. The schedule changes (never drastically) every few weeks outside the peak season so double-check your preferred departure. See p380 for more on ferry travel.

Train

Vancouver's **Pacific Central Station** (Map pp58-9; 1150 Station St) serves **VIA Rail** (☎ 888-842-7245; www.viarail.ca) trains travelling to the rest of Canada, while **Amtrak** (☎ 800-872-7245; www.amtrak.com) links Vancouver – through Seattle – to the US.

GETTING AROUND
To/From the Airport

The mint-green **Vancouver Airporter** (☎ 604-946-8866, 800-668-3141; www.yvrairporter.com; adult/ child $12/5, round-trip adult/child $18/10; ☯ 5:30am-11:45pm) stops at Pacific Central Station and all major hotels. Tickets can be purchased from the airport office or your hotel desk.

The length of the journey varies with traffic and your ultimate destination. If Granville St is jammed – not unlikely – and your hotel is last on the route, it can take over 90 minutes.

An hour-long trip to the airport by **Translink** (adult/child $3/2) takes No 98 south on Granville St to Airport Station where you'll transfer onto No 424 to the airport.

If you're driving, as you head over the Arthur Lang Bridge from the airport, you can take the Granville St exit, or follow Marine Dr to Cambie St. Cambie has less traffic and the tree-lined central median makes it a more pleasant drive.

A taxi ride to the airport should be $25.

To/From the Ferry Terminals

To bus (adult/child $4/3) from downtown to Tsawwassen ferry terminal, take No 601 on Howe St to the Ladner Exchange, then No 640 to the ferry terminal. Allow about 75 minutes for the trip. To bus (adult/child $3/2) to the Horseshoe Bay terminal, take No 250 or 257 on Georgia St. A cab ride to either terminal should be around $35.

Bicycle

Vancouver is a great cycling city. Several secondary-street bikeways run across town, giving people the option of traveling by cycle away from the main arteries. The Adanac Bikeway, for example, runs 5.5km from downtown to the eastern city limits; others include the Seaside Bike Route and the Cassiar Bikeway. For more information, call the Bike Hotline ☎ 604-871-6070. Bikes are allowed on the SeaBus, as well as on the ferries across False Creek. See Activities (p70) for more information.

Car

Vancouver's traffic system was 20 years out of date 20 years ago, and it hasn't been improved. Vancouver is also the master of the bottleneck and it's not uncommon for the three-lane road you're on to narrow down to two...and then to one.

There are no expressways in or near downtown, which is a glass half-full, half-empty phenomenon; a spaghetti tangle of concrete interchanges don't corrupt the natural beauty and splendor of the city, but everyone must travel on surface streets. Congestion is a big problem and traffic can back up for blocks during rush hours (7am to 9am and 4pm to 7pm). Try to avoid driving at these times but if you must, pay attention to the time restrictions for left-hand turns posted at intersections.

Then there's parking; if you're patient, the spots will come. Residential areas will have at least a few streets of free parking, limited to one or two hours, but parking in some areas can be as much as $2 for 15 minutes. If you'll be downtown for the day, use the parking lot of your hotel, consider parking away from town and taking transit, or park in one of the guarded lots south of Georgia St, as they're generally cheaper than those to the north.

All major car rental companies have offices downtown and at the airport. See p382 in the Directory for contact info.

Ferry

Two companies operate mini-ferry shuttles across False Creek.

Aquabus (☎ 604-689-5858; $2-5; ☼ 7am-10:30pm, 7am-9pm winter) Travels between Downtown, Granville Island, Yaletown, Stamp's Landing and Science World.

Burrard Water Taxi (☎ 604-293-1160) Offers a 24-hour water-taxi service to the greater Vancouver maritime region.

The False Creek Ferries (☎ 604-684-7781; $2-5; ☼ 7am-10pm, 7am-9pm winter) Travels between Vanier Park, Vancouver Aquatic Centre, Granville Island, Stamp's Landing and Science World.

Public Transit

Public transportation in Vancouver used to be government-operated but things didn't run right so a private company took over their routes and equipment. **Translink** (☎ 604-953-3333; www.translink.bc.ca; adult/child $2/1.50, Daypass $8/6) now runs city buses; the SkyTrain automated light-rail system and SeaBus ferries to North Vancouver.

If you're staying within Vancouver, you need only worry about one-zone travel, but the transit system expands to three zones as you move further out in to the 'burbs. Ask the driver for a transfer when you pay with exact change and travel is good for 90 minutes. If you're staying longer than a couple days, you might want to consider purchasing 10-trip FareSaver tickets or monthly FareCards.

Translink produces *Discover Vancouver on Transit*, an excellent booklet that out-

lines bus, SkyTrain and SeaBus routes to all area attractions, parks, recreational sites and shopping districts. It's available for free at the info center and on some buses.

SkyTrain connects downtown Vancouver with greater Vancouver via the Expo line and the newly completed Millennium line. The passenger-only SeaBus catamarans zip across Burrard Inlet between Waterfront Station downtown and Lonsdale Quay in North Vancouver. For both, try to avoid rush hours, when many commuters crowd aboard.

Taxi

Flagging a cab on the street shouldn't take too long downtown, but it's easiest to get your hotel to call you one. Companies include:

Black Top & Checker Cabs (☎ 604-731-1111)
Vancouver Taxi (☎ 604-871-1111)
Yellow Cab (☎ 604-681-1111, 604-876-5555)

THE LOWER MAINLAND

Vancouver is the main draw for this corner of the world and is deserving of center stage. But there is a supporting cast who have their own role in the area around Vancouver, known as 'the Lower Mainland', and have some interesting qualities in their own right.

East of Kitsilano, north–south Boundary Rd is the border between Vancouver and the city of Burnaby. Southeast of Burnaby is New Westminster, once the capital of BC and now an industrial area along the Fraser River. Southwards across the Fraser, are Delta, Surrey, White Rock, Langley and the Fraser Valley.

NORTH VANCOUVER
pop 125,220

'North Van' takes over the north shore east of the Lions Gate Bridge, where forested mountains rise suddenly from Burrard Inlet and reach heights of over 1000m. Development over the decades has seen swaths of trees removed and housing climb further and further up these hills, but there is still some natural beauty up there to be explored and enjoyed.

The sights up in the hills are too far to walk to, but if you plan on sticking close to shore, the SeaBus makes North Van just a boat-ride away.

Sights & Activities
GROUSE MOUNTAIN RESORT
The Skyride gondola takes people up 1100m to the **Peak of Vancouver** (☎ 604-984-0661; 6400 Nancy Greene Way; adult/child $25/14; ✇ 9am-10pm), the city's most convenient ski area and a popular summer destination with outstanding views of Vancouver and plentiful activities. Once you're up here, some premier hiking and mountain biking is to be had.

You can also hoof it to the top via the Grouse Grind, a 3km route almost straight up the 850m ascent that's more of an outdoor Stairmaster than a nature hike. Not that it's a bad idea, but be prepared for little being offered in the way of views until you get to the top, and hordes of people on the trail. Fit people make it in an hour, for those taking smoke-breaks, allow 90 minutes. Hiking is free but if your knees are shaking, catch the Skyride ($5 one-way) down.

If you came for the snow, being able to ski **Grouse's** (☎ 604-980-9311; adult/child $42/18) The Cut – especially at night – while looking down at the city is pure bliss. Winter activities also include cross-country skiing, ice-skating and sleigh rides and if it's a clear night, head up to enjoy the city lights while sipping a hot chocolate.

Head north over Lions Gate Bridge and veer right on Marine Drive, then turn left (north) onto Capilano Rd.

MT SEYMOUR PROVINCIAL PARK
Lesser known but just as fun – no city-views, though – **Seymour** (☎ 604-924-2200) has some good hiking and mountain biking featuring several lakes and lots of forest. Some areas are very rugged, so visitors on overnight trips should register with park rangers. **Mt Seymour Resorts** (☎ 604-986-2261; www.mountseymour.com; adult/child $34/18) operates a downhill ski area in the winter that doesn't get as crowded as the other local mountains. To get to Seymour, take the Mt Seymour Parkway exit east, then turn north on Mt Seymour Rd.

LONSDALE QUAY MARKET
At the center of the North Shore SeaBus terminal complex, this lively **marketplace** (☎ 604-985-6261; ✇ 9:30am-6:30pm, 9:30am-9pm Fri) features a lower floor devoted to fresh and cooked food, with outdoor seating and frequent entertainment, and an upstairs area with specialty shops and several sit-down restaurants. A booth in the ferry terminal offers information on North Shore attractions.

LYNN CANYON PARK
While thousands flock to the Capilano suspension bridge (below), the suspension bridge in this **park** (☎ 604-984-3149; ✇ 7am-dusk), although shorter and not as high, remains relatively un-walked. It makes for a more realistic experience since it's possible for you to be the only one on the wobbly 90-year-old span. The park also includes some great hiking trails, plus picnic and swimming spots.

The **Lynn Canyon Park Ecology Centre** (☎ 604-981-3103; 3663 Park Rd; ✇ 10am-5pm, noon-4pm Sat & Sun Oct-May) can educate you about the biology of the area through dioramas, films and slide shows.

To get to the park, take the Lynn Valley Rd exit off Hwy 1, then turn right (east) on Peters Rd, where you'll see signs that point the way.

CAPILANO SUSPENSION BRIDGE
The original cedar and hemp bridge was built over a century ago; the current **pedestrian bridge** (☎ 604-985-7474; 3735 Capilano Rd; adult/child $17/4; ✇ 8am-dusk, 9am-5pm Sep-May) was built in 1956 using wire cables and cement, so don't worry, it's not going to break. The 1333-person capacity bridge – 140m long and 70m above the Capilano River – isn't the only thing to experience here; other attractions include a totem-pole carving house, nature trails, historical exhibits and guided tours every half-hour. It can get very busy here; another option is the less-touristy, free Lynn Canyon Park (see above).

Head north over Lions Gate Bridge and veer right on Marine Drive, then turn left (north) onto Capilano Rd.

CAPILANO RIVER REGIONAL PARK
Excellent and convenient hiking is possible through the cedars in this **park** (☎ 604-224-5739; ✇ 8am-dusk). The Capilano River is also good for whitewater kayaking, but only if

you're experienced, as the canyon gets very narrow in places.

Capilano Salmon Hatchery (☎ 604-666-1790; 4500 Capilano Rd) is most interesting from July to November when, through the glass walls, you can see adult salmon jump up the ladders to reach spawning grounds upstream. Exhibits explain life-cycle of these purely instinctive fish.

Cleveland Dam creates Capilano Lake, which supplies much of Vancouver's drinking water. There are picnic grounds and great views of the Lions, two peaks of the Coast Mountains. The site is also a hot spot for film crews, largely due to the easily accessed forest on the other side of the dam.

Sleeping

Lonsdale Quay Hotel (Map pp54-5; ☎ 604-986-6111, 800-836-6111; www.lonsdalequayhotel.bc.ca; 123 Carrie Cates Court) A definite naval theme with an aquamarine color scheme and dark wood furniture, but why not, since it's right on the waterfront with great views of Vancouver.

Canyon Court Motel (Map pp54-5; ☎ 604-988-3181, 888-988-3181; www.canyoncourt.com; 1748 Capilano Rd; $129; P ☒ ☜) has a chalet-like appearance and good, clean rooms surrounding an outdoor courtyard. Across the street, **Grouse Inn** (Map pp54-5; ☎ 604-988-7101, 800-779-7888; www.grouseinn.com; 1633 Capilano Rd; r $99-145, ste $145-179; P ☒ ☜) is another good option. Both are near the Lions Gate Bridge and include continental breakfast.

A Lynn Canyon House B&B (Map pp54-5; ☎ 604-986-4741; 333 Robinson Rd; www.vancouverinn.com $75-145; P ☒ ☜) Looking like a gingerbread house, this place is right near the entrance to Lynn Canyon Park. Once you step inside it quickly takes the form of a charming English inn. It has the elegance of antique furnishings, classic coverings and warm hospitality, and the modern conveniences of goose-down quilts and an outdoor hot tub.

Thistledown House B&B (Map pp54-5; ☎ 604-986-7173, 888-633-7173; www.thistle-down.com; 3910 Capilano Rd; $135-250; P ☒) Decide if you'd rather have the sleigh bed and stained glass of 'Sweet Tibby's' or the crisp, white comfort and private balcony of 'Mulberry Peak'.

Right by the Lions Gate Bridge, **Capilano RV Park** (Map pp54-5; ☎ 604-987-4722; 295 Tomahawk Ave; tent/RV $27/34) has a pool, showers and laundry. Wilderness camping is permitted at **Mt Seymour Provincial Park** (☎ 604-986-2261;

DETOUR: DEEP COVE

Take the Dollarton Hwy exit off Hwy 1 and go east, right if you just crossed Second Narrows Bridge, left if you're driving towards it. Stop in Cates Park, if you'd like to enjoy the views of Belcarra Regional Park across the waters of the Burrard Inlet/Indian Arm intersection, or follow the road as it turns left and becomes Deep Cove Rd.

The road will pass close to some incredible pieces of property before making a right turn, leading you down through the quaint hamlet of Deep Cove and the protected waters of...Deep Cove. It's a completely relaxed part of the Lower Mainland where you can grab lunch or a snack at **Honey's** (☎ 604-929-4988; 4373 Gallant St; mains $4-8) or rent from **Deep Cove Canoe & Kayak Centre** (☎ 604-929-2268; 2156 Banbury Rd) for a paddle up Indian Arm.

To get back to Vancouver, retrace your steps.

---

www.mountseymour.com; adult/child $34/18), but there are no facilities.

Eating

Grab a quick bite from any of the many food vendors at Lonsdale Quay Market.

Grouse Mountain has three dining options with views from up high. **The Observatory** (Map pp54-5; ☎ 604-998-4403; mains $18-30; ☽ dinner) is a fine dining choice offering dishes as good as the view. **Altitudes Bistro** (☎ 604-984-0661; mains $7-15) is more casual, but still fun and trendy where you can enjoy pub-style food. **híwus feasthouse** (Map pp54-5; ☎ 604-980-9311; adult/child $65/29; ☽ dinner) is an event in a traditional longhouse where the feast is only part of the experience. Stories are told, dances are danced and legends are explained with First Nations storytelling, music and dancing

Sailor Hagar's Brew Pub (Map pp54-5; ☎ 604-984-3087; 86 Semisch Ave; mains $7-12; ☽ lunch & dinner) A couple of blocks up and over from the quay, Hagar produces some excellent beer and serves in a traditional pub setting. Solid wood furniture and a definite nautical décor are apt for the good pub food.

Ship of the Seven Seas (Map pp54-5; ☎ 604 987-3344; foot of Lonsdale Avenue; mains $7-12; ☽ Tue-Sun dinner) A historic ferry that used to cross

Burrard Inlet, before the Lions Gate Bridge was built, is now a floating seafood restaurant specializing in fresh seafood, including a 50-item buffet, and steak dinners.

WEST VANCOUVER
pop 41,400

This suburb claims to have the highest per-capita income in Canada and is also the birthplace of Canada's first mall, Park Royal Shopping Centre. But West Vancouverites have more than money at their disposal; several lovely public parks, beaches and trails still exist amid the chic homes, shops and restaurants.

Parks
CYPRESS PROVINCIAL PARK

This **park** (☎ 604-924-2200), 8km north of West Vancouver off Hwy 99, competes with Grouse (p93) for activity-popularity. It has good trails for hiking and mountain biking, and is a popular ski destination. **Cypress Bowl Ski Area** (☎ 604-926-5612; www.cypressmountain.com; adult/child $42/19) has downhill skiing and a network of cross-country trails. It usually has more snow, and is a little drier than Grouse.

LIGHTHOUSE PARK

Some of Vancouver's largest trees live within this **park** (☎ 604-925-7200), which includes a rare stand of original coastal forest including arbutus trees. About 13km of hiking trails wind through the park; the most popular leads to Point Atkinson Lighthouse, and its view of the inlet from its rocky perch. To get here, turn west (left) on Marine Drive after crossing Lions Gate Bridge.

AMBLESIDE PARK

Right on the north shore of Burrard Inlet, and hidden behind Park Royal, this **park** (15th Ave & Marine Dr) has awesome views of Stanley Park and a myriad of activities. Trails, ponds, beaches, playgrounds, picnic areas and green lawns are what you'll find here, not to mention the hundreds of people having fun.

Sleeping & Eating
Park Royal Hotel (Map pp54-5; ☎ 250-926-5511, 877-926-5511; www.parkroyalhotel.com; 540 Clyde Ave; r/ste $99/169; P ✗) The small 30-room inn has almost become part of the beautiful garden as ivy, bushes and flowers grow along its walls. The rooms are charmingly pastel and suggest an English country inn.

Salmon House on the Hill (☎ 604-926-3212; 2229 Folkestone Way; mains $20-30; ⊗ dinner) With Vancouver at your feet, it's tough to beat this place when it comes to views. And with a chef who specializes in fresh catches, it's also hard to beat when it comes to seafood.

Wilderness camping is permitted in **Cypress Provincial Park** (☎ 604-924-2200; parking $5), but there are no facilities.

HORSESHOE BAY & BOWEN ISLAND

The small coastal community of Horseshoe Bay (pop 1000) marks the end of the North Shore and the start of trips to Whistler via The Sea to Sky Hwy (Hwy 99), to Vancouver Island or the Sunshine Coast via the ferry terminal. Ferries also travel to Bowen Island (pop 2950), which is considered a 'Gulf Island' but is only a stone's throw from the mainland. Both occupy pretty locations, with great views across the bays to distant glaciated peaks.

Whytecliff Park, at the far end of Marine Drive, attracts scuba divers to its protected waters, hikers to its rocky trails and rock climbers to its granite cliffs. It's also a fun place for families and kids to visit as there are plenty of picnic areas and views of the marine activity.

Hiking trails and picnic grounds are found all over Bowen, be it the five-minute stroll near early-20th century buildings to the tables at Snug Cove, or the 45-minute trek from the ferry dock to Killarney Lake, itself encircled by a 4km trail. Several short kayaking tours are offered by **Bowen Island Sea Kayaking** (☎ 604-947-9266, 800-605-2925; www.bowenislandkayaking.com; ferry dock; rental $50, tours from $50).

Doc Morgan's Inn (☎ 604-947-0808; ferry dock; mains $8-12) On Bowen, the wooden patios overlooking the park and the harbor make time seem irrelevant – and it also gives a great vantage point for the terminal so you don't miss your ferry. Pub grub is the main focus of the menu, but they also have some good seafood entrées.

The Boathouse (☎ 604-921-8188; 6695 Nelson Ave; mains $10-20; ⊗ lunch & dinner) This is a Horseshoe Bay landmark. Sitting prominently to the west of the ferry terminal with its big cedar-framed windows looking out over the bay, it's a wonderful place for some west coast seafood.

Getting There & Around

BC Ferries (☎ 604-921-7414; adult/child $6/3, car $19; ☣ 5:35am-10:05pm) travels 16 times daily between Bowen and Horseshoe Bay.

BURNABY
pop 194,000

Burnaby, the city immediately east of Vancouver, is a city of residence, industry and parks, and home to one of BC's largest shopping complexes.

Sights & Activities

Atop Burnaby Mountain, a 1965 institution, **Simon Fraser University** (SFU; Map pp54-5; ☎ 604-291-3111), was designed by noted Canadian architect Arthur Erickson. His unusual use of space and perspective remains controversial, and though the university was a laughing stock at first, it has a unique campus and has been graduating brilliant and creative minds for decades. Some of the worthwhile attractions here include the **Museum of Archaeology & Ethnology** (☎ 604-291-3325; admission free; ☣ 10am-4pm Mon-Fri) and the **SFU Art Gallery** (☎ 604-291-4266; admission free ☣ noon-6pm Mon, 10am-4pm Tue-Fri). To get to campus follow Hastings St east.

Draped around SFU, Burnaby Mountain Park offers some grand views of Greater Vancouver through the deciduous trees and foliage, and includes several trails that are excellent for mountain biking. Inside the park is Kamui Mintara ('Playground of the Gods') featuring sculptures of more than a dozen poles carved by the father-son team of Nuburi and Shusei Toko.

Offering a peaceful environment minus the hectic energy of downtown, Deer Lake Park has paths that crisscross the meadows and woodlands, and circle the lake where fowl and other wildlife frequent. Inside the park, **Burnaby Village Museum** (Map pp54-5; ☎ 604-293-6501; 6501 Deer Lake Ave; adult/child $6.60/3.95, carousel $1; ☣ 11am-4:30pm late Apr–mid-Sep) recreates the atmosphere of a southwestern BC town circa 1925. The replica village contains establishments of the time, along with a working steam-train model and a wonderfully restored 1912 carousel built in Leavenworth, Kansas, recently retro-fitted for wheelchair access. To get there take the Sperling Ave exit off Hwy 1 and follow the signs to the museum.

A continually growing monstrosity of commercialism is made up of **Metrotown** (☎ 604-438-2444) Shopping Centre, Metropolis at Metrotown, and Crystal Mall. Savvy shoppers usually head out early in the morning to beat the crowds and get back sometime the following week. Fortunately, non-shoppers don't have to stand outside the stores waiting. They can head to **Playdium** (☎ 604-433-7529) which features dozens of interactive games, virtual-reality rides and enough sensory overload to put the average person into a coma.

Sleeping & Eating

Kingsway Blvd (p78), just west of Boundary is a motel strip.

Mountain Shadow Inn (Map pp54-5; ☎ 604-291-9322, 800-667-9901; 7147 Barnett Rd; mains $6-11; ☣ lunch-late) An old mansion and the most charismatic sports bars in the Lower Mainland, with jerseys and posters adorning the walls. Dark wood banisters and stairs lure you to the central fireplace upstairs. They serve pub grub, with daily happy-hour specials.

Burnaby Cariboo RV Park (Map pp54-5; ☎ 604-420-1722; camping@bcrvpark.com; 8765 Cariboo Place; tent/RV $25/36.50) is near Exit 37 off Hwy 1.

RICHMOND
pop 164,350

Richmond has become closely identified with British Columbia's recent influx of Hong Kong Chinese. Some argue this is cleaner, cheaper, safer and better than Vancouver's Chinatown, but it doesn't have Chinatown charm.

The No 3 Rd has become the main artery that leads to the modern collection of shopping malls known as Asia West. Yaohan Centre and Parker Place are two of the better shopping centres featuring gleaming Chinese stores filled with Chinese products and mostly Chinese shoppers, along with excellent Chinese food at very reasonable prices.

Canada's largest temple, the **Buddhist temple** (Map pp54-5; ☎ 604-274-2822; 9160 Steveston Hwy; donation; ☣ 9:30am-5pm) has tiled roofs, marble statues, peaceful gardens, tranquil ponds and colorful murals that are as authentic as you can get. Visitors are always welcome to come and experience serenity.

Sleeping

Being the airport city that it is, Richmond is packed with hotel chains – they're all here. See p367 for major hotels.

Richmond RV Park (Map pp54-5; ☎ 604-270-7878; richmondrv@aol.com; 6200 River Rd; tent/RV $17/24; ✍ Apr-Oct) is a mini-community of camping near the wonderfully developed riverfront.

Steveston

In Richmond's southwest corner sits the old fishing village of Steveston. You can smell the salt in the air as you stroll past the docks, checking out the local catches. A pleasant bike- and pedestrian-only trail winds north and east of the village.

Britannia Heritage Shipyard National Historic Site (Map pp54-5; ☎ 604-718-8050; 5180 Westwater Dr; donation) This walk-through park gives a fascinating look at the industries that made Steveston what it is. Restored cannery, shipyard buildings and residences stand where they were built and you can still watch shipbuilders restore old boats using techniques used by pioneers.

Gulf of Georgia Cannery National Historic Site (Map pp54-5; ☎ 604-664-9009; 12138 4th Ave; adult/child $6.50/3.25; ✍ 10am-5pm summer, closed Nov-Feb) This cannery dates from 1894 and was left as it was – well, they did clean out the fish guts – to display this once-powerful industry in informative and fun fashion.

Dave's Fish & Chips (Map pp54-5; ☎ 604-271-7555; 3460 Moncton St; $6-8) A visit to Steveston without fish and chips would be a crime and not getting them from Dave's would be grand larceny. Eat in the dining room or order from the take-out window.

From Vancouver, take the 'Steveston Hwy' exit west off Hwy 99.

DELTA
pop 96,950

Vancouver's forgotten child is a fertile flatland of farms, greenhouses, and 'that place between the border and Vancouver'; but there's more for those who venture off Hwys 99 or 91.

North Delta

Known as 'the bog', the largest estuarine raised-peat bog on the west coast of the Americas, Burns Bog is habitat to unique animal and plant species specially adapted to the wet and acidic conditions. Access is limited to the Delta Nature Reserve section, and the enthusiastic **Burns Bog Conservation Society** (☎ 604-572-0373; www.burnsbog.org; adult/child $15/10; ✍ noon every 3rd Sat) leads three-hour walking tours.

The wet and cool vegetation in Watershed Park has some great walking trails and is popular with mountain-bikers, too.

To get to North Delta, take Hwy 99 south to Hwy 91 and follow the 'North Delta' signs over the Alex Fraser Bridge.

Tsawwassen

Serving as a gateway to Vancouver Island through its BC Ferries terminal, Tsawwassen (suh-wah-sen) also receives the most sunshine of any place in the Lower Mainland.

Long stretches of beach, excellent bird-watching and warm water for swimming at high tide make Centennial Beach Park, fronting Boundary Bay, one of Greater Vancouver's best-kept secrets. Off Hwy 17, turn left on 56th St, and then left on 12th Ave to Boundary Bay Rd.

Park Canada RV Inns (☎ 604-943-5811; www.parkcanada.com; 4799 Nulelum Way; tent/RV $20/28) beside Splashdown park has free showers.

Ladner

Ladner is a quaint, pretty, pioneer-days town considered one of the aesthetic hidden gems of the Lower Mainland.

Reifel Migratory Bird Sanctuary (☎ 604-946-6980; 5191 Robertson Rd; adult/child $4/2; ✍ 9am-4pm) could be called a nature stroll for ornithologists. This wetland is a huge stopover for migrating birds that is most populated in the fall, and extremely fun in the spring when the ponds may be still slightly frozen. You owe it to yourself to watch a duck try and land on a frozen pond.

Off Hwy 17, turn right on Lander Trunk Rd and follow it through Ladner to River Rd. Turn right on Westham Island Rd, go over the bridge and follow it to the sanctuary.

Tsawwassen and Ladner are both reached by taking Hwy 99 south through the George Massey tunnel, then exiting right to Hwy 17.

GOLDEN EARS PROVINCIAL PARK

You're engulfed by evergreens flanking the winding road before you pass the wooden sign with the mountain goat that says, 'Golden Ears Provincial Park'. As you enter the **park** (☎ 604-795-6169; wlapwww.gov.bc.ca/bc parks) the strange sensation you get as urban growth disappears is serenity; it will last for the duration of your stay. At 55,900 hectares, Golden Ears Provincial Park is smaller than its northern neighbor, Garibaldi Provincial Park, but is still among BC's largest, and it's hard to believe you're less than an hour from Vancouver. The park is named for Mt Blanshard's twin peaks, which sometimes glow in the sun like the ears of a golden retriever.

Pretty Alouette Lake is Golden Ears' centerpiece and a perfect spot for fishing, swimming, canoeing, windsurfing and waterskiing.

Hikers of all abilities should find something suitable in the 65km of trails. If time is short, the **Spirea Nature Trail** can take an hour for the whole information-plaque-lined route, or 20 minutes for the short loop. For a deeper appreciation of the park's wonders, the strenuous root-entangled **Alouette Mountain Trail** (10km, 1000m elevation change) is most rewarding in June when the meadows are green and Mount Robie Reid still has enough snow to make the view worthwhile. Easier trails that still explore the bounty of the park:

Alouette Valley Trail 7km, minimal elevation gain.

Lower Falls Trail 2.7km, minimal elevation gain. Popular hike, follows Gold Creek to a 10m waterfall; impressive views of jagged mountains and good sunbathing spot halfway.

Mike Lake 4.2km, 100m elevation gain. Also a popular horseback trail so watch your step if you're not saddled up.

At **Alouette**, **Gold Creek** (☎ 800-689-9025; www .discovercamping.ca; site $22) and **North Beach Campgrounds** ($14), tall hemlock and fir trees protect the 400 campsites in the park. Back-country camping is also permitted ($5).

Take Lougheed Hwy (Hwy 7) east through Maple Ridge and turn left on 232nd St. Turn right on Fern Cres just after Maple Ridge Park; serenity sinks in 2km later.

FORT LANGLEY

pop 2,600

Tiny Fort Langley's tree-lined streets and 19th-century storefronts make it as picturesque a village as you'll find in the Lower Mainland. It's the kind of place where you feel compelled to indulge in an ice-cream cone and explore the museums and shops.

DETOUR: WHITE ROCK

Follow Hwy 99 south and just before the US border take the '8th Ave West' exit and turn right on 8th. One kilometer later, Semiamhoo Bay reveals itself on your left; if the tide's in, the water will be on the other side of the train tracks, if the tide's out, you'll see hundreds of meters of sandy beach and countless tide pools. Welcome to **White Rock**, where Vancouverites daytrip.

Park the car (free parking can be had a few blocks from the beach, but only if you're lucky; otherwise, parking meters are in effect from 6am to 2am) and stroll along the beach and down the famous pier by the big white rock (yes, it's painted).

If you're here for breakfast or lunch, you're lucky. On your right, **Poultry in Motion** (☎ 604-538-8084; 15491 Marine Dr; mains $5-8; ☻ breakfast & lunch) is a little hole-in-the-wall café that's an absolute gem. It serves standard breakfasts with friendly serviced. If you're in a rush, the huge muffins are a hit.

Or grab some fish and chips from any of the take-out places and eat them on the beach with your back against a log and the sun on your face.

Take your time, but when you're ready to leave, retrace your steps back to town, or continue south on Hwy 99 to the US.

CROSSING THE FRASER

The other side of the mighty Fraser River seems so close and as you drive through the valley east of Greater Vancouver, but there are limited crossings (east to west):

- **Port Mann Bridge** (Trans-Canada Hwy, Hwy 1) Surrey to Coquitlam.

- **Albion Ferry** (free; every 15 minutes 4:30am to 12:30pm, then every 30 minutes until 1am) Fort Langley to Maple Ridge; midday multiple-sailings waits are not uncommon.

- **Mission Bridge** (Hwy 11) Abbotsford to Mission.

- **Agassiz-Rosedale** Bridge (Hwy 9) Rosedale to Agassiz, access to Harrison Hot Springs; last crossing until Hope.

The 4km **Fort-to-Fort Trail** is a leisurely walk that follows the Fraser River from the present location of the fort to the site of the original Fort Langley in Derby Reach Regional Park. The **Visitor Info Centre** (☎ 604-888-1477; 23245 Mavis St; ⏰ 9am-6pm May-Oct) is an old Canadian National Railway station.

Fort Langley National Historic Site

During the early-to-mid 1800s, Fort Langley burned down and changed locations, yet still served as an important link between interior fur-trade posts and international markets. But gold fever and an influx of thousands of prospectors from California in the 1850s put the fear in James Douglas of an American takeover. On November 19, 1858, he stood in the Big House and read the proclamation creating the colony of British Columbia, giving Fort Langley a legitimate claim to the birthplace of BC.

Later that same year, paddle wheelers made it possible to travel further up the Fraser River, eliminating the fort's importance along the supply-chain and the place was eventually abandoned. In 1923 the federal government realized the historical importance and this **site** (☎ 604-513-4777; www.parkscanada.gc.ca/langley; 23433 Mavis Ave; adult/child $5.75/3; ⏰ 10am-5pm Mar-Oct) is now a museum with a feel of pioneer days. The fort hosts several special events each year, including an old-fashioned Canada Day bash on July 1.

MISSION

pop 31,300

Originally the home of the Stó:lo, the name Mission comes from a much later Catholic attempt to convert the people. The town sits on Lougheed Hwy and the **Visitor Info Center** (☎ 604-826-6914; 34033 Lougheed Hwy) is east of town.

Xá:ytem (*hay*-tum) **Longhouse Interpretive Centre** (☎ 604-820-9725; www.xaytem.museum.bc.ca; 35087 Lougheed Hwy; ⏰ noon-4pm Mon-Fri Sep-Jun, 11am-5pm Jul-Aug; adults/seniors & children/family $6/5/13) The site of this BC Heritage site was actually being cleared for housing when small tools were discovered. Further excavations produced artifacts as old as 9000 years. The center focuses on Stó:lo spirituality, archeology and history, and the centerpiece is the huge Hatzic Rock, thought to be three tribal leaders turned to stone.

Westminster Abbey (☎ 604-826-8975; 33224 Dewdney Trunk Rd; free; ⏰ 1:30-4pm Mon-Fri, 2-4pm Sun) The bell tower offers sweeping views of the Fraser Valley. The stained glass windows of the church are views in their own right and it's interesting to learn how the Benedictine Monks have created a life of self-sufficiency.

Motorheads will dig watching drag-racing at **Mission Raceway Park** (☎ 604-826-6315; www.missionracewaypark.com; $8; ⏰ Mar-Oct), or maybe racing their own street-legal car ($23; ⏰ 5pm Fri).

Whistler & the Sunshine Coast

CONTENTS

WHISTLER & THE SUNSHINE COAST

It's hard to imagine genuine outdoor adventures are just an hour or two north of cosmopolitan Vancouver, but it's a fact. You've got a couple of choices. From Horseshoe Bay you can head north on the beautiful Sea to Sky Hwy through mountain scenery that rivals the Rockies. The goal of many who travel this highway is Whistler-Blackcomb, one of the world's premier ski spots. Even those who don't ski will enjoy the ambience of Whistler Village, with its restaurants, nightlife and relaxed atmosphere. In summer, the lifts transport visitors to lovely alpine hikes.

For even more natural wonders, you could catch the ferry to Langdale and travel up the jagged and stunning Sunshine Coast. The weather here is some of the warmest in Canada. Kayaking and diving are fantastic, and the ferry ride itself is spectacular – you might see eagles and myriad sea life. The friendly little towns along the way are great for day trips or overnight stops.

What you'll discover during either journey is forested or marine splendor that's guaranteed to stimulate the part of your mind that makes you say, 'Wow!' It's truly awesome country. Whether it's green valleys through the Coast Mountains or the drive along Hwy 101 that flirts with the mountains and the beaches of the Sunshine coast, you won't be sorry you made this trip.

HIGHLIGHTS

- Skiing 7000 acres at **Whistler-Blackcomb** (p108)
- Climbing **'The Chief'** (p103) near Squamish, or watching in amazement as others scale it
- Hiking through alpine meadows to gorgeous **Garibaldi Lake** (p105)
- Watching ocean rapids at **Skookumchuck Narrows** (p117)
- Exploring the beaches of **Savary Island** (p118), 'Hawaii of the North'

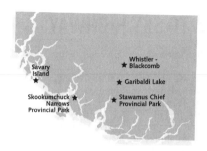

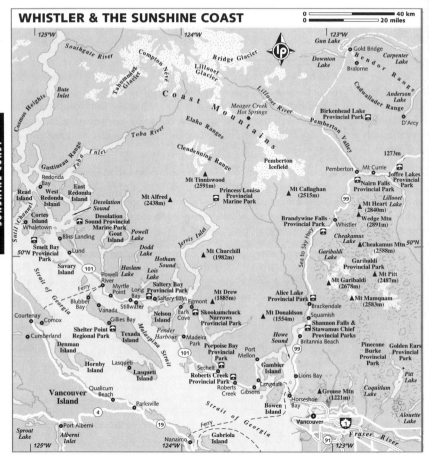

WHISTLER & THE SUNSHINE COAST

SEA TO SKY HIGHWAY

The Sea to Sky Hwy (Hwy 99) defines the border between land and water along the west coast of Howe Sound to Squamish, and then defines mountainous beauty on its way through the Coast Mountains all the way to Lillooet. All along its route is a natural playground perfect for outdoorsy types who appreciate recreation.

Of course, a place of such renowned beauty so close to the metropolitan area of Vancouver means it's also consistently populated with activity-seekers. It's hard, though not impossible, to find yourself alone here; but the crowds matter little – most people will be there for the same reasons you are; to just enjoy it.

The highway closes a few times in winter due to weather, and its two lanes often get packed in early morning and evening. A new highway is being punched through to be ready in time for the 2010 Olympics, but this will undoubtedly makes things worse before they get better with closures for construction. 'The Mountain' radio station (107.1 FM in Squamish, 102.1 FM in Whistler) provides helpful reports on traffic and road conditions every 20 minutes.

LIONS BAY

You'll find some of Howe Sound's best **scuba diving** near Lions Bay. Prime spots include Porteau Cove Marine Park, Christie Islet, Pam Rocks, Kelvin Grove and Bowyer Island. **Sea to Sky Ocean Sports** (☎ 604-892-3366; 37819 2nd Ave, Squamish) rents equipment and offers lessons and charter trips in these waters.

SQUAMISH & AROUND
pop 14,250

Situated halfway between Vancouver and Whistler, Squamish enjoys an incredible natural setting at the meeting of ocean, river and alpine forest. The monolith of the Stawamus Chief flanks the town to the southeast, its bulk nearly as great as Gibraltar, and Howe Sound creeps in from the south, creating the Squamish River Estuary.

Squamish's reputation as an excellent place for recreation has been gaining momentum, overshadowing the town's traditional role as a forestry hub. A diverse group of rock climbers, windsurfers, railroad history buffs and bird-watchers all make time to stop here.

If you're coming from Vancouver, turn left off Hwy 99 at the signal to reach Cleveland Ave and Squamish's small downtown. The well-stocked **Visitor Info Centre** (☎ 604-892-9244; www.squamishchamber.bc.ca; 37950 Cleveland Ave; 🕙 9am-6pm Jun-late Sep, 9am-5pm Dec-Feb, 9am-5pm Mon-Fri 10am-2pm Sat & Sun) is near the far end of the street. For medical emergencies, go to **Squamish General Hospital** (☎ 604-892-5211; 38140 Behrner Dr).

Parks

Squamish is blessed with numerous natural surroundings that the provincial government deems worthy of protecting.

At **Shannon Falls Provincial Park**, 2km south of Squamish and accessed by a short hiking trail, the 335m Shannon Falls ranks among Canada's highest and most beautiful waterfalls. A few picnic tables make this a good stopping point for lunch. In winter when the falls freeze, ice climbers pick and pull their way to the top.

Stawamus Chief Provincial Park is home to the 650m, granite, flat-faced monster 'The Chief.' Just looking at this natural climbing wall is awe-inspiring; looking out from on top of it is awe-striking. If you don't have the skills to climb it, there are hiking routes to the top so you can also enjoy the views.

Alice Lake Provincial Park (☎ 604-898-9680) is the spot for families. Alice Lake is an excellent swimming hole with two sandy beaches, wharfs and picnic tables. The Four Lakes Trail (6.5km) takes about two hours to trek, but if you don't have that long you can hike around Stump Lake.

West Coast Railway Heritage Park (☎ 604-898-9336; www.wcra.org/heritage; 38645 Government Rd; adult/child $8/7, train $2; 🕙 10am-5pm, trains 11am-4pm), the final resting place of the world-famous *Royal Hudson* steam engine, is an outdoor museum and mini pioneer town featuring 12 acres of historic rolling stock. Around 65 railcars have been converted to walk-through exhibits, including the three-car display depicting the painstaking and often tedious work involved in railroad car restoration. A 1/8 scale train is a fun way to get around the park.

BC Museum of Mining

It looks like a collection of old decrepit warehouses, but under the surface this **museum** (☎ 604-896-2233; www.bcmuseumofmining.org; adult/child $13/11; 🕙 9am-4:30pm May-Oct, 10am-4:30pm Mon-Fri Apr-Nov, tours hourly) south of town tells the story of the Britannia Mine. It was once the largest copper producer in the British Empire and had produced 650,000 tons of copper before society began to hate the penny and the mine closed in 1974.

A small train takes visitors into one of the mine's 360m tunnels, where you'll see demonstrations on ore extraction. During the tour you can also pan for gold and see the huge Concentrator, itself a National Historic Site, along with a 235-ton 'super' mine truck.

Activities

Casting its millennia-old, stone-faced gaze over Squamish, 'The Chief' is a **rock climbing** destination of international proportions. It has over 200 climbing routes and it's dotted with seemingly insignificant humans in the summer. For information, guides or instruction, call **Squamish Rock Guides** (☎ 604-898-1750; from $175). Other outfitters include:
Slipstream Rock & Ice (☎ 604-898-4891; 800-616-1325; 5010 Cheakamus Valley Rd, Brackendale; from $175; 🕙 9:30am-5:30pm)
Vertical Reality Sports Store (☎ 604-892-8248; 38154 2nd Ave; rentals $20 per day; 🕙 8:30am-6pm)

The Coast Salish didn't name this place 'Mother of the Winds' for nothing. Thermal inflows cause 60km/h winds to blow up Howe Sound and into Squamish Harbour, creating great windsurfing. For information on weather and water conditions, call the **Squamish Windsurfing Society** (☎ 604-892-2235; www.squamishwindsurfing.org).

The 100 or so trails around Squamish draw a lot of enthusiasts for mountain biking. Stop at **Corsa Cycles** (☎ 604-892-3331; 38128 Cleveland Ave; ☽ 9:30am-5:30pm) or **Tantalus Bike Shop** (☎ 604-898-2588; 40446 Government Rd; half-/full-day $15/35; ☽ 9:30am-5:30pm) for information on the best routes.

Sleeping & Eating

Howe Sound Inn & Brewing Company (☎ 604-892-2603, 800-919-2537; www.howesound.com; 37801 Cleveland Ave) The rooms are earthy and inviting and the duvets are thick enough to bounce off, but the best part of this inn is how unbelievably quiet it is. Not that Squamish is a rambunctious center of chaos, but you'll experience serenity here that's uncompromised.

Attached to the inn is the equally earthy and inviting brewpub. The outdoor patio tries (in vain) to stare down 'The Chief' but does give a good vantage for watching climbers. The chalet-like post-and-beam constructed interior does away with traditional furniture and uses worn and rustic tables, chairs and couches. They make their own beer and bread and make up their own menu as they go, depending on the season and the mood; ingredients in all three are fresh, resulting in excellent tastes. This is where you want to stop if traffic from Whistler to Vancouver is horrible.

Squamish Hostel (☎ 604-892-9240, 800-449-8614; www.squamishhostel.com; 38220 Hwy 99; dm/r $19.50/39) Completely rebuilt, yet still casual and friendly, this hostel is bright, colorful and plush by hostel standards. They organize rock-climbing and rafting trips. Amenities include bikes to borrow, a small rock-climbing wall, fully equipped kitchen, a laundry and a rooftop deck. It's an easy walk from downtown.

Dryden Creek Resorts (☎ 604-898-9726, 877-2379336; www.drydencreek.com; cnr Hwy 99 & Depot Rd; tent/RV/s/d $20/26/79/89) If you need a place to crash after conquering the winds, the sea and the earth, then this is the place. The

kitchenettes are well equipped and the rooms are clean. There's also camping by the creek.

Camping is available at **Alice Lake Provincial Park** (☎ 800-689-9025; www.discovercamping.ca; sites $22) and **Stawamus Chief Provincial Park** (http://wlapwww.gov.bc.ca/bcparks; site $9) has 15 drive-in and 47 walk-in sites popular with climbers.

Yanni's Taverna (☎ 604-892-9696; 38043 Cleveland Ave; mains $8-13; ☽ lunch & dinner) This little Greek place can't really be called a hidden gem, since it's always crowded and obviously popular, but it's definitely nondescript from the outside. Inside is a different story: the atmosphere is fun and light and full of good people having good times. And the food melts in your mouth just before the spices and tangy flavors kick in.

Roadhouse Diner (☎ 604-892-5312; cnr Hwy 99 & Darryl Bay; mains $7-12) South of town on Hwy 99, you'll enjoy views of Shannon Falls at this atypical roadhouse diner. The inside is clean and wood-covered and the food isn't greasy-spoon type stuff. They do have burgers and sandwiches and standard breakfast, but also serve pasta and seafood dishes.

North of town, the **Sunrise Japanese Restaurant** (☎ 604-898-2533; 40022 Government Rd; mains $9-12; ☽ dinner Tue-Sun) offers sashimi and noodle dishes for $7 and dinner combinations for $13.

Getting There & Away

Greyhound (☎ 604-898-3914; www.greyhound.ca; adult/child $9.50/4.75) operates about seven daily buses from Vancouver between 5:30am and 8:10pm.

GARIBALDI PROVINCIAL PARK

East of Hwy 99, 195,000-hectare **Garibaldi Provincial Park** (☎ 604-898-3678; backcountry sites $5) is known for its hiking. With more than 67km of developed trails and backcountry campsites throughout, there's plenty to explore. You're not limited to exploring only in shorts-and-t-shirts weather: trails become marked cross-country ski routes in the winter. Garibaldi has five main developed areas, directions to each are clearly marked by the blue and white signs off Hwy 99. Unfortunately Fido must stay at home; dogs aren't allowed in the park. The park also restricts the use of mountain bikes to certain trails.

MARK NEWMAN

Migrating orca, **Johnstone Strait** (p169), Vancouver Island

MARK LIGHTBODY

Male elk, **Rocky Mountains** (p257)

FRANK CARTER

Goose, Esquimalt Harbour, **Vancouver Island** (p120)

Brown bear, the **Yukon** (p336)

ERNEST MANEWAL

Rafting, **Tatshenshini-Alsek Provincial Wilderness Park** (p335)

Ice walking, **Maligne Canyon** (p285)

Hiking, **Garibaldi Provincial Park** (p104)

Sea kayaking, **Clayoquot Sound** (p158), Vancouver Island

DETOUR: BRACKENDALE (THE EAGLES HAVE LANDED)

As you head north from Squamish along Hwy 99 you'll see a sign at Depot Rd with a bunch of local businesses advertising themselves pointing east to Brackendale – follow it. Brackendale is the kind of town you can't help but like.

There's nothing super fancy here, but if you turn left on Government Rd, you'll notice it's a charming little town in a quiet river setting and that's its main draw – that and the thousands of bald eagles that come here each winter to feed on the salmon in the river.

The main viewing site is at Eagle Run, beside Government Rd north of Garibaldi Way and south of Depot Rd. Volunteer interpreters often staff the site on Saturday and Sunday afternoons during eagle season (early November to late February).

The **Brackendale Art Gallery** (☎ 604-898-3333; www.brackendaleartgallery.com; cnr Government & Depot Rds) offers helpful information about the eagle migration. While you're there, check out owner Thor Froslev's creations.

Diamond Head

The hiking and mountain-biking trail to Elfin Lakes (11km, three to five hours one way) is a beautiful and relatively easy day hike. The trail continues on to the extinct volcano of Opal Cone if you're into some overnight hiking. There's a first-come, first-served overnight shelter once you reach Elfin and backcountry camping is available at Red Heather (5km from parking lot). The parking lot is 16km of logging roads east of Hwy 99.

Garibaldi Lake

This area features beautiful alpine meadows and scenic mountain vistas. The trek to Garibaldi Lake (9km, three to four hours) is an outstanding crash-course in Beautiful BC. The indescribable aqua color of the undisturbed lake contrasts the dark, jagged peak of Black Tusk rising behind it. Backcountry campsites are on the west shore of Garibaldi Lake further up the trail at Taylor Meadows.

Cheakamus Lake

The hike to Cheakamus Lake (3km, 45 minutes to one hour) is among the park's most popular. It's relatively easy with minimal elevation gain; many people portage a canoe or kayak. Also in this area and just outside the provincial park, the BC Forest Service's 3000-hectare **Whistler Interpretive Forest** offers a wide variety of summer activities, ranging from hiking and mountain biking to kayaking and fishing. The trailhead is 8.5km from Hwy 99 opposite Function Junction at the south end of Whistler.

Singing Pass

The trail to Singing Pass (11km, four hours) leaves from the Whistler ski area and is a wonderful alpine hike. The trail leads up Fitzsimmons and Melody Creeks to the pass. From there it's another 3km to Russett Lake, where backcountry campsites are available. Mountain bikes are not allowed on this trail.

Wedgemount Lake

The hike to Wedgemount Lake (7km, four to six hours) is a steep, knee-burner of a climb, but the emerald glacial lake and views of the 300m waterfall of Wedgemount Creek are just reward. Wedge Mountain (2891m), the highest in the park, rises to the south and this hike offers your best chance to see wildlife in the area.

BRANDYWINE FALLS PROVINCIAL PARK

A popular day-use area 9km south of Whistler, this **park** (parking $3, site $14) features a spectacular 70m waterfall. A short trail in the park leads to the falls' brink, which makes a relaxing picnic spot.

Another 7km trail leads through dense forests and lava beds to a suspension bridge near BC Forest Service's Cal-Cheak Confluence Recreation Site (p111).

There are 15 drive-in campsites, and though the gate is closed in winter, you may still walk in for winter camping.

WHISTLER

pop 8900

'Whistler' is common nomenclature for the resort village and the Whistler-Blackcomb ski area that has brought fame to this region, 123km north of Vancouver. It has been called the best ski destination in North America many times over, its summertime popularity has begun to rise and it's officially on the 'trendy places to visit' list. Its appeal is understandable. With all the money that's been pumped into the area over the last few decades, the temptation to go completely commercial must have been huge, but instead they did it right. The architecture is the way a mountain resort should be, with lots of stone and logs. Even though mega-chain businesses are located here, you can't tell by looking at the buildings that line the cobblestone pedestrian malls.

It's this nonconformist image and the countless activities on offer that draw people from all walks of life. You can see a girl with a snowboard, a muddied-up biker, and a woman in a business suit all within 15m of each other.

Orientation

Whistler is made up of four neighborhoods: Whistler Creekside, Whistler Village, Village North and Upper Village. Approaching town from the south, you'll enter at Whistler Creekside, the original Whistler base and site of recent major redevelopment.

The other three areas, 4km north past Alta Lake, tend to blur into one large village. From Hwy 99, turn right (east) onto Village Gate Blvd, which divides Whistler Village (base of Whistler Mountain, on your right) from Village North. At the end of the road, parking lots are on the other side of Blackcomb Way, which divides the other two areas from Upper Village (base of Blackcomb Mountain).

Whistler Village is the center of most commercial activity, and the usual starting point for exploration.

Information

BOOKSTORES
Armchair Books (☎ 604-932-5557; 4205 Village Sq)

INTERNET ACCESS
Electric Daisy (☎ 604-905-2980; 4314 Main St; 22¢ per min)
HotBox (☎ 604-905-5644; 109-4369 Main St; $4 per 15 min)

LAUNDRY
The Laundromat at Nesters Square (☎ 604-932-2960; 7009 Nesters Rd)
Laundromat at Creekside Plaza (☎ 604-932-3980; 2010 Innsbruck Dr)

MEDIA
Two free weekly newspapers are available throughout Whistler and Squamish. *Pique Newsmagazine* offers news and entertainment listings and the *Whistler Question* is a more traditional weekly newspaper.

MEDICAL SERVICES
Whistler Health Care Centre (☎ 604-932-4911; 4380 Lorimer Rd)
Town Plaza Medical Clinic (☎ 604-905-7089; 40-4314 Main St)

MONEY
ATMs are widely available in Whistler. Exchange money at:
Custom House Currency Exchange (☎ 604-938-6658; 4227 Village Stroll)
Thomas Cook (☎ 604-938-0111, 800-252-8232; visitor info centre area)

POST
Mail can be sent from **Whistler Canada Post Office** (☎ 604-932-5012; 106-4360 Lorimer Rd; ☽ 8am-5pm Mon-Fri, 8am-noon Sat).

TOURIST INFORMATION
Activity & Information Centre (☎ 604-938-2769, 877-991-9988; 4010 Whistler Way; ☽ 8am-6pm)
Visitor Info Centres (☎ 604-932-5922 ext 17; www.mywhistler.com); Welcome Centre (4230 Gateway Dr; ☽ 8am-8pm, 9am-6pm Nov–mid-Jun); Village North Kiosk (☽ 11am-6pm summer); Upper Village Kiosk (☽ 10am-6pm summer)
Whistler 2010 Info Centre (☎ 877-408-2010; 4365 Blackcomb Way; ☽ 11am-5pm) Information of Olympic proportions.

Whistler Museum & Archives

In Village North this **museum** (☎ 604-932-2019; www.whistlermuseum .com; 4329 Main St; ☽ 10am-4pm, Thu-Sun Sep-Jun) features exhibits on regional history and the area's draw to adventure seekers from as early as the 1910s. Word began to spread about remote Alta Lake and its surrounding mountains and more people arrived. Whistler's fame took off in the 1970s and the rest, as they say, is still-being-written history.

WHISTLER

0 ———————— 300 m
0 ———————— 0.2 miles

INFORMATION	
Activity & Information Centre	(see 9)
Armchair Books	**1** A5
Central Reservation Service	(see 9)
Custom House Currency Exchange	**2** B6
Electric Daisy	**3** B5
Hot Box	**4** B5
Police Station	**5** B5
Post Office	**6** A4
The Laundromat at Nesters Square	(see 33)
Thomas Cook	(see 9)
Town Plaza Medical Clinic	**7** B5
Upper Village Info Kiosk	**8** C5
Village North Info Kiosk	(see 10)
Visitor Info Centre	**9** B5
Whistler 2010 Info Centre	**10** B4

Whistler Health Care Centre	**11** B4
Whistler Public Library	**12** A5

SIGHTS & ACTIVITIES	(pp106-9)
Cougar Mountain Adventures	**13** B5
Cross-Country Skiing Ticket Booth	(see 46)
Lost Lake Cross-Country	
Connection	(see 46)
Mountain Adventure Centre	**14** C5
Mountain Adventure Centre	(see 39)
Outdoor Adventures at Whistler	**15** A5
Whistler Conference Centre	**16** A5
Whistler Museum & Archives	**17** A5
Whistler River Adventures	**18** B6
Whistler/Blackcomb Lift Tickets &	
Guest Services	**19** B6

SLEEPING	(pp110-11)
Cascade Lodge	**20** A5
Chalet Luise	**21** C3
Edelweiss Pension	**22** B2
Fairmont Chateau Whistler	**23** C5
Shoestring Lodge	**24** B2
Valhalla	**25** A4

EATING	(pp111-12)
Auntie Em's Kitchen	**26** A4
Bearfoot Bistro	**27** A6
Black's Pub & Restaurant	**28** B6
Caramba	**29** B5
Citta's Bistro	**30** A5
La Brasserie des Artistes	**31** B5
Mogul's Coffee	**32** A5
Nesters Market	**33** B2
Sushi Ya	**34** A4
Whistler Noodle House	**35** A5
Zeuski's	**36** B5

DRINKING	(p112)
Boot Pub	(see 24)
Brewhouse Restaurant & Pub	**37** B4
Buffalo Bill's Bar & Grill	**38** A5
Dubh Linn Gate Old Irish Pub	**39** B6
Garfinkel's	**40** B5
Longhorn Saloon & Grill	**41** B6
Maxx Fish	**42** B5
Merlin's Bar & Grill	**43** C5
Moe Joe's	**44** A5
Savage Beagle	**45** B5

ENTERTAINMENT	(pp112-13)
Maurice Young Millennium	
Place	**46** B5
Rainbow Theatre	(see 16)
Village 8 Cinema	**47** B5

TRANSPORT	(p113)
Bus Stop	**48** A5

WHISTLER & THE
SUNSHINE COAST

To Riverside RV Resort
& Campground (500m);
Nicklaus North Golf &
Country Club (500m);
Pemberton (30km);
Lillooet (120km)

Nesters Rd

Nancy Greene Dr

Fitzsimmons Dr

Fitzsimmons Creek

Lost Lake

Lost Lake Trail

Chateau
Whistler
Golf Club

Village
North

Lorimer Rd

Blackcomb Way

Lot 4
Lot 4a

Whistler's
Marketplace

Blackcomb Way

Lot 5

Northlands Blvd

Main St

Village Gate Blvd

Lot 3

Upper
Village

Chateau Blvd

Speedhead Dr

Rebagliati
Park

Lot 2

Wizard Express

Village
Square

Whistler
Village

Lot 1

Glacier Dr

Magic Chair

Whistler Way

Mountain
Square

Skier's Plaza

Whistler
Golf Club

Driving
Range

Whistler Village Gondola

Fitzsimmons Express

To Whistler Creekside (4km);
Vancouver (123km)

To Whistler
Mountain

Blackcomb
Mountain

Excalibur Gondola

'SINGLE!'

As with any other major mountain, your chances are better for getting to the top quicker if you split up at the chair-lifts and use the singles' line. 'How you doing?' is kind of passé, so try something fresh like, 'Come here often?' or, 'What gorgeous scenery…and the mountains look good, too' to try and get the cute boy or girl at the front of the line to let you in their group. If that fails, get in the queue for single skiers and rendezvous with your group at the top.

Winter Activities

The mild Pacific air flowing around the mile-high peaks delivers reliable snowfall to the area without it getting too cold. Intrawest Corporation owns and operates both the Whistler and Blackcomb Mountains ski areas, and makes the most of the setting nature has provided.

SKIING & SNOWBOARDING

Whistler-Blackcomb (☎ 604-932-3434, 800-766-0449; www.whistlerblackcomb.com; adult/child $68/34; ☽ 8:30am-3pm Nov-late Jan, 8:30am-3:30pm late Jan-Mar, 9am-4pm Mar-season end) has over 7000 acres of skiable terrain and 200 longer-than-average trails, and that doesn't include the backcountry. The typical season runs from mid-November until late April on Blackcomb and until June on Whistler, with the bulk of the crowds showing up from December through late March. And it does get crowded. The five major bases (Whistler Creekside, Whistler Village, Excalibur Village, Excalibur Base II and Upper Village Blackcomb) and all the available terrain allow skiers to spread out. High-speed lifts make exceptionally long lines move relatively quickly, but prepare yourself for half-hour waits on weekends.

Mountain Adventure Centres (Whistler ☎ 604-905-2252, Blackcomb ☎ 604-938-7737; www.whistlerblackcomb.com/rentals; adult/child from $32/21) has its two main offices in Whistler and Blackcomb. Fourteen other locations (scattered around Whistler Village, Upper Whistler and Whistler Creekside) also rent gear and there are even more pick-up locations if you reserve equipment online.

To access the untouched powder of backcountry peaks, **TLH Heliskiing** (☎ 250-558-5379, 800-667-4854; www.tlhheliskiing.com; from $1932) has multi-day trips and **Whistler Heli-Skiing** (☎ 604-932-4105, 888-435-4754; www.heliskiwhistler .com; 3-4241 Village Stroll; from $640) has day trips.

CROSS-COUNTRY SKIING & SNOW SHOEING

Whistler Municipality (Lot 4A off Lorimer Rd; adult/child $10/5; ☽ 8am-9pm Nov-Mar) grooms more than 30km of cross-country ski trails through serene Lost Lake Park and the valley. **Lost Lake Cross-Country Connection** (☎ 604-905-0071; www.crosscountryconnection.bc.ca; rentals adult/child $24/16, tours from $28; ☽ 9am-8pm Mon-Sat, 9am-5pm Sun), beside the ticket booth, rents equipment and runs tours. **Cougar Mountain Adventures** (☎ 888-297-2222; www.cougarmountain.ca; 4314 Main St; from $49; ☽ 10:30am-3pm) also leads tours.

Outdoor Adventures at Whistler (☎ 604-932-0647; 4205 Village Sq; from $59; ☽ 7am-2pm) offers various snowshoeing tours, with all equipment included.

Summer Activities

Whistler is a playground for all seasons. The increasing popularity of mountain biking and alpine hiking have allowed the area to be just as popular a destination in the summer as skiing and snowboarding allow it to be in the winter.

MOUNTAIN BIKING

It doesn't get any easier than riding the **Whistler Gondola** (adult/child lift $35/17, bike rental $59/29; ☽ 10am-5pm Jun-Sep) to mid-mountain and enjoying a gravity-fed adrenaline rush down. Opportunities range from easy trails for recreational riders to hard-core mountain descents for experienced cyclists. Whistler is also expanding its traditional coverage by adding more terrain accessed via the Fitzsimmons chair, resulting in a total of 1100m of vertical.

HIKING

To experience some alpine hiking the easy way, take the lifts to the top of **Whistler** (adult/child $20/15; ☽ 8am-5pm late Jun-Aug) and access the 48km of trails – the views go forever.

SKIING & SNOWBOARDING

It's getting to the point where it's laughable to label skiing and boarding as winter-only

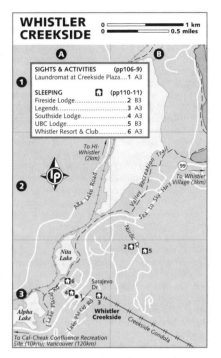

WHISTLER CREEKSIDE

0 — 1 km
0 — 0.5 miles

SIGHTS & ACTIVITIES	(pp106–9)
Laundromat at Creekside Plaza....1	A3

SLEEPING	(pp110–11)
Fireside Lodge.............................2	B3
Legends......................................3	A3
Southside Lodge.........................4	A3
UBC Lodge.................................5	B3
Whistler Resort & Club.................6	A3

To HI-
Whistler
(2km)

99

To Whistler
Hwy Village (3km)

Nita
Lake

Sarajevo
Dr

Alpha
Lake

Whistler
Creekside

Creekside Gondola

To Cal-Cheak Confluence Recreation
Site (10km); Vancouver (120km)

activities since **Horstman Glacier** ($39/32; noon-3pm Jun 7-Aug 1, lift opens at 11am) on the top of Blackcomb (1609m) is open until August. Obviously there won't be any powder but if you feel like strapping on the planks in high summer, knock yourself out. Blackcomb base bustles with activity in summer, too; check out the climbing wall, trapeze swing and social scene.

GOLFING
Whistler is the site of some of the most prestigious and sought after golf courses in the province. **Nicklaus North Golf & Country Club** (☎ 604-938-9898, 800-386-9898; 8080 Nicklaus North Blvd; $165), designed by Jack Nicholson – er, Nicklaus – is the best known. Other options include:
Whistler Golf Club (☎ 604-932-3280, 800-376-1777; 4001 Whistler Way; adult/child $136/59)
Chateau Whistler Golf Club (☎ 604-938-2092, 877-938-2092; 4612 Blackcomb Way; adult/child $185/25)

Tours
HORSEBACK
Saddle up. Most ranches are north of town and two-hour trips typically head up Cougar Mountain for views of Mount Robie Reid.
Whistler River Adventures (☎ 888-932-3532; www.whistlerriver.com; Whistler Gondola; $60)
Whistler Outdoor Experience Co (☎ 604-932-3389; www.whistleroutdoor.com; $44)

GLACIER AIR TOURS
Glaciers seen from afar are impressive enough, but a half-hour flight above them reveals the astonishing mass and strength of these shields of ice.
Whistler Air Services Ltd (☎ 888-806-2299; www.whistlerair.ca; from $99)
Glacier Air Tours (☎ 604-898-9016, 800-265-0088; www.glacierair.com; from $75)

Festivals & Events
Whistler stages events year-round:
Big Mountain Experience Come out and play; manufacturers showcase their new gear; photographers

---

WORKING AT WHISTLER-BLACKCOMB

Being a 'liftie' is considered a pretty sweet gig by those who can't get enough of the white stuff. **Whistler-Blackcomb** (☎ 604-938-7366; www.whistler-blackcomb.com; Whistler-Blackcomb, 4896 Glacier Dr, Whistler BC, V0N 1B4, Canada) makes that dream a little closer to reality by hiring several thousand people each year for seasonal jobs ranging from ski-lift operators to food service personnel. Most jobs go to Canadian residents or people with Canadian work authorization, such as Australians and New Zealanders on working holiday visas who make a living rotating winters between Canada and Australia. But don't let that stop you from chasing the dream. October–November and February–March are the peak recruiting times. Hourly wages range from about $7.50 to $12, plus good benefits: a season ski pass to both mountains, food discounts of 50% and free ski and snowboard lessons.

Once you get a job, finding cheap enough housing in Whistler can be pretty difficult. The resort makes some rooms available through its Glacier Residence program; rental rates range from $8.25 to $15 per person, per night. Call ☎ 604-938-7500 for information.

WHISTLER & THE SUNSHINE COAST

showcase their latest shoots and Whistler-Blackcomb showcases new ways to play and party (January).

Altitude Gay & lesbian ski/snowboard fest (early Febuary).

TELUS World Ski & Snowboard Festival Concerts and sports (mid-April).

Summit Concert Series Lovely outdoor location for live music (mid-April).

Whistler Jazz & Blues Weekend (mid-June)

Whistler Arts Experience Showcase of artistic talents (early July).

ArtRageous Multi-disciplinary event with exhibits, performances and fun interactive crafts (early July).

Oktoberfest Can it get any more perfect than a beer and sausage harvest festival in an alpine setting? (mid-October)

Cornucopia Fine wine and fine dining (mid-November).

Sleeping

Whistler has plenty of accommodations of all shapes and sizes. Prices at most places can double in the winter and there's a huge spike in rates from mid-December to early January so you'll want to book well in advance. Summer doesn't have the same sense of urgency but the area is gaining popularity as a summertime destination.

Central Reservation Service (☎ 604-664-5625, 800-944-7853; fax 938-5758) can book a room at almost any of the area's hotels, lodges and condominiums (but not budget lodgings or B&Bs). Ask about package deals that can help cut the cost of accommodations and activities.

HOTELS & CONDOMINIUMS

Whistler has dozens of stone-and-log resorts with forest-green rooms and natural wood furnishings. Not to say that every place follows the same concept, but to fit in with the image of mountain retreat, there is a certain architectural uniformity to follow. Most of the big-name hotel chains also have places here.

Fairmont Chateau Whistler (☎ 604-938-8000, 800-441-1414; www.fairmont.com; 4599 Chateau Blvd; summer/winter from $459/759; 🐾 ➡️) Watching over the base of Blackcomb from the north, this castle is enormous but somehow doesn't take away from the surrounding natural beauty. The rooms, hallways and lobbies are adorned in deep, rich colors and tastefully furnished. Added to this elegance is convenience, as you'll enjoy ski-in/ski-out proximity to the lifts.

Whistler Resort & Club (☎ 604-932-2343; reserve@rainbowretreats.com; 2129 Lake Placid Rd; r/ste summer $70/85, winter $99/130; ✖️) In Whistler Creekside the 1970s appeal comes from the days of Whistler's conception as a resort. It hasn't given in to the lure of modernization and captures the essence of Whistler's yester-decade with red brick fireplaces, wood paneling and pull-down Murphy beds in some rooms. The nice amenities include a whirlpool and sauna and free use of canoes, tennis courts and bicycles in summer.

Legends (☎ 604-689-8816, fax 682-7842; 2036 London Lane; ste $139-229; ✖️ 🐾 ➡️) For the ultimate convenience, this resort has the Creekside Gondola right next to the lobby. Ski-in/ski-out access allows you to spend more time on the slopes, in the hot tub and in your modern-rustic suite.

Valhalla (☎ 604-985-8484, 800-967-1319, fax 985-8470; Village North; summer/winter from $165/325; ✖️) This townhouse complex is in a quiet area of Village North. The units are built the way ski chalets should be: stacked together, steep roofs and wood siding. It's a good place for families as there's plenty of space inside, and they're all decorated to create a 'make yourself at home' atmosphere.

Cascade Lodge (☎ 604-905-4875, 866-580-6643; www.whistler-cascadelodge.com; 4315 Northlands Blvd; r/ste summer $89/109, winter $251/350; ✖️ 🐾 ➡️) What sets this lodge apart is that it occupies a quiet location that's not stacked between other businesses. Its stone and wood-beam construction fits in with the Whistler vibe, and though it's away from the heart of things it's still within walking distance.

Carleton Lodge (☎ 604-932-2343; reserve@rainbow retreats.com; 4290 Mountain Lane; summer $85-155, winter $275-450; ✖️) This is a suite-only complex with emphasis on 'sweet'. Run by the same good folks as Whistler Resort & Club, it sits at the nadir where Whistler meets Blackcomb and has easy access to both mountains. The rooms are fully furnished, equipped with kitchens and have plenty of space to throw your gear about.

B&BS

The info center can provide information on the B&Bs and has a good brochure listing most of them.

Chalet Luise (☎ 604-932-4187, 800-665-1998; www.chaletluise.com; 7461 Ambassador Cres; summer $125-160, winter $170-220; ✖️) This country-style inn with country-style hospitality doesn't seem out of place among the mountains of Whistler. It's within walking distance of Whistler Village and the lifts, and the Jacuzzi is welcome after a day on the hills.

Edelweiss Pension (☎ 604-932-3641, 800-665-2003; www.pensionedelweiss.com; 7162 Nancy Greene Dr; summer $95-125, winter $125-275) Genuine and personal Irish hospitality is what you get here. Close to the village, each of the eight rooms are different, and all of them are charming, bright, and inviting. The sun-splashed dining room hosts true European-style breakfast; you're served until you can no longer eat, and then offered more.

HOSTELS & LODGES

In Nordic Estates off Hwy 99 between Whistler Creekside and Whistler Village, **Fireside Lodge** (☎ 604-932-4660; 2113 Nordic Dr; $25) and the **UBC Lodge** (☎ 604-932-6604, ☎ 822-5851 in Vancouver; 2124 Nordic Dr; summer/winter $30/21.25) both offer dormitory-style accommodations.

Shoestring Lodge (☎ 604-932-3338, fax 932-8347, shoe@direct.ca, 7124 Nancy Greene Dr; dm/r summer $21/80, winter $31/125) This is the place to party; it's a 15-minute walk from the village. The Boot Pub attracts the rowdies, with exotic dancers and bands making regular appearances. The motel-style rooms and dorms are cleaner than you'd expect.

Hostelling International-Whistler (☎ 604-932-5492; whistler@hihostels.ca; 5678 Alta Lake Rd; dm $19.50) It's remote, but enjoys a beautiful setting on Alta Lake, 4km from Whistler Village, with awesome views of Blackcomb. It only has 32 beds, so it's a good idea to book ahead, especially during ski season.

Southside Lodge (☎ 604-932-3644; fax 932-0551; 2121 Lake Placid Rd; night/week $25/100) This is by far the closest hostel to the lifts, right across Hwy 99 from Whistler Creekside. The slightly faded building has 30 beds inside, with two bunk beds per room. Each room comes with its own bathroom and shower, cable TV and VCR.

CAMPING

BC Forest Service's **Cal-Cheak Confluence Recreation Site** (site $10; ☺ May-Oct) is 10km south of Whistler on Hwy 99. The Cal-Cheak suspension bridge is a short walk from the south site.

Riverside RV Resort & Campground (☎ 604-932-5469, 877-905-5533; www.whistlercamping.com; 8018 Mons Rd; tent/RV $30/45, cabin summer/winter $150/175) Just north of Whistler Village sits this resort that looks tacky from afar, but is actually a respectable place. Sure they have a mini-golf course, but the holes are real putting greens. Sure it looks like a wide spot in the road reminiscent of tourist-traps, but a closer look reveals a hot tub, playground, laundry, showers, well-maintained sites and cute little log cabins.

Eating

Restaurateurs in Whistler know you came for the sights and activities and not the food. They also know that after a day of activity you don't really feel like dressing up and acting proper, so you'll find a large percentage of eateries are the pub-food, burgers, sandwiches, pizza, tapas, have-a-good-time-on-the-patio sort. Of course this is great for families as well as single 20-somethings. Prices are slightly higher here than in other areas outside of Vancouver.

BUDGET

Whistlerites shop for groceries at **Nesters Market** (☎ 604-932-3545; 7019 Nesters Rd). For quick bites, **Auntie Em's Kitchen** (☎ 604-932-1163; 4340 Lorimer Rd; $5-8) serves sandwiches and salads. **Mogul's Coffee** (☎ 604-932-4845; 203-4204 Village Square; $2-6) is the coffeehouse where locals go with its vantage point to watch the bustle of the square.

MID-RANGE

Citta's (chee-tahs) **Bistro** (☎ 604-932-4177; 4217 Village Stroll) The patio right on the edge of Village Square means there's no shortage of activity. This place is always lively and serves up good, creative food like the Jim Beam-and-garlic steak.

Black's Pub & Restaurant (☎ 604-932-6408; 4270 Mountain Square; mains $8-15) Known for its pizzas and selection of 99 beers, it's a popular spot among Whistlerites and a good spot for non-residents because of the upstairs patio. Enjoy a whiskey or hot toddy while watching skiers coming down the slopes to Whistler base.

Roundhouse Lodge (☎ 604-932-3434; Whistler Mountain; mains $5-20) The complex at the top of the Whistler Village Gondola is a great place for non-skiers to meet their skiing traveling partners for lunch, or to just go up and watch other non-skiers crash into each other. Aside from an outdoor grill, it houses cafeteria-style Pika's; an open-air market with a selection of international dishes at The Marketplace; the casual, full-service restaurant Steeps; and the semi-formal Italian restaurant Paloma's. It's a concrete and wood monster of a building perched at mid-mountain with some amazing views of the valley.

La Brasserie des Artistes (☎ 604-932-3569; mains $7-12) This is the place to go for breakfast, with several versions of eggs Benedict and the kind of vibe that gets you pumped for the day ahead. It's also a good spot to kick back and have a beer and a sandwich on the patio in the afternoon.

Dubh Linn Gate Old Irish Pub (☎ 604-905-4047; 170-4320 Sundial Cres; mains $10-20) A wee luck o' the Irish at the base of Whistler. This place has a vibrant social scene with folksy Gaelic songs resounding through the stone and wood dining room.

Whistler Noodle House (☎ 604-932-2228; 9-4330 Northlands Rd; mains $8-12; ⓨ lunch & dinner) Nothing delivers comfort like a hearty bowl of hot soup after playing in the snow. This place gives you that in a relaxed and casual setting. The bowls are huge and there are plenty of vegetarian options.

Caramba (☎ 604-938-1879; 12-4314 Main St; mains $10-18; ⓨ lunch & dinner) The Mediterranean fare comes highly recommended by visitors and locals alike. The pastas and rotisserie main dishes are tantalizing.

Sushi-Ya (☎ 604-905-0155; 230-4370 Lorimer Rd; mains $10-20; ⓨ lunch & dinner) This popular sushi spot is a hopping place with avocado and salmon that dissolve on your tongue almost before you get a chance to swallow it.

TOP END
Major hotels at Whistler contain a semi-fancy dining room or two, but aren't the only upscale options.

Bearfoot Bistro (☎ 604-932-3433; 4121 Village Green; mains $15-30) This place attracts attention with wild-game specialties like moose and venison. It's got a solid, woodsy feeling on the inside, and a casual atmosphere.

Zeuski's (☎ 604-932-6009; mains $16-26; ⓨ lunch & dinner) This is a good place to go for a nice, quiet meal. It's along the pedestrian mall at town plaza and has an outside patio, but the place never seems to get too noisy. Great mezes and tasty broiled salmon.

Drinking
After a day on the slopes what the body needs is some good partying, but a little recuperation time is in order first. Aprés is time to swap tales and injuries over a couple of drinks and appetizers:

Buffalo Bill's Bar & Grill (☎ 604-932-6613; 4122 Village Green) 30-and-older crowd.

Longhorn Saloon & Grill (☎ 604-932-5999; 4290 Mountain Square) Attracts crowds off the slopes at Whistler base.

Merlin's Bar & Grill (☎ 604-938-7700; Upper Village, base of Blackcomb) Sit out on the patio and watch your ski-buddies come down Blackcomb.

PUBS
Brewhouse Restaurant & Pub (☎ 604-905-2739; 4355 Blackcomb Way) This place makes its own beer on the premises and like any artistic work, the natural surroundings inspire brew masterpieces like 'Twin Peaks Pale Ale' and 'Lifty Lager'. It's a great pub away from the huge crowds and the place to go to just have fun.

Boot Pub (☎ 604-932-3338) Live bands play frequently in the Shoestring Lodge's pub, but the exotic dancers of 'Das Boot Ballet' draw the rowdy crowds several nights a week.

Entertainment
A lot of eateries also have live music after the sun goes down. Stroll around the village and trust your ears.

NIGHTCLUBS
Garfinkel's (☎ 604-932-2323; 1-4308 Main St) This club of choice among residents and regular visitors is a good place to hang out. It's the usual stop for touring musical acts, and on other nights people dance to hip-hop and dance music with a little old-fashioned rock n' roll thrown in. Other places to pop-n-lock:

Maxx Fish (☎ 604-932-1904; 4232 Village Stroll) College crowds and wild parties.

Moe Joe's (☎ 604-935-1152; Whistler Village) Ladies' night Thursday.

Savage Beagle (☎ 604-938-3337; 4222 Village Square) Top 40 and younger crowds.

CINEMA & THEATER
Rainbow Theatre (☎ 604-932-2422; 4010 Whistler Way; $5) has discount screenings for second-run movies. **Village 8 Cinema** (☎ 604-932-5833; Whistler Village; $8) is for first-run flicks.

Maurice Young Millennium Place (☎ 604-935-8410; 4335 Blackcomb Way) MY Place is the community center where plays and other events take place.

Getting There & Away

Most people get to Whistler via ground transportation from Vancouver, which is the only option in winter.

AIR

Whistler Air (☎ 888-806-2299; www.whistlerair.ca; $135) offers float-plane service at 8:30am and 4pm June to September from Green Lake to Vancouver.

Helijet (☎ 800-665-4354; www.helijet.com; $179) flies helicopters between Vancouver and Whistler.

BUS

Greyhound Canada (☎ 604-932-5031, 800-661-8747; www.greyhound.ca; adult/child $22.50/12.25) makes seven daily trips from Vancouver to Whistler between 5:45am and 9:30pm. The first Vancouver departure and the 3pm Whistler departure are express buses with limited stops.

Perimeter Tours (☎ 604-266-5386, 877-317-7788; www.perimeterbus.com; adult/child $58/39) runs buses from Vancouver hotels to Whistler hotels.

Bigfoot Adventure Tours (☎ 888-244-6673; www.bigfoottours.com; one-way/return $27/49) runs a shuttle between central Vancouver and Whistler twice daily between 6:30am and 5pm. They also organize and offer discounts on Whistler activities.

Getting Around

The **WAVE** (☎ 604-932-4020; adult/child $1.50/free) is the Whistler area's public transit; buses are equipped with outside ski and bicycle racks. The shuttle between Whistler Village, Village North and Upper Village is free.

Sea to Sky Taxi (☎ 604-932-3333) provides taxi service.

If you want to ride in style, call **Town & Country Chauffeurs** (☎ 604-932-6468).

PEMBERTON

pop 1650

Just a short drive (30km) north of Whistler on Hwy 99, takes you into the cowboy country of Pemberton. For local information stop at the **Visitor Info Centre** (☎ 604-894-6175) across from the Petro Canada station.

Nairn Falls Provincial Park (www.gov.bc.ca/bcparks) is 6km south of Pemberton along Hwy 99. Unlike other falls that spill over the edge of abrupt cliffs in one great plunge, Nairn Falls collects, gurgles and sprays its way down the mountain like an aqua-ballet before continuing on as the Green River. The trail to the falls (3km round-trip) winds along steep banks of the river. Another trail (4km roundtrip) leads to One Mile Lake.

As you'd expect from the cowboy hats in town, horseback riding is a popular pastime. **Poole Creek Stables** (☎ 604-932-8666; from $49) and **Adventures on Horseback** (☎ 604-894-6269; from $58) offer trail rides and pack trips.

After a day of exercise, or to rest your weary soul, soak in **Meager Creek Hot Springs** (☎ 604-898-2100; BC Forest Service; $5), 47km north of Pemberton via the Upper Lillooet River Rd. This world-class soaking site features regularly drained and cleaned Japanese-style bathing pools and interpretive trails. Geological hazards occasionally close Meager Creek, so inquire at the info center or call before setting out.

Joffre Lakes Provincial Park (www.gov.bc.ca/bcparks), 15km east of town on Hwy 99, has some great hiking to the first lake, or follow a much more ambitious trail to the upper backcountry. Mountain peaks rise up from Lower Joffre Lake and tell their glacial tale through U-shaped valleys and cirques. The trail continues on to Joffre Lakes, and though it's a little more challenging, it's a lot more rewarding as time seems to move at a glacial pace in the stillness of the lake's surface.

Birkenhead Lake Provincial Park (www.gov.bc.ca/bcparks), 55km from Pemberton, has excellent wildlife watching, canoeing, fishing and swimming.

Sleeping & Eating

The Farmhouse B&B (☎ 604-894-6205, 888-394-6205; www.pembertonbandb.com/The_Farmhouse.htm; 7611 Meadows Rd; s/d $65/75; ☒ ☎) Sleep in country comfort on 10 acres of pastoral bliss in this 1920s farmhouse. You don't have to get up and do chores at 5am, but you can get up at your leisure and enjoy a fantastic full breakfast.

For information on the other 10 or so B&Bs in the area check www.pembertonbandb.com or the visitor center.

Nairn Falls Provincial Park and **Birkenhead Lake Provincial Park** (☎ 800-689-9025; www.discover camping.ca; site $14) have camping.

Pony Espresso (☎ 604-894-5700; 1426 Portage Rd; snacks $5-8) This funky little café on the way into the town center is popular with everyone from Whistler commuters to long-time Pemberton locals.

Getting There & Away

Greyhound Canada (☎ 604-932-5031, 800-661-8747; www.greyhound.ca; adult/child $24.50/12.25; ☻ 8am-7pm) operates four daily bus trips from Vancouver.

The Sea to Sky (Hwy 99) turns to Duffey Lake Rd as it continues north past Duffey Lake Provincial Park through dense forest and beautiful scenery to Lillooet (p193).

DETOUR: GOLD BRIDGE

From Pemberton, follow the Upper Lillooet River Rd through the acres of farmland along the Lillooet River. Cross the bridge and turn right on the Lillooet River Forest Service Rd (if you want to visit Meager Creek Hot Springs, keep going straight then backtrack to this point and turn left). You're then on a gravel road that crosses through the stark contrasts of the clear-cut forests and the forested hills. Keep your eyes open for deer and black bears as you follow the signs to Gold Bridge.

Keep right as you round the western end of Carpenter Lake and go through town to Bralorne; go through Bralorne and follow the switchbacks to a real-life ghost town where the residents just up and left once mining in the area went bust.

Double-back to Gold Bridge and stop in at the info center. Follow the signs to Gun Lake for some excellent hiking, biking, fishing, swimming and picnicking, and a visit to the extravagant **Tyax Mountain Lake Resort** (☎ 250-238-2221; www.tyax.com). Follow the well-maintained Lillooet Pioneer Rd No 40 east along the north shore of beautiful Carpenter Lake. There are a few free campsites along the road if you feel like stopping for the night. You'll pass by the Terzaghi Dam and through some jagged mountain and river valley scenery on the way to Lillooet.

SUNSHINE COAST

Stretching from Langdale to Lund, the Sunshine Coast is a geographical orphan, separated from the rest of the Lower Mainland by the formidable Coast Mountains. Sunshine Coasters make full use of their scenic maritime location, enjoying everything from cruises into majestic Princess Louisa Inlet to kayaking and scuba diving in world-class settings.

Hwy 101 winds nearly the length of the coast, interrupted by water between Earls Cove and Saltery Bay; BC Ferries bridges the gap. Powell River, the region's largest town, is the jumping-off point for ferries to Comox on Vancouver Island, and the Langdale terminal near Gibsons takes travelers to the mainland. Although it is possible to travel between Langdale and Powell River (including the ferry crossing) in about three hours, give yourself a bit more time for the unexpected little things like stopping for the spectacular scenery, day-long hikes or week-long kayak trips.

GIBSONS

pop 3900

Gibsons is the gateway to the Sunshine Coast and served as the setting for *The Beachcombers*, a popular CBC series filmed here in the 1970s. Relic, one of the characters of the show, no longer lives here but the town he loved so faithfully is still worthy of admiration.

Orientation & Information

Gibsons Landing is the visitor-oriented part of town and the commercial strip known as 'Upper Gibsons' is farther up the hill along Hwy 101 (the Sunshine Coast Hwy).

The **Visitor Info Centre** (☎ 604-886-2325; www.gibsonschamber.com; ☻ 9am-5pm) is inside the Sunnycrest Mall, just off Hwy 101 in Upper Gibsons. There's also a seasonal **Info Centre** (417 Marine Dr; ☻ 9am-6pm summer) at Gibsons Landing.

Sights & Activities

A walk down **Gower Point Rd** in Gibsons Landing will show you what this seaside town is all about. The cute shops and storefronts blend nicely with that smell of sea air.

For a swim or a picnic, try **Armours Beach**, just northeast of the village below Marine Drive, or **Chaster Park**, around the point on Ocean Beach Esplanade (follow Gower Point Rd).

The sheltered harbors and islands of Howe Sound make an idyllic setting for sea kayaking. Rentals, lessons and a variety of tours are available from **Sunshine Kayaking** (☎ 604-886-9760; www.sunshinekayaking.com; Molly's Lane; rentals from $28).

Maritime & Elphinstone Pioneer Museum (☎ 604-886-8232; 716 Winn Rd; admission by donation; ✆ 10:30am-4:30pm Tue-Sat) This two-in-one museum displays an eclectic collection of bottles, period costumes, Native Indian baskets, seashells, a collection of model ships and other nautical exhibits.

Sleeping & Eating

Ritz Inn (☎ 604-886-3343, 800-649-1138; www.ritz inn.com; 505 Gower Point Rd; $72-92; ⊠ ⊠ ⊠) Set back by the marina, this white motel has balconies facing the water. The well-priced, large rooms make it a good spot for families.

Bonniebrook Lodge (☎ 604-886-2887, 877-290-9916; www.bonniebrook.com; 1532 Oceanbeach Esplanade; $150-190; ⊠) Set away from the harbor, with a lot more ocean to look at, this B&B provides an incredibly relaxed setting and supreme hospitality. Enjoy your room with a view and your delicious hearty breakfast by the stone-hearth fireplace.

You can buy fresh seafood right off the wharf, or visit **Gibsons Fish Market** (☎ 604-886-8363; 292 Gower Point Rd; mains $5-8) for fish and chips.

Molly's Reach (☎ 604-886-9710) This greasy-spoon cafeteria with the huge sign hasn't changed since it starred in *The Beachcombers* in the 1970s. It's got nostalgia, which lends vicarious charm. The food is hearty, but it's the character, the memorabilia and the view that will draw you.

Gramma's Pub (☎ 604-886-8215; 412 Marine Dr; mains $7-15; ✆ lunch & dinner) This downstairs pub has a small glassed-in patio with a great view of the harbor and marine activity. This is where Gibsons residents hang out to unwind and tell their stories of life on the water. The interior and the food are pub-esque.

Howl at the Moon (☎ 604-886-8881; 450 Marine Dr; mains $9-13) At the end of the strip, the décor in this place is Tex-Mex, but meals are from all over the map. It's a super-casual place that's good for families and has huge windows at the back for great harbor views.

Opa Japanese Restaurant (☎ 604-886-4023; 281 Gower Point Rd; mains $10-13; ✆ dinner) Walk through the huge wooden doors at this Japanese restaurant and you'll be treated to a delight of the senses. The sushi is excellent, mainly due to the same-day catch. The wooden interior with the bay windows creates instant marine ambience.

Getting There & Around

BC Transit's **Sunshine Coast Transit System** (☎ 604-885-6899; www.suncoastcentral.com; adult/child $1.50/1) serves the Lower Sunshine Coast from Langdale to Secret Cove.

Malaspina Coach Lines (☎ 877-227-8287; $15.50/23) travels between Vancouver and Gibsons and the cost includes the ferry crossing.

BC Ferries (☎ 604-886-2242, 888-223-3779; www.bcferries.com; adult/child $8.25/4.25, car $28.75; ✆ 6:20am-10:10pm) travels eight to 11 times daily from Langdale to Horseshoe Bay. This fare covers either a roundtrip between Horseshoe Bay and Langdale, or a one-way-trip from Horseshoe Bay through to Saltery Bay.

ROBERTS CREEK

pop 3100

Some draft-dodgers who fled to Canada during the Vietnam War era decided this place on the coast was as good as any and took up residence. Thirty years later, the area still retains a strong counterculture feel.

Roberts Creek Rd, off Hwy 101, leads to the anti-commercial, rural center of town. Check the placards around town or www.robertscreek.com to see what's happening at the community hall.

Follow the road through the village to **Roberts Creek Park** and have yourself a picnic or walk out to the spit. **Roberts Creek Provincial Park**, just west of town off Hwy 101, is also a good place for a quick stop or day at the beach.

Sleeping & Eating

Moon Cradle Backpackers Retreat (☎ 604-885-0238, 877-350-5862; mooncradle@uniserve.com; 3125 Hwy 101; dm/s/d $25/40/55) This place has captured the hostel mood perfectly by creating a welcoming home in the woods. The bunks are handcrafted cedar beds and amenities include an all-organic continental breakfast, shoulder massage, kitchen access (vegetarian food only) and drum circles and bonfires in summer.

Roberts Creek Provincial Park (☎ 604-885-3714; site $14; ☽ May-Sep) has 21 sites; the gate is locked in winter, but you can walk in if you'd like.

Gumboot Garden Café (☎ 604-885-4216; 1057 Roberts Creek Rd; mains $7-14) Definitely the earthy, wooden kind of establishment you'd expect to find in a place like Roberts Creek. It's a super loose and open café, serving home-made granola, veggie sandwiches, burritos, and such fine-dining fare as organic chicken with lemon-ginger dipping sauce.

Creekhouse (☎ 604-885-9321; 1041 Roberts Creek Rd; mains $20-25; ☽ dinner Fri-Sun) One of the Sunshine Coast's most upscale choices serves *pêche du jour* in its elegant white house in the pretty little garden.

Getting There & Away
Malaspina Coach Lines (☎ 604-886-7742, 877-227-8287) runs buses to Vancouver.

SECHELT
pop 7800
Being located alongside the narrow gateway to the Sechelt Peninsula, Sechelt has water to the south and to the north and mountains that rise steeply from all its coastlines. It's the second-largest town on the Sunshine Coast and has long been an important stronghold of the Coast Salish people; in 1986, the Sechelt Band became the first in modern Canada to attain self-government.

Sechelt's downtown area is centered around the intersection of Hwy 101 and Wharf Ave. From here, if you're coming from Roberts Creek, turn right for Porpoise Bay or left for Halfmoon Bay and the Earls Cove ferry. The **Visitor Info Centre** (☎ 604-885-0662; 5755 Cowrie St; ☽ 8:30am-5pm Mon-Fri, 8:30am-12:30pm Sat) is in Trail Bay Mall.

The **post office** (☎ 604-885-2411; ☽ 8:30am-5pm Mon-Fri, 8:30am-12:30pm Sat) is at the corner of Dolphin and Inlet Sts. The **Daily Roast** (☎ 604-885-4345; 5547 Wharf St; 10¢ per min) offers email access and good Java.

Sights & Activities
Take a walk down the long pier to fish or go for a swim at **Davis Bay** beach, on the south side of Sechelt. With a good kayak launch and a sandy beach, **Porpoise Bay Provincial Park** (☎ 604-898-3678), 4km north of Sechelt, makes an ideal base camp for paddlers and cyclists exploring the Sunshine Coast.

House of Hewhiwus (☎ 604-885-8991; 555 Hwy 101) The Sechelt First Nations band has its headquarters at the southern end of town. This complex includes **Tems Swiya Museum** (Our World Museum; ☎ 604-885-8991), with its impressive gallery of First Nations art and artifacts, and the **Raven Theatre** (☎ 604-885-4597).

Because of Sechelt's unique geographical location, it can appease activity seekers of all kinds. The mountains to the east and the west provide some excellent hiking and mountain biking. The info center has detailed descriptions of dozens of hikes in the area and **On the Edge** (☎ 604-885-4888, 877-322-4888; www.ontheedgebiking.com; 5644 Cowrie St; from $30 per day) rents bikes and leads guided mountain-biking trips in the spring and summer.

Suncoast Diving & Watersports (☎ 604-740-8006; www.suncoastdiving.com; 5643 Wharf St; rentals $75; dives from $135; ☽ 9am-6pm) makes picking the scuba-dive site that's right for you from the dozen in the area easy. **Pedals & Paddles** (☎ 604-885-6440; from $38 per day), at Tillicum Bay on Sechelt Inlet, has stubbornly left the 'Pedals' in its name, but offers kayak rentals, tours and advice on the wonderfully tranquil waters of the inlet.

Sleeping & Eating
The info center has extensive details of the many B&Bs in the area; rooms typically cost $90 to $120.

Driftwood Inn (☎ 604-885-5811; www.driftwoodmotorinn.com; 5454 Trail Ave; s/d $79/89; ✗) On the waterfront downtown, this red brick motel has some outstanding views and easy beach access.

Upper Deck Hostel (☎ 604-885-5822; upperdeck@wuts.nu; 5653 Wharf St; dm/r $20/35) Set above some shops in an industrial looking part of town, you wouldn't expect to find a hostel, but here it is. The huge sundeck that leads to the glass patio doors is covered in potted plants and the kitchen, lounge and rooms are as welcoming as your friend's apartment.

South of Sechelt, **Wilson Creek Campground** (☎ 604-885-5937, 800-565-9222; 4314 Hwy 101; site $15.50) offers 37 sites year-round. **Porpoise Bay Provincial Park** (☎ 800-689-9025; www.discover camping.ca; site $12) features a separate area set aside for hikers and cyclists, plus regular sites for everybody else ($17.50).

Old Boot Eatery (☎ 604-885-2727; 5330 Wharf St; mains $10-13; ☽ lunch & dinner) The name refers to its Italian menu, rather than its charm. This popular restaurant smells better than an old boot too – and the aroma from the kitchen and the huge portions of pasta grab your attention immediately.

Beach Buoy Restaurant (☎ 604-885-3715; 4774 Hwy 101; mains $6-8; ☽ lunch & dinner) This fish and chips and burger joint is across the street from Davis Beach. It's perfect for getting your grease intake on the patio, or you can take away and walk out onto the pier.

Getting There & Away

Malaspina Coach Lines (☎ 604-885-2217, 877-227-8287) runs buses to Vancouver.

EGMONT & EARLS COVE

These communities at the top of the Lower Sunshine Coast are often overlooked, but are excellent access points for trips up Jervis Inlet to the rugged fjords of **Princess Louisa Inlet** and **Chatterbox Falls**. **Malibu Yacht Charters** (☎ 604-883-2003) and the **Egmont Water Taxi** (☎ 604-883-2092) lead tours.

For a good hike to a natural wonder, the trail in **Skookumchuck Narrows Provincial Park**, near Egmont, leads to an inlet so narrow that water forced through during tides can cause rapids as fast as 30km/h.

BC Ferries (☎ 604-487-9333, 888-223-3779; www.bc ferries.com; adult/child $8.25/4.25, car $28.75) offers eight daily sailings between Earls Cove and Saltery Bay (6:30am to 10:10pm); the fare covers either a roundtrip between Earls Cove and Saltery Bay or a through-trip from Saltery Bay to Horseshoe Bay.

POWELL RIVER

pop 13,000

Powell River, 31km north of the Saltery Bay ferry terminal, is an honest town built in 1910 for the sole purpose of providing housing for mill workers. Rather than dismissing it as an industrial outpost, visitors who stay find an excellent array of recreational opportunities.

> ### DETOUR: PENDER HARBOUR
>
> From Hwy 101, head east on Garden Bay Rd and follow its winding path through the woods and around Garden Bay Lake's north shore. Veer right onto Irvine's Landing Rd and watch for deer, eagles and the wonderfully jagged coast that can be seen through clearings in the trees. The road will take you to **Irvine's Landing**, the original settlement site in the Pender Harbour area, affectionately known as 'Venice of the North'. Get out and stretch your legs along the beaches and rocky shore, checking tide pools for unbelievably colored sea critters. When you're ready, follow your path back to Hwy 101.

Hwy 101 becomes Marine Ave through downtown and leads north to The Townsite area, home to the huge Pacific Paper mill. From there, Hwy 101 continues on to its terminus at Lund, 23km north.

The **Visitor Info Centre** (☎ 604-485-4701; 4690 Marine Ave; ☽ 9am-5:30pm) stays open year-round. Buy stamps from the **post office** (☎ 604-485-5552; 4812 Joyce Ave; ☽ 8:30am-5pm Mon-Fri). Access email at the **Powell River Public Library** (☎ 604-485-4796; 4411 Michigan Ave; ☽ closed Sun & Mon). For medical emergencies, go to **Powell River General Hospital** (☎ 604-485-3211; 5000 Joyce Ave).

Sights & Activities

Willingdon Beach, west of downtown, has a childrens' playground and pleasant views of Vancouver Island.

Powell River Museum (☎ 604-485-2222; adult/child $2/1; ☽ 9am-5pm Mon-Fri Sep–mid-Jun) across Willingdon Ave from the beach, contains a replica of a shack once occupied by Billy Goat Smith, a hermit who lived (with his goats) in the area in the early 20th century. Ask about times for the museum's treasure hunt if you're traveling with children.

Patricia Theatre (☎ 604-483-9345; 5848 Ash St) In Townsite, this reminder of the great days of theater is Canada's longest running movie house. It offers a great glimpse of the past while showing first-run movies. Check out the carousel at the back.

Hike all or part of the 180km **Sunshine Coast Trail** (www.sunshinecoast-trail.com) that wanders through the forests and marine environments from Saltery Bay to Sarah Point.

Check with the info center for the excellent *Powell River Visitor Map* ($2), which also details the 57km **Powell Forest Canoe Route** that connects 12 lakes via easily portaged trails.

For information on the ample scuba diving around Powell River, **Don's Dive Shop** (☎ 604-483-3456; www.donsdiveshop.com; 4552 Willingdon Ave) leads guided dives and rents gear. **Taw's Cycle & Sports** (☎ 604-485-2555; 4597 Marine Ave) rents bikes and offers sound advice on local mountain biking, campsites and hiking. **Powell River Sea Kayak** (☎ 604-485-2144; 6812E Alberni Pl) rents boats and leads a range of kayaking tours, from two-hour paddles to multi-day trips into Desolation Sound.

Sleeping

Westview Centre Motel (☎ 604-485-4023, 877-485-4023; fax 485-7736; 4534 Marine Ave; r $62-75; ✗) As you head up the steep driveway to these bungalow motel rooms, your back is to the ocean, but when you turn around, the view is amazing. The front windows of rooms here look at the same view.

Old Courthouse Inn & Hostel (☎ 604-483-4000, 877-483-4777; oldcourthouseinn@armourtech.com; 6243 Walnut St; r $20-75) In the Townsite section, this beautifully restored courthouse and police station is so cool. Tell your friends you spent the night in jail, or in the judge's chambers or constable's office. In keeping with the historic theme, the rooms are nicely decorated with antique furnishings.

At **Willingdon Beach Campsite** (☎ 604-485-2242, 4845 Marine Ave; tent/RV $15/20) the facilities include showers, laundry and a large plastic Popeye.

Eating

Small Planet Whole Foods (☎ 604-485-9134; 4449 Marine Ave; mains $4-8) is a vegetarian deli/café. **Captain Billy's Old Fashioned Fish and Chips** (☎ 604-485-2252; mains $6-8; ☽ Apr-Nov) has been dishing the fish at the ferry terminal for more than 25 years.

Rocky Mountain Pizza & Bakery (☎ 604-485-9111; 4471 Marine Ave; snacks $2-5, pizza $6-9) This little coffeehouse and bakery is a popular spot among the locals. The tables for two and chairs outside are always occupied.

La Casita (☎ 604-485-7720,4578 Marine Ave; mains $7-12; ☽ lunch & dinner Tue-Sun) This colorful and energetic Mexican restaurant has some delicious combo plates that nicely complement the blue and orange decor.

Chiang Mai (☎ 604-485-0883; 4463 Marine Ave; mains $7-13; ☽ lunch & dinner) The linoleum floors and light wooden tables and chairs are nothing special to look at, but this Thai place is about the food, not image. The pad thai and seafood dishes are tasty and spicy.

Shinglemill Pub (☎ 604-483-2001; 6233 Powell Place; mains $7-12; ☽ lunch & dinner) On Powell Lake north of the Townsite, this woodsy pub offers good pub grub accompanied by great views.

Getting There & Around

Powell River airport (7576 Duncan St), 2km from downtown, services **Pacific Coastal Airlines** (☎ 800-663-2872; www.pacific-coastal.com) flights to Vancouver.

BC Ferries (☎ 604-485-2943, 888-223-3779; www.bc ferries.com; adult/child $7.75/4, car $26) offers four daily 75-minute sailings to Comox on Vancouver Island between 8:10am and 8:45pm. The boats are often overloaded, especially on the midday sailing, so plan to arrive at least an hour before departure if you're driving.

Malaspina Coach Lines (☎ 604-485-5030, 877-227-8287) runs buses to Vancouver.

BC Transit's **Powell River Regional Transit System** (☎ 604-485-4287; adult/child $1.50/1) handles local bus services. For taxi service, call **Powell River Taxi** (☎ 604-483-3666).

LUND & BEYOND

Lund (populaton 265), at the northern end of Hwy 101, serves as a staging point for trips to **Desolation Sound** and tropical-like **Savary Island**. Desolation Sound got its name from Captain George Vancouver, who thought the region's seascapes seemed remote and forbidding. With its many sheltered bays, 8256-hectare Desolation Sound Provincial Marine Park offers plenty of boating, fishing, kayaking and swimming opportunities.

Savary Island, aka 'Hawaii of the North', features pristine, white sandy beaches surrounded by turquoise and emerald water. It's in the rain shadow of the Coast Mountains, so it's very sunny here and the water is unusually warm.

To get to the island, call **Lund Water Taxi** (☎ 604-483-9749; adult/child $6.50/3.25). When you arrive visit **Savary Island Bike Rental & Repair**

(☎ 604-414-4079) to help you get around. There's no car ferry and no paved roads, so it's pretty peaceful – perfect for a quiet weekend on the beach. For accommodations and a short rundown of the few services on the island, visit www.savary.ca.

Sleeping & Eating

Desolation Resort (☎ 604-483-3592; www.desolation resort.com; 2694 Dawson Rd; r $129-209, chalet $229-249) North of Lund on Okeover Inlet, the cedar chalets peer out onto the water through the trees like they're part of the scenery, or at least as if they don't want to spoil what nature created. Like snowflakes, no two cabins are alike and all are fully furnished, rustic and colorfully decorated.

Lund Hotel (☎ 604-414-0474; 1436 Hwy 101; s/d from $70/85) The outside is blue and white and has a certain marine quality to it and the pub inside is definitely nautical by nature, but the rooms are lightly colored and fresh.

Laughing Oyster (☎ 604-483-9775; 10052 Malaspina Rd; mains $12-30; ☽ lunch & dinner) The views are stunning enough to illicit laughs of disbelief, but the food prepared in this wooden restaurant is serious. Seafood and steaks are prominent on the menu. This is a great example of excellent west coast dining in a spectacular west coast setting.

Nancy's Bakery (☎ 604-483-4180; $3-7; ☽ break-fast & lunch), on the Lund Pier, is known for gooey cinnamon rolls.

Vancouver Island

CONTENTS

Vancouver Island is the largest island off the coast of the Americas and a model of Pacific Northwest climates and ecologies. The coastline is rocky and tempestuous in some places, sandy and calm in others; it rains only 65cm a year in Victoria but 750cm a year 75km north in Port Alberni. Vancouver Island could be described in a word as 'green'; it's 450km long and only 100km wide, and the Island Mountain Range stretching down its spine is covered in evergreens and old-growth forests.

Some of the mildest climates in Canada are making the Island increasingly popular, and it's now home to more than 500,000 people, most living along the southeast coast. Natural resources have always driven the main industries, but recent tariffs in lumber and depleted fishing stocks have forced many small communities to find other ways of survival. Tourism has worked for most communities, though with varying degrees of commercial success.

Vancouver Island is increasing in popularity as a travel destination, especially in late summer. To avoid crowds consider coming in spring, when flowers are in full bloom and spring run-off feeds the vegetation making everything a rich green; or in autumn, when wild winds, semi-rough seas and scattering leaves show off Vancouver Island's magnificence.

VANCOUVER ISLAND

HIGHLIGHTS

- Enjoying old-world elegance in **Victoria** (p124), the Garden City

- Taking **afternoon tea** – English style in Victoria (p137) or Salish style (p145)

- Experiencing First Nations heritage at a T'sasala dance performance in **Alert Bay** (p171)

- Riding the *Lady Rose* down from Port Alberni, through the Broken Group Islands to the tiny village of **Bamfield** (p156)

- Walking the boardwalks and watching for whales in **Telegraph Cove** (p169)

VANCOUVER ISLAND

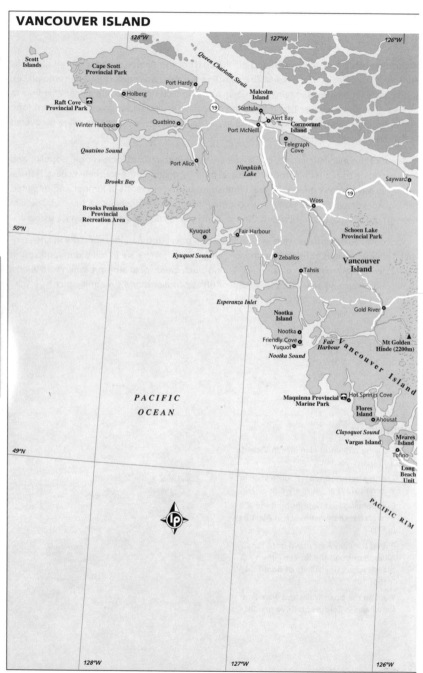

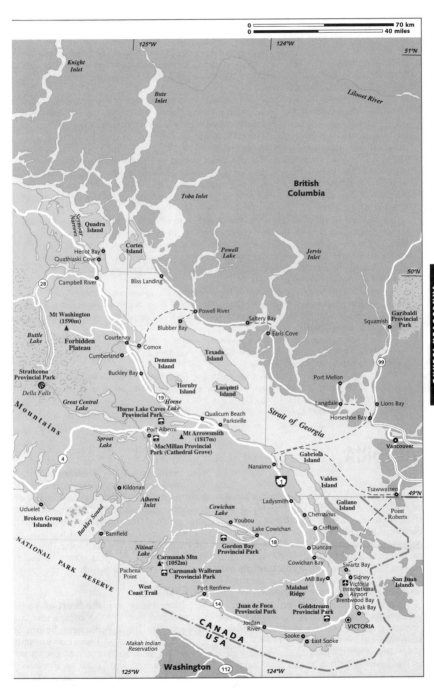

ISLAND TIME, ISLAND TALK, ISLAND LIVING

On Vancouver Island time moves at about half the speed of the mainland, and people who live there wouldn't have it any other way. Island residents, on the whole, don't feel comfortable west of Nanaimo and only head over when absolutely necessary. 'Too many people, too fast' are the common reasons for their uneasiness.

It's a reverse effect the other way, and for those used to the chaos of major urbanity it may take a day or two to adapt. But once you get used to it, 'island time' fits like a pair of well-worn jeans. Those accustomed to big-city living should start their trip in Victoria to reduce shock to the system. Victoria is about three-quarter time and after a day or so you'll be sufficiently acclimatised and 'island time' won't feel so foreign.

You look at your watch less on the Island; two o'clock, six o'clock – gone. It's lunchtime or nighttime or breaktime or time to go fishing or time to go hiking or time to go swimming or time for a beer. The day doesn't seem all that important, either – until it's time to leave – as if it's always Saturday. It's stress-free living at its finest; nobody's in a rush and everyone's got time to stop and talk.

The only real exception to this rule is the recently completed Inland Highway (Hwy 19) from Nanaimo to Campbell River. The Island Hwy (now 19A) was once the only north–south route, but with the new highway a few kilometers inland, people have discovered that their right foot goes a little closer to the floor and it's not uncommon to be traveling 130km/h and still get passed. But for the most part, island residents have the enviable mindset that there's no hurry and we'll get there when we get there.

Once you feel like you could get used to island time, take it up a notch and learn 'island talk'. Call it 'the Island' instead of 'Vancouver Island'. 'Up-island' is north and 'down-island' is south, relative to your position; if you're in Victoria, Ladysmith is up-island but if you're in Parksville, Ladysmith is down-island.

For the most part you can drop 'Port' from town names and 'Island' from island names - Port Hardy is now 'Hardy' and Gabriola Island is 'Gabriola.' Port Alice and Port Alberni are exceptions, for whatever reason they keep the 'Port'.

Practice before you go. Tuck away your watch and when someone asks where you're going, say: 'Over to the Island. The ferry lands in Nanaimo and from there it's up-island to McNeill, with maybe a stop at Denman and Hornby.'

Now you're ready for 'island living'.

VICTORIA

pop 74,000

Victoria is British Columbia's provincial capital, and lies at the southeast end of Vancouver Island, 90km southwest of Vancouver. Although bounded on three sides by water, the shelter of Olympic Peninsula (across the Strait of Juan de Fuca, in Washington State) makes Victoria an anomaly in the Pacific Northwest as it receives a third less rain than Vancouver or Seattle.

Hanging flower baskets on the lampposts, impeccable gardens on public and private grounds and plants in bloom all year make an easy case for 'The Garden City' title. Victoria likes to think of itself as traditionally British, rather than Anglophilically snobby, yet the broad range of international settlers, and their customs, has allowed it to blossom from a place to visit your grandma to a city as cosmopolitan as any you'll find. Plenty of travelers come to Victoria for its heavily publicized major attractions: high tea at the Empress or shopping on Government St. But many others use Victoria as a springboard for outdoor adventures, including kayaking the Inner Harbour, diving the clear waters or hiking the West Coast Trail further up the coast.

ORIENTATION

The Inner Harbour is the heart of Victoria, watched over by the complementary Empress Hotel and Parliament Buildings. From there, Wharf St leads northwest to Bastion Sq, and Government St goes north to tourist-haven and south to the ocean. A block east, Douglas St (Hwy 1, aka

Trans-Canada Hwy) is downtown's main north–south thoroughfare and your likely entrance into the city. The southern terminus marks 'Mile 0'; if you do an about face to head up-island to Nanaimo – roughly ˙8000km later you'll be in Newfoundland. One-way Fort St heads east up the hill, then along Oak Bay Ave, through the 'tweed curtain' to the wealthier, very British area of Oak Bay, 3km from downtown.

Blanshard St is the other northern entrance/exit to/from the city, leading to the Patricia Bay (Pat Bay) Hwy (Hwy 17) and the Saanich Peninsula, with Sidney and the Swartz Bay BC Ferries terminal. Hwy 1A is an alternate route, via Gorge and Craigflower Rds, to either the Trans-Canada or Hwy 14 – the road to Sooke and Port Renfrew.

Maps

The *Official Victoria Free Map* includes discounts to local attractions. AAA/CAA and MapArt both publish good street maps. BC Transit's free *Explore Victoria By Bus* leaflet tells you how to get to attractions by public transportation.

INFORMATION
Bookstores

Take a walk down Johnson St between Douglas and Wharf to peruse the dozens of new and used bookstores:

Chapters (☎ 250-380-9009; 1212 Douglas St) Local outpost of mega-chain.
Crown Publications (☎ 250-386-4636; 521 Fort St) Government books and maps.
Munro's Books (☎ 250-382-2464; 1108 Government St) More than just a bookstore, it's an institution.

Internet Access

Get a visitor's card at the **Greater Victoria Public Library** (☎ 250-382-7241; 735 Broughton St; ☺ 9am-6pm Mon-Sat, 9am-9pm Tue & Thu, 1-5pm Sun) for two free daily half-hour Internet sessions, or try:
James Bay Coffee & Books (☎ 250-386-4700; 143 Menzies St; $4 per hr; ☺ 7:30am-9pm)
Stain Internet Café (☎ 250-382-3352; www.staincafe .com; 609 Yates St; $3 per hr; ☺ 11am-2am)

Media

The *Times Colonist* is the daily island newspaper. *Monday Magazine* (www.monday mag.com) is a weekly magazine featuring arts and entertainment. Some of the radio stations on offer include:
CBC (90.5 FM)
The Q (100.3 FM) Classic and contemporary rock.
The Ocean (98.5 FM) Easy listening.

Medical Services

Royal Jubilee Hospital (☎ 250-595-9200, 250-595-9212 for emergencies; 1900 Fort St; ☺ 24hrs)
Downtown Medical Centre (☎ 250-380-2210; 622 Courtney St; ☺ 9am-6pm)

Money

Most downtown businesses accept US dollars, and some take other foreign currency, but exchange rates are more favorable via ATMs, which are everywhere.

Major banks have branches along Douglas St.

Places to exchange currency include:
American Express (☎ 250-385-831; 1213 Douglas St)
Custom House Currency Exchange (www.custom house.com); Main Branch (☎ 250-389-6007; 815 Wharf St); Inner Harbour (☎ 250-385-6002; 812 Wharf St, below Info Centre; ☺ 10am-10pm May-Sep 15); Bastion Square (☎ 250-389-6076; 19 Bastion Sq); Victoria International Airport (☎ 250-655-0385)

Post

Look for the red and blue signs of postal outlets in businesses around town.
Main post office (☎ 250-953-1352; 706 Yates St; ☺ 8am-5pm Mon-Fri)

Tourist Information

Visitor Info Centre (☎ 250-953-2033; fax 382-6539; www.tourismvictoria.com; 812 Wharf St; ☺ 8:30am-6pm) At the Inner Harbour.
BC Ferries Information Office (☎ 250-386-3431; 1112 Fort St)

DANGERS & ANNOYANCES

Victoria is an incredibly safe city – even at night there's rarely any kind of disturbance. The homeless and the drunks hang out near the water by the Johnson St Bridge, but pose no threat save for the odd panhandler.

SIGHTS

The majority of Victoria's sights are clustered around the Inner Harbour.

Parliament Buildings

Like a king, all-knowing and powerful, the stone and copper **Parliament Buildings**

VANCOUVER ISLAND

VICTORIA

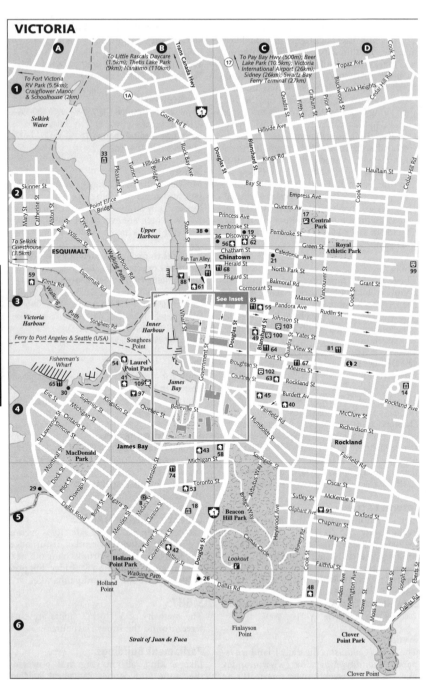

A   **B**   **C**   **D**

To Little Rascals Daycare
(1.5km); Thetis Lake Park
(9km); Nanaimo (110km)

To Pay Bay Hwy (500m); Beer
Lake Park (10.5km); Victoria
International Airport (26km);
Sidney (26km); Swartz Bay
Ferry Terminal (27km)

To Fort Victoria
RV Park (5.5km);
Craigflower Manor
& Schoolhouse (2km)

Trans Canada Hwy

Topaz Ave

Cook St

Vista Heights

Blackwood St

Cedar Hill Rd

Gorge Rd E

Graham St

Prior St

Fifth St

Quadra St

Selkirk
Water

Hillside Ave

Kings Rd

Skinner St

Douglas St

Rock Bay Ave

Hillside Ave

Bridge Rd

Turner St

Pleasant St

Bay St

Haultain St

Cedar Hill Rd

Empress Ave

Cook St

Mary St

Catherine St

Alston St

Tyee Rd

Wilson Rd

Bay Rd

Point Ellice
Bridge

Queens Av

Upper
Harbour

Princess Ave

17

**Central
Park**

Store St

38

Pembroke St

Discovery St
19

Pembroke St

Green St

**Royal
Athletic Park**

To Selkirk
Guesthouse
(3.5km)

ESQUIMALT

Harbour Rd

Walking Path

Esquimalt Rd

Fan Tan Alley

36

56

62

Chatham St

Caledonia Ave

21

Chinatown

Herald St

North Park St

Vancouver St

Grant St

59

Kimta Rd

Walking Path

71

68

Fisgard St

Balmoral Rd

Mason St

Cook St

88

Cormorant St

See Inset

85

Pandora Ave

Rudlin St

99

Victoria
Harbour

Songhees Rd

Walking Path

**Inner
Harbour**

61

Wharf St

55

Johnson St

103

49

100

Blanshard St

Yates St

81

Ferry to Port Angeles & Seattle (USA)

Songhees
Point

Douglas St

64

View St

2

Fisherman's
Wharf

54

**Laurel
Point Park**

Government St

Broughton St

Fort St

63

67

Quadra St

Meares St

Courtney St

Rockland Ave

14

65

41

109

**James
Bay**

Belleville St

102

Rockland Av

45

Burdett Av

40

Rockland

30

97

Superior St

Quebec St

Humboldt St

McClure St

Erie St

Kingston St

Michigan St

Fairfield Rd

Richardson St

St Lawrence St

Ontario St

Simcoe St

Fairfield Rd

Southgate St

Arbutus Way

MacDonald
Park

Montreal St

James Bay

43

58

Michigan St

Oscar St

Sutley St

McKenzie St

Dock St

Prior St

Oswego St

Menzies St

74

Toronto St

91

Oxford St

29

Dallas Road

Boyd St

Niagara St

Madina St

Clarice St

53

18

Bridge Way

Heywood Ave

Oliphant Ave

Chapman St

Dallas Rd

May St

**Beacon
Hill Park**

1

Camas Circle

Nursery Rd

Cook St

Faithful St

Linden Ave

Wellington Ave

Howe St

Moss St

Olive St

Joseph St

Eberts St

Dallas Rd

**Holland
Point Park**

S Turner St

Battery St

42

Walking Path

Lookout

Finlayson
Point

Holland
Point

Douglas St

Dallas Rd

26

Strait of Juan de Fuca

48

**Clover
Point Park**

Clover Point

VANCOUVER ISLAND

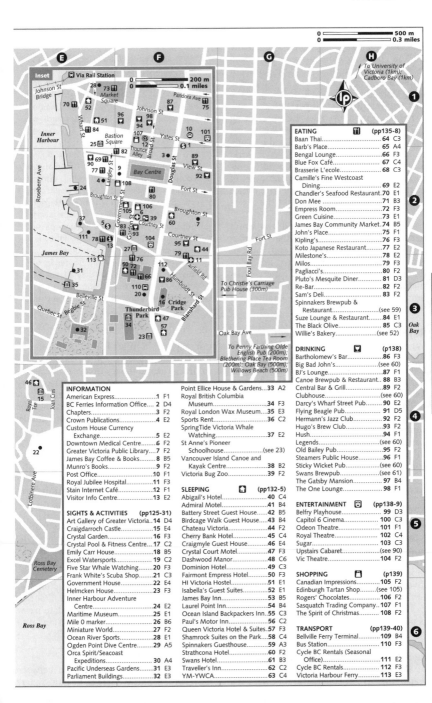

(☎ 250-387-1400; 501 Belleville St; free tours Jun-Sep; ☽ 8:30am-5pm) keep a watchful eye on the harbor and stare you down as you head south on Government St. The statue of Captain George Vancouver sits atop the main dome, reminding all that he was the first to circumnavigate the island.

Francis Rattenbury knew he was creating something important and when his multi-turreted buildings were completed in 1898, he must have been in awe of his own work. Marble floors and brass trim inside complement the exterior and the paintings of Canadian history and industries are a nice touch. The 3000 lightbulbs make the buildings a spectacular sight at night

Tours last half an hour and you won't need much more time than that. Provincial legislature is made here, and you can watch the debates (although rare, fist-fights do break out) from the public gallery when members try and take it to the house. Session times vary but are generally from September to March.

Royal British Columbia Museum

Who says museums have to be boring? This **museum** (☎ 250-356-7226, 888-447-7977; 675 Belleville St; adult/child $13/10; ☽ 9am-5pm) did it right and is well worth a few hours or even half a day.

The 2nd floor hosts the temporary exhibits (an Egyptian exhibit is planned for summer 2004) and the permanent 'Living Land, Living Sea' gallery. If you ignore the glass, the life-sized dioramas make it appear as if you're actually hanging with the animals in the seashore, forest, river or Arctic environments. If you can't get to a tide pool in person, mingle with sea stars and anemones and if you can't get to a real woolly mammoth, check out the one here. 'Open Ocean' mimics an undersea voyage in a silly little movie and presentation that was unbelievably left off the Oscar ballot, though the story is based on actual deep-sea dives and sheds some light on the darkness of the deep ocean.

The First Peoples exhibit on the 3rd floor is packed with carvings, canoes, beadwork and basketry. Visitors can wander through the displays of totem pole sections, a model of the 19th-century Haida village of Skedans and a re-creation of Nawalag-watsi, 'the cave of supernatural power'. It's

---

WAXING NOSTALGIC

When you first walk into the lobby of the Royal London Wax Museum you'll see an old man in a chair wearing an old-man hat; nothing really out of the ordinary. Ask what he's doing and you'll be told he's waiting for his wife. Look a little closer and you realize he's not moving. You ask yourself if he's wax, but he looks very real.

It turns out Mr. Peabody is a wax figure, but for years the old man in an old-man hat would sit in the lobby unmoving, causing visitors to wonder and stare. He would convince them he wasn't real, then pick the right moment to blink or smile and cause jaws to drop and hearts to stop. He has since passed away, and the figure now in the lobby is a wax re-creation and fitting tribute.

Be aware that there are figures in the museum that aren't what they appear. See if you can spot the posing impostors – and stop staring at the topless Cleopatra, she's wax.

---

not impossible to get lost on this floor, so don't panic thinking you've traveled back in time. The old town displays on the gold-rush, coal-mining and early 20th-century era are meant to impress. Captain Vancouver (he preferred 'Captain Van') will be upset if you miss the walk-through model of his *Discovery*.

The museum includes the **National Geographic IMAX Theatre** (☎ 250-953-4629; www.imax victoria.com; adult/child $9.75/3.50; ☽ 8am-10pm) and its larger-than-life screen. Discounts available for joint IMAX & museum admission.

Royal London Wax Museum

Making a look-alike of a person from a wick-less candle is pretty impressive. The displays in the **wax museum** (☎ 250-388-4461; 470 Belleville St; adult/child $9/4.50; ☽ 9am-7:30pm mid-May–Sep, 9:30am-6pm Sep-Dec, 9:30am-5pm Jan–mid-May) do it dozens of times, depicting Napoleon, Cleopatra, Prince Charles, Gordie Howe and Little Red Riding Hood, to name a few. More than 300 wax models stand motionless, waiting to be stared at.

Bastion Square

On the site of old Fort Victoria between Government and Wharf Sts, Bastion Square once held the courthouse, jail, gallows and a brothel, but the square's old buildings have since turned into restaurants, nightclubs, boutiques, galleries and offices. You can purchase handcrafted local creations at the open-air market **Bastion Square Festival of the Arts** (☎ 250-413-3144; 🕙 10:30am-5:30pm Wed-Sun & holidays).

In the 1889 building that was BC's first provincial law court, the **Maritime Museum** (☎ 250-385-4222; www.mmbc.bc.ca; 28 Bastion Sq; adult/child $8/3; 🕙 9am-5pm summer) explores Vancouver Island's seafaring past and present. Exhibits include more than 400 model ships dating back to 1810, displays on piracy, shipwrecks and navigation, and the *Tilikum*, a converted dugout canoe in which John Voss sailed almost completely around the world from 1901 to 1904.

Chinatown

Small but charismatic, this area has all the inexpensive restaurants and authentic Asian markets you'd expect to find in a Chinatown. Set on the northern edge of downtown, it's the oldest in Canada. Look for **Fan Tan Alley**, a narrow passageway between Fisgard St and Pandora Ave, which was the place to buy opium in the 1800s.

Miniature World

For those who like to pretend to be giants, those who appreciate detail, or those who just like cool stuff, there's **Miniature World** (☎ 250-385-9731; www.miniatureworld.com; 649 Humboldt St; adult/child $8/7; 🕙 8:30am-9pm Jun-Aug, 9am-5pm Sep-May). It should be more interesting to children than adults, but it's not – both are enchanted. Dickens' stories, future space stations, the civil war and a cross-country history of the Canadian Railway are among the 80 scenes depicted in incredible detail.

Victoria Bug Zoo

Just plain creepy. All kinds of critters, from giant desert hairy scorpions to perpetually pregnant Australian stick insects to leafcutter ants, live in a sprawling Plexiglas tube-maze at the **Victoria Bug Zoo** (☎ 250-384-2847; 631 Courtney St; adult/child $6/4; 🕙 9am-9pm Jul-Aug, 9:30am-5:30pm Sep-Jun). Informative guides explain how the bugs eat, mate and give birth. If looking isn't enough, you can touch and even hold some of them; or why

not just go all the way and take a tarantula ($100) home with you. Your kids would love it.

Crystal Garden

Fashioned after London's Crystal Palace by architect Francis Rattenbury, the 1925 **greenhouse** (☎ 250-381-1213; 713 Douglas St; adult/child $9/5; 🕙 9am-9pm Jul-Aug, 9am-6pm Sep-Jun) puts on a show with colorful tropical-style gardens and exotic animals, including the world's smallest monkeys and waves of free-flying butterflies.

Craigdarroch Castle

A man's home is his castle, but poor Robert Dunsmuir never got to experience his **castle** (☎ 250-592-5323; 1050 Joan Cres; adult/child $10/3.50; 🕙 10am-4:30pm daily, 9am-7pm Jun 15-Labor Day) as his home. It was completed in 1889, just months after the millionaire coal-mogul died. Now restored, it's so fascinating you'll just want to unpack and move in. The staircase in the main tower keeps going up and up and the restored furniture and displays are a nice touch.

Government House

East of the city center, the aptly named **Government House** (☎ 250-387-2080; 1401 Rockland Ave) is the official residence of the province's lieutenant governor (representative of the Queen). It's closed to the public, but visitors are welcome to stroll the extensive gardens which are open from dawn to dusk. When the flag is flying from the flagpole the lieutenant governor is home – resist the urge to moon the windows.

Art Gallery of Greater Victoria

East of downtown, just off Fort St, the **art gallery** (☎ 250-384-4101; www.aggv.bc.ca; 1040 Moss St; adult/child $6/4; 🕙 10am-5pm Fri-Wed, 10am-9pm Thu) features a permanent Emily Carr exhibition and temporary exhibits that rarely disappoint. The way the gallery sets up the exhibits is a work of art in itself. Check the website for exhibitions occuring during your visit.

Fisherman's Wharf

Though overrun by colossal condominium complexes of impossible geometric shapes, Fisherman's Wharf hasn't lost its identity. Just west of the Inner Harbour, it bustles with fishing boats and pleasure craft. Buy fresh seafood from the boats, or stop by Barb's Place for fish and chips (p136).

Starting from Fisherman's Wharf, the **Scenic Marine Drive** skirts the coast along Dallas Rd and Beach Dr. Plenty of parks and beaches dot the coastline along the way, though access to the shore is restricted in many places because of private homes. You can also begin the drive at Beacon Hill Park.

Beacon Hill Park

An easy walk south from downtown via Douglas St, this 61-hectare park offers gardens, ponds and playing fields. You'll find the world's second-tallest totem pole, a 100-year-old cricket pitch, a wildfowl sanctuary and children's petting zoo. The southern edge overlooks the ocean, which you can reach via steps down to the beach across Dallas Rd. The intersection of Dallas Rd and Douglas St marks Mile 0 of the Trans-Canada Hwy.

Pacific Underseas Gardens

It's pretty small but the 'Underseas' part of this **garden** (☎ 250-382-5717; 490 Belleville St; adult/child $7/6.25; ☽ 10am-7pm Jul-Aug, 10am-5pm Sep-Jun) is worth a visit. There's a show where you get to see a diver play with an octopus.

Thunderbird Park

This downtown park is one of Victoria's most popular landmarks. Photograph the people photographing other people posing with the totem poles as if they're movie stars, or simply take pictures of the poles themselves. Famed carver Mungo Martin oversaw the initial plans for the park and the restoration of many of these poles. In summer, it's possible to watch First Nations' artists do their thing in the carving shed.

Emily Carr House

South of the Inner Harbour, a short walk leads to **Emily Carr House** (☎ 250-383-5843; www.emilycarr.com; 207 Government St; entry by donation; ☽ 10am-5pm mid-May–mid-Oct), birthplace of BC's best-known painter. It has been restored to its original state and features displays on her life and work, including her paintings, many of which incorporated subject matter drawn from the culture of Vancouver Island's coastal First Nations people.

Point Ellice House & Gardens

The social elite of the gold-rush days used to hobnob in the 1861-built and beautifully kept **house** (☎ 250-380-6506; 2616 Pleasant St; adult/child $7/5, afternoon tea & tour $19.95; ☽ noon-5pm mid-May–mid-Sep). Near the Point Ellice Bridge, it retains a superb collection of Victorian furnishings and decorations.

Helmcken House

Since 1852, unassuming **Helmcken House** (☎ 250-361-0021; 10 Eliot Sq; adult/child $5/3; ☽ 10am-5pm May-Oct) has sat in Eliot Square. The one-time residence of the Helmcken's (an early town doctor and James Douglas' daughter), it's the oldest house in the province to remain unchanged.

St Anne's Pioneer Schoolhouse

Also in Eliot Square, this schoolhouse is one of the oldest buildings in Victoria still in use. Built sometime between 1840 and 1860, it was moved from the grounds of St Anne's Academy to its present site in 1974.

Craigflower Manor & Schoolhouse

Built in 1856, the restored Georgian-style farmhouse **Craigflower Manor** (☎ 250-383-4627; adult/child $5/3; ☽ noon-4pm Wed-Sun Jun 10-Labour Day), at Craigflower and Admirals Rds northwest of the city, was once the central home in the first farming community on Vancouver Island.

Fort Rodd Hill National Historic Site

The protection of Esquimalt Harbour and the Royal Navy yards rested squarely on the sturdy, concrete shoulders of Fort Rodd Hill in the late-19th to mid-20th century. Now the gun batteries and barracks at the **Fort Rodd Hill National Historic Site** (☎ 250-478-5849; 603 Fort Rodd Hill Rd; adult/child $4/2; ☽ 10am-5:30pm March-Nov, 9am-4:30pm Apr-Oct), 11km northwest of the city, off Ocean Blvd, can be toured. The site also contains **Fisgard Lighthouse**, Western Canada's first. It's been in continuous use since 1860.

ACTIVITIES

While Victoria may be old, it's not geriatric – all kinds of activities exist within a 30km radius. The **Inner Harbour Adventure Centre** (☎ 250-995-2211, 800-575-6700; www.marine-adventures.com; 950 Wharf St; ☽ 9am-6pm), on the docks at the foot of Broughton St, runs its own expeditions and houses several other charter and tour companies. This is a good place if you want to take care of all your activities under one roof. **Sports Rent** (☎ 250-385-7368; www.sportsrentbc.com; 1950 Government St) is an excellent place for all equipment rentals.

Whale-Watching

Around 90 resident orcas (killer whales) think April to October is Miller Time in the waters just off the island's southern tip, making Victoria an excellent place for whale-watching. Some see this as a cash cow, so about a dozen outfitters offer trips out into Georgia Strait and they all claim to be the best. Check at the info centre (p125) for something that matches your taste, keeping in mind a three-hour excursion shouldn't cost more than $79 to $89 per adult. Each company has its own territory and sometimes whales are there, sometimes they're not. Sighting success rates should be posted but if they're not, ask; if they stall or give an answer other than a number, move on.

The more successful companies include:
Five Star Whale Watching (☎ 250-388-7223, 800-634-9617; www.5starwhales.com; 706 Douglas St; adult/child $89/59; 9am-5pm)
Orca Spirit/Seacoast Expeditions (☎ 250-383-2254, 888-672-6722; www.orcaspirit.com;146 Kingston Rd; adult/child $79/59; 9am-5pm) Ocean Pointe (45 Songhees Rd)
SpringTide Victoria Whale Watching (☎ 250-386-6016, 800-470-3474; www.springtidecharters.com; adult/child $89/59; 9am-6pm) Delta Ocean Pointe Resort (45 Songhees Rd); Inner Harbour (950 Wharf St) 99% sighting-success rate.

Scuba Diving

Victoria's nutrient-rich waters support a diverse underwater ecosystem and are amazingly clear.

Good shore dives include:
10 Mile Point Near Cadboro Bay.
Ogden Point Breakwater Just south of Beacon Hill Park.
Race Rocks Superb scenery both above and below the water 18km southwest of Victoria Harbour.
Saanich Inlet Contains Willis Point Park.
Saxe Point Park Off Esquimalt Rd.

In-town dive shops include:
Frank White's Scuba Shop (☎ 250-385-4713; 1855 Blanshard St; 9am-6pm) Offers $45 package.

Ogden Point Dive Centre (☎ 250-380-9119; www.divevictoria.com; 199 Dallas Rd; 9am-6pm) Offers $49 package.

Kayaking

A peaceful paddle in the protected waters just off the coast gives a different perspective on Victoria's beauty. Most companies offer tours ranging from one- to seven-days with varying prices.

Recommended operators (prices are for 24-hour rentals) include:
Ocean River Sports (☎ 250-381-4233, 800-989-4233; www.oceanriver.com; 1827 Store St; kayak $52; 9am-5:30 Mon-Thu & Sat, 9:30am-8pm Fri, 11am-5pm Sun)
Sports Rent (☎ 250-385-7368; www.sportsrentbc.com; 1950 Government St; kayak/canoe $29/24) No tours offered but the best deal if you want to paddle solo.
Vancouver Island Canoe and Kayak Centre (☎ 250-361-9365, 877-921-9365; www.canoeandkayakcentre.com; 575 Pembroke St; kayak/canoe $52/50; 9am-5:30pm Mon-Sat)

Windsurfing

The winds whipping through Juan de Fuca Strait aren't as strong as those you'll find further up the island's west coast, but they're enough to catch some air. Boardsailing is big in **Cadboro Bay**, near the university, and at **Willows Beach** in Oak Bay. **Excel Watersports** (☎ 250-383-8667; www.excel-sports.com; 2001 Douglas St; 9am-5:30pm) doesn't offer rentals, but will help with information on getting blown away.

Swimming

Crystal Pool & Fitness Centre (☎ 250-361-0732; 2275 Quadra St; adult/child $4.50/2.50, senior & student/family $3.50/9; 5:30am-10:30pm Mon-Fri, 6am-6pm Sat, 8:30am-6pm Sun) contains a pool, sauna and whirlpool. Of course, there's this thing called the ocean and the fine, white sand and protected waters make **Willows Beach** a favorite spot. **Thetis Lake Municipal Park**, off the Trans-Canada Hwy, and **Beaver Lake Municipal Park**, off Hwy 17, both north of town, are good swimming holes.

VICTORIA FOR KIDS

When the kids are restless and don't feel like looking at flowers anymore, you've got options. The info centre has *Kid's Guide Victoria* and www.kidsinvictoria.com has exhaustive lists of kid-friendly resources. Beaver Lake (above) is the only outdoor swimming spot with a lifeguard but **Willows Beach** is always loaded with families and an ideal place for kids to burn off energy while mom and dad relax.

The Royal British Columbia Museum (p128) has plenty of hands-on exhibits and kids find the Victoria Bug Zoo (p129) and Miniature World (p129) fascinating.

The Art Gallery of Greater Victoria (p129) has 'Family Sunday' every third Sunday from October to March, where kids literally take the exhibits into their own hands and are given the chance to be inspired and show off their artistic flair.

Most hotels will offer or recommend childcare services; or take the children to **Little Rascals Daycare** (☎ 250-727-6817; rascals4@ telus.net; 629 Sedger Rd).

TOURS

Gray Line (☎ 250-388-5248; www.grayline.ca; 700 Douglas St; adult/child from $19/9.50) Classic double-decker bus tours start in front of the Fairmont Empress Hotel (p134). Tours start with the basic 90-minute trip but there are a dozen others.

Tally-Ho Sightseeing (☎ 250-383-5067, 866-383-5067; www.tallyhotours.com; trolley adult/child $15/7, carriage 30/60/90min $70/120/180) Tours in large, horse-drawn trolley or small six-seat carriage. Leaves from Menzies St near Belleville St.

Victoria Carriage Tours (☎ 250-383-2207; 877-663-2207; www.victoriacarriage.com; trolley adult/child $12/6, carriage 30/45/60/90min $70/95/120/180) Tours board from Menzies St near Belleville St.

Victoria Harbour Ferry (☎ 250-708-0201; harbor tour adult/child/senior $14/12/7) Little bathtub-like boats that bounce around the Inner Harbour taking people on their tours or to scheduled stops (p140).

Walking Tours

Victoria Bobby Walking Tours (☎ 250-995-0233; $15; ☼ 11am May 1-Sep 15) 75-minute city walk led by a retired, uniformed London Bobby (police officer) who is also a history buff. Reservations are recommended.

Bird's Eye View Walking Tours (☎ 250-592-9255; $7; ☼ 10am May-Oct) Guided strolls through the secrets of the Empress Hotel.

Ghostly Walks (☎ 250-384-6698; adult/child/senior or student/family $12/6/10/30; ☼ departs info centre 7:30pm Jul & Aug) Echoes of hangings and murders can still be heard and ghosts can make their presence known.

FESTIVALS & EVENTS

Major events in Victoria happen year-round, but the bulk of the activity is from May to September. Check the info centre or *Monday Magazine* for a calendar of events; www.vicfun.com is another good resource.

To solidify Victoria's image as the 'Garden City', the **Victoria Flower & Garden Festival** (www .flowerandgarden.net) happens in mid-June. Breweries from around the world put their creations to the test at the **Great Canadian Beer Festival** (www.gcbf.com) in a Labour Day weekend of debauchery. In late May at the **Swiftsure International** (www .swiftsure.org), sailboats and their crews test themselves against the rough seas and each other. The Inner Harbour gets a little prettier in early September at the **Classic Boat Festival**.

Arts

Folkfest (www.icafolkfest.com) Victoria's longest running multicultural arts festival (late June).

Jazzfest International (www.vicjazz.bc.ca) Held in late June.

TerrifVic Jazz Party (www.terrifvic.com) Occurs mid-April.

Victoria Shakespeare Festival From mid-July through mid-August.

Victoria Fringe Theatre Festival (www.victoriafringe .com) Late August.

Heritage

Victoria Day Third weekend in May, affectionately known as 'Two-four long weekend' – it's normally centered on May 24 and involves many 2-4s (cases) of beer. The parade along the Inner Harbour is excellent and a little more family-oriented.

Canada Day The whole country lets loose on July 1. Victoria is no exception.

First People's Festival First weekend in August.

SLEEPING

Victoria is a busy place, especially in summer, so make reservations as soon as you know your travel plans. Tourism Victoria's **room-reservation service** (☎ 250-663-3883) and www.tourismvictoria.com can help.

Motels & Hotels

Rates plummet, almost across the board, by as much as 40% to 50% in the off-season and Victoria is just as charming in the winter as it is in summer.

BUDGET

Victoria's increasing popularity correlates to a decrease in budget-level motels downtown, but if you're the sort who feels a-room-is-a-room-is-a-room, the Gorge Rd area northwest of downtown features several lower-cost motels.

Paul's Motor Inn (☎ 250-382-9231, 866-333-7285; www.paulsmotorinn.com; 1900 Douglas St; r/ste $89/109) It's just itching to be a set in a 1970s movie; maybe a car-chase or shootout backdrop. Not sleazy-70s, the rooms are big and clean and the service is great, but walking through the big glass doors under the overhang just makes a person want to strut.

Crystal Court Motel (☎ 250-384-0551; martin.scott@crystalcourt.ca; 701 Belleville St; r $95; P ⊠) This quaint blue and white motel is dwarfed by larger buildings and easily overlooked, but is one of the best-value places in the center of town. The rooms are typical motel-style and unremarkable but a good option if you just need a place to crash.

Cherry Bank Hotel (☎ 250-385-5380, 800-998-6688; cherrybank@pacificcoast.net; 825 Burdett Ave; r with private/shared bathroom $69/99; P ⊠) It dates back to 1897 and this one-time brothel won't suit everyone. While the place isn't a fleabag, the rooms are barren, faded and old. Breakfast is included, TVs and telephones aren't.

Traveller's Inn (☎ 250-381-1000; 888-753-3774; www.travellersinn.com; 1850 Douglas St; s/d $99/109; P ⊠ ⊠) The flagship of 10 Victoria locations, some on the same block, it has attained chain-status over the last couple years, but has been more concerned with reputation than image. Highly recommended by visitors it is great value for those just looking for a room.

MID-RANGE

Swans Hotel (☎ 250-361-3310, 800-668-7926; www.swanshotel.com; 506 Pandora Ave; studio/1-/2-bedroom $99/129/179; ⊠) The former rotting, ugly-duckling of an old brick-warehouse building has been converted into the beautiful swan of one of Victoria's most comforting and spacious hotels. Most of the 30 two-story suites have high ceilings and the woodbeam construction is accentuated with modern features. All rooms are incredibly inviting and the penthouse suite ($695) is, in a word, amazing.

Dominion Hotel (☎ 250-384-4136, 800-663-6101; www.dominion-hotel.com; 759 Yates St; s/d/ste $119/129/149; P ⊠) As the oldest hotel in Victoria, this heritage building recently underwent a much-needed facelift. It maintained its

---

SEE YOU AT THE STRATH

Although it's not the city's fanciest hotel, the clean rooms with the dark green carpets, comfortable beds and cherry wood furniture at the **Strathcona Hotel** (☎ 250-383-7137, 800-663-7476; www.strathconahotel.com; 919 Douglas St; r $89-119; P ⊠) are pleasant enough. It doesn't have the most character, though as one of Victoria's earliest hotels it's got enough to hold its own. What the Strath does have, and is not ashamed to flaunt, are three bars and a restaurant under one roof, and two sandpit beach volleyball courts on top of it – not your typical hotel-lobby type places, either.

- **Sticky Wicket Pub** has a rooftop patio and kitchen, two games rooms, four dining areas, several hundred feet of bar and enough sporting memorabilia to start a museum, you don't need to know what a sticky wicket is to enjoy yourself.

- **Big Bad John's** is a true hillbilly bar where the welcome sign says 'Sorry, we're open'.

- **Legends** is a popular nightclub booking big-name acts.

- **Clubhouse** alters between power-lunch/cocktail-lounge by day, dance club by night.

---

character with marble floors, dark wood trim and chandeliers while giving the rooms a fresh look. It is a family-oriented hotel, but those traveling without kids can still come and appreciate the charm.

Admiral Motel (☎ 250-388-6267, 888-826-4725; 257 Belleville St; s/kitchenette/ste $165/195/245; P ⊠) A locally-owned and operated place on the southwest shore of the Inner Harbour with no computer check-ins or technology to get in the way. Instead, you get efficient staff and a nice, clean room in the white-and-blue building on the quiet side of the harbor. The suites are brighter and have the best views.

James Bay Inn (☎ 250-384-7151, 800-836-2649; 270 Government St; r $110-150; ste $177-226; P ⊠) It's close enough to the Inner Harbour to walk, and far enough so that it's quiet. There are a dozen different room configurations and all of them are inviting. The light streaming through the windows in the south-facing rooms provides a nice contrast to the dark carpets and furnishings.

Shamrock Suites on the Park (☎ 250-385-8768, 800-294-5544; www.shamrocksuites.com; 675 Superior St; studio/1-bedroom $135/165; P ⊠) Enjoys a great location across from Beacon Hill Park and big windows from which to see it.

TOP END

Fairmont Empress Hotel (☎ 250-348-8111, 800-441-1414; www.fairmont.com; 721 Government St; small/standard/deluxe $389/449/549 P ⊠ ⊠ ⊠) What the Plaza is to New York City, the Empress is to Victoria. Francis Rattenbury must have looked at his creation, the Parliament Buildings (p125), and said to himself, 'Somewhere a king has no wife...but not here' before he built a companion. She sits to the right of her king, as she has done since the first guests arrived in 1908. Despite her stone-faced façade, she's a good-looking woman for almost 100 years old and a softie on the inside. Everywhere you look, there's some luxurious detail. Unadvertised – but somehow becoming popular (maybe due to all the travel-writers) – attic rooms accessed via a hidden 7th-floor stairway can be had if you ask at check-in. They're decorated with original furniture and are actually larger than some of the standard rooms.

Laurel Point Inn (☎ 250-386-8721, 800-663-7667; www.laurelpoint.com; 680 Montreal St; d/ste $229/279; P ⊠ ⊠ ⊠ ⊠) Like a spaceship that smashed into a 30-year-old hotel, this then-and-now resort guards the entrance to the Inner Harbour. The original brick hotel still stands where it was built, but the new aero-dynamically-shaped addition takes your attention. Inside, the simple elegance of marble and brass is decorated with artifacts and art. You may feel like checking your room for secret compartments or buttons that activate James Bond-style gadgets, but you should really concentrate on the views outside on the patio.

Queen Victoria Hotel & Suites (☎ 250-386-1312, 800-663-7007; www.queenvictoriainn.com; 655 Douglas St; r/ste with kitchen $185/215; P ⊠ ⊠) Apartments offer good views above the 5th floor and the **Chateau Victoria** (☎ 250-382-4221, 800-663-5891; www.chateauvictoria.com; 740 Burdett Ave; r $150; P ⊠ ⊠) is just up the hill.

B&Bs

Victoria is literally packed with B&Bs – contact **Victoria Vacationer B&B** (☎ 250-382-9469; 1143 Leonard St, Victoria, BC V8V 2S3) for details.

Spinnakers Guesthouse (☎ 250-384-2739, 877-383-2739; www.spinnakers.com; 308 Catherine St; r/ste $179/249; P ⊠) On the northwest side of the harbor - the perfect vantage point for admiring the city lights - you'll find lavish garden suites and heritage-style rooms at the brewery of the same name (p138). The modern comforts of a queen-sized bed, Jacuzzi tub and fireplace are melded with the old-style charm of restored colors and décor.

Dashwood Manor (☎ 250-385-5517, 800-667-5517; www.dashwoodmanor.com; 1 Cook St; r $145-285; P ⊠) It'll be hard to pick your favorite from the 14 rooms in this Tudor mansion, although the views and spaciousness of The Chelsea ($255) won't disappoint. They take a bit of a twist on traditional B&B, and stock the mini-fridge in your room so you can self-cater your own breakfast. Pastries are delivered in the morning, as is wine and cheese in the evening

Isabella's Guest Suites (☎ 250-381-8414; www.isabellasbb.com; 537 Johnson St; night/wk $135/700; ⊠) In an excellent location down Waddington Alley, the two apartment-like suites are right in the modern romantic verve of one of Victoria's busiest bar-hopping and dining areas. With hardwood floors and windows throughout, the units are open

---

AUTHOR'S CHOICE

Abigail's Hotel (☎ 250-388-5363, 800-561-6565; www.abigailshotel.com; 906 McClure St; $279-389; P ⊠ ⊠) With 22 individually-themed rooms, you just might want to stay for 22 nights. Not the cheapest place in town, but it pulls all the stops, giving you a personal and romantic touch you don't find in hotel rooms. The bright, airy rooms are classically (but not excessively) decorated in a combination that has never seen paisley and earth tones look so good together. The fresh flowers are a nice touch to rooms that include fireplaces, huge bathrooms and goose-down duvets. And when you think things can't get any better, the breakfast is a three-course deal (served in your room, if you like) and evening hors d'oeuvres are part of the package.

and airy and include huge beds, full kitchens, claw-foot tubs and classy furnishings. Week-long stays are the norm, so nightly stays are harder to come by.

Battery Street Guest House (☎ 250-385-4632; www.batterystreetguesthouse.com; 670 Battery St; s/d $105/125; P ☒) This 1898 heritage house has three rooms and they all pass the B&B litmus-test for having pastel colors. Located in a pleasant, quiet neighborhood, it's close enough to the ocean and downtown.

Birdcage Walk Guest House (☎ 250-389-0804, 877-389-0804; birdcagebnb@hotmail.com; 505 Government St; s/d $85/105; P ☒) Probably Victoria's most conveniently located B&B; Inner Harbour to the north, ocean to the south, Beacon Hill Park to the east. The rooms are nicely decorated with antiques and include cooking facilities, though breakfast is delivered to your room.

Craigmyle Guest House (☎ 250-595-5411; 1037 Craigdarroch Rd; s/d/tw/f/ste $65/90/100/155/170; P ☒) Right next to Craigdarroch Castle (p129), it was originally built on the castle grounds as a guesthouse. Dark wood is the overriding theme here. Some rooms are suitable for small families.

Hostels

Victoria is a hosteller's dream town. In true hostel fashion, they all offer discounts with local activity outfitters.

Ocean Island Backpackers Inn (☎ 250-385-1785, 888-888-4180; www.oceanisland.com; 791 Pandora Ave; dm/s/d/f $22/26/34/52; ☒) If you're looking for plain ol' fun, staying at this super colorful hostel near downtown is a good start. The big building is seemingly undergoing constant renovations and rooms pop up in some funny places; if a window is crucial to you, let the friendly, attitude-free staff know when you book. There are 210 beds, spacious kitchen facilities, a bathroom on each floor and a fridge in each room. There's also free morning coffee and a café downstairs.

HI Victoria Hostel (☎ 250-385-4511, 888-883-0099; www.hihostels.ca; 516 Yates St; d $21; ☒) This old converted warehouse near the Inner Harbour offers bunks in the barracks-style (not as bad as it sounds) dorm rooms. Reservations are a must.

Selkirk Guest House (☎ 250-389-1213, 800-974-6638; www.selkirkguesthouse.com; 934 Selkirk Ave; dm $20, r $75-90; ☒) Part hostel, part B&B, this place is just over the Johnson St Bridge in Esquimalt. A family atmosphere in the country but close to town (half-hour walk or short drive to downtown). It's got a tree house, trampoline, waterfront hot tub and dock on the Gorge Waterway with boats for use.

YMCA-YWCA (☎ 250-386-7511; 880 Courtney St; dm $40; P ☒) With both Y's in the same building, one is compelled to ask why the residence is for women only; that's just the way it is. Because it's often fully booked with long-term boarders, reservations well in advance are essential. The rooms are basic and guests enjoy free use of the swimming pool and other fitness facilities. No kitchen privileges, but you can buy cheap breakfasts and lunches in the cafeteria downstairs.

Camping

Fort Victoria RV Park (☎ 250-479-8112; info@fortvicrv.com; 340 Island Hwy; RV/tent $29/23), on Hwy 1A, is the closest campground (6.5km from downtown). **Thetis Lake Campground** (☎ 250-478-3845; petisa@home.com; 1938 W Park Lane; RV/tent $8/6) has a good swimming hole.

Southern Vancouver Island (p140) has more camping options in the Victoria vicinity.

EATING

Victoria is the kind of town where afternoon tea can be followed by a big steak dinner; where vegetarians and carnivores can dine at the same place; where you can have Thai one night and Greek the next. In short, you won't run out of excellent options.

Victoria's price levels are on a relative scale compared with other areas. Budget is considered around the $10 mark or less; mid-range places will charge $10 to $20 for a meal; for top-end places, bring more than a $20 bill per person.

Budget

John's Place (☎ 250-389-0799; 723 Pandora Ave; mains $7-11) Exactly how a greasy-spoon should be run – without the greasy. You will not leave with an empty stomach, a bad taste, or complaints about the service. The menu is traditionally dineresque, prepared the way simple food should be.

Sam's Deli (☎ 250-382-8424; 805 Government St; $7-8; ☺ breakfast & lunch) It's not just its proximity to the Inner Harbour that makes this fuel-up spot an institution – they also make darn good sandwiches.

Blue Fox Café (☎ 250-380-1683; 101-919 Fort St; mains $6-9; ☙ breakfast & lunch) Tiny and popular means queues, but they're worth it at this granola hole-in-the-wall. Come for the hearty food, not the overworked service.

Pluto's Mesquite Diner (☎ 250-385-4747; 1150 Cook St; mains $7-11; Ⓟ) If the A-Team had included Mad Max and someone with style, they couldn't have done a better job in converting an old garage into a trendy-tacky, post-present eatery. The grill is always on, cooking breakfast, chicken or beef burgers. There are Mexican dishes, and while the food is never bad, it's hit-or-miss between great and good.

Willie's Bakery (☎ 250-381-8414; 537 Johnson St; mains $6-10; ☙ breakfast & lunch) Where breakfast is served for Isabella's Guest Suites (p134). Grab-and-go or enjoy a full breakfast on the cobblestone patio

Green Cuisine (☎ 250-385-1809; 560 Johnson St; $6.50 per lb) Inside Market Square this is a vegetarian buffet, pay-by-weight, cafeteria-style place.

Barb's Place (☎ 250-384-6515; 310 St Lawrence St; mains $7-9) Authentic fish and chips from a shack on Fisherman's Wharf; nothing more need be said.

Victoria will never win awards for best street food but the food carts at Market Square, at the corner of Johnson and Wharf Sts, are decent for a quick bite. **James Bay Community Market** (☎ 250-381-5323; 547 Michigan St; ☙ 9am-3pm Sat) is an excellent farmers' market.

Mid-Range

Suze Lounge & Restaurant (☎ 250-383-2829; 515 Yates St; mains $10-13; ☙ dinner-late) The architecture is old, but the place is hip – the kind of place where nine-to-fivers come after work and the next thing they know it's 1am. The lively kitchen serves good pizzas and pastas but the majority of the crowd has an appetizer in front of them and a martini or glass of wine in hand.

The Black Olive (☎ 250-384-6060; 739 Pandora Ave; lunch $9-10, dinner $16-20; ☙ lunch & dinner) 'Mediterranean and Italian influenced West Coast dining' could be a recipe for disaster, but this place has recipes that are anything but. If you tried to mix beef, pasta and cranberries at home you'd probably gag,

---

AUTHOR'S CHOICE

Pagliacci's (☎ 250-386-1662; 1011 Broad St; mains $8-12; ☙ lunch & dinner) Hands down the most oft-visited restaurant by regular Victoria visitors, and a favorite for locals as well. Pagliacci's is a little cramped, but doesn't cramp your style because it's such a fun place. Popularity hasn't gone to its head, either; loyalty is rewarded with a delicious and inventive menu featuring Italian 'famous' dishes like Hemingway Short Story (beef-stuffed tortellini) or Souper Bowl.

---

but here beef and cranberry pappardelle is a flavor-explosion. The atmosphere is not your typical Mediterranean exuberance, but instead a more relaxed, semi-formal crispness.

Baan Thai (☎ 250-383-0050; 1117 Blanshard St; mains $8-12; ☙ lunch & dinner) They say Thai cuisine is an art form refined over centuries, but this place must have taken a crash course because it hasn't been around long and the food is excellent. The aroma when you walk in is mouth-wateringly confusing and it may take a while before your olfactory and taste senses agree on a dish.

Re-Bar (☎ 250-360-2401; 50 Bastion Sq; mains $7-12; ☙ lunch & dinner) A happening, primarily-vegetarian spot with an eclectic, international menu – try the almond burger. It's also got a juice bar and bakery and is a hangout for all walks of life.

Don Mee (☎ 250-383-1032; 538 Fisgard St; mains $10-13, dim sum $9-15; ☙ closed 2:30-3pm) Climb the stairs to the huge green-and-black eating area and the noise and activity is the first thing you notice; second is the smell from the kitchen. It's a fun place to eat and the food is as good as you'd expect from a family that's been serving for 80 years. They claim duck is their specialty but the seafood is also fantastic.

Milos (☎ 250-382-5544; 716 Burdett Ave; mains $10-14; ☙ lunch & dinner) Of Victoria's many Greek restaurants, this ranks among the most popular – either for the roast lamb or the nightly belly dancers.

Koto Japanese Restaurant (☎ 250-382-1514; 510 Fort St; mains $15-20; ☙ lunch & dinner) Large wooden tables and Japanese screens set the stage for the live cooking at your table in

DONALD C. & PRISCILLA ALEXANDER EASTMAN

Queen Elizabeth Park (p69), Vancouver

RICHARD CUMMINS

Marina, **Granville Island** (p63), Vancouver

LEE FOSTER

Capilano Suspension Bridge (p93), Vancouver

Evening view, **Stanley Park** (p61), Vancouver

RICHARD CUMMINS

RICHARD CUMMIN

Butchart Gardens (p142), Victoria, Vancouver Island

RICHARD CUMMINS

Parliament Buildings (p125),
Victoria, Vancouver Island

Historic **Fairmont Empress Hotel** (p134), Victoria,
Vancouver Island

ANN CEC

Fisherman's Wharf (p129), Victoria, Vancouver Island

RICHARD CUMMINS

the main dining room. In the sushi room, the chef takes food preparation seriously and it pays off as the rolls melt in your mouth.

Milestone's (☎ 250-381-2244; 812 Wharf St; mains $7-11; ☀ lunch & dinner) A trendy place right on the water and a good option for those who can't make up their minds or those travelling in groups with varied tastes.

Top End

Fittingly, Victoria's classiest lady looks after Victoria's finest restaurants. The **Fairmont Empress Hotel** (☎ 250-348-8111, 800-441-1414; www .fairmont.com; 721 Government St) is the top-tier dining spot in town, with the following three options. Reservations are required.

Kipling's, (mains $20-25) Yes, as in Rudyard. Not really unrefined but more like the kid who would rather play in the mud than wear a suit – you can get away with 'smart-casual attire' here and it's the most casual choice in the Empress. Most people opt for the buffet but an á la carte menu is available.

Bengal Lounge (mains $20-30; ☀ lunch & dinner Sun-Thu) The tiger skin above the blazing fireplace and ample leather furniture may inspire you into a bit of foxhunting. Before making a fool of yourself on the front lawn, enjoy the curry buffet for lunch ($20) or sample other curried dishes.

Empress Room (3-course $60, prix-fixe $58; ☀ dinner) So refined and formal; back straight, grab the glass thusly, pinky finger out and sip. You won't get the boot if you don't show your best table manners but you'll get some crook-eyes and 'ahems.' The three-course menu is the more popular.

Some other top-end options include **Brasserie L'ecole** (☎ 250-75-6260; 1715 Government St; $18-26) High ceilings of an old Chinese schoolhouse combined with French bistro furnishings converge here. The atmosphere occupies a niche between semi-casual and semi-snobby and the steaks and seafood are so well-presented they almost look better than they taste.

Camille's Fine Westcoast Dining (☎ 250-381-3433; 45 Bastion Sq; mains $18-20; ☀ dinner) Head underground to Victoria's most inventive restaurant. The seasonally changing menu combines Northwest ingredients with eclectic, international cuisine.

Chandler's Seafood Restaurant (☎ 250-385-3474; 1250 Wharf St; lunch $10-13, dinner $18-25;

VANCOUVER ISLAND

PUT A LITTLE ENGLISH ON IT

Afternoon tea with a beer chaser? The British do it better than anyone. Outside of England, Victoria probably offers the most authentic examples of afternoon tea anywhere. It's more than a bunch of old biddies jabbering about whatever between sips – it's an event for everyone, involving pastries, finger sandwiches, fruit...and tea. The always prim and proper **Empress Hotel** (☎ 250-348-8111, 800-441-1414; www.fairmont.com; 721 Government St; afternoon tea $49.95) is a mainstay, where mouthwatering scones, fresh berries in Devonshire cream and decadent pastries are all on the menu. Reserve at least two weeks in advance during the busy season.

The Empress doesn't hold the monopoly on tea though. Other choices include:

- **Blethering Place Tea Room & Restaurant** (☎ 250-598-1413; 2250 Oak Bay Ave; $16.95) The name means 'voluble, senseless talking' but don't act like a blethering idiot.
- **Point Ellice House & Gardens** (☎ 250-380-6506; 2616 Pleasant St; $16.95 ☀ noon-5pm mid-May–mid-Sep) Fancy a game of croquet?
- **The Gatsby Mansion** (☎ 250-663-7557; 309 Belleville St; $21.95) Great view of the Inner Harbour.

You can't have virtue without vice and Victoria also has some British-style pubs striving to put you in the old country. The **Penny Farthing Olde English Pub** (☎ 250-370-9008; 2228 Oak Bay Ave) is the most authentic choice, with three fireplaces and no detail overlooked in creating the traditional experience. Other choices:

- **Bartholomew's Bar** (☎ 250-388-5111; 777 Douglas St)
- **Christie's Carriage House Pub** (☎ 250-598-5333; 1739 Fort St)
- **Flying Beagle Pub** (☎ 250-382-3301; 301 Cook St)
- **Old Bailey Pub** (☎ 250-389-0232; 777 Courtney St)

VANCOUVER ISLAND

lunch & dinner) Great food, outstanding views, good service and a pleasant nautical atmosphere; that pretty much sums up what this restaurant has been doing since 1862. They make a variety of tasty sauces but if you want to know what good fish tastes like, just order it sautéed.

DRINKING
Brewpubs
Mmmm, beer. The golden ales and dark stouts of the micro-brewed beers in Victoria are some of BC's finest. Not only do micro-brews taste better than most commercially produced beers, they're better for you – some even argue they're good for you.

Spinnakers Brewpub & Restaurant (☎ 250-386-2739; 308 Catherine St) The pioneer of Victoria brewpubs. Over a dozen taps line the bar and they've found dozens of ways to use almost every unused molecule from the beer-brewing process in their food. It's away from the action but the deck with great views has you in no rush to get back.

Canoe Brewpub & Restaurant (☎ 250-361-1940; 450 Swift St) It's a huge brick warehouse but surprisingly intimate, though on a nice day you'll want to sit on the patio.

Swans Brewpub (☎ 250-361-3310; 506 Pandora St) Takes up half the main floor of Swans Hotel. Only the oatmeal stout has anything in it other than hops, yeast and water.

Hugo's Brew Club (☎ 250-920-4844; 625 Courtney St) Dimly lit with dark wood and a semi-formal atmosphere, this steakhouse-lounge doesn't look or act like your traditional brewpub, but the beer is definitely traditionally made.

ENTERTAINMENT
Check out *Monday Magazine's* calendar to see what's happening.

Live Music
Hermann's Jazz Bar & Grill (☎ 250-388-9166; 753 View St) Everything a jazz club should be. The acoustics are amazing and the dimly lit room is perfect for sipping on a single-malt scotch. Sunday is traditional Dixie.

Steamers Public House (☎ 250-381-4340; 570 Yates St) They have local bands on the weekends and open-mic or live jazz during the week.

Darcy's Wharf Street Pub (☎ 250-380-1322; 1127 Wharf St) With a welcoming and casual atmosphere this is the kind of place where you can just hang out. Crowds line up Thursday to Saturday to see the cover band.

Bands rolling through town usually rock at **Legends** (☎ 250-383-7137; 919 Douglas St) or **Central Bar & Grill** (☎ 250-361-1700; 708 View St).

Nightclubs
Clubs in Victoria change as often as the drink specials and cover charges. Check www.clubvibes.com or follow your ears and the crowds around Bastion Square.

Some Victoria standards:

BJ's Lounge (☎ 250-388-0505; 642 Johnson St) The spot for gays and lesbians; it's open every day with DJs spinning on the weekend.

Hush (☎ 250-385-0566; 1325 Government St) Victoria's up-and-coming club is making an impact with great music and staff, and no attitude.

Sugar (☎ 250-920-9950; 858 Yates St) Only open weekends – but it gets packed.

The One Lounge (☎ 250-384-3557; 1318 Broad St) Fun early-20s crowds, top 40, R&B and hip-hop; the illuminated bars are pretty cool.

Upstairs Cabaret (☎ 250-385-5483; 15 Bastion Sq) More like a rave scene with DJs Tuesday to Saturday.

Theatre & Performing Arts
McPherson Playhouse (☎ 250-386-6121; www.rmts .bc.ca; 3 Centennial Sq) and **Royal Theatre** (☎ 250-386-6121; 805 Broughton St) are the elegant mainstages of Victoria – think velvet ropes and curtains, marble floors and wood carvings. The latter is the home of the **Victoria Symphony** (☎ 250-385-6515; www.victoriasymphony.bc.ca) and the **Pacific Opera Victoria** (☎ 250-386-6121; www.pov.bc.ca).

The **Belfry** (☎ 250-385-6815; www.belfry.bc.ca; 1291 Gladstone Ave), and the **Phoenix Theatre** (☎ 250-721-8000), on the University of Victoria campus, are noteworthy for live independent theater.

Cinemas
You will find generally lower prices for matinees.

Vic Theatre (☎ 250-383-1998; 808 Douglas St; adult/ child $8.50/5) This old theater is not without a sense of style and shows lesser-known first-run movies in its single theater.

Cinecenta (☎ 250-721-8365; adult/child $6.25/4.75) On the University of Victoria campus, Cinecenta features recently released and classic independent films in the Student Union Building.

The first-run cinemas downtown are **Capitol 6 Cinema** (☎ 250-384-6811; 805 Yates St; $7.95) and **Odeon Theatre** (☎ 250-383-0513; 780 Yates St; $8.25).

SHOPPING

Trounce Alley, between Government and Broad Sts north of View St, is tucked away but lined with clothing and European fashion shops. Fort St east of Blanshard St is known as 'Antique Row'. The **Bay Centre** (☎ 250-382-7141), bounded by Government, Douglas, Fort and View Sts, is Victoria's mall-rats hangout.

Government St is the main shopping street with an interesting mix of chain retailers and locally owned shops. Try:

Rogers' Chocolates (☎ 250-384-7021; 913 Government St) Tiny store but oh-so-good chocolates.

Canadian Impressions (☎ 250-383-2641; 921 Government St) First Nations crafts.

Edinburgh Tartan Shop (☎ 250-953-7788; 909 Government St)

Sasquatch Trading Company (☎ 250-386-9033; 1233 Government St) Hand-knitted Cowichan sweaters – unique to BC.

The Spirit of Christmas (☎ 250-385-2501; 1022 Government St) Get your Christmas decorations all year.

GETTING THERE & AWAY
Air

Regional and Seattle flights depart Victoria International airport (YYJ) in Sidney, 26km north of the city via Hwy 17. **Harbour Air Seaplanes** (☎ 250-384-2215, 800-665-0212; www.harbour-air.com; $99) and **West Coast Air** (☎ 250-388-4521, 800-347-2222; www.westcoastair.com; $99) offer seaplane flights from the Inner Harbour to Vancouver Harbour.

Boat
CAR FERRIES

BC Ferries (☎ 250-656-5571; www.bcferries.com; adult/child $10/5, car $34.75, reservation $15) operates services to the mainland from Swartz Bay, 27km north of Victoria via Hwy 17 (hourly from 7am to 10pm June 9 to September 12, varies in off-season). Ferry schedules are widely available around town, or check their information office (p125).

It's a 95-minute sailing from Swartz Bay to Tsawwassen, near Vancouver – an absolutely beautiful trip through the Gulf Islands. Reservations are highly recommended in summer, especially on Friday and Sunday afternoons; it's not uncommon to arrive for the 4pm ferry and not get on a boat until 7pm. The schedule changes slightly every few weeks outside the peak season so double-check your preferred departure.

BC Ferries also operates between Swartz Bay and the southern Gulf Islands (adult/child $6.50/3.50, car $22.25). Schedules only make sense to the schedule-maker and vary by season and destination, with more frequent sailings in July and August.

BC Ferries is not your only way off the island; ferries to the great state of Washington depart from the **Belleville Ferry Terminal** (254 Belleville St). US change is given, but Canadian money is accepted at their exchange rate.

Black Ball Transport (☎ 250-386-2202; adult/child US$9/4.50, car US$33.50; ⏲ 6:10am, 10:30am, 3pm & 7:30pm) operates the *MV Coho* to Port Angeles (90 minutes).

PASSENGER-ONLY FERRIES

Victoria Express (☎ 250-361-9144; www.victoria express.com; adult/child US$12.50/7.50, bicycles US$3) One-hour journey to Port Angeles (9:45am & 6:15pm mid-May–mid-Jul & Sep, also 2pm Jul 19-Sep 1) .

Clipper Navigation (☎ 250-382-8100; www.victoria clipper.com; adult/child US$76/70) *Victoria Clipper* and *Victoria Clipper II* make the three-hour journey to Seattle (11:30am & 7pm mid-May–Jun, also 5:30pm Jun-Sep) in water-jet-propelled catamarans.

Victoria-San Juan Cruises (☎ 250-443-4552; www .whales.com; adult/child US$79/34.50) *Victoria Star* goes to Bellingham (5pm).

Bus

Long and short-range bus trips depart from the **bus station** (700 Douglas St). Though Greyhound (☎ 250-385-5248) doesn't serve Vancouver Island, there's an office in the station to purchase tickets for Vancouver buses.

Train

VIA Rail (☎ 250-842-7245; www.viarail.ca) runs trains – the *E&N Railiner* or the *Malahat* – up-island to Courtney and back (8:15am & 12:50pm Mon-Sat, noon Sun); the **station** (450 Pandora Ave; ⏲ 7-11am & 12:30-2:30pm Mon-Sat, 8am-noon Sun) is only open when trains are arriving or departing.

GETTING AROUND

Since Victoria is concentrated around the Inner Harbour, it's a walking town.

To/From the Airport

AKAL Airport Shuttle Bus (☎ 250-386-2525; adult/child $14/7; ☼ 4:30am-midnight) provides services between the airport and all area hotels and B&Bs.

A taxi to the airport from downtown costs about $45. BC Transit's No. 70 goes to the airport at peak times and passes within 1km other times.

Bicycle

Cycle BC Rentals (☎ 250-380-2453, 866-380-2453; bicycle/scooter/motorcycle per day $19/45/99) Main office (747 Douglas St); Seasonal office (950 Wharf St)

Sports Rent (☎ 250-385-7368; www.sportsrentbc .com; 1950 Government St; road/mountain bike per day $25/20)

Bus

BC Transit (☎ 250-382-6161; www.bctransit.com; day-pass $1.75/2.50/5.50) buses run frequently and cover a wide area – two-zone travel ($2.50) will take you into the suburbs to places such as Colwood or Sidney. Use exact change. Day-passes aren't sold on buses but are available from convenience stores and the info centre (p125).

Car

All major rental companies have offices at the airport and in the downtown area; the info centre sometimes has discount coupons.

Ferry

Victoria Harbour Ferry (☎ 250-708-0201; adult/child from $3.50/1.75) provides scheduled service to the Inner Harbour, Ocean Pointe Resort, Songhees Park (Spinnakers Brewpub), Fisherman's Wharf and other stops up the Gorge waterway. Fares vary with distance traveled.

Taxi

Two-seater, human-powered pedicabs of **Kabuki Kabs** (☎ 250-385-4243; $1 per min) are fun, if only to hear the 'driver' spin a yarn.

If you are looking for the more traditional kind, at $1.40 per kilometer try:
Blue Bird Cabs (☎ 250-382-3611)
Empress Taxi (☎ 250-381-2222)

SOUTHERN VANCOUVER ISLAND

Southern Vancouver Island's attractions range from world-famous gardens to tide pools, with plenty of coastal hiking trails and excellent cycling routes for outdoor types. Beyond Victoria the Southwest Coast is an amazingly overlooked destination – amazing that it gets overlooked and also simply amazing. The wildlife here is abundant, and you can expect to see orcas in the water and bald eagles in the sky. The forests and rugged coastline are inspiring.

SIDNEY

pop 11,000

Situated at the north end of the Saanich Peninsula near the airport and ferry terminal, 'Sidney by the Sea' is a small town with boats and books – possibly the most bookstores per capita in BC. It has an offshore provincial park and is also the northern terminus of the Lochside Regional Trail (see the boxed text, p143).

Sidney has two **Visitor Information Centres** (☎ 250-656-0525; 10382 Patricia Bay Hwy; ☼ 8:30am-5:30pm summer), one on **Ocean Ave** (☎ 250-656-3260; 2295 Ocean Ave; ☼ 10am-2pm & 4-7pm summer). **Tanners** (☎ 250-656-2345; 2436 Beacon Ave) is the biggest of Sidney's bookstores, with an excellent map department and thousands of magazine titles.

Sights & Activities

Sidney Spit Provincial Marine Park is a great spot for swimming, sunbathing and beachcombing. Get there by passenger **ferry** (☎ 250-474-5145; adult/child $11/8; ☼ 10am-5pm Mon-Thu, 10am-6pm Fri-Sun late-Jun–early-Sep).

It's nothing fancy, but at the **Marine Ecology Centre** (☎ 250-655-1555; Port Sidney Marina; adult/child $4/3; ☼ noon-5pm summer) you can view a whole range of live sea critters and their habitats, some in hands-on touch tanks.

Rent a bike at **True Value Hardware** (☎ 250-656-8611; 2488 Beacon Ave; $25 per day) for cycling the Lochside Regional Trail.

Sleeping & Eating

Shoal Harbour Inn (☎ 250-656-6622, 877-956-6622; www.shoalharbourinn.com; with sea/garden views $219/199; P ☒ ☐) All rooms are suites and are

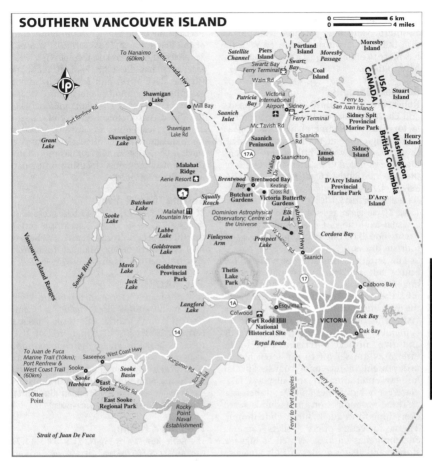

SOUTHERN VANCOUVER ISLAND

bright and spacious in this chalet-like hotel. Relax in earth tones and country furnishings while the sea breeze blows in through the open balcony door.

Waterfront Hotel Sidney (☎ 250-656-1131, 888-656-1131; 2537 Beacon Ave; with/without view $105/120; P X) has clean rooms and is close to the marina.

Camping is available at **McDonald Provincial Park** (☎ 250-825-4212; $14), near the Swartz Bay ferry terminal, and **Sidney Spit Provincial Park** (www.gov.bc.ca/bcparks; $5) offers fine white sand as your mattress.

Maria's Souvlaki (☎ 250-656-9944; 9812 2nd St; mains $7-11; ☺ lunch & dinner) The name says souvlaki, but they cover the whole Greek gambit with zest and flavor. Locals agree it

stands out as a favorite, complete with got the requisite checkered tablecloths.

Mary's Bleue Moon Café (☎ 250-655-4450; 9535 Canora Rd; mains $7-12) Across the highway from town, near the end of the airport runway, Mary's is a locally-popular spot with the look and feel of an ex-pilot's basement; wood paneled walls, old wooden furniture and old pictures on the wall.

Getting There & Away

Washington State Ferries (☎ 250-381-1551; 888-808-7977; www.wsdot.wa.gov/ferries; 2499 Ocean Ave; adult/child $13.10/6.50, car $44.25; ☺ 11:40am) offers a service from Sidney on a two-hour cruise through the US San Juan Islands to Anacortes on the Washington mainland.

SAANICH PENINSULA

Southern Vancouver Island's transportation hub, this peninsula north of Victoria has more to offer than just a way to get from here to there.

Butchart Gardens

Robert Butchart noticed limestone deposits and chose this site in 1904 for his cement factory; his wife Jennie planted sweet peas and a single rose at the nearby residence, though she knew very little about gardening. One hundred years later, 20 hectares of the elaborate **Butchart Gardens** (☎ 250-652-5256, 866-652-4422; www.butchartgardens.com; 800 Benvenuto Ave; adult/youth/child $21/10.50/2; ☼ 9am-10:30pm Jun 15-Aug 31, closing time varies at other times) provide a visual explosion of color and texture in Brentwood Bay, one of the province's top tourism draws.

The length of the average visit is 1½ hours, but avid gardeners may want to linger much longer. If time is short, don't miss the impressive Sunken Gardens and the peaceful Japanese Garden. Consider visiting in the evenings from June 15 to September 15, when the grounds are lit and live musical entertainers perform. Fireworks are set off to music each Saturday night in July and August. Special holiday entertainment and displays take place every November and December.

Three restaurants on the grounds serve everything from quick bites to fine dining. The visitor centre offers strollers, cameras and umbrellas on loan, as well as luggage storage and visitor guides in 19 languages.

Located 23km north of Victoria via Patricia Bay Hwy (Hwy 17), the gardens can be reached via bus No 75 from downtown Victoria, though it's a slow trek. Better to take **Gray Line** (☎ 250-318-0818; www.grayline.ca/victoria; express includes admission $28, tour adult/child $44.50/14.25).

Victoria Butterfly Gardens

On the way to Butchart Gardens, this lesser-known collection of **aviaries** (☎ 250-652-3822, 877-722-0272; www.butterflygardens.com; 1461 Benvenuto Ave; adult/child $8.75/5; ☼ 9am-5:30pm summer) features more than 300 free-flying butterflies from 30 species. Watching the variety of colors flutter through the air is a visual delight and makes the world seem lighter.

Centre of the Universe

Perched on Little Saanich Mountain, **Centre of the Universe** (☎ 250-363-0012; 5071 W Saanich Rd; adult/child $7/5; ☼ 10am-6pm, till 11pm weekends summer) has the 1.8m Plaskett Telescope (in use since 1918) and features hands-on exhibits and a mini-planetarium. At **Star Parties** (☼ 7-11pm Sat Apr-Oct), members of the Royal Astronomical Society of Canada and their telescopes are at your disposal for inquisitions and explanations. **Stargazer Sundays** (☼ 7-11pm Sun Jul & Aug) has more family-oriented programs, focusing on planets and meteor-showers.

Getting There & Away

BC Ferries (☎ 250-223-3779; www.bcferries.com; adult/child $4.50/2.25, car $11.50; ☼ 7:30am-5:55pm) runs a marine shortcut from Brentwood Bay to Mill Bay, north of The Malahat if you're in a rush to get up-island.

THE MALAHAT

Just north of Victoria on the Island Hwy, this mountainous area makes a scenic daytrip from Victoria. **Goldstream Provincial Park** (☎ 250-391-2300), 19km north of Victoria, is best known for its chum salmon spawning season (late-October to December). You'll also find good fishing and hiking, along with human and natural history exhibits at the park's **Freeman King Visitor Centre** (☎ 250-478-9414; ☼ 9am-4:30pm).

Sleeping & Eating

The Aerie Resort (☎ 250-743-7115, 800-518-1933; www.aerie.bc.ca; 600 Ebedora Lane; with/without Jacuzzi $295/325, ste $395-775; ⓟ ⓧ ⓧ ⓡ) This Mediterranean-style villa high on the hill offers 29 rooms, none of them the same. The views of southern Vancouver Island and Finlayson Arm are amazing. Windows everywhere and fluffy white coverings lend an inviting, cool comfort to the rooms. The Aerie is close enough to Victoria to drive, and its acclaimed dining (mains $15 to $25) is a high-flying affair with several tasting menus (vegetarian/farmers' market $75/85 seafood $85, discovery $115) that sample seasonal dishes, all expertly prepared using local ingredients. Ask about the chef-led Cowichan Valley farm tours.

Considered the nicest campground near Victoria, **Goldstream Provincial Park** (☎ 250-391-2300; sites $18.50) has 160 sites (above).

Malahat Mountain Inn (☎ 250-478-1979, 800-913-1944; 265 Trans-Canada Hwy; breakfast & lunch $8-15, dinner $10-20) The sign says 'Fine Dining', there's a neon martini in the window and purple napkins on the table. But the menu isn't as outrageous as the décor and the view from the patio, combined with the ocean breezes, is relaxing. The food is casual and tasty, and there are good vegetarian options to go with the steaks and burgers.

SOOKE

pop 8700

It's easy to neglect this small community 31km east of Victoria, but it occupies a happy place between ocean and rainforest and is worth a visit. If you're traveling west, there are no gas stations between Sooke and Port Renfrew, so fill up.

Island-renowned swim spot **Sooke Potholes**, a 5km drive from Hwy 14 (turn-off is east of town), is good for picnicking and the cool, clear waters are great for swimming or tube-floating. The **Sooke Visitor Info Centre** (☎ 250-642-6351; 2070 Phillips Rd; ☾ 9am-5pm) runs the **Sooke Regional Museum** which has a collection of forestry artifacts, tools and displays that show how life was 'back then'.

East Sooke Regional Park offers outstanding hikes that exemplify beautiful BC: waves crashing against a bluff one minute, the peaceful canopy of Douglas fir the next. From short strolls to the beach to the rough six-to-eight-hour, 10km Coast Trail, this park is a must for nature-lovers. To get here from Sooke, you must travel around the harbor; there is no ferry.

Sooke Adventures (☎ 250-646-2820; www.sookeadventures.com) leads tours on water and land, as does **Rush Adventures** (☎ 250-642-2159; www.rush-adventures.com; 5449 Sooke Rd), which also rents kayaks (half-/full-day $40/50) and gives lessons ($55-95).

Cycle the Galloping Goose Trail (see the boxed text, above) after you've rented a bike at **Sooke Cycle & Surf** (☎ 250-642-3123; 6707 West Coast Rd; 3hrs/full-day $13/25).

Sleeping & Eating

Sooke has more than 60 B&Bs, averaging $65 to $85. Check at the info centre to see the posted displays.

Sooke Harbour House (☎ 250-642-3421; www.sookeharbourhouse.com; 1528 Whiffen Spit Rd; ste from $399; Ⓟ ✖) Like old country-house meets artist's garage sale, elegance and rustic appeal come together without getting in each other's way at this hotel. Of the 28 rooms, 27 have ocean views; all come with stone-hearth fireplaces, full breakfast and picnic, and inspired individual decor. The seaside **dining room** (reservation-only, prix-fixe $69.95) is open to the public for dinner and features a constantly-changing menu focused on local ingredients and tastes.

Just up Phillips Rd from the museum, **Sooke River Flats Campsite** (☎ 250-642-6076; tent/RV $15/17) has coin-op showers that hikers will appreciate. **French Beach Provincial Park** (☎ 250-474-1336; sites $14), 20km west of Sooke, has 69 sites – no showers – that also fill up with hikers.

Mom's Cafe (☎ 250-642-3314; 2036 Shields Rd; mains $6-11) A throwback to the days of the classic café, with blue vinyl seats, Formica tabletops and old-school coke glasses. It's busy, you seat yourself and the all-day breakfasts, soups, sandwiches and burgers are tasty.

JUAN DE FUCA PROVINCIAL PARK

While the West Coast Trail (WCT; p158) is still considered BC's favorite long-distance

---

THE GALLOPING GOOSE

Starting north of Sooke, The Galloping Goose Trail – named for a noisy gas railcar that ran between Victoria and Sooke in the 1920s – is a 55km bike and walking path to Victoria on abandoned railway beds. If you're not wiped out by the end, you can ride 29km up the Saanich Peninsula to Sidney on the Lochside Regional Trail. It's long been said that some of the best scenery is seen from the window of a train, and that's true here. This route goes a step further by getting cyclists off the highways and into some unseen backcountry.

Getting on and off the trails is easy since four bus lines along both routes are bikerack equipped. For a brochure with maps or more information, ask at area Visitor Info Centres or call the **Capital Region District Parks** (☎ 250-478-3344). The Greater Victoria Cycling Coalition's website (www.gvcc.bc.ca) is a good place to look for regional cycling information.

VANCOUVER ISLAND

coastal hike, the 47km **Juan de Fuca Marine Trail** in **Juan de Fuca Provincial Park** (☎ 250-391-2300) is an up-and-comer. Unlike the WCT, the Juan de Fuca doesn't require hiking reservations and it features several access points so you can tramp for a day without having to go all the way.

From east to west, access points from Hwy 14 are **China Beach**, **Sombrio Beach**, **Parkinson Creek** and **Botanical Beach**. There are six established campsites ($5, cash-only, pay at trailheads) and most through-hikers take four days to make the complete trek. The most difficult stretch is from Bear Beach campsite to China Beach, but any part can be a major struggle, with slippery tree roots, mud and unpredictable weather.

It's not as grueling as WCT, but Juan de Fuca isn't a cakewalk either, so be prepared. Contact **BC Parks** (☎ 250-391-2300; www.gov.bc.ca /bcparks) or visit www.juandefucamarinetrail .com for detailed information on planning a trip. **West Coast Trail Express** (☎ 250-477-8700; China Beach/Port Renfrew $30/35; ⏱ 6:40am) runs shuttle services between Victoria and the trailheads.

Rush Adventures (☎ 250-642-2159; www.rush -adventures.com; 5449 Sooke Rd one-/two-/three-/four-day $90/190/300/380) and **Sooke Adventures** (☎ 250-646-2820; www.sookeadventures.com; 2 people $725) lead guided treks along the Juan de Fuca.

China Beach (☎ 250-689-9025; www.discover camping.ca; sites $14) is an especially nice spot. It's popular with families and has vehicle-accessible campsites. An easy 15-minute walk from the parking lot ($3 parking) leads to a sandy beach and water warm enough for wading. There's a waterfall at the western end of the beach.

PORT RENFREW
pop 190

As the southern node of the West Coast Trail (p158) and the northern node of the Juan de Fuca Marine Trail (above), Renfrew busts out of its sleepy shell from May through to September. The 'Jewel of the West Coast' at the end of Hwy 14 hums with activity as hikers prepare to tackle (or recuperate from) their hikes.

Check in at the **Visitor Info Centre** (www.portrenfrew .com; ⏱ 10am-6pm) on your left as you get into town.

Those looking for a hike will enjoy the 2.7km **Botanical Loop**, connecting Botanical

Beach and Botany Bay, both known for their amazing tide pools and sandy beaches. Allow about 90 minutes, and go at low tide. The nearby **Mill Bay Trail** accesses a small pebble-and-shell beach on an easy walk. Go through town and follow the blue signs to Botanical Beach.

Sleeping & Eating

West Coast Trail Hotel (☎ 250-647-5565, 877-299-2288; www.westcoasttrailmotel.com; Parkinson Rd; r $72, with kitchenette $85; P ✗) Clean and basic motel-style rooms and an outdoor hot tub.

Arbutus Beach Lodge (☎ 250-647-5458, 866-772-8887; www.arbutusbeachlodge.com; s/d $65/75, cabin $105; P ✗) On the waterfront, this lodge has a hot tub. The pink and turquoise rooms are basic but the beds are comfy; the 'Seaview' is your best bet with more room and not much less view.

Many hikers stay at **Pacheedaht Campground** (☎ 250-647-0090; WCT trailhead; $5-20) on the Pacheedaht Reserve.

Coastal Kitchen Cafe (☎ 250-647-5545; Hwy 14; mains $9-12) Almost out of place in the surroundings of Renfrew, this café serves fresh salads and sandwiches, and cooks up burgers and pizzas. Hikers, either replenishing or fuelling up, are often outside on the picnic tables under the trees.

Lighthouse Neighbourhood Pub & Restaurant (☎ 250-647-5543; Parkinson Rd; mains $8-11) This red-roofed pub serves good appetizers, burgers, pasta and seafood in the family dining room, in the pub or on the patio.

COWICHAN VALLEY

Just over the Malahat from Victoria, this valley is home to the Cowichan First Nations group, for whom Cowichan means 'land warmed by the sun'.

DUNCAN
pop 4700

Duncan town leaders and the Cowichan people worked together in the 'City of Totems' to display several dozen examples of this West Coast art form along its streets.

The **Visitor Info Centre** (☎ 250-746-4636; 381 Trans-Canada Hwy; ⏱ 9am-5pm mid-Apr–mid-Oct) can direct you (if you really want) to the 61,000-pound **World's Largest Hockey Stick and Puck**.

Quw'utsun' Cultural & Conference Centre

An extremely well-put-together First Nations attraction, the **Quw'utsun' Cultural & Conference Centre** (☎ 250-746-8119; www.quwutsun.ca; 200 Cowichan Way; adult/child $15/6.60; ☺ 9am-6pm May-Sep, 10am-5pm Oct-Apr) will immerse you in the Cowichan Tribe's culture, especially if you come for the **Midday Salmon BBQ and Cultural Tour** (adult/senior or student/child $35/32/26; ☺ noon Thu-Sat Jul-Sep). Try your hand at carving or beading, learn about the importance of salmon and see the tribe's 'Great Deeds'. The **River Walk Café** has an entirely First Nations' menu serving Hul'qumi'nun' Steen'uq (hull-keem-nun steen-ook; Feast; $33), or Meh'wulp (may-wulp; Salish afternoon tea; $17).

BC Forestry Discovery Centre

This **centre** (☎ 250-715-1113; www.bcforestmuseum.com; 2892 Drinkwater Rd; adult/child $9/5; ☺ 10am-6pm May–early-Sep, reduced hours other times), 3km north of Duncan, features both indoor and outdoor exhibits on its 40 hectares. Stroll through a stand of 200-year-old, 55m-tall Douglas firs, take rides on a working steam train, visit the bird sanctuary, hike nature trails or view a replicated logging camp.

COWICHAN LAKE & AROUND

Cowichan Lake is the largest freshwater lake on Vancouver Island, 22km west of Duncan via Hwy 18.

Small Lake Cowichan (pop 2900) maintains a **Visitor Info Centre** (☎ 250-749-3244; 125-C South Shore Rd; ☺ 9am-5pm Tue-Sat, 10am-2pm Sun & Mon), behind which lies **Kaatza Station Museum** (☎ 250-749-6142; $2; ☺ 9am-4pm, closed mid-Dec–Feb), an incredible museum for such a small town, with realistic walk-through displays of pioneer life.

Cowichan River Provincial Park is a reserve stretching from the Glenora area south of Duncan to the village of Lake Cowichan. Highlights include a 20km hiking trail (the western stretch east from Skutz Falls makes a good short hike) and advanced-level kayaking in Marie Canyon.

Gordon Bay Provincial Park (☎ 250-474-1336), 14km from Lake Cowichan on South Shore Rd, is excellent for swimming, fishing and boating. **Nitinat Lake** (nit-nat), 68km west of Cowichan Lake over logging roads, is a die-hard windsurfing community during the

---

DETOUR: COWICHAN BAY

Heading up-island (north) on Hwy 1 The Malahat, turn right where the 'S Side Route' signs direct you. You're c your way along a scenic drive to the small, working waterfront village of Cowichan Bay. It doesn't have any huge attractions to brag about, but doesn't need any, either. The pretty town by the bay has well-used houses, shops and cafés along the water. Stop for fish and chips or a cup of coffee, enjoy the surroundings and follow the signs back to Hwy 1.

---

summer and people literally spend weeks at the **Nitinat Campsite** ($10). They welcome outsiders, so visit the Nitinat Windsurfing Society's website (www.island.net/~nitinat) for details.

Pachena Bay Express (☎ 250-728-1290) runs shuttles to and from Nitinat by reservation only; call for schedules and fares.

Sleeping & Eating

South Shore Motel (☎ 250-749-6482; 266 South Shore Rd; with/without kitchenette $50/45; [P] [X]) Located in town, this has basic motel rooms, but the service is first-rate.

Greendale Riverside Cabins (☎ 250-749-6570; www.greendalecabins.com; 8012 Greendale Rd; $65-110; [P] [X]) Five individual cabins in a park-like setting with wildlife and river access. The cabins are pretty spacious (the one-bedroom 'Rainbow Room' excepted) and have kitchens and rustic furnishings.

Sahtlam Lodge and Cabins (☎ 250-748-7738; www.sahtlamlodge.com; 5720 Riverbottom Rd W; $150-180; [P] [X]) Between Lake Cowichan and Duncan, this lodge offers slightly more upscale cabins in the woods. It's in a convenient location near the Cowichan River and Trans-Canada trails; the third night and beyond is 30% off.

Lakeview Park Municipal Campground (☎ 250-749-3350; www.town.lakecowichan.bc.ca/camping.shtml; 885 Lakeview Park Rd; sites $20), on the southern shore of Cowichan Lake, has showers, toilets and free firewood. **Gordon Bay Provincial Park** (☎ 250-474-1336; sites $22) has 126 sites.

Trail's End Pub (☎ 250-749-4001; 109 South Shore Rd; mains $7-10) Right on the lake and with an outdoor patio, this place features pub food a step above normal grub as they add seafood

s and nachos. It's
...t Thursday and
...ttle wild.
9-6350; 72 Cowichan
...nted restaurant

....ANAH WALBRAN PROVINCIAL PARK

BC Parks' newest member, **Carmanah Walbran Provincial Park** (☎ 250-474-1336; backcountry $5) is home to some of Vancouver Island's oldest residents.

Some of the last remaining old-growth forest exists in this 16,450-hectare park. With tall, moss-covered spruce trees (including Canada's largest tree, at 95m) and 1000-year-old cedars, the whole place feels old and mythical, almost forgotten. Carmanah can only be reached via active logging roads; pick up a forestry or recreation map from any of the area info centres and bring a spare tire.

For those without a map: follow South Shore Rd from Lake Cowichan to Nitinat Main Rd and bear left. Then follow Nitinat Main to Nitinat Junction and turn left onto South Main. Continue to the Caycus River Bridge and, just south of the bridge, turn right and follow Rosander Main (blue and white BC Parks signs reassuringly point the way) for 29km to the park. From Port Alberni follow Bamfield Rd to South Main, bear left and follow the directions above.

Despite its remote location, the trails are well maintained and easy to follow. Once you're there, it's a half-hour walk down the valley into the tallest trees. Campsites with tent pads, tables and water are provided at the trailhead, and dedicated campsites and food stashes are found up the trail. The closest phone and gas station are on the Didtidaht Reserve, at Nitinat Lake.

CHEMAINUS
pop 4500

Chemainus' main attractions are the many depictions of Chemainus. The sawmill shut down in 1983, but rather than submit to a slow death, town officials commissioned a large outdoor mural of local history. People took notice, and 33 murals now adorn 'The Little Town That Did'.

Check out the **Visitor Info Centre** (☎ 250-246-3944; 9796 Willow St; 🕙 9am-5pm May-Oct, 10am-5pm Mon-Fri Nov-Apr) or look for information exhibits across the street in **Waterwheel Park**.

Chemainus Theatre (☎ 250-246-9820, 800-565-7738; www.ctheatre.bc.ca) puts on magnificent performances that rival big-city theaters. The classic architecture and marble, brass and velvet interior make going to a show the event it should be. The theater has been a mainstay in Chemainus for years.

Renovations to add a colossal resort got underway in 2003 and will continue until 2005.

Chemainus Tours (☎ 250-246-5055; adult/child $7/3) has horse-drawn carriages leading 30-minute mural tours.

Sleeping & Eating

Bird Song Cottage (☎ 250-246-9910; 9909 Maple St; s/d $80/105; P ✗) Not only are the rooms in this old Victorian luxuriously romantic, the service is top rate. The breakfasts look almost too elegant to eat and the rooms are cozy as in 'cozy,' not as in 'small'.

Fuller Lake Chemainus Motel (☎ 250-246-3282; 9300 Smiley Rd; r/ste $70/85; P ✗) The studio-like rooms are clean and nothing to write home about, but the huge yard and garden sets this place apart.

Bonnie Martin Eats (☎ 250-246-1068; 2877 Mill Rd; mains $7-12) It's where the locals eat and the family feel comfortable and good home-cooking is probably why.

VANCOUVER ISLAND

A FITTING LEGACY

Randy Stoltmann ranks high among the mythical figures of BC's backcountry. Stoltmann stumbled on the giant trees of the Carmanah Valley on a 1988 hiking trip. Learning they were slated to be logged, he argued for the preservation of these majestic trees, and his determined efforts led to the establishment of the Carmanah Walbran Provincial Park in 1990. Stoltmann died in a mountaineering accident in 1994, but his legacy lives on in Carmanah's Randy Stoltmann Commemorative Grove. He was also an author and wrote several notable hiking guides, including *Hiking the Ancient Forests of British Columbia & Washington*.

LADYSMITH
pop 7000

Right on the 49th parallel, Ladysmith is one of the prettiest small towns you'll see. Contrary to its name, and despite the fact that the town produced model-turned-actor Pamela Anderson, the main industry is not crafting ladies. Its real industries have included coal and forestry, and the latest is tourism. Revitalized First Ave's restored 19th and 20th century buildings entice you off the highway and up the hill.

The **Visitor Info Centre** (☎ 250-245-2112; 26 Gatacre St; ☉ 9am-6pm) is adjacent to the **Black Nugget Museum** (☎ 250-245-4846; 12 Gatacre St; ☉ 9am-3:30pm Jul & Aug) – a hidden treasure-trove of memorabilia in the former Jones Hotel. **Transfer Beach Park** attracts lots of swimmers and picnickers; visit **Sealegs Kayaking** (☎ 250-245-4096, 877-529-2522; www.sealegskayaking.com; from $50; ☉ May-Oct) for a tour.

NANAIMO & AROUND

NANAIMO
pop 73,000

The second largest city on Vancouver Island, the 'Harbour City' offers plenty of sights and recreation right around town, with many more attractions only a short drive or ferry ride away.

A number of First Nations bands once shared the area which was called *Sne-Ny-Mos* – a Salish word meaning 'meeting place'. Coal was discovered in 1852, and mining was the dominant industry for 100 years. It has since declined in importance and tourism and forestry have taken over. Nanaimo's Marine Festival and World Championship Bathtub Race take place each July.

Orientation

Nanaimo, 110km north of Victoria, has done a superb job revitalizing its downtown waterfront. Eateries and shops lining the promenade and a completely redone Mafeo-Sutton Park have added life and verve around the inner harbor, extending from the Boat Basin Marina area near Harbour Park Mall to Departure Bay. The city center lies behind the harbor, with most shops on Commercial St and Terminal Ave. Old City Quarter, a small section up the hill from downtown bordered by Fitzwilliam,

> **DETOUR: FOLLOW THE YELLOW POINT ROAD**
>
> From Hwy 1, head east on Yellow Point Rd north of Ladysmith. You'll wind in and out of valleys and through farmland and forest on your way to the coast where the road turns left and heads north at **Yellow Point Lodge** (☎ 250-245-7422; www.yellowpointlodge.com; 3700 Yellow Point Rd; s/d $100/181, cottage $89-122). The log lodge and cabins in this adults-only inclusive resort look out over the rocky point onto Georgia Strait. Activities include kayaking, tennis, swimming, and mountain biking.
>
> Continue north along Yellow Point Rd to the **Crow & Gate** (☎ 250-722-3731; 2313 Yellow Point Rd; mains $7-10). Set back in the countryside, this is arguably the most authentic British-style pub west of the Atlantic Ocean. The low-sloped roof and white walls with dark trim on the outside complement the well-used wooden furniture and brickwork inside. Pints of Guinness, poured the proper way, and beef and kidney pie enjoyed in the impeccable back garden are the perfect way to spend an afternoon.
>
> Follow the Yellow Point Rd north through the town of Cedar – stopping for a dip in the river if you'd like – and onto Nanaimo.

Selby and Wesley Sts, has recently been spruced up to reflect old-city charm.

Nicol St, the southern extension of Terminal Ave, leads south to the Trans-Canada Hwy and Hwy 19 (Inland Hwy) and BC Ferries Duke Point terminal. Heading north, Terminal Ave forks: the right fork becomes Stewart Ave (Hwy 1), leading to BC Ferries Departure Bay terminal; the left fork becomes Hwy 19A (Island Hwy), heading up-island. Island Hwy is lined with shopping malls and commercial activity so if you're in a rush, take the Inland Hwy which skirts the city's west side.

Information
BOOKSTORES

There are several good used bookstores along Commercial St.

Literacy Nanaimo Bookstore (☎ 250-754-8982; 19 Commercial St) Profits go to helping people learn to read.
Chapters (☎ 250-390-0380; Woodgrove Centre, North Island Hwy) North of downtown.

Nanaimo Maps & Charts (☎ 250-754-2513, 800-665-2513; 8 Church St) Excellent selection of activity/travel guides and maps.

Spiritwood Books (☎ 250-753-2789; 99 Commercial St) Good selection of New Age and metaphysical titles.

INTERNET ACCESS

Literacy Nanaimo Bookstore (☎ 250-754-8982; 19 Commercial St; $3 per hr)

Vancouver Island Regional Library (☎ 250-753-1154; 90 Commercial St; $1 per 30 min)

MEDICAL SERVICES

Nanaimo Regional General Hospital (☎ 250-754-2121; 1200 Dufferin Cres) Northwest of downtown.

MONEY

Major banks are located on **Commercial St**. **Money Mart** (☎ 250-753-1440; 164 Nicol St) exchanges currency.

POST

Post office (☎ 250-267-1177; Harbour Park Mall ⊗ 8:30am-5pm Mon-Fri)

TOURIST INFORMATION

Visitor Info Centre (☎ 250-756-0106, 800-663-7337; www.tourismnanaimo.com; 2290 Bowen Rd; ⊗ 8am-7pm May-Sep, 9am-5pm Mon-Fri 10am-4pm Sat & Sun Oct-Apr) Curiously located away from downtown but extremely helpful.

Information kiosk (⊗ 9am-6pm summer) Located in The Bastion.

Tourism Vancouver Island (☎ 250-754-3500; www.islands.bc.ca; 335 Wesley St, 2nd floor) Headquarters in Old City Quarter.

Sights

Get your map at the info centre or follow the color-coded walks to see the remarkable **Jeff King's Murals** on building walls around town. **Mafeo-Sutton Park** is a great place for kids with its man-made tidal pool and Children's Play Dock, an Island-inspired playground. Just across the inlet, **Newcastle Island Provincial Marine Park** (☎ 250-753-5141, 250-755-1132) offers picnicking, cycling, hiking and beaches. Walks or hikes range from a 1km stroll to the 7.5km perimeter hike. Get here on a 10-minute **ferry** (adult/child $7/6; ⊗ 10am-7pm May 1–mid-Oct).

Petroglyph Provincial Park, 3km south of Nanaimo on Hwy 1, is unfortunately seldom used although the old-school First Nations sandstone carvings are neat. Most

are now barely visible, but kids like making rubbings from recreated castings.

Overlooking downtown, the **Nanaimo District Museum** (☎ 250-753-1821; 100 Cameron Rd; adult/child $2/0.75; ⊗ 10am-5pm mid-May–early Sep, Tue-Sat Sep-May) traces the growth of the city, from its First Nations heritage to its Hudson's Bay Company days.

The Bastion (cnr Front & Bastion Sts; $1; ⊗ 9am-5pm Wed-Sun summer) was built by the Hudson's Bay Company in 1853 for protection, though it was never used save for the odd cannon firing to simmer-down ruckuses. It still fires daily at noon.

Bungy Zone (☎ 250-753-5867, 800-668-7771; www.bungyzone.com; 35 Nanaimo River Rd; from $50), set on a bridge spanning the Nanaimo River south of town, offers a buffet for thrill-seekers. If you opt for the jump, go the extra distance and get your head wet. Become a lifetime member for $100 and get jumps for $25 apiece. There's camping on the premises (tent per person if no-one jumps is $10) and free pick-up from either local BC Ferry terminal if someone pays for a jump.

Activities

Nanaimo and its nearby islands offer some of the best scuba diving in BC. Dive enthusiasts recently sunk the World War II supply ship *Cape Breton* northwest of Gabriola Island, creating the area's newest and largest artificial reef. For information on dive sites, or for guides, lessons or equipment, visit **Ocean Explorers Diving** (☎ 250-753-2055, 800-233-4145; www.oceanexplorersdiving.com; 1956 Zorkin Rd; from $50).

Kayak Shack (☎ 250-753-3234; from $25; ⊗ 9am-6pm) offers sea-kayaking lessons, rentals and tours from its headquarters near the Departure Bay terminal.

Parkway Trail extends 20km along Hwy 19, and offers opportunities for cycling, in-line skating, jogging and walking. The trail accesses many parks, including **Buttertubs Marsh Sanctuary** and **Morrell Sanctuary**, both good for bird-watching. The trail map from the info centre is excellent.

Sleeping

MOTELS & HOTELS

Nicol St south of town is lined with plenty of basic, plain-but-clean motels. Follow the rule of getting a room as far above ground level as you can: better views.

NANAIMO

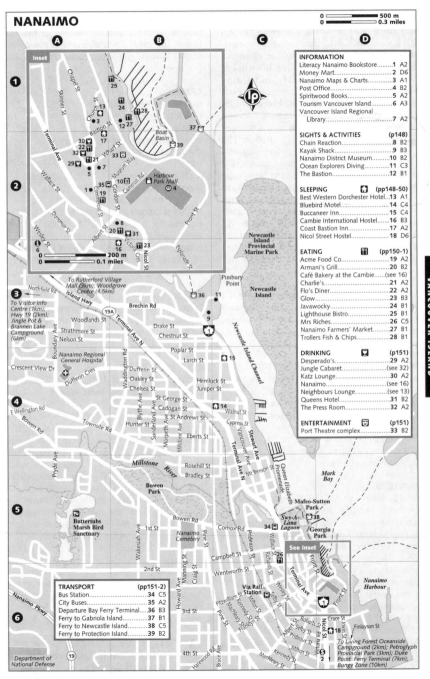

0 —————— 500 m
0 —————— 0.3 miles

Inset

Boat Basin

Harbour Park Mall

0 —————— 200 m
0 —————— 0.1 miles

VANCOUVER ISLAND

Newcastle Island Provincial Marine Park

Newcastle Island

Pimbury Point

Brechin Rd

To Rutherford Village Mall (3km); Woodgrove Centre (4.5km)

Northfield Rd

To Visitor Info Centre (1km); Hwy 19 (2km); Jingle Pot & Brannen Lake Campground (6km)

Woodlands St

Strathmore St
Nelson St

Nanaimo Regional General Hospital

Crescent View Dr

Dufferin Cres

Drake St
Chestnut St

Poplar St
Larch St

Hemlock St
Juniper St

St George St
Cadogan St
St Andrews St

Hunter St
Eberts St

Walnut St
Cypress St

Newcastle Island Channel

Millstone River

Rosehill St
Bradley St

Bowen Park

Buttertubs Marsh Bird Sanctuary

Bowen Rd

Nanaimo Cemetery

Comox Rd

Mark Bay

Mafeo-Sutton Park

Swy-A-Lana Lagoon

Georgia Park

Campbell St
Wentworth St

See Inset

Nanaimo Harbour

1st St

2nd St

Via Rail Station

3rd St

4th St

Nanaimo Pkwy

Department of National Defense

To Living Forest Oceanside Campground (2km); Petroglyph Provincial Park (3km); Duke Point Ferry Terminal (7km); Bungy Zone (10km)

Best Western Dorchester Hotel (☎ 250-754-6835, 800-661-2449; 70 Church St; r/ste $99/129; P X) It's been refurbished but the hallways running at funny angles couldn't be changed, nor could its historic character. It's still got Victorian moldings, a library and sitting rooms on the southwest corners of each floor which are nice when the breeze comes off the water.

Buccaneer Inn (☎ 250-753-1246; www.thebuccaneerinn.com; 1577 Stewart Ave; s/d $65/70; P X) The closest motel to Departure Bay terminal welcomes divers to its comfortable rooms. Up on a hill, it has awesome views of Newcastle Island and they'll be more than happy to help you arrange any activities in the area.

Bluebird Motel (☎ 250-753-4151; www.thebluebirdmotel.com; 995 N Terminal Ave; s/d $49/58; P X) Yep, it's blue alright, powder blue at that. This throwback-style motel – two stories high, hundreds of feet long, outdoor walkways – has clean rooms.

Coast Bastion Inn (☎ 250-753-6601, 800-663-1144; www.coastbastion.com; 11 Bastion St; r/ste $110/200; P X X) Nanaimo's high-rise and high-end option has some excellent views from its upper floors.

B&BS

Whitehouse on Longlake B&B (☎ 250-758-5010, 877-956-1185; www.nanaimobandb.com; 231 Ferntree Pl; r $75-99; P X) As the name would suggest, it's on Long Lake, north of Nanaimo via Hwy 19A. Huge south-facing windows face the lake but if you'd rather do more than look, take the canoe, kayak or paddle-boat out there. The fireplace beside the Jacuzzi tub adds the romantic touch.

HOSTELS

Nicol St Hostel (☎ 250-753-1188; gmurray@island.net; 65 Nicol St; tent/dm/r $10/15/40) The views are amazing from the backyard of John and Moni Murray's home on the hill, and it may be where you'll spend most of your time. The hostel is a five-minute walk from downtown, it's great for families and has an airy outdoor shower, barbecue facilities and a fun mural created by past guests.

Cambie International Hostel-Nanaimo (☎ 250-754-5323, 877-395-5335; nanaimo@cambiehostels.co; 63 Victoria Cres; dm/r $20/40) The crowds that hang around the downstairs café and pub at this central place appear to be the seedy type but are really fun. Each dorm room

has its own toilet. There are no cooking facilities, but Cambie throws in free breakfast at the café. The pub can get rowdy at night; you might want to be away from the noise.

CAMPING

Newcastle Island Provincial Marine Park (☎ 250-753-3481; site summer/winter $12/9) has only 18 walk-in sites, no reservations and no services, but hey, you're on an island.

Campgrounds with showers and laundry include:

Brannen Lake Campsites (☎ 250-756-0404, 866-756-0404; 4228 Briggs Rd; tent/RV $18/22) Camp on a working farm with hay rides and a petting zoo.

Jingle Pot Campsites & RV Park (☎ 250-758-1614; 4012 Jingle Pot Rd; tent/RV $14/21) 120 sites and plenty of activities like badminton and bocce ball.

Living Forest Oceanside Campground & RV Park (☎ 250-755-1755; 6 Maki Rd; tent/RV $19/28) 193 sites and closest campground to town.

Eating

It wouldn't be entirely accurate to call Nanaimo a 'dining' town, but it can be said that it has plenty of places to eat good, honest meals.

BUDGET

Pioneer Waterfront Plaza, near The Bastion, hosts **Nanaimo Farmers' Market** (☼ 10am-2pm Fri May-Oct).

Café Bakery at the Cambie (☎ 250-754-5323; 63 Victoria Cres; mains $3-5) Nanaimo's best bet for breakfast – $3.50 buys bacon, eggs, hash browns and toast. They've also got good sandwiches and a fun vibe, not to mention an outstanding version of the town's signature sweet, Nanaimo bar.

Troller's Fish & Chips (☎ 250-741-7994; mains $7-10) Nothing beats the ambience of Troller's when it comes to grubbing on some fish and chips. This shack on the docks at the boat basin always cooks fish caught that morning.

Javawocky (☎ 250-753-1688; 90 Front St; snacks $2-5) The locally popular coffeehouse on the waterfront. It's a Nanaimo tradition to get a coffee and sit outside, watching the ships come in, and then watch them roll away again.

Charlie's (☎ 250-753-7044; 123 Commercial St; mains $5-6) They open all the street-side windows here so it's light and airy. A hugely popular place for breakfast and lunch – the daily specials are a sure bet.

Flo's Diner (☎ 250-753-2148; 187 Commercial St; mains $6-10) Home of the 'Big-Ass Breakfast'. This place is intentionally in-your-face rude so when they ask 'What the hell do you want?' don't be terrified. The hearty home-cooked food is worth a little in-your-faceness.

MID-RANGE & TOP END

Armani's Grill (☎ 250-754-5551; 22 Victoria Cres; burgers $6-11) They're not just burgers, they're works of art. Armani uses ground sirloin, not chuck, and hand makes each patty after you order. There's 3oz of Jack Daniels in the Jack Burger and the Mushroom Burger has enough mushrooms to tap a small farm's entire crop.

Dinghy Dock Floating Pub (☎ 250-753-2373; mains $7-12) The name is no lie; this restaurant floats offshore from Protection Island. See Nanaimo from the outside and enjoy pub food or seafood. The 10-minute **ferry** (☎ 250-753-8244; roundtrip adult/senior $4/3) leaves from Nanaimo harbor.

Mrs Riches (☎ 250-753-8311; 199 Fraser St; mains $7-11) It's like stepping into a comic book about a carnival, but that's their shtick. It's a family-oriented place with good burgers and pasta, knick-knack strewn walls, and a fun atmosphere.

Acme Food Company (☎ 250-753-0042; 14 Commercial St) The diner on the corner is always packed. The food is good, the menu is varied and has a lively atmosphere.

Glow (☎ 250-741-8858; 7 Old Victoria Rd; mains $16-20) Located in the old brick firehall, the dark tones and receded lighting add a mysterious and secluded atmosphere. The menu combines traditional seafood dishes with Asian accents and local ingredients.

Lighthouse Bistro (☎ 250-754-3212; 50 Anchor Way; mains $10-30) This white-linen bistro is located on the waterfront and features a selection of dishes including pastas, lamb and veal schnitzel. The pub upstairs has lower prices and a more casual atmosphere. There's an excellent view of the harbor from either floor.

Drinking

Katz Lounge (☎ 250-753-5280; 121 Bastion St; ⏰ 6pm-1am) is an upscale cocktail lounge for martinis and Manhattans.

Neighbours Lounge (☎ 250-716-0505; 70 Church St), in the basement of the Dorchester Hotel, caters to the gay and lesbian community. For live music by local and regional bands stop at the **Queens Hotel** (☎ 250-754-675; 34 Victoria Cres).

Entertainment

The **Port Theatre** (☎ 250-754-8550; 125 Front St) presents local and touring fine-arts performances.

As a general rule, **The Press Room** (☎ 250-716-0030; 150 Skinner St) is the most happening nightclub, but **Desperado's** (☎ 250-753-8787; 240 Skinner St) and **Jungle Cabaret** (☎ 250-754-1775; 241 Skinner St) come close. Look for the biggest crowds to help you choose.

Major movie houses include the 10-screen **Avalon Cinema Centre** (☎ 250-390-5021; Woodgrove Centre, 6631 North Island Hwy) and the **Galaxy Cinemas** (☎ 250-741-9000; Rutherford Village Mall, 4750 Rutherford Rd).

Getting There & Away

AIR

Nanaimo has a seaplane terminal right on the harbor. **Baxter Aviation** (☎ 250-661-5599) and **Harbour Air** (☎ 250-714-0900, 800-665-0212) fly to Vancouver and other regional destinations.

Nanaimo Collishaw Air Terminal (☎ 250-245-2157) is 18km south of town on Hwy 1. **Canadian Western Airline** (☎ 866-835-9292) and Air Canada offer scheduled flights to and from Vancouver.

BUS

Vancouver Island Coach Lines (☎ 250-318-0818; 1 North Terminal Ave; www.grayline.ca/victoria/schedules/main_schedule.shtml) connects Nanaimo with up- and down-island.

FERRY

BC Ferries (☎ 250-753-1261; www.bcferries.com; adult/child $10/5, car $34.75, reservation $15; ⏰ 6:30am-9pm) sails from Departure Bay to Horseshoe Bay about 16 times daily, and from **Duke Point** (☎ 250-722-018; ⏰ 5:15am-10:45pm) eight times daily to Tsawwassen. See p380 for more on ferry travel.

TRAIN

VIA Rail (☎ 250-842-7245; www.viarail.ca; 321 Selby St; Victoria $22), aka the *E&N Railiner*, passes through the station once daily in each

VANCOUVER ISLAND

direction. Tickets can be purchased from the conductor.

Getting Around

The waterfront promenade was designed for walking, and downtown is easily accessed on foot, but after that the city spreads out and vehicular transport or strong bike legs will make things easier.

Pick up a transit guide at the tourist office. **BC Transit** (☎ 250-390-4531; trip/daypass $1.75/4.50) buses stop along Gordon St, west of Harbour Park Mall. No 2 goes to the Departure Bay ferry terminal; no city buses run to Duke Point.

Nanaimo Seaporter (☎ 250-753-2118; Departure Bay/Duke Point $6/14) provides door-to-door service. For a taxi, call **AC Taxi** (☎ 250-753-1231; Departure Bay/Duke Point $8/25).

Chain Reaction (☎ 250-754-3309; 12 Lois Lane), down the steps between Victoria Cres and the Harbour Park Mall, rents bicycles and offers good information on local cycling.

GABRIOLA ISLAND

The most northerly of the Southern Gulf Islands, Gabriola makes a fun daytrip from Nanaimo. Hundreds of artists live on the island, but it's also known for its scenery and recreation.

For local information, 'Gabriola Gertie' will most likely be handing out island maps and brochures on the Nanaimo ferry dock. The **Visitor Info Centre** (☎ 250-247-9332, 888-284-9332; www.gabriolaisland.org; 575 North Rd; ☷ 9am-5pm May-Sep) is on your second left after you leave the ferry.

Sights & Activities

Gabriola Sands Provincial Park (☎ 250-248-9460) includes shaded Taylor Bay Beach and sandy Pilot Bay Beach, separated by a grassy field and picnic area. It's also home to **Malaspina Galleries**, known for its wave-like, wind-and-tide-carved sandstone caves. On the island's southeast end, **Drumbeg Provincial Park** offers good swimming, while Brickyard Beach features tide pools and clam-digging.

About a dozen Gabriola artists open their studios to the public; find out who, what, where and when from the info centre, figure out why when you visit. **FOGO Folk Art** (☎ 250-247-8082; www.fogoart.com; 3065 Commodore Way) features Bob and Dee Lauder's practical, sometimes profane and always whimsical wooden carvings – 'Gabriola Gertie' is theirs.

Getting There & Away

BC Ferries (☎ 250-223-3779; www.bcferries.com; passenger/car $5/12.75; ☷ 5:45am-10:25pm) travels 16 times daily from Gabriola to the Nanaimo dock north of Harbour Park Mall.

CENTRAL VANCOUVER ISLAND

The midsection of Vancouver Island includes some great recreation and visual pleasures, be it on the wind-swept and storm-tossed west coast, the serene and sandy east coast, or in the mountainous, forest-covered areas in between.

PARKSVILLE, QUALICUM BEACH & AROUND

What used to be a stopover to the north and west parts of Vancouver Island, Parksville (pop 10,300) and Qualicum Beach (pop 7000) – collectively known as Oceanside – have quietly become a legitimate travel destination in their own right. Protected by the Beaufort Mountain Range, the climate and water temperature are more akin to that of central California than central Canada.

Check out either of the **Visitor Info Centres** Parksville (☎ 250-248-3613; 1275 E Island Hwy; 9am-5pm Mon-Fri, 10am-4pm Sat); Qualicum Beach (☎ 250-752-9532; 2711 W Island Hwy; 9am-5pm Mon-Fri) or visit www.oceansidetourism.com.

For that stubbed toe, the **Walk-in Clinic** (☎ 250-248-5757; 154 Memorial Ave; ☷ 9am-5pm Mon-Fri) and the **After-Hours Clinic** (☎ 250-248-7200; ☷ 5-9pm Mon-Fri; 9am-9pm Sat) are in the same complex in Parksville.

Sights & Activities

At **Butterfly World & Gardens** (☎ 250-248-7026; 1080 Winchester Rd; adult/child $15.95/10.95; ☷ 9am-5pm Mon-Sat, 1-5pm Sun; Apr-Oct) you can walk through a tropical garden filled with butterflies and birds.

North Island Wildlife Recovery Centre (☎ 250-248-1274; 1240 Leffler Rd; adult/child $3/2) is dedicated to teaching about the importance of BC's wildlife. It includes a wildlife museum and exhibits on its efforts to rehabilitate bald eagles and black bears.

On the surface, **sea kayaking** and **sailing** are popular activities on the ocean; delve a little deeper for some fantastic **salmon fishing** or witness the underwater ecology that made Jacques Cousteau call Oceanside the second best cold-water **diving** destination in the world.

Take advantage of the **biking** and **walking** paths along the beaches, or set aside the day to hike **Mount Arrowsmith**, 40km west, and take in the view.

Paradise Adventure Fun Park (☎ 250-248-6612; 375 West Island Hwy; adult/child $6.25/4.25) is the place to practice your short game, where holes are silly, a giant shoe blocks the view and the windmill is in play.

Sleeping

Maclure House B&B Inn (☎ 250-248-3470; www .maclurehouse.com; 1015 E Island Hwy; $110-150) Pamper yourself like Rudyard Kipling did in this Tudor house set among perfectly manicured gardens. The rooms are instantly welcoming and the staff put together some great seasonal packages that include all meals.

Tigh Na Mara Resort Hotel (☎ 250-248-2072, 800-663-7373; www.tigh-na-mara.com; 1095 E Island Hwy; from $110; P X R) Set amid forests yet close to the beach, this resort has become Oceanside's favorite darling over the last few years. Rooms of all types are available – lodge rooms, cottages and condos – and they are just as rustically luxurious on the inside as they look on the outside.

Pacific Shores Nature Resort (☎ 250-468-7121; www.pacific-shores.com; 1-1600 Stroulger Rd; from $80; P X R) This place took a page from other resorts and built a resort to blend with nature, but then added a page of their own by sprucing it up. The only earth tones in the well-furnished rooms are in the wood, everything else is brightly decorated.

In a tribute to loading up the wood-paneled station wagon, **Parksville Beach Motel** (☎ 250-248-6789, 888-248-6789; www.parksvillebeach motel.com; 161 W Island Hwy; $115-160; P X), **Sea Edge Motel** (☎ 250-248-8377; www.seaedge .com; 209 W Island Hwy; $105-150; P X), and **Paradise Sea Shell Motel & RV Park** (☎ 250-248-6171, 877-337-3529; www.bctravel.com/ci/seashell .html; 411 W Island Hwy; r/ste $60/150; P X) are within three blocks of each other and any could serve as the backdrop for your

---

> **CRAZY FOR CAVES**
>
> **Horne Lake Caves Provincial Park** (☎ 250-248-7829; rental $5, adult/child tour from $15/12; ☉ tours 10am-5pm Jul & Aug, weekends May-Sep), Twelve kilometers north of Qualicum Beach off Hwy 19 are some spelunking delights. Of the 1000 caves on the island, the limestone creations here are easily accessible. Two caves are open to the public, or you can take a guided tour of the protected **River-bend Cave**. Tours range from a 90-minute interpretive guide to five-hour excursions for the more experienced. Bring warm clothing, even if it's mild weather; sturdy shoes, even if you have strong ankles; and at least two flashlights, even if you're not scared of the dark.

favorite fun-in-the-sun flick. All have rooms facing the water and yep, you guessed it, floral print bedcovers.

Popular **Rathtrevor Provincial Park** (☎ 250-248-9460, 800-689-9025; www.discovercamping.ca; summer/winter $14/9), 3km south of downtown, has 200 wooded campsites just a short walk from the beach. There are full services including hot showers in summer, none in winter. **Riverbend Resort** (☎ 250-248-3134, 800-701-3033; www.riverbendresort.bc.ca; 1-924 E Island Hwy; tent/RV $16/22) has campsites and your very own cottage with fireplace ($65). **Park Sands Beach RV Resort** (☎ 250-248-3171, 877-873-1600; www.parksands.com; 105 E Island Hwy; tent/RV $16/18) is close to town and the beach.

Eating

Coombs Old Country Market (☎ 250-248-6272; 2326 Alberni Hwy, Coombs; mains $5-8) The goats on the roof are real, as are the locally made jams and jerkeys under it at this spot 8km west of Parksville. Indulge in an ice cream, grab a burger, sandwich or samosa or load up with everything you need for a picnic.

Saigon Garden (☎ 250-548-5667; 118 Craig St; mains $7-9) A hidden gem in Parksville, this place is tucked away but offers good, hot and spicy Vietnamese cuisine with vegetarian options.

The Rod & Gun Cafe (☎ 250-954-1881; 163 Alberni Hwy; mains $7-15) One of Parksville's oldest buildings is still young at heart. This restaurant was established in 1898 and the new outdoor patio and indoor modifications

VANCOUVER ISLAND

haven't detracted from the look and feel of an old-time saloon.

Lefty's (Parksville ☎ 250-954-3886; 101-280 E Island Hwy; Qualicum Beach ☎ 250-752-7530; 710 Memorial Ave; mains $8-14) You'll find little else but fun and casual dining at this place that started out vegetarian but has seen chicken and beef creep into the menu. Funky colors emphasize the 'fresh' ideals they seek in their Left Coast dishes.

Fish Tales Café (☎ 250-752-6053; 3336 E Island Hwy; mains $8-15) Fish and chips are the centerpiece of the menu, but the seafood without chips is delicious. The setting is unbeatable; sit in the Tudor house or admire it from outside on the front lawn.

Getting There & Away

Vancouver Island Coach Lines (☎ 250-318-0818; www.grayline.ca/victoria/schedules/main_schedule.shtml; Victoria $28, Nanaimo $8.40) run buses to both Parksville and Qualicum Beach. **VIA Rail** (☎ 250-842-7245; www.viarail.ca) runs the *E&N Railiner* from Victoria to both Parksville ($28) and Qualicum Beach ($30).

PORT ALBERNI

pop 17,800

The gateway to Vancouver Island's west coast, Port Alberni was built on natural resources, namely fishing and forestry. Since both those industries have been hit hard lately, so too has 'Port'. It's sad to see that it's not the town it once was, but rather than decaying into nothingness, the waterfront and historical attractions have been revitalized to attract visitors.

The **Alberni Valley Visitor Info Centre** (☎ 250-724-6535; www.avcoc.com; 2533 Redford St;

8am-6pm) is a great facility with helpful information on the area. For medical help, go to **West Coast General Hospital** (☎ 250-723-2135; 3841 8th Ave).

Sights & Activities

Lady Rose Marine Services (☎ 250-723-8313, 800-663-7192; www.ladyrosemarine.com; 5425 Argyle St) has day trips down Alberni Inlet on the 100-passenger MV *Lady Rose* or 200-passenger MV *Frances Barkley*.

The working packet freighters make stops en route to deliver mail and supplies, with a 60- to 90-minute layover before returning. This trip is an enjoyable, scenic way to spend a day, as well as a practical means of returning from the West Coast Trail's north end at Bamfield (p156).

The route taken to **Bamfield** ($23; departs 8am Tue & Thu-Sun Jul & Aug) depends on the day and season. There's also a separate run to **Ucluelet** ($25; depart 8am Mon Wed & Fri Jun-Sep) and the Broken Group Islands. Reserve at least a week in advance and bring a sweater or jacket, even if it's warm in Port Alberni.

From October to May, kayakers and canoeists can request stops at the Broken Group Islands. The transplanted office building-turned-**Whaling Station Lodge** (s/d $100/155) at Sechart rents canoes or kayaks ($35).

Keep your eyes gazing at the sky, looking out for the **Martin Mars Water Bombers**, huge cargo planes converted to hold tons of water scooped up from lakes and used to fight forest fires. **Harbour Quay**, at the foot of Argyle St, is a good place to start your Port Alberni visit as it's home to shops and cafés.

NATURE VS NURTURE

Between Parksville and Port Alberni lies **MacMillan Provincial Park** (☎ 250-248-9460) home to Cathedral Grove. You'll know it when you see the dense forest of giant evergreens lining the roads like centuries-old centurions guiding your way – they will not lead you astray, for they are old and wise.

On January 1, 1997, Mother Nature unleashed herself on herself in a moment of self-inflicted fury – perhaps hungover from too much New Years' champagne – and blew a wild storm through the area. Enormous trees were felled and tossed like toothpicks and now lie on the forest floor. Of course, she is also a model of efficiency and the decomposition of these logs provides nutrients for another generation of growth.

Park your car at the wide spot in the road and take self-guided interpretive trails to learn more about the cycles of nature and see the largest tree still standing – 800 years old and 3m in diameter.

DOING DELLA FALLS

At 440m tall, Della Falls is the highest in Canada, and getting there can be a tall task in itself. Though set deep within Strathcona Provincial Park, the 'easiest' way to reach Della is from Port Alberni.

Take Hwy 4 13km west of town to Great Central Lake Rd. You'll then need to cross 35km Great Central Lake; before you begin to don your swim gear, plan on seven to 12 hours in a canoe or consider taking a shuttle (see below) to the trailhead. It's then a 16km, five- to eight-hour, 510m-elevation-gain scramble through the woods and up steep slopes to the falls. Set aside a minimum of two days for the trip (four in you're canoeing) but once you're there – 'Whooooo boy!' prepare to be amazed.

Ark Resort (☎ 250-723-2657; www.arkresort.com; 11000 Great Central Lake Rd, Port Alberni; campsite/r $21.50/65) offers water-taxi service ($90) to the trailhead. The resort also rents boats, canoes and camping gear for Della-bound trekkers.

Alberni Pacific Railway Steam Train (adult/child incl admission to mill $22/5) runs between the restored 1912 mini-museum **Railway Station** and **McLean Mill Historic Site** (☎ 250-723-1376; adult/child $6.50/4.50; ⏲ 10am-5pm mid-Jun–Sep), the only steam-operated sawmill in Canada.

Alberni Valley Museum (☎ 250-723-2181; 4255 Wallace St; admission $3; ⏲ 10am-5pm Tue-Sat, 10-9pm Thu) features impressive exhibits, including beautifully woven goods and a spectacular Chinese paper lion headdress.

The Maritime Discovery Centre (☎ 250-723-6164; Industrial Rd; adult/child $5/3; ⏲ 10am-5pm mid-Jun–Sep) was made from an actual coastal lighthouse and exhibits maritime history.

Sleeping

Somass Motel (☎ 250-724-3236, 800-927-2217; www .somass-motel.ca; 5279 River Rd; r/kitchenette/ste $75/85/ 115; P ☒ ☣) The rooms are nice, bright and comforting in this little motel with a private garden.

Cedar Wood Lodge (☎ 250-724-6800, 877-314-6800; www.cedarwood.bc.ca; 5895 River Rd; s/d $125/135; P ☒) You feel relaxed immediately upon entering this B&B, nestled under the canopy of trees in a garden by the Somass River. The colors are soft, the furnishings are comfortable and the breakfasts are delicious.

Arrowvale Campground (☎ 250-723-7948; 5955 Hector Rd; site $15, cottage 1/2 nights $120/150) Situated on the Somass River, 6km west of Port Alberni, the Arrowvale has showers, swimming, a playground, farm tours and laundry. The two deluxe riverview cottages feature vaulted timber-trussed ceilings, fireplaces and full kitchens.

Stamp River Provincial Park (☎ 250-689-9025; www.discovercamping.ca; site $14) A small wooded campground near a waterfall where salmon migrate in late August lies 14.5km west on Beaver Creek Rd.

Sproat Lake Provincial Park (☎ 250-689-9025; www.discovercamping.ca; site $17) Popular with boaters; the lower campground is on the lake and has showers.

Eating

Blue Door Café (☎ 250-723-8811; 5415 Argyle St; mains $3-8) This hole-in-the-wall opens at 5am and draws an early-morning crowd of fisherfolk; it's a handy spot to grab breakfast before boarding the *Lady Rose*.

Clam Bucket (☎ 250-723-1315; 4479 Victoria Quay; mains $8-14; ⏲ lunch & dinner) Known more for its seafood – try any of the surf 'n' turf – Clam Bucket also makes huge sandwiches and gourmet burgers. Funky oranges and blues provide a casual atmosphere indoors, or eat on the patio with a view of the inlet.

Getting There & Around

Vancouver Island Coach Lines (☎ 250-318-0818; www .grayline.ca/victoria/schedules/main_schedule.shtml; Victoria $33.60, Nanaimo $14) runs a once-daily bus.

AUTHOR'S CHOICE

J & L's (☎ 250-723-6331; 4422 Gertrude St; $3-7) The drive-in has not died. The carhops here don't wear roller-skates or pink mini-skirts, and they don't really like being called carhops either, but you get served cheeseburgers, onion rings and ice cream in your vehicle – vehicle not included. It's fun and one of life's simple pleasures. For the automobile-less, there are picnic tables under the trees.

BAMFIELD
pop 245

Gateway to the West Coast Trail, the Pacific Ocean, and layover spot for the *Lady Rose* (p154), tiny, remote and ever-popular Bamfield lies on both sides of Bamfield Inlet. Bamfield East is your arrival after the 100km drive from Port Alberni and Bamfield West is your boardwalked *Lady Rose* layover. The **Visitor Info Centre** (☎ 250-728-3006; www.bamfieldchamber.com; Grappler Rd; ⊙ 9am-6pm) is in Bamfield East.

Brady's Beach Trail in Bamfield West is a good short stroll. **Broken Island Adventures** (☎ 250-728-3500, 888-728-6200) specializes in scuba throughout Barkley Sound.

West Coast Trail Express (☎ 250-477-8700; www.trailbus.com; $55; ⊙ May 1-Sep 30) shuttles to Bamfield from Victoria and Nanaimo.

Sleeping & Eating
Bamfield Trails Motel (☎ 250-728-3231; fax 250-728-3215; bamotel@port.island.net; r/kitchenette $99/129; P ✗) Near the dock at Bamfield East, it's popular with West Coast Trail hikers and Pacific Ocean salmon fishers. There are several room options to accommodate groups of all sizes. The adjacent **Hawk's Nest Pub** (mains $7-10) is where Bamfield relaxes – or gets more riled-up.

Marie's Bed & Breakfast (☎ 250-728-3091; fax 250-728-2000; 468 Pachena Rd; s/d $50/80) Marie has rooms in her wooden house up the hill. The rooms face west so the views are amazing.

Bamfield Lodge and Cottages (☎ 250-728-3419; cottage/house $100/250; ✗) This place on the boardwalk at Bamfield West has appealing wood-paneled cottages that sleep up to four. For caffeine and hickory simultaneously there's an espresso bar in the lodge and a barbecue pit outside.

The First Nations-run **Pachena Bay Campground** (☎ 250-728-1287; sites $15), 3km east on Port Alberni Rd, features a splendid setting and, more importantly, has showers.

PACIFIC RIM NATIONAL PARK RESERVE
With rainforests of huge cedar and fir trees and tremendous waves rolling in from across the ocean, **Pacific Rim National Park Reserve** (☎ 250-726-7721; pacrim.info@pc.gc.ca) has become one of BC's top attractions. The 50,000-hectare park includes three units: the Long Beach area between Tofino and Ucluelet, the Broken Group Islands in Barkley Sound and the famous West Coast Trail.

For casual visits to the Long Beach Unit, you won't need anything beyond the map in this book and perhaps a stop at the park information centre on Hwy 4 just inside the southern boundary. You don't have to pay to drive through, but parking fees (day/annual $10/45) must be paid at the Wickaninnish Centre or at parking lots.

For trips to the **Broken Group Islands** or the **West Coast Trail**, get detailed information from **Parks Canada** (☎ 250-726-7721; parkscanada .pch.gc.ca/pn-np/bc/pacificrim).

Long Beach Unit
Easily accessed by Hwy 4, the Long Beach Unit attracts the largest number of visitors in the park. Stop at the interpretive exhibits on the park's cultural and natural history at **Wickaninnish Centre** (⊙ 9am-6pm mid-Mar–mid-Oct), named for a chief of the Nuu-chah-nulth tribe, who have lived in the Long Beach area for centuries. Then try one or more of the trails ranging from 100m to 5km:

Bog Trail (800m) Loop around a moss-layered bog.
Long Beach Easy walking at low tide and great scenery along the sandy shore.
Radar Hill (100m) Climb to a former World War II installation.
Rainforest Trail (1km) Two interpretive loops through old-growth forest.
Schooner Cove (2km) Through old- and second-growth forests with beach access.
Spruce Fringe (1.5km) Loop trail featuring hardy Sitka spruce trees.
South Beach (1km) Through forest to a pebble beach.
Wickaninnish Trail (5km) Shoreline and forest trail.

The usual safety precautions apply here: tread carefully over slippery rocks and roots and in the water never turn your back on the surf. Avoid swimming near rocks or in areas where water currents seem to push you offshore.

SLEEPING & EATING
Green Point Campground (☎ 250-689-9025; sites drive-in/walk-in $20/14) This campground on Hwy 4 is the only park-run site. The 94 drive-in sites can be reserved three months ahead; it's first-come, first-served for the 20 walk-in sites. Another camping option within the park is the privately-run **Long Beach Golf Course Campground** (☎ 250-725-3332; site $25) near Grice Bay.

PACIFIC RIM NATIONAL PARK RESERVE – LONG BEACH UNIT

INFORMATION
Pacific Rim Information Centre....**1** D4
Tofino Visitor Info Centre............**2** B2
Warden Office...........................**3** C3
Wickaninnish Centre..................**4** C4

SIGHTS & ACTIVITIES   (pp159; 160)
Live to Surf...............................(see 5)
Surf Sister.................................**5** A2
Tofino Botanical Gardens...........**6** A1

SLEEPING   (pp156; 161)
Bella Pacifica Resort &
 Campground.........................**7** A1
Crystal Cove Beach Resort..........**8** A2
Green Point Campground............**9** C3
Long Beach Golf Course
 Campground.......................**10** B2

EATING   (p162)
Beaches.....................................(see 5)
So Bo..(see 5)

VANCOUVER ISLAND

Wickaninnish Centre Restaurant (☎ 250-726-7706; mains $10-15; ⓥ 11am-10pm Mar-Oct) Enjoy superb dining on fresh and delicious local seafood while overlooking the crashing surf of Long Beach. This place is also a good place to go for a cup of coffee and dessert for the view alone.

GETTING THERE & AWAY
Vancouver Island Coach Lines (☎ 250-318-0818; www
.grayline.ca/victoria/schedules/main_schedule.shtml; Victoria $53.20, Nanaimo $33.60) runs a once-daily bus.

Broken Group Islands
Broken Group includes about 100 islands scattered about the entrance to Barkley Sound. **Broken Island Adventures** (☎ 250-728-3500,

888-728-6200; broken@island.net; Sechart/ Bamfield $38/85) runs sightseeing trips which include lunch.

The Broken Group is an increasingly popular kayaking destination, but visitors must be experienced or sign on with a guided trip. **Eco West Adventures** (☎ 250-748-0511, 888-326-9378; 5-day $700) and **Wildheart Adventures** (☎ 250-722-3683, 877-722-3683; www.kayak bc.com; 4-day $649) lead tours.

Kayakers should travel in groups of three or more and thoroughly read Parks Canada's information sheets on potential hazards. Don't go beyond your limits; know how to use a compass, plot a chart, and navigate in the fog. Canadian Hydrographic Service marine charts 3670 and 3671 are essential, they're available at marine shops or **Nautical Data International, Inc** (☎ 250-563-0634; www.digitalocean.ca; $20).

Designated primitive camping areas ($8 per site) are located on eight islands: Hand, Turret, Gibraltar, Willis, Dodd, Clarks, Benson and Gilbert. The maximum stay in Broken Group is 14 nights and no more than four nights at the same site. The camp-sites have solar composting toilets, but you must pack out your garbage.

GETTING THERE & AWAY
Toquart Bay is the principal launching spot, accessed via 16km of gravel logging road off Hwy 4, 12km northeast of the Pacific Rim Hwy junction. There's a BC Forest Service campsite at the launch.

Lady Rose Marine Services (☎ 250-723-8313, 800-663-7192; www.ladyrosemarine.com; 5425 Argyle St, Port Alberni; $12-35) runs a water taxi from Sechart and Toquart Bay to several of the Broken Group Islands in addition to its services to Sechart.

West Coast Trail
The third and most southerly section of the park contains the 75km West Coast Trail, one of Canada's best-known and toughest hiking routes. There are two things you need to know before you think about completing this hike: you'll break you back (or your butt) completing it; and once won't be enough. It's a magnificent natural stage that never puts on the same show twice; people who have done it five or more times still aren't through with it yet.

Originally constructed as an escape route for shipwreck survivors, the trail runs between **Pachena Bay** (☎ 250-728-3234), near Bamfield on the north end, and **Gordon River** (☎ 250-647-5434), near Port Renfrew on the south. Hikers must be able to manage rough terrain, rock-face ladders, stream crossings and adverse weather conditions. Plan on six to eight days to hike the entire route.

Overnight hikers must have a permit. Reservations are through **Super Natural British Columbia Reservation Service** (☎ 250-387-1642, 604-663-6000, 800-663-6000; reservation $25, permit $90) and only 52 people can begin the hike per day, 26 in each direction. You can begin to reserve spots on the first day of the month, two months prior to your desired

departure date. Sign up as early as 3:30pm the day before your hike but call ahead if you'll be later than 1pm on hike-day

Permits also are available through a waiting-list system; five of each day's 26 available spaces are set aside at 1pm to be used on a first-come, first-served basis at each trailhead. If you win this lottery you can begin hiking that day, but keep in mind hikers might wait three days to get a permit this way.

Overnight hikers must attend a one-hour **orientation session** (⏱ 9:30am, 1:30pm, 3:30pm, also noon at Gordon River) before hiking. Fees for both ferries ($28) along the trail are payable at the registration centre.

Pack reliable gear and break in your boots before you start. Practice low-impact, pack-in, pack-out camping. On the trail, be prepared to carry – and read – tide tables; treat or boil all water; and cook on a lightweight backpackers' stove. Filling, nutritious and low-odor foods are ideal. Hikers can camp at any of the designated sites along the route, most of which have solar-composting outhouses. Theoretically, supplies are unattainable on the trail, though soda, beer and food are sometimes available at the Nitinat Narrows Ferry and the store just south of the Carmanah Lighthouse.

Some people do a day hike or hike half the trail from Pachena Bay, considered the easier end of the route. Overnight hikers who only hike this end of the trail can leave from Nitinat Lake. Day hikers are allowed on the trail from each end, but need a free day-use permit available from the registration centres. Permits are not issued to children six and under.

GETTING THERE & AWAY
See Bamfield (p156) and Port Renfrew (p144).

TOFINO & AROUND
At the north terminus of Hwy 4, Tofino (pop 1450) is definitely not a dead-end town. Activity-packed and ecologically-friendly, it's on Vancouver Island's west coast in a setting both serene and spectacular. It sits on Clayoquot (clay-kwot) Sound where forested mounds rise from the water and crescent beaches greet well-traveled waves in front of a mountainous backdrop. It's also a top place to go for moving scenery: whales, sea lions and other

GOING GREEN

A major center for environmental activism, Tofino is home to **Friends of Clayoquot Sound** (☎ 250-725-4218; www.ancientrainforest.org; 331 Neill St), a grassroots organization working to defend rainforests and marine ecosystems in Clayoquot Sound and Vancouver Island's West Coast. Efforts to curb indiscriminate logging haven't been in vain; 10 years after massive protests in Clayo-quot, major forestry companies' logging rates in the area have dropped almost 80%. The group also concerns itself with salmon farming and these operations' practices in regards to sewage, antibiotics use and other impacts on Clayoquot's fragile ecosystem. For more information, write to Box 489, Tofino, BC V0R 2Z0.

The **Raincoast Interpretive Centre** (☎ 250-725-2560; www.tofinores.com; 451 Main St; ☺ noon-5pm Wed-Sun summer) is a project of The Raincoast Education Society, part of a growing international network to explore sustainable forest management. Visit the centre to learn about the Clayoquot Sound and its ecosystems.

Planned for an October 2004 opening, **Cedar Corner** (cnr Fourth & Cambie Sts; www.cedarcorner.com, www.tofinobrewhouse.com) has a story. It started with an abandoned lot, an organic grocery store that needed a home, a moderately successful and ecologically aware businessman and a timber-salvager. James Rodgers got the wood (originally milled in 1881) from the timber-salvager, and the 9000-sq-ft project was started with a focus on creating minimal environmental impact. It will be built from 100% recycled timber and be home to the grocery store and Tofino Brewhouse.

maritime creatures are often found in the surrounding waters.

Tofino is 122km west of Port Alberni via the winding Hwy 4. Make the drive in the daytime, both for safety's sake and for the pleasure of enjoying the scenery.

Information

The **Visitor Info Centre** (☎ 250-725-3414; www .island.net/~tofino; 1426 Pacific Rim Hwy; ☺ 10am-6pm May-Sep) is 6km south of town and has detailed listings and photos of area accom-modations, although finding last-minute places can be difficult. The staff can help you with the hot surf spots or recommend some good hikes. Pick up a copy of the local newspaper *Tofino Time* and the help-ful *Long Beach Maps* brochure.

The main **post office** (☎ 250-267-1177; 161 First St) is half a block north of the **Tofino Hospital** (☎ 250-725-3204; 261 Neill St). **Long Beach Laundry** (☎ 250-725-4252; 448 Campbell St) has pay showers.

Sights

A lot of Tofino's sights are north of Tofino, in Clayoquot Sound; see Tours (p161) on how to reach them.

HOT SPRINGS COVE

One of the more sought-out day-trips from Tofino, **Hot Springs Cove** is the central attraction for **Maquinna Provincial Marine Park**, 37km north of Tofino. Sojourners travel by Zodiac boat or seaplane, watching for whales and other sea critters en route. From the boat landing, 2km of boardwalks lead to a series of natural hot pools that rejuvenate the soul.

MEARES ISLAND

Visible from Tofino, Meares Island is home to the **Big Tree Trail**, a 400m-board-walk through old-growth forest, including a 1500-year-old red cedar. The island was the site of the key 1984 anti-logging protest that kicked off the modern environmental movement in Clayoquot Sound.

AHOUSAT

Located on remote Flores Island, Ahou-sat is home to the spectacular **Wild Side Heritage Trail**, a moderately difficult path that traverses 10km of forests, beaches and headlands between Ahousat and Cow Bay.

TOFINO BOTANICAL GARDENS

Cleverly and artistically laid out – even borderline abstract – these **gardens** (☎ 250-725-1237; www.tofinobotanicalgardens.com; 1084 Pacific Rim Hwy; 3-day pass adult/child $10/2, $1 less without vehicle; ☺ 8am-dusk) display the unique plants of Clayoquot Sound and other rainforests

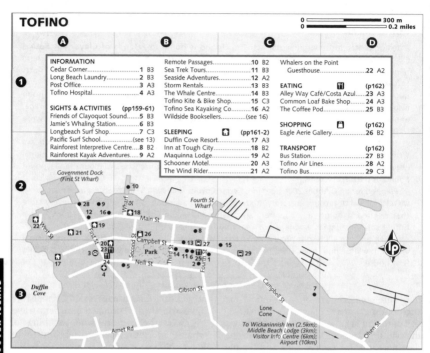

TOFINO

0 ——— 300 m
0 ——— 0.2 miles

INFORMATION
Cedar Corner...........................1 B3
Long Beach Laundry.................2 B3
Post Office................................3 A3
Tofino Hospital........................4 A3

SIGHTS & ACTIVITIES (pp159-61)
Friends of Clayoquot Sound......5 B3
Jamie's Whaling Station............6 B3
Longbeach Surf Shop................7 C3
Pacific Surf School.............(see 13)
Rainforest Interpretive Centre...8 B2
Rainforest Kayak Adventures....9 A2

Remote Passages.....................10 B2
Sea Trek Tours........................11 B3
Seaside Adventures.................12 A2
Storm Rentals.........................13 B3
The Whale Centre....................14 B3
Tofino Kite & Bike Shop...........15 C3
Tofino Sea Kayaking Co...........16 A2
Wildside Booksellers............(see 16)

SLEEPING (pp161-2)
Duffin Cove Resort..................17 A3
Inn at Tough City....................18 B2
Maquinna Lodge.....................19 A2
Schooner Motel.......................20 A3
The Wind Rider.......................21 A2

Whalers on the Point
Guesthouse.........................22 A2

EATING (p162)
Alley Way Café/Casta Azul......23 A3
Common Loaf Bake Shop.........24 A3
The Coffee Pod.......................25 B3

SHOPPING (p162)
Eagle Aerie Gallery.................26 B2

TRANSPORT (p162)
Bus Station.............................27 B3
Tofino Air Lines......................28 A2
Tofino Bus.............................29 C3

---

from around the world. Kids will enjoy the playground and grown-ups will enjoy the tree house and several themed gardens and bird-watching blinds.

Activities

KAYAKING

Rainforest Kayak Adventures (☎ 250-725-3117, 877-422-9453; 316 Main St; from $615) Specializes in four- to six-day guided tours and courses for beginners and intermediates.

Tla-ook (☎ 250-725-2656; www.tlaook.com; trips 2/4/6 hrs $44/58/140) Learn about First Nations culture while paddling an authentic dugout canoe.

Tofino Sea Kayaking Co (☎ 250-725-3330; www.tofino-kayaking.com; 320 Main St; day-/half-day $48/35) Paddles to Meares Island, offers lessons and rentals; home to Wildside Booksellers.

SURFING

With nothing between Japan and Vancouver Island's west coast to slow waves down, the sandy beaches south of Tofino make excellent surf spots.

Nearby surf shops include:
Longbeach Surf Shop (☎ 250-725-3800; 630 Pacific

Rim Hwy; board/wetsuit 24hrs $20/20) A no-nonsense shop that gets you in, out and on the water fast.

Live to Surf (☎ 250-725-4464; www.livetosurf.com; 1180 Pacific Rim Hwy; $25/20) Tofino's first surf shop; useful website.

Pacific Surf School (☎ 250-725-2155, 888-777-9961; www.pacificsurfschool.com; 440 Campbell St; 3-hour $79)

Storm Rentals (☎ 250-725-3344; www.stormsurf shop.com; 444 Campbell St; $20/20)

Surf Sister (☎ 250-725-4456, 877-724-7873; www.surfsister.com; 1180 Pacific Rim Hwy) All-female surf school offers daily lessons ($75) to boys and girls but no dudes allowed in multiple-day courses (from $195).

WHALE-WATCHING

Whale-sightings can happen on any trip to Hot Springs Cove or Flores Island, or even from shore in Tofino, but there are trips devoted to their pursuit. Whales migrate through the area from March to May, though many linger through summer.

Recommended outfitters include the following:

The Whale Centre (☎ 250-725-2132; 411 Campbell St; $60) Headquarters has a small museum displaying gray whale skeletal pieces.

Jamie's Whaling Station (☎ 250- 725-3919, 800-667-9913; www.jamies.com; 606 Campbell St; adult/child $65/50)

Remote Passages (☎ 250-725-3330, 800-666-9833; www.remotepassages.com; adult/child $64/49)

STORM-WATCHING

From mid-October through March, Tofino has a front-row seat to the most spectacular storms on the North American West Coast. Many visitors are content to watch the pounding surf from their hotel rooms, but **Long Beach Nature Tours** (☎ 250-726-7099; half-day $160) offers guided hikes to spots where it is safe to watch the spectacle.

Tours

Rainforest Boatshuttle (☎ 250-725-3793; $20) One- or two-hour trip to Meares Island and hike the trail.

Remote Passages (☎ 250-725-3330, 800-666-9833; 71 Wharf St; adult/child $99/69) Seven-hour Hot Springs tours; guides are well versed in natural history of Clayoquot Sound.

Sea Trek Tours (☎ 250-725-4412, 800-811-9155; www.seatrektours.bc.ca; 411B Campbell St; adult/child $25/5) Operates 90-minute trips in a glass-bottom boat.

Tofino Air Lines (☎ 250-725-4454, 866-486-3247; 3/6 people $369/534) Scenic tours over beautiful Clayoquot Sound.

Walk the Wild Side (☎ 250-670-9586, 888-670-9586; adult/child $75/25) Guided hikes of Ahousat.

Sleeping

Tofino's ever-increasing popularity means you'll want to book way ahead. Most accommodations offer package deals with area activities so ask when you're making inquiries.

MOTELS & RESORTS

Duffin Cove Resort (☎ 250-725-2448, 888-629-2903; www.duffin-cove-resort.com; 215 Campbell St; r/ste/cabin $190/245/245; P ✖) Deeply wooded and secluded cabins and suites are perched on the hills above Tofino's western shoreline. Fall asleep in front of the fire to the sound of rhythmic crashes of waves on the shore.

Inn at Tough City (☎ 250-725-2021; 877-725-2021; www.toughcity.com; 350 Main St; r $140-175; ✖) Taking a page from *The Three Little Pigs*, this house was made out of brick. The courtyard, wrap-around deck and rustic furnishings combine country-ambience with waterfront location.

The InnChanter (☎ 250-670-1149; www.innchanter .com; r $98-110) A heritage vessel moored near Hot Springs Cove has been restored and refitted to include sleeping cabins. There's no surly captain here – instead this makes for a memorable stay. Rates included breakfast and dinner.

Middle Beach Lodge (☎ 250-725-2900; www .middlebeach.com; Mackenzie Beach; r/ste/cabin from $105/215/225; P ✖) The forested grounds on this beach-site south of town are more reminiscent of a lodge than a resort, giving a greater feeling of seclusion. Room types range from adults-only 'At-the-Beach' to the family-oriented 'At-the-Headlands', and luxury and charm don't take a back seat in any of them.

Wickaninnish Inn (☎ 250-725-3100, 800-333-4604; www.wickinn.com; Chesterman Beach; r without/with $280-620; P ✖) Embodies nature with recycled old-growth furniture, natural stone tiles and the atmosphere of a place grown rather than constructed. Guest rooms feature push-button gas fireplaces, two-person hot tubs and private balconies.

Your basic motel options in town are **Schooner Motel** (☎ 250-725-3478; www.schooner motel.net; 315-321 Campbell St; r/kitchenette $95/125), where the 2nd floor has better views of the bay, and **Maquinna Lodge** (☎ 250-725-3261, 800-665-3199; fax 250-725-3433; 120 First St; r without/with view $120/130) which sits on the hill above the docks.

HOSTELS

Whalers on the Point Guesthouse (☎ 250-725-3443; www.tofinohostel.com; 81 West St; dm/r $26/75; P ✖) Built specifically as a hostel in 1999, this HI affiliate is the Cadillac of hostels. It has a secluded waterfront location with huge windows and bright and airy common rooms, but with all the commotion and camaraderie you expect in a hostel.

The Wind Rider (☎ 250-725-3240, 877-725-3240; www.windrider.org; 231 Main St; r shared/private $25/60) A nonprofit, women-only retreat house best suited to groups of women traveling together, although individual backpackers are welcome. Kitchen facilities and linen are provided, and there's a Jacuzzi on the deck.

CAMPING

Bella Pacifica Resort & Campground (☎ 250-725-3400; tent/RV $28/41) is 3km south of Tofino on Pacific Rim Hwy. **Crystal Cove Beach Resort**

VANCOUVER ISLAND

(☎ 250-725-4213; 1165 Cedarwood Place; tent/RV/cottage $37/47/220) also rents log cottages.

Eating

For self-catering, **Beaches** (☎ 250-725-2270; 1184 Pacific Rim Hwy) is a grocer with a good range of organic products.

So Bo (☎ 250-725-2341; 1180 Pacific Rim Hwy; lunch $4-5; ⏱ closed Tue) This isn't your typical roach-coach. Locally renowned chefs Lisa and Aaron prepare and serve gourmet salads, soups and tacos in their construction-site-lunch-wagon behind Beaches Grocery. Lisa's daily creations are varying specials and the fish tacos are phenomenal.

The Coffee Pod (☎ 250-725-4246; 151 Fourth St; mains $4-7; ⏱ breakfast & lunch) The huge deck outside is always full of locals, especially in the morning, so you can eavesdrop – or ask – to find out where the hot surf/dive/fishing spots are that day. Coffees, pastries and a good selection of full breakfasts – the Pod Burrito is a particular favorite – are all on the menu.

Alley Way Café/Costa Azul (☎ 250-725-3105; behind 305 Campbell St; mains $8-10) This schizophrenic eatery, tucked behind the intersection of First and Campbell Sts, serves all-day breakfasts, vegetarian and non-vegetarian lunches by day, and Mexican dinners by night. It's a colorful spot in a garden-like setting with a very, very casual vibe.

Common Loaf Bake Shop (☎ 250-725-3915; 180 First St) A low-key local gathering spot with a tree-house-like 2nd-floor atrium and tasty home-made muffins, cookies, smoothies and sandwiches.

Pointe Restaurant (☎ 250-725-3100; Wickaninnish Inn; lunch $10-20, dinner $25-40, prix-fixe veggie/non-veggie $70/50) The wrap-around windows in this restaurant on the cliff look out over the Pacific surf. Reservations are essential for dinner because the Smoked Albacore is that good.

Shopping

The longhouse-style **Eagle Aerie Gallery** ☎ 250-725-3235; 350 Campbell St) displays work by noted artist Roy Henry Vickers, who lived in Tofino for many years.

Beside Surf Sister surf school (p160), **Keith Plumbley** works in his shack and sells his wood-carvings and burls-turned-bowls worldwide.

Getting There & Around

Tofino airport (☎ 250-725-2006) is south of town off the Pacific Rim Hwy. **Canadian Western Airline** (☎ 250-866-835-9292) and **North Vancouver Air** (☎ 250-228-6608) fly to Vancouver year-round. **Northwest Seaplanes** (☎ 250-690-0086) runs scheduled high-season floatplane services between the Seattle, Washington area and Tofino.

Vancouver Island Coach Lines (☎ 250-318-0818; www.grayline.ca/victoria/schedules/main_schedule.shtml; Victoria/Nanaimo $53.20/33.60) runs a once-daily bus.

Tofino Bus (☎ 250-725-2871, 866-986-3466; www.tofinobus.com; 564 Campbell St) also runs to Nanaimo ($32.71, 8:15am & 2:50pm in summer) and Victoria ($50).

Long Beach Link (☎ 250-726-7779, 877-954-3556; one-way/roundtrip $9/12) shuttles passengers between Tofino and Ucluelet with stops at the Tofino airport and within Pacific Rim National Park (Long Beach, Greenpoint and Wickaninnish Centre). See schedules posted locally.

For taxis, call **Tofino Taxi** (☎ 250-725-3333). **Tofino Kite & Bike Shop** (☎ 250-725-1221; 441A Campbell St) rents and repairs bicycles. Water taxis to take you up the sound can be flagged down at the government dock; there's also a **seabus** ($12; ⏱ 10:30am-4pm) to Ahousat.

UCLUELET

pop 1550

Ucluelet (yew-klew-let) has long been unfairly pegged as Tofino's ugly and less-charming sibling. While Ucluelet may be less popular and seen as a little more rugged, it shares the same scenery and the same activities, and is generally cheaper and more accessible. Besides, nature is, by definition, naturally beautiful and rugged at the same time, so if you've come to explore the Island's west coast, Ucluelet allows you to do that without fighting crowds.

The **Visitor Info Centre** (☎ 250-726-4641; 100 Main St; ⏱ 9am-5pm) is near the government wharf.

The tide pools, seashells and kelp beds make **Big Beach** a great spot to discover and to make you wonder what else is out there. The 8.5km **Wild Pacific Trail** winds through rainforests and along the wild coastline with views of the Broken Islands and Barkley Sound, or nothing but the Pacific Ocean as far as the eye can see.

Subtidal Adventures (☎ 250-726-7336; www.sub tidaladventures.com; 1950 Peninsula Rd adult/child $65/45) and **Canadian Princess Resort** (☎ 250-726-7771, 800-663-7090; fax 250-598-1361; www.canadian princess.com; 1948 Peninsula Rd; adult/child $39/25) offer whale-watching trips. **Majestic Ocean Kayaking** (☎ 250-726-2868; www.majestic.bc.ca; 1786 Peninsula Rd; half-day/day $55/105) leads sea-kayaking trips. **Pristine Adventures** (☎ 250-726-4477; www.alberni.net/pristine; from $125) offers guided canoeing and black bear-watching trips.

Inner Rhythm Surf Camp (☎ 250-726-2211; www.innerrhythm.net; 2490 Pacific Rim Hwy; from $69) teaches posers how to surf.

Sleeping

Thornton Motel (☎ 250-726-7725; www.thornton motel.com; 1861 Peninsula Rd; s/kitchenette/ste $89/104/165) The rooms are spacious and the suites have two bedrooms which are great for families.

Canadian Princess Resort (☎ 250-726-7771, 800-663-7090; fax 598-1361; www.canadianprincess.com; 1948 Peninsula Rd; stateroom s/d $105/115, r/ste $180/200; P ⊠) Tiny but cool, share-everything staterooms are on a survey ship moored in Ucluelet Harbour, also the site of the resort's restaurant (mains $7 to $10) and bar. Landlubbers can go for bright, comfortable rooms or suites in the lodge. This hotel has great 'fish and stay' packages.

A Snug Harbour Inn (☎ 250-726-2686, 888-936-5222; www.awesomeview.com; 460 Marine Dr; r $230-310) This is an upscale and romantic waterfront inn with an outdoor hot tub on the cliffs above the ocean. All six of the rooms are nice; The Valhalla ($230) has a nautical theme to complement the amazing views

Ucluelet Campground (☎ 250-726-4355; 260 Sea-plane Base Rd; tent/RV $26.75/32.10) has hot showers and flush toilets.

Eating

Gray Whale Ice Cream & Delicatessen (☎ 250-726-2113; 1950 Peninsula Rd; mains $5-8) Sandwiches, salads, pastries and everything you'd expect from a deli is here. They also do a fisher-men's picnic, available for pick-up as early as 5.30am. Of course, they've also got ice cream, but not gray-whale flavored.

Blueberries Café (☎ 250-726-7707; 1627D Penin-sula Rd; mains $7-15) Crab cakes with curried raisin mayo and dill linguine? It's actually

pretty good. This unassuming little café is known for good breakfasts, and is also a popular spot for innovative lunches and dinners.

Matterson Restaurant (☎ 250-726-6600; 1682 Peninsula Rd; mains $6-15) This farmhouse-turned-restaurant features a refined country atmos-phere with lace curtains and home-baked goods. Breakfasts include build-your-own omelets.

Getting There & Away

Vancouver Island Coach Lines (☎ 250-318-0818; www.grayline.ca/victoria/schedules/main_schedule.shtml; Victoria/Nanaimo $30.80/50.40) runs a once-daily bus.

DENMAN & HORNBY ISLANDS

Both Denman and Hornby have light-hearted and welcoming atmospheres with artistic offerings and plenty of out-door activities. These are acoustic-guitar-around-the-campfire, take-it-easy type places. Both islands publish annual map brochures, available at area info centres, or on the ferry (see below); visit www.denman island.com and www.hornbyisland.com for more information.

Denman has three provincial parks: **Fil-longley**, with easy hiking and beachcomb-ing; **Boyle Point**, with a beautiful walk to the lighthouse; and **Sandy Island**, only accessible by water from Denman's northern tip. Of Hornby's provincial parks, **Tribune Bay** fea-tures a long sandy beach with safe swim-ming, while **Helliwell** offers notable hiking. **Ford's Cove**, on Hornby's south coast offers the chance for divers to swim with six-gill sharks.

For kayaking rentals, contact **Denman Island Sea Kayaks** (☎ 250-335-2505; 1536 North-west Rd). **Hornby Ocean Kayaks** (☎ 250-335-2726; hikayak@telus.net) will come to where you are.

Sleeping & Eating
DENMAN ISLAND

Ships Point Inn (☎ 250-335-1004, 877-742-1004; www.shipspointinn.com; 7584 Ships Point Rd; $125-175) On Fanny Bay, this seaside home occupies a happy place between forest and ocean. But the beauty doesn't stop there – the six rooms and common areas are colorfully and tastefully decorated.

Denman Island Guest House (☎ 250-335-2688; 3806 Denman Rd; dm/s/d $20/40/50) Up the hill and on the left from the ferry landing, is this 1912 farmhouse, a combination hostel/ B&B. The rate drops to $15 for the third night of a stay. You can rent bikes, including one with a kid-trailer.

Denman Island Bakery & Pizza (☎ 250-335-1310; Northwest Rd; mains $7-11; ☾ closed Sun) This little café in the village is the local hangout. Try one of their excellent slices of pizza or talk to some of the local artists over a cuppa and a muffin.

Camp at **Fillongley Provincial Park** (☎ 250-689-9025; www.discovercamping.ca; $17).

HORNBY ISLAND

There are some terrific options on Hornby.

Breatheasy Vacations (☎ 250-335-2944; 6580 Central Rd; bunk/cottage $50/125) This unique resort is aimed at adults who enjoy camping but hate the hassles. Five weatherproof cedar 'bunkies' with two twin beds share an outdoor kitchen, privy, shower facilities and a glassed-in guest pavilion with an ocean view. Guests need to bring their own bedding and food. Private cottages are also available.

Sea Breeze Lodge (☎ 250-335-2321; www.sea breezelodge.com; adult/child $172/61) At Tralee Point, this 12-acre resort features cottages overlooking the ocean. It's got the feel of a Spanish villa with a Pacific Rim twist, and few things are more peaceful than sitting on the patio or in the hot tub with the sea breeze in your face.

Wheelhouse Restaurant (☎ 250-335-0136; mains $6-12) Near the ferry, this place has its boardwalk patio on ground level, among gardens and hanging baskets, with no need for annoying railings to get in the way of the incredible view. Summer evenings feature a barbecue buffet and the ambience is super-casual.

Camp on Hornby at **Ford's Cove** (☎ 250-335-2169; Ford's Cove; tent/RV $14/22).

Getting There & Away

BC Ferries (☎ 250-223-3779; www.bcferries.com; adult/ child $5/2.50, car $12.25; ☾ 7am-11pm) makes 17 sailings from Buckley Bay terminal, 75km north of Nanaimo, to Denman and 12 trips from the other side of Denman to Hornby (departs 7:45am to 6:35pm Sunday to Thursday and Saturday, 7:45am to 10:35pm Friday). No boats run between 8am and 9am Sundays.

COMOX VALLEY

Comox, Courtenay and tiny Cumberland make up the Comox Valley. Mt Washington, 32km west of Courtenay, and Strathcona Provincial Park make fun day-trips, or spend an afternoon or two traipsing around the harbors and town.

The **Visitor Info Centre** (☎ 250-334-3234, 888-357-4471; www.comox-valley-tourism.ca; 2040 Cliffe Ave; ☾ 9am-6pm) is in Courtenay and distributes information on the surrounding area. Courtenay is also home to the main **post office** (☎ 250-334-4341; 333 Hunt Pl), **Joe Read's Bookstore & Internet Café** (☎ 250-334-9723; 2760 Cliffe Ave) and **Courtenay Centre Home Style Laundry** (☎ 250-334-0875; 4-2401 Cliffe Ave).

Sights & Activities

Mt Washington Alpine Resort (☎ 250-338-1386; www.mt washington.bc.ca; adult/child lift ticket $44/23, tubing $15) is known as the place to ski on Vancouver Island. This resort features 50 alpine ski runs, a snowboard park, cross-country and snow-shoe trails as well as a snow-tubing park.

Mt Washington stays open year-round and summer activities (lift ticket adult/ child/bike $10/8/15) include **horseback riding**, **fly-fishing**, **hiking** and **mountain-biking**. For an easy, rewarding hike into adjacent Strathcona Provincial Park (p168), take the 2.2km **Paradise Meadows Loop Trail** from the Nordic ski area parking lot. Lodging (☎ 888-231-1499) restaurants and cafés are open year-round on the mountain.

Courtenay & District Museum (☎ 250-334-0686; www.courtenaymuseum.ca; 207 4th St; $3; ☾ 10am-5pm daily May-Sep, Tue-Sat Oct-Apr) in Courtenay is best known for its life-size replica of an elasmosaur, a prehistoric marine reptile first discovered in this area. You can also hunt for your very own fossils on their **palaeontology tours** (adult/child $20/12.50; ☾ 9am-noon & 1-4pm daily Jul & Aug, weekends Apr-Jun).

Comox Air Force Museum (☎ 250-339-8162; 19 Wing Comox; ☾ 10am-4pm) is jam-packed with exhibits from Canada's aviation history and is an excellent find for enthusiasts and casual fans of air history.

Miracle Beach Provincial Park (☎ 250-755-2483), 22km north of Courtenay, contains hiking trails and sandy beaches. For scuba diving, contact **Pacific Pro Dive & Watersports** (☎ 250-338-6829; 2270 Cliffe Ave) in Courtenay, a full-service shop with trips, tours, lessons and gear.

Sleeping

River Heights Motel (☎ 250-338-8932; 1820 Cliffe Ave; s/d/ste $60/70/82; **P** ☒ ☒) In Courtenay, this motel on the river plays a little game and leaves the guidebook writer guessing if the bedcovers will be white, green or violet; otherwise, the rooms are all similar. The suites share a huge outside deck and there are discounts for extended stays.

Mt Washington Guest House (☎ 250-898-8141; www.mtwashingtonguesthouse.com; 1203 Fosters Pl; dm/r $22/60) This chalet-turned-hostel with six rooms and four bathrooms has nature right outside the door.

Courtenay Riverside Hostel (☎ 250-334-1938; wandstar@yahoo.com; 1380 Cliffe Ave; dm/r $16/35) It's in a good location close to parks and downtown; ask about free pick-up service from the Powell River ferry and discount ski packages for Mt Washington.

Comox Lake Hostel (☎ 250-338-1914; comoxlakehostel@telus.net; 4787 Lake Trail Rd; camping/dm $10/17; ☒) A homey place, 6km west of Courtenay, makes a fine rural retreat. You can literally hike into Strathcona Provincial Park, or take one of the shorter walks to the Puntledge River, waterfalls and swimming holes.

Riding Fool (☎ 250-313-3665; 2705 Dunsmuir St; dm/r $18/45; ☒) This funky hostel in Cumberland, with hardwood floors, central kitchen with stone countertops, and open common rooms also has places to store your boards and bikes.

Eating

The Atlas Café (☎ 250-338-9838; 250 6th St; mains $10-13) In Courtenay, the hip yellow and orange restaurant has a varied international menu specializing in Italian and Mediterranean dishes; it also has some Mexican plates as well as vegetarian options.

Thai Village Restaurant (☎ 250-334-3812; 2104 Cliffe Ave; mains $10-15; ☽ dinner Tue-Sun) In Courtenay, this place makes good authentic pads. Local ingredients and seafood are combined with traditional Thai flavors to make dishes that aren't too spicy.

Black Fin Pub (☎ 250-339-5030; 132 Port Augusta St; mains $8-12) In Comox, this is a semiformal place with a great view of the harbor and the hills behind it. **Edge Marine Pub** (☎ 250-339-6151; 1805 Beaufort Ave; mains $7-11) is a more casual spot right on the wharf on the other side of the marina.

Getting There & Around

Comox Valley Regional Airport (☎ 250-897-3123) services **West Jet** (☎ 250-937-8538; www.westjet.com) flights to Calgary and **Pacific Coastal** (☎ 250-663-2872) flights to Vancouver.

Vancouver Island Coach Lines (☎ 250-318-0818; www.grayline.ca/victoria/schedules/main_schedule.shtml; Victoria/Nanaimo $39.20/19.60) run buses to Courtenay.

Courtenay is the end of the line for the **VIA Rail** (☎ 250-842-7245; www.viarail.ca; $43) *E&N Railiner* from Victoria.

BC Ferries (☎ 250-890-7800, 888-223-3779; www.bcferries.com; adult/child $7.75/4, car $26) makes four daily 75-minute trips from Little River terminal near Comox to Powell River on the mainland. There are no reservations, so arrive early to ensure boarding.

BC Transit (☎ 250-339-5453; www.bctransit.com; adult/child $1.25/1) operates local buses.

CAMPBELL RIVER

pop 28,500

Vancouver Island's northernmost city and trading center, Campbell River is a hot spot for salmon fishing and scuba diving, as well as a supply depot for adventures in the wilderness areas to the north and west and the main departure point for Strathcona Provincial Park.

For local information, stop at the **Visitor Info Centre** (☎ 250-287-4636; www.campbellrivertourism.bc.ca; 1235 Shoppers Row; ☽ 9am-7pm). Access the Internet at **Online Gourmet** (☎ 250-286-6521; 970 Shoppers Row) or the **library** (1240 Shoppers Row; $1 per ½ hr). The coin-op **laundry** (☽ 7am-11pm) behind the Rip Tide Pub has showers.

Sights & Activities

The well-done **Museum at Campbell River** (☎ 250-287-3103; 470 Island Hwy; adult/child $7.50/2.50; ☽ 10am-5pm Mon-Sat, noon-5pm Sun mid-May–Sept, noon-5pm Tue-Sun Oct-May) features a good collection of First Nations masks, an 1890 pioneer cabin and video footage of the world's largest-ever artificial, non-nuclear blast that destroyed Ripple Rock – a submerged mountain in Seymour Narrows north of Campbell River that caused more than 100 shipwrecks before it was blown apart in 1958.

Campbell River lives up to its 'Salmon Capital of the World' billing with some excellent **fishing**. You can wet a line right off the downtown Discovery Pier. The info centre has lists of deep-sea outfitters and can match something to your requirements; or just stroll down to the dock to see what's available.

The artificial reef provided by HMCS *Columbia*, sunk near Campbell River, is a major draw for scuba diving. Contact **Beaver Aquatics Limited** (☎ 250-287-7652; 760 Island Hwy) for information, gear and lessons. July through October, **Paradise Found Adventure Tours** (☎ 250-923-0848, 800-897-2872; www.paradisefound.bc.ca; $89) leads snorkeling trips to see migrating salmon in the shallow pools and slow-running waters of the Campbell River.

Sleeping & Eating

Hotel Bachmair (☎ 250-923-2848, 888-923-2849; fax 250-923-2849; www.hotelbachmair.com; 492 S Island Hwy; s/d/ste $89/99/120; P ✗) If you feel like a fancier place with European décor and hospitality, this is your spot. All the rooms have balconies and the gardens are especially lovely.

Rustic Motel (☎ 250-286-6295, 800-567-2007; www.rusticmotel.com; 2140 N Island Hwy; s/d $100/110; P ✗ ✿) North of downtown, this place sits quietly in the trees by the river – away from the bustle of Campbell River the town.

Painter's Lodge Holiday & Fishing Resort (☎ 250-286-1102, 800-663-7090; www.painterslodge .com; 1625 MacDonald Rd; r $189-229, ste $275, cabin $245-255; P ✗ ✿ ☐) More than just a place to stay, though the spacious rooms with sunken sleeping areas are bright and cheery, this resort wants to take you out to sea on its guided fishing trips and wildlife tours.

Hwy 19's south entrance to town is lined with motels with views of Discovery Passage and they all get booked up in summer.

Camping (☎ 250-689-9025; www.discovercamping .ca; site $14) is available at **Elk Falls Provincial Park**, 10km west of Campbell River on Hwy 28; **Loveland Bay Provincial Park**, 19km northeast at Campbell Lake; and **Morton Lake Provincial Park**, (☎ 250-337-8550), 19km north on Hwy 19.

Bee Hive Café (☎ 250-286-6812; 921 Island Hwy; mains $7-12) In business since 1929, this waterfront diner-like place has better-than-diner food. Breakfast, lunch and dinner are on the menu and historical photos of Campbell River are on the walls.

Dick's Fish and Chips (☎ 250-287-3336; 1003-G Coast Marina; mains $6-9) A fish and chips place on the dock can't get away with being a fraud and Dick's isn't. They also serve burgers and have indoor seating but you'll want to eat their specialty outside.

Getting There & Around

Pacific Coastal (☎ 250-663-2872; www.pacific-coastal .com) provides scheduled air service to/from Vancouver, as does **Air Rainbow** (☎ 250-287-8371, 888-287-8366), which uses a floatplane. **Kenmore Air Float Planes** (☎ 250-543-9595; www.ken moreair.com) operates flights to/from Seattle.

Vancouver Island Coach Lines (☎ 250-318-0818; www.grayline.ca/victoria/schedules/main_schedule.shtml; Victoria/Nanaimo $25.20/44.80) runs buses.

BC Transit (☎ 250-287-7433; www.bctransit.com; adult/child $1.25/1) operates local buses.

See below for ferry information to Quadra and Cortes Islands.

QUADRA & CORTES ISLANDS

Quadra Island is a quick hop from Campbell River; Cortes Island is a bit more remote. Together they're the 'Discovery Islands', either for their location in the Discovery Passage, or the fact they offer condensed versions of the natural and ecological splendors of the area, with much to discover.

Each island's annual map/brochure is available at area info centres and on the ferries; *The Discovery Islander* is a free newspaper distributed on both islands. The **visitor information booth** (☎ 250-286-1616; ☯ 9am-4:30pm Jun-Sep) is behind the **Quadra Credit Union** (☎ 250-285-3327; 627 Harper Rd). Information is also available at www.discoveryislands .ca, www.quadraisland.ca and www.cortes island.com.

Sights & Activities

Located at Quadra's Cape Mudge, the acclaimed **Kwagiulth Museum and Cultural Centre** (☎ 250-285-3733; adult/child $3/1; ☯ 10am-4:30pm Mon-Sat, noon-4:30pm Sun Jun-Sep) features a fascinating collection of items used in potlatches, along with early photos of traditional Kwakwaka'wakw villages.

Hollyhock (☎ 250-933-6339; www.hollyhock.ca; tent/dm/s/d $66/143/165/177), a retreat center at Manson's Landing on Cortes, offers innovative workshops on yoga, meditation, massage, songwriting and many other topics. The location in the forest and on the shores is definitely relaxing and inspirational.

Replace the evergreens with palm trees, and Quadra's **Rebecca Spit Provincial Park** could be a Caribbean postcard. The sandy beaches and clear waters offer excellent swimming and boating access. On Cortes, **Manson's Landing Provincial Park** boasts abundant shorebirds and shellfish, and **Smelt Bay Provincial Park** is a great place to watch sunsets. Nearby **Mittlenatch Island Nature Park**, called the 'Galapagos of Georgia Strait' for its natural diversity, can be seen on guided walks led by longtime area guide **George Sirk** (☎ 250- 935-6926).

The map/brochure shows the hiking trails of varying length that wind their way around Quadra. Newton Lake trail will take you through a two-hour presentation of Quadra's natural wonders. **Quadra Sun Rentals** (☎ 250-285-3601; day $30) offers canoe rentals to tour the island's chain of freshwater lakes. Main Lake Provincial Park offers an outstanding multi-day tour with campsites along the way that let you take it at your own pace.

Coast Mountain Expeditions (☎ 250-287-0635; www.coastmountainexpeditions.com; rental/daytrip $65/95) or **Coastal Spirits Sea Kayak Tours** (☎ 250-285-2895; www.kayakbritishcolumbia.com; 1069 Topcliff Rd; daytrip $40-60) do sea kayaking tours.

Abyssal Diving Charters & Lodge (☎ 250-285-2420, 800-499-2297; www.abyssal.com), just up the hill from the Quathiaski Cove ferry dock, is Quadra's source for scuba diving.

Sleeping

Cortes Island Motel (☎ 250-935-6363; Seaford Rd; s/d $59/69) Set amid tall trees at Manson's Landing, this is good value, with basic rooms.

Heriot Bay Inn & Marina (☎ 250-285-3322; www.heriotbayinn.com; tent/RV/r/cottage $14/18/80/115; P ⊠) This historic waterfront resort and B&B is located near the ferry to Cortes. The country-farmhouse look is prominent in the rooms and the cottages are pure rustic and fancy-free. There is also a restaurant (mains $7-12) in the main lodge.

Tsa-Kwa-Luten Lodge (☎ 250-285-2042; 800-665-7745; www.capemudgeresort.bc.ca; 1 Lighthouse Rd; r/loft/cottage $125/130/175; P ⊠) This First Nations-owned resort on Quadra's southern tip features Native art and architecture. Set in 1100 acres of lush green forest with views

of Discovery Passage, you'll feel at one with nature here.

Coastal Spirits (☎ 250-285-2895; www.coastal spirits.bc.ca; 1069 Topcliff Rd; $79; P ⊠) This huge house is in a secluded and private property on Quadra's east coast of undisturbed rainforest. The rooms are well looked after; you'll sleep well and wake up energized.

Quadra Island Backpackers' Hostel (☎ 250-285-3557; 1225 Heriot Bay Rd; tent/dm $10/16) Though Quadra is already pretty well off the beaten path, this hostel in a big farmhouse gets off even it more. There's 33 acres of farmland and forest surrounding the house.

Cortes camping is at **Smelt Bay Provincial Park** (☎ 250-337-8550; $14) or **Gorge Harbour Marina Resort** (☎ 250-935-6433; tent/RV $14.50/20.50, s/d $55/60) on Hunt Rd; the latter also has guest suites, coin-op laundry and showers.

Eating

Aroma (☎ 250-285 2404; 685 Heriot Bay Rd; mains $4-5) This coffeehouse takes coffee very seriously and mixes beans from around the world to make their own blends. They are only slightly less obsessive about their sandwiches and pastries.

The Tak (☎ 250-935-8555; 7 Sutil Point Rd; mains $7-12; ☯ lunch & dinner) In Manson's Landing on Cortes, this is the choice for good food and good fun. Burgers are on the menu and so are specials such as snapper fillet with roasted red pepper sauce.

Floathouse Restaurant (☎ 250-935-6631; Hunt Rd; mains $9-14; ☯ lunch & dinner) The restaurant at Gorge Harbour Marina serves excellent seafood dishes.

The small shopping plaza near Quathiaski Cover ferry dock on Quadra has pizza at **Lovin' Oven II** (☎ 250-285-2262) and good Mexican food at **Wacko Taco** (☎ 250-285-2777).

Getting There & Around

BC Ferries (☎ 250-286-1412, 888-223-3779; www.bc ferries.com) runs 17 times daily from Quathiaski Cove on Quadra to Campbell River (adult/child $5/2.50, car $12.50; ☯ 6:15am to 11pm), and from Heriot Bay (adult/child $6/3, car $15; ☯ 6:15am to 11pm), the other side of Quadra, to Whaletown on Cortes six times.

The Cortes Connection (☎ 250-935-6911; $12 plus ferry) provides shuttle bus service from Campbell River to Cortes Island via the ferry. It runs six times a week in summer (not Sundays) and three times a week the rest of the year. Reservations are advised.

Both Quadra and Cortes are fairly large islands, so it's something of a challenge to get around without a car. Check if your accommodations offer pick-up from the ferry. **Island Cycle** (☎ 250-285-3627; Heriot Bay; 1-/3-day $25/65) has bike rentals. For a taxi, call **Quadra Taxi** (☎ 250-285-3598).

STRATHCONA PROVINCIAL PARK

By far the largest provincial park on Vancouver Island, 250,000-hectare **Strathcona Provincial Park** (☎ 250-337-2400) is BC's oldest protected area. Campbell River is the main access point, and Hwy 28 between Campbell River and Gold River cuts across the Buttle Lake district. The Forbidden Plateau area is reached via Courtenay, as is the Mt Washington alpine resort area. The park is centered around Mt Golden Hinde (2200m), the highest point on Vancouver Island.

Strathcona is a hiker's park. In the Forbidden Plateau area, notable trails include the **Paradise Meadows Loop** (2.2km, 45 minutes), an easy walk through wildflower meadows; the summit of **Mt Albert Edward** (6.5km, five hours); and **Mt Becher** (5km, two hours), with great views of the Comox Valley, the Strait of Georgia and the Coast Mountain Range. The 9km, unmaintained **Comox Glacier Trail** sounds like quite an adventure – and it is – but it's not advised unless you're an advanced hiker or mountaineer.

In the Buttle Lake area, easy walks include **Lady Falls** (900m, 20 minutes) and the trail along **Karst Creek** (2km, 45 minutes), which winds past sinkholes, disappearing streams and beautiful waterfalls. For a more challenging hike, try the **Flower Ridge Trail** (6km, five hours) for its great alpine scenery.

Strathcona has two campgrounds in the Buttle Lake area. **Buttle Lake Campground** ($17) offers both first-come-first-served and reservable sites. The swimming area and the nearby playground make this a good choice for families. There are also some marine camping sites ($8). **Ralph River Campground** ($12), 26km south of the Hwy 28 junction, has first-come, first-served sites. Backcountry sites ($5) are available throughout the park.

Strathcona Park Lodge

Begun in 1959 as an outdoor education center, this family-run **lodge** (☎ 250-286-3122; www.strathcona.bc.ca; r $119-144; 1-/2-/3-bedroom cabins $169/195/255) on Hwy 28, and still takes teaching as its mission. It has rooms with a bathroom and lakeview.

Strathcona runs a variety of programs from daily adventures (half-/full-day adult $35/63 child $25/44) of scheduled classes in land and marine activities, to Nootka family adventures ($895) with five days of kayaking in Nootka Sound.

The casual atmosphere of the Whale Room is where buffet meals (breakfast/lunch/dinner $9.50/9.50/17) are served, as well as à la carte dishes ($7 to $13) during summer.

GOLD RIVER

pop 1350

This small burg is a relative newcomer to Vancouver Island. Built in the 1960s for workers in the now-defunct pulp mill, it's a hidden-gem of a launching spot for sports fishing and a base camp for outdoor activities.

Gold River is at the end of Hwy 28, 89km west of Campbell River. The **Visitor Info Centre** (☎ 250-283-2418; 9am-6pm mid-May–Labour Day) is at the corner of Hwy 28 and Scout Lake Rd.

Sights & Activities

Typically people come with their own boats to go fishing. If you're without, **Nootka Sound Sports Fishing** (☎ 877-283-7194; www.nootkasoundfish.com) runs charters.

Ask at the Visitor Info Centre about organized and self-guided **caving tours** to the 450m of passages and 16 known entrances of **Upana Caves**, north of town on the gravel road toward Tahsis.

If you're in town the first Saturday in June, the **Gold River–Tahsis Great Walk** (☎ 250-934-6570) is labeled as North America's toughest walkathon.

Nootka Sound Service (☎ 250-283-2325; www.mvuchuck.com) uses the *Uchuck III*, a converted WWII mine-sweeper, to deliver supplies and packages to remote villages and settlements up-island. Year-round, passengers can go on overnight trips up Nootka Sound to Zeballos (single/double/child $175/275/40, 9am Mon-4pm Tue) or further up the coast through the open waters of the Pacific to Kyuquot (single/double/child/transportation-only $210/325/75/55; 7am Thu-5pm Fri). Overnight accommodations and breakfast are included, and this is a great way to see some otherwise inaccessible scenery.

Also offered are day trips to **Friendly Cove** (adult/child $40/20 ☺ 10am-4pm Wed & 10am-5:30pm Sat summer), where Captain Cook first met Chief Maquinna and the Mowachaht people in 1778.

Sleeping & Eating

Ridgeview Motor Inn (☎ 250-283-2277, 800-989-3393; 395 Donner Court; r $89-125) This hotel-lodge up on the hill has impressive views of the inlet. It features upscale rooms and a hospitality room where guests can do some light cooking. The attached **Ridge Neighbourhood Pub** (☎ 250-283-2600; mains $8-12) has better-than-average pub food and excellent seafood.

Camping is available alongside the river at **Lions Club Campground** ($10, pay at the gate) on the south side of town. For B&Bs, the info centre will help find one to suit you.

Manila Grill (☎ 250-283-7779; mains $6-10) In all respects this place is a diner until you look at the menu. Vegetarian dishes and stir-fries are listed right along with traditional breakfasts, sandwiches and burgers.

NORTH VANCOUVER ISLAND

Only 5% of the population live north of Campbell River, an area covering nearly half of Vancouver Island. That math leads some to argue there is 'nothing up there to see' – how wrong they are. This is god's (or whatever deity's) own country. Rather than cheapen it with fanciness and frills, North Island is presented as the naturally rugged, raw and rough-around-the-edges place that it is.

SAYWARD & WOSS

The 200km stretch of Hwy 19 between Campbell River and Port McNeill has plenty to see (keep your eyes open for wildlife and stop at the lookout for **Seymour Narrows** and **Ripple Rock**, 14km north of Campbell River), but only Sayward (pop

380) and Woss (pop 400) have services. The **Sayward Info Centre** (☎ 250-282-3265), at Sayward Junction, has detailed infomation about the area. It's 12km on a rough road from Hwy 19 south of Woss to **Schoen Lake Provincial Park** (☎ 250-954-4600). There are only 10 primitive sites ($10) but it's an absolute gem of a spot, perfect for those looking for a quiet lakeside setting surrounded by forested hills. The **Rugged Mountain Motel** (☎ 250-281-2280; $55; P ☒) in Woss is a popular stopping place for those biking around Vancouver Island. The rooms are basic motel-style with comfy beds.

If it's meal-time when you get to Sayward, the **Original Cable Cookhouse** (☎ 250-282-3433; 1741 Sayward Rd; mains $7-11) has good home-cooking and puts a Pacific spin on classic dishes like west coast salmon Wellington. The restaurant was built from 2700m of used logging cables and has all kinds of old logging trinkets scattered about the property.

TELEGRAPH COVE

In 1911 it was a lonely telegraph station 190km north of Campbell River, but today the creatively named Telegraph Cove is a privately owned boardwalk resort-community and a major base for wildlife-watching tours.

The **Whale Interpretive Centre** (☎ 250-928-3129; www.killerwhalecentre.org; donation) is worth a visit to see the Bones Project, including the skull of a gray whale, which aims to increase awareness about these fascinating creatures.

Hundreds of orcas migrate through Johnstone Strait each year to see the thousands of people who come to 'the community on stilts'. It's easier for them to see you on one of the daily whale-watching trips with **Stubbs Island Whale Watching** (☎ 250-928-3185, 800-665-3066; www.stubbs-island.com; 4-hr trip adult/child $65/59, lunch $8) to **Robson Bight Ecological Reserve**, where they hang out from July to September.

Grizzly bears don't care much about seeing people, but from August through October, **Tide Rip Tours** (☎ 250-339-6294, 888-643-9319; www.tiderip.com; from $145) leads trips up Knight Inlet to see them. **Discovery Expeditions** (☎ 250-758-2488, 800-567-3611; www.orcaseakayaking.com from $850) offers kayak rentals and four- to six-day sea-kayaking tours from Telegraph Cove and elsewhere in BC.

Telegraph Cove Resorts (☎ 250-928-3105, 800-200-4665; www.telegraphcoveresort.com; tent $18-23, d $95-175, cabins from $105; P ✂) A chunk of land was recently sold where condominiums now occupy the eastern shore of the inlet, but these characteristic private cabins prove it's better to be original. Former residences from the 1920s to 1940s, when the sawmill was running, range from a simple room for two in the old air force mess hall to a cabin for eight people. There are vintage hotel-style rooms with antique furnishings in the 1912 Wastell Manor and a huge deck with a magnificent view of the strait. The resort also has 120 campsites; E96 & E98 offer the most seclusion.

The **Killer Whale Café** (☎ 250-928-3155; mains $7-12) and adjacent **Old Saltery Pub** share the same kitchen and are owned by the resort. The café is open for breakfast, and both are open for lunch and dinner. The outside deck, central fireplaces, old-time photos, and maybe the fact they're the only restaurants in Telegraph Cove, make them popular spots.

PORT MCNEILL
pop 2800

Civic pride is displayed on the sign that welcomes you to Port McNeill: 'Home of NHLer Willie Mitchell'. McNeill is the kind of town that knows what it has and is proud to show it. Its front-and-center seat to the marine highway of Broughton Straight shows that marine activities are not far away.

The log cabin **Visitor Info Centre** (☎ 250-956-3131; www.portmcneill.net; 351 Shelley Crest; ☺ 9am-5pm) can help you plan your helicopter tours, diving or fishing trips.

Learn about the trees you've spent hours looking at and logging procedures at the **North Island Discovery Centre** (☎ 250-956-3844; www.island.net/~nifctour). There's a decommissioned yarding span, a self-guided interpretive trail and popular six-hour guided tours are available July to September. Guaranteed as something you've never seen before, the 350-year-old **world's largest burl**, removed from a 260ft spruce, sits at the entrance to Weyerhauser's offices north of town.

Seeview B&B (☎ 250-956-4818; www.island.net/~seeview; 2291 Quatsino Cres; s/d $65/80; P ✂) The bedrooms aren't exactly huge, but the living rooms, kitchen and rec-room are spacious

and inviting. You'll get a full breakfast, hot tub, sauna and excellent views.

Haida-Way Motor Inn (☎ 250-956-3373; fax 250-956-4710; www.portmcneillhotels.com; 1817 Campbell Way; s/d $80/96; P ✂ 🖳) has the most rooms in town. The brick wall separating the rooms has an institutional feel but they're spacious and clean. The **café** ($5-9; ☺ closed 2pm-5pm) is decent and serves good meals and sandwiches. Its **Northern Lights Restaurant** (☎ 250-956-3262; $15-25) is dinner-only and a little more formal, with more intricate meals like steak and prawns or vegetarian kebabs.

Getting There & Away
Air Rainbow (☎ 250-956-2020) offers floatplane service to and from Vancouver and Seattle. **Vancouver Island Coach Lines** (☎ 250-318-0818; www.grayline.ca/victoria/schedules/main_schedule.shtml; Victoria/Nanaimo $84.75/$65.15) runs one bus daily.

The **BC Ferries** (☎ 250-956-4533, 888-223-3779; www.bcferries.com; adult/child $6/3, car $15; ☺ 6:45am-10:40pm) schedule between Port McNeill, Alert Bay and Sointula seems confusing, but it's designed for regular users. Check the schedule carefully; the first and last sailings visit all three locations, then alternating round-trips between each island and Port McNeill occur throughout the day. See p380 for more on ferry transport.

ALERT BAY & SOINTULA
The village of Alert Bay (pop 580) on Cormorant Island has an aura that seems both mythical and ancient. Its First Nations community and traditions are prevalent, but its blend with an old fishing settlement makes the place a fascinating day trip. Malcolm Island and the town of Sointula (pop 635) is a one-time socialist commune founded in 1901 by Finns, for whom the town's name meant 'harmony'.

Alert Bay's **Visitor Info Centre** (☎ 250-974-5024; www.alertbay.ca; 116 Fir St; ☺ 9am-4:30pm Mon-Fri) has enthusiastic and knowledgeable staff.

The **U'Mista Cultural Centre** (☎ 250-974-5403; www.umista.org; ☺ 9am-5pm Jun-Aug, Mon-Fri Sep-May; adult/child $5/1) immaculately presents its impressive collection of Kwakwaka'wakw masks and other potlatch items originally confiscated by the federal government in the 1920s (see p18 for more information).

Singing, dancing and barbecues often take place in a scaled-down big house. Modern-day totem pole carvers can usually be seen working out front; ask questions and don't be shy, they love their work. The fascinating dance performances are held during the summer months.

At 53m, the world's tallest **totem pole** is appropriately placed on the front lawn of the enormous **Big House** (☎ 250-974-5403; 🕑 1pm Thu-Sun; $15) which hosts traditional dances; ask if it's possible to pop your head inside as the construction is truly impressive.

Amazing tranquility is the highlight of this lovely, mossy walk through giant cedar trees at **Alert Bay Ecological Park** (also known as Gator Gardens); an excellent interpretive guide is available at the info centre. While Sointula is not as tourist-oriented as Alert Bay, it does have some great hiking.

Seasmoke/Sea Orca Expeditions (☎ 250-974-5225, 800-668-6722; www.seaorca.com; adult/child $75/55) offers a whale-watching sailing experience aboard its classic yacht, including afternoon tea.

PORT HARDY
pop 4600
'The highway ends and the adventure begins' in this small town at the northern end of Vancouver Island, best known as the gear-up spot for Cape Scott and the arrival/departure point for BC Ferries trips through the Inside Passage. The **Visitor Info Centre** (☎ 250-949-7622; 7250 Market St; 🕑 9am-5pm) also operates the small **museum** (7110 Market St; 🕑 10am-5pm Mon-Sat).

Activities
The weather is often cloudy, foggy and wet but the area has lots of activities for those hardy enough. The **Port Hardy Adventure Centre** (☎ 250-902-2232, 866-902-2232; www.adventurecenter.ca; 8635 Granville St) is a one-stop-shop for activities and the website is an excellent resource.

CAVING
The caves in the area around Port Hardy draw international attention among spelunkers. Reappearing rivers, sinkholes and land bridges are examples of what to expect at sites like **Eternal Fountain** and **Disappearing River**. Contact **Vancouver Island**

Nature Exploration (☎ 250-902-2662; www.nature-exploration.com) or the info centre for details.

SALMON FISHING & DIVING
The **Port Hardy Charter Boat Association** (☎ 250-949-2628) has extensive listings of charters in the area.

Recommended operators include:
North Island Diving & Watersports (☎ 250-949-2664; 8295 Hastings St) Rents equipment and runs courses.
Catala Charters (☎ 250-949-7560, 800-515-5511; www.catalacharters.net; 6170 Hardy Bay Rd) Offers a variety of options.
Sea Legend Charters (☎ 250-949-9525; www.sea legend.com) Operates a variety of adventure tours for divers, hikers and sightseers.

KAYAKING
Odyssey Kayaking (☎ 250-902-0565, 888-792-3366; www.odysseykayaking.com)
North Island Kayak (☎ 250-949-7707; www.kayak bc.ca; 8635 Granville St)

WILDLIFE-WATCHING
It would be odd if you didn't see deer or elk on the drive up and it's not uncommon to spot black bears or cougars within town limits. But **Great Bear Nature Tours** (☎ 250-949-7707, 888-221-8212; www.greatbeartours.com; $390) boats you through whale and dolphin areas to bear country and flies you back on an 11-hour day trip offered from June to mid-October.

Sleeping & Eating
Port Hardy fills up most nights from June through September, so book ahead.

Catala Bed & Breakfast (☎ 250-949-7560, 800-515-5511; www.catalacharters; 6170 Hardy Bay Rd; from $75) The two rooms are decorated in true Port Hardy fashion in this big brown house right on the inlet. The rooms can sleep up to five ($150), but more than three adults ($100) would be pretty cramped.

Quarterdeck Inn (☎ 250-902-0455; fax 250-602-0454; www.quarterdeckresort.com; 6555 Hardy Bay Rd; s/d/ste $95/115/125, 🅿 ✖) A suite gives you a lot more room and is worth the extra $10. The waterfront rooms on the upper floors have excellent views once the clouds burn off.

Glen Lyon Inn (☎ 250-949-7115; fax 250-919-7415; www.glenlyoninn.com; 6435 Hardy Bay Rd; s/d/ste from $85/95/125 🅿 ✖) This blue-roofed, newly renovated hotel has large rooms with balconies and a decidedly aqua color scheme.

VANCOUVER ISLAND

Campers head to **Quatse River Campground** (☎ 250-949-2395; 5050 Hardy Bay Rd; tent/RV $14/18).

IV's Quarterdeck Pub (☎ 250-949-6922; 6555 Hardy Bay Rd; mains $8-13) They'll cook your catch any way you like at the IV (eye-vee), but with the evidence on your plate you won't be able to exaggerate like the others swapping tales on the enclosed patio. There may be more locals than visitors in the pub, decked out like a ship, and while the afterthought of a family dining room isn't flattering, it serves its purpose.

High Tide Restaurant (☎ 250-949-7122; mains $6-11) In the Glen Lyon Inn, this restaurant is open for lunch and dinner, but is best enjoyed at breakfast as you sit with local fisherman and look out the wrap-around windows at the mist dancing on the inlet waters.

Getting There & Around

Pacific Coastal Airlines (☎ 250-949-6353, 800-663-2872; www.pacific-coastal.com; $200) offers air service to/from Vancouver. **Vancouver Island Coach Lines** (☎ 250-318-0818; www.grayline.ca/victoria/schedules/main_schedule.shtml; Victoria/Nanaimo $94.15/74.55) runs buses from down-island. **North Island Transportation** (☎ 250-949-6300; nit@island.net; $5.25) runs a shuttle to/from the ferry terminal.

BC Ferries (☎ 250-949-6722, 888-223-3779; www.bcferries.com; adult/child $102.50/51.25, car $241.50; ☯ mid-May–mid-October) sails the *Queen of the North* up the Inside Passage to Prince Rupert on spectacular, 15-hour daylight trips. Also from Port Hardy, the **Discovery Coast Passage** (adult/child $106.25/53.25, car $212.50; ☯ summer) goes to Bella Coola. See p380 for more on ferry transport.

CAPE SCOTT PROVINCIAL PARK & AROUND

Pristine beaches and challenging hikes await in Cape Scott Provincial Park, 70km west of Port Hardy over an active logging gravel road. **San Josef Bay**, a 2.5km walk along a well-maintained trail, is easily accessible and its undisturbed beach and crashing Pacific waves are only a glimpse of the park's offerings. Beyond this, however, it's no stroll in the park. The 24km slog to Cape Scott, an old Danish settlement at the park's far end, is a mud-fest and sort of rite-of-passage among hikers. If you mentally prepare for knee-high mud and stuck feet, and physically prepare for unpredictable storms with strong winds and freezing rain, rewards such as waking up on the fine, white sand of Nels Bight Beach and the endless views at Cape Scott will leave you awestruck.

This is the epitome of backcountry camping ($3, pay at trailhead); leave nothing but footprints and take nothing but pictures and memories.

Raft Cove Provincial Park has similar rewards, with considerably less effort; a 2km hike over rough, but passable, territory brings you to the crescent beach and beautiful lagoons of **Raft Cove**. This is an excellent alternative for those who don't have the time for Cape Scott and want more privacy than San Josef; at best you'll have the entire 1.3km of beach to yourself, at worst you'll have a few hundred meters. Small blue signs point to the trailhead along the logging roads.

Along the road to the parks, keep your eyes open for the crushed car under the huge log with the sign that reads, 'Anything can happen'; the boot-tree decorated with footgear of Cape Scott returnees; and **Ronning's Garden**, an extreme version of the Sesame Street song, 'One of these things doesn't belong'. Bernt Ronning picked this place-of-all-places to plant dozens of foreign seeds in 1910 and create a garden that includes Monkey trees. After his death the place became overgrown with rainforest, but was rediscovered and is now cared for by Ron and Julia Moe. Signs lead the way to the trailhead of the 500m walk to the gardens.

Southern Gulf Islands

CONTENTS

While the west coast of Vancouver Island is storm-tossed, wild and rugged, the protected southeast coast creates a tranquil oasis and mild climate that's home to a series of green, forested islands that rise from the Georgia Strait. The Southern Gulf Islands are seemingly always on vacation and best characterized as open, artsy and stress-free. The relaxed, unhurried pace is easy to get used to, yet a glut of activities make the islands a popular destination for kayaking, cycling, hiking, scuba diving and gallery hopping. Deer travel around the islands with little concern for their surroundings, hundreds of species of birds use them as a home or stopover, and whales migrate through the area in spring and fall.

Even just getting to the Southern Gulf Islands is a treat: you must either take a plane or ride one of the wonderful ferries that ply the waters between the islands. The routes are premier voyages, each through channels and passages that seem impossibly narrow for such large vessels sailing just a stone's throw from forested and rocky shorelines.

Though not really in a gulf, the Gulf Islands name is used for any body of land between Vancouver Island and the mainland; the area northeast of Victoria and southwest of Tsawwassen contains the 200 or so Southern Gulf Islands. Most are small and uninhabited, but five of the larger ones are serviced by regular BC Ferries and have attracted many retirees, artists and counterculture types who shun the nine-to-five grind of mainland life.

HIGHLIGHTS

- Shopping the Ganges **Saturday market** (p177)
- Watching the crashing waves at **Georgina Point** (p183) on Mayne
- Visiting artists in their studios on **Pender** (p181)
- Watching whales from **Saturna** (p182)
- Seeing **Galiano** (p184) from the outside in a kayak

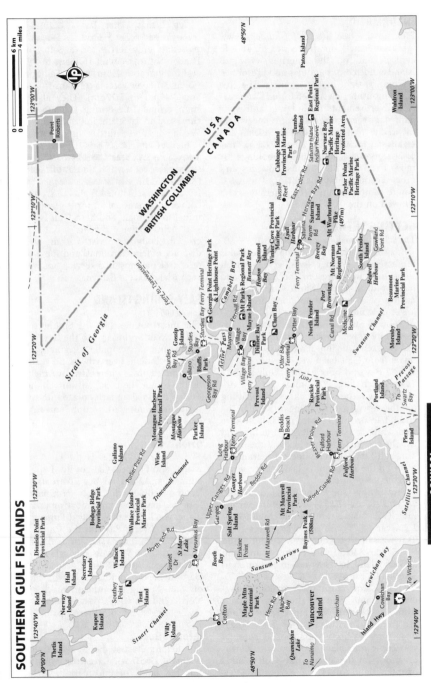

SOUTHERN GULF ISLANDS

SOUTHERN GULF ISLANDS

INFORMATION

Pick up the free the *Gulf Islander* (www
.gulfislands.net) on the ferries or at info
centres, and on the Internet www.gulf
islandsguide.com is another good resource.
Lodging is tight in the summer. The free
twice-monthly newspaper *Island Tides* carries advertisements for lodgings and www
.gulfislandvacationrentals.com specializes
in private rentals. **Canadian Gulf Islands Reservations** (☎ 250-539-3089, 888-539-2930; holidays@
gulfislandsreservations.com) handles bookings for
more than 100 B&Bs, inns, cottages and
other accommodations. Bring a stove if
you're camping, campfires generally aren't
allowed on the Gulf Islands.

GETTING THERE & AROUND

The schedule-makers for **BC Ferries** (☎ 888-223-
3779; www.bcferries.com) were probably calculus
professors in former lives; give yourself
some time to figure out their genius and
plan your itinerary. More sailings occur
during peak travel times, but prices are
lower in winter and midweek in summer.

Though Swartz Bay, near Victoria, offers more travel to the Gulf Islands than
Tsawwassen on the mainland, you can
travel from Gulf Island to Tsawwaseen via
Swartz Bay and only pay the Gulf Island–
Tsawwassen fare. You must get a date-
stamped voucher from either (depending
on the ferry) a dispensing machine, the
snack bar, or ship's Mate. You'll then have
to disembark at Swartz Bay, get in line and
use the voucher to buy a ticket at the lower
'through-fare' rate. This doesn't guarantee a
place on the Swartz Bay–Tsawwassen ferry,
just the lower fare.

Swartz Bay–Gulf Island fares (adult/child
$6.50/3.25, car $22.25) are roundtrip while
inter-Gulf Island fares (adult/child $3.75/
1.25, car $7.75) are one-way. Fares from
Tsawwassen to a Gulf Island (adult/child
$10/5, car $36.50) are higher than from
a Gulf Island to Tsawwassen (adult/child
$4.50/2.25, car $18.75).

Gulf Island commuters make Friday-
evening and Sunday-afternoon ferries
from Tsawwassen very busy. Reservations
are free, and mandatory, for Tsawwassen
departures so book your spot as soon as
you know your plans. You can't make reservations for the Swartz Bay–Gulf Islands
or inter-island routes.

Gulf Islands Water Taxi (☎ 250-537-2510;
one-way/return $15/20; ☺ school days Sep-Jun) runs
passenger-only ferries on a Salt Spring–
Pender–Saturna circuit (6:45am to 8:55am
and 3:45pm to 5:45pm) and a Salt Spring–
Galiano–Mayne circuit (6:45am to 8:40am
and 3:45pm to 5:22pm). They also do a
summertime Salt Spring–Galiano–Mayne
run (9am to 10:50am and 3pm to 4:50pm
Wednesday and Saturday, June to August).

Harbour Air (☎ 800-665-0212; www.harbour-air
.com; one-way $69), **Seair** (☎ 800-447-3247; www.seair
seaplanes.com; one-way $80) and **Pacific Spirit Air**
(☎ 800-665-2359; www.tofinoair.ca/sched.htm; one-way
$66) all have scheduled flights to/from Van-
couver International airport's seaplane terminal to the main Southern Gulf Islands.

It helps to have a vehicle, but it's not
crucial. Lodgings exist within walking
distance of ferry terminals and some places
offer free pickups; taxi service operates on
each island except Saturna.

SALT SPRING ISLAND

pop 10,000

The most populous of the Southern Gulf
Islands, Salt Spring is also the largest (180
sq km) and most popular. Originally settled
by Salish Indians over a thousand years ago,
it became a place where African Americans
fled to escape the racial tensions in the US.
Today, it's an artsy-fartsy place with studios
scattered about and a confident-but-not-
cocky quality.

Orientation

The village of Ganges is the heart of the
island, and Fulford–Ganges Rd, Long Harbour Rd and Vesuvius Bay Rd are its aortas
leading to BC Ferries' three terminals. Unless you have your own boat or arrive by
plane, you'll hit Salt Spring at Fulford Harbour (via Swartz Bay) on the south; Long
Harbour (via Tsawwasen or Gulf Island)
on the east; or Vesuvius Bay (via Crofton)
on the west. Beaver Point Rd, near Fulford
Harbour, leads to Ruckle Provincial Park
on Salt Spring's southeast reach, while
North End Rd winds past St Mary's Lake
toward the island's northern tip.

Information

The helpful staff at the Ganges **Visitor Info
Centre** (☎ 250-537-5252; 121 Lower Ganges Rd; ☺ 9am-
4pm) has loads of information, including

THE BEST $150 CRUISE EVER

For frequent riders, the ferry may have lost some of its charm, but newbies are in for a treat. Rounding North Pender and navigating the untamable waters between Galiano and Mayne is as enlivening as it is peaceful. Not only do the islands offer spectacular scenery, but there's a distinct possibility of seeing migrating whales from May to October.

BC Ferries (☎ 888-223-3779; www.bcferries.com/res/sailpass.html; 4/7 days $119/149; ☼ summer, must reserve 5 days in advance) has introduced the SailPass, a multi-day pass good for two passengers and a vehicle for roundtrip travel on each of the Mainland-Vancouver Island routes, and unlimited travel on Gulf Islands and Sunshine Coast sailings. This is an excellent and hassle-free way to see this part of the world, where the favorite route is the seven-day circle Tsawwassen–Gulf Islands–Victoria–Comox–Powell River–Sunshine Coast–Vancouver. A little hint: fares aren't collected from Langdale (on the Sunshine Coast) to Horseshoe Bay, so you can make this your fifth or eighth day and not be charged extra.

---

hiking guides, a beach-access map and extensive accommodations listings.

The weekly newspaper, *The Driftwood*, also publishes the free *Salt Spring Visitor*, available on the ferries and most shops on the island. **Salt Spring Books** (☎ 250-537-2812; 104 McPhillips Rd, Ganges; 10¢ per min) offers email access. **Lady Minto Hospital** (☎ 250-538-5545; 135 Crofton Rd) serves Salt Spring's medical needs. Major banks have branches in Ganges and ATMs can be found at pubs and shops around the island. Post services are at **Ganges** (☎ 800-267-1177; 109 Purvis Lane; ☼ 8:30am-5:30pm Mon-Fri, 8:30am-noon Sat) and **Fulford Harbour post office** (☎ 800-267-1177; 101 Morningside Rd; ☼ 8:45am-5pm Mon-Fri, 8:45am-12:15pm Wed & Sat).

Ganges

Ganges, nestled at the north end of Ganges Harbour, is the vibrant focal point of Salt Spring's activity. Not just a sleepy village by the sea, it has a creative and artistic vibe, without the hurry-up of other major tourist centers.

Market in the Park (☎ 250-537-4448; www.salt springmarket.com; Centennial Park; ☼ 8:30am-3:30pm Sat Apr–mid-Oct) has evolved from the farmers' market for locals to an internationally famous colossal event featuring the creations of local artists, craftspeople and farmers. Non-residents are known to come to Salt Spring specifically for the market, where everything is locally grown, baked or made.

ArtSpring (☎ 250-537-2102; www.artspring.ca; 100 Jackson Ave) is a theater with a full calendar of performing arts events. **Festival of the Arts** (☎ 250-537-4167) in July is where local and touring artists present music, theater and dance performances.

Parks & Beaches

Mt Maxwell Provincial Park (☎ 250-539-2115), south of Ganges via Cranberry and Mt Maxwell Rds, offers a very accessible and very captivating viewpoint. Baynes Peak (588m) climbs far above sea level, even above soaring eagles, and makes Georgia Strait seem like a bathtub dotted with small, green islands.

Ruckle Provincial Park (☎ 250-539-2115; parking $3) is a gem occupying Salt Spring's southeast corner – a place of seashores, forests and farmlands. Henry Ruckle settled on what is now one of the oldest, and still active, family farms in British Columbia (established in 1872) and still has some of the original buildings. The Ruckles donated most of their land to the government and this now makes up the park's forested hiking trails and shorelines of tidal pools filled with marine life.

Ganges' parks include **Rotary Maritime Park**, on Ganges Harbour, where you can launch kayaks and other small boats, and **Mouat Park**, behind the ArtSpring center, which features walking trails and a frisbee-golf course.

Popular beaches include **Southey Point** at the island's north end and **Beddis Beach** on the island's east side, noted for good swimming and sunbathing; head to **Erskine Bay** or **Vesuvius Bay** for vivid sunsets.

Activities

Available from the info centre, *Salt Spring Out Of Doors* ($3.95) details hiking trails, beach-access points, historic sites and more. The narrow, winding and steep roads present more of a challenge than a deterrent for cycling; *Cycling Map of Salt*

WHAT'S IN A NAME?

The body of water in which the Gulf Islands sit can be called a strait, channel, passage, sound, archipelago or even canal, but one of the last things it can technically be called is a 'gulf'. In 1792, when Captain George Vancouver was making his way through the area, he made the brief notation 'gulf' before continuing on his way to fame and greatness. Apparently, his brilliance was not to be questioned and the name 'Gulf Islands' stuck.

In less fraudulent fashion, original settlers of Salt Spring (the Salish Indians) named the island for the saltwater springs on the north end; Ganges, the town, takes its name from HMS *Ganges*, the 1857 British Royal Navy ship; Saturna Island was named after the Spanish ship *Saturina*; and Spanish explorer Dionisio Galiano took vanity a step further by naming that island after himself.

The HMS *Plumper* perhaps has the most claims to Gulf Island namesakes. Dispatched in 1858-1859 to fact-check a few 'discrepancies', residents coined the name Plumper Pass for the waters between Mayne and Galiano. Captain Richard Mayne, wanting to give credit where credit was due, renamed the passage as Active Pass after the *US Active*, the first steamship to navigate the waters (perhaps an act of foreshadowing, as these waters are the most traveled today). He then named Mayne Island after himself, Pender Island after his second in command and Plumper Pass now labels the water between Saturna and Pender.

In all, there probably isn't a park, point, mountain, bay, harbor or channel name on any of these islands that doesn't have historical significance.

Spring Island (50¢) shows the best routes.

Salt Spring Kayaking (☎ 250-653-4222; www.saltspringkayaking.com; 2923 Fulford–Ganges Rd, Fulford Wharf; hr/day $5/25, delivery/pick-up $15) rents bikes if you arrive without.

Kayaking the calm waters and beautiful shorelines of any of the Gulf Islands is amazing, but Salt Spring has a certain ominous quality to it. **Salt Spring Kayaking** (☎ 250-653-4222; www.saltspringkayaking.com; 2923 Fulford-Ganges Rd, Fulford Wharf; tours from $35, rentals hr/day $12/45) offers the popular two-hour sunset or full-moon harbor tours, as well as day or multi-day trips. **Sea Otter Kayaking** (☎ 250-537-5678, 877-537-5678; 149 Lower Ganges Rd; 2hr/day rentals $20/45, tours from $35) rents kayaks and offers trips from the foot of Rainbow Rd at Ganges Harbour.

Salt Spring Guided Rides (☎ 250-537-5761; $35/hr) leads horseback riding on Mt Maxwell.

Sleeping

The info centre will help with the dozens of B&B choices.

Salt Spring Spa Resort (☎ 250-537-4111, 800-665-0039; www.saltspringspa.com; 1460 North Beach Rd; chalet from $239; ☒) This place is for those who are looking to relax beyond the cerebral relaxation of sea-air and ocean views. Austrian mud baths, massages and back scrubs are among the á la carte services you can order, or just enjoy your private cedar chalet and its immaculate views.

Beachcomber Motel (☎ 250-537-5415; 770 Vesuvius Bay Rd; s/d/r with kitchenette $89/99/119; ☒) This place on the hill facing east towards Vancouver Island has your basic motel rooms, but it's conveniently located by the Vesuvius terminal and the nearby restaurants.

Seabreeze Inn (☎ 250-537-4145, 800-434-4112; reservations@seabreezeinns.com; 101 Bittancourt Rd; r with kitchenette $115/135; ☒) This standard motel overlooking Ganges Harbour does its best to provide a non-standard motel stay. With an outdoor hot tub, patio, barbecue, bikes for guests and communal feel, this is a great place for those in large groups, with families or who just like making new friends.

Lakeside Gardens (☎ 250-537-5773; lakesidegardens@saltspring.com; 1450 North End Rd; site/cabana/cottage $25/65/125; ☒) and **Cottage Resort** (☎ 250-537-2214; pearl@saltspring.com; 175 Suffolk Rd; cottage $95-220), both on St Mary's Lake, have huge willow trees and wood-built cabins and cottages are a reminder that naturally-occurring luxury can't be outdone. Both are great places for families, with ample swimming for the kids and Adirondack chairs for the non-kids.

Seido-En Forest House (☎ 250-653-2311; www.seido-en.com; seido-en@uniserve.com; 124 Meyer Rd; 2-nights/wk $330/990) This Japanese-style dwelling combines old-world tradition with new-world convenience. It looks like it belongs among tall bamboo trees, and yet doesn't seem out of place among the conifers of Salt Spring's southeast coast.

Salt Spring Island Hostel (☎ 250-537-4149; hostel@saltspring.com; 640 Cusheon Lake Rd; dm/r/ treehouse/caravan $21/60/70/70) This hostel is more like a retreat in the woods. The requisite dorms and rooms are in the main house, but what sets this place apart from your typical hostel are the camping tipis, charming tree houses and a gypsy caravan built for more intimate accommodations.

Ruckle Provincial Park (☎ 250-539-2115; site $14) has walk-in campsites right on the beach where you can wake up to sunrises of unbelievable colors.

Eating

Treehouse Café (☎ 250-537-5379; 106 Purvis Lane; mains $5-11) This hip outdoor café in the heart of Ganges' action is the kind of place where a hobbit would feel at home. Enjoy a sandwich, espresso or pint on the terrace under the plum tree on a sunny afternoon, or come on a summer evening, when they feature 123 consecutive nights of live music.

Moby's Marine Pub (☎ 250-537-5559; 124 Upper Ganges Rd) Placed on the rocky shore, Moby's is up there among Salt Spring's most popular eateries, mainly due to the lively atmosphere, excellent views of Ganges Harbour and good food. The menu features usual pub grub with seafood cameos. On Sunday, come for brunch in the morning or live jazz in the evening.

Salt Spring, like most islands, is a pub kind of place; **Fulford Inn** (☎ 250-653-4432; 2661 Fulford–Ganges Rd; mains $7-12) on the south end and **Vesuvius Inn Pub** (☎ 250-537-2312; 805 Vesuvius Bay Rd; mains $7-10) on the west coast serve you honestly with few surprises, attracting locals and visitors alike.

Calvin's Bistro (☎ 250-538-5551; 133 Lower Ganges Rd; mains $10-20) West Coast cuisine mixes with a little European flavor in this cottage look-alike by the Ganges Harbour. It has Gulf Island atmosphere and old European charm with a menu that combines the same tendencies in its food with dishes like Swiss toast or halibut fillet.

Embe Bakery (☎ 250-537-5611; 174 Fulford–Ganges Rd; snacks $3-5; ☷ 5am-lunch) The bakery that was formerly a creamery serves scrumptious muffins, breads and other baked treats.

Rose's Café (☎ 250-653-9222; Fulford ferry landing; mains $5-10) Arrive for your ferry early so you'll have time for one of Rose's delicious sandwiches or breakfasts.

Shopping

If you're looking to browse many local artisans' creations at once, you'll want to be here for the Saturday market (p000), but most smiths do have open studios; the info centre has a free self-guided map. For atypical souvenirs, **Mouat's Trading Co** (☎ 250-537-5551, 877-490-5593; 106 Fulford–Ganges Rd) is home to the batik jackets and hand-painted rain boots of Mouat's Clothing Co, and the Housewares Store, an old-fashioned hardware emporium. Next door, **Pegasus Gallery of Canadian Art** (☎ 250-537-2421, 800-668-6131; 104 Fulford–Ganges Rd) offers an extensive selection of paintings, jewelry, basketry and carvings.

Getting There & Around

BC Ferries (☎ 888-223-3779; www.bcferries.com; Vancouver Island adult/child $6.25/3.25, car $20) has three terminals in Salt Spring, all serving different destinations; the fare from here to Vancouver Island is lower than the other islands. **Long Harbour** (☎ 250-537-5313; ☷ 6am-4pm) handles sailings to the other Gulf Islands and Tsawwassen. **Fulford Harbour** (☎ 250-653-4245; ☷ 6:20am-8pm) departures sail direct to Swartz Bay. **Vesuvius Bay** (☷ 7am-9:40pm) boats sail straight across to Crofton, north of the Malahat. See p380 for more on ferry travel in general and p176 for more on Gulf Island travel.

Harbour Air (☎ 800-665-0212; www.harbour-air .com; one-way $74) flies between Vancouver Harbour and Ganges in addition to its normal YVR flight.

It's best to have a car on Salt Spring, but **Silver Shadow Taxi** (☎ 250-537-3030) offers cab service and **Ganges Faerie** (☎ 250-537-5305, 250-537-6758) shuttles between ferry terminals, Ganges, the hostel and Ruckle and anywhere en route. **Marine Drive Car & Truck Rentals** (☎ 250-537-5464; 122A Upper Ganges Rd; $50 per day), at the Ganges Marina, rents cars and has free ferry pick-up.

NORTH & SOUTH PENDER ISLANDS
pop 1900

The Pender Islands fall in the geographical center of the Gulf and San Juan Islands, which obviously makes them the center of the universe. It's not that the Penders or their inhabitants are necessarily snobby; it's just that they're not really designed for someone who's never been there before. The mood is a sort of laissez-faire attitude – they're neither happy nor disappointed that you decided to come. Pender life is just about enjoying the surrounding spectacularity at your own pace.

Information

If the **Visitor Info Centre** (☎ 250-629-6541; 2332 Otter Bay Rd; ☽ 9am-5pm late Jun–Labour Day, Wed-Sun mid-May, Thu-Mon Jun) on North Pender isn't open when you arrive, look at the information board listing locations and phone numbers of lodgings and other businesses. There are also free brochures and maps available on the ferry and at other info centres.

At **Driftwood Centre** (4605 Bedwell Harbour Rd) shopping plaza you'll find an ATM, the **post office** (☎ 800-267-1177; ☽ 8:30am-4pm Mon-Fri, 8:30am-noon Sat) and **Driftwood Auto Centre** (☎ 250-629-3005), which has a 24-hour laundromat and showers. For medical emergencies, **Pender Island Health Care Society** (☎ 250-629-3242; 5715 Canal Rd) is near the bridge connecting the islands.

Sights & Activities

The map published by **Galloping Moon Gallery** (☎ 250-629-6020; 4450 Hooson Rd) is nothing if not detailed. It shows beach access points, of which some of the more popular are **Medicine Beach**, **Clam Bay** on North Pender and **Gowlland Point** on the east coast of South Pender.

Just over the bridge to South Pender is **Mt Norman Park**, and the hike up its namesake (255m) rewards you with grand views of the San Juan and Gulf Islands and a feeling of omnipotence. The trail can be accessed via Ainslie Point Rd (1km hike) or Canal Rd (2.5km hike).

Kayak Pender Island (☎ 250-629-6939, 877-683-1746; www.kayakpenderisland.com; 2319 MacKinnon Rd; lesson from $54, adult/child tour from $39/25) at Otter Bay Marina on North Pender, offers guided kayaking tours, which are pretty spectacular around the many harbors and inlets of the islands.

A lot of accommodations have bikes available to guests to cycle the winding,

narrow roads of islands. **Pender Island Golf & Country Club** (☎ 250-629-6659; 2305 Otter Bay Rd; $26) on North Pender, is open to the public.

Sleeping
NORTH PENDER

Inn on Pender Island (☎ 250-629-3353; 800-550-1572; 4709 Canal Rd; s/d/cabin $79/89/139) This small motel is located on seven acres of wooded property. Rooms in the lodge are bright and comfortable and the log cabins are fully appointed and popular with cyclists. There's an outdoor hot tub for lodgers and the cabins get their very own private tub.

Betty's Bed & Breakfast (☎ 250-629-6599; bettys b-b@direct.ca; 4711 Buccaneer Rd; r $90; ☒) This pink B&B run by Betty is in a wonderful garden setting on the shores of Magic Lake. Take the rowboat for a paddle on the lake or the bikes for a pedal on the islands after you've devoured your full breakfast chosen from the menu.

Oceanside Inn (☎ 250-629-6691; www.pender island.com; 4230 Armadale Rd; r $125-259; ☒) This adults-only, upscale B&B has three tastefully appointed rooms with amazing views from the north coast. To stimulate more than just your sense of sight, sit outside on the deck enjoying your breakfast or soak in the hot tub, taking in the sea air as well as the views.

Arcadia-by-the-Sea (☎ 250-629-3221, 877-470-8439; peterortessa@arcadiabythesea.com; 1329 MacKinnon Rd; cottage $95-185; ☒ ☺) Close to the ferry landing, this adults-only place could stand in as the backdrop for *The Great Gatsby*. The self-contained cottages are nice, bright and cheery, and the grounds are lush and perfect for strolling.

Prior Centennial Park (site $14) has 17 campsites set in thick forest close to Medicine Beach. **Port Browning Marina Resort** (☎ 250-629-3493; 4605 Oak Rd; site/r/cabin $15/50/80; ☒ ☺) has camping near the shore, rooms are in its hardwood-floor beach house and self-contained cabins.

Eating

If you're waiting for your BC Ferries ship to come in, grab a sandwich or hamburger at **The Stand** (☎ 250-629-3292; 1371 Otter Bay Rd; mains $5-9) at the terminal.

Pender Island Bakery Café (☎ 250-629-6453; Driftwood Centre; ☽ breakfast & lunch) The local coffeehouse and fuel-up spot has great breakfast sandwiches as well as ciabatta sandwiches and pizzas. They also brew a mean pot of coffee.

Memories at the Inn (at Inn on Pender Island; ☎ 250-629-3353; 800-550-1572; 4709 Canal Rd; mains $8-13; ☽ 5:30-8pm) This restaurant specializes in pizzas, but is also successful at creating seafood dishes like wild spring salmon or crab cakes. The dining room is small, but inviting, and there are tables on the patio.

Islanders Restaurant (☎ 250-629-6811; 1325 MacKinnon Rd; mains $15-30; ☽ dinner) Everything about this place is local: the art on the walls, the music from the speakers, the chef in the kitchen, and the ingredients on the menu – except for the wild Arctic musk ox. The small and refined dining room isn't 'shush' quiet, but reflective and pensive 'enjoy-the-food-on-your-plate-and-views-out-the-window' quiet.

Seaside Pub & Bistro (Poets Cove; mains $7-15) It has an upscale and shipshape look, but a casual and laid back feel. Microbrews and daily fresh seafood specials make appearances on the typical pub menu, and the views from the deck are some of the most serene in the Gulf Islands.

Shopping

Galloping Moon Gallery (☎ 250-629-6020; 4450 Hooson Rd) features local arts and crafts, including clothes, candles, gargoyles, gift foods, and linens. Shop around, or just grab a cup of coffee and sit in the garden. Most artists open their studios to the public and the island map brochure will tell you who, where and when. **'In Toon' Productions** (☎ 866-422-8666; www.getintoon.com; 4527 Bedwell Harbour Rd; $45; ☽ closed Tue) will put you in the funny pages by drawing your face, or someone from a picture, onto a comic book cover with incredible detail.

Getting There & Around

BC Ferries (☎ 250-537-5313, 888-223-3779; www.bcferries.com; ☽ 7am-8:30pm, 7am-9:30pm Fri-Sun) departs from Otter Bay on North Pender. Sailings to Salt Spring are always non-stop and it's possible to get a non-stop trip to Tsawwassen, Swartz Bay or another island, depending on the time and day. See p380 for more on ferry travel in general and p176 for more on Gulf Island travel.

Having a car isn't crucial since there are several lodgings close to the ferry. If you

---

PARK IT

Over 200 years after George Vancouver put the area under British protection, the Southern Gulf Islands are finally getting protected status. The Pacific Marine Heritage Legacy was conceived in 1995 and officially launched in 2000 when the magnificent viewpoint of Narvaez Bay Pacific Marine Heritage Protected Area and the heritage stone house, sandstone quarry and barge docks at historic Taylor Point Pacific Marine Heritage Park on Saturna Island were covered under the act.

On May 9, 2003, the **Gulf Islands National Park Reserve** (☎ 250-654-4000; www.pc.gc.ca/pn-np/bc/gulf) was created, covering 33 sq km on 16 islands. It will be a park in transition for some time as land needs to change hands, but the federal-provincial plan has been well received by residents who don't want the beauty that drew them here to be overrun with urban development.

---

don't have wheels, and your host can't pick you up, catch a ride with **Pender Island Taxi** (☎ 250-629-6516).

SATURNA ISLAND
pop 350

Saturna Island makes a strong case for the argument that glamour translates to popularity. As the least accessible of the major southern Gulf Islands, Saturna is an untrodden gem ripe with naturally beautiful environments waiting to be explored. It's also home to the first chunks of land protected under the Pacific Marine Heritage Legacy (see the boxed text, above).

The annual Saturna Island map brochure lists all the accommodations and activities and can be picked up on the ferry, or see www.saturnatourism.com. The **post office** (☎ 800-267-1177; 101 Navarez Bay Rd; ☽ 9am-3pm Tue-Sat) is in the Saturna General Store. Get some cash before you come and try not to get hurt while you're here – as there are no ATMs and the **medical clinic** (☎ 250-539-5553, 250-539-5423; 185 East Point Rd; ☽ Tue) has limited hours.

Sights & Activities
Winter Cove Provincial Marine Park, on the island's northern side, has a fine white, sandy

beach with access to fishing, boating and swimming. The hiking trail that wanders between forest and coastline is especially nice in the spring, when wild flowers bloom and cover the ground in pinks and golds. At the top of **Mt Warburton Pike** (497m) you'll find a wildlife reserve with goats and pleasant views of Georgia Strait, countless islands and a jumble of telecommunications equipment.

Saturna Island Vineyards (☎ 250-539-5139, 877-918-3388; 8 Quarry Rd; ☯ 11:30am-4:30pm May-Oct) offers tastings and tours though its beautiful vineyards and post-and-beam built winery.

Whales migrating through Georgia Strait typically travel between the Gulf and San Juan Islands; since Saturna is the easternmost of the Gulf Islands, some of the best whale-watching – without getting on a boat – can be seen from the shores of **East Point Regional Park**. Near the ferry, **Saturna Sea Kayaking** (☎ 250-539-5553; 121 Boot Cove Rd; half-/full-day $35/45, tours from $50) offers kayaking lessons and rentals, along with good paddling advice for Saturna and surrounding islands.

Saturna hasn't been left off the 'places where artists live' list; the tourism map brochure lists those who invite visitors to their studios, usually by appointment.

Sleeping & Eating

There are no campgrounds on Saturna Island and it's not the kind of place where you can just show up and get a room, so reserve ahead of time. All eateries on Saturna close by 8pm, so be prepared if you're the midnight-snack kind of person.

East Point Resort (☎ 250-539-2975; 187 East Point Rd; cottage $85-115) Six individual cottages sit on these 80 acres of forested land on the east coast of the island. Private sandy beaches or patios facing the water are excellent places for watching whales. There's a seven-day minimum stay in high season and two-day in the low-season.

Saturna Lodge (☎ 250-539-2254, 888-539-8800; www.saturna-island.bc.ca; 130 Payne Rd; r $135-195, dinner $30; ☯ restaurant dinner) Unpretentious elegance is found in the seven unique rooms at this lodge on the grounds of the vineyards. The country furnishings contrast the coastal setting, but the result is relaxing harmony. A gourmet breakfast is included for guests but nonguests aren't exempt from enjoying

a delicious meal here. Fixed-price dinners blend fresh seafood with locally grown produce and locally-raised lamb.

Pick up picnic goodies at **Saturna General Store** (☎ 250-539-2936; 101 Navarez Bay Rd; snacks $4-7) featuring locally made Haggis Farm baked goods, fresh produce and deli items, or grab some soup or a wrap at the small café. The **Lighthouse Pub** (☎ 250-539-5725; 102 East Point Rd; mains $7-10) at the Saturna Point Store is another popular spot for a quick bite.

Getting There & Around

BC Ferries (☎ 250-537-5313, 888-223-3779; www.bc ferries.com; ☯ 6:30am-4:30pm, 6:30am-9:30pm Victoria sailings) departs from Lyall Harbour on Saturna and most sailings stop first at Mayne Island. There is no direct sailing to/from Tsawwassen so expect a two- to four-hour trip that transfers at Mayne or Swartz Bay. See p380 for more on ferry travel in general and p176 for more on Gulf Island travel.

You don't absolutely need a car on Saturna, since some lodgings are near the ferry terminal, but there is no taxi or bus service.

MAYNE ISLAND
pop 900

Geographers and anthropologists will appreciate the historical necessity and geographic turmoil of Mayne Island. Situated halfway between Vancouver Island and the mouth of the Fraser River, it served as an important stopover for gold-rushers. It also fronts Active Pass, the narrowest channel between Vancouver Island and the mainland, resulting in a tight squeeze before the dawn of the age of ocean liners. Today, Mayne Island is where a number of resident artists, musicians, writers, and professional people call home, though for some it's a second (or third) home.

Information

The ferry has free copies of the Mayne Island brochure, which contains a good map and current listings of places to stay, eat and play. You'll also find an information panel set up just past the Village Bay ferry terminal on the right-hand side. For more local information, visit www.mayneisland.com.

There are no ATMs on Mayne Island. The **post office** (☎ 800-267-1177; 472 Village Bay Rd;

9am-6pm Mon-Fri, 9am-noon Sat) is at Tru Value Foods, and the **Mayne Library** (☎ 250-539-2673; 11am-3pm Wed, Fri & Sat) is across the street. Next door, **Miners Bay Books** (☎ 250-539-3112; 400 Fernhill Rd) carries a good selection of new and used books for adults and children.

The **Health Centre** (☎ 250-539-2312; cnr Fernhill & Felix Jack Rds) is there for your boo-hoos.

Sights & Activities

The **Plumper Pass Lock-up** (☎ 250-539-5286; 11am-3pm Fri-Mon late Jun–early Sep) is a tiny museum that once served as a jailhouse for late-19th-century rowdies. Grab the *Mayne Island Arts & Crafts Guide and Map* on the ferry to visit the **artists' studios** around the island. **Treefrog Gallery** (☎ 250-539-3551; 574 Fernhill Rd) in Fernhill Centre, between Miners Bay and Bennett Bay, features local creations.

Dinner Bay Park, on Mayne's south shore, has a nice sandy beach, and recently added an incredibly authentic and tranquil **Japanese Garden**, commemorating the Japanese who lived on the island in the first half of the 20th century until WWII. It's an immaculate garden in a very unlikely place.

Georgina Point Heritage Park, at the north end of the island, is home to the lighthouse that was established in 1885 and staffed until 1997. The lighthouse and the keeper's house are still there and it's an invigorating place to be when the waves are pounding against the shore.

The forested hike to the top of **Mt Parke** will reward you with 360-degree views of Active Pass that make the islands seem insignificant. The trailhead is at the end of Montrose Drive, near Fernhill Centre.

Mayne Island Canoe & Kayak Rentals (☎ 250-539-2667; 250-539-0077; www.maynekayak.com; 411 Fernhill Rd; 2hr/day $26/45) rents kayaks and offers free ferry pick-ups; they'll also drop you and then come get you at different bays around the island.

Mayne offers leisurely back-road cycling; most accommodations have bikes for guest use. **Island Charters** (☎ 250-539-5040; maynemistral@ gulfislands.com; tours from $135) offers full- or half-day sailboat cruises aboard a 33ft (10m) vessel.

Sleeping & Eating

Mayne Inn Hotel (☎ 250-539-3122; 494 Arbutus Dr; r $70-80) This waterfront hotel on Bennett Bay has eight bright and spacious rooms with outstanding east-facing views. There's a sand volleyball court outside and funky, owner-created pottery caricatures for sale in the lobby. The restaurant and bar downstairs serve up the usual family-dining and seafood options but the huge deck outside has possibly one of the calmest views on the island.

Oceanwood Country Inn (☎ 250-539-5074; www.oceanwood.com; 630 Dinner Bay Rd; r $159-329, dinner $48; ☒) Hidden behind tall trees and nestled against the rocky coast sits this unassumingly luxurious inn. All rooms are plush, spacious and the views of Navy Channel are incredible. Rates include breakfast and afternoon tea in the downstairs restaurant, which is also open to nonguests for dinner.

The dining room itself is an intimate, saffron-colored pocket of cozy. The glass doors are opened on summer evenings, allowing you to see the view. The menu is an ever-changing prix-fixe four-course affair focused on local meat, seafood and produce, with vegetarian options.

Tinkerers B&B (☎ 250-539-2280; tinkerers@gulfnet .sd64.bc.ca; 417 Sunset Pl; $90-115; ☒) Along Sunset Place in Miners Bay, this charming house overlooking Active Pass has rooms of various configurations in an excellent garden setting. Language and knife-sharpening tutorials are offered, or you can take the 'I'm on vacation' route and laze in the hammock, enjoy the sea views or go for a bike ride. The upstairs rooms share a shower, but they've got the best views.

Springwater Lodge (☎ 250-539-5521; spring waterlodge@netscape.net; r/cabin $40/95, mains $7-13) This white pioneer-days hotel (established 1890) could possibly be the oldest continuously operating hotel in BC. The rooms in the lodge share a bathroom and are basic but the old furniture and hardwood floor gives them character. There are also two-bedroom, fully furnished cabins with sun decks.

The dining room, with a distinct seafaring heritage and the ocean front deck, invites loyal locals and visitors to enjoy a meal. The Springwater burger is a common favorite and the seafood is as delicious as you'd expect from a place right on the ocean.

Cobworks (☎ 250-539-5253; 640 Horton Bay Rd; site/cobhouse $15/80, tour/course $5/200-2600; tour

2pm last Sun May-Aug) This campground's big draw is a stay in a cobhouse – made from a mixture of sand, clay and straw. The company's main focus is creating dwellings made from natural materials and offers seminars where you learn to build your own dirt-cheap house. Only the one house can be rented and even if it's not available (it's often booked far in advance) the tour of other cobhouses on Mayne is pretty interesting.

Mayne Island Eco Camping Tours & Charters (☎ 250-539-2667; 359 Maple Dr; sites per person $12), at Miners Bay, offers forested sites on the coast and a hot tub and showers.

Miners Bay Café (☎ 250-539-9888; 417 Fernhill Rd; mains $4-10) This earthy café features lots of vegetarian options and excellent pizzas; kick back on the couches on the front deck under birch trees. **Dolphins** (☎ 250-539-3324) offers short-order and tasty food at the Village Bay ferry.

Getting There & Around

BC Ferries (☎ 250-537-5313, 888-223-3779; www.bc ferries.com; ☽ 7:20am-9:10pm) sails from Village Bay, on Mayne's west side. Sailings to Galiano are always nonstop, sailings to other destinations vary. See p380 for more on ferry travel in general and p176 for more on Gulf Island travel.

Mayne is a fairly large island and getting around on foot will take a while if you want to spread out beyond Miner's Bay. Most accommodations have bikes for guests but if you're not the pedaling type, **MIDAS Taxi Company** (☎ 250-539-3132, 250-539-0181) offers taxi service.

GALIANO ISLAND
pop 1000

Long and narrow Galiano Island has an uncrowded feel, though it's the closest island to the mainland and oft-visited. It supports the most natural and ecological diversity of the main Gulf islands and offers a bounty of activity for marine enthusiasts and landlubbers alike.

Information

As always, grab the island map brochure on the ferry; the **Galiano Chamber of Commerce** (☎ 250-539-2233; www.galianoisland.com) has an information shack on your right-hand side as you leave the ferry.

Galiano Island has no banks but there's an ATM at the Hummingbird Pub (p185). Gulf Islands Insurance, near the ferry, houses the **post office** (☎ 800-267-1177; 23 Madrona Rd; 9am-4:30pm Mon-Fri, 9am-2pm Sat). The **Health Care Centre** (☎ 250-539-3230; 908 Burrill Rd; 9am-noon & 1:30-4:30pm Mon, Tue, Thu & Fri) keeps regular hours but will also respond to emergencies.

Parks & Beaches

The sheltered peninsula of **Montague Harbour Provincial Marine Park** (☎ 250-539-2115) allows you to enjoy both relaxing sunrises and sunsets. A trail leads through the ecological hodgepodge of white shell beaches, open meadows, tidal lagoons, towering forests and the cliff carved by glacial movements.

Bluffs Park boasts great views of Active Pass, along with 5km of hiking paths. Known for its abundant and colorful bird life, **Bodega Ridge Provincial Park** contains the sheer drop-off Lovers' Leap viewpoint. **Bellhouse Park**, the island's easternmost point, looks on Active Pass from the shallow granite slope at sea level.

Activities

Alcala Point and its friendly wolf eels; Race Point's and Baines Bay's anemone walls; the cave at Matthews Point; and the sunken Point Grey tugboat make Galiano a good spot for scuba diving. For gear and tours, contact **Galiano Island Diving** (☎ 250-539-3109; 1005 Devina Dr; rental $49).

Galiano's sandstone cliffs can really only be appreciated from offshore; the protected waters of Trincomali Channel and the chaotic waters of Active Pass appease paddlers of all kayaking skill-levels. **Gulf Island Kayaking** (☎ 250-539-2442; www.seakayak.ca; Montague Marina 3hr/full-day rental $28/48, tours from $40) will help with rentals and specializes in multi-day tours.

Bodega Trails (☎ 250-415-0913; $30) owner Steve Oscko will tell you stories and take you horseback riding through the pastoral lands on the ridge. Cycling the island's narrow, hilly roads is thrilling and **Galiano Bicycle Rental & Repair** (☎ 250-539-9906; 36 Burril Rd; 4hr/full-day $23/28), near Sturdies Bay, has the equipment you'll need. For moped rentals **Galiano Adventures** (☎ 250-539-3443, 877-303-3546; 300 Sticks Allison Rd; hr/day $20/99) at Montague Marina, is the spot.

Sleeping

Bodega Resort (☎ 250-539-2677; 120 Cook Rd; r/cabin $80/100; ✗) This pastoral farmland setting up on the ridge has incredible views onto Trincomali Channel, or take the short trail up the hill for some truly panoramic views. The fully equipped, two-story log cottages are furnished in rustic country fashion, as are the two B&B rooms on the lodge. Help yourself to the fruits of the apple, fig, plum trees and blackberry bushes and feel free to play with the sheep.

Island Time B&B (☎ 250-539-3506, 877-588-3506; www.gulfislands.com/islandtime; 952 Sticks Allison Rd; $135-215; ✗) It's enough that this place enjoys a spectacular setting of wooded seclusion right on the west coast; but hospitality and comfort are taken up a notch when you wake up in your bright, comfortable room and wander to the breakfast nook to enjoy a four-course breakfast, made from scratch. The east-facing wall is seemingly made from glass and you may spend the bulk of your visit in the house or the outdoor hot tub watching and listening to the pounding surf.

Galiano Inn (☎ 250-539-3388, 877-530-3939; www.galianoinn.com; 134 Madrona Dr; r $325) This Mediterranean-looking villa on Sturdies Bay employs a West Coast feel. The plush rooms include fireplaces and patios to enjoy the views of Active Pass.

Montague Harbour Provincial Marine Park (☎ 800-689-9025; www.discovercamping.ca; site $17) has 25 drive-in and 15 walk-in campsites. Site Nos 34 to 38 are on a cliff above the harbour and are only a five-minute walk from the parking lot. Kayakers and hikers appreciate **Dionisio Point Provincial Park** (☎ 250-539-2115; backcountry/frontcountry $5/14) at the island's far northwest end; the park can only be reached by boat or via the hiking trail from Devina Drive.

Eating

Max & Moritz Spicy Island Food House (☎ 250-539-5888; mains $3.50-8) From this trailer at the ferry terminal, you can grab some delicious Indonesian and German food. Get to the ferry early to sample some curried dishes or tantalizing *scaschliktasche* (sha-she-shlatz-kee) – grilled meat and vegetables in a pita.

Hummingbird Pub (☎ 250-539-5472; 47 Sturdies Bay Rd; mains $8-12) This is where locals and regular visitors come to hang out and enjoy a beer or an honest meal. The huge log columns and well-used outdoor deck lend the pub an earthy feel and the dining room, hummingbird trivia and play area make it a favorite for families.

Harbour Grill (☎ 250-539-5733; Montague Marina; mains $8-20) This restaurant on the deck of Montague Marina makes standard breakfasts and pick-your-meat dinners.

Getting There & Around

BC Ferries (☎ 250-537-5313, 888-223-3779; www.bcferries.com; ☺ 6:30am-9pm) sails from Sturdies Bay, on Galiano's east end, which is the usual first stop from Tsawwassen, before continuing on to Swartz Bay via other islands. See p380 for more on ferry travel in general and p176 for more on Gulf Island travel.

Go Galiano Island Shuttle (☎ 250-539-0202; $4; ☺ ferry arrivals daily in summer, Fri-Sun May, Jun & Sep) meets the ferries for island transport and also makes evening runs to the Hummingbird Pub.

Fraser-Thompson Region

East of Vancouver, British Columbia's legendary topography becomes apparent: mountains rise up, beautiful green valleys drop down and rivers rush through it all. At the eastern edge of the Thompson Valley, the climate begins to dry out, and the wildlife you see will be more of the livestock variety, as the area supports some of BC's biggest farms. Throughout the region, outdoor activities abound. It was on the route of gold prospectors who rushed through the area on their way to the Cariboo.

The towns here are generally small and friendly. An exception is Kamloops, which is big and friendly and has a fantastic First Nations cultural center and museum. The area offers many great bases for exploring, either on hikes through the provincial parks or on white-water rafting trips down the Fraser, Chilliwack, Thompson or Nahatlatch Rivers. This is the high country and skiing is also a big draw.

These areas are both drive-throughs and destinations. You'll notice that the highways can be crowded (which will become a distant memory if you're following Hwy 1 north), and the services are generally plentiful. If you're staying a while, you might get a chance to see a heritage farm near Harrison Hot Springs, a great music festival in Merrit, a powwow in Kamloops, spawning sockeye in Roderick Haig-Brown Provincial Park or the sights made famous in the film *First Blood* in Hope.

HIGHLIGHTS

- Hiking the Paintbrush Nature trail through lupine meadows at **EC Manning Provincial Park** (p191)

- Whitewater rafting untamed rivers near **Lytton** (p193) – you'll crash, bang, get soaked and have a blast

- Renting a houseboat and floating away a weekend with your pals on scenic **Shuswap Lake** (p200)

- Visiting **Secwepemc Museum & Heritage Park** (p196) to see how First Nations people thrived in the area for centuries

- Skiing **Sun Peaks Resort** (p198) with the whole family – kids will love the Adventure Park here

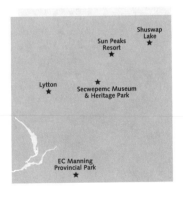

FRASER-THOMPSON REGION

THE FRASER CANYON & THOMPSON VALLEY

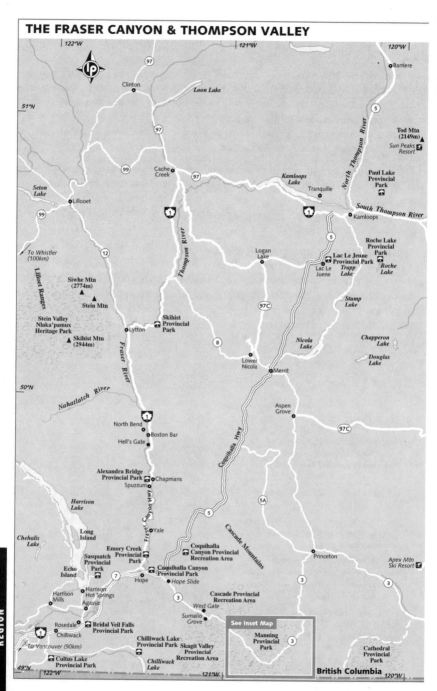

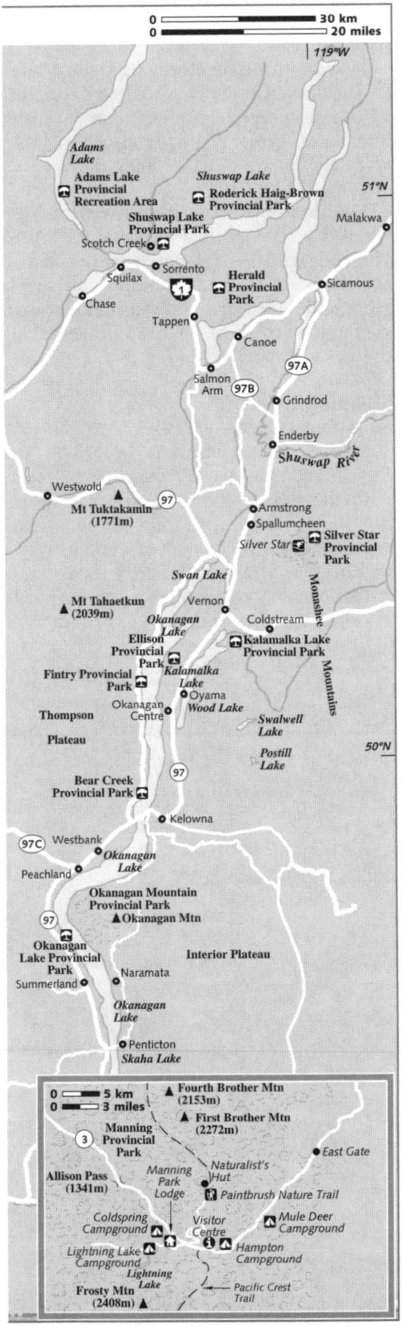

FRASER CANYON

A mighty river has carved a dramatic canyon between the Coast and Cascade Mountains, before taking an odd buttonhook west near Hope, creating a flat, wide valley bottom on its way towards the Pacific Ocean. Simon Fraser (fray-zer, not 'Frasier' like the TV show) explored it in 1808 and had such an adventurous time that the river, canyon and valley now bear his name. In order to have an equally good time, you'll have to do the opposite of most travelers who rip through, desperate to get to the coast or the interior; stop, smell the roses, take in the sights and enjoy the ride. The small towns, deep canyons, wild rivers and accessible wilderness areas make excellent day- or weekend-trips from Vancouver.

HOPE

pop 6200

Many theories exist on how this former Hudson's Bay Company fort got its name, but Vancouverites will say once you head north or east of here you're literally 'beyond Hope'. The northwest corner of town is framed by the scenic valley.

Hwys 1, 3 and 5 converge east of town making it an usual pit stop on the way to or from the interior, but there's enough Hope to warrant a longer stay.

Information

The **Visitor Info Centre** (☎ 604-869-2021; 919 Water Ave; 9am-5pm) has helpful staff inside and information kiosks outside if you arrive after hours. The **post office** (☎ 800-267-1177; 777 Fraser St; 8:30am-5pm Mon-Fri) will help with your mailing needs. **Blue Moose Café** (☎ 604-896-0729; 322 Wallace St; 8am-10pm; $1 per 20min) is a hip place to get a coffee and a muffin and check email. For medical help, there's **Fraser Canyon Hospital** (☎ 604-869-5656; 1275 7th Ave).

Sights

Most people head towards **Memorial Park** in the town center with its **Friendship Garden** built by local Japanese-Canadians, and **chainsaw carvings** created by local artist Pete Ryan, but riverside **Centennial Park** has peaceful views of the Fraser. Built in 1861, **Historic Christ Church** (☎ 604-869-5402; 681 Fraser St)

HOPE & PROSPERITY

The obvious star of bullet-riddled and carnage-heavy *First Blood*, first of the *Rambo* movies, was Sylvester Stallone, but a nod for best supporting actor should go to the town of Hope. In the fall of 1981 a crew of Hollywood set designers arrived with tools and American flags in hand to create buildings and false fronts to convert Hope into the small-town American birthplace of John Rambo. Fortunately, not all Hope was lost; the old southern entrance to town, Flood Hope Rd, still runs under the 'Welcome to Hope' sign seen in the opening scenes of the movie. Canyons, rivers, even the Othello Tunnels played a significant role, and the natural beauty of the area got real ugly. Other movies have been filmed in Hope since, but this movie has such a cult-like following that a copy of *First Blood* can be viewed in the museum, and the info centre has directions for self-guided tours of shooting, pun intended, locations.

is the oldest church on BC's mainland still used for regular services.

A walk through **Othello Quintette Tunnels** in **Coquihalla Canyon Provincial Park** (parking $3 per day) reveals awesome canyon-views and engineering genius, considering they were cut for the Kettle Valley Railway between 1911 and 1919.

Decide for yourself if you want to stop where four people were buried in a 1965 landslide and two planes have crashed in the years since, but thousands of people stop, look and learn without incident each year at the **Hope Slide**, 20km southwest along the Crowsnest Hwy.

Sleeping & Eating

Swiss Chalets (☎ 604-869-9020; fax 604-869-7588; 456 Trans-Canada Hwy; s/d $49/55; ✗ ✗) A cute little place that doesn't seem out of place with the mountainous backdrop. The individual chalets with dark brown trim, wood-paneled walls – not in a cheesy way – and fireplaces make for a cozy stay.

Old Hope-Princeton Way is a motel strip with reasonable prices and plenty of rooms:

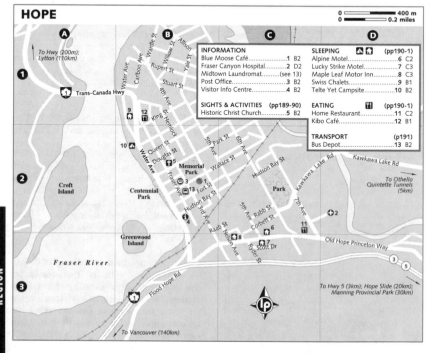

HOPE

| | 0 ————— 400 m |
| | 0 ▬▬▬▬ 0.2 miles |

INFORMATION	
Blue Moose Café	1 B2
Fraser Canyon Hospital	2 D2
Midtown Laundromat	(see 13)
Post Office	3 B2
Visitor Info Centre	4 B2

SIGHTS & ACTIVITIES	(pp189–90)
Historic Christ Church	5 B2

SLEEPING 🏠 🏠	(pp190–1)
Alpine Motel	6 C2
Lucky Strike Motel	7 C3
Maple Leaf Motor Inn	8 C3
Swiss Chalets	9 B1
Telte Yet Campsite	10 B2

EATING 🍽	(pp190–1)
Home Restaurant	11 C2
Kibo Café	12 B1

TRANSPORT	(p191)
Bus Depot	13 B2

To Hwy (200m); Lytton (110km)

Trans-Canada Hwy

Croft Island

Centennial Park

Greenwood Island

Fraser River

Memorial Park

Kawkawa Lake Rd

To Othello Quintette Tunnels (5km)

Park

Old Hope Princeton Way

To Hwy 5 (3km); Hope Slide (20km); Manning Provincial Park (30km)

Flood Hope Rd

To Vancouver (140km)

Maple Leaf Motor Inn (☎ 604-869-7107; mapleleaf inn@uniserve.com; 377 Old Hope Princeton Way, with/ without kitchenettes $55/65; ✗ ✗)
Lucky Strike Motel (☎ 604-869-5715; 504 Old Hope Princeton Way; $60; ✗ ✗ ✗)
Alpine Motel (☎ 604-869-9931; alpinemotel2001@ hotmail.com; 505 Old Hope-Princeton Way; $60; ✗ ✗)

Telte Yet Campsite (☎ 604-869-9481; 600 Water Ave; site $12-19) on the river, has showers, laundry and a play area.

Home Restaurant (☎ 604-869-5558; 665 Old Hope Princeton Way; mains $7-11) It's away from the town center, but the name says it all. Popular enough that you may have to stand in line for a table, the huge portions and tasty, home cooking make it worth the wait.

Kibo Café (☎ 604-869-7317; 267 King St; mains $8-10) A pleasant surprise in a town you might not expect good Japanese food. The tempura is delicious and though the sushi selection is limited, the California rolls taste great. There's a patio, so eat outside if the weather is nice.

Getting There & Away
Greyhound (☎ 800-661-8747; www.greyhound.ca; adult/child $21.45/10.75) runs five buses from Vancouver to the **Midtown Laundromat** (☎ 604-869-9715; 800 3rd Ave, No 1) daily.

HARRISON HOT SPRINGS & AROUND
pop 1350

The small, sandy beach at the southern end of **Harrison Lake** has made this town a resort area since the 1880s. This is also Sasquatch country, keep your eyes peeled – the obligatory claims of 'I saw Bigfoot' are made every summer.

The **Visitor Info Centre** (☎ 604-796-3425; 499 Hot Springs Rd; ☼ 9am-5pm May-Oct) is on the way into town. The **hot springs** are a five-minute walk west of the lake but aren't open to the public; its waters, however, are pumped into the **Harrison Public Pool** (☼ 9am-9pm; adult/child $9/7).

Kilby Store & Farm (☎ 604-796-9576; www.kilby.ca; adult/child $6/5) Harrison Mills (pop 100) is known for its restored and impressive 1920s general store. Feed the farm animals, do some chores that make mowing the lawn seem like a cake-walk, try on some period clothing and enjoy a cup and scone ($2 to $6) in the charming tearoom.

Harrison Lake has been steadily growing in popularity for **boating** and **water-skiing**.

If you don't have your own, **Harrison Water Sports** (☎ 604-796-3513; www.harrisonwatersports .com), at the marina on the beach, will take care of that with their rentals and charters.

Sleeping & Eating
Bungalow Motel (☎ 604-796-3536; www.bungalow motel.com; 511 Lillooet Ave; $70-95) The 12 individual cabins, most with kitchens, are bigger than they look. It's close enough to the beach to walk, but far enough so you've got your own space.

Harrison Hot Springs Resort (☎ 604-796-2244, 800-663-2266; www.harrisonresort.com; 100 Esplanade; r with/without view $180/150, cottage $239; ✗ ✗ ✗) On the west end of the beach and off the beaten path, this hotel rises above the treetops and watches over the lake with its 75-year-old all-knowing presence. Featuring its own outdoor mineral pools, there are nice cottages available, but if it's your first time here, you'll want a room with a view of the lake.

Sasquatch Provincial Park (☎ 800-689-9025; www.discovercamping.ca; site $14) is 6km north of town via Hwy 7. Closer to town, **Bigfoot Campgrounds** (☎ 604-796-9767, 800-294-9907; 670 Hot Springs Rd; $15-28) has showers and laundry.

Charlie's on the Lake & Harry's Cabaret (☎ 604-796-2695; 234 Esplanade) If Charlie and Harry were brothers or roommates, Charlie would be the successful businessman and Harry would be 'between jobs'. Charlie's is a dinner-only place with a formal atmosphere featuring steak and seafood (mains $12 to $18) whereas Harry's is more hip and casual, serving burgers and appetizers ($6 to $11) on the rooftop patio overlooking the lake.

EC MANNING PROVINCIAL PARK
Named after former Chief Forester Ernest C Manning, this 70,844-hectare provincial **park** (☎ 604-795-6169; wlapwww.gov.bc.ca/bcparks), 30km southeast of Hope via Hwy 3, is a model of diversity. Habitat for over 200 species of birds and 60 species of mammals, its climates range from arid valley-bottoms to alpine country above the trees. Manning marks the end of the 4240km Mexico-to-Canada **Pacific Crest Trail,** and hikers can often be found swapping tales inside Manning Park Resort's **Bear's Den Pub.**

The **Visitor Info Centre** (☼ 8:30am-4:30pm Jun-Oct, 8:30am-4pm Mon-Fri Oct-May) has detailed

hiking descriptions and a 3D relief model of the park. People may look at you funny, but fill your bottles with fresh mountain-water at the faucet near the resort parking lot.

Good hiking choices include:

Dry Ridge Trail (3km roundtrip) Crosses from dry interior to alpine climate. Excellent views and wildflowers.

Heather Trail (21km one-way; 300m elevation gain) Usually an overnight hike through premier alpine country and lupine meadows; first half makes great day-hike; bring the bug spray.

Lightning Lake Loop (9km roundtrip)

Paintbrush Nature Trail (1.5 km) The short first leg of Heather Trail.

Sumallo Grove Trail (700m roundtrip) Wheelchair-accessible trail lined by impressive stands of western red cedar and Douglas fir.

If you don't have time to hike, take the five-minute drive to the spectacular views of bioclimatology and geomorphology and such stuff at **Cascade lookout**.

Motorized boats aren't allowed, so the lakes are excellent for fishing, swimming, canoeing and kayaking.

Rather than hibernate, Manning puts on its parka and stares winter in the face. **Manning Park Resort** (250-840-8822, 800-330-3321; www.manningparkresort.com; adult/child lift-ticket $33/21.50) runs a downhill ski and snowboard area, and 100km of groomed trails for cross-country skiing and snowshoeing.

The **resort** (r/cabin/chalet from $69/115/189) is the only indoor lodging in the park. The rooms in the lodge are comfy, or try a private cabin or chalet. All rooms are well furnished but don't go overboard. The chalets and cabins are placed in an unfortunate parking-lot setting, but your gaze will almost always be fixated up at the mountains anyway.

Stay outdoors at **Coldspring**, **Hampton** or **Mule Campgrounds** (800-689-9025; www.discover camping.ca; site $14) or the more popular, maybe due to the showers, **Lightning Lake Campground** (800-689-9025; www.discovercamping.ca; site $22).

Greyhound (800-661-8747; www.greyhound.ca; adult/child $35/17.55) buses stop five times daily from Vancouver.

HOPE TO LYTTON

North of Hope, Hwy 1 takes a field-trip through the impressive steep-sided scenery and glacial creations of the Fraser Canyon. Use the many pullouts to stop and enjoy

the view. It's traditional to honk your horn while passing through the **Seven Canyon Tunnels** that were blasted through the mountains between Yale and Boston Bar.

Founded by – big surprise – the Hudson's Bay Company, **Yale** (pop 17) marked the furthest point that paddle wheelers could go during the gold rush, and at its peak claimed to be the largest city north of San Francisco and west of Chicago. **The Yale Museum** (604-863-2324; 31187 Douglas St; adult/child $4.50/2.50; 10am-5pm May-Oct) is jammed with history and trinkets from the time.

Alexandra Bridge Provincial Park (604-795-6169; wlapwww.gov.bc.ca/bcparks/explore/parkpgs/alexandra.htm) The historical 1861 **Alexandra Bridge** can be admired as it still spans the Fraser – though traffic now uses the 1926 replacement to cross. The toll for the first bridge was $7.40/ton but in an odd case of reverse-inflation, these days it's free.

Hell's Gate Airtram (604-867-9277; adult/child $12/6.50; 9am-6pm Jun-Sep, varies other times) Simon Fraser declared, 'Surely we've arrived at the gate of Hell' when he arrived at this narrow spot in the canyon in 1808. You may feel like muttering the same at this carnivalesque tourist-trap 31km north of Yale. However, beyond the tackiness are some genuinely educational displays and interesting information on the upriver struggles of historical people and modern-day salmon. The tram is neither scary nor exhilarating, and if you can't justify the cost, it is possible to walk down a steep 1km switchback to the bridge. There is a warning at the bottom of the trail that the train tracks you must cross are private property and trains can arrive without warning, so please do be careful.

LYTTON
pop 320

Lytton is a quiet town located where the clear-running Thompson River meets the silt-laden Fraser in a dramatic aqua-battle that the mighty Fraser wins before continuing to the Pacific. Lytton justifiably claims to be the rafting capital of BC; it also serves as the gateway to the Stein Valley. The helpful staff at the **Visitor Info Centre** (250-455-2523; 400 Fraser St; 10am-4pm May, Jun & Sep, 9am-5pm summer, 11am-2pm Oct-May) offers heaps of information on area recreation.

Stein Valley Nlaka'pamux (nuh-la-ka-pa-mux) **Heritage Park** (wlapwww.gov.bc.ca/bcparks/explore/parkpgs/steinvly.htm) is ecologically diverse and relatively unlogged, and offers some truly superb hiking. Weekend hikes are possible, but to experience semi-desert valleys and alpine glaciers in the same journey, check the website or check out *Stein Valley: Wilderness Guidebook* by Gordon R White, and plan ahead for a multi-day hike. The free **ferry** (☻ 6:30am-10:15pm) north of Lytton heads over the Fraser to the park's entrance.

Whitewater Rafting

There are many adventure outfitters who can gear you up for a raft trip in the high country. One-day trips cost $80 to $120 per adult and most places offer discounts on Sundays. Lytton-based **Kumsheen Raft Adventures** (☎ 800-663-6667; www.kumsheen.com; day-trips $122, site/cabin $9/79), 6km east of town, offers both power trips (hang on, the motor does the work) and paddle trips (dig in and use your pipes); either way, you'll get soaked. After-rafters can after-party at the campsites or furnished four-person cabin tents.

Other rafting companies are based outside of town and shun motorized trips:
Fraser River Raft Expeditions (☎ 800-363-7238; www.fraserraft.com; $105) Runs the lesser-known but very fast Nahatlatch River.
Hyak River Rafting (☎ 800-663-7238; www.hyak.com; $109)
REO Rafting Adventure Resort (☎ 800-736-7238; www.reorafting.com; $125) Also runs the Nahatlatch River.

Sleeping & Eating

Totem Motel & Lodge (☎ 250-455-2321, fax 250-455-6696; www.angelfire.com/bc2/totemmotel; 320 Fraser St; from $50; ⊠ ⊠) This cute place has red and white cottages that sit on a cliff above the Fraser and three motel-style rooms in a 1912 lodge. All rooms are nice and clean and the owners have done their best to keep the original look.

Skihist Provincial Park (☎ 250-315-2771; site $17), east on Hwy 1, made the most of a mostly barren landscape with private sites.

Acacia Leaf Café (☎ 250-455-2101; 437 Main St; mains $7-10) Not quite a greasy-spoon but the Formica table tops and linoleum floor make it pretty close. Good food made by good people with no surprises.

Getting There & Away

Greyhound (☎ 800-661-8747; www.greyhound.ca; adult/child $35/17.55) buses pass through twice daily from Vancouver.

LILLOOET
pop 2750

The 64km stretch of Hwy 12 between Lytton and Lillooet (lil-*oo*-ett) winds through steep rocky canyons, rolling grasslands and flat river valleys of prospector and cowboy country. Lillooet's semi-arid microclimate sees some of the hottest temperatures in Canada, resulting in a landscape akin to northern New Mexico.

Pick up a copy of the informative *Visitor's Guide* at the **Visitor Info Centre** (☎ 250-256-4308; 790 Main St; ☻ 9am-5pm summer, closed Nov–mid-May), which is inside a converted church that also serves as the **museum**.

Gravity Fed Adventures (☎ 250-256-7947; www.gravityfedadventures.com; daytrip/heli-biking/multi-day from $40/200/300; ☻ summer, hrs vary) organize excellent mountain-biking tours through the backcountry: day-trips, multi-day cabin-to-cabin treks, or helicopter trips to the mountains where all you do is hop off and hold on.

Fraser River Jet Boat Adventures (☎ 250-256-4180; adult/child $30/20; ☻ May-Oct) show why paddling is for suckers. Take a jet boat on a river trip for some wild action and the chance to see some wildlife.

THOMPSON VALLEY

The spectacular North Thompson and South Thompson Rivers converge at Kamloops and become the Thompson River. These aquatic gems have supported and transported humans for eons and help explain why this entire area is rich in Shuswap ('shoe-swap') First Nations history and culture. It is a place where lakes and rivers converge, highways connect and cattle thrive. East of Kamloops, just north of the Okanagan Valley, is the Shuswap, an area known for houseboating and summer fun on scenic Shuswap Lake. West of Kamloops, the Thompson River passes through rolling green hills and beautiful ranchlands to Ashcroft, Cache Creek and Logan Lake.

Kamloops is the major town and anchors the area with services and culture. As you head south the land becomes drier and you might feel like you've walked into an old western movie.

KAMLOOPS

pop 77,300

Sitting at the confluence of the North Thompson, South Thompson and Thompson Rivers, Kamloops (or 'Loops', as it's called by the locals) has always served as an important crossroad. The Shuswap Natives used the rivers and many lakes for transportation and salmon fishing. Fur traders arrived in 1811, trading European goods with Shuswaps all along the riverbanks. The Canadian Pacific Railway arrived in 1885, and by 1890 Kamloops had become a bustling transportation center.

The highways took over where the rivers left off. The Trans-Canada Hwy (Hwy 1) cuts east–west through town, the Yellowhead Hwy (Hwy 5) heads north to Jasper, Hwy 5A travels south and the Coquihalla Hwy (Hwy 5) heads southwest to Vancouver.

With its strategic location, the city has grown rapidly since the late 1960s and has turned into a major service and industrial center, thanks to forestry, agriculture and manufacturing.

Kamloops is spread over a large area of lakes and dry, rolling hills. The downtown is delightful and entertaining. Stroll the shops and restaurants of Victoria St and then head down to Riverside Park for a view of the confluence of the rivers.

Orientation

The Thompson River is separated by very busy train tracks from the downtown area. The principal shopping street is Victoria St. The Trans-Canada Hwy runs through the hills above the center. You can reach the north shore of town via the Overlander Bridge (called Blue Bridge by the locals) or the Red Bridge on the north end of downtown. Over the pedestrian bridge from Lansdowne St and 3rd Ave is Riverside Park, a pleasant spot for a picnic or stroll, which has live music some summer nights.

Information

BOOKSTORES

Merlin Books (☎ 250-374-9553; 448 Victoria St; ⓨ 8:30am-7pm Mon-Sat, noon-5pm Sun) Great local

bookstore with regional books, maps, magazines and newspapers.

LAUNDRY

McCleaners Laundry (☎ 250-372-9655; 437 Seymour St; ⓨ 7am-8pm weekdays, 10am-6pm Sat & Sun)

LIBRARY

Public library (☎ 250-372-5145; 465 Victoria St; ⓨ 10am-5pm Mon, Fri & Sat, 10am-9pm Tue-Thu & noon-4pm Sun winter only) Large; has Internet access.

MEDICAL SERVICES

Royal Inland Hospital (☎ 250-374-5111; 311 Columbia St; ⓨ 24hr)

POST

Post office (☎ 250-374-2444; 217 Seymour St; ⓨ 8:30am-5pm Mon-Fri)

TOURIST INFORMATION

Visitor Info Centre (☎ 250-374-3377, 800-662-1994; www.adventurekamloops.com; 1290 W Trans-Canada Hwy, exit 368; ⓨ 8am-6pm daily summer, 9am-6pm Mon-Fri winter) Great view of the town and rivers.

Sights & Activities

Many brick and stone buildings in the downtown core date back to the late 1800s, including the restored 1887 **St Andrews Presbyterian Church**, now the oldest public building in town. Pick up a copy of the Kamloops *Heritage Walking Tour* from the Visitor Info Centre to see additional delights.

The **Kamloops Museum** (☎ 250-828-3576; 207 Seymour St at 2nd Ave; donation; ⓨ 9am-4:30pm Tue-Sat) explores the area history, from the early Shuswaps to the missionaries, from the Overlanders (who passed through on their way to find gold in the Cariboo) to the arrival of the railroad. The video library includes the history of mapmaker and river namesake David Thompson.

Kamloops Art Gallery (☎ 250-828-3543; 465 Victoria St; adult/child $3/2; ⓨ 10am-5pm Tue, Wed & Fri, 10am-9pm Thu, noon-4pm Sat & Sun) in the same industrial-style building as the public library, features an impressive collection of local, regional and national artists.

The **British Columbia Wildlife Park** (☎ 250-573-3242; adult/child $8.95/5.95; ⓨ 8am-4:30pm, 8am-8:30pm Jul & Aug), 17km east of Kamloops on the Trans-Canada Hwy; contains an interesting population of wild things, mostly native to the province.

KAMLOOPS

(pp194–6)

INFORMATION	
Post Office	1 C2
Royal Inland Hospital	2 C3

SIGHTS & ACTIVITIES	(pp194–6)
Kamloops Art Gallery	3 D2
Kamloops Heritage Railway	4 D2
Kamloops Museum	5 C2
McCleaners Laundry	6 C2
Merlin Books	7 D2
Paramount Cinema	8 D2
Public Library	(see 3)
Spoke 'n Motion	9 C2
Sport Mart Place	10 C2
Wanda Sue Paddlewheeler	11 E2

SLEEPING	(pp196–7)
Coast Canadian Hotel	12 C2
Fountain Motel	13 D3
Grandview Motel	14 B2
HI Kamloops	15 C2
Plaza	16 C2
Riverland Motel	17 F2
Silver Sage Tent & Trailer Park	18 D1
Thompson Hotel	19 D2

EATING	(p197)
Kelly O'Bryan's	20 C2
Magnums	21 C2
Peter's Pasta	22 D2
Sanbiki	23 D2
Zach's	24 C2

SHOPPING	
Thompson Park Mall	25 B3

TRANSPORT	(p197)
Greyhound Bus Depot	26 A4

See the Thompson River from the restored **Wanda Sue Paddlewheeler** (☎ 250-374-7447; 1140 River St; adult/child $13.50/7.50; ⏰ times vary, May-Sep). The boat leaves from the terminal at the Old Yacht Club at the foot of 10th Ave. For historic fun on land, ride the **Kamloops Heritage Railway** (☎ 250-374-2141; 510 Lorne St in the old CN station; adult/child $13.50/9; ⏰ times vary, Jul & Aug, also some holidays). The 1912 vintage steam engine pulls vintage cars along the rivers.

Hikers and beach-lovers flock to **Paul Lake Provincial Park**, which is 5km north from Kamloops on Hwy 5, then 19km on Pinantan Rd. Mountain bikers like to do the 20km trip around Paul Lake, while fisher types try for Gerard or rainbow trout. This is a protected habitat for falcons, bald eagles, coyotes and mule deer, so keep your eyes peeled. The 213-hectare **Lac Le Jeune Provincial Park**, 37km south of Hwy 5 is popular for camping, swimming and rainbow-trout fishing on Lac Le Jeune (French for 'the young lake'). In winter the park connects to the Stake Lake cross-country ski trails.

Sleeping

Try to stay downtown so you can easily enjoy Kamloops' nightlife.

MOTELS & HOTELS

Plaza (☎ 250-377-8075, 877-977-5292; www.plaza heritagehotel.com; 405 Victoria St; s/d $99/109; P ✷) Built in 1927 to the then-soaring height of six stories, the Plaza is the pick of Kamloops lodging. Beautifully maintained, its rooms boast period furnishings and each is decorated differently. Good views of the rivers from high floors are perfect for sunsets; you can also ponder the sunrise from the coffee shop.

Riverland Motel (☎ 250-374-1530, 800-663-1530; 1530 River St; s/d $75/85; P ✷ ✷) Overlooking the Thompson River, this pleasant place features good-sized rooms, plus an indoor pool and hot tub. Most rooms have kitchenettes. It's a nice stroll to the center.

Modern, central, comfortable but distinctly unclassic accommodation can be had at the **Thompson Hotel** (☎ 800-561-5253; www.vipresorts.kamloops.com; 650 Victoria St; s/d $89/109; P ✷ 🖳 ✷) and the **Coast Canadian Hotel** (☎ 250-372-5201, 800-663-1144; www.coasthotels.com; 339 St Paul St; s/d $165/175; P ✷ 🖳 ✷). Across

from the hospital, the **Fountain Motel** (☎ 250-374-4451, 888-253-1569; www.fountain.kamloops.com; 506 Columbia St; s/d $44/48; P ✷) offers basic rooms.

Scores of chain motels lurk amidst the strip malls on Columbia St, west of the downtown area. A notable standout, the **Grandview Motel** (☎ 250-372-1312, 800-210-6088; www.grandviewmotel.com; 463 Grandview Terrace; s/d $69/75) features the eponymous view and a large patio with outdoor barbecues. It's a classic, well-maintained motor lodge.

East of town, another passel of motor inns lines the Trans-Canada Hwy. Most are older properties but combine good value with good maintenance. Typical is the **Courtesy Inn Motel** (☎ 250-372-8533, 800-372-8533; www.courte symotel.kamloops.com; 1773 Trans-Canada Hwy; s/d $55/68; P ✷ ✷) which features an indoor pool, sauna and very comfortable rooms.

HOSTELS

HI Kamloops (☎ 250-828-7991, 866-782-9526; www .hihostels.ca; 7 W Seymour St; dm members/non-members $17/21, r $45; P 🖳) Grandly housed in a beautiful old 1909 courthouse close to downtown, it opened as a hostel in 1992.

Common areas include a lounge and dining room in the original courtrooms, where you can sit in the jury box and reenact the sentencing of outlaws like Billy Minor. The hostel is often full in summer, so it's a good idea to reserve ahead. From the Greyhound bus depot, take local bus No 3 to the corner of Seymour St and 3rd Ave, then walk two blocks west, or you can walk the entire way in about 30 minutes.

CAMPING

Quiet, shady and plain describes **Silver Sage Tent & Trailer Park** (☎ 250-828-2077, 877-828-2077; 771 Athabasca St E; tent site \$20-25). You can see across the river to downtown, which is walkable from the campground. The facilities include a coin laundry and showers.

You can also camp in the two nearby **provincial parks** (☎ 250-851-3000). Paul Lake Provincial Park (tent site \$14) offers nice sites on the north end of Paul Lake. The park is 24km northeast of Kamloops on a marked road off Hwy 5; Lac Le Jeune Provincial Park (tent sites \$18) has 144 sites, each with a picnic table and fire pit. There are no showers. The park is 37km south of Kamloops off Hwy 5.

Eating

Along and around Victoria St, numerous places offer meals or just coffee.

Start your day with a cup of joe from **Zach's** (☎ 250-347-6487; 377 Victoria St; coffee \$1.50; ☽ 7am-11pm). A local hub, it has sidewalk tables that are almost always busy (although snow is their downfall, as it were). There's an in-house bakery cranking out good bagels etc.

Peter's Pasta (☎ 250-372-8514; 149 Victoria St; meals \$10; ☽ lunch & dinner Mon-Sat) Very popular with locals, Peter dishes up treats throughout the day. There's a full coffee bar and Italian ice in summer. Dishes include all the classics – can't go wrong with the meatballs. The owners are justifiably proud of their homemade pasta.

Sanbiki (☎ 250-377-8857; 476 Victoria St; meals \$12; ☽ lunch & dinner Tue-Sun) is a bright and refreshing little Japanese restaurant which is also known for its good sushi brought in daily from Vancouver. The patio is heated.

Minos (☎ 250-376-2010; 262 Tranquille Rd; meals \$19; ☽ lunch & dinner Mon-Sat, dinner Sun) Fittingly,

the owner's name is George and, even more fittingly, Greek can be heard wafting over the top of the booths at this excellent Greek restaurant. Everything is as it should be: from the warm welcome to the buttery soft, marinated lamb chops. A five-minute drive across the river from downtown; take the Overlander Bridge.

Entertainment

Magnum's (☎ 250-377-7700; 357 Victoria St; ☽ noon-late) is a locally owned club that spans several high-concept floors. One level has a fireplace and couches, another has dance music. Theme nights range from acid jazz to hip hop to house. Upscale bar snacks served until 11pm.

Kelly O'Bryans (☎ 250-828-1559; 244 Victoria St; burgers \$8; ☽ noon-late) is a merry Irish pub that mixes up its Celtic charm by putting its male employees in kilts (we should say 'unhappily in kilts').

Kamloops Blazers (☎ 250-828-3339; www.kam loopsblazers.bc.ca; adult/child \$14/11) are the arch-rivals of the Kelowna Rockets in the Western Hockey League. They take to the ice at Sport Mart Place, a modern arena across the tracks from downtown.

Getting There & Away

Seven km northwest of town on Kamloops' north shore is **Kamloops Airport** (YKA; ☎ 250-376-3613). Air Canada Jazz flies to/from Vancouver several times daily.

Greyhound bus depot (☎ 250-374-1212; 725 Notre Dame Dr) is southwest of the downtown area off Columbia St W. The building has a cafeteria and luggage lockers. Many buses leave daily for Vancouver, Calgary, Jasper, Edmonton, Prince George and Kelowna.

VIA Rail station (☎ 800-561-8630), 11km north of town off the Yellowhead Hwy, is only open 30 minutes prior to departures. Every week, three trains go south to Vancouver, and three trains go east to Jasper, Edmonton and beyond.

Getting Around

Most of the city is covered by **Kamloops Transit Service** (☎ 250-376-1216; www.city.kamloops.bc.ca /transportation/transit/; one-way fare adult/child \$1.50/ free) The main stop, where you can catch any bus, is at the Thompson Park Mall, at Lansdowne St and 6th Ave.

For a taxi, call **Yellow Cabs** (☎ 250-374-3333).

AROUND KAMLOOPS

Heading west on Hwys 1 & 97, you'll hit **Cache Creek**, a tiny town prospectors rushed through on their way to find gold in the Cariboo. The story goes that the miners would hide their gold or cache in a nearby creek. Locals insist that there are still unclaimed stashes of gold buried deep in the creek bed. If you want to hear local boosterism at its most fervent, tune to 105.9 FM.

Just south is **Ashcroft** (pop 1900), a charming, little cattle-ranching community surrounded by sagebrush and tumbleweeds. When the railroad rolled through in the 1880s, Ashcroft was already a small farming community settled by gold-prospectors, who realized early that they weren't going to find any gold. From here, avoid the road through **Logan Lake** unless you want to see open-pit copper mining at its most frightening and dramatic.

Sun Peaks Resort

You can have a blast at **Sun Peaks Resort** (☎ 250-578-5474, 800-807-3257; www.sunpeaksresort .com; lift tickets adult/child $55/29), built on Tod Mountain 53km northeast of Kamloops. It's a year-round recreation spot, though it rarely looks more picturesque than in winter, when snow blankets the small village, full of restaurants and shops. The mountain boasts 117 runs, 10 lifts, a snowboard park and 881m of vertical rise. BC Olympian Nancy Greene is director of skiing. More than 70% of the runs are novice or intermediate, making the resort more family-oriented. The Kids Adventure Park has pint-sized snowmobiles, toboggan runs and more, in a specially monitored area. Shuttles run to Kamloops and the Kelowna Airport.

Ski rentals are available on the mountain or in Kamloops at **Spoke 'n Motion** (☎ 250-372-3001; 194 W Victoria St; snowboard packages from $25), a bike rental shop that also has a wide selection of equipment.

In summer the quad chair keeps running (adult $12, child $9), taking hikers and mountain bikers up top to play around on the snowless runs.

Skiers will like **Sun Peaks International Hostel** (☎ 250-578-0057; www.sunpeakshostel.com; 1140 Sun Peaks Rd; beds from $20; ⌨), which is right in the ski village by the lifts.

MERRITT

pop 3100

Nestled in the pretty Nicola Valley 115km north of Hope, Merritt offers the only services along the Coquihalla Hwy (Hwy 5) between Hope and Kamloops.

Motels sprang up with the building of the highway, and that's pretty much all the action Merritt sees today – car traffic. Until July, that is, when the toe-stompin' **Merritt Mountain Music Festival** (☎ 250-860-5989; www.mountainfest.com) two-steps into town. This four-day country music festival attracts up to 100,000 hootin' and hollerin' cowboy-hat-clad dudes who camp on the festival grounds. Beware that motels fill up during this week. At other times of the year you can put your foot on the spirit of the event by following the **Walk of Stars** downtown, a collection of bronze stars set in cement bearing the handprints of past festival performers such as Johnny Cash, the Dixie Chicks, Merle Haggard and about 30 more.

From Merritt, Hwy 97C heads east to Kelowna and the Okanagan or northwest to the Cariboo. Before continuing on, stop by the excellent **Visitor Info Centre** (☎ 250-315-1342; www.merritt-chamber.bc.ca; junction of Hwys 5 & 97C; ☉ 9am-7pm summer, 9am-5pm weekdays winter) which has extensive regional information. However its popularity also means that the conditions in the toilets will leave you hankering for a bush.

It's also a good idea to check road conditions before going south or north, as road conditions on the Coquihalla can get nasty any time of year. Be forewarned that there's a toll booth on the Coquihalla midway between Merritt and Hope; cars pay $10.

Standing out from the plethora of motels, the 1908 **Coldwater Hotel** (☎ 250-378-2821; 1901 Voght St; basic r $40) has a great bar popular with cowboys. The burgers ($6) are good too.

THE SHUSWAP

The area around the Shuswap lakes is picturesque, with green, wooded hills and farms, although the town of **Salmon Arm** is at best merely a functional stop. The grazing cattle and lush, cultivated land make a pleasant change of scenery no matter which direction you're coming from. Many provincial parks dot the area offering an abundance of water-related activities.

SALUTING THE SOCKEYE

Sockeye salmon are some of the most hard-core travelers around. These wily fish travel from the Adams River to the Pacific Ocean and back again in what is one of nature's most miraculous and complete cycles of life. It all starts on the shallow riverbed in Roderick Haig-Brown Provincial Park, a massive breeding ground for sockeye salmon. Since glaciers carved out river valleys, pairs of male and female sockeye have fought starvation, currents and grueling rapids to return from the ocean to the place of their birth. In early fall, the lower Adams River hosts a frenzy of spawning salmon.

Each spawning female lays about 4000 eggs; many of which are unsuccessfully fertilized or munched on by rainbow trout and other predators. The ones that do survive spend the winter tucked into the gravel on the riverbed, waiting out frost and weather while slowly growing in the soft, jelly-like casing of the eggshell. In spring the eggs hatch and tiny salmon fry – measuring about 2.5cm in length – emerge and float downriver to spend their first year in Shuswap Lake. Though the calm lake water keeps the fry safe from the rushing currents of the river, only one out of four fry eludes the hungry jaws of predators. Survivors of that ordeal grow in the lake, becoming smolt. These hardy fish, up to 10cm long, then begin the long journey to the mouth of the Fraser River, which they follow all the way to the Pacific Ocean. Once in the salty water, the salmon grow up to 3kg, needing size and agility to escape more ravenous predators like killer whales, seals and commercial fishing nets. Once they've reached maturity, about four years after their birth, a biological signal as sharp as intuition takes hold and the salmon know it's time to make the great journey back home.

Of every 4000 eggs produced at Roderick Haig-Brown Provincial Park, only two fish survive long enough to make the long, grueling journey home to spawn. When the internal alarm rings, the sleek, silvery ocean sockeye stop eating as they reach the Fraser's freshwater mouth. From here on, for the next 21 days, the fish rely on body fat and protein to energize their 29km-a-day swim over rocks and raging rapids.

Scraped, beaten and torn, the fish slowly turn a bright crimson red, a color they'll carry like cloaks until they reach the spawning grounds. There, the red heads turn a deep green, the male's snout elongates and his teeth get sharper, ready to fend off intruders as he and the female, now heavy with eggs, search for a place to nest. But good real estate on the shallow riverbed is hard to come by, and the pairs of fish fight like crazed parents to find a sheltered spot. The female digs her nest by furiously flopping her tail while simultaneously laying eggs. The male quickly swims by, dropping a shower of milt to fertilize the eggs. The female then covers the nest with gravel. Upon completion of this exhausting ordeal of procreation, the hardy couple quietly dies, leaving their eggs to follow this incredible journey.

Though the salmon spawn annually, every four years a mass migration occurs (the next one is 2006) that far overshadows the intermittent-year spawns. In these years, up to four million sockeye return home. The best time for viewing is in October, check with the Salmon Arm VIC for the best times each year.

Accommodations are tight in the height of summer, so if you're coming in July and August, reserve ahead.

Shuswap Lake squiggles about a series of valleys, looking like a mutant spider. The top right arm of the lake is Seymour Arm, and below it is Anstey Arm. At the bottom left is Salmon Arm (also the name of the town). The top left of the lake thickens into Little Shuswap Lake. Salmon Arm, on the Trans-Canada Hwy, is the main service center at the lake, though nearby Sicamous proclaims itself the 'houseboat capital of Canada'. On the north shore of the lake, you'll find two excellent provincial parks, more camping and accommodations.

Salmon Arm contains the area's main **Visitor Info Centre** (☎ 250-832-2230, 877-725-6667; www.sachamber.bc.ca; 751 Marine Park Dr NE at Harbourfront Dr; ⊗ 9am-7pm summer, 9am-5pm Mon-Fri winter). There is a smaller VIC in Sicamous (☎ 250-836-3313; 110 Finlayson St).

The Salmon Arm **Greyhound bus depot** (☎ 250-832-3962; 50 10th St SW) is one block north of the Trans-Canada Hwy. You can use the luggage lockers if you need to store some stuff. Buses leave daily going east and west.

FRASER-THOMPSON REGION

Roderick Haig-Brown Provincial Park

This **provincial park** (☎ 250-851-3000) on the north shore of Shuswap Lake takes its name from Roderick Haig-Brown (1908–1976), a British Columbian naturalist and angler who devoted much of his life to conserving sockeye salmon. Look for his many books (among his best: *The Seasons of a Fisherman*) in BC bookstores. The 1059-hectare park protects either side of the Adams River from the northwest side of Shuswap Lake to Adams Lake. If you're here in October, you'll see the bright red sockeye running upriver to spawn (see boxed text, p199). The fish population peaks every four years, when as many as four million fish crowd the Adams' shallow riverbeds. The next big spawn is set for 2006, although other salmon – as many as two million – spawn in other years. Interpretive displays tell all about this great event. You can hike in the park but camping is not permitted.

Activities

Whitewater rafting is popular on the Adams River, which is mostly a Class 3 river (which means it'll get your adrenaline pumping but won't send you into cardiac arrest). **Adams River Rafting** (☎ 250-955-2447, 888-440-7238; 3993 Squilax-Anglemont Rd, Scotch Creek; 2hr floats adult/child $48/38) operates an exciting four-hour expedition for adult/child $75/45.

Houseboating can be a fun way to explore the Shuswap, especially during the height of summer, when the lake looks like a little village with a bunch of floating houses. Most houseboats are totally self-contained, with kitchens and running water. Some even come with hot tubs and waterslides. Most rent by the week, can sleep about 10 people and cost from $2000 for the week. Fuel is extra, and you have to bring your own food. If you want to rent houseboats, your best bet is to get a list of rentals from the Visitor Info Centres in Salmon Arm or Sicamous.

Sleeping

Many motels line the Trans-Canada Hwy on either side of Salmon Arm. But the closer you can get to nature, the more you will enjoy yourself.

The beautiful **Quaaout Lodge Resort** (☎ 250-679-3090, 800-663-4303; www.quaaout.com; 8km east of Chase on Hwy 1; r from $120; P ⚡ ⚡) on Little Shuswap Lake, was designed and built by the Little Shuswap Band, a part of the Shuswap First Nations. The building that contains the entrance area and dining room resembles a *kekuli*, or winter house, which is usually buried in the ground. First Nations art decorates the hotel, and the kitchen serves up gourmet meals based on traditional foods and cooking methods. Even if you are not staying here, it is a good place for lunch.

The **HI Squilax General Store Hostel** (☎ 250-675-2977; www.hihostels.ca; dm members/non-members $16/20; P ⚡) is about 10km east of Chase and 45km west of Salmon Arm on Hwy 1. Get your head around the rustic charm and this hostel can make a good rural hub for exploring the area. Plus, if you've ever wanted to explore the rear of a train, here's your chance: the dorm-style beds are in three old cabooses.

All Shuswap provincial parks have the same phone number for **information** (☎ 250-851-3000). **Herald Provincial Park**, 25 minutes northwest of Salmon Arm, sits on the homestead of one of the Shuswap's first farmers. It features sandy beaches, waterfalls and 51 sites ($22). To get there, turn off the Trans-Canada Hwy onto Sunnybrae Rd. **Shuswap Lake Provincial Park**, on the north shore at Scotch Creek, offers excellent wooded sites on the lake and no shortage of them: the park contains a whopping 272 campsites ($22). Both parks have the same **reservation information** (☎ 800-689-9025; www.gov.bc.ca/bcparks/wlap/). You can also camp by the water at **Silver Beach Provincial Park**, which sits at the head of Seymour Arm near the old gold-rush town of Seymour City. With only 35 sites, it's a little quieter.

Eating

Sample the fruits of the many orchards at the **Salmon Arm Farmers Market** (Piccadilly Place Mall; ☉ mornings Tue & Fri). The Mall is at 1151 10 Ave SW, south of Hwy 1 and just west of the town center. Many of the farms also have well-marked produce markets.

Salmon Arm has many basic cafés. For classic old-world baked goods and soup, try **Penkert's Bakery** (☎ 250-832-4610; 420 4th St NE; meals under $4; ☉ lunch, closed Sun). Enjoy the vintage copies of *Mad* magazine on offer.

Okanagan Valley

CONTENTS

Summer travelers coming to the dry, hot Okanagan Valley from the Lower Mainland marvel at the seemingly impossible shift in climate. Just when you thought it wasn't going to happen, wham-o – you find summer and have to put away your raincoat and bust out the shorts. This fertile valley, dominated by orchards, wineries and warm lakes, gets more than 2000 hours of sunshine a year. When it rains, it doesn't last long and the splash is actually refreshing after you've spent days lolling around on the hot beach. Three 'sister cities' – Penticton, Kelowna and Vernon – attract the majority of visitors. Like migrating birds, tourists and British Columbians alike flock here in summer – to sip wine, play golf, hike or mountain bike in the dry hills, or simply flake out on one of the many sandy beaches. In winter, when dry, fluffy snow falls, the climate stays mild, the sun still shines and snow sports take over.

Of course all this fine weather comes at a price: the lack of rain makes the entire valley prone to fires during the summer. This was horribly demonstrated during the summer of 2003 when several major fires scorched hundreds of square kilometers; especially hard-hit was the area around Kelowna. However most of the valley's wineries and orchards were spared, so the Okanagan is as welcoming as ever.

The region is incredibly scenic, with rolling, scrubby hills, narrow blue lakes and clear skies. Near Osoyoos, close to the US border, cactuses grow on desert slopes that receive only 250mm of rain a year. Warm lakes, fresh fruit and sandy beaches draw people to Penticton and Kelowna. Vernon, with a smaller population and fewer tourists, is surrounded by excellent provincial parks.

HIGHLIGHTS

- Organic orchard-hopping in **Oliver** (p206)
- Eating a freshly picked **Penticton** peach (p209)
- Discovering **Okanagan Valley** wineries (p210)
- Sampling cultural **Kelowna** (p214)
- Testing the legendary powder at **Apex** (p214) and **Big White** (p222)

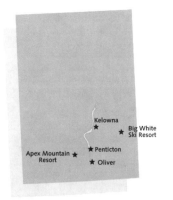

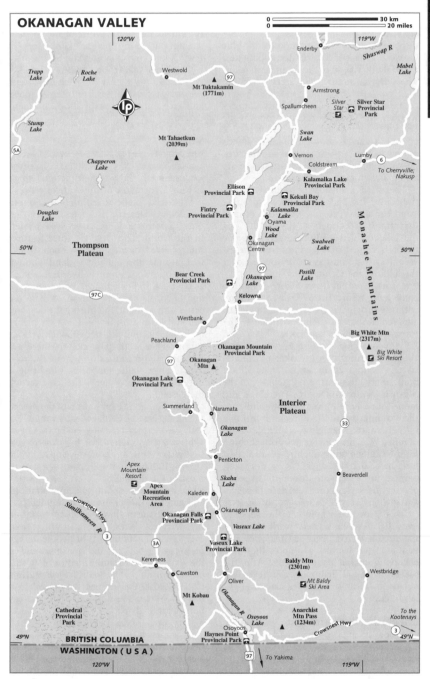

OKANAGAN VALLEY

0 — 30 km
0 — 20 miles

120°W   119°W

Enderby   Shuswap R

Trapp Lake   Roche Lake   Westwold   Mabel Lake

Mt Tuktakamin (1771m)   97   Armstrong

Spallumcheen   Silver Star   Silver Star Provincial Park

Stump Lake   Swan Lake

5A   Mt Tahaetkun (2039m)   Vernon   Lumby   6

Chapperon Lake   Coldstream   To Cherryville; Nakusp

Kalamalka Lake Provincial Park

Ellison Provincial Park   Kekuli Bay Provincial Park

Douglas Lake   Fintry Provincial Park   Kalamalka Lake

Oyama
Wood Lake

50°N   Thompson Plateau   Okanagan Centre   Swalwell Lake   50°N

Bear Creek Provincial Park   Okanagan Lake   Postill Lake

97C   97   Kelowna

Westbank   Big White Mtn (2317m)

Peachland   Okanagan Mountain Provincial Park   Big White Ski Resort

97   Okanagan Mtn

Okanagan Lake Provincial Park

Summerland   Naramata   Interior Plateau

Okanagan Lake   33

Apex Mountain Resort   Penticton   Beaverdell

Apex Mountain Recreation Area   Skaha Lake

Kaleden

Okanagan Falls Provincial Park   Okanagan Falls

Vaseux Lake

3   Vaseux Lake Provincial Park

3A   Baldy Mtn (2301m)   Westbridge

Keremeos   Mt Baldy Ski Area

Crowsnest Hwy   Cawston   Oliver

Similkameen R

Mt Kobau   Anarchist Mtn Pass (1234m)   To the Kootenays

Cathedral Provincial Park   Osoyoos Lake   Crowsnest Hwy   3

49°N   Osoyoos

Haynes Point Provincial Park

BRITISH COLUMBIA

WASHINGTON (USA)

120°W   97   To Yakima   119°W

OSOYOOS

pop 4400

Osoyoos sits at the edge of dark-blue Osoyoos Lake, amid stark, dry, rolling hills at the southern end of the Okanagan Valley. The skies are sunny, the waters warm and the air dry, which is quite a shocker if you're coming from the coast. With its hot, dry weather, the Osoyoos region produces the earliest and most varied fruit and vegetable crops in Canada. Look for roadside stands selling – often organic – cherries, apricots, peaches, apples and other fruit. There are also many vineyards in the area.

The word 'Osoyoos' is a butchering of the Native Indian word 'soyoos', meaning 'sand bar across', for the thin strip of land that almost cuts Osoyoos Lake in half. Why the 'O' got added is a little uncertain; some boosters suggest that it comes from the involuntary 'oh' you gasp as you come over the hill into the scenic valley.

A small town at heart, Osoyoos has become a big resort. In 1975, in cooperation with the provincial government, the locals adopted a Spanish theme to beautify the town – with limited success.

Osoyoos' 'pocket desert', which runs about 50km northward to Skaha Lake and stretches about 20km across at its widest point, marks the northern extension of the Mexican Sonoran Desert. The flora and fauna found here are remarkably similar to their counterparts (at 600m elevation) two borders south. Averaging less than 200mm of rain a year, the area creates prime habitat for the calliope hummingbird (the smallest bird in Canada), as well as rattlesnakes, painted turtles, coyotes, numerous species of mice and various cactuses, desert brushes and grasses. This is Canada's only desert.

In a province where all the superlatives that describe scenery work overtime, the stretch of road between Osoyoos and Penticton has to rank as one of the more deserving recipients of praise. And the scenery isn't too shabby as you head west out of town, toward the Okanagan Highlands, either.

Orientation & Information

Osoyoos is at the crossroads of Hwy 97, heading north to Penticton, and the Crowsnest Hwy (Hwy 3), running east to the Kootenay region and west to Hope. The US border, cutting through Osoyoos Lake, is 5km to the south. Most of the town is strung out along several kilometers of Hwy 3, known locally as Main St.

The **Visitor Info Centre** (☎ 250-495-7142, 888-676-9667; 9912 Hwy 3 at Hwy 97; ☾ 9am-5pm summer, weekdays only other times) has free Internet access and excellent hiking maps and recommendations.

Sights

The **Desert Centre** (☎ 250-495-2470; www.desert.org; 3km north of Osoyoos off Hwy 97; adult/child $6/3; ☾ 9am-7pm summer only) is a top attraction which sits on 27 hectares of the Antelope Brush ecosystem, a fragile extension of the Sonora and Mojave Deserts. Estimates suggest that only 9% of this endangered ecosystem is left in the world. The Desert Centre features interpretive kiosks along raised boardwalks that meander through the dry land. Though plenty of unique animals live here – such as Great Basin pocketmice, spadefoot toads and tiger salamanders – most of them are active only at night. But during the day, you can still learn a lot, as well as hear plenty of birdsong and the occasional tickle of a rattlesnake's tail. The center offers 90-minute guided tours throughout the day. You'll get a shade umbrella, but bring a hat and drinking water – this is, after all, the desert.

Continuing the exploration of the desert, the **Nk'Mip Desert & Heritage Centre** (☎ 250-495-7901; www.nkmipdesert.com; 1000 Rancher Creek Rd, off 45th St north of Hwy 3; adult/child $7/4; ☾ 9am-7pm May-Sep, less often winter) has been developed by the Osoyos Indian Band, who control access to most of the remaining desert. This worthwhile stop features cultural demonstrations and guided tours of the sandy highlights.

The climate makes **Osoyoos Lake** among the warmest lakes in the country, and every summer thousands of people lounge on the sandy beaches and splash around in the water. If you're sunburned or plain sick of the hot sun, the small **Osoyoos Museum** (☎ 250-495-2582; Gyro Community Park off Hwy 3; adult/child $3/1; ☾ 10am-3:30pm Jun-Sep) will fill a shady hour with its displays on natural and local history, orchards and irrigation.

In winter, take the rough Camp McKinney Rd from Oliver east to the **Mt Baldy Ski Area** (☎ 866-754-2253; www.skibaldy.com; one-day lift ticket adult/child $36/25). This small resort has

FRUIT ORCHARDS & VINEYARDS

The region's fertile soil and heavy irrigation, combined with the relatively warm climate (summers tend to be hot and dry), have made the Okanagan the country's top fruit-growing area. Its 100 sq km of orchards represent 85% of Canada's total.

During April and May, the entire valley comes alive with blossoms. In late summer and autumn, the orchards drip with delicious fresh fruit. Stands dotting the roads sell the best and cheapest produce in Canada.

So-called 'agri-tourism' has become very popular – you can visit farms, orchards and wineries throughout the valley. *Tours of Abundance*, a widely distributed free guide, lists the many orchards and wine tastings. The drive north along Hwy 97 from Osoyoos passes an almost endless succession of orchards, farms and fruit stands. You'll have plenty of time to smell the apples, peaches and, yes, even the roses. The entire region fills with visitors in summer, so throughout July and August expect all types of accommodation to be tight.

It's hard to tell which is growing faster in Okanagan, the number of people or the number of wineries. Dozens of vineyards line the hills and welcome visitors for tasting (and purchasing...). See Okanagan Wineries (p210) for details.

If you wish to tie your trip to a specific fruit, the approximate harvest times are as follows:

- **Strawberries** mid-June to early July
- **Cherries** mid-June to mid-August
- **Peaches** mid-July to mid-September
- **Apples** early September to late October
- **Raspberries** early July to mid-July
- **Apricots** mid-July to mid-August
- **Pears** mid-August to late September
- **Grapes** early September to late October

cross-country trails and 11 downhill runs with a vertical drop of 420m. It boasts that it doesn't have high-speed lifts or long lines.

On the south side of Hwy 3, 8km west of town, look for the **spotted lake**, a weird natural phenomenon. In the hot summer sun, the lake's water begins to evaporate, causing its high mineral content to crystallize, leaving white-rimmed circles of green on the water.

Three kilometers further west along Hwy 3, look for a gravel Forest Service road that will take you to the summit of **Mt Kobau**, where you'll enjoy superb views of the town and desert to the east, the **Similkameen Valley** to the west and the US border to the south. The bumpy road to the summit is 20km long, but the views are well worth it. Amateur and professional astronomers flock here every August for the **Mt Kobau Star Party** (www.mksp.ca), during which they set up telescopes, use red lights only and marvel at the night sky.

Sleeping
MOTELS
Central beachside motels line motel row on Main St (Hwy 3) at the eastern end of town. Most of them drastically drop their rates from September to June.

Holiday Inn Sunspree Resort (☎ 250-495-7223, 877-786-7773; www.holidayinnosoyoos.com; 7906 Main St; s/d from $120/140; P ✗ ☐ ☒) The pick of motels locally, the Holiday Inn has a prime lakefront location. It boasts its own little island complete with resort amenities like barbecues and that perennial fave: shuffleboard. Rooms have private balconies from which you can view your own boat moored at the private pier – if you have one.

Desert Motor Inn (☎ 250-495-6525, 877-495-6525; www.desertinn.ca; 7702 Main St; s/d $90/95; P ✗ ☒) The large indoor/outdoor pool comes with a water slide, yeehaw! Let the Jacuzzi bubbles work the grains of sand from the private beach out of your crevices.

Poplars Motel (☎ 250-495-6035; www.poplars motelthe.supersites.ca; 6404 Cottonwood Dr; r from $85; P ✗) Every room at this older but nice beachfront property has a kitchenette.

Away from the lake but right in the center of town, the **Avalon Inn** (☎ 250-495-6334; 800-264-5999; www.avaloninn.com; 9106 Main St; s/d from $70/79; P ✗ ☐) has free high-speed Internet and new suites with private decks.

CAMPING
Haynes Point Provincial Park (☎ 250-494-0321, 800-689-9025; www.discovercamping.ca; 2km south of the center off Hwy 97; tent sites $22) This is the most

sought-after campground. In fact, you're not likely to get one of the 41 sites until next year unless you reserved early. The park has beaches, nature trails and much more.

Out near the desert, the **Nk'Mip Resort Campground & RV Park** (☎ 250-495-7279; www .campingosoyoos.com; off 45th St north of Hwy 3; tent sites $21) is on the Osoyoos Indian Reserve and offers laundry facilities, watersports rentals and good beach access.

Eating & Drinking

Wildfire Grill (☎ 250-495-2215; 8526 Main St; meals $15-20; 🕑 lunch & dinner, brunch Sun) A range of global cuisines is produced in the bustling open kitchen in this excellent restaurant right in the center of town. The ingredients are mostly local and the menu changes often. Pastas feature prominantly, but expect food from the waters of BC to the remote islands of Indonesia. The décor is warm and romantic and the courtyard is a treat.

For classically good and classically Italian fare in town, try **Campo Marina** (☎ 250-495-7650; 5907 Main St; meals $10-25; 🕑 dinner Tue-Sun). Authentic Italian pasta dishes are complemented by fresh bread from their own bakery as well as one of the best wine lists in the valley. The steaks are delightful, as is the plant-filled patio.

Grab a beer and pub food at the **Burrowing Owl Pub** (☎ 250-495-3274; 7603 Spartan Ave; meals $7-15; 🕑 noon-late) where a patio overlooks the lake. The burgers and everything else are large.

Getting There & Away

Greyhound (☎ 250-495-7252; Chuckers Convenience Store; 6615 Lakeshore Dr) is located at the east end of the motel strip. Buses run daily to Vancouver and Calgary and north up the valley to Penticton and Kelowna.

AROUND OSOYOOS

Cathedral Provincial Park (☎ 250-494-6500) is a 33,272-hectare mountain wilderness area characterized by unusual basalt and quartz rock formations. The park offers excellent backcountry camping and hiking around wildflower meadows and turquoise lakes. To reach the park, go 30km west of Osoyoos on Hwy 3 to Ashnola River Rd and then another 21km.

Three steep trails lead to the park's core area around Quiniscoe Lake and the

---

AUTHOR'S CHOICE

Toasted Oak (☎ 250-498-4867; 34881 97th St, Osoyoos; meals $10-25; 🕑 lunch & dinner) is a major local addition. The restaurant serves tapas, salads, sandwiches and more complex meals that feature local products. The 'Wine Information' sign and the well-stocked public cellar are evidence that this is an excellent stop for sampling valley vintages. It's a great place to sit outside and enjoy a glass or two of wine on the long summer nights.

---

gorgeous **Cathedral Lakes Lodge** (☎ 250-492-1606, 888-255-4453; www.cathedral-lakes-lodge.com; 2 nights from $320). The lodge operates a shuttle service for guests (and wilderness campers) from the parking area at the base of the mountain.

OLIVER
pop 3200

The drive from Osoyoos north to Oliver along Hwy 97 is alone worth the trip. The oodles of ripe hanging fruit are matched by the oodles of fruit stands selling same. Many offer samples and will let you pick your own. The small and charming town of Oliver is right in the midst of the Okanagan's bounty.

North of Oliver to Penticton, the orchards and vineyards abate a bit and the scene is dominated by mountains, rock formations and forests.

VASEUX WILDLIFE CENTRE

Just south of Okanagan Falls, watch for the small sign for **Vaseux Wildlife Centre** (☎ 250-494-6500; free; 🕑 dawn-dusk) at the north end of Vaseux Lake off Hwy 97. You'll see lots of birds here, and you might catch a glimpse of bighorn sheep or the northern Pacific rattlesnake. From the center, you can hike to the Bighorn National Wildlife Area and the Vaseux Lake National Migratory Bird Sanctuary, where more than 160 bird species nest. There are also nature trails of varying lengths.

You can **camp** (sites $14) at one of the 12 year-round sites on the east side of the lake, popular for bass fishing, swimming and canoeing in summer. In winter, people head to the lake for skating and ice fishing.

PENTICTON

pop 34,200

Penticton, the southernmost of the three Okanagan sister cities, sits directly between Okanagan Lake and Skaha Lake, which are connected by the Okanagan River Channel.

To the Salish, Pen-Tak-Tin means 'place to stay forever', an idea that many people took to heart. Popular with retirees, the town still exudes a young, sporty feel, generated perhaps by the plethora of annual festivals that draw tourists en masse. Maybe it's the excellent mountain biking and the world-class climbing on Skaha Bluffs or maybe it's just the long, sunny, lakeside days. In Penticton the sun shines for an average of 600 hours in July and August – about 10 hours a day – and that's more than it shines in Honolulu! It's not surprising, then, that the number-one industry is tourism.

Penticton became an official town in 1892, while several nearby mine claims were being developed. But over the next 100 years, orchards and tourism came to dominate. The downtown is undergoing something of a revival, particularly along the small Front St. Close by, Okanagan Beach boasts about 1300m of long sandy beach, with average summer water temperatures of about 22°C, making this a good spot to cool your heels for a day or two.

Orientation

The attractive downtown area extends for about 10 blocks southward from Okanagan Lake along Main St. It has a full range of shops, banks and services. Go further, however, and you'll encounter strip malls, sprawl and the like. So don't.

At the southern end of town, you'll find the 1.5km-long Skaha Beach, with sand, trees and picnic areas.

Information

BOOKSTORES

Book Shop (☎ 250-492-6661; 242 Main St) Huge collection of secondhand books.
Okanagan Books (☎ 250-493-1941; 233 Main St) Good selection of regional books and magazines.

INTERNET ACCESS

Penticton Library (☎ 250-492-0024; 785 Main St; ☺ 10am-5pm Mon-Sat, until 9pm Tue & Thu, 1-5pm Sun) Free.

LAUNDRY

Laundry Basket (☎ 250-493-7899; 976 Eckhardt Ave W; ☺ 8am-5pm)

MONEY

ATMs and banks abound along Main St.

MEDICAL SERVICES

Penticton Regional Hospital (☎ 250-492-4000; 550 Carmi Ave; ☺ 24hr)

POST

Gallop's Flowers (☎ 250-492-0615; 187 Westminster Ave W; ☺ 9am-6pm Mon-Sat)

TOURIST INFORMATION

BC Wine Information Centre, (☎ 250-493-4055, 800-663-5052; 888 Westminster Ave W next to the convention center; ☺ 8am-8pm summer, 9am-5pm Mon-Fri, 11am-5pm Sat & Sun other times) Information & tastings.
Visitor Info Centre (☎ 250-493-4055, 800-663-5052; 888 Westminster Ave W next to the convention center; ☺ 8am-8pm summer, 9am-5pm Mon-Fri, 11am-5pm Sat & Sun other times) May be moving to the corner of busy Eckhardt Ave W & Power St.

Sights

SS Sicamous (☎ 250-492-0403; 1099 Lakeshore Dr W; adult/child $5/1; ☺ 9am-9pm summer, 9am-4pm Mon-Fri winter) An old stern-wheeler, the SS *Sicamous* hauled passengers and freight on Okanagan Lake from 1914 to 1936. Now nicely restored, it has been joined by the equally old SS *Naramata*, a tug boat.

If you want to take some time out to smell the roses, you can stroll around the **Penticton Rose Garden**, beside the SS *Sicamous*, for free. The paved **Okanagan River Channel Biking & Jogging Path** follows the channel from lake to lake. It's great for running, walking, cycling or in-line skating.

The **Art Gallery of Southern Okanagan** (☎ 250-493-2928; 199 Front St; $2; ☺ 10am-5pm Tue-Sat) displays an excellent collection of regional, provincial and national artists. Exhibits change regularly.

The **Penticton Museum** (☎ 250-490-2451; 785 Main St; donation; ☺ 10am-5pm Tue-Sat) is an excellent small-town museum with well-done, delightfully eclectic displays, including the *de rigueur* natural-history exhibit with stuffed animals and birds. Check out the history of the Peach Festival and pick up the excellent historic walking brochures.

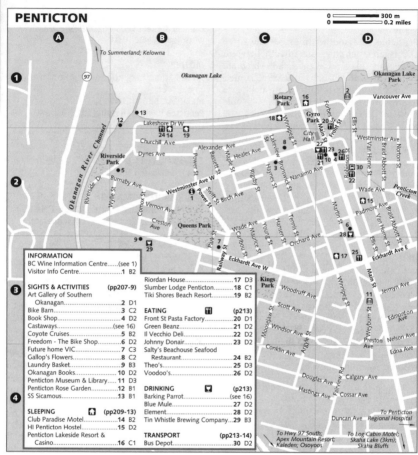

PENTICTON

| | 0 | 300 m |
| 0 | | 0.2 miles |

To Summerland; Kelowna

Okanagan Lake

Okanagan Lake Park

Vancouver Ave

Okanagan River Channel

Lakeshore Dr W

Churchill Ave

Dynes Ave

Riverside Park

Burnaby Ave

Wylie St

Westminster Ave W

Vernon Ave

Creston Ave

Queens Park

Alexander Ave

Healeys Ave

Westminster Ave W

Birch Ave

Wade Ave

Eckhardt Ave W

Rotary Park

Gyro Park

City Hall

Westminster Ave

Wade Ave

Penticton Creek

Padmore Ave

Orchard Ave

Eckhardt Ave E

Kings Park

Woodruff Ave

Scott Ave

Windsor Ave S

Conklin Ave

Douglas Ave

Hastings Ave

Cossar Ave

Calgary Ave

Jermyn Ave

Edmonton Ave

Nelson Ave

Preston Ave

Edna Ave

To Penticton Regional Hospital

To Hwy 97 South;
Apex Mountain Resort;
Kaleden; Osoyoos

To Log Cabin Motel;
Skaha Lake (3km);
Skaha Bluffs

INFORMATION	
BC Wine Information Centre......(see 1)	
Visitor Info Centre.....................**1** B2	

SIGHTS & ACTIVITIES	(pp207-9)
Art Gallery of Southern	
Okanagan.............................**2** D1	
Bike Barn.................................**3** C2	
Book Shop...............................**4** D2	
Castaways...........................(see 16)	
Coyote Cruises........................**5** B2	
Freedom - The Bike Shop.........**6** D2	
Future home VIC.....................**7** C3	
Gallop's Flowers......................**8** C2	
Laundry Basket........................**9** B3	
Okanagan Books.....................**10** D2	
Penticton Museum & Library....**11** D3	
Penticton Rose Garden............**12** B1	
SS Sicamous...........................**13** B1	

SLEEPING	(pp209-13)
Club Paradise Motel................**14** B2	
HI Penticton Hostel.................**15** D2	
Penticton Lakeside Resort &	
Casino.................................**16** C1	

Riordan House........................**17** D3
Slumber Lodge Penticton.........**18** C1
Tiki Shores Beach Resort..........**19** B2

EATING	(p213)
Front St Pasta Factory..............**20** D1	
Green Beanz...........................**21** D2	
Il Vecchio Deli........................**22** D2	
Johnny Donair.........................**23** D2	
Salty's Beachouse Seafood	
Restaurant...........................**24** B2	
Theo's...................................**25** D3	
Voodoo's...............................**26** D2	

DRINKING	(p213)
Barking Parrot.....................(see 16)	
Blue Mule..............................**27** D2	
Element.................................**28** D2	
Tin Whistle Brewing Company...**29** B3	

TRANSPORT	(pp213-14)
Bus Depot...............................**30** D2	

The **BC Wine Information Centre** (☎ 250-493-4055, 800-663-5052; 888 Westminster Ave W next to the convention center; ☻ 8am-8pm summer, 9am-5pm Mon-Fri, 11am-5pm Sat & Sun other times) gives tastings, sells quality wines from local vineyards and dispenses lots of information.

The **Farmer's Market** (☎ 250-770-3276; Gyro Park in the 100 block of Main St; ☻ 8:30am-noon Sat, May-Oct) has large numbers of local organic producers.

Activities

WATERSPORTS

Both Okanagan and Skaha Lakes enjoy some of the best sailboarding and boating conditions in the Okanagan Valley. **Castaways** (☎ 250-490-2033; Penticton Lakeside Resort, 21 Lakeshore Dr; kayaks $19 per hr) rents just about anything

that floats. A full day's rental of a ski boat is $470. Gear for towing the kids is extra.

Coyote Cruises (☎ 250-492-2115; 215 Riverside Dr; rental & shuttle $12) rents inner tubes that you can float on all the way down the Okanagan River Channel to Skaha Lake. The trip takes nearly two hours; Coyote Cruises buses you back.

MOUNTAIN BIKING

The dry climate and rolling hills around the city combine to offer some excellent mountain biking terrain. Get to popular rides by heading east out of town, toward Naramata. Follow signs to the city dump and Campbell's Mountain, where you'll find a single-track and dual-slalom course, both of which aren't too technical. Once you get there, the riding is mostly on the right side, but once you pass the cattle guard, it opens up and you can ride anywhere.

In summer, the fast quad chairlift (adult/child $10/5) at **Apex Mountain Resort** zips riders and their bikes to the top of the mountain (p214). You can explore the backcountry or simply get a rush from following a trail down again.

Rent bikes and pick up a wealth of information at either of Penticton's well-stocked bike shops. Both rent bikes for $35 per day.

Bike Barn (☎ 250-492-4140; 300 Westminster Ave W)

Freedom – The Bike Shop (☎ 250-493-0686; 533 Main St)

ROCK CLIMBING

Drawn by the dry weather and compact gneiss rock, climbers from all over the world come to the Skaha Bluffs to enjoy a seven-month climbing season on more than 400 bolted routes. The rock is compact but still has plenty of holes to make the climbing excellent for experienced and novice climbers. You'll need a car or a ride to get to the Bluffs. Follow S Main St toward Skaha Lake. Just before the playground and beach parking lot, turn right on Crescent Hill Rd and then right again onto Valleyview Rd. Proceed for a few kilometers until you see a dirt road on the right and a sign directing you to the parking area. From there, you'll see the bluffs, though most of the climbing happens on the back side of the rock, so you'll have to follow the well-marked trail around.

Skaha Rock Adventures (☎ 250-493-1765; www .skaharockclimbing.com; one-day courses from $110) offers advanced, technical instruction and introductory courses for anyone venturing into a harness for the first time.

Festivals & Events

Penticton is the city of festivals, which happen almost nonstop throughout the summer.

JULY

Beach Blanket Film Festival (www.beachblanket filmfest.ca) Bring a lawn chair or blanket and kick back to watch the movie screen, which is set up on Skaha Lake.

EARLY AUGUST

Peach Festival (☎ 800-663-5052; www.peachfest .com) The city's premier event is basically a weeklong party that has taken place since 1948. The festivities include sports activities, novelty events, street music and dance, nightly entertainment and a major parade that's held on Saturday.

BC Square Dance Jamboree (☎ 250-492-5856) Attracts about 3500 dancers who kick it up on an enormous dance floor in Kings Park from 8pm to 11pm six nights in a row.

LATE AUGUST

Ironman Triathlon (☎ 250-490-8787; www.ironman .ca) More than 1800 athletes swim 3.9km, cycle 180km and then, just for the heck of it, run a full marathon (42km). You, however, can sit in the shade, watch the action and munch a peach.

Sleeping
MOTELS & HOTELS

Lakeshore Drive W and S Main St/Skaha Lake Rd contain most of the local motels.

Penticton Lakeside Resort & Casino (☎ 250-493-8221, 800-663-9400; www.rpbhotels.com; 21 Lakeshore Dr W; s/d from $150/160; P ⊠ ☐ ☎) This large high-rise located on the edge of the lake features extensive facilities, including a restaurant, bar and a Vegas-style casino. Like the architecture, the rooms are pretty straightforward.

Slumber Lodge Penticton (☎ 250-492-4008, 800-663-2831; www.slumberlodge.com; 274 Lakeshore Dr W; r from $90; P ⊠ ☎) Modern place right across from the beach.

Club Paradise Motel (☎ 250-493-8400; clubpara dise.penticton.com; 1000 Lakeshore Dr; r from $60; P ⊠) sits across the street from the Okanagan Lake beach, though the rooms are behind Salty's Beach House (p213). Still, the accommodations are clean and a fairly raucous vibe is often in the air.

Tiki Shores Beach Resort (☎ 250-492-8769, 866-492-8769; www.tikishores.com; 914 Lakeshore Dr; condos from $100; P ⊠ ☎) Another lively place at this end of the beach; all the units have separate bedrooms and kitchens. Throw your own toga party in one of the 'Roman theme units'.

Log Cabin Motel (☎ 250-492-3155, 800-342-5678; www.logcabinmotel.penticton.com; 3287 Skaha Lake Rd; s/d from $75/85; P ⊠ ☎) One of the better places at the Skaha Lake end of town, the Log Cabin has very nice grounds and has some units with kitchenettes.

OKANAGAN VALLEY WINERIES

Wine lovers agree that there's nothing more wonderful than wandering around a lush orchard on a hot summer day, sipping wine and admiring the view. Well, welcome to casual connoisseur heaven. With lots of sunshine and fertile soil, the Okanagan is BC's largest and oldest wine-producing region. The area is known for its white wines, especially Pinot Grigio, produced mostly in Kelowna and North Okanagan. It also has a fine reputation for classic reds, Merlot in particular, made in South Okanagan, mainly around Penticton and along the 'Golden Mile' in Oliver.

Festivals

In 1979, the first Fall Wine Festival was held. Over the years, this celebration of valley wine grew in popularity to where it lasted more than a week and was a virtual nonstop orgy of banquets, special tastings, parties and more. Lots of people came, so many in fact that now there are festivals in winter, spring and summer as well.

Although frustrated by a lack of a fifth season, the Okanagan wineries know how to put on a party. Expect vintners to premier special vintages, hold tastings of rare wines, host special tasting dinners and more. You can check up on the seasonal happenings at the valley's very good **festival website** (www.owfs.com).

The festivals:

- **Fall** – early October
- **Spring** – early May
- **Winter** – late January
- **Summer** – early August

Information

There are two good sources of information on Okanagan Valley wines:

BC Wine Information Centre (☎ 250-493-4055, 800-663-5052; 888 Westminster Ave W, Penticton; ⚇ 8am-8pm summer, 9am-5pm Mon-Fri,11am-5pm Sat & Sun other times) Information and tastings. Next to the convention center but may be moving to the corner of busy Eckhardt Ave W & Power St.
Wine Museum (☎ 250-868-0441; 1304 Ellis St, Kelowna; free; ⚇ 10am-5pm Mon-Sat, noon-5pm Sun) Knowledgeable staff can recommend tours and wines.

At each of these places, you can get guidance if you are looking for wineries specializing in certain types of wines.

Tours

There are several companies that let you do the sipping while they do the driving. See the Kelowna section (p218) for details.

VISITING THE WINERIES

At all the wineries open for visitors, you can expect to taste wine, but the quality of the experience varies widely. Some establishments are simple, with just a couple of wines on offer. Others are grander affairs with dozens of vintages ready for your attention. Some tasting rooms seem more like glorified sales areas, other have magnificent views of the vines, valley and lakes. And some wineries have restaurants, others cafes and others just bowls of bread for cleansing your palette.

At last count, there were more than 50 wineries in the Okanagan Valley. Here are a few we've chosen for various qualities that make them especially worth a visit (listed north to south).

Quails' Gate Estate Winery (18; ☎ 250-769-4451; www.quailsgate.com; 3303 Boucherie Rd, Kelowna; ⚇ 10am-5pm) A small winery with a huge reputation; known for its Pinot Noir, Sauvignon Blanc and its superb Totally Botrytis Affected Optima dessert wine. One of the best places for a visit.
Calona Vineyards (2; ☎ 250-762-3332; 1125 Richter St, Kelowna; ⚇ 9am-7pm summer, 10am-5pm winter) One of the oldest – 1932 – and largest wineries in the valley.

St Hubertus Estate Winery (21; ☎ 250-764-7888; www.st-hubertus.bc.ca; 5225 Lakeshore Rd, Kelowna; ☼ 10am-5:30pm summer, phone for winter) A family-run winery where you are likely to be given tastings by the owner.

CedarCreek Estate Winery (3; ☎ 250-764-8866; www.cedarcreek.bc.ca; 5445 Lakeshore Rd, Kelowna) Known for excellent tours as well as Pinot Blanc.

Mission Hill Family Estate Winery (16; ☎ 250-768-7611; www.missionhillwinery.com; 1730 Mission Hill Rd, Westbank; ☼ 10am-5pm) Go for a taste of the 2000 Cabernet Sauvignon Reserve; open year-round, great education on tasting, too.

Sumac Ridge Estate Winery (22; ☎ 250-494-0451; www.sumacridge.com; 17403 Hwy 97, Summerland; ☼ 9am-9pm, until 5pm Jan & Feb) Another excellent family-run winery with good personal tours; try the Cabernet-Merlot, unoaked Chardonnay & Okanagan Blush.

Jackson-Triggs Vintners (13; ☎ 250-498-4981; 38619 Hwy 97, Oliver; ☼ 9am-4:30pm Mon-Fri) The small Okanagan vineyard of this large Canadian label was named Winery of the Year in 2003, so it's a good thing that a grand, new tasting facility was set to premier in 2004. Try the Grand Reserve Meritage, Viognier, Merlot, Shiraz and the sweet and alluring Reisling ice wine.

Inniskillin Okanagan Vineyards (12; ☎ 250-498-6663; www.inniskillin.com; Rd 11 W, Oliver; ☼ 10am-5pm, until 3pm winter) Renowned for its ice wines, including the Vidal and Riesling.

Aside from the favorites we list above, there are many, many more wineries you can visit. The following list we recommend (north to south) isn't exhaustive, so you'll have to make a few discoveries on your own, you lucky devils.

Okanagan Centre
Gray Monk Estate Winery (7; ☎ 250-766-3168; 1055 Camp Rd)

Kelowna
Pinot Reach Cellars (17; ☎ 250-764-0078; 1670 Dehart Rd)
Slamka Cellars (20; ☎ 250-769-0404; 2815 Ourtoland Rd)
Summerhill Pyramid Winery (23; ☎ 250-764-8000; 4870 Chute Lake Rd)

Peachland
Hainle Vineyards Estate Winery (8; ☎ 250-767-2525; 5355 Trepanier Bench Rd)

Penticton
Hillside Estate (11; ☎ 250-493-6274; 1350 Naramata Rd)

Naramata
Lake Breeze Vineyards (14; ☎ 250-496-5659; 930 Sammet Rd)
Lang Vineyards (15; ☎ 250-496-5987; 2493 Gammon Rd)
Red Rooster Winery (19; ☎ 250-496-4041; 910 De Beck Rd)

Okanagan Falls
Hawthorne Mountain Vineyards (9; ☎ 250-497-8267; Green Lake Rd)
Wild Goose Vineyards (25; ☎ 250-497-8919; 2145 Sun Valley Way)

Oliver
Burrowing Owl Vineyards (1; ☎ 250-498-0620; 100 Burrowing Owl Place)
Domaine Combret Estate Winery (4; ☎ 250-498-6966; 32057 Rd No 13)
Gehringer Brothers Estate Winery (5; ☎ 250-498-3537; Road No 8)
Golden Mile Cellars (6; ☎ 250-498-8330; 13140 316A Ave)
Hester Creek Estate Winery (10; ☎ 250-498-4435; 13163 326th Ave)
Tinhorn Creek Vineyards (24; ☎ 250-498-3743; 32830 Tinhorn Creek Rd)

OKANAGAN VALLEY

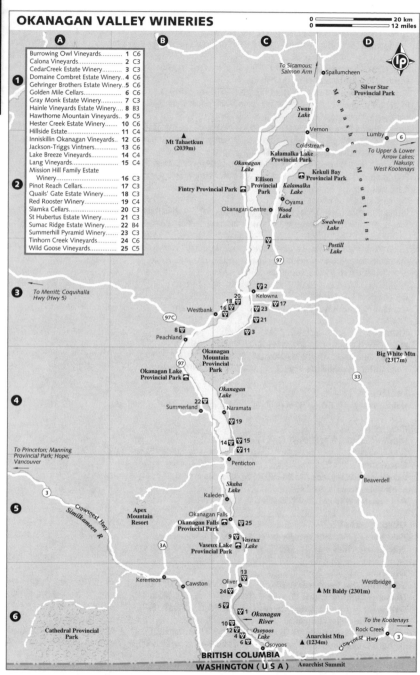

OKANAGAN VALLEY WINERIES

B&BS

The Visitor Info Centre keeps a long list of local B&Bs.

A long-time Penticton family runs the historic **Riordan House** (☎ 250-493-5997; www .icontext.com/riordan; 689 Winnipeg St; r from $50; P), which features four rooms filled with antiques.

Many of Penticton's B&Bs are in nearby Kaleden, which can be reached by following Hwy 97 south. Nature lovers will like the reclusive **Three Gates Farm B&B** (☎ 250-497-6889; threegates@img.net; s/d $85/95; P). The log house sits on 77 acres amid pine trees and flowering meadows. Call for directions.

HOSTELS

HI Penticton Hostel (☎ 250-492-3992; www.hihostels.ca; 464 Ellis St; members/non-members $17/21; P ⊠ ▯) This hostel is near downtown in a worn but sorta charming large old house. Facilities include private rooms, kitchen, laundry and a decent patio. Guests qualify for discounts on activities and meals. The hostel also arranges a wine tour.

CAMPING

You'll find many tent and trailer parks in the area, especially south of town, around Skaha Lake. Many are just off Hwy 97. Most charge about $17 to $25 for two people in a tent. This is in no way like wilderness camping, but it's a cheap place to stay. The beach closes at midnight and stays that way until 6am.

Eating & Drinking

Penticton definitely has its share of good eats. Stroll around Main and Front Sts and you will find numerous choices.

Voodoo's (☎ 250-770-8867; 67 E Nanaimo Ave; meals $8-12; ☿ 5pm-late) While away your night in this stylish space which is known for its interesting and inventive small plates like the evocative apricot chicken balls. Or just have one of the fine burgers. The long bar can mix anything – and does. On many nights there's live blues or other music.

Front St Pasta Factory (☎ 250-493-5666; 75 Front St; meals $11-18; ☿ lunch & dinner) features excellent Italian food and a patio with a good view of funky Front St. This is a good place to bring the kids.

Theo's (☎ 250-492-4019; 697 Main St; dinner $10-18; ☿ dinner) Another place where kids will want to do more with the food than just throw it is this classic Greek dinner house. The food's great and you can avoid the perils of retsina and wash down your souvlaki with local wines.

Salty's Beachouse Seafood Restaurant (☎ 250-493-5001; 1000 Lakeshore Dr; mains $12-22; ☿ dinner April-Oct). Can't get to Aruba? Try this open air seafood joint at the fun end of the beach. It dishes up all manner of fresh seafood, with a changing menu to reflect what's been caught. It's lively – what do you expect from a place that boasts about its 'cold beer'? – and fun.

Il Vecchio Deli (☎ 250-492-7610; 317 Robinson St; sandwiches $4; ☿ lunch Mon-Sat) For the best sandwich in town, go to this old Italian deli where you can almost dine on the aromas alone.

Green Beanz (☎ 250-493-8085; 218 Martin St; meals $6; ☿ 8am-5pm) is a slightly funky coffeehouse with couches and tables outside. The salads and wraps are good; the coffees and teas organic.

Johnny Donair (☎ 250-770-1913; 219 Main St; meals $7; ☿ lunch Mon-Sat) For a quick lunch downtown, try any of the veggie options on offer here; there are also various grilled meat treats.

Tin Whistle Brewing Company (☎ 250-770-1122; 954 W Eckhardt Ave; ☿ 11am-5pm) brews its own ales and offers free tours and tastings.

Entertainment

Barking Parrot (☎ 250-493-8221; Penticton Lakeside Resort, 21 Lakeshore Dr W; ☿ noon-late summer) attracts a local crowd that lounges around at the outdoor tables and snacks on food and drinks. There's frequent live music and comedy.

Element (☎ 250-492-0241; 535 Main St; cover $5; ☿ 7pm-late) is a hot dance club with hip-hop DJs, that also attracts top touring acts like the West Coast's Swollen Members.

Blue Mule (☎ 250-493-1819; 218 Martin St; cover varies; ☿ 8pm-late Sat & Sun) features country music, classic rock and dancing.

Getting There & Around

Penticton regional airport (YYF; 250-492-6042) is served by Air Canada Jazz, which has daily flights to Vancouver.

The Greyhound Bus Company offers services within the Okanagan Valley as well as operating routes to Vancouver, Prince George and Calgary. Its **depot** (☎ 250-493-4101; 307 Ellis St) is downtown.

The lake-to-lake shuttle bus of **Penticton Transit** (☎ 250-492-5602; www.busonline.ca; $1.75, day-pass $4) runs hourly along both water-fronts from 9am to 6:50pm.

APEX MOUNTAIN RESORT

Skiiers and snowboarders of all abilities head to **Apex Mountain Resort** (☎ 877-777-2739, conditions 250-487-4848; www.apexresort.com; 33km west of Penticton off Green Mountain Rd; lift tickets adult/child $48/29), one of Canada's best small ski resorts. It features over 60 downhill runs, but the mountain is known for its plethora of double-black-diamond and technical runs (the drop is over 600m). The crowds are smaller than at nearby Big White Mountain in Kelowna (p222), and the high-speed quad chair hauls skiers and boarders up quickly, keeping the lines short. Close to the village you'll find 30km of cross-country trails.

Apex is also a popular summer spot, when the downhill trails open up to horse-back riders, hikers and mountain bikers.

SUMMERLAND

pop 11,700

A small lakeside resort town 18km north of Penticton on Hwy 97, Summerland features some fine 19th-century heritage buildings. **Kettle Valley Steam Railway** (☎ 877-494-8424; 18404 Bathville Rd; adult/child $16/10; ☯ trains at 10:30am & 1:30pm Sat & Sun & holidays mid-May–mid-Oct) features an old logging steam locomotive and open-air cars. The views of the countryside are good and amateur thespians will empathize with the spirit of the 'robbers' who attack the train. From Hwy 97 take Prairie Valley Rd west out of town to Doherty Ave, then Bathville Rd.

Summerland Trout Hatchery (☎ 250-494-0491; 13405 Lakeshore Dr; free; ☯ 8:30-11:30am & 1:30-4:30pm) is one of the few BC hatcheries that are used to stock lakes. This one focuses on rainbow, eastern brook and kokanee trout. While you're in town, head to **Giant's Head Mountain**, an extinct volcano south of the downtown area, for great views of Okanagan Lake.

Agricultural Research Station (☎ 250-494-6385; free; ☯ 8am-dusk), 7km south of Summerland on Hwy 97, was designed for the study of fruit trees, their growth, diseases and production. You can enjoy your lunch on picnic grounds surrounded by an ornamental garden displaying a wide variety of plants and trees.

PEACHLAND

pop 2300

This lakeside town just south of Kelowna on the west bank of Okanagan Lake lives up to its lovely and evocative name. In fact, go for a quick stroll among the views and shops along the waterfront and you'll soon feel warm and fuzzy like a ripe peach.

KELOWNA

pop 103,000

The Okanagan's major city, Kelowna is an excellent base of exploration. It has a pretty lakefront, thriving downtown nightlife and numerous cultural institutions. The rounded, scrubby hills typical of the valley encircle Kelowna, gradually growing greener the closer you get to town, which (unusually) is the greenest area around, thanks to its many gardens and parks (65!). Beneath skies that are almost always clear, terraced orchards and bright green golf courses line the slopes of Kelowna's rolling hills, and sandy beaches rim the dark-blue water of the lake.

Throughout the summer, scores of tourists come through to sip wine, play in the lake, hike the hills or simply laze around in the ample sunshine. Summer days are usually dry and hot, the nights pleasantly cool. Winters are snowy but dry, making nearby Big White a big attraction for skiers and snowboarders. Kelowna's popularity as a tourist destination lends the town a distinct resort feel. Even the fires of 2003 have not dampened the spirit of 'the Okanagan Tiger', although hundreds of expensive homes burned south of town and Okanagan Mountain Provincial Park was destroyed.

The town's population has more than doubled in the last 30 years, partly due to its thriving economy. The combination of excellent weather and agricultural prowess make Kelowna the biggest producer of BC wines. Along with tourism and agriculture, high-tech manufacturing now helps drive the economy. Even without the tourists, there are plenty of people around to spend money, play golf and sip wine. In fact, more millionaires per capita reportedly live in Kelowna than anywhere else in Canada.

History

Kelowna, an Interior Salish word meaning 'grizzly bear', owes its settlement to a number of missionaries who arrived in 1858, hoping to convert the Natives. One of the priests, Father Charles Pandosy, established a mission in 1859 and planted the area's first apple trees along the banks of L'Anse au Sable, now known as Mission Creek. He is Canada's lesser-known equivalent of the USA's Johnny Appleseed.

An increasing trickle of settlers followed his lead, as this was ideal pioneer country, with lots of available timber to build houses, a freshwater creek and prime, grassy lands that were just begging for the cattle to come munching.

In 1892 the town of Kelowna was established; it quickly became an economic hub. The next decades saw prosperity based on the orchards and other natural resources of the area.

With the completion of the Okanagan Lake Floating Bridge in 1958, Kelowna experienced yet another growth spurt. Growing pains are evident in the barrage of motels and strip malls that plague the eastern end of town along Hwy 97. Ignore all that and you'll find that the lakeside, downtown area and surrounding orchards make Kelowna a stunning, surprisingly cosmopolitan city.

Orientation

Kelowna sits midway between Vernon and Penticton along the east side of 136km-long Okanagan Lake. Starting from City Park, Bernard Ave runs east and is the city's main drag. Ellis St, running north–south, is important and parallels the Cultural District.

Hwy 97, called Harvey Ave in town, marks the southern edge of the downtown area; it heads west over the bridge toward Penticton. East of downtown, Harvey Ave becomes a 10km strip lined with service stations, shopping malls, motels and fast-food restaurants. Past the sprawl, Harvey Ave is again called Hwy 97 and heads northeast toward Vernon.

Information

The central business district all but shuts down on Sundays.

DO WE NEED THE OGOPOGO?

What with all the fruit, the wine and the weather, does Kelowna really need a mythical monster in the lake called an Ogopogo? Given that Loch Ness would seem to lack an identity without Nessie, would Okanagan Lake really suffer without the legend of Opopogo? Granted there are tales of people centuries ago supposedly tossing hapless animals into the lake as offerings; granted it does give illustrators a chance to draw strange, sinuous, fanciful creatures, albeit ones with smiley faces; and granted it does offer parents a chance to tell their kids: 'Now if you're nice while mommy and daddy visit the vineyard, you can play on the Ogopogo statue in Kelowna'. But is it really necessary? You decide.

BOOKSTORES

First Try Books (☎ 250-763-5364; 426B Bernard Ave) Used bookstore whose bookmark reads 'In literature as in love, we are astonished at what is chosen by others'.

Kelowna Tobacco & Gifts (☎ 250-762-2266; 521 Bernard Ave) Big assortment of magazines, newspapers and Cuban cigars.

Mosaic Books (☎ 250-763-4418; 411 Bernard Ave) Sells maps (including topographic ones), atlases, travel and activity guides, plus books on Native Indian history and culture. Good selection of magazines and a coffee bar. There is a bargain branch nearby at 441 Bernard Ave.

Ted's Paperbacks & Comics (☎ 250-763-1258; 269 Leon Ave) Used books and an eclectic mix of collector comics.

INTERNET ACCESS

Kelowna Library (☎ 250-762-2800; 1380 Ellis St; ☺ 10am-5:30pm Mon, Fri & Sat, 10am-9pm Tue-Thu, 1-5pm Sun Oct-Mar) Online access is free with registration. The building is cleverly designed to look like an open book – albeit a huge one.

MEDICAL SERVICES

Kelowna General Hospital (☎ 250-862-4000; 2268 Pandosy St at Royal Ave; ☺ 24hr)

MONEY

Most of the town's banks are on Bernard Ave, between Water and Ellis Sts.

POST

Post office (☎ 250-868-8480; 591 Bernard Ave; ☺ 8:30am-5:30pm Mon-Sat)

KELOWNA

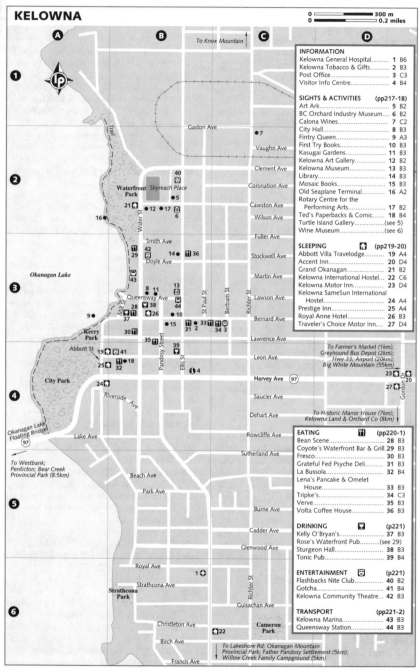

0 ————— 300 m
0 ————— 0.2 miles

INFORMATION
Kelowna General Hospital.........	1	B6
Kelowna Tobacco & Gifts.........	2	B3
Post Office................................	3	C3
Visitor Info Centre....................	4	B4

SIGHTS & ACTIVITIES (pp217-18)
Art Ark...................................	5	B2
BC Orchard Industry Museum..	6	B2
Calona Wines.........................	7	C2
City Hall................................	8	B3
Fintry Queen.........................	9	A3
First Try Books......................	10	B3
Kasugai Gardens....................	11	B3
Kelowna Art Gallery..............	12	B2
Kelowna Museum..................	13	B3
Library..................................	14	B3
Mosaic Books........................	15	B3
Old Seaplane Terminal..........	16	A2
Rotary Centre for the		
Performing Arts................	17	B2
Ted's Paperbacks & Comic..	18	B4
Turtle Island Gallery.............(see 5)		
Wine Museum.....................(see 6)		

SLEEPING (pp219-20)
Abbott Villa Travelodge..........	19	A4
Accent Inn.............................	20	D4
Grand Okanagan....................	21	B2
Kelowna International Hostel..	22	C6
Kelowna Motor Inn................	23	D4
Kelowna SameSun International		
Hostel...............................	24	A4
Prestige Inn..........................	25	A4
Royal Anne Hotel..................	26	B3
Traveler's Choice Motor Inn...	27	D4

EATING (pp220-1)
Bean Scene............................	28	B3
Coyote's Waterfront Bar & Grill.	29	B3
Fresco....................................	30	B3
Grateful Fed Psyche Deli........	31	B3
La Bussola.............................	32	B4
Lena's Pancake & Omelet		
House................................	33	B3
Tripke's.................................	34	C3
Verve....................................	35	B3
Volta Coffee House................	36	B3

DRINKING (p221)
Kelly O'Bryan's.....................	37	B3
Rose's Waterfront Pub........(see 29)		
Sturgeon Hall.......................	38	B3
Tonic Pub..............................	39	B4

ENTERTAINMENT (p221)
Flashbacks Nite Club..............	40	B2
Gotcha...................................	41	B4
Kelowna Community Theatre...	42	B3

TRANSPORT (pp221-2)
Kelowna Marina.....................	43	B3
Queensway Station................	44	B3

To Knox Mountain

Gaston Ave
Vaughn Ave
Clement Ave
Coronation Ave
Cawston Ave
Wilson Ave
Fuller Ave
Smith Ave
Stockwell Ave
Doyle Ave
Martin Ave
Queensway Ave
Lawson Ave
Bernard Ave
Lawrence Ave
Leon Ave
Harvey Ave (97)
Saucier Ave
Dehart Ave
Rowcliffe Ave
Sutherland Ave
Beach Ave
Park Ave
Burne Ave
Cadder Ave
Glenwood Ave
Royal Ave
Strathcona Ave
Guisachan Ave
Christleton Ave
Birch Ave
Francis Ave

Waterfront Park
Skyreach Place
Okanagan Lake
Kerry Park
Abbott St
City Park
Riverside Ave
Lake Ave
Strathcona Park
Cameron Park

Water St
St Paul St
Bertram St
Richter St
Pandosy Street
Ellis St
Mill St
Gordon Dr

To Westbank;
Penticton; Bear Creek
Provincial Park (8.5km)

Okanagan Lake
Floating Bridge
(97)

To Farmer's Market (1km);
Greyhound Bus Depot (2km);
Hwy 33; Airport (20km);
Big White Mountain (55km)

To Historic Manor House (7km);
Kelowna Land & Orchard Co (8km)

To Lakeshore Rd; Okanagan Mountain
Provincial Park; Father Pandosy Settlement (5km);
Willow Creek Family Campground (5km)

TOURIST INFORMATION

Visitor Info Centre (☎ 250-861-1515, 800-663-4345; 544 Harvey Ave near the corner of Ellis St; ⊗ 8am-7pm summer, 8am-5pm Mon-Fri, 10am-3pm Sat & Sun winter) Pick up the impressive brochure for a self-guiding tour of the Cultural District.

Sights

THE CULTURAL DISTRICT

The **Kelowna Art Gallery** (☎ 250-979-0888; 1315 Water St; admission free; ⊗ 10am-5pm Tue-Sat, 10am-9pm Thu, 1-5pm Sun) features the work of local artists, of which there are many. The light, airy gallery has a vibrant collection and regular special exhibits. Nearby are two worthwhile art galleries. **Art Ark** (☎ 250-862-5080; 1295 Cannery Lane; ⊗ 10am-5pm, later in summer) shows and sells a wide range of works (paintings, sculpture, photography, mixed media and so on) by Okanagan artists. Great space to view art. Next door, the smaller **Turtle Island Gallery** (☎ 250-717-8235) sells works by First Nations artists.

Located in the old Laurel Orchards packinghouse, the **BC Orchard Industry Museum** (☎ 250-763-0433; 1304 Ellis St; admission by donation; ⊗ 10am-5pm Mon-Sat) recounts the conversion of the Okanagan Valley from ranch land to orchards. The exhibits show just about everything you can do with fruit, from seeds to jam. Note the displays of beautiful old packing crate labels – many of which are works of art in their own right. Especially appealing is the one for Laurel Canadian Pears. In the same building is the **Wine Museum** (☎ 250-868-0441; admission free; ⊗ 10am-5pm Mon-Sat, noon-5pm Sun). The knowledgeable staff can recommend tours, steer you to the best wineries for tastings and help you fill the trunk of your car with examples of the myriad local wines on sale.

A part of the civic center complex, the **Kelowna Museum** (☎ 250-763-2417; 470 Queensway Ave at Ellis St; admission by donation; ⊗ 10am-5pm Tue-Sat) showcases Kelowna's ethnographic and natural history. A much-needed facelift seems forever delayed but in the meantime there are good special exhibits along with the regular collection.

Behind the museum, **Kasugai Gardens** (admission free; ⊗ 9am-6pm) are good for a lovely peaceful stroll around the beautifully manicured grounds. The Circle of Friendship sculpture marks the entrance to the Japanese garden, which also has pools of lazy koi.

CITY PARK & PROMENADE

City Park & Promenade, the central downtown park, is excellent. Slide into the water from the sandy **Hot Sands Beach**, read under one of the many shade trees or just marvel at the flower gardens blooming with tulips and enjoy the soothing view across **Okanagan Lake**. Given the bucolic setting and the warm lake water (just slightly cooler than the summer air), it's no wonder would-be fruit pickers are sitting around picking only guitars.

At 650m long, the **Okanagan Lake Bridge**, just west of City Park, is Canada's longest floating bridge; it's supported by 12 pontoons and has a lift span in the middle so that boats up to 18m high can pass through.

From Bernard Ave, the lakeside promenade extends north past the marina, lock and artificial lagoon to The Grand Okanagan and a condominium complex that boasts a blend of Canadian and Spanish architectural styles. The promenade is good for a stroll, skate or jog in the evenings. The promenade joins City Park with the equally bucolic Waterfront Park, just to the north.

You'll find several **beaches** south of Okanagan Lake Bridge along Lakeshore Rd. Gyro Beach, at the south end of Richter St, attracts lots of locals. The **Okanagan Shuswap Nudist Society** (osnswebmaster@shaw.ca) provides information on local buff beaches.

The 10.5-sq-km **Okanagan Mountain Provincial Park** (☎ 250-494-6500; www.elp.gov.bc.ca/bcparks), south of Kelowna off Lakeshore Rd, was 95% burned by the fires, but BC Parks has plans to offer programs showing how the land recovers from the conflagration. See Tours, p218.

About 8.5km northwest of Kelowna, **Bear Creek Provincial Park** (☎ 250-494-6500; www.elp.gov.bc.ca/bcparks) offers opportunities for hiking as well as windsurfing, fishing, swimming, and wilderness camping. From Kelowna, cross the floating bridge and go right (north) on Westside Rd.

OTHER SIGHTS

An easy stroll from the Cultural District, **Calona Wines** (☎ 250-762-9144; www.calonavineyards.ca; 1125 Richter St; ⊗ 9am-6pm) is one of BC's largest producers and was the first in the Okanagan Valley; it started in 1932. This is a great place for tastings as you can avoid worrying about getting back in your car.

The **Farmer's Market** (☎ 250-878-5029; corner Springfield Rd & Dilworth Dr off Hwy 97; ☟ 8am-1pm Wed & Sat May-Oct) has over 100 stands, including many with prepared foods.

The major historic site in the area is the **Father Pandosy Settlement** (admission free; ☟ 8am-dusk Apr-Oct), where some original buildings survive on the spot where the priest set up his mission in 1859. The church, school, barn, one house and a few sheds from what was the first White settlement in the Okanagan have been restored. The site is small, well away from the center of town and rather quiet, you may feel compelled to proselytize. To get there, go south along Lakeshore Rd, then east on Casorso Rd to Benvoulin Rd.

Activities

The weather makes Kelowna a great spot for outdoorsy stuff, lots of it centered around the lake.

WATER SPORTS

Fishing is possible on Okanagan Lake and many of the 200 lakes near Kelowna. You can rent speedboats (starting at $55 per hour), arrange fishing trips and cruises or rent windsurfing gear at **Kelowna Marina** (☎ 250-861-8001; lake end of Queensway Ave). Windsurfers take to the water from the old seaplane terminal, near the corner of Water St and Cawston Ave.

HIKING & MOUNTAIN BIKING

You'll find great hiking and fat-tire riding all around town. To get started, pick up the excellent *Heritage Walking Tour* brochure from the VIC. While you're there, ask for directions to **Mission Creek Greenway**, a meandering, 18km wooded path following the creek. It makes for a nice, mellow bike ride. Hike or ride up **Knox Mountain**, which sits at the northern end of the city. Along with bobcats and snakes, the mountain has good trails and rewards you with excellent views from the top.

The fires of 2003 were devastating to the **Kettle Valley Railway**, with 14 of the 18 historic trestles being destroyed. The old line, which affords fantastic views of the Myra Canyon, had been a highly popular trail since its closure to rail traffic. The route follows the old railway tracks through tunnels and over old trestles. To reach what remains, follow Harvey Ave (Hwy 97) east to Gordon Drive. From there, turn right on KLO Rd and follow it all the way to the end of McCulloch Rd. About 2km after the pavement ends, you'll come to a clearing where power lines cross the road. Turn right on the Myra Forest Service Rd and follow it for 8km to the parking lot. You'll see the trailhead along with current news about conditions. There has been significant community interest in rebuilding the route in some form, although cost estimates are upwards of $15 million. Follow news of rebuilding plans at the website (members.rogers.com/kettlevalley/).

Kelowna for Kids

At the foot of Bernard Ave, behind the model of Ogopogo, the old ferry boat **Fintry Queen** (☎ 250-763-2780; lake cruises adult/child $15/10; ☟ May-Oct) is docked in the lake. Kids love the old-boat atmosphere and the 90-minute cruises are a good way to escape the heat on land on sultry days and there's a restaurant on board – if you just have to eat.

Kelowna Land & Orchard Co (☎ 250-763-1091; 3002 Dunster Rd; orchard tours adult/child $6/free; ☟ 10am-4pm May-Oct, tour times vary seasonally) is the largest of local orchards open for tours. The tours aboard open wagons are fun for all ages. You can also buy fruit and baked goods here; the fresh-pressed apple juice is addictive. Kids will want to pet the llamas.

Tours

Monashee Adventure Tours (☎ 250-762-9253, 888-762-9253; www.monasheeadventuretours.com) offers biking or hiking tours of the valley, parks and wineries. Tours are accompanied by local guides, who give excellent historical accounts of the area. Prices, which average $100, include a bike, lunch and shuttle to the route.

Selah Outdoor Explorations (☎ 250-762-4968, 866-695-2972; half-day tours from $33) offers ecological tours by canoe to see the fire's destruction and nature's recovery along the shore of Okanagan Mountain Provincial Park.

WINERY TOURS

Numerous Kelowna companies offer tours to many of the region's wineries. There are a myriad of programs that last from a few hours to a full day, with various eating options as well. Tour prices usually include pick-up at hotels and motels.

Club Wine Tours (☎ 250-762-9951, 866-386-9463; www.clubwinetours.com; 4hr/7hr tour $49/95)

Okanagan Wine Country Tours (☎ 250-868-9463, 866-689-9463; 4hr tour $52) Available tours include all-day with a gourmet lunch for $110.

Tasteful Tours (☎ 250-769-1929; 3hr tour $35)

Wildflower Trails and Wine Tours (☎ 250-979-1211, 866-979-1211; www.wildflowersandwine.com; day tour $95) Combines a lovely hike through the wildflower-covered hills of the valley with lunch and an afternoon of wine tasting.

Festivals & Events

JULY

Kelowna Regatta (☎ 250-860-0529; www.kelowna regatta.com) Hundreds of boat owners celebrate boat ownership.

SEPTEMBER

Dragon Boat Festival (☎ 250-868-1136) Local teams race the Chinese boats on the lake then party afterwards.

OCTOBER

Okanagan Fall Wine Fest (☎ 250-861-6654; www .owfs.com) You thought they wouldn't have one of these? Are you drunk?

Sleeping

As in the rest of the Okanagan Valley, accommodation here can be difficult to find in summer; it's best to book ahead or arrive early in the day.

MOTELS & HOTELS

Grand Okanagan (☎ 250-763-4500, 800-465-4651; www.grandokanagan.com; 1310 Water St; r from $180; P ✗ ⌨ ⌘) The ever-growing Grand boasts a premier position on the lake in the Cultural District. This is a top-notch property with artwork in the common areas, a spa, a damn fine pool area and much more, all attended to by an engaging staff. Aim for one of the rooms with a private balcony. Should you need to empty your pockets, there's a small casino.

Prestige Inn (☎ 250-860-7900, 877-737-8443; www.prestigeinn.com; 1675 Abbott St; r from $150; P ✗ ⌨ ⌘) This modest-sized place has a great location across from City Park. If weather makes the lake uninviting, try the indoor pool and Jacuzzi. The decent rooms

have free high-speed Internet access, and refrigerators.

Abbott Villa Travelodge (☎ 250-763-7771, 800-578-7878; www.travelodge.com; 1627 Abbott St; s/d $109/119; P ✗ ⌘) Also well located across from City Park, right downtown, this renovated motel is good value, offers free breakfast and has a nice outdoor pool.

Royal Anne Hotel (☎ 250-763-2277, 888-811-3400; 348 Bernard Ave; s/d from $89/99; P ✗) The decent rooms look better on the inside than the hotel does on the outside but the location is unassailable.

If you can't stay at one of the well-located places above, consider the following motels, which are about a 10-minute walk from the center yet not fully in the thick of strip mall hell on Hwy 97.

Traveler's Choice Motor Inn (☎ 250-762-3221, 800-665-2610; www.travellerschoice.org; 1780 Gordon Dr; r from $66; P ✗ ⌘) features VCRs in the rooms if you can't bear another moment of cable. The good-sized rooms have balconies.

Accent Inn (☎ 250-862-8888, 800-663-0298; www .accentinns.com; 1140 Harvey Ave; r from $99; P ✗ ⌨ ⌘) is a well-run place with comfortable rooms. Highly recommended.

Kelowna Motor Inn (☎ 250-762-2533, 800-667-6133; www.kminn.bc.ca; 1070 Harvey Ave; s/d from $85/89; P ✗ ⌘) is clean and has a small spa.

B&BS

Kelowna contains more than 60 B&Bs, which range from luxurious lakeside retreats to farmhouses in the middle of vineyards. The VIC keeps a substantial list of all the B&Bs affiliated with the Chamber of Commerce.

For an excellent lesson in Kelowna history, visit the **Historic Manor House** (☎ 250-861-3932; www.manorhouseokanagan.com; 2796 KLO Rd; s/d from $89/115; P) Only a 10-minute drive from town, this beautiful heritage home sits on a still-working apple orchard – one of Kelowna's first.

HOSTELS

Kelowna SameSun International Hostel (☎ 250-763-9814, 877-562-2783; www.samesun.com; 245 Harvey Ave; dm/r $20/40; P ✗ ⌨) Perfectly located near the corner of Hwy 97 and Abbott St. The building is downright spiffy and has all the usual amenities. The young crowd enjoys barbecues year-round and other delights like 'party boat trips' in the summer. The hostel offers free pick-up at the bus depot as well as shuttles to its Big White and Silver Star ski resort hostels.

The **Kelowna International Hostel** (☎ 250-763-6024; www.kelowna-hostel.bc.ca; 2343 Pandosy St; dm from $13; P ☐) is about 12 blocks from downtown. An old, spiffed-up house, the place feels relaxed and neighborly. There's free transport to the bus station.

CAMPING
Camping is the cheapest way to stay in the area, though you'll be a fair way from town. The best place is **Bear Creek Provincial Park** (☎ 250-494-0321; tent sites $22; P), on the west side of the lake 9km north of Kelowna off Westlake Rd. The campground offers 122 shady sites close to the park's 400m-long beachfront area.

Numerous privately owned places surround Kelowna, especially in Westbank and south along Lakeshore Rd. The grounds are usually crowded and the sites close together. To get to Westbank, head west along Hwy 97 over Okanagan Lake Bridge and then turn off at Boucherie Rd. Follow this for quite a while and you'll hit the so-called 'resort area'. This area is quite far from town – you'll need a car. Sites cost $15 to $25.

Closer to town, **Willow Creek Family Campground** (☎ 250-762-6302; willowcreekcampground@shaw.ca; 3316 Lakeshore Rd; sites $22; P) boasts its own beach, a fire pit and proximity to shops and restaurants.

Eating
Because of the abundance of local wine and produce, Kelowna is a great place to eat out.

RESTAURANTS
Fresco (☎ 250-868-8805; 1560 Water St; meals $35; dinner Tue-Sat) Noted BC chef Ron Butters has racked up much acclaim with his signature restaurant. Seasonal and regional ingredients are used to superb effect in the dramatic open kitchen. Elsewhere the dining room is both spare in detail yet warm in décor. The ever-changing menu usually has at least a few of the dishes that made Butters famous such as roasted Dungeness crab cappuccino (a frothy soup). Other favorites are roast pork smoked over

fruitwood and anything made with wild salmon or halibut. Reserve.

La Bussola (☎ 250-763-3110; 234 Leon Ave; meals $25; dinner Tue-Sat) Since 1974 Franco and Lauretta Coccaro have worked the kitchen preparing every dish served in their slightly elegant yet fun Italian dinner house. The nautical theme comes from the name, which means 'compass' in Italian. Fresh pasta is complemented by regional ingredients. Great wine list.

Coyote's Waterfront Bar & Grill (☎ 250-860-1226; 1352 Water St; steaks $24; lunch & dinner) There are great lake views from this upstairs place on the water. The menu is vaguely Southwestern but really concentrates on huge steaks and ribs.

Lena's Pancake & Omelet House (☎ 250-861-5531; 533 Bernard Ave; meals $6; breakfast & lunch) Don't let the plain exterior fool you (or the interior for that matter), Lena's serves classic breakfast specials and all types of pancakes, omelets and sandwiches.

CAFÉS
Join the hip and happenin' locals and start your morning off with a coffee and muffin from the **Bean Scene** (☎ 250-763-1814; 274 Bernard Ave; coffee $2; 6:30am-10pm). There's a great bulletin board to check up on local happenings – or ask one of the voluble patrons.

Tripke's (☎ 250-763-7665; 567 Bernard Ave; meals $5; 8am-5:30pm Mon-Sat) A classic European bakery with a little café area for a light lunch.

Volta Coffee House (☎ 250-868-3919; 1387 Ellis St; light lunch 7$; 7am-5:30pm Mon-Sat) Across from the library, this tiny café serves only organic and fair-trade coffees. And in case the coffee puts a spring in your step, they sell professional dancing shoes as well – the owner's a dancer.

Grateful Fed Psyche Deli (☎ 250-862-8621, 509 Bernard Ave; sandwiches $5; 7am-9pm Mon-Sat, later in summer) Lots of folks hang out at the tables outside, and they can still hear the continually playing music by the…oh, you know who.

Verve (☎ 250-860-8086; 345 Lawrence Ave; meals $10; 7am-10pm) Part café, part bistro, part performance venue, Verve is a fun and ever-changing hip place downtown. If the theme one week is Cuban, there will be Cuban dance lessons at night to go with the black beans.

Drinking

Drinking establishments in Kelowna are usually open from noon to late.

Rose's Waterfront Pub (☎ 250-860-1141; 1352 Water St) is a popular beer-swilling spot for the locals with standard pub fare (burgers for $8). The lakefront patio is a delight, with heaters overhead to extend the season.

Kelly O'Bryan's (☎ 250-861-1338; 262 Bernard Ave) features a popular upstairs 'paddy-o' and Guinness on tap. It has views of the lake.

Sturgeon Hall (☎ 250-860-3055; 1481 Water St) is home to the fanatical fans of the local Kelowna Rockets hockey team. After the game it gets mobbed with a mood that clearly reflects the outcome of the game. Score a hat trick with a Rocket burger ($9) and a few brews.

Tonic Pub (☎ 250-860-2997; 1654 Ellis St) is a new place that is already a classic pub. Gets a good, fun crowd.

Entertainment

CLUBS

Downtown Kelowna boasts several clubs. For anyone who fondly remembers the tight jeans and big hair of the '80s, **Flashbacks Nite Club** (☎ 250-861-3039; 1268 Ellis St; cover varies; 7pm-late Wed-Sun) in a former cigar factory, brings those halcyon days back. You can play pool or enjoy the live music.

Gotcha (☎ 250-860-0800; 238 Leon Ave; cover varies; 7pm-late Tue-Sat) is one of three clubs on this stretch of Leon. Some people bounce between the three all night, others decide after seeing who's playing and/or DJ'ing at each.

PERFORMANCE & ART

Rotary Centre for the Performing Arts (☎ 250-717-5304, tickets ☎ 250-763-1849; 421 Cawston Ave) This impressive new building anchors the Cultural District and has galleries, a theatre, a café and more.

Kelowna Community Theatre (☎ 250-762-2471; 1375 Water St) hosts music and theatre.

The **Sunshine Theatre Company** (☎ 250-763-4025) stages a range of productions at both of the above venues.

Free **concerts**, featuring everything from rock to classical music, take place in downtown's Kerry Park on Friday and Saturday nights during summer and in City Park on Sunday afternoons in summer.

SPORTS

Kelowna Rockets (☎ 250-860-7825; www.kelownarockets.com; tickets from $10) are the much beloved local WHL hockey team. They play in 6000-seat Skyreach Place (☎ 250-979-0888; www.skyreachplace.com; Water St & Cawston Ave).

Getting There & Away

Kelowna airport (YLW; ☎ 250-765-5125; www.kelownaairport.com) is now Canada's 11th busiest, thanks to the arrival of discount carrier Westjet, which serves Vancouver, Victoria, Edmonton and Calgary with nonstop cheap flights. Air Canada Jazz – with newly lowered fares from Kelowna – serves Vancouver and Calgary. Horizon Air provides international service and connections to Seattle. The airport is a long 20km north on Hwy 97 from Kelowna.

Greyhound bus depot (☎ 250-860-3835; 2366 Leckie Rd) is north of the downtown area, off Hwy 97. Daily buses travel to other points in the Okanagan Valley, as well as Kamloops, Vancouver, Calgary and Prince George. The station contains a restaurant and coin lockers. To get there, take city bus No 10 from Queensway station, Queensway Ave between Pandosy and Ellis Sts. It runs every half hour, roughly, from 6:30am to 9:45pm. From the depot, use the free phone to request a pick-up from where you're staying.

Getting Around

TO/FROM THE AIRPORT

There are two buses connecting with the airport. **Kelowna Airporter bus** (☎ 250-765-0182; one-way $20) and **Vernon Airporter** (☎ 250-542-7574). A one-way taxi fare is about $28.

BUS

Pick up a copy of Kelowna Regional Rider's Guide from the Visitor Info Centre, or try **Kelowna Regional Transit Systems** (☎ 250-860-8121; www.busonline.ca). There are three zones for bus travel, and the one-way fare in the central zone is $1.50. A day pass for all three zones costs $4.25. All the downtown buses pass through Queensway station, on Queensway Ave between Pandosy and Ellis Sts. Some of the buses are London-style double-deckers.

CAR & TAXI

All the major car rental companies operate from Kelowna airport.

Taxi companies include:
Kelowna Cabs (☎ 250-762-4444, 250-762-2222)
Checkmate Cabs (☎ 250-861-1111, 250-861-4445)

BIG WHITE SKI RESORT

Known for its incredible powder, **Big White Ski Resort** (☎ 250-765-8888, 800-663-2772, snow report ☎ 250-765-7669; www.bigwhite.com; 55km east of Kelowna off Hwy 33; one-day lift passes adult/child $56/30) is one of BC's best ski resorts. Non-locals know about the powder as well, and the resort's popularity grows every year. The highest ski resort in the province, it features 840 hectares of runs, which are covered in the noted deep dry powder for excellent downhill and backcountry skiing, and deep gullies that make for killer snowboarding. The drop is 777m. There is also night skiing. Because of Big White's distance from Kelowna, most people stay up here. The resort includes numerous restaurants, bars, hotels and hostels.

Big White has hotels, condos, rental homes and a hostel. Contact **central reservations** (☎ 800-663-2772; www.bigwhite.com) for full details and pricing. One of their nicer properties is **Chateau Big White** (r $150-180; P 🖵), which has a spa, great public spaces and ski runs right outside the door.

SameSun Ski Resort Hostel (☎ 250-765-7050, 877-562-2783; www.samesun.com; in the Alpine Center; dm from $20, r from $60; 🖵) lets you ski to and from the runs right from the hostel. If you're looking for rest and lots of sleep, don't count on it here, as the hostel is known for its party atmosphere. There are daily shuttles to/from the Kelowna Same-Sun International Hostel (p219).

VERNON

pop 33,200

Vernon, the most northerly of the Okanagan's 'Big Three', lies in a scenic valley encircled by three lakes: the Okanagan, Kalamalka and Swan. But unlike Penticton and Kelowna, Vernon developed because of its roads, not its lakes. Once the hub of the Okanagan Valley, Vernon used to be a major crossroads town that connected the valley with the rest of the interior. Fur traders first used its strategic location, followed by an onslaught of gold prospectors streaming up the valley to the Cariboo district. Later, cattle were brought in, and in 1891 the railway arrived. But it was in 1908, with the introduction of large-scale irrigation, that the town took on an importance that was more than transitory. Soon the area was covered in orchards and farms.

With a friendly and artsy community and stunning Kalamalka Lake, Vernon is possibly the most underrated city in the Okanagan. Its growth has been slower than that of its sister cities, so it hasn't been hit as hard by the blight of urban sprawl. Though forestry remains the city's primary industry, Vernon's population is surprisingly cosmopolitan, with a multicultural bent provided by populations of Germans, Chinese and First Nations people, the last of whom occupy a reserve to the west of town.

Downtown Vernon is interesting and compact, and an ongoing community project to paint murals depicting the area's history is a colorful attraction, popular with both locals and visitors.

Orientation

Surrounded by rolling hills, downtown Vernon is a clean, neat, quiet place on Hwy 97. Main St, also called 30th Ave, rarely bustles. At 25th Ave, Hwy 6, which leads southeast to Nelson and Nakusp, meets Hwy 97, which runs north–south, becoming 32nd St in Vernon and bisecting the city. On 32nd St, north of 30th Ave, you'll find a commercial strip with service stations, motels and fast-food outlets.

All the downtown sights are within easy walking distance of each other.

Information
BOOKSTORES

Bookland (☎ 250-545-1885; 3400 30th Ave) Topo maps, travel guides and books on activities in the Okanagan Valley and BC. Excellent selection of magazines and newspapers.

INTERNET ACCESS

Vernon Public Library (☎ 250-542-7610; 3001 32nd Ave; ☼ 10am-5:30pm Mon, Thu-Sat, 10am-4pm Tue & Wed) Free access; next to the Vernon Museum.

LAUNDRY

Aloha Coin Wash (☎ 250-545-8022; 2800 34th St) For a little Hawaiian vibe while you watch your clothes go round and round.

MEDICAL SERVICES
Vernon Jubilee Hospital (☎ 250-545-2211; 2101 32nd St; ☑ 24hr)

POST
Main post office (☎ 250-545-8239; 3101 32nd Ave & 31st St)

TOURIST INFORMATION
Vernon has two **Visitor Info Centres** (☎ 250-542-1415, 800-665-0795; www.vernontourism.com; 6326 Hwy 97 N, near the southeastern shore of Swan Lake & 701 Hwy 97 S about 5km north of town; ☑ 8:30am-6pm summer; 8:30am-4:30pm Mon-Fri, 10am-4pm Sat & Sun winter) that cover the main entrances and exits to town.

Sights & Activities
DOWNTOWN VERNON
Vernon has over 30 **murals** that have been painted by local artists with help from school kids and other volunteers. These are not your usual faded-flag-with-a-poorly-drawn-national-icon murals either. Rather, these are building-sized works of art. Pick up a copy of the *Downtown Vernon Directory* at the Visitor Info Centres. It has full descriptions of each work along with a handy map. You can walk and study all of them in under 90 minutes. A **trompe l'oeil scene** (3306 30th Ave) looks through the building wall to see orchard workers busily packing fruit. **The World Wars** (3202 32nd St) is a moving study of war and its effects. Note the text of the telegram carrying news families dread in wartime. **Multiculturalism** (3101 32nd St) turns a humdrum building into a thing of beauty. Really, the architect should send a check to the artists.

Built entirely of local granite, the **Provincial Courthouse** (☎ 250-549-5422; 30th Ave & 27th St) sits majestically at the eastern end of downtown. **Polson Park**, off 25th Ave next to 32nd St, bursts with spring and summer flowers. If it's hot outside, this is a good, cool rest spot, thanks to the shade and trickling Vernon Creek. The Japanese and Chinese influence is evident in the gardens and the open, cabana-like structures dotting the park, at one end of which is a floral clock.

Behind Polson Park is a **skateboard park** and the **Okanagan Science Centre** (☎ 250-545-3644; 2704 Hwy 6; adult/child $7/4; ☑ 9am-5pm Tue-Sat, 1-5pm Sun) where science buffs and little kids can check out interactive science exhibits. Check out the one on local air quality.

The **Vernon Museum** (☎ 250-542-3142; 3009 32nd Ave at 31st St; free; ☑ 10am-5pm Tue-Sat) displays historical artifacts from the area, including old carriages and clothes, a good antique telephone collection and lots of archival photos of the area and the locals. The library is right next door.

The **Vernon Art Gallery** (☎ 250-545-3173; 3228 31st Ave; donation; ☑ 10am-5pm Tue-Fri, 11am-4pm Sat) boasts impressive exhibits and knowledgeable staff. Ask them about their favorite artworks for an impromptu tour.

Named for wildlife painter Allan Brooks, who lived in Vernon before he died, the **Allan Brooks Nature Centre** (☎ 250-260-4227; adult/child $4/3; ☑ 10am-5pm Tue-Sun May–mid-Oct) features interactive displays on the North Okanagan's diverse ecosystems. To get there, follow 34th St until it becomes Mission Rd. Follow that for about 2km, then turn left onto Allan Brooks Rd. Follow the signs to the center. It's in a very pretty setting, housed in an old weather station. There are numerous walks in the area.

Davison Orchards (☎ 250-549-3266; 3111 Davison Rd; free; ☑ daylight hrs May-Oct) is one of many orchards in the area, but outpaces its competition in the visitor-friendly category. Fragrant orchards surround a café and small produce store where you can sample the myriad variety of apples grown on the farm. This is a good time to find out that an Arlet is possibly the crispest apple, while Empires are mighty fine for eating. On many weekends there are games for the kids and wagon rides through the trees. Take 30th Ave west until it becomes Bella Vista Rd, then watch for the orchards.

Right next to Davison Orchards is another natural treat, one with a sting. **Planet Bee** (☎ 250-542-8088; 5011 Bella Vista Rd; free; ☑ daylight hrs May-Oct) is a working honey farm with extensive visitor facilities that include an indoor hive you can study up close (you'll see that males really are just a bunch of drones) as well as a production area where you can see the honey go from hive to jar. The shop sells no end of bee-derived products. You can sample diverse honeys made from various types of nectar.

Vernon Farmer's Market (☎ 250-546-6267; 2200 58th Ave; ☑ 4-8pm Fri) is held at a salubrious time. Unfortunately the same cannot be said for the location: the parking lot of Wal-Mart.

PROVINCIAL PARKS
Kalamalka Lake
This 8.9-sq-km park lies on the eastern side of warm, shallow Kalamalka Lake (simply called 'Kal' by the locals), south of town. The park offers great swimming at Jade and Kalamalka beaches, good fishing and public picnic areas. A network of mountain biking and hiking trails takes you to places like **Cougar Canyon** (apparently a bit of a misnomer as no one has ever reported seeing a cougar), where the rock climbing is excellent. There are no campgrounds in the park. To get there from downtown, follow Hwy 6 east to the Polson Place Mall, then turn right on Kalamalka Lake Rd and proceed to Kal Beach. You can also ride bus No 1 from downtown.

Ellison
A 15-minute drive takes you to this beautiful park on Okanagan Lake, 16km southwest from Vernon on Okanagan Landing Rd. Ellison includes campsites, more hiking and biking trails and the only freshwater marine park in western Canada. Scuba divers can plunge into the warm water to explore a sunken wreck or come face to face with a giant perch. You can rent scuba gear in Vernon at the dive shop **Innerspace Dive & Kayak** (☎ 250-549-2040; 3103 32nd St). Ellison is also known for its world-class rock climbing. To get to Ellison from downtown, go west on 25th Ave, which soon becomes Okanagan Landing Rd. Follow that and look for signs to the park.

Sleeping
MOTELS & HOTELS
You'll find many, many motels in and around Vernon, especially north of downtown along 32nd St (Hwy 97).

If you've done your laundry at Aloha Coin Wash (see Information above) you may want to continue your tropical vibe at **Tiki Village Motel** (☎ 250-503-5566, 800-661-8454; www.tikivillagevernon.com; 2408 34th St; r $79-89; P ⊠ ⓡ). This authentic retro-motel boasts lovely grounds, a large outdoor pool and faux tiki torches. The quiet rooms have their own patios or balconies, making the Tiki a fine place to stay on a warm summer evening.

Travelodge (☎ 250-545-2161, 800-578-7878; www.travelodge.com; 3000 28th Ave; s/d $64/69; P ⊠ ⓡ)

The location is good, right downtown near the restaurants and pubs. The rooms hold no surprises – even if you look under the bed.

North on 32nd St around 42nd Ave is a thicket of chain motels. You'll be a short drive or a long walk from town. The **Super 8** (☎ 250-542-4434, 866-542-4434; www.super8.com; 4204 32nd St; r $95-150; P ⊠ ⓡ) features an indoor pool and whirlpool.

Best Western Vernon Lodge (☎ 250-545-3385, 800-663-4422; www.rpbhotels.com; 3914 32nd St; s/d from $104/114; P ⊠ ⓡ) has convention facilities as well as an indoor pool where tipsy conventioneers can get tipped in. The rooms are standard and comfortable.

B&BS
Vernon has lots of B&Bs, many located on the surrounding hills and on local farms. Get a complete listing from the VIC. Close to downtown, **Tuck Inn** (☎ 250-545-3252; www.pixsell.bc.ca/bcbbd.htm; 3101 Pleasant Valley Rd; s/d from $45/65; P) is in a large, white Victorian house. The second 'B' in B&B consists of large gourmet vegetarian breakfasts.

HOSTELS
The beautiful **HI Lodged Inn** (☎ 250-549-3742, 888-737-9427; www.hihostels.ca; 3201 Pleasant Valley Rd; members/nonmembers $16/20; P ⊠) is just a few minutes' walk from downtown. The hostel works with local organizations to arrange paragliding, skydiving, climbing and hiking trips, plus winery tours and interpretive tours of the area's flora and fauna. You can rent bikes.

CAMPING
By far the best campground is at **Ellison Provincial Park** (☎ 800-689-9025, information only ☎ 250-494-6500; www.discovercamping.ca), 16km southwest of Vernon on Okanagan Landing Rd. The park features a developed beach, underwater marine park and good hiking and biking trails. Its 71 campsites ($17) fill up early, so it's a good idea to make a reservation.

Kekuli Bay Provincial Park (☎ 800-689-9025, information only ☎ 250-494-6500; www.discovercamping.ca), which opened in 2000, is 11km south of Vernon off Hwy 97. Though trees have been planted, it'll take a few years before they'll offer any shade. As a result, the 69 sites ($22) are fully exposed to the scorching summer sun. The park is, however, right on the western shore of Kalamalka Lake.

There are lots of privately owned campgrounds that may lack a knee-deep-in-wilderness experience but offer easy access to Kalamalka and Okanagan Lakes. These, too, get crowded in the height of summer. One of the closest campgrounds to town is **Swan Lake RV Park** (☎ 250-545-2300; www.swanlakecampground.com, 7255 Old Kamloops Rd; tent sites $18; P), 5km north of Vernon, which has nicely landscaped grounds.

Eating
For a small town, Vernon abounds with good eateries.

RESTAURANTS
A favorite with locals, **Eclectic Med** (☎ 250-558-4646; 3117 32nd St; meals $10-25; lunch & dinner Mon-Fri, dinner Sat & Sun) consistently wins awards in valley competitions. The menu lives up to its name, with diverse foods from around the world. Feast on everything from Tuscan tuna to red coconut curry to seafood gumbo. Excellent vegetarian dishes are complemented by a superb wine list.

Amarin Thai (☎ 250-542-9300; 2903 31st St; meals $9-15; lunch & dinner Mon-Fri, dinner Sat) doesn't skimp on the spice or the flavor, the green curry is pungent and fragrant. The classic Thai cooking is set off by the almost elegant yet inviting décor.

Little Tex Cafe & Bistro (☎ 250-558-1919; 3302B 29th St; meals $7-10; 11am-8pm Mon-Sat) is small, but the portions are big. So is the flavor (especially the salsa). The long list of Mexican standards is augmented by salads, Southwestern sandwiches and lots of vegetarian items. Tables outside have good views of the train tracks. Bring the kids here.

A little north of town and an easy walk from the chain motels, **Tita's Italian Bistro** (☎ 250-545-1950; 3002 41st St; meals $10; lunch & dinner Mon-Fri, dinner only Sat) is a local institution that has been run by the same family for 40 years. The freshly made pasta is excellent – as is the sausage. Good veggie options, too.

CAFÉS
Whether you're craving caffeine or a solid dose of local gossip, **Bean Scene** (☎ 250-558-1817; 2923 30th Ave; coffee $2) is definitely the place to be. The hub of what's happening in town, the café offers good coffee and teas served by a friendly staff. It has sidewalk tables.

Bean to Brew (☎ 250-260-7787; 3202 31st Ave; muffins $2; 6am-10pm Mon-Fri, 8am-4pm Sat & Sun) has a good outdoor area that is heated when it's cold. There's a range of muffins – try the blueberry, made with local berries.

SELF CATERING
Simply Delicious (☎ 250-542-7500; 3419 31st Ave; 9am-5:30pm) has a good selection of natural and organic foods to go with all the great local produce. It's a good place to stock up for a picnic.

Entertainment
For a lively pub atmosphere in town, try **Sir Winston's Pub** (☎ 250-549-3485; 2705 32nd St; pizza $10; noon-late) with fine beer choices and a cool patio. The pub menu is long and the food is a cut above the norm. Sir Winston would have approved of the fish and chips.

Each of the local lakes boasts a great waterfront pub. The best outdoor patio in town sits right on Kalamalka Lake at **Alexander's Beach Pub** (☎ 250-545-3131; 12408 Kalamalka Rd; 11am-late summer), right beside the beach. **Blue Heron Waterfront Pub** (☎ 250-542-5550; 7673 Okanagan Landing Rd; 11am-late Apr-Oct) has a perfect perch on Okanagan Lake.

One of the few nightclubs in town, **Impact** (☎ 250-549-7448; 2900 29th Ave; cover varies; 7pm-late Thu-Sun) is where the younger set boogies the night away.

Getting There & Around
There's a restaurant and baggage storage at the **Greyhound bus depot** (☎ 250-545-0527; 3102 30th St at 31st Ave), though there are no lockers. Buses depart south down the valley as well as for Vancouver, Kamloops, Prince George, and Calgary.

Buses of the **Vernon Regional Transit System** (☎ 250-545-7221; $1.50) leave downtown from the bus stop at 31st St and 30th Ave. For Kalamalka Lake, catch bus No 1 or 6; for Okanagan Lake, bus No 7. A day pass costs $3; service is infrequent.

If you want to catch a cab, call **Vernon Taxi** (☎ 250-545-3337).

AROUND VERNON

The **O'Keefe Historic Ranch** (☎ 250-542-7868; adult/child $7/4; ◷ 9am-5pm May-Sep), 12km north of Vernon on Hwy 97, Spallumcheenl, was home to the O'Keefe family from 1867 to 1977. Among other things, you'll see the original log cabin, a general store, old farm machines and St Ann's, probably the oldest Roman Catholic church in the province. The ranch offers an introduction to life in the valley before the region was taken over by the fruit-growing industry. This is a good stop for folks of any age.

On Hwy 97A, 23km north of Vernon, you'll come across **Armstrong** (pop 3950), known mostly for its cheese and excellent **farmer's market** (☎ 250-546-1986; IPE Grounds downtown; ◷ 8am-12:30pm Sat May-Oct). It's the valley's oldest market, running since 1973. While in town, check out the manicured tracks of the rail line right through the heart of the charming old center.

Thirteen kilometers further north is **Enderby** (pop 3000), on the banks of the Shuswap River. Rock climbers scale the vertical rocks at Enderby Cliffs, north of town. The Enderby **Visitor Info Centre** (☎ 250-838-6727, 877-213-6509; www.enderby.com/chamber; 706 Railway St) has climbing info.

East of Vernon on Hwy 6, farms and forests line the road to **Lumby** (population 1900) and **Cherryville** (pop 1000), about 20km and 48km from Vernon, respectively. Outdoor opportunities abound, and the many lakes draw lots of anglers. From Cherryville, you can drive northeast on the Sugar Lake Rd to the backcountry wonderland of remote **Monashee Provincial Park**. Hwy 6 also heads east over a scenic road to **Needles**, where you catch the ferry to the Kootenays (p000).

SILVER STAR

A provincial park 22km northeast of Vernon, Silver Star doubles as a year-round resort. Boasting a built-up Victorian-style village, hotels, lots of great restaurants and more than 1100 hectares of snowy terrain, **Silver Star Mountain Resort** (☎ 250-542-0224, 800-663-4431, snow report ☎ 250-542-1745; www.silverstarmtn.com; one-day lift pass adult/child $56/30) attracts every level of skier and snowboarder from late October to early April. The vertical drop is 760m and there are 11 lifts. The powder is vaunted by locals in the know.

At the end of June – the official start of the summer season – the chairlifts begin operating again, and ski runs become excellent hiking and mountain-biking trails. Stunning views let you see all the way west to the Coast Mountains.

To get to Silver Star, take 48th Ave off Hwy 97, just northeast of downtown Vernon.

Sleeping

Putnam Station Inn (☎ 250-542-2459, 800-489-0599; www.putnamstation.com; r $119-170; P) This comfy lodge has a train station theme. The one question you'll have after a night in the fun-filled pub and a soak in the hot tub is who wants to play the engine and who wants to be the caboose!

Samesun Budget Lodge (☎ 250-545-8933, 877-562-2783; www.samesun.com; 9898 Pinnacles Rd; dm/d $20/49; P ☐) is a new place with good but cheap rooms and dorms. Can get rowdy but rarely are there debates about who gets to play the engine and caboose. There is also all manner of accommodation at the Resort. **Silver Star Mountain Resort** (see above for contact details).

The Kootenays

Mountain-lovers take note: the Kootenay region of BC is dominated by four mountain ranges – the Selkirks and Monashees in the west and the Rockies and Purcells in the east. Almost anywhere you look, you'll see snow-covered peaks. Wedged between the parallel mountain chains is an incredibly scenic series of lakes, rivers and thinly populated valleys. Dense populations of grizzly and black bears, elk, moose and deer thrive here, so you stand a good chance of seeing wildlife. National and provincial parks throughout the area preserve much of the varied terrain and make it accessible for visitors.

Traversing the high mountain passes has always been both a challenge and a necessity. Evidence shows that First Nations people crossed the snowy peaks and canoed turbulent river waters to trade with neighboring tribes more than 10,000 years ago. Later, starting in the early 1800s, European explorers fought treacherous conditions to conquer, then map, the craggy passes.

During the 1890s prospectors found rich mineral deposits, and boom towns sprang up like daisies in the silver-rich Slocan Valley and around Rossland, where the mountains were studded with gold, as well as near Kimberley, where prosperous claims of lead and zinc populated the area. Soon stern-wheelers plied the Kootenays' long lakes, carrying minerals to smelters or to waiting trains.

Today people still come here to explore the region's rich natural bounties. Visitors travel to the Kootenays to soak in the area's many hot springs, to ski and snowboard at spectacular mountain resorts, to relive the mining history or to play in the rivers and lakes. And mountain-lovers simply rejoice.

HIGHLIGHTS

- Hitting the pristine powder in the hills around **Revelstoke** (p232)
- Soothing your sore muscles in the warm waters of **Nakusp Hot Springs** (p237)
- Plucking guitars or dancing to the bongo beats in groovy **Nelson** (p240)
- Getting goose bumps rafting the roaring **Kicking Horse River** (p255)
- Hanging out with history in fabulous **Fernie** (p249)

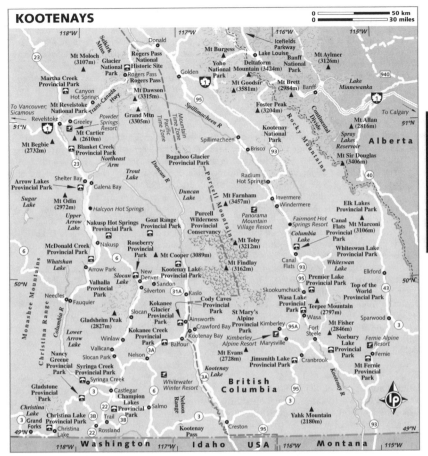

KOOTENAYS

WEST KOOTENAYS

East of the busy Okanagan Valley, the western boundary of the West Kootenays follows the 230km-long Arrow Lake. The eastern boundary follows the 145km-long Kootenay Lake, which is nestled in the scenic valley between the Selkirk and Purcell Mountains. Several free ferries across lakes and rivers connect highways throughout the region (see the boxed text, p237).

Stern-wheeler transportation on the long lakes in the late 1800s and early 1900s connected the area to the US via rivers and lakes. Later, trains added to the transportation network by carrying goods

to and from the stern-wheeler ports. Busy ports included pretty Nakusp on Upper Arrow Lake and Kaslo on Kootenay Lake, where today you can visit the world's oldest surviving stern-wheeler. The Slocan Valley boomed with silver mines during the late 1800s, and during WWII more than 20,000 Japanese Canadians were forced into internment camps throughout the valley (see the boxed text, p238). Today the Slocan Valley is one of the most picturesque parts of the province.

The area around Castlegar and Grand Forks is rich in Russian Doukhobor history (p244), and Rossland's Red Mountain, once famous for gold discoveries, is now one of the province's best ski areas. Revelstoke,

---

AVALANCHE!

As you marvel at all the snowy peaks, take a second to realize that you are in the pumping heart of avalanche country, where heavy slides of falling snow have enough power and weight to crush an entire city. An avalanche – the name is derived from the French verb 'avaler' (to swallow) – occurs when a slab of snow separates from more stable snow or ground cover. This most often happens when there's a dramatic shift in temperature or when there's a heavy snowfall or, for that matter, heavy snowmelt.

Watching a distant avalanche is perhaps one of the most spectacular sights in nature. Up close, an avalanche can be the most thunderous and frightening exertion of power you'll ever encounter – and you want to be well out of the way. Avalanches kill more people in BC each year than any other natural phenomenon, a statistic that has been even more true recently. In January 2003 seven heli-skiers were killed in an avalanche near Revelstoke. Not far away two weeks later, seven Calgary high school students were killed by an avalanche in Glacier National Park. You'll see effects of these tragedies: every outdoor gear shop in Revelstoke now rents avalanche gear, including the vital homing beacons that assist rescuers. The entire town was shocked and saddened by the deaths, but trips to the backcountry continue despite high avalanche risk.

Whether you're backcountry ski-touring or simply hiking in the alpine, you should definitely find out conditions before you venture into unknown terrain. The worst month is March, although avalanches occur year-round.

In Revelstoke, the Canadian Avalanche Centre is operated by the **Canadian Avalanche Association** (CAA; ☎ 250-837-2435, ☎ 800-667-1105 24hr info; www.avalanche.ca). It analyzes avalanche trends, weather patterns and avalanche accidents. A highly visible advocate for the group is Justin Trudeau, son of the former prime minister and brother of Michel Trudeau, who was killed in an avalanche in 1998.

If you're planning on doing any trips in the backcountry, you'll want to contact the CAA first. In late 2003 the BC government agreed to greatly increase CAA funding in order to improve public awareness.

---

at the north end of the West Kootenays, is one of the world capitals for heli-skiing and the gateway to Mt Revelstoke and Glacier National Parks. The striking town of Nelson, the center of the region, boasts an active artist community, and more than one third of the town's buildings have been restored to their Victorian glory.

REVELSTOKE
pop 7500

This small mountain city near the Trans-Canada Hwy (Hwy 1), 70km east of Sicamous, is nestled between the Monashee and Selkirk mountain ranges and sits at the confluence of the rushing Illecillewaet River and the wide, slow-moving Columbia River. It perches on the western edge of Mt Revelstoke National Park, which is about halfway between the Okanagan Valley and the Rocky Mountains. Revelstoke's natural landmarks make it a picturesque, outdoorsy place, with a recreational splendor not lost on the active, friendly community. Neat

wooden houses and tiny gardens line the quiet residential streets. An effort to revitalize downtown heritage buildings paid off, giving the alpine community a sense of historical dignity.

Originally known to First Nations people as 'Big Eddy', for the respite it offered canoe travelers, the town was later named for Edward Charles Baring (Lord Revelstoke), the British financier who came through with a much-needed cash advance that saved the Canadian Pacific Railway (CPR) from bankruptcy. The coming of the CPR in the 1880s and the opening of the Trans-Canada Hwy in 1962 made Revelstoke a viable transportation hub. Today more and more people use the town as a base from which to venture to the mountains to ski and snowboard, hike, bike or simply gaze at snowy peaks and alpine meadows.

Orientation & Information

Revelstoke is south of the Trans-Canada Hwy. Victoria Rd runs parallel to the very busy railway tracks that run along the northeast end of town. The main streets include 1st St and Mackenzie Ave.

BOOKSTORE
Grizzly Book & Serendipity Shop (☎ 250-837-6185; 208 Mackenzie Ave) Offers magazines, a wide selection of metaphysical literature and regional books.

LAUNDRY
Family Laundry (☎ 250-837-3938; 409 1st St; 8am-8pm Mon-Sat, 8am-5pm Sun)

LIBRARY
Revelstoke Library (☎ 250-837-5095; 605 Campbell Ave; noon-8pm Tue, 10am-5pm Wed-Sat)

MEDICAL SERVICES
Queen Victoria Hospital (☎ 250-837-2131; 6622 Newlands Rd; doctor on call 24hrs)

POST
Post office (☎ 250-837-3228; 313 3rd St)

TOURIST INFORMATION
Friends of Mt Revelstoke & Glacier (☎ 250-837-2010; www.friendsofmtrevelstokeandglacier.bc.ca) In the same building as Parks Canada. Distributes books and maps of the parks, although the staff are often tied up typing their web address.
Parks Canada Regional Office (☎ 250-837-7500; revglacier.reception@pc.gc.ca; 301 3rd St; 8am-4:30pm Mon-Fri) Offers information about Mt Revelstoke National Park (www.parkscanada.gc.ca/Revelstoke) and Glacier National Park (www.parkscanada.gc.ca/glacier).
Visitor Info Centre (☎ 250-837-5345, 800-487-1493; www.seerevelstoke.com; 206 Campbell Ave; 8:30am-4:30pm Mon-Fri) Internet access available. In summer a second and larger VIC opens, usually in the center of town and it's open daily; look for signs.

Sights

Grizzly Plaza, between Mackenzie and Orton Aves, is a pedestrian precinct and the heart of downtown, where free live music performances take place in the evenings throughout July and August. Life-size bronze grizzly bears flank the plaza. The paved **Revelstoke River Trail** (an excellent place to walk or jog) runs along the river at the south end of town.

Revelstoke Railway Museum (☎ 250-837-6060, 877-837-6060; adult/child $6/3; 9am-8pm summer, 9am-5pm Mon-Fri winter) Situated on Long St across the tracks from the town center

and within a beautiful building right off Victoria Rd downtown, this great museum contains restored steam locomotives, including one of the largest steam engines ever used on CPR lines. Photographs and artifacts document the construction of the CPR, pay tribute to its hardy workers and relate the railway's original financial woes. Volunteer railway engineers are often on hand to recount stories about the heyday of rail travel. Check out the museum's website at www.railwaymuseum.com.

The museum bookstore carries a vast selection of books about the building of the CPR, which was instrumental – if not essential – in linking Canada (see the boxed text, p236).

Revelstoke Museum (☎ 250-837-3067; 315 1st St; adult/child $2.50/1; 10am-5pm Mon-Sat summer, 1-4pm Mon-Fri winter) This interesting museum holds a permanent collection of furniture and historical odds and ends, including mining, logging and railway artifacts that date back to the town's establishment in the 1880s. Also look for the many historical plaques mounted on buildings around town.

Canyon Hot Springs (☎ 250-837-2420; 35km east of Revelstoke on the Trans-Canada Hwy; daypass adult/child $8.50/7; 9am-9pm May-Sep, 9am-10pm Jul & Aug) These springs make a great spot for a quick visit. The site consists of a hot pool (42°C) and a larger, cooler swimming pool (32°C). You can rent a bathing suit and towel.

Between Revelstoke and Sicamous lie many kitschy roadside attractions of the kind that were popular several decades ago. Some prime examples, all on the Trans-Canada Hwy, include **Three Valley Gap Heritage Ghost Town** (☎ 250-837-2109; www.3valley.com; 19km west of Revelstoke; r from $100); the **Enchanted Forest** (☎ 250-837-9477; 32km west of Revelstoke); and **Beardale Castle Miniatureland** (☎ 250-836-2268; 42km west of Revelstoke). The first combines historical buildings, a stage show, a motel and more in a large frilly complex; the second involves numerous fairies and other figures, including a crafty pirate, scattered around a forest; the third displays handcrafted tiny towns and teensy trains. If you're in the mood to buy trinkets or hunks of fudge, you'll get your fill at any of these places. All these roadside attractions are open roughly May to September.

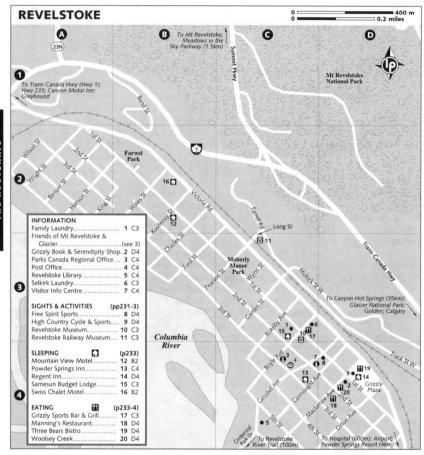

REVELSTOKE

To Mt Revelstoke;
Meadows in the
Sky Parkway (1.5km)

Mt Revelstoke
National Park

To Trans-Canada Hwy (Hwy 1);
Hwy 235; Canyon Motor Inn;
Greyhound

Farwel
Park

Long St

Columbia
River

Moberly
Manor
Park

To Canyon Hot Springs (35km);
Glacier National Park;
Golden; Calgary

Grizzly
Plaza

To Revelstoke
River Trail (100m)

To Hospital (600m); Airport;
Powder Springs Resort (4km)

INFORMATION		
Family Laundry	1	C3
Friends of Mt Revelstoke &		
Glacier	(see 3)	
Grizzly Book & Serendipity Shop	2	D4
Parks Canada Regional Office	3	C4
Post Office	4	C4
Revelstoke Library	5	C4
Selkirk Laundry	6	C3
Visitor Info Centre	7	C4

SIGHTS & ACTIVITIES	(pp231-3)	
Free Spirit Sports	8	D4
High Country Cycle & Sports	9	D4
Revelstoke Museum	10	C3
Revelstoke Railway Museum	11	C3

SLEEPING		(p233)
Mountain View Motel	12	B2
Powder Springs Inn	13	C4
Regent Inn	14	D4
Samesun Budget Lodge	15	C3
Swiss Chalet Motel	16	B2

EATING		(p233-4)
Grizzly Sports Bar & Grill	17	C3
Manning's Restaurant	18	D4
Three Bears Bistro	19	D4
Woolsey Creek	20	D4

Activities

Sandwiched in between the vast but relatively lesser-known Selkirk and Monashee mountain ranges, Revelstoke draws serious snow buffs looking for untracked powder and no crowds.

SKIING & SNOWBOARDING

Whether you ski, board or just like to romp around in the snow, Revelstoke's long, snowy winter season and experienced tour operators give you plenty of options.

For downhill skiing, head to **Powder Springs Resort** (☎ 250-837-5151, 877-991-4455; www.catpowder .com/indexsprings.html; one-day lift tickets adult/child $28/ free). This small ski hill on Mt Mackenzie, just 4km southeast of Revelstoke, lacks the

multiple chairlifts of bigger resorts, but its heavy snowfall (up to 12m), access to backcountry slopes and small crowds make it a spectacular spot. Tickets cost $24 on weekdays and $28 on weekends, and kids always ski free. You can get further deals if you stay at the Powder Springs Inn (p233).

A popular but expensive way to find fresh powder is by heli-skiing, where a helicopter takes you high into the alpine to ski or snowboard steep slopes, deep powder and even glaciers. **Selkirk Tangiers Helicopter Skiing** (☎ 250-837-5378, 800-663-7080; www.selkirk -tangiers.com) runs three-, five- and seven-day trips ranging from $2100 to $6300.

Though sometimes called the poor man's heli-skiing, snow-cat skiing isn't exactly

STEPHEN SAKS

Outdoor mural, **Chemainus** (p146), Vancouver Island

Nelson (p240), West Kootenays

FRANK CARTER

SUSAN RIMERMAN

Dawson City (p357), the Yukon

STEPHEN SAKS

O'Keefe Historic Ranch (p226), Okanagan Valley

FRANK CARTER

'Ksan dancer, **'Ksan Historical Village** (p317), New Hazelton

JOHN ELK III

Totem-pole carver, **Quwn'utsun' Cultural and Conference Centre** (p145), Duncan

FRANK CARTER

Indian longhouse and totem pole, **Thunderbird Park** (p130), Victoria

Totem pole at the **Malahat** (p142) summit, Vancouver Island

JONATHAN SE

cheap. Snow cats are large, heated tractors that easily navigate ice and snow, allowing you to reach some pretty pristine alpine conditions. **CAT Powder Skiing** (☎ 250-837-5151, 800-991-4455; www.catpowder.com) offers packages, including accommodations and meals at Powder Springs Inn (below). Prices range from $1000 to $2500 (two to five days).

For **cross-country skiing**, head to the Mt MacPherson Ski Area, 7km south of town on Hwy 23. You'll pay $5 to use the 22km of groomed trails.

Free Spirit Sports (☎ 250-837-9453; rctvonline.net/freespirit; 203 1st St W) rents a wide-variety of winter gear including essential avalanche equipment.

WHITEWATER RAFTING
Apex Rafting Company (☎ 250-837-6376, 888-232-6666; adult/child $69/59) With an office at Canyon Hot Springs, Apex runs mellow, two-hour guided trips on the Illecillewaet River in spring and summer. The trips are perfect for first-time rafters or for anyone wanting to just kick back and enjoy the scenery.

MOUNTAIN BIKING
Once the snow melts, ski runs become excellent mountain-biking trails. Pick up a copy of the *Biking Trail Map* from the VIC or **High Country Cycle & Sports** (☎ 250-814-0090; 118 Mackenzie Ave) where you can also rent bikes.

Sleeping
Revelstoke has a good selection of places to stay in all price ranges.

MOTELS & HOTELS
Regent Inn (☎ 250-837-2107, 888-245-5523; www.regentinn.com; 112 1st St W; r $99-169; ✷ ▫) The best place in town, this is where a lot of the heli-skiers stay in winter. The renovated and historic hotel contains a spa, sauna, restaurant and lively bar.

Powder Springs Inn (☎ 250-837-5151, 800-991-4455; www.catpowder.com; 200 3rd St W; r $42-75; ▫) This place is part of the empire that includes the ski resort and the snow-cat skiing operation (above). Great-value packages abound and this motel has become a hub for skiers and snowboarders. Fun bar.

Mountain View Motel (☎ 250-837-4900; revmtn viewmotel@hotmail.com; 1017 1st W; s/d $45/52; ✷)

This motel has basic large rooms that come with a fridge.

Swiss Chalet Motel (☎ 250-837-4650, 888-272-4538; www.swisschaletmotel.com; 1101 Victoria Rd; s/d $59/64; ✷ ▫) This motel has newly renovated rooms and is close to town.

You'll find a collection of big chain motels and hotels along the Trans-Canada Hwy. However, a good bet if the town is full is **Canyon Motor Inn** (☎ 250-837-5221, 877-837-5221; www.revelstokecc.bc.ca/snow/teasers/canmotel-ts.htm; 1911 Fraser Dr; s/d $70/80; ✷ ▫). This older but well-maintained property has large rooms and free high-speed Internet. The staff are very friendly.

HOSTELS
SameSun Budget Lodge (☎ 250-837-4050, 877-562-2783; www.samesun.ca; 400 2nd St W; dm/d $20/49; ▫) In a nicely restored but somewhat labyrinthine building, the lodge offers various deals for local activities.

CAMPING
Blanket Creek Provincial Park (☎ 800-689-9025; www.discovercamping.ca; sites $14) This park, 25km south of Revelstoke along Hwy 23, includes 64 campsites with flush toilets and running water but no showers. You'll find the same facilities and 25 sites at **Martha Creek Provincial Park** (☎ 250-825-4421; sites $14), 16km north of town on Hwy 23.

Many private campgrounds lie east and west of Revelstoke along the Trans-Canada Hwy. **Canyon Hot Springs Resort** (☎ 250-837-2420; www.canyonhotsprings.com; 35km east of Revelstoke; sites $22; ☣) offers full facilities and a grocery store.

Eating
Woolsey Creek (☎ 250-837-5500; 212 MacKenzie Ave; meals $6-12) This is a great choice for a meal, with everything from omelets to oatmeal in the morning followed by great salads and sandwiches at lunch and at night an interesting and changing fusion menu with lots of seafood and pasta. It's open for breakfast, lunch and dinner daily – or have a beer on one of the comfy chairs out front. Has a full coffee bar and Internet access.

Three Bears Bistro (☎ 250-837-9575; 114 Mackenzie Ave; meals $6; ☽ lunch Mon-Sat) Three Bears features a good outdoor patio on the plaza where you can consume sandwiches and big salads. Enjoy the many soups during the long winter. It's also open for dinner some nights in summer.

Manning's Restaurant (☎ 250-837-3200; 302 Mackenzie Ave; meals $9; ☺ noon-9pm) Manning's is a throwback to the 1950s right down to its classic neon sign out front. The Chinese food is pretty good.

Grizzly Sports Bar & Grill (☎ 250-814-1002; 314 1st St W; meals $8; ☺ noon-late) Here you'll find a fun sports bar with good pub food. The fish and chips are excellent. They have the full line of the very fine locally brewed Mt Begbie beers on tap.

Getting There & Away
Greyhound (☎ 250-837-5874; 1899 Fraser Dr) is west of town, just off the Trans-Canada Hwy. It has storage lockers. Buses go east to Banff and Calgary, and west to Kamloops, Kelowna and beyond.

MT REVELSTOKE NATIONAL PARK
This relatively small (260 sq km) national park, just northeast of Revelstoke in the Clachnacudainn Range of the Selkirk Mountains, comes alive with blankets of wildflowers in summer. The Selkirks are known for their jagged, rugged peaks and steep valleys. From the 2223m summit of Mt Revelstoke, the views of the mountains and the Columbia River valley are excellent. To get to the summit, take the 26km **Meadows in the Sky Parkway**, 1.5km east of Revelstoke off the Trans-Canada Hwy. Open when enough snow melts (usually not until July, although officially it is June to September), the paved road winds through lush cedar forests and alpine meadows and ends at Balsam Lake, within 2km of the peak. From here walk to the top or take the shuttle, which runs from 10am to 4:20pm daily.

Umbrella-sized leaves are just some of the highlights of the **Skunk Cabbage Trail**, 28km east of Revelstoke on Hwy 1. A 1.2km boardwalk along the Illecillewaet River gives an up-close view of the eponymous skunk cabbage, the marshes and myriad birds.

There are several good hiking trails from the summit. You can camp only in designated backcountry campsites, and you must have a $8 Wilderness Pass camping permit (in addition to your park pass), which is available from **Parks Canada** (☎ 250-837-7500) in Revelstoke or

from the **Rogers Pass Centre** (☎ 250-814-5233; www.parkscanada.gc.ca/revelstoke) inside Glacier National Park. There are no 'front country' campsites in the park. Much of the summer is rainy, so check your tent for leaks.

There's good cross-country skiing and snowshoeing in the very long winters, but avalanches and bad weather require you to have the right gear and be prepared for anything. Be sure to stop off at the Parks Canada office before venturing out into the backcountry. Admission to both Mt Revelstoke and Glacier National Parks (the two are administered jointly) is adult/child $5/2.50 per day.

GLACIER NATIONAL PARK
About halfway between Revelstoke and Golden lies this 1350-sq-km park that contains more than 430 glaciers. If you think the other mountain parks have been wet, then you'll like this place. It only rains here twice a week – once for three days and then again for four. It's the same in winter; it snows nearly every day, and the annual snowfall can be as much as 23m. Because of the sheer mountain slopes, this is one of the world's most active avalanche areas. For this reason, skiing, caving and mountaineering are closely regulated; you must register with the park warden before venturing into the backcountry.

Around Rogers Pass, you'll notice the many snow sheds protecting the highway. With the narrow road twisting up to 1330m, this is a dangerous area, sometimes called Death Strip; an unexpected avalanche can wipe a car right off the road. Still, the area is carefully controlled, and sometimes snows are brought tumbling down with artillery before they fall by themselves. Call for a daily **avalanche report** (☎ 250-837-6867) in season.

In summer the road is clear of snow, though you can encounter rains even on the sunniest of days. Whether you travel by car, bus, trail or bicycle (more power to you), Rogers will likely rank as one of the most beautiful mountain passes you'll ever have the pleasure of traversing.

At the east side of the park is the dividing line between Pacific Standard and Mountain Standard time zones, which means that if it's noon in the park, it's 1pm just outside the east gate (heading into Alberta).

Definitely plan to spend some time at the informative **Rogers Pass Centre** (☎ 250-814-5233; www.parkscanada.gc.ca/glacier; 72km east of Revelstoke; ☽ 8am-7pm summer, 9am-5pm spring & fall, 9am-7pm winter). The center shows films on the park and organizes guided walks in summer. Also check out the CPR displays documenting the railway's efforts to conquer the pass. Next door the **Best Western Glacier Park Lodge** (☎ 250-837-2126; www.glacierparklodge.ca; r $100-250; ☒ ☒) has a 24-hour coffee shop.

Not far from here are the park's two campsites: **Illecillewaet Campground** ($17) and **Loop Brook Campground** ($17). Both have running water and flush toilets. Backcountry campers must stick to designated backcountry sites and must have an $8

Wilderness Pass camping permit (in addition to your park pass), which is available from the Parks Canada regional office in Revelstoke or from the Rogers Pass Centre.

NAKUSP
pop 1700

Charmingly frayed around the edges, quiet Nakusp sits about midway up the long Upper Arrow Lake. It is the main town in the valley south of Revelstoke. The dry, picturesque valley follows a chain of lakes between the Monashee and Selkirk mountain ranges. Nakusp, a First Nations word meaning 'sheltered bay', was a major steamship port during the Slocan mining

THE KOOTENAYS

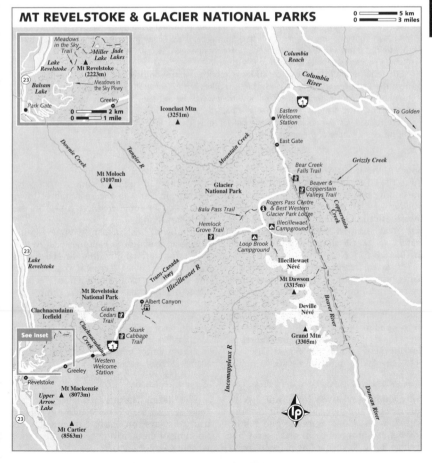

MT REVELSTOKE & GLACIER NATIONAL PARKS

CANADIAN PACIFIC RAILWAY'S IRON LINK

British Columbia had an almost separate existence from the rest of Canada until 1885, when the Canadian Pacific Railway (CPR) made its way over the treacherous Rockies. These tracks for the first time linked the disparate territories of the west and east and played an instrumental role in cementing the unity of the nation.

Running the rails through the Rockies was an enormous challenge that was accomplished by the work of thousands of immigrant laborers who endured harsh conditions to complete the dangerous job. Hundreds of workers were killed by disease and accident. Among the challenges they faced were the horrific avalanches of Rogers Pass, which swept away people and trains like toys. Eventually huge tunnels and snow sheds were laboriously constructed to protect the trains. East of the town of Field in Yoho National Park (p260), the gradients were so steep that any braking problem caused trains to run away down the hill, where they would eventually fly off the tracks and kill passengers. To solve this problem, two huge spiraling tunnels were built inside the granite mountains so that the grades were cut in half to a much more manageable 2.2%. These remain in use and are an internationally recognized engineering marvel.

Along with the trains, the CPR built grand hotels in Calgary, Banff, Lake Louise, Vancouver and elsewhere to encourage tourists and business travelers to ride the line and explore the region. People jumped at the chance to experience such rugged wilderness and still sip tea in luxury. The line was completed on November 7, 1885, and it carried passengers for over a hundred years until government stinginess cut back on rail services. Today the route is still traversed by CPR freight trains and the occasional Rocky Mountaineer cruise train. West of Calgary, the Trans-Canada Hwy runs parallel to much of the route.

There are three excellent places to learn about the history of this rail line in BC: a lookout from the Trans-Canada Hwy 8km east of Field offers a good view of the lower of the two spiral tunnels, with explanatory displays on how they work; the museum area inside the Rogers Pass Centre in Glacier National Park shows the hazards of avalanches and features a model of the entire route over the Rockies; and the railway museum in Revelstoke (p231) documents the construction history of the entire CPR.

---

boom in the 1890s. Steamships carried ore up to the CPR tracks in Revelstoke. When the boom subsided and new highways took business away from the stern-wheelers, the economy shifted to forestry. The last great stern-wheeler to ply the lake's waters was the SS *Minto*, which was retired in 1954.

The lakes were forever changed by the dams built as part of the Columbia River energy and flood control projects in the 1950s and 1960s. The level of Upper Lake was raised and several small towns were flooded in the process. This is why even today you see little of the shoreline development you might expect. Hwy 23 between Nakusp and Revelstoke is rather desolate.

This very attractive section of the province enjoys a relatively low profile, so it's surprisingly and refreshingly not overrun with tourists. Good camping and hiking areas, pleasant travel roads and nearby hot springs make Nakusp a fine place to spend a couple of days. If you're in the area on a Wednesday night in summer, stop by Recreation Park on the east side of town and listen to some free live music in the park bandstand.

Southwest of Nakusp, Hwy 6 splits, heading southwest to Fauquier past Arrow Park, the official dividing line between Upper and Lower Arrow Lakes, and to the free ferry from Fauquier to Needles. Once on the other side, you'll climb over the 1189m-high Monashee Pass en route to Vernon (p222) in the Okanagan Valley. You'll pass a few small provincial parks along this route.

Nakusp Visitor Info Centre (☎ 250-265-4234, 800-909-8819; www.nakusphotsprings.com; 92 W 6th Ave; ☽ 9am-5pm summer, 11am-5pm Mon-Fri winter) has good hiking information for the area.

The **Nakusp Museum** (next to the Visitor Info Centre; admission free; ☽ 9am-5pm summer) houses neat displays on early settlement, the flooding of the Arrow Lakes and the stern-wheeling days.

Hot Springs

The springs get a diverse crowd of families, aging hippies, backpackers and others who want to chill out in the hot water.

The tranquil **Nakusp Hot Springs** (☎ 250-265-4528; www.nakusphotsprings.com; 12km northeast of Nakusp off Hwy 23; adult/child $8.50/free; ☼ 9:30am-10pm summer, 10am-9:30pm winter) are a mere 2km from the spring's source. Though the squeaky clean pools tend to ruin some of the natural vibe, the gorgeous scenery reminds you that you are steeping deep in nature. Instead of driving you might want to make the beautiful 8km hike on the Kuskanax Interpretive Trail from Nakusp. The VIC has a detailed brochure with the route. There are cramped tent sites for camping ($15).

The resort **Halcyon Hot Springs** (☎ 250-265-3554; www.halcyon-hotsprings.com; 32km north of Nakusp on Hwy 23; daypass adult/child $9.50/6.50; ☼ 8am-10pm, 8am-11pm summer) caters to every budget, with accommodations that range from campsites ($18) and camping cabins ($74 for two) to luxurious chalets ($178). You don't need to stay here to enjoy the hot springs, which sit high on a balcony above Upper Arrow Lake.

Anyone wishing to soak for free should ask around about two nearby natural hot springs: **St. Leon's**, a favorite with locals for its seclusion and kidney-shaped pools, and **Halfway**, 24km north on Hwy 23. Getting to both undeveloped springs requires driving on logging roads and a little hiking. Ask at the VIC for specific directions as these spots are, after all, secluded.

Sleeping & Eating

The **Kuskanax Lodge** (☎ 250-265-3618, 800-663-0100; www.kuskanax.kootenays.com; 515 Broadway; s/d $55/70) is a good choice and it has a fun sports bar.

Nakusp International Hostel (☎ 250-265-3069; 1950 Hwy 23 N; dm $20; family r $45) has a killer location on the lake across from Hot Springs Rd. Enjoy the quiet on one of the many hammocks. They have good area hiking information. The historic **Leland Hotel** (☎ 250-265-4221; 96 4th Ave) overlooks the lake but the entire place could be the focus of one of those home improvement TV shows.

Besides the hot springs, you can camp right in town at the **Village of Nakusp Campsite** (☎ 250-265-4019; cnr 8th Ave & 4th St; sites $15; ☼ Apr-Oct). The facilities include flush toilets, showers and wooded sites for $15.

One of the friendliest places in town, **Broadway Deli & Bistro** (☎ 250-265-3767; 408 Broadway St; meals $6; ☼ 8am-5pm) serves good breakfasts (super oatmeal!), plus salads, sandwiches and yummy burritos. Look for the big pink pig. **Wylie's Pub** (☎ 250-265-4944; 401 Broadway St; meals $8; ☼ noon-late) is the place for beer and burgers.

NEW DENVER & AROUND

Southeast of Nakusp, Hwy 6 rolls 47km to New Denver (pop 600), Silverton, Sandon and the lovely Slocan Valley. There are no gas stations on this stretch of highway.

A major boomtown in the heyday of the Silvery Slocan Mines and originally named

---

KOOTENAY FERRIES

The long Kootenay and Upper and Lower Arrow Lakes necessitate some ferry travel. All **ferries** (www.th.gov.bc.ca/bchighways/inland ferryschedule/ferryschedule.htm) are free.

Upper Arrow Lake Ferry (☎ 250-837-8418) runs year-round between Galena Bay (49km south of Revelstoke) and Shelter Bay (49km north of Nakusp) on Hwy 23. The trip takes 20 minutes and runs from 6am to 11pm every hour on the hour from Shelter Bay and every hour on the half-hour between 6:30am and 11:30pm from Galena Bay.

Needles Ferry (☎ 250-837-8418) crosses Lower Arrow Lake between Fauquier (57km south of Nakusp) and Needles (135km east of Vernon) on Hwy 6; the trip takes five minutes. The ferry runs every day, leaving from Fauquier every 30 minutes on the hour and the half-hour from 5am to 10pm. From Needles it runs on the quarter and three-quarter hour between 5:15am and 9:45pm. After hours the ferry travels on demand only.

Kootenay Lake Ferry (☎ 250-229-4215) sails between Balfour on the west arm of Kootenay Lake (34km northeast of Nelson) and Kootenay Bay. Its 45-minute crossing makes it the world's longest free car ferry. In summer the ferry leaves Balfour every 50 minutes between 6:30am and 9:40pm, and from Kootenay Lake from 7:10am to 10:20pm. In winter the sailings are less frequent.

Eldorado, New Denver grew quickly with seemingly endless potential, enough (it was felt) to rival the also-booming Colorado town. This optimism shrank as the boom subsided, and New Denver is now just a twinkle in its namesake's eye. But greatness is a subjective thing; New Denver's quiet, progressive and artistic community lives surrounded by gorgeous mountain peaks on the shoulder of beautiful Slocan Lake. Ask anyone who lives here and they'll tell you, it doesn't get better than this. Nearby Silverton (pop 220) also boomed but went bust. The pretty spot is scarcely more than a ghost town now.

There is no visitor info centre in New Denver, but the Chamber of Commerce runs a de facto information booth in summer, though its location changes every year. The best place to get information is at the Valhalla Inn (p239).

Sights & Activities

The **Silvery Slocan Museum** (202 6th Ave; ☼ 10am-5pm summer, weekends only spring & fall) in the historic Bank of Montreal building features well-done displays from the booming mining days, including a rare bank vault.

RELOCATION CAMPS

In 1942 more than 22,000 Japanese Canadians where forced from their coastal homes, herded into animal stalls at Vancouver's Hastings Park, then sent to remote 'relocation camps' throughout BC's interior.

The **Nikkei Internment Memorial Centre** (☎ 250-358-7288; www.newdenver.ca/nikkei/nikkei.php; 306 Josephine St, New Denver; adult/child $4/2; ☼ 9am-5pm Jun-Sep) sits on the site of one of 10 former internment camps in the Slocan Valley. Today it is a peaceful place built and cared for by the Kyowakai Society, which a group of internees formed in 1943. The center includes a beautiful Japanese garden and remains the only internment camp organization still in operation; a few internees still live in the area. Three of the old huts remain, two furnished to show how the internees lived. Note the efforts to try to make the walls a little warmer. In the large central hall are exhibits documenting the entire sad affair.

Sandon (☼ 10am-6pm summer), a ghost town on Hwy 31A between New Denver and Kaslo, features historic buildings restored to reflect the exciting and greedy days when the silver mines boomed. Check out where the action happened at **Molly Brown's Brothel**, have a snack at the **Tin Cup Café** (☎ 250-358-2606) or peruse the **Sandon Museum** in the historic general store building.

Near Sandon you can get one of the best views of the Slocan Valley from the **Idaho Lookout**, a 2244m-high viewpoint above the ghost town. A rough logging road leads up to a parking lot. From there an easy 30-minute (one-way) hike takes you to this awesome vista. In July and August spare your poor car from navigating the bumpy road and take the shuttle from Sandon. Ask at the museum for information. For less of a hike, try the **K&S Railway Historic Trail**, which also starts in Sandon. The 5km trail dallies along, passing interpretive signs, old mine shafts and remnants of the railway. You'll also get good views of the surrounding mountains.

Valhalla Provincial Park

A stunningly scenic position in the verdant Slocan Valley, along with lakeside seclusion, makes this 49,600-hectare area one of the province's best parkland jewels. Southwest of New Denver just east of Hwy 6, the park encompasses most of the Valhalla Range of the Selkirk Mountains. The range takes its name from the Norse mythological palace for slain warriors. Ochre rock paintings along the shoreline are believed to represent the dreams and visions of ancient Arrow Lakes Indians, who treasured the natural sanctuary.

You can drive 30km along Hwy 6 and marvel at the jaw-dropping vistas of the Valhallas' sharp, snow-covered peaks. Or you can enjoy even better views by packing your backpack for a day hike or overnight trip. Slocan Lake serves as the park's eastern boundary; its other sides butt up against more rugged peaks and dense forest. You can only access the main areas of the park by boat or commercial water taxi; these travel across Slocan Lake from three points along Hwy 6: New Denver, northeast of the park; Silverton, to the east; and Slocan, to the southeast. In New Denver **Valla Venture** (☎ 250-358-7775) offers water-taxi services to the Nemo Creek trailhead, a good point of departure for day hikes. Other trailheads are served as well.

Valhalla was protected as parkland in 1983, mostly due to the intense efforts of the **Valhalla Wilderness Society** (☎ 250-358-2333; www.vws.org; 307 6th St; ✆ hours vary), an advocacy group that formed in the 1970s to save the Valhalla Range from logging. Since then the now-thriving group has also successfully campaigned to protect the Khutzeymateen Grizzly Sanctuary near Prince Rupert and the nearby White Grizzly Wilderness. A current focus is the commercialization of BC's parks. When open, the office is a great place to learn more about current issues and to get excellent park topographic maps and helpful trail information.

Sleeping & Eating

The **Valhalla Inn** (☎ 250-358-2228; inn-valhalla .com; 509 Slocan Ave; s/d from $55/60) is somewhat of a hub, with a lively pub, a restaurant and good-sized rooms.

Camping with flush toilets and showers is available at the **Village of New Denver Municipal Campground** (☎ 250-358-2316; waterfront tent sites $13-16). It's near the marina at the bottom of 3rd Ave.

On 6th Ave in New Denver you'll find two good stops for breakfast or lunch. **The Apple Tree** (☎ 250-358-2691; 210 6th Ave; meals $6; ✆ 7am-4pm), beside the museum, attracts friendly locals who lounge on the outdoor patio. The motto is: 'Up to the minute gossip and financial advice'. A little further east is the **Panini Bistro & Delicatessen** (☎ 250-358-2830; 306 6th Ave; meals $6; ✆ 9am-6pm Tue-Sun) where you can order a European breakfast or a filled baguette.

KASLO

pop 1030

Unlike what happened in surrounding towns in the Slocan Valley, it was timber, not silver, that lured the first European settlers to Kaslo. But it was the fervor in the nearby mines that prompted the first timber-claim holders to sell off small parcels of what is now the Kaslo townsite.

In 1895 the Kaslo & Slocan Railroad, backed by the US-based Great Northern Railroad, brought Kaslo out of isolation by linking it with the silver mines in the Slocan Valley. With the building of hotels,

bars and brothels, the population boomed along with the mines.

Once the mining slowed, Kaslo became a thriving fruit-growing community noted especially for its cherries, some of which were said to be the size of plums. During WWII the *New Canadian*, a newspaper serving all the Canadian Japanese internment camps, was published in Kaslo.

Today Kaslo's tree-lined streets, restored Victorian buildings and access to outdoor activities make it an excellent stop for travelers. The downtown on Front St is both vibrant and picturesque. It has a good mix of shops, bakeries, organic markets and more. Nearby, the drive on Hwy 31A to New Denver is a treat of white water and waterfalls.

The helpful staff at the **Visitor Info Centre** (☎ 250-353-2525; www.klhs.bc.ca; 324 Front St; ✆ 9am-5pm mid-May–mid-Sep) can give you great information on hiking and mountainbiking trails in the area.

The complex also serves the 1898 **SS Moyie** (adult/child $5/2), the world's oldest surviving stern-wheeler. In its early days, Kaslo's isolated location on the north arm of Kootenay Lake made steamship travel to Nelson significant. Now a National Historic Site, the SS *Moyie* is moored permanently on the downtown lakeside and has a good museum.

The **Kootenay Star Museum** (☎ 250-353-2115; 402 Front St; donation; ✆ 9am-6pm) is like a garage sale of old artifacts from the mines. It has a good café with homebaked items. The beautifully restored **Langham Cultural Centre** (☎ 250-353-2662; 477 A Ave) features displays by local artists and live music performances.

Discovery Canada Outdoor Adventure (☎ 250-353-7349, 800-300-4453; www.discoverycanada.ca) runs outdoor activities including guided hiking tours (starting at $75), mountaintop concerts by moonlight ($40) and courses on mountaineering. The staff can tell you almost anything you'd want to know about hiking in the Selkirk or Purcell Mountains or kayaking on the lakes.

Sleeping & Eating

For B&B listings, pick up a copy of *North Kootenay Lake B&B Directory* from the visitor info centre.

Mariner Inn (☎ 250-353-7171; 430 Front St; r from $55; ✆) As well as a bed, here you'll find a

THE KOOTENAYS

pub and restaurant with a patio overlooking the lake. The rooms are small but clean.

Kaslo Motel (☎ 250-353-7603; www.kaslomotel .com; 330 D Ave; s/d $52/62; 💽) This motel has a pretty garden and simple but nice rooms.

Kootenay Lake Backpackers Hostel (☎ 250-353-7427; klhostel@pop.kin.bc.ca; 232 B Ave; dm $18; r from $27; 🖳) This lovingly built and cozy European-style hostel has a big common kitchen, patio and vegetable garden. You can rent kayaks, canoes and bikes.

Kaslo Municipal Campground (☎ 250-353-2311; Vimy Park; sites $13) Its bare-bones sites are at least close to town.

Mirror Lake Campground (☎ 250-353-7102; sites $16) This campground has shady sites, a store, lake access and more. It is 5km south of Kaslo on Hwy 31.

NELSON

pop 9300

Nelson, surrounded by the Selkirk Mountains and snug up against the west arm of Kootenay Lake, is both the highlight and the heart of the Kootenays. Regardless of what activity you're after, be it kayaking on the lake, skiing at Whitewater or checking out local arts, Nelson makes a great base for exploring the region.

The town was born in the late 1800s, when two down-on-their-luck brothers from Washington sat bemoaning their bad fortune on top of Toad Mountain, just southwest of what is now Nelson. While the brothers rested, some of their party found the copper-silver deposit that later became the Silver King Mine. A town began to build up around the ore-rich mine, and its mass production prompted two transcontinental railways to serve Nelson in order to carry the goods away to smelters. When this proved too costly, the mining company built its own smelter, which only lasted as long as the ore. Finally the smelter buildings were destroyed in a massive fire in 1911, and like most mined-out towns Nelson turned to its forests.

In 1977 Nelson was chosen for the government's project on heritage conservation. Lucky choice. Today the picturesque town nestled in the hillside boasts more than 350 carefully preserved and restored late-19th-to early-20th-century buildings.

The town's charm and location lure many people who are seeking city culture but small-town lifestyle. The active, artsy community fancies itself as sophisticated, eccentric and lucky enough to live in paradise. The renowned Kootenay School of the Arts, the Selkirk School of Music and a school of Chinese medicine draw an interesting and eclectic mix.

The town's friendly, laid-back character is inviting. At any given time you can hear people talking about spirituality or tofu. And that sweet smell in the air? Yup, you guessed it – Nelson is renowned (unofficially, of course) for its excellent pot.

Orientation

Nelson sits on the west arm of Kootenay Lake. Traveling from the north, Hwy 3A becomes a series of streets before heading west to Castlegar. Hwy 6, skirts the west side of downtown, and goes to Castlegar or south to the small lumber town of Salmo before connecting with Hwy 3 and heading to Creston and the East Kootenays.

Baker St is the main drag and has many shops and restaurants. (And who couldn't love a town with a corner of Josephine and Baker?)

Information

For a good sense of the local scene, pick up a copy of the *Daily News*. You'll find events listings posted at the Kootenay Co-Op at 295 Baker St (p244). And given the local vibe, you shouldn't be surprised that Nelson has its own community-run radio station, CKCR 93.5FM.

BOOKSTORES

Otter Books (☎ 250-352-7525; 398 Baker St) Excellent selection of local books, topographic maps and magazines.

Packrat Annie's (☎ 250-354-4722; upstairs at 411 Kootenay St) Good array of used books.

INTERNET ACCESS

Nelson Library (☎ 250-352-6333; 602 Stanley St; 🕑 1-8pm Mon, Wed & Fri, 10am-6pm Tue & Thu, 11am-6pm Sat) Free Internet access.

LAUNDRY

Plaza Laundromat (☎ 250-352-6077; 616 Front St; 🕑 8am-6pm)

MEDICAL SERVICES

Kootenay Lake District Hospital (☎ 250-352-3111; 3 View St; 🕑 24hr)

POST

Post office (☎ 250-352-3538; 514 Vernon St; ⏱ 8:30am-5pm)

TOURIST INFORMATION

Visitor Info Centre (☎ 250-352-3433, 877-663-5706; www.discovernelson.com; 225 Hall St; ⏱ 8:30am-8pm daily summer, 8:30am-5pm Mon-Fri winter)

Sights

Almost a third of Nelson's buildings have been restored to their high- and late-Victorian architectural splendor, so you'll definitely want to pick up the superb *Heritage Walking Tour* leaflet from the VIC. It gives details on 26 buildings in the center and offers a good lesson in Victorian architecture. Highlights include the 1899 **Burns Building** (560 Baker St), which has a carved cow-head over the door courtesy of its cattle-baron builder. The companion *Architectural Heritage Motoring Tour* highlights treasures further afield.

Lakeside Park is a popular spot where you can hang out or walk along the trail that runs through the park. In summer brave souls swim in chilly, glacier-fed Kootenay Lake. **Streetcar No 23** (adult/child $3/2; noon-6pm summer, weekends spring & fall), one of the town's originals, has been restored and now follows a 2km track from under the bridge (at the north end of Lakeside Park) to the wharf at the foot of Hall St.

THE KOOTENAYS

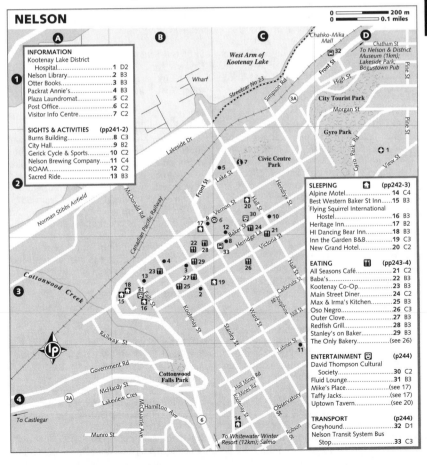

NELSON

INFORMATION
Kootenay Lake District
Hospital.........................1 D2
Nelson Library......................2 B3
Otter Books.........................3 B3
Packrat Annie's.....................4 B3
Plaza Laundromat...................5 C2
Post Office..........................6 C2
Visitor Info Centre.................7 C2

SIGHTS & ACTIVITIES (pp241-2)
Burns Building......................8 C3
City Hall............................9 B2
Gerick Cycle & Sports............10 C2
Nelson Brewing Company......11 C4
ROAM..............................12 C2
Sacred Ride.......................13 B3

SLEEPING (pp242-3)
Alpine Motel......................14 C4
Best Western Baker St Inn......15 B3
Flying Squirrel International
Hostel...........................16 B3
Heritage Inn......................17 B2
HI Dancing Bear Inn.............18 B3
Inn in the Garden B&B...........19 C3
New Grand Hotel.................20 C2

EATING (pp243-4)
All Seasons Café..................21 C2
Baba's............................22 B3
Kootenay Co-Op...................23 B3
Main Street Diner.................24 C2
Max & Irma's Kitchen.............25 B3
Oso Negro........................26 C3
Outer Clove......................27 B3
Redfish Grill.....................28 B3
Stanley's on Baker...............29 B3
The Only Bakery................(see 26)

ENTERTAINMENT (p244)
David Thompson Cultural
Society..........................30 C2
Fluid Lounge.....................31 B3
Mike's Place....................(see 17)
Taffy Jacks.....................(see 17)
Uptown Tavern.................(see 20)

TRANSPORT (p244)
Greyhound.......................32 D1
Nelson Transit System Bus
Stop.............................33 C3

For more history, go to the **Nelson & District Museum** (☎ 250-352-9813; 402 Anderson St; $2; ⏰ 1-6pm summer, 1-4pm Mon-Sat winter) northeast of town, which features displays on the early indigenous population, settlers, the Silver King Mine and boating history. The museum hopes to move to the present **city hall** in the next few years.

Beer lovers will want to check out the **Nelson Brewing Company** (☎ 250-352-3582; 402 Anderson St; 512 Latimer St). Call to find out about the frequent tours and tastings. Their many top-notch brews are served all over town; the Wild Honey Ale is a treat.

One of the biggest events is the **Nelson International Street Performers & Arts Festival** (☎ 250-352-7188; www.streetfest.bc.ca). Known by locals as 'Streetfest', the three-day affair, which happens the third weekend in July, features a variety of street artists, from buskers and mimes to poets and craft-makers. Baker St becomes a pedestrian mall, and performers from all over the world do their thing on the crowd-lined streets.

Activities
KAYAKING
All that lake water is just waiting to be rippled by a kayak. **ROAM** (☎ 250-354-2056, 877-229-4959; www.roamthekootenays.com; 579 Baker St) is a large outfit dedicating to kayaking locally. A three-hour guided trip costs $55, or you can rent kayaks (single $60 per 24 hours). They also arrange higher-end rafting and white-water kayaking expeditions around the province.

HIKING & MOUNTAIN BIKING
The two-hour climb to Pulpit Rock, practically in town, affords fine views of Nelson and Kootenay Lake. Find the trailhead on your right at the end of Johnstone Rd (in the northern part of town). Excellent hikes abound at **Kokanee Creek Provincial Park**, 20km northeast of town off Hwy 3A. Stop in at the park's **visitor centre** (☎ 250-825-4212) for information on specific hikes, including the Canyon Trail, which winds through lush forest to views of waterfalls spilling off Kokanee Glacier. Eight trails begin right at the visitor centre. Lake-filled **Kokanee Glacier Provincial Park** (☎ 250-825-3500 for trail conditions) boasts 85km of some of the area's most superb hiking

trails. The two-hour hike to Kokanee Lake is wonderful and can be continued to the glacier.

Most of this area's mountain-biking trails wind up from Kootenay Lake along steep and rather challenging hills, followed by stomach-emptying downhills. Trail names like 'Boneyard' and 'Fat Chance' make the whole idea a little daunting for anyone other than advanced riders, but there are some intermediate trails for those wishing to end the day free of open wounds. The best way to find out about trails is by chatting to the folks at one of the bike shops. **Gerick Cycle & Sports** (☎ 250-354-4622, 877-437-4251; 702 Baker St; rentals from $20) rents road and mountain bikes. **Sacred Ride** (☎ 250-362-5688, 888-296-5688; 213 Baker St) has knowledgeable staff. Both of the shops sell *Your Ticket to Ride*, an extensive trail map, for $10.

SKIING & SNOWBOARDING
Known for its heavy powdery snowfall, which averages 1050cm per year, **Whitewater Winter Resort** (☎ 250-354-4944, 800-666-9420, snow report ☎ 250-352-7669; one-day lift tickets adult/child $42/26) features good skiing and boarding. Unlike more commercial places, Whitewater maintains its small-town charm. Whitewater has only two double chairs and a rope tow, but they can take you to an elevation of 396m and some great powdery snow. Several snow-cat operators can take you to virgin territory from $375 for the day. There are 11 groomed Nordic trails. The resort is 12km south of Nelson off Hwy 6.

You can rent equipment at the resort or from the two sporting goods shops listed above under Hiking & Mountain Biking.

Sleeping
Whatever you do, try to stay in town to fully enjoy Nelson.

MOTELS & HOTELS
New Grand Hotel (☎ 250-352-7211, 888-722-2258; www.newgrandhotel.ca; 616 Vernon St; s/d $55/60; 🖭) This renovated classic has good views of the lake from high floors. The vibe is casual and stylish and there's almost a whiff of Ian Schrager in the air. Its Uptown Tavern is the place to be (p244).

Heritage Inn (☎ 250-352-5331, 877-568-0888; www.heritageinn.org; 422 Vernon St; s/d $65/70; 🖭)

With a pub, restaurant and nightclub (Mike's Place, p244), this hotel is somewhat of a hub, whether you stay here or not. As with most heritage buildings – this one dates from 1898 – the rooms are small but clean and full of character.

Best Western Baker St Inn (☎ 250-352-3525, 888-255-3525; www.bwbakerstreetinn.com; 153 Baker St; r $120-260; 🞬 🖳) A typical business-class hotel, it offers free, high-speed Internet in the rooms, which are comfortable. But don't settle for one of the rooms with a view of a wall.

You can find a variety of motels at the highway intersections. Best is the lovely **Alpine Motel** (☎ 250-352-5501, 888-356-2233; www .alpine-motel.com; 1120 Hall Mines Rd; s/d from $55/60; 🞬). The grounds are lovely and there is a fine view of the lake from the hot tub. The rooms are a good size. The motel is near Observatory St up the hill south of the center.

B&BS
Inn the Garden B&B (☎ 250-358-3226, 800-596-2337; www.innthegarden.com; 408 Victoria St; r $80-200; 🞬) Right downtown, this B&B offers guest rooms in a lovingly restored Victorian home. The yard and patio are bedecked with flowers and the rooms feature comfy wicker furniture. The VIC has many more B&B listings.

HOSTELS
HI Dancing Bear Inn (☎ 250-352-7573, 877-352-7573; www.dancingbearinn.ca; 171 Baker St; dm members/non-members $17/20, r from $40; 🖳) This is a beautifully renovated hostel with quiet and immaculate rooms. The comfortable living room makes a great place to read a book or find out about local happenings.

Also named after active animals, **Flying Squirrel International Hostel** (☎ 250-352-7285; www.flyingsquirrelhostel.com; 198 Baker St; dm/r $20/49; 🖳) is a decent choice with a lively bar filled with lively locals on its ground floor.

CAMPING
The Redfish and Sandspit Campgrounds at **Kokanee Creek Provincial Park** (☎ 800-689-9025; www.discovercamping.ca; sites $22), 20km northeast of Nelson off Hwy 3A, contain 132 wooded sites with toilets and showers. The park has its own visitor center and offers daily interpretive programs, especially on the

land-locked kokanee salmon that spawn in the creek.

Eating
Along with Kelowna, Nelson may have the best choice of places to eat east of Vancouver. But don't let the cosmopolitan selection fool you: outside of tourist season the trendy restaurants often pull the shades by 8:30pm, just like any other small town.

RESTAURANTS
Redfish Grill (☎ 250-352-3456; 491 Baker St; meals $4-15) Always bustling and always good, Redfish serves excellent cuisine through the day. The breakfast special ($4) includes all the bacon, eggs, toast and hash browns you can eat. Lunch features tasty soups and salads while dinner has an array of fusion items like the curry mushroom bowl and South African chicken.

The **All Seasons Café** (☎ 250-352-0101; 620 Herridge Lane; meals $20-30; 🕑 dinner Mon-Sat) is easily one of the finest spots in town. Set back on a quiet tree-lined alley, the restaurant has a heated patio. The menu features local ingredients and dishes that change by the season, although the salmon is always good. Bring someone special to help you manage the beguiling wine list.

Baba's (☎ 250-352-0077; 445 Baker St; meals $10; 🕑 lunch & dinner) This bright and lively place lives up to its boast of providing an 'authentic taste of India'. It may help that the owners/chefs hail from the subcontinent. It has a lot of veggie options on the menu and, for a real treat, hit the Monday-night veggie buffet.

Max & Irma's Kitchen (☎ 250-352-2332; 515A Kootenay St; meals $10-15; 🕑 lunch & dinner Mon-Sat) It serves pizzas and pasta dishes but try the grilled wild salmon, and when it's nice, sit out on the patio.

Garlic lovers should head straight to the **Outer Clove** (☎ 250-354-1667; 536 Stanley St; meals $8-15; 🕑 dinner Mon-Sat), where spicy and delicious dinners include a good vegetarian selection.

Stanley's on Baker (☎ 250-354-4458; 402 Baker St; meals $5-10; 🕑 7am-3pm) Enjoy omelets made with organic free-range eggs at this high-quality breakfast spot.

People-watching is best on the sidewalk patio at **Main Street Diner** (☎ 250-354-4848; 616 Baker St; burgers $10; 🕑 lunch & dinner). Although the menu leans towards Greek, there's also good hamburgers and Belgian fries.

CAFÉS
There's always a crowd hanging put in front of **Oso Negro** (☎ 250-532-7761; 522 Victoria St; 7am-5pm), which brews the best coffee this side of Vancouver. This locally owned 'micro-roaster' serves up over 18 blends of socially conscious organic coffee – and it's strong and delicious. In the same building, pick up a boiled bagel or muffin from **The Only Bakery** (☎ 250-354-1200).

SELF-CATERING
Kootenay Co-op (☎ 250-354-4077; 295 Baker St; 8am-7pm Mon-Sat) Worth a visit is this fantastic natural foods market with a deli and local organic produce. The bakery makes its own bagels.

Entertainment
Nelson has its share of places to pound a pint or party down. Most are within walking distance of each other.

PUBS
Uptown Tavern (☎ 250-352-7211; 616 Vernon St in the New Grand Hotel; noon-late) This tavern has DJs some nights, hockey other nights and a good vibe most nights.

Mike's Place (Heritage Inn; meals $10; 11am-late) Mike's is a classic with dark paneling and a good mix of visitors and locals alike (one of the latter describes it using the over-used *Cheers* but in this case he's right). Good pub food can be washed down by the full complement of Nelson Brewing Co beers.

Bogustown Neighbourhood Pub (☎ 250-354-1313; 712 Nelson Ave; noon-late) Featuring a fun, relaxed atmosphere, pub food, pool tables and a good patio, it's just far enough from the center to make it a good excursion.

CLUBS
Taffy Jacks (Heritage Inn; cover varies; 8pm-late) has Top-40 music dancing nightly, and the **Fluid Lounge** (☎ 250-354-4603; 198 Baker St; cover varies; 8pm-late Wed-Sat) has DJs spinning punk, acid jazz and more depending on the night.

THEATER
David Thompson Cultural Society (☎ 250-352-1888; 373 Baker St) A Nelson institution that has its roots as a center for local college students. It is now home to a variety of performances, art installations and lectures. Stop by to see what's on. Some nights there's a cutting edge dance club the society calls Charlotte's.

Getting There & Around
The closest airport with commercial service to Nelson is in Castlegar.

Greyhound (☎ 250-352-3939; 1112A Lakeside Dr) In the Chahko-Mika Mall. Buses depart for Calgary via Fernie and for Vancouver via Kelowna.

Nelson Transit System Buses (☎ 250-352-8228) The main stop is on the corner of Ward and Baker Sts. Bus No 2 will take you to the Chahko-Mika Mall or Lakeside Park. No 10 goes to the North Shore and to the Kootenay Lake ferry. On some days there's **regional service** (☎ 250-265-3674) to Kaslo & Nakusp.

Queen City Limousine (☎ 250-352-9829; www.queencitylimo.com; one-way $23) Reserve in advance.

CASTLEGAR
pop 7300
Castlegar, a sprawling town known primarily as a highway junction (Hwys 3 and 3A merge here), sits on the Kootenay and Columbia Rivers. It's a vital hub, even if it is not a vital stop.

Castlegar's history centers around the more than 5000 Doukhobors, members of a Russian Christian pacifist sect who followed their leader, Peter Verigin, west from Saskatchewan between 1908 and 1913. The Doukhobors, small groups of peaceful, communal-living people, had begun to reject the teachings of the Russian Orthodox Church during the 18th century. They refused ritual worship, believing instead that god's spirit lived within each individual and that it was up to individuals, not an outside god, to have peaceful and harmonious lives. The church shunned the Doukhobors, exiling them to cold, barren corners of Russia, where the church hoped the group would fizzle out. But the Doukhobors thrived and, in 1898 and 1899, 7500 members immigrated to Canada, first to Saskatchewan and then to Castlegar and nearby Grand Forks.

If the town of Castlegar is a bit of a letdown, the Columbia River Valley to the south is stunning. Beautiful in all seasons, it comes alive with golden colors when the leaves change in the fall. North of town, however, you'll see a huge pulp mill on the Columbia. Over on the Kootenay River, **Keenleyside Dam** is a major source of hydroelectric power.

Head to the north end of Columbia Ave to see the strip of stores known as downtown Castlegar. In the southern part of town, you'll find the year-round **Visitor Info Centre** (☎ 250-365-6313; www.castlegar.com; 1995 6th Ave at 20th St; ✆ 9am-5pm summer, Mon-Fri winter), which is a good source of regional information.

Check out the Doukhobor legacy at **Zuckerberg Island Heritage Park** (☎ 250-365-6440; donation; ✆ dawn-dusk). The island was the home of Alexander Feodorovitch Zuckerberg, a Russian teacher brought in to educate the Doukhobor children. Today the park contains a suspension bridge, trails and restored buildings, including the former chapel house. This is a good stop if the kiddies in the back seat are turning in to Cossacks.

The **Castlegar Museum** (☎ 250-365-6440; 400 13th Ave; donation; ✆ 10am-5pm Mon-Sat) is housed in the old CPR train station. It features an interesting display on the history of the West Kootenay Power & Light Company, including diving gear used by early company workers. Upstairs is a well-done display of early Castlegar inhabitants.

Skip the reconstructed **Doukhobor Historical Village**, on the east side of the Columbia River off Hwy 3A by the airport. It's little more than a couple of buildings, a statue of Tolstoy and a small museum that you can afford to miss.

If you're going to stay overnight, the **Super 8** (☎ 250-365-2700, 888-828-5331; www .super8.com; 651 18th St; r $89; 🐾) has standard and comfortable rooms and it is close to the airport.

Syringa Creek Provincial Park (☎ 800-689-9025; www.discovercamping.ca; sites $17; ✆ Apr-Oct) sits on Lower Arrow Lake, 17km northwest of Castlegar off Broadwater Rd on the north side of the Columbia River. It offers 60 campsites, a long beach, swimming and good hiking.

Though everyone claims to have the best borscht in town, the winner appears to be **Weezie's Borscht Hut** (☎ 250-304-2633; 2816 Columbia Ave; borscht $6; ✆ breakfast & lunch),

at the south end of Castlegar. The small restaurant serves up Russian specialties like meat-filled cabbage rolls.

Getting There & Away

Castlegar Airport (YCG; ☎ 250-365-5151) is on Hwy 3A southeast of town. It is the major airport for the region. Air Canada Jazz has daily flights to Vancouver and Calgary. Major rental car firms have offices in the terminal. Nelson is 41km northeast. **Queen City Transportation** (☎ 250-352-9829; $25) meets all flights but reserve in advance for the service to/from Nelson.

ROSSLAND

pop 3700

This gorgeous mountain town is perched high in the Rossland Mountains, a southern buttress of the Monashee Range.

At 1023m, this high-elevation town sits in the eroded crater of an ancient mineral-rich volcano. The area was first encountered by Europeans in 1865, when builders of the historic Dewdney Trail passed by and simply marveled at the reddish mineral stains on nearby Red Mountain. Prospectors didn't come sniffing around for another 25 years. It wasn't until 1890 that a guy named Joe Moris decided to do more than marvel and finally tapped into the incredibly rich gold deposits that induced Rossland's birth. After old Joe's discovery, the town built up quickly. Sourdough Alley (today's Columbia Ave) became the province's wildest and roughest main thoroughfare, and by 1895, 7000 residents and hundreds of prostitutes could take their pick of 42 saloons. By 1929 most of the claims were mined-out, and the boom shrank to a whisper, but in less than 45 years Rossland had produced $165 million worth of gold.

Today Rossland has become a cool small town whose sporty inhabitants take full advantage of the area's bounty. Skiing has long been a top attraction, and the Red Mountain Resort boasts some of the best technical trails in the world. Canadian Olympic gold medalists Kerrin Lee-Gartner and Nancy Greene hail from Rossland.

Information

Gold Rush Books & Espresso (☎ 250-362-5333; 2063 Washington St)

Visitor Info Centre (☎ 250-362-7722, 888-448-7444; www.rossland.com; ☺ 9am-5pm mid-May–mid-Sep) Located in the museum building, at the junction of Hwy 22 and Hwy 3B.

Sights & Activities

With its excellent displays on mining history, the **Rossland Museum** (☎ 250-362-7722; adult/child $9/6; ☺ 9am-5pm mid-May–mid-Sep, mine tours 9:30am-3:30pm), beside the Visitor Info Centre on the site of the former Black Bear Mine, merits a stop. The 45-minute tour of the mine gives you a good idea of the toil the early hard-rock miners had to endure.

Dubbed 'Canada's Mountain Bike Capital', Rossland features a well-developed and extensive trail system that radiates right from downtown. Much of the **mountain biking** is for hard-core types who refer to themselves as 'Rubberheads', but there are mellower trails also accessible from town. As usual, bike shops are the best places to go for information. **Powderhound** (☎ 250-362-5311; 2044 Columbia Ave) offers bike rentals from $35 per day depending on how much suspension you want. The **Sacred Ride** (☎ 250-362-5688; 2123 Columbia Ave) has friendly staff, sponsors a local bike club and rents bikes for $35 to $45. At both shops pick up a copy of *Trails of the Rossland Range* ($8).

Only 5km north of downtown on Hwy 3B, **Red Mountain Ski Resort** (☎ 250-362-7384, 800-663-0105, snow report ☎ 250-362-5500; www .ski-red.com; one-day lift pass adult/child $48/25) includes 1590m-high Red Mountain and 2040m-high Granite Mountain, making a total of 485 hectares of powdery terrain. Geared mostly toward intermediate and advanced skiers and snowboarders, the area is known for its steep, tree-filled runs (83 at last count). There are five lifts and a drop of 880m.

Ski and snowboard rentals are available on the mountain at **Le Rois Sports Shop** (☎ 250-362-7124; full-day ski package $23). In town you can get full-day ski packages from $40 at **Powderhound** (☎ 250-362-5311; 2040 Columbia Ave).

Across the highway from Red Mountain, **Black Jack Cross Country Area** (☎ 250-362-9465; www.skiblackjack.ca; day-pass adult/child $9/5) boasts 25km of groomed skating and classic trails.

Sleeping & Eating

The ski resort has detailed listings of the many places to stay near the slopes. The following rates cover the peak season, which means winter in Rossland. Unlike much of British Columbia, summer here is low season.

Ram's Head Inn (☎ 250-363-9577, 877-267-4323; www.ramshead.bc.ca; r $60-150) A large common room with vaulted ceilings and a hefty stone fireplace, an outdoor hot tub, a games room and cozy guest rooms make a stay here a real treat. It has a beautiful forest setting 3km west of Rossland on Red Mountain Rd off Hwy 3B at the base of the ski resort.

The **Uplander Hotel** (☎ 250-362-7375, 800-667-8741; www.uplanderhotel.com; 1919 Columbia Ave; r $60-110; ☒) contains two dining rooms, the popular Powder King Pub and basic but comfortable rooms. The ones with kitchenettes are best.

Join the mountain bikers for coffee and a good $5 breakfast at **Clansey's** (☎ 250-362-5273; 2042 Columbia Ave; meals $5-8; ☺ breakfast & lunch). For great views and delicious pub food, head to **The Flying Steamshovel** (☎ 250-362-7323; 2003 2nd Ave; meals $7; ☺ noon-late). It's two blocks uphill from Columbia Ave.

AROUND ROSSLAND

West of Rossland, the lovely **Christina Lake** is a good place to stay for a day or two, especially if you're camping at **Gladstone Provincial Park**. The Texas Creek Campground (☎ 800-689-9025; www.discovercamping.ca) in the park, on the north end of Christina Lake, offers reservable campsites for $14 year-round. It lies 10km east of Christina Lake off Hwy 3 and can be tricky to find, so keep a good eye out for the signs for East Lake Drive and then follow it for a kilometer to the campground.

Further west you'll hit the pretty border town of **Grand Forks**, known for its borscht and relatively abundant sunshine. The town was a by-product of the Phoenix Mine, once the biggest copper-producing smelter in BC. Some of the Doukhobors who settled in Castlegar came here, and their influence still lends character and good food to the town.

Going east from Rossland you go downhill in every sense of the word. The smokestacks on the skyline belong to the industrial town of **Trail**, where even the hospital has a big smokestack. The good-sized town has traded a potentially scenic

CHECK YOUR WATCH

Like Alberta and Idaho, the East Kootenays lie in the Mountain Time Zone, unlike the West Kootenays and the rest of BC, which fall in the Pacific Time Zone. If you're heading west on the Trans-Canada Hwy (Hwy 1) from Golden, the time changes at the east gate to Glacier National Park. Or, as you travel west on the Crowsnest Hwy (Hwy 3), the time changes between Cranbrook and Creston. Mountain Time is always an hour ahead of Pacific Time. For example, when it's noon in Golden and Cranbrook, it's 11am in Glacier National Park and Creston.

spot on the Columbia River for an economy based on a vast smelting plant. Faux-cheery lamppost banners (Trail: It's all here!) miss any irony.

CRESTON

pop 4900

Following the Crowsnest Hwy 3 east from Trail as it skirts the US border, you'll climb over the scenic 1774m Kootenay Pass and roll down into Creston, the center of a green, fruit-growing district. The fertile soil and mild weather create perfect growing conditions for apples. Other thriving crops include asparagus, peaches and canola. Lapin cherries (large, juicy and dark red) are becoming a big deal as farmers realize that they can bring in 10 times the profit of your average apple crop.

Only 11km north of the US border, Creston serves as a gateway to the Kootenays from Washington and Idaho in the US. The **Visitor Info Centre** (☎ 250-428-4342; www .crestonbc.com/chamber; 711 Canyon St; 9am-5pm summer, 8:30am-4:30pm Mon-Fri winter) is both helpful and delightful. The bathroom wall is a very good read.

Sights & Activities

The interesting **Creston & District Museum** (☎ 250-428-9262; 219 Devon St; $2; 10am-3pm May-Sep) is a thick-walled idiosyncratic stone structure with animal heads (fake) and even car windshields embedded into the walls.

Beer connoisseurs will want to take the free hour-long tour through the **Columbia Brewery** (☎ 250-428-9344; 1220 Erickson St; admission free; tours 9:30am & 11am, 1pm & 3pm Mon-Fri mid-May–mid-Sep) where BC's famed Kokanee beer is brewed and bottled. It's just south of the center.

An absolute must-see is the **Creston Valley Wildlife Management Area** (☎ 250-428-3259;

admission free; dawn-dusk), 11km west of Creston along Hwy 3. These 6900 hectares of internationally recognized prime waterfowl habitat sit on protected provincial land. More than 100,000 migrating birds use the area to nest and breed. The fertile floodplain is filled with birdsong, and the marshy wetlands attract the province's largest populations of black terns, white-fronted geese and blue herons. You can walk along a 1km boardwalk to a watchtower. An interpretive center is open for varying hours from April to mid-October, admission is $3.

Sleeping & Eating

Creston Hotel & Suites (☎ 250-428-2225; www.creston hotel.com; 1418 Canyon Rd; s/d $50/60;) A really good locally owned place that's right in the center, it has free high-speed Internet in the rooms and an outdoor patio.

Downtowner Motor Inn (☎ 250-428-2238, 800-665-9904; www.crestonvalley.com/downtowner; 1218 Canyon St; s/d $45/55;) Comfortable rooms and right next to a bowling alley – what more could you want? Except maybe a pitcher of Kokanee to help you roll a strike.

Scottie's RV Park & Campground (☎ 250-428-4256, 800-982-4256; scottiesrv@telus.net; 1409 Erickson Rd; sites $17), right in town across from Columbia Brewery, offers non-secluded but convenient sites (especially for beer-tasting). More bucolic, **Little Joe's Campground & Fruit Stand** (☎ 250-428-2954; faye@kootenay.net; 4020 Hwy 3; sites $17), about 5km east of town, features very nice sites surrounded by grand old cedar trees.

Munro's (☎ 250-428-7222; 1403 Canyon St; meals $10-18; lunch & dinner) is the pick of Creston with its great salad bar, thick steaks and propensity to lace everything with garlic.

Annette's Delicate 'Essen' & Coffee House (☎ 250-428-0500; 1130A Canyon St; sandwiches $6; 9am-5pm Mon-Fri, 10am-4pm Sat) puts the 's' in 'essen' with her super German-style baked goods, sandwiches and coffee.

EAST KOOTENAYS

The East Kootenays has become a world-class ski and snowboard area, with substantial resorts popping up at Fernie, Kimberley, Panorama and Golden. The town of Fernie itself is a highlight of the region.

The East Kootenays are strategically located between the Purcell Mountains in the west and the Rocky Mountains in the east. Golden, in the north, sits between Glacier and Yoho National Parks, while Cranbrook, in the south, serves as the major highway crossroads. The area teems with creeks and lakes that are perfect for fly-fishing. The 16km-long Columbia Lake, at Canal Flats, is the source of the great Columbia River, which winds around BC and Washington State before spilling into the Pacific Ocean in Oregon.

CRANBROOK

pop 19,000

Despite its position at the base of the Steeples Range of the Rocky Mountains and in the rolling foothills of the Purcells, this city, which lies 106km northeast of Creston, is not a very attractive place. The comely yet sleepy downtown core is overshadowed by 'the Strip', a 2km slice of Hwy 3 called Cranbrook St as it runs through town, which is dominated by fast-food chains, auto-parts stores, malls and roadside motels.

The **Visitor Info Centre** (☎ 250-426-5914, 800-222-6174; www.cranbrookchamber.com; 2279 Cranbrook St N; ☺ 8:30am-6pm Mon-Fri, 9am-5pm weekends summer, 8:30am-4:30pm Mon-Fri winter) has the usual array of great info. There's a **summer-only Info Centre** (☺ 9am-5pm Mon-Fri Jun-Aug) at the south end of town on Hwy 3.

All of Cranbrook whoops it up for **Sam Steele Days** (☎ 250-426-4161), a four-day party, on the third weekend in June. The whole town comes out in costume to celebrate the hardy founder of Fort Steele. Events include a parade, logger sports and the Sam Steele Sweetheart Pageant.

Sights

Fort Steele Heritage Town (☎ 250-426-7342; www.fortsteele.bc.ca; adult/child $19.25/2.25; ☺ 9:30am-5pm May-Oct, 9:30am-6pm Jul & Aug) This worthy

sight is 14km north of Cranbrook on Hwy 93/95. It was named for the diplomatic North West Mounted Police (later to become the RCMP) superintendent Samuel Steele, who worked to ease tensions between gold seekers and the Ktunaxa First Nations during the East Kootenay gold rushes in the late 1800s. Fort Steele became a boomtown, but after it was bypassed by the railway it fell into obscurity. Today the town has over 60 restored buildings that are populated by characters in historical dress. Unlike most tourist traps, it is well done and always a fave with kids.

Sleeping

The Strip (Hwys 3 and 95) is littered from end to end with motels; most of the chains are here and finding a room should not be a problem.

Lazy Bear Lodge (☎ 250-426-6086, 888-808-6086; 621 Cranbrook St N; s/d from $50/60; ☒ ☒) This lodge is very nicely maintained and has good-sized rooms. The heated outdoor pool can be a welcome relief at the end of a long hot day.

Jimsmith Lake Provincial Park (☎ 250-422-4200; sites $14) Off Hwy 3 at the southern end of Cranbrook, this park has 29 good, shady sites and beach access although there are only pit toilets and no showers.

Eating

You can find any kind of fast food and standard diners along the Strip – surprise! However, the best places to eat are downtown. A very popular spot with locals is the **Cottage Restaurant** (☎ 250-426-6516; 13 9th Ave S; meals $6; ☺ breakfast & lunch Mon-Sat). The food's fresh, the baked goods good and the borscht yummy.

Heidi's European & International Cuisine (☎ 250-426-7922; 821C Baker St; meals $10-20; ☺ 11am-9pm) serves large portions of vegetarian spaetzle and Wiener schnitzel. The weekend-only prime rib is sought after.

Join the locals outside at **Kootenay Roasting Company** (☎ 250-489-0488; 821 Baker St; coffee $1.50; ☺ 7am-6pm) where the heady scents confirm that they roast their own coffee.

Getting There & Around

Cranbrook Airport (YXC; ☎ 250-426-7913) Just north of town on Hwy 95A; Air Canada Jazz flies daily to Vancouver & Calgary. Major car rental firms are here.

Greyhound (☎ 250-489-3331; 1229 Cranbrook St N) Buses to Vancouver & Calgary.

Star Taxi (☎ 250-426-3888)

FERNIE

pop 5100

A beautiful little town with an active preservation and arts movement, Fernie delights in the unusual. Where else would they have a nudist ball to raise money for bear (that's 'bear' as in big teeth and bigger claws, not 'bare') preservation?

The area's history was tied to mining, but when the mines closed many years ago the town went to sleep. All the better as now there's real appreciation for what at the time must have seemed like just a bunch of old brick buildings. Certainly BC has enough towns that were decimated in the name of progress. You can find plenty of old miners about town, many more than happy to share harrowing tales of life underground. These days you can also find plenty of folks around town ready to share harrowing tales of their exploits on the slopes of the Fernie Alpine Resort. In the non-ski season, Fernie seems to be half-full of people lazing about and keeping one eye cocked for the first sign of snow.

THE KOOTENAYS

THE TRUTH ABOUT TROUT

Fishing types who visit BC boast about the eager schools of fish that practically leap out of the water, onto fishing lines and into garlic- and butter-soaked cooking pans. They bolster this talk with day-dreamy visions of sitting in a boat on a glassy early-morning lake or of delicately dancing a fly rod on a babbling brook, all of which add to the romantic notion that BC lakes are stocked with fish. Well, in fact, they are, though not as naturally as you might think.

Few people realize that the provincial government's **Ministry of Water, Land and Air Protection** (wlapwww.gov.bc.ca/wld/fishhabitats/index.html) plays a major role in keeping the fish count up. Anglers catch an estimated nine million freshwater fish every year. To keep up with angler demand, more than 1100 lakes and streams are augmented with 12 million fish born and raised in metal containers in fish hatcheries throughout the province. Five major hatcheries produce inland fishes, including steelhead trout, anadromous cutthroat, brook char, land-locked kokanee salmon, rainbow trout and westslope cutthroat.

Before stocking lakes or streams, biologists need to consider factors such as how many people are fishing in a certain lake, how the increase in fish will impact vegetation or other animals such as the fish's predators or its prey. Fish are transported in special trucks that feed the fish into the stream through a large pipe. Helicopters and small airplanes carry fish to higher-elevation lakes or to streams inaccessible by road.

Learn more about this fascinating augmentation of nature by visiting one of the freshwater fish hatcheries.

The **Kootenay Trout Hatchery** (☎ 250-429-3214; admission free; ☺ 8am-4pm), 45km east of Cranbrook along the Bull River, raises about three million rainbow, brook and cutthroat trout a year, mostly to stock the area's lakes. Here you'll see how the fertilized eggs are captured and raised from fry to fish until they're able to return to local rivers and lakes. You may even get the chance to feed a few. To get there from Cranbrook, take Hwy 3 toward Fernie and turn left onto the Fort Steele–Wardner Rd. Look for signs.

Happily, constant winter storms travel over the Rockies and dump vast amounts of snow on the area, making it a powdery paradise for skiers and snowboarders. In summer the run-off means great rafting on local rivers.

Orientation & Information

Downtown Fernie lies southeast of Hwy 3. Many shops and services can be found on 7th Ave, which runs parallel to the highway. The old town is bounded by 3rd and 7th Sts and 4th and 1st Aves.

Fernie District Hospital (☎ 250-423-4453; 1501 5th Ave; ☒ 24hr)

Fernie Heritage Library (☎ 250-423-4458; 492 3rd Ave; ☒ 11am-8pm Tue-Fri, noon-5pm Sat & Sun Nov-Mar) In the 1907 Post Office & Customs House, free Internet access.

Polar Peek Books (☎ 250-423-3736; 592 2nd Ave) A beautiful little store with a good selection of regional history and adventure books.

Visitor Info Centre (☎ 250-423-6868; www.fernie chamber.com; 102 Commerce Rd; ☒ 9am-7pm summer, 9am-5pm Mon-Fri winter) East of town off Hwy 3, just past the Elk River crossing.

Sights

Fernie experienced a devastating fire in 1908, which resulted in a brick-and-stone building code. Thus, today you'll see many fine **early-20th-century buildings**, many of which were built out of local yellow brick, giving the town an appearance unique in the East Kootenays. Get a free copy of *Heritage Walking Tour*, a superb booklet produced by the **Fernie & District Historical Society** (☎ 250-423-7016). It's available at the VIC and various businesses around town. The map highlights buildings where you can enter and see exhibits on Fernie's history.

Give yourself a couple of hours to stroll historic Fernie. Add time at one of the cafés or pubs as well as some shopping and you'll fill much of a day. In the old CPR train station is the **Arts Station** (☎ 250-423-4842; 601 1st Ave), which has a small theatre, galleries and studios for some of the many local artists. Opening hours depend upon what's on. On summer Sunday mornings, the **Mountain Market** is held in Rotary Park at 7th St and Hwy 3. It's a fun and eclectic mix of artists, bakers, gardeners, musicians and more.

Fernie Alpine Resort

A five-minute drive from downtown Fernie, 'BC's fastest-growing ski resort', which is meant to eventually rival Whistler, gets a whopping 875cm of snow per year on average. The **Fernie Alpine Resort** (☎ 250-423-4655, 877-333-2339; snow conditions ☎ 250-423-3555; www.skifernie.com; one-day lift pass adult/child $58/19) is undergoing massive resort-style growth to turn it into a year-round attraction. For now, its 107 runs, five bowls and almost endless dumps of powder draw droves of skiers and snowboarders looking for unspoiled terrain. Thirty percent of the runs are rated expert.

To get to the resort from town, follow Hwy 3 west and turn right onto Ski Hill Rd. Most hotels run shuttles daily. Rent ski or snowboard equipment in town from $25 per day at **Fernie Sports** (☎ 250-423-3611; www.ferniesports.com; 1191 7th Ave). This is the place recommended by locals. The resort charges from $25 per day for skis and snowboard packages.

Heavy snowfalls dramatically increase avalanche danger. If you are planning on doing any backcountry touring, it is important to stop by the **Guides Hut** (☎ 250-423-3650; www.theguideshut.com; 671 2nd Ave), where you can get the scoop on weather, rent avalanche kits, get topographic maps and find out about organized backcountry tours.

Activities
WHITEWATER RAFTING

Whether you're looking to soak up some rays or get soaked by the river, two rafting companies offer trips on the Bull and Elk Rivers. **Canyon Raft Company** (☎ 250-423-7226, 888-423-7226; www.canyonraft.com) and **Mountain High River Adventures** (☎ 250-423-5008, 877-423-4555; www.raftfernie.com) both offer day trips on either river for about $90 or half-day floats for about $50. The trips include all the gear and lunch.

HIKING

Great hiking trails radiate in all directions from Fernie. The excellent and challenging Three Sisters hike winds through forests and wildflower-covered meadows, along limestone cliffs and scree slopes. The 2744m summit offers incredible 360-degree views of the Elk Valley, Fisher Peak and surrounding lakes. From the Visitor Info Centre, take Dickens Rd to Hartley Lake Rd and follow it to the lake. Turn left onto the dirt track and hike 3km to the trailhead. Allow at least four hours each way. Another hike affording spectacular views, the Hosmer Mountain Trail, is also off Hartley Lake Rd (there is a parking area and a well-marked trailhead). This moderate hike takes about 2½ hours one-way.

MOUNTAIN BIKING

The best thing about mountain biking in Fernie is the choice of terrain, from easy toodles along trails in Mt Fernie Provincial Park to steep granny-gear uphills and log-jumping downs. The *Secret of Single Track* is a good local map with trail descriptions. Pick it up at bike shops or at the Visitor Info Centre. Get the lowdown from local riders at Fernie Sports (p250), where you can rent front-suspension bikes from $29 per day.

Sleeping

Being a big ski town, Fernie's high season is the winter.

Royal Hotel (☎ 250-423-7750; www.fernieroyal hotel.com; 501 1st St; s/d $90/110) This may be the funkiest place you stay on your trip. Built in 1909 the hotel was run for many years by the Quail family and their spooky family photos still line the walls. The rooms have been freshened and are comfortable but basic. However, you stay here for the goofy atmosphere and the proximity to one of the best bars in town (see below).

Best Western Fernie Mountain Lodge (☎ 250-423-5500, 800-937-8376; www.bestwestern fernie.com; 1622 7th Ave; s/d $120/140; ⊠ ☐ ☎) A comfortable and modern place close to the historic center, it boasts a large indoor pool. Get a room with a balcony and a view.

Snow Valley Motel (☎ 250-423-4421, 877-696-7669; www.snowvalleymotel.com; 1041 7th Ave; s/d $64/69; ⊠) The rooms here are large and clean. There's an eight-person hot tub and a nice barbecue patio.

Griz Inn Sport Hotel (☎ 250-423-9221, 800-661-0118; www.grizinn.com; 5369 Ski Hill Rd; r $100, ste from $200; ⊠ ☐ ☎) A very enjoyable place to stay near the base of the resort, the Griz Inn has a pool inside and two hot tubs outside. Rooms have VCRs and the many suites can sleep numerous weary skiers.

HI Raging Elk Hostel (☎ 250-423-6811; www.hi hostels.ca; 892 6th Ave; dm members/non-members $18/22) Though the rooms are not a complete delight, the hostel enjoys a central location.

Three kilometers west of town, **Mt Fernie Provincial Park** (☎ 800-689-9025; www.discover camping.ca; sites $14) offers 38 sites, flush toilets, waterfalls, a self-guided interpretive trail and access to mountain-bike trails.

Eating & Drinking

The Saloon (☎ 250-423-7750; 501 1st St; meals $8; ☺ noon-late) The old corner bar in the Royal Hotel is a beguiling place with great characters, food and a full range of the tasty local beers from the Fernie Brewing Company. There are animal heads on the wall, each with its own story to tell.

Blue Toque Diner (☎ 250-423-4637; 500 Hwy 3; meals $8; ☺ 8am-3pm Thu-Tue) A long and fresh menu features lots of seasonal standards. You can have a coffee out on the platform or a delicious sandwich or salad inside, it is in the Arts Station next to the galleries.

Rip 'n' Richards Eatery (☎ 250-423-3002; 301 Hwy 3; meals $9; ☺ lunch & dinner) The quesadillas draw raves from local aficionados. You'll agree but you'll also probably rave about the view of the river from the deck. The varied menu also has pizza, jambalaya, burgers and more.

Jamochas Coffee House & Bagel Co (☎ 250-423-6977; 851 7th Ave; coffee $2; ☺ 7am-7pm) The staff take heed of the motto, 'Life's too short to drink bad coffee'. It's a good spot to read the paper and plan your day – just be sure to turn off that cell phone or you'll make a major faux pas should somebody ring.

Getting There & Around

Greyhound (Park Place Lodge, 742 Hwy 3) Buses in each direction to Vancouver and Calgary.

Kootenay Taxi (☎ 250-423-4408)

Rocky Mountain Sky Shuttle (☎ 403-762-5200, 888-762-8754; www.rockymountainskyshuttle.com) Service to Cranbrook Airport one-way adult/child $52/32.50, Calgary International airport return $124/62.

KIMBERLEY

pop 6700

At 1113m Kimberley can claim to be the highest city in Canada (at 1397m, Banff in Alberta is higher, but it's technically a town, not a city), as well as one of the nicer stops in the East Kootenays.

The discovery of rich minerals in 1891 prompted the birth of the North Star Mine. The following year, on the other side of Mark Creek, another claim staked out what would grow to become the largest lead and zinc mine in the world, the Sullivan Mine. Mark Creek Crossing was renamed Kimberley in 1896, after the successful South African diamond mine. In 1909 Cominco took over operations, drawing more than 162 million tons of ore out of the Sullivan, though the metal isn't worth as much as diamonds. The mine's closure was anticipated years in advance and the town, with help from Cominco, has been busily diversifying into tourism.

Before 1973 Kimberley looked like what it is – a small mountain mining town. Since then it has been revamped to resemble a Bavarian alpine village. Most of the downtown section, the **Platzl**, was transformed, with city planners paying enough attention to detail to make it interesting. Kimberley's mascot, Happy Hans, lives in a huge cuckoo clock in the center of the Platzl. Every hour on the hour, people will stand in awed anticipation waiting for old Hans to pop out and yodel. All of the town's fire hydrants have been hand-painted to look like little people wearing lederhosen. While slightly ridiculous, the Bavarian theme serves Kimberley well: it has prevented out-of-control sprawl and has spawned several good restaurants, jolly beer-drinking events and an overall sense of fun. Though this Bavarianism, combined with the new, rapidly growing ski resort, brings lots of camera-happy people to Kimberley, it still remains a quiet alpine town.

Information

Internet Access (☎ 250-427-3112; 115 Spokane St at the east end of the Platzl; 🕑 10am-5pm Tue-Sat, 10am-8pm Thu) Internet access $1 per hour.

Visitor Info Centre (☎ 250-427-3666; 350 Ross St; 🕑 9am-4:30pm Mon-Sat summer, 1-4pm Mon-Fri winter) Currently located with the mining railway but should be moving to location off Platzl.

Sights & Activities

Take a 13km ride on the **Bavarian City Mining Railway** (☎ 250-427-3666; 🕑 noon-5:30pm summer) as it chugs through the steep-walled Mark Creek Valley toward some incredible mountain vistas. Recent extensions take the

train right to the base of the chairlift for the Kimberley Alpine Resort, from where you can ride to the top for great views (combined train and lift tickets adult/child $16.05/7.49). The station is about 1km north of the Platzl off Gerry Sorensen Way.

You can learn about mining history at the **Kimberley Heritage Museum** (☎ 250-427-7510; 115 Spokane St; admission free; 🕑 9am-4:30pm Mon-Sat summer, 1-4pm winter), which is beside the library at the east end of the Platzl.

The 12-acre **Cominco Gardens**, beside the hospital above Kimberley, are full of roses, tulips and gnomes. If you're walking from town, take the stairway and trail at the west end of Howard St. It takes about 15 minutes.

The extensive network of trails (100km worth) of the **Kimberley Nature Park** wind around Kimberley. You can cross-country ski or walk along the well-marked trails while observing the active wildlife. Get a copy of *Kimberley Nature Park Trail Guide* ($3) at the VIC.

Just west of town, in the nearby community of Marysville, take the short walk to see the **Marysville Waterfalls**. Park at the Mark Creek bridge where Hwy 95A becomes 304 St and follow the boardwalk along the creek. It takes about 10 minutes.

Kimberley Alpine Resort

The Resorts of the Canadian Rockies have spent millions building up the **Kimberley Alpine Resort** (☎ 250-427-4881, 877-754-5462; www.skikimberley.com; one-day lift pass adult/child $48/16). The results show the effort and the resort boasts 728 hectares of skiable terrain, mild weather and 67 runs. There are 10 lifts and 45% of the runs are intermediate. A new high-speed quad-lift serves the 8200m Main Run, which has a 609m drop and is fully lit for night skiing. Ski package rentals start at $29 per day.

Festivals & Events

The Platzl is the perfect place to have a party, and Kimberley certainly has its share.

FEBRUARY

Winterfest With winter bocce, hockey and snow golf.

JULY

Kimberley International Old Time Accordion Championships (yikes!)

Julyfest A week of dancing, parades and lots of beer.

SEPTEMBER
International Folkdance & Octoberfest When there's lots of entertainment and more beer.

Sleeping

As attractive as the Platzl is, most of Kimberley's accommodations are at the ski resort, which runs a central **reservations service** (☎ 877-754-5462; www.skikimberley.com). **Polaris Inn** (☎ 250-427-0090;301 Northstar Blvd; r from $100; ☒) lets you ski on and off the slopes from your front door. The large rooms are a good place to relax and the suites have nice kitchens.

Crazy Chef Bernard has his finger in many strudels. He runs the **Chef Bernard's Platzl Inn** (☎ 250-427-4820, 800-905-8338; www.cyberlink.bc.ca/~chefbernards; 170 Spokane St; r from $60), above his restaurant on the Platzl. Prices vary wildly when demand is high or low. When the inn is full, the fine chef can supply you with accommodations at one of his condos up at the Kimberley Alpine Resort. If you want to score points ask to read his bio. Also question him on his fondest memory...

Right in the middle of the Platzl, above the Ozone Pub, is the **Kimberley SameSun Budget Lodge** (☎ 250-427-7191, 877-562-2783; www.samesun.com; 275 Spokane St; dm/r $20/49). The excellent location and modern, clean rooms make this a good place to stay, especially in the ski season. The hostel runs a shuttle to the ski hill in winter.

The massive **Happy Hans Riverside RV Resort** (☎ 250-427-2929, 877-999-2929; www.happyhans.com; sites from $16; ☒) features 140 sites with amenities that include a water park. To get there, turn off Hwy 95A in Marysville and follow the St Mary Lake Rd for 2.9km.

Eating

The most notable places to eat are in the Platzl where almost every place has tables out front over-looking the action. You'll hear the music and see the vast collection of trinkets spilling out the door over at **Chef Bernard's Restaurant** (☎ 250-427-4820; 170 Spokane St; meals $12-22; ☽ lunch & dinner). Besides the mandatory schnitzel and strudel, the chef cooks up a long and good Thai menu.

Bypassing the Bavarian theme, the **Snowdrift Cafe** (☎ 250-427-2100; 116 Spokane St; meals $7; ☽ lunch) on the northwest side of the Platzl has a mostly vegetarian menu featuring salads and veggie burgers.

Below SameSun, the **Ozone Pub** (☎ 250-427-7744; 275 Spokane St; ☽ noon-late) is big with ski bums who play pool and await the occasional live band.

On the way up to the ski resort, **The Old Bauernhaus** (☎ 250-427-5133; 280 Norton Ave; meals $10-16; ☽ lunch & dinner Thu-Mon) offers Bavarian favorites in a 350-year-old farmhouse, moved here piece by piece from Germany. The stone patio has delightful views.

Getting There & Away

Greyhound (☎ 250-427-3722; 1625 Warren Ave), east of Kimberley, runs buses daily to Calgary and Vancouver.

KIMBERLEY TO RADIUM HOT SPRINGS

Hwy 95A heads northeast out of Kimberley and connects up with Hwy 93/95. Just south of the junction on Hwy 95 is **Wasa Lake Provincial Park** (☎ 800-689-9025; sites $15), home to the warmest lake in the Kootenays. The popular campground contains 104 sites, 50 of which can be reserved, and offers good lake access, interpretive programs and flush toilets. The park protects an increasingly rare chunk of BC's grassland, most of which has been turned into golf courses or farmland. A paved path meanders around the lake, giving you a good chance to check out this ecosystem from a bike, in-line skates or a wheelchair. For information on Wasa Lake or any of the area's provincial parks, call ☎ 250-422-4200.

After Wasa, Hwy 93/95 continues north along the scenic Kootenay River. At **Skookumchuck**, 18km north of Wasa, the Lussier and Skookumchuck Rivers join the Kootenay. You'll find little more than a gas station and coffee shop here. Continue 41km northeast to **Whiteswan Lake Provincial Park**, where the rustic **Lussier Hot Springs** lie 17km into the park. The loose-gravel road that branches off the highway is bumpy but navigable for most cars. A well-marked trailhead leads you down to the springs, which, despite their remoteness, can get downright crowded in summer. Past the springs are Whiteswan and Alces Lakes, both popular with anglers. The four campgrounds in the park all contain pit toilets and good sites for $12.

THE KOOTENAYS

To access the remote **Top of the World Provincial Park**, follow the Whiteswan Rd for 52km off Hwy 95. Once you get to the end of the bumpy road, it's an easy 6km hike or mountain-bike ride to Fish Lake, so named for its thick population of Dolly Varden and cutthroat trout. You can camp at one of the backcountry sites at Fish Lake or stay in the large rustic cabin often used by anglers.

Fairmont Hot Springs Resort

If you head north of Canal Flats on Hwy 95, you'll come to what is essentially a giant sinkhole for vacationer dollars. This resort community, centered around some natural hot springs, is for people who just want to get away and not have to worry about much at all. There's nothing inherently wonderful about Fairmont Hot Springs Resort to make it worth a stop.

Windermere Valley

This narrow valley between the Purcell and Rocky Mountains has long been a well-used transportation route, first for the Ktunaxa and Kinbasket First Nations people. Pioneer David Thompson began his exploration of the Columbia River here in 1807. The towns of **Windermere** and **Invermere** are often overlooked by visitors heading to the national parks, but they are both worthwhile stops for stocking up on supplies before heading into the backcountry.

Panorama Mountain Village Resort

Taken over in 1993 by Intrawest, the same folks who own Whistler-Blackcomb, the **Panorama Mountain Village Resort** (☎ 250-342-6941, 800-663-2929; www.panoramaresort.com; one-day lift pass adult/child $59/27) went from being an understated, local skiers' mountain to a major, full-service resort. Boasting a 1220m drop, the resort has over 100 immaculately groomed runs, plus a gondola that shuttles people from the upper to lower villages. And, with an endless array of new services and condos, Panorama is fast becoming a built-up and exclusive resort. Panorama Mountain is at the end of an 18km drive up a winding road from Invermere.

RADIUM HOT SPRINGS

pop 600

Radium Hot Springs is a major gateway to all four Rocky Mountains national parks: Kootenay, Banff, Jasper and Yoho. It lies just outside the southwest corner of Kootenay National Park.

The town sits in the Rocky Mountain Trench, with the spires of the Purcells to the west and the Rocky Mountains directly east. Radium was so named after a government test conducted in 1914 showed small levels of radioactivity in the nearby hot springs. The surrounding Columbia River wetlands north of Radium attract more than 100 species of birds, including migrating waterfowl traveling along the Pacific Flyway. Radium boasts a large resident population of Rocky Mountain bighorn sheep, which often wander through town during much of the year – an attraction in itself.

The biggest draw in Radium, however, is the famed hot springs, which are located at the park's southern end (p263).

The **Kootenay National Park & Radium Hot Springs Visitor Info Centre** (☎ 250-347-9331, 800-347-9704; www.rhs.bc.ca; 7556 Main St East – Hwy 93/95; ☿ 9am-7pm daily summer, 9am-5pm Mon-Sat winter) includes Parks Canada information for the nearby parks.

Sleeping & Eating

Radium Hot Springs contains more than 30 motels, most of which borrow heavily from Bavarian schtick. Despite all the accommodations though, it's a good idea to arrange accommodations ahead of time in July and August. The best camping is in the park (p264).

Misty River Lodge (☎ 250-347-9912; www.radium hostel.bc.ca; 5036 Hwy 93; dm/r $21/45) Right outside the park gate, this lodge and hostel has a good homey atmosphere plus a communal kitchen and large sunny patio with views of the Purcells. The owners can make detailed recommendations on area activities. Bikes and canoes may be rented.

Motel Tyrol (☎ 250-347-9402, 888-881-1188; www .moteltyrol.com; 5016 Highway 93; 4872 McKay St; r $60-80; ▨ ▨) Rooms have fridges and are quite comfortable, and there's a large outdoor heated pool; the bar's good too.

Rocky Mountain Springs Lodge & Restaurant (☎ 250-347-9548, 877-457-1117; www.milliondollar view.com; 5067 Madsen Rd; r $69-99; ☿ restaurant 5:30-9pm; ▨) The web address says it all for this simple place that boasts one of the best restaurants in the area. Debate which is better: the schnitzel or the view from the

THE STORY OF THE KICKING HORSE

With a burning desire to 'open up the west', the Canadian government started looking for ways to push the railway over the high, icy Rocky Mountains. In 1858 it sent a scientific and exploratory expedition out to survey the land and return with suggestions for a feasible route over the Rockies. Led by John Palliser, the expedition was accompanied by a geologist named Sir James Hector, who is credited for finding the Kicking Horse Pass, albeit by rather unfortunate circumstances.

Fatigued and cold after a long day hiking in the mountains, Hector camped with his cohorts near the Continental Divide. Just as the beginnings of sleep finally closed Sir James' eyelids, one of the packhorses escaped across the river. In fear of losing valuable gear, Sir James jumped in the chilly river waters and swam after the horse. He dragged it back to camp, tied it up next to his own horse, and before long the two horses started biting each other. (Poor James wasn't getting much sleep.) Finally he intervened, and for his troubles his horse delivered a swift kick square to his abdomen. The kick broke three ribs and left him unconscious for so long that the Native Americans he was traveling with presumed he was dead.

They dragged his corpse to a gravesite in a valley away from camp. Just before they threw him into the ground, Sir James revived – apparently not dead after all. Once he healed, he set off to explore the pretty valley and stumbled onto the pass that would become the CPR's route to connecting the west.

patio. Madsen Rd turns off Hwy 93 near the entrance to the park. Look for the wood-carving attraction.

Helena's Stube (☎ 250-347-0047; 7547 Main St; meals $13-18; ☺ dinner, closed Tue & Wed winter) The place looks simple but the food isn't. The pasta, steaks and hearty fare like beef roulade are good. There's a good patio with tables.

GOLDEN
pop 4000
Sandwiched between the Purcell and Rocky Mountains and surrounded by six national parks, this is the first town of any size you encounter if you're coming west from Alberta. Golden sits near the confluence of the Columbia and Kicking Horse Rivers.

Before prospectors came rolling into the area in search of gold, the town was referred to as the 'Cache' because it was little more than a storage spot for supplies. It was later renamed Golden City (the 'City' was later dropped) to compete with Silver City, a nearby, momentary boomtown where someone had planted decoy deposits of silver ore.

Later, with the advent of tourism in the Rockies, the Canadian Pacific Railway hired Swiss guides to lure rich Europeans to explore the pristine mountain peaks. To make the guides feel at home, the CPR housed them in Swiss-style chalets just above Golden. You can still see remnants of the village.

Many guidebooks and highway tourists give Golden a bad rap. If you never venture off the Trans-Canada Hwy, it looks like an unattractive commercial strip of motels, fast-food restaurants and service stations. But once you get off the highway and discover the year-round outdoor opportunities, you might change your mind. Whitewater rafting is incredibly popular. The areas mountains beckon skiers, boarders and hikers, while other brave souls launch hang gliders off Mt 7, so named for the way snow falls on the ridge – in the shape of a seven.

Information
The center of town lies 2km south of the highway; many businesses are along 10th Ave.

Visitor Info Centre (☎ 250-344-7125, 800-622-4653; www.goldenchamber.bc.ca; 500 10th Ave North; ☺ 9am-5pm daily Jul & Aug, Mon-Fri winter)

Activities
WHITEWATER RAFTING
Golden is the center for whitewater rafting trips on the turbulent and chilly Kicking Horse River. Powerful Class 3 and 4 rapids and breathtaking scenery along the sheer walls of the Kicking Horse Valley make this rafting experience one of North America's best. The fainter of heart can take a mellow but equally scenic float trip on the upper river. Many operators run the river in the

busy summer season, sometimes making it resemble a traffic jam.

Strict BC rafting regulations and training ensure each company employs qualified, experienced staff. **Glacier Raft Company** (☎ 250-344-6521; www.glacierraft.com) and **Wet 'n' Wild** (☎ 250-344-6546, 800-668-9119; www.wetn wild.bc.ca) both offer a range of trips from mellow floats to wild whitewater adventures that cost from $55.

MOUNTAIN BIKING
For easy riding in town, you can bike along the trails following the Kicking Horse River or head across the Columbia River to the West Bench, where you can tool around on 40km worth of trails. Hard-core types with good lungs peddle the steep trails up Mt 7 and then scream down technical single track.

Summit Cycle (☎ 250-344-6600; 1007 11th Ave S; bikes from $30/day) has knowledgeable staff and a tech shop if you need your bike tuned.

Kicking Horse Mountain Resort
Big plans are underway for Golden's Whitetooth Mountain. The growing **Kicking Horse Mountain Resort** (☎ 250-439-5400, 866-754-5425; www.kickinghorseresort.com; one-day lift pass adult/child $53/23) has a gondola and three lifts; a lodge near the gondola is set to open in 2004. A challenging 60% of its 96 runs are rated Advanced or Expert. With 1260 vertical meters and a relatively snow-heavy, wind-free position between the Rockies and the Purcells, the resort is a future contender in the race for ski-resort tourist dollars. Kicking Horse Resort is 14km from Golden on Kicking Horse Trail.

Sleeping
There are scores of motels on Hwy 1.

Mary's Motel (☎ 250-344-7111, 866-234-6279; www .marysmotel.com; 603 8th Ave N; r $59-90; ❂ ⚐) In town right along the river, Mary's is tidy inside and out. It offers indoor and outdoor pools, two hot tubs, and balconies/patios with the rooms.

Sportsman Lodge (☎ 250-344-2915, 888-989-5566; www.sportsmanlodge.net; 1200 12th St N; s/d

from $44/54; ❂ ⚐) Kick back in the lodge's indoor pool, which has that accoutrement loved by kids everywhere: a water slide. Older kids will enjoy the hot tub.

Golden Rim Motor Inn (☎ 250-344-2216, 877-311-2216; www.rockies.net/~goldrim; 1416 Golden View Rd; r $59-100; ❂ ⚐ ⚐) Another place with a water slide and indoor pool, it also boasts a sauna and hot tub. The secret here is to look past the expansive parking lot: the rooms are nice.

Golden contains a good selection of mountain lodges – from rustic to lavish – that are worth checking out. **Beaverfoot Lodge** (☎ 250-344-7144; www.rockies.net/~beaverft; r $85-105) has a beautiful main building with a fine porch. All meals are included and feature many ingredients grown on the ranch. For something different you can sleep in a covered wagon. The ranch is on Beaver Foot Forestry Rd 13km off Hwy 1 near the Yoho Park Gate.

Sander Lake Campground (☎ 250-344-6517; www.rockies.net/~bsander; sites $11-14), 12km southwest of Golden off Hwy 95, has a very pretty location amid trees and hills. Cabins cost $75.

Eating
Kicking Horse Grill (☎ 250-344-2330; 1105 9th St S; meals $20-30; ⏲ lunch & dinner Tue-Sat) This is Golden's best place for a fun yet very fine meal. The ever-changing menu concentrates on simple foods prepared well. There's steak, fish and highlights such as Madagascar pork in a peppercorn sauce. The dining room has a sort of elegantly rustic feel. Kids will love the menu: they get to order pretty much anything they want – the kitchen will sort it out.

Check your email and grab a coffee right in the center of town at **Jenny's Java Express/ Internet Café** (☎ 250-344-5057; 506 N 9th Ave; snacks $3; ⏲ 7am-7pm). The menu includes the requisite muffins as well as soups, salads, sandwiches and pizza by the slice.

Stock up on organic and other healthy foods at **Living Well Market** (☎ 250-344-4848; 828 10th Ave S; ⏲ 9am-6pm Mon-Sat) before you head into the parks.

The Rockies

CONTENTS

The entire Rocky Mountains area is a place of spectacular beauty, with some of the best scenery, climbing, hiking and skiing in the world. The national parks offer jagged, snow-capped glacier-covered mountains, peaceful valleys, rushing rivers, natural hot springs and alpine forests. The opaque emerald-green or milky-turquoise color of many Rocky Mountains lakes will have you doubting your eyes. The parks also feature both modern conveniences and plenty of backcountry trails. Wildlife abounds, particularly in Jasper National Park.

The Rocky Mountains, the world's fourth-highest mountain chain, sit on the easternmost part of the Canadian Cordillera, the name for all the mountains in western Canada. Starting as stubby knobs in central Mexico, the Rockies quickly rise into the majestic peaks that run through New Mexico, Colorado, Wyoming and Montana, before crossing the US border into Canada at Glacier National Park (in the US) and Waterton Lakes National Park (in Canada). The Canadian Rockies then act as a natural boundary between Alberta and BC. All told, the Canadian Rockies stretch almost 1500km.

Alberta's Banff and Jasper National Parks and BC's Kootenay and Yoho National Parks, together with British Columbia's Mt Robson and Mt Assiniboine Provincial Parks and Alberta's Hamber Provincial Park, compose the Canadian Rocky Mountain Parks Unesco World Heritage area, one of the largest protected areas in the world. Banff and Jasper lie in the province of Alberta, BC's eastern neighbor.

To preserve the region, Parks Canada controls the impact of visitors by designating specific park areas for campgrounds, picnic sites, service centers and town sites. The towns of Banff, Lake Louise and Jasper act as service centers where you can pick up supplies and information. For many people, a trip to these parks is truly a trip of a lifetime.

HIGHLIGHTS

- Rejuvenating your soul in **Radium** (p263), **Miette** (p285) or **Banff Hot Springs** (p269)

- Wandering through the massive and elegant **Banff Springs Hotel** (p272)

- Driving or cycling the spectacular, glacier-filled **Icefields Parkway** (p278)

- Watching for bears and moose and listening for the sounds of rutting elk in **Jasper National Park** (p279)

- Hiking on the many trails surrounding the turquoise-colored **Lake O'Hara** (p260) in **Yoho National Park** (p260)

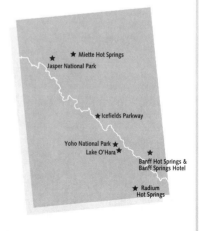

THE ROCKIES

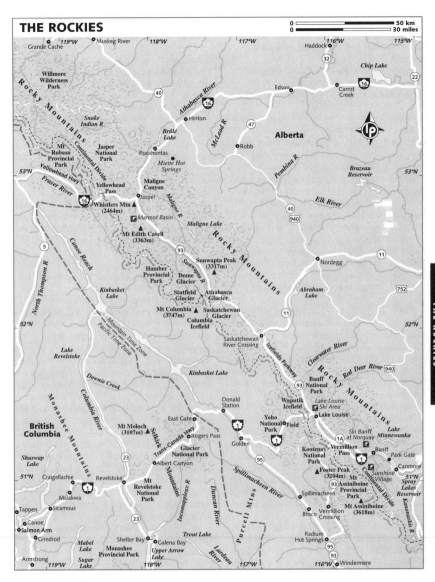

INFORMATION

On entering Banff and Jasper National Parks, you'll be given the excellent *Mountain Guide*. As well as outlining policies for the parks, the guide is full of information including what not to do when you see an elk in the middle of mating fever. There is more information available at the various park visitor's centers. Booklets outlining the myriad hikes and other activities as well as backcountry guides are highly useful.

Parks Canada offers links to all of the country's national parks from its website (www.parkscanada.ca). For more information, call or write to the parks.

Banff National Park (☎ 403-762-1550; Box 900, Banff, AB T1L 1K2)
Jasper National Park (☎ 780-852-6176; Box 10, Jasper, AB T0E 1E0)
Kootenay National Park (☎ 250-347-9505; Box 220, Radium Hot Springs, BC V0A 1M0)
Yoho National Park (☎ 250-343-6783; Box 99, Field, BC V0A 1G0)

FEES
You have to buy a park pass upon entry into any national park. The cost of **daypasses** (adult/child/group of up to 7 people $7/3.50/14) quickly adds up, especially if you're spending a few days in the parks. It may make more sense to buy an **annual pass** (adult/child/group $45/22/89). Not only will this save you money but it will give you unlimited admission to Canada's 27 national parks.

Other fees, such as for camping, are outlined in the appropriate sections throughout the chapter. However, note that none of the park campsites accept reservations.

BOOKS
It seems like there are endless books about the Rockies, but a few stand out from the crowd. The bible for the region is the encyclopedic *Handbook of the Canadian Rockies* by Ben Gadd. For fun, scholars try to find errors in this incredible work about the geology, history, flora and fauna in the Rockies. They rarely succeed.

Recommended hiking guides include the discerning *Don't Waste Your Time in the Rockies* by Kathy and Craig Copeland, with good maps and trail descriptions, and the longtime, solid guide *Classic Hikes in the Canadian Rockies* by Graeme Poole. *Canadian Rockies Access Guide* by John Dodd and Gail Helgason will also help lead you off the beaten path.

History buffs should check out *The Canadian Rockies: Early Travels & Explorations* by Esther Fraser or *A Hunter of Peace* by Mary Schaffer, about her early travels in the Malign Valley.

If you're looking for a novel to read while in the Rockies, *Icefields* by Thomas Wharton is a beautifully written book that offers excellent insight into Victorian-era exploration of the Columbia Icefields.

For a detailed look at Banff, Jasper and Glacier National Parks, look to Lonely Planet's *Banff, Jasper & Glacier National Parks*.

YOHO NATIONAL PARK

Established in 1886, waterfall-filled Yoho National Park is the smallest of the four national parks in the Rockies, with an area of merely 1310 sq km. Still, with its mountain peaks, river valleys, glacial lakes and beautiful meadows, it's an awe-inspiring place, as befits the park's name (Yoho means 'awe' in Cree). The park is adjacent to the Alberta border and Banff National Park to the east and Kootenay National Park to the south. Not as busy as Banff, Yoho often has campsite vacancies when Banff is full, though its position on the west side of the Rockies means that Yoho experiences more wet or cloudy days than Banff. The rushing Kicking Horse River flows through the park.

FIELD
The very small town of Field, which lies in the middle of the park along the Kicking Horse River, is the last town in BC as you head east along the Trans-Canada Hwy from Golden (see p255). Many of its buildings date from the early days of the railways, when it was the Canadian Pacific Railway's headquarters for exploration and, later, for strategic planning when engineers were trying to solve the problem of moving trains over the Kicking Horse Pass.

At the **Yoho National Park Information Centre** (☎ 250-343-6783; ☉ 9am-4pm, 9am-5pm May, Jun & Sep, 9am-7pm Jul & Aug), Tourism BC and Alberta Tourism staff their own desks in summer. The center also contains an interesting display on the Burgess Shale. While you're there, pick up the free *Backcountry Visitors' Guide*; its map and trail descriptions make it an excellent resource for exploring the park.

In town the **Siding General Store** (☉ 8am-8pm) can provide you with supplies if you're going to stay in the park. Its pleasant little café serves homemade food. The Greyhound bus also stops in Field coming west from Lake Louise and east from Golden along the Trans-Canada Hwy.

LAKE O'HARA
Nestled high in the mountains east of Field, this somewhat exclusive beauty spot more than lives up to its exalted reputation. The excellent walking trails definitely make it

THE ROCKIES

YOHO NATIONAL PARK

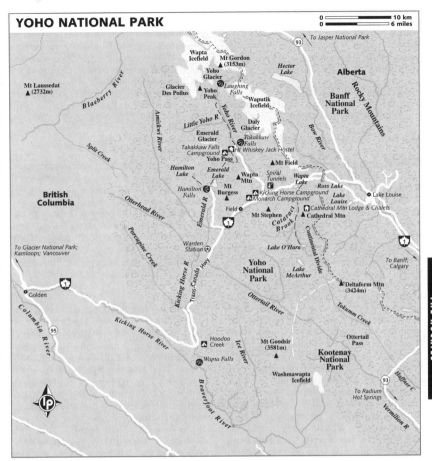

0 — 10 km
0 — 6 miles

To Jasper National Park
93

Wapta Icefield

Mt Gordon (3153m)

Yoho Glacier

Hector Lake

Alberta

Mt Laussedat (2732m)

Blaeberry River

Glacier Des Poilus

Yoho Peak

Laughing Falls

Waputik Icefield

Banff National Park

Rocky Mountains

Amiskwi River

Little Yoho R

Yoho River

Daly Glacier

Emerald Glacier

Takakkaw Falls

Bow River

Split Creek

Takakkaw Falls Campground

HI Whiskey Jack Hostel

Yoho Pass

British Columbia

Hamilton Lake

Emerald Lake

Mt Field

Spiral Tunnels

Wapta Lake

Ross Lake

Lake Louise

Hamilton Falls

Emerald R

Wapta Mtn

Mt Burgess

Kicking Horse Campground

Monarch Campground

Lake Louise

Field

Cathedral Mtn Lodge & Chalets

Otterhead River

Mt Stephen

Cataract Brook

Cathedral Mtn

To Glacier National Park; Kamloops; Vancouver

Porcupine Creek

Warden Station

Lake O'Hara

Continental Divide

1

Golden

Kicking Horse Hwy

Trans-Canada Hwy

Yoho National Park

Lake McArthur

To Banff; Calgary

Deltaform Mtn (3424m)

Columbia River

95

Kicking Horse River

Ottertail River

Tokumm Creek

Ice River

Hoodoo Creek

Mt Goodsir (3581m)

Ottertail Pass

Wapta Falls

Kootenay National Park

Washmawapta Icefield

Haffner C

Beaverfoot River

To Radium Hot Springs

93

Vermilion R

worth the sizable hassle involved in reaching this place, an encapsulation of the whole Rockies. Compact wooded hillsides, alpine meadows, snow-covered passes, mountain vistas and glaciers are all concentrated around the stunning lake.

A simple day trip is definitely worthwhile, but more trails (most fairly rigorous) are accessible if you stay overnight in the backcountry. The very fine Alpine Circuit trail (12km) offers a bit of everything.

To reach the lake, you can take the **shuttle bus** (adult/child $15/7.50; ☺ mid-Jun–early Oct) from the Lake O'Hara parking lot, 15km east of Field on the Trans-Canada Hwy. This is prime grizzly bear habitat and a major wildlife corridor. In an effort to

alleviate human pressure on the trails, park officials have come up with a quota system that governs bus access to the lake and limits permits for the popular backcountry campsites. You can freely walk the 13km from the parking area, but no bikes are allowed.

Make reservations for the **bus trip** (☎ 250-343-6433) or for **camping** (backcountry permit adult $8) up to three months in advance. Given the popularity of Lake O'Hara, reservations are basically mandatory (unless you want to walk). However, if you don't have advance reservations, six day-use seats on the bus and **three** to five campsites are set aside for 'standby' users, but you need to show up in person at the park information center in Field the day *before* you want to go. In high season a long line often forms before the doors open at 8:30am. The area around Lake O'Hara usually remains snow-covered or very muddy until mid-July.

ELSEWHERE IN THE PARK

East of Field on the Trans-Canada Hwy is the **Takakkaw Falls road** (late-Jun–early Oct) – at 254m, Takakkaw Falls is one of the highest waterfalls in Canada. Takakkaw is a Cree word for 'magnificent,' and it certainly is. From here **Iceline**, a 20km hiking loop, passes many glaciers and spectacular scenery.

The beautiful green **Emerald Lake**, 10km north off the Trans-Canada Hwy, features a flat circular 5.2km walking trail with other trails radiating from it. The lake gets its incredible color from light reflecting off the fine glacial rock particles, deposited into the lake over time by grinding glaciers. In late summer the water is just warm enough for a quick swim. Look for the turnoff west of Field.

The **Burgess Shale World Heritage Site** protects the amazing Cambrian-age fossil beds on Mt Stephen and Mt Field. These 515-million-year-old fossils preserve the remains of marine creatures that were some of the earliest forms of life on earth. (The Royal Tyrrell Museum in Drumheller, Alberta, contains a major display on these finds.) You can only get to the fossil beds by guided hikes, which are led by naturalists from the **Yoho-Burgess Shale Foundation** (www.burgess-shale.bc.ca). The 10-hour hike to **Burgess Shale** in **Walcott's Quarry** (adult/child $55/26; Jun-Sep 15) covers 20km, and the more strenuous six-hour jaunt to **Mt Stephen** and the **fossil beds** (adult/child $25/15; Jun-Sep 21) covers a steep 6km. You need to be in good shape for either, and you must make **reservations** (800-343-3006; burgshal@rockies.net) well ahead of time.

The famous **spiral tunnels** – the engineering feat that enabled Canadian Pacific Railway trains to navigate the challenging Kicking Horse Pass – lie 8km east of Field along the Trans-Canada Hwy. When the railway was completed, it demanded that trains climb the steep 4.5% grade, the steepest railway pass in North America. Many accidents occurred when the trains lost control either hauling themselves up

or down the tricky pass. In 1909 the spiral tunnels were carved into the mountain, bringing the grade to a more reasonable 2.2%. If you time it right, you can see trains twisting in on themselves as they wind through the spirals.

Near the south gate of the park, you can reach pretty **Wapta Falls** via a 2.4km trail. The easy walk takes about 45 minutes each direction.

SLEEPING

Yoho National Park has four campgrounds. The small town of Field contains several B&Bs and a lodge; ask for details at the park information center.

Cathedral Mountain Lodge & Chalets (250-343-6442; www.cathedralmountain.com; r $200-400) This place is highly recommended and pleasantly rustic. Situated 4km east of Field on Yoho. Valley Rd, it offers luxurious cabins at the base of Cathedral Mountain and alongside the river. Many of the rooms contain antiques.

HI Whiskey Jack Hostel (403-762-4122, 866-762-4122; www.hihostels.ca; dm member/non-member $15/19;) Fifteen kilometers off the Trans-Canada Hwy on Yoho Valley Rd just before the Takakkaw Falls Campground, this hostel offers 27 dorm-style beds. It's open only from June to September. The daily shuttle bus between Banff and Jasper takes a detour off the Icefields Parkway to pick up and drop off people at the hostel.

The campgrounds within Yoho all close during winter. Only the **Kicking Horse Campground** (sites $22) has showers, making its 92 sites the most popular. Interpretive programs run on summer nights. To get there, drive 3.2km east of Field on the Trans-Canada Hwy, then proceed 1km along the Yoho Valley Rd. Nearby, right at the turnoff to Yoho Valley Rd, the quieter **Monarch Campground** (sites $14) offers 46 basic sites. No fires are allowed.

Near the park's south entrance, the wooded **Hoodoo Creek Campground** (sites $17) offers 106 sites and flush toilets. **Takakkaw Falls Campground** (site $14), 13km along the gravel Yoho Valley Rd, has 35 walk-in campsites for tents only. The sites are only a five-minute walk from the designated parking area. The absence of cars around the campsites is a rarity in the Rockies – it's a nice treat.

KOOTENAY NATIONAL PARK

Kootenay National Park, in BC but adjacent to Alberta's Banff National Park, runs south from Yoho National Park. Encompassing 1406 sq km, the park was born during the building of the expensive Banff–Windermere Hwy (Hwy 93). When funding for the highway ran dry, the federal government stepped in and offered to finance the highway's completion in return for land on either side. It became parkland in 1920. Today Hwy 93 travels down the center and is really the only road in the park, other than a few gravel trails. Between the northern entrance at Vermilion Pass and Radium Hot Springs at the park's southern end, there are four campgrounds, plenty of points of interest, hiking trails and views of the valley along the Kootenay River. Most attractions lie just off the highway. Note that fires in 2003 burned almost 13% of the park; recovery efforts are ongoing.

Kootenay experiences a more moderate climate than the other Rocky Mountain parks and, in the southern regions especially, summers can be hot and dry. It's the only national park in Canada to contain both glaciers and cactuses.

INFORMATION

Kootenay National Park is on Mountain Time, one hour ahead of most of BC.

Kootenay National Park Information Centre
(☎ 250-347-9505, 800-347-9704; 7556 Main St
E - Hwy 93/95; ☼ 9am-5pm mid-May–Jun & 1-15 Sep,
9am-7pm Jul & Aug, 9am-5pm 16 Sep-15 Oct Fri & Sat)
Inside the Visitor Info Centre in the town of Radium
Hot Springs.

Kootenay Park Lodge Visitor Centre (☼ 10am-7pm
summer, 11am-6pm Fri-Sun spring & fall) At Vermillion
Crossing, 63km from Radium.

SIGHTS

The park boundary between Banff and Kootenay National Parks marks the **Continental Divide**, which runs through Yellowhead, Kicking Horse, Vermilion and Crow Nest Passes. At the Divide, rivers flow either west to the Pacific or east to the Atlantic.

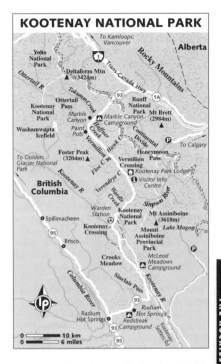

KOOTENAY NATIONAL PARK

For an adrenaline rush, head to **Marble Canyon**, where a short trail begins at the parking lot just off the highway and follows the rushing Tokumm Creek, crisscrossing it frequently on small wooden bridges. As you climb higher, the drop below gets narrower and deeper as the roaring water rages through the limestone and dolomite (not marble) canyon walls. Hang onto your camera, sunglasses and small children while looking down.

Some 2km further south on the main road is the short, easy trail through forest to ochre pools known as the **Paint Pots**. For years first the Kootenay people and then European settlers collected this orange-and red-colored earth. They'd shape it into patties, dry it, grind it, then mix it with fish or animal oil to make paint. Today you can walk past the muddy red pools and read panels describing the mining history of this rusty earth.

Long gone are the days when Native Indians and trappers soaked in the natural hot pools, but built-up **Radium Hot Springs** (☎ 250-347-9485; adult/child $6.50/5.50; ☼ 9am-11pm

THE ROCKIES

summer, noon-9pm winter), 3km north of the town of Radium Hot Springs, is always worth a visit. Even though they are the largest hot springs pools in Canada, the pools can get very busy in summer; early and late are the times least crowded. The facilities include showers and lockers. The water comes from the ground at 44°C, enters the first pool at 39°C and hits the final one at 29°C.

Sleeping

Radium Hot Springs contains lots of motels, many in alpine style. Outside of Radium Hot Springs you'll also find suitable accommodations.

Kootenay Park Lodge (☎ 403-762-9196; www.kootenayparklodge.com; r $89-125; mid-May–Sep) If you're looking for a roof over your head, this lodge at Vermilion Crossing offers cozy rooms and log cabins with fireplaces and puffy duvets.

The **Marble Canyon Campground** ($17), 88km from Radium Hot Springs and about 8km from the park's east gate, offers flush toilets but no showers with its 61 sites. With similar facilities and 98 sites, **McLeod Meadows Campground** ($17) features good, wooded sites along the Kootenay River. **Redstreak Campground** (tents $22), near the park's west gate, contains 242 sites (154 tent sites and 88 partial- and full- hookup sites for RVs) and offers full services, including flush toilets, showers and nightly interpretive programs. Ask for a list of the park's backcountry campsites at the visitor info centres.

AROUND KOOTENAY NATIONAL PARK

Mt Assiniboine Provincial Park

Between Kootenay and Banff National Parks lies this lesser-known and smaller (39 sq km) provincial park, part of the Rockies' Unesco World Heritage area. The craggy summits of Mt Assiniboine (3618m), often referred to as Canada's Matterhorn, and its near neighbors have become a magnet for experienced rock-climbers and mountaineers. The park also attracts lots of backcountry hikers.

This park takes its name from the Assiniboine (ass-*in*-a-boyne) Native Indians, who are also referred to as 'Stoney' for the way they cook some foods – by putting hot stones in pots of water to warm them up. The park's main focus is Lake Magog, which is reachable only by a gravel road. At the lake there's the commercially operated **Mt Assiniboine Lodge** (☎ 403-678-2883; r per person incl all meals from $180), a **campground** ($5) and some **Naiset cabins** ($30), which may be reserved through the lodge. There's wilderness camping in other parts of the park.

The only way in is on foot. From Hwy 93, two hiking trails start near the road at Vermilion Crossing in Kootenay National Park, and both are close to 30km to Magog Lake. Another hiking trail begins at Sunshine Village Ski Resort in Banff National Park; allow a good eight hours to make this 27km trek to Magog Lake.

BANFF NATIONAL PARK

Banff is by far the region's best-known and most popular park. The tall peaks here make for world-famous skiing and climbing, and the spectacular beauty is enchanting. Modern conveniences and backcountry trails appeal to coffee-sippers and hikers equally.

Established in 1885 and named for two Canadian Pacific Railway (CPR) financiers who hailed from Banffshire in Scotland, Banff National Park became Canada's first national park, built around the thermal sulfur springs at what has become the Cave & Basin National Historic Site. It covers an area of 6641 sq km and contains 25 mountains of 3000m or more in height.

BANFF

pop 7000

Banff, 138km west of Calgary and 90km east of Field, is Canada's number one resort town in both winter and summer and as such is really the center of the Rockies. The town, built in a rustic-alpine style, is surrounded by unbeatable scenery. Despite attracting several million visitors a year, Banff is small, consisting essentially of one main street, so it can get crowded. In July and August the normal population swells by 25,000. Although this can cause problems, the many vacationers create a relaxed and festive atmosphere. Many of those smiling young workers in and around town were once visitors themselves. They now enjoy the low pay and rustic living conditions that enable them to make their home in the Rockies.

MARY L PEACHIN

Rainbow Range (p297), Tweedsmuir Provincial Park

Long Beach Unit (p156), Pacific Rim
National Park

FRANK CARTER

DONALD C. & PRISCILLA ALEXANDER EASTMAN.

Marble Canyon (p263), Kootenay
National Park

DONALD C. & PRISCILLA ALEXANDER EASTMAN.

Reflections in Balsam Lake,
Mt Revelstoke National Park (p234)

MICHAEL LAANELA

View of **Meares Island** (p159) in Clayoquot Sound, Vancouver Island

DOUG MCKINLAY

Ice formations, **Joffre Lakes Provincial Park** (p113)

Bear sculpture, **Grouse Mountain Resort** (p93), Vancouver

PRAMOD MI

MICHAEL LAANELA

Graham Island (p329), Queen Charlotte Islands

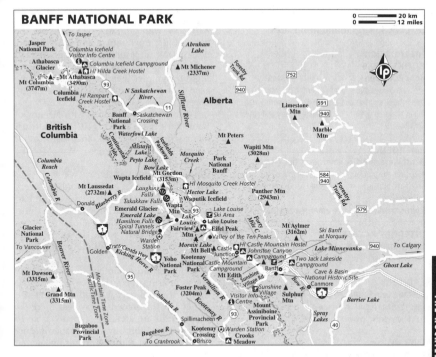

BANFF NATIONAL PARK

History

Born because of the CPR company's dream to build a health spa town in the middle of the park, Banff was destined to draw tourists from its beginnings in the 1880s. The growth happened quickly. Wealthy, well-traveled Victorian adventurers flowed into the park on the CPR trains, ready to relax in the rejuvenating hot springs or hire one of the many outfitters to take them up the mountains. In 1912 the decision to allow cars in Banff opened up the area to auto travelers. Soon, people other than rich Victorians wanted to check out the scene, and the town began pushing its boundaries. The south side of the river, with the Banff Springs Hotel, catered to the wealthy crowd. The north side of the river, however, resembled more of a prairie town, with small lots zoned in a grid system. This class-distinctive boundary is still evident today.

Banff continues to face conflicts over its growth. Many people complain that the townsite is too crowded and argue that it should build more hotels and streets to accommodate all the camera-clicking tourists. But at what size does Banff start losing its charm? It's a classic conundrum faced by desirable places the world over. But without protective measures from the government, Banff could become a sprawling city. With Banff's popularity continuing to grow, the debate will only intensify. Meanwhile the strains are evident in the charming town center where small buildings are slowly being replaced by enclosed low-rise malls filled with a full complement of shops such as the Body Shop, Gap and Starbucks.

Orientation

Banff Ave, the main street, runs north–south through the whole length of town, then heads northeast to meet the Trans-Canada Hwy.

South of town past the Bow River Bridge, Mountain Ave leads south to Sulphur Mountain and the hot springs, while Spray Ave leads east to the Banff Springs Hotel, the townsite's most famous landmark. To the west, Cave Ave goes to the Cave & Basin

THE ROCKIES

National Historic Site, which contains the first hot springs found in the area.

Information

BOOKSTORES

Book & Art Den (☎ 403-762-3919; 94 Banff Ave; ☺ 9am-9pm summer, 9am-7pm winter) Features comfortable quarters and a good selection, with a wall full of books on the area's mountains, history and outdoor activities.

EMERGENCY

Banff Warden Office emergency line (☎ 403-762-4506) For any problems in the backcountry, be it hiking accidents, avalanche scares, missing persons or grizzly sightings.
Police, medical and fire emergencies (☎ 911)

INTERNET ACCESS

Underground (☎ 403-760-8776; 211 Banff Ave; ☺ 9am-midnight) In the Park Ave Mall.

LAUNDRY

Cascade Coin Laundry (☎ 403-762-3444; 317 Banff Ave; ☺ 8am-10pm) On the lower level of Cascade Plaza, has a good public posting board.

LIBRARY

Banff Public Library (☎ 403-762-2661; 101 Bear St; ☺ 10am-8pm Mon-Thu, 10-6pm Fri, 11am-6pm Sat, 1-5pm Sun Oct-Apr) Internet access for email $1 per 15 minutes; reserve in advance.

MEDICAL SERVICES

Mineral Springs Hospital (☎ 403-762-2222; 301 Lynx St; ☺ 24hr) Treats 15,000 emergency patients each year.

MONEY

Freya's Currency Exchange (☎ 403-762-4652; 110 Banff Ave; ☺ 9am-8pm summer, 9am-6pm winter) In the Clock Tower Village Mall.

POST

Main post office (☎ 403-762-2586; 204 Buffalo St; ☺ 9am-5:30pm Mon-Fri)

TOURIST INFORMATION

Parks Canada (☎ 403-762-1550; www.parkscanada .pch.gc.ca) and the **Banff/Lake Louise Tourism Bureau** (☎ 403-762-8421; www.banfflakelouise.com) both maintain counters inside the historic **Visitor Info Centre** (224 Banff Ave; ☺ 8am-8pm summer, 9am-5pm winter). Before doing any hiking, check in here; Parks Canada publishes a detailed map, and the staff will tell you about

specific trail conditions and hazards. Anybody who's hiking overnight in the backcountry must sign in and buy a wilderness permit. Free naturalist programs and guided hikes take place regularly and each night in summer there is a lecture on some aspect of the area. There's even a handy drop box to pay your parking tickets.

To stay up-to-date, tune into Friends of Banff Park radio station (101.1FM), which has park news, specials and many other fascinating features.

Dangers & Annoyances

The police are strict in Banff, and it is a very bad idea to drive after a night at the bar; not only are you putting yourself and others at risk, but after 1am police often check cars for drunk drivers and drugs. The fines are heavy. Less severe but more prolific are parking tickets.

As for all those photogenic elk you may see wandering the streets, remember that they're wild animals and will charge at you if they feel threatened. Every year there are people who are attacked. It's advisable to stay at least 100m away, particularly during the autumn rutting and spring calving seasons.

Sights

The stretch of Banff Ave between Wolf and Buffalo Sts is lined with hotels, stores,

---

THE ULTIMATE MOUNTAIN MAN

Entering Banff, you'll see the town's signs adorned with the image of a rugged-looking man. It's Bill Peyto, a legendary character who explored much of the wilderness around Banff after his arrival from England in 1886. His exploits in the high peaks were matched by his high-jinks around town: his cabin featured a set bear-trap to thwart burglars; he brought a wild lynx into a bar and then sat back with a drink while chaos reigned; and so on. Generally regarded as the hardiest of the hardy breed that first settled high in the Rockies, he died in 1943 at age 75. In his honor, one of the region's most beautiful lakes is named for him. So, perhaps most appropriately, is a bar in Banff – Wild Bill's Legendary Saloon.

restaurants and gift shops, many of which cater to the large Japanese tourist trade. Toward the south end of Banff Ave is **Central Park**, where you can stroll along the mellow Bow River. Still further south across the Bow River Bridge is the **Park Administration Building**, a good place for a view and a photo of the town. Behind the building, **Cascade Gardens** burst with flowers. A stream, ponds and a few benches dot the gardens. In summer the Siksiki Nation erects a **tepee** with displays of traditional culture and dance exhibitions.

BANFF PARK MUSEUM

The **park museum** (☎ 403-762-1558; 93 Banff Ave; adult/child $4/3; ☺ 10am-6pm summer, 1-5pm winter), near the Bow River Bridge at the southern end of town, sits in an old wooden building, built by the CPR in 1903 before Banff had electricity. Before trails first led curious wildlife watchers into the bush, the museum also housed a zoo and aviary, so Victorian visitors to Banff could catch a safe glimpse of the park's wildlife. The museum, declared a National Historic Site, contains a collection of animals, birds and plants found in Banff National Park, including two small stuffed grizzlies and a black bear, plus a tree carved with graffiti dating back to 1841. A visit here is just like stepping back to 1914.

WHYTE MUSEUM OF THE CANADIAN ROCKIES

The **Whyte Museum complex** (☎ 403-762-2291; 111 Bear St; adult/child $6/3.50; ☺ 10am-5pm) features an art gallery and a vast collection of photographs telling the history of early explorers, artists and the Canadian Pacific Railway. The archives also contain manuscripts, oral history tapes and maps. On the property are four log cabins and two Banff heritage homes, one dating from 1907 and the other from 1931. The museum conducts tours of the complex and walking tours of the town year-round; check for details.

BUFFALO NATIONS LUXTON MUSEUM

This **museum** (☎ 403-762-2388; 1 Birch Ave; adult/child $6/4; ☺ 10am-7pm summer, 1-5pm winter) is in the fort-like wooden building to the right as you head south over the bridge. Worth your visit, it mainly explores the history of

---

AUTHOR'S CHOICE

Since it was completed in the 1920s, the **Fairmont Banff Springs Hotel** (☎ 403-762-2211; 405 Spray Ave; public areas free), an 800-room baronial palace 2km south of downtown, has posed for thousands of postcards and millions of snapshots. The spectacular design includes towers, turrets and cornices, giving the impression that the hotel is full of hidden secrets. Within its thick granite walls are myriad public spaces, bars and restaurants. At any given time, a dozen or more restaurants and bars inside the hotel are busily serving guests. Even if you're not staying here, it's a fascinating place to wander around. Mt Stephen Hall is a grand space with views. Have a seat and soak it in. FYI: all locals drop the Fairmont from the name, considering the chain a mere interloper.

---

the Native Indians of the Northern Plains and the Rockies but also covers indigenous groups from all over Alberta. Through life-size displays, models and re-creations, it depicts traditions such as buffalo hunts. Note the woven porcupine quills, the old photographs and the human scalp.

CANADIAN SKI MUSEUM WEST

Under the guise of a shopping mall, this **museum** (☎ 403-762-8484; 317 Banff Ave; admission free; ☺ 7am-11pm) in the Cascade Plaza chronicles Banff's ski history through bronze statues of skiers and panels describing the evolution of the sport and its growth in Banff. As you wander amid the boutique stores, you can learn about everyone from the charming Swiss guide Bruno Engler to modern national ski greats like Ken Read and Karen Percy.

BANFF GONDOLA

In less than 10 minutes, the **Banff Gondola** (☎ 403-762-2523; adult/child $21.50/10.75; ☺ approximately 10am-dusk) – formerly and still commonly known as the 'Sulphur Mountain Gondola', which makes one wonder if it had been called, say, the Lavender Mountain Gondola would they have renamed it? – lofts you up to the 2285m summit for spectacular views over the surrounding mountains, Bow River and Banff townsite. You can hike up

THE ROCKIES

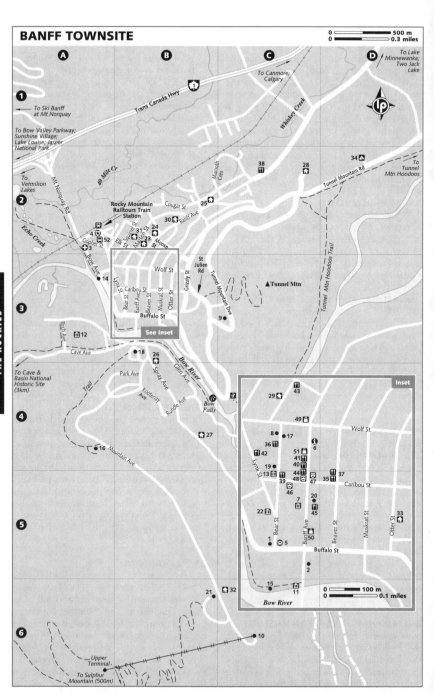

BANFF TOWNSITE

the steep east side of the mountain in about two hours one-way. You will be aptly rewarded with great views and a free lift down; tickets are only needed going up. The trail starts from the Upper Hot Springs parking lot. Or just hike down.

The lower terminal is just over 3km south of Banff on Mountain Ave; it's adjacent to the Upper Hot Springs pool. A cab ride costs about $12.

LAKE MINNEWANKA
The largest reservoir in the national park, Lake Minnewanka is 11km east of the Banff townsite. Forests and mountains surround this scenic recreational area, which features plenty of hiking, swimming, sailing, boating and fishing opportunities.

Lake Minnewanka Boat Tours (☎ 403-762-3473; adult/child $30/13; ☎ mid-May–Sep) offers 90-minute cruises on the lake to **Devil's Gap**. To get to the lake from the townsite, take Banff Ave east over the Trans-Canada Hwy to Minnewanka Rd and turn right.

CAVE & BASIN NATIONAL HISTORIC SITE
This is the birthplace of Banff. The discovery of hot sulfur springs in a cave here led to the creation of Banff National Park. The **complex** (☎ 403-762-1557; adult/child $4/3; ☎ 9am-6pm summer, 11am-4pm Mon-Fri, 9:30am-5pm weekends), southwest of town at the end of Cave Ave, has been rebuilt in the original style of 1914, but you're not allowed to bathe at the site. Visitors can see (and smell) the cave and sulfurous waters, as well as view exhibits

and a 30-minute film. The **Middle Springs** further down the hill are closed to visits to protect their delicate waters.

You can stroll around the attractive grounds, where you'll see both natural and artificially made pools, for no charge. It's a good place for picnics, as there are tables, a fine view and a snack bar. Several pleasant **short walks** begin here: the 400m Discovery Trail, the 2.7km Marsh Loop and the 3.7km Sundance Trail.

UPPER HOT SPRINGS
You'll find a soothing hot pool and steam room at the **Upper Hot Springs spa** (☎ 403-762-1515; adult/child $7.50/6.50; ☎ 9am-11pm, 10am-10pm winter), 3km south of town on Mountain Ave. Besides soaking in the balmy pool (where water temperatures average 40°C), you can also indulge in a massage or aromatherapy treatment. Admission to the pool is $7/6 for adults/students. You can rent bathing suits ($2), lovely sulfur-colored towels ($2) and lockers ($1). Note the heated floors in the changing rooms.

OTHER MUSEUMS & GALLERIES
Banff has a thriving arts community thanks to the twin influences of (a) money and (b) lots of resident artists.

Banff Centre (☎ 403-762-6300; www.banffcentre.ca; 107 Tunnel Mountain Dr) Off St Julien Rd east of downtown, the center contains one of Canada's best-known art schools, complete with facilities for dance, theater, music and the visual arts. Exhibits, concerts and various

THE ROCKIES

other events take place regularly. During the Festival of the Arts, which happens throughout the summer, students and internationally recognized artists present pieces in workshops and performances. The **Walter Phillips Gallery** (admission free; noon-5pm Tue-Sat, noon-9pm Thu) shows changing displays of contemporary art that are at times thought-provoking.

AURAStudio Gallery (403-760-6102; 111 Banff Ave; 11am-8pm) An eclectic gallery, it features the works of painter Jan Kabatoff and sculptor Buck Vander Kooi among others. The group of artists who run the studio focus on interpreting nature.

Canada House Gallery (403-762-3757; cnr Caribou & Bear Sts; 9am-7pm) This is a large private gallery that only sells work by Canadian artists and those from the Rockies in particular.

Activities

HIKING

You'll find many good short hikes and day walks around the Banff area. Parks Canada publishes an excellent brochure, *Day Hikes in Banff National Park*, outlining hikes accessible from the townsite. For longer, more remote hiking, pick up the helpful brochure *Backcountry Visitors' Guide*, which contains a simple map showing trails throughout the whole park.

You can take a pleasant, quiet stroll by **Bow River**, just three blocks west of Banff Ave beside Bow Ave. The trail runs from the corner of Wolf St along the river under the Bow River Bridge and ends shortly after on Buffalo St. If you cross the bridge, you can continue southwest through the woods along a trail to nearby **Bow Falls**.

For a good short climb to break in your legs and to view the area, walk up stubby **Tunnel Mountain**, east of downtown. A trail leads up from St Julien Rd; you can drive here, but it's not a long walk from downtown to the start of the path. From the southern end of Buffalo St, a short interpretive trail between Bow River and Tunnel Mountain heads north and east toward the **Tunnel Mountain Hoodoos**. The term 'hoodoo' refers to the distinctive vertical pillar shapes carved into the rock face by rainfall and glacial erosion.

Just west of downtown, off Mt Norquay Rd, is the 2km **Fenland Trail** loop, which goes through marsh and forest and connects the town with First Vermilion Lake.

Some excellent hiking trails meander off the Bow Valley Parkway (Hwy 1A), northwest of Banff. The Parkway branches off from, but finally rejoins, the Trans-Canada Hwy en route to Lake Louise. Pick up the Parks Canada brochure for details on specific trails.

CANOEING

You can go canoeing on **Lake Minnewanka** and nearby **Two Jack Lake**, northeast of Banff. The **Vermilion Lakes**, three shallow lakes connected by narrow waterways, attract lots of wildlife and make excellent spots for canoeing. To get to the lakes, head northwest out of town along Lynx St and follow signs toward Hwy 1. Just before the highway, turn left onto Vermilion Lakes Dr, and you'll soon come to small parking areas for the lakes.

In town your best bet is the Bow River. **Bow River Canoe Rentals** (403-762-3632; $16/hr, $40/day; 10:30am-6pm) rents out canoes from the prosaically named Canoe Dock, on the corner of Bow Ave and Wolf St near the river.

CYCLING

You can cycle on the highways and on some of the trails in the park. Excursions of all varieties are possible, whether you're looking to ride for a few hours, a day or several days with overnight stops at campgrounds, hostels or lodges. Two good, short cycling routes close to Banff run along **Vermilion Lakes Drive** and **Tunnel Mountain Drive**. For a longer trip, try the popular and scenic 24km **Bow Valley Parkway**, which connects Banff and Lake Louise.

Ski Stop (403-760-1650; www.theskistop.com; 203A Bear St; one-day bike rentals $25-35; 9am-9pm summer, 7:30am-9pm winter) runs popular and good mountain-biking trips that cost from $20 to $70. There is a second location in the Fairmont Banff Springs Hotel. Numerous other companies around town provide similar services at the same hours including **Bactrax** (403-762-8177; www.snowtips-bactrax.com; 225 Bear St; 8am-8pm summer, 7am-9pm winter).

Parks Canada publishes a brochure, *Mountain Biking and Cycling Guide Banff National Park*, that describes trails and regulations.

HORSEBACK RIDING

Horseback riding is a great way to explore the area. In Banff the most popular routes lie south of Bow River. **Holidays on Horseback** (☎ 403-762-4551; www.horseback.com), which operates out of the **Trail Riders Store** (132 Banff Ave; 9am-9pm), offers a variety of horse-riding trips on trails around town, which include an hour-long ride along Spray River ($29), a three-hour Bow Valley Loop ($58) and a full-day ride up Sulphur Mountain with a down-home barbecue ($115).

ROCK CLIMBING

Banff's rocky crags and limestone peaks present almost endless opportunities for good climbing. In fact many of the world's best climbers live in nearby Canmore so that they can enjoy easy access to this mountain playground. This is not terrain for unguided novice climbers; even experienced climbers wanting to go it alone should first talk to locals, read books and get the weather lowdown before venturing out.

Inexperienced climbers will find quite a few companies offering climbing courses and organized tours into the mountains. **Mountain Magic** (☎ 403-762-2591; www.mountainmagic.com; 224 Bear St; 9am-9pm) has an indoor climbing wall and a staff ready to share local expertise. **Banff Adventure Centre** (☎ 403-762-8536, 800-760-8539; www.mountainguide.com) offers lessons and guided climbs including a half-day rock climb ($69).

SKIING & SNOWBOARDING

Three excellent mountain resorts with spectacular scenery are accessible from Banff; together they offer 227 trails.

Ski Banff at Norquay (☎ 403-522-3555, 800-258-7669; www.banffnorquay.com; one-day lift pass adult/child $49/16) Just 10 minutes from downtown Banff on Mt Norquay Rd is the area's oldest resort. It has 77 hectares of skiable area and a drop of 503m.

Sunshine Village (☎ 403-762-6500, 877-542-2633; www.skibanff.com; one-day lift pass adult/child $64/21.50) Sunshine is 22km southwest of Banff. It has a drop of 1070m and 1282 hectares of skiable runs.

Lake Louise Ski Area (☎ 403-522-3555, 800-258-7669; www.skilouise.com; one-day lift pass adult/child $58/19) Near the Samson Mall, this ranks among Canada's largest ski areas, boasting a 1000m

drop and 28.5 sq km of terrain spread over four mountain faces.

At each resort you can purchase a variety of passes good at all three (check out www.skibig3.com). These start at adult/child $168/60 for a three-day pass.

Numerous stores in Banff and the various ski resorts rent equipment. One of the better is **Ski Stop** (☎ 403-760-1650; www.theskistop.com; 203A Bear St; one-day ski package rentals $25-49; 7:30am-9pm winter).

HELI-SKIING

Canadian Mountain Holidays (CMH; ☎ 403-762-7100, 800-661-0252; www.cmhski.com) specializes in four- to 10-day heli-skiing trips to some of the best and most remote regions in the western mountain ranges. These superb trips cost around $6000 for one week.

Quirky Banff
CANADA PLACE

This odd **museum** (☎ 403-760-1338; Park Administration Building, 1 Cave Ave; admission free; 10am-6pm summer, 1-4pm winter) almost seems like a response to *South Park* and their 'Blame Canada' song, but this high-concept,

---

BEST BETS FOR KIDS

Banff is a good place for kids. There's all the fun outdoors, lots of things to do and plenty of fun shops to run into. Banff Ave alone holds great allure in its many ice-cream and candy stores.

Above everything else, the Gondola (p267) scores high on the fun-meter. Also in the running is the Buffalo Nations Luxton Museum (p267) with its many displays about its big, hairy namesake buffalo. Then there are the silly exhibits in Canada Place (above).

The VIC (p266) can help with various short hikes aimed at kids, and in winter the area's three ski resorts each have programs aimed at kids – from special ski schools to fun groups where kids dine together and you dine, well, not with them.

And if they've been really good, guide their Banff Ave culinary adventures to **Welch's Chocolate Shop** (☎ 403-762-3737; 126 Banff Ave; 9am-10pm). It's a local favorite where you can run amok among oodles of treats.

government-sponsored attraction touts the nation's history, people, culture, maple syrup and more through a series of interactive and at times goofy exhibits. Keep your eyes peeled for the hidden beaver.

NATURAL HISTORY MUSEUM

This crammed, private **museum** (☎ 403-762-4652; 110 Banff Ave, 2nd fl Clock Tower Village Mall; admission free; ☻ 11am-7pm summer, variable other times) features displays on the geological history of the area, from the formation of hoodoos to the telling tales of fossils. Another exhibit includes a model of Sasquatch, the elusive, abominable snowman of the Rockies and other places in need of tourist icons. This character is said to be about 3m tall and to have been sighted upwards of 500 times. Of course, many of those who claim sightings also claim to have been abducted by aliens.

Tours

WALKING

There are several excellent walking tours of Banff and its environs offered by various organizations.

The **Whyte Museum** (☎ 403-762-2291; 111 Bear St) in summer offers daily guided walks and tours of Historic Banff ($7) and Heritage Homes ($7).

The **Friends of Banff** (☎ 403-762-8911; donations; ☻ 10am Tue-Sat summer) offers a walk at Vermilion Lakes that focuses on the area's wildlife. Call for details.

BUS

Something of a legend in the Banff area, **Brewster** (☎ 403-762-6767, 877-791-5500; www.brewster.ca) began helping develop tourism in the area over 100 years ago. It offers a three-hour **Discover Banff tour** (adult/child $43/21.50). The bus goes to the Hoodoos, Tunnel Mountain Drive, Sulphur Mountain and Cave & Basin National Historic Site. Brewster also runs tours to Lake Louise ($55/27.50), a return trip to the Columbia Icefield ($95/47.50), a one-way trip to Jasper ($95/47.50) that stops at the ice field and many other trips. The tours depart from the **Banff Bus Station** (☎ 403-762-1092; 100 Gopher St) and various hotels.

Bigfoot Adventure Tours (☎ 888-244-6673; www.bigfoottours.com; $95) offers a fun, two-day trip from Banff to Jasper and back that's aimed at travelers in their twenties. It includes just about every sight between the two towns.

Festivals & Events

Banff/Lake Louise Winter Festival (☎ 403-762-8421) Annual town-wide party held in late January since 1919 with much mirth and merriment.

Banff Mountain Film & Book Festival (☎ 403-762-0270; www.banffmountainfestivals.ca) International stories and movies about mountain adventure are honored in early November.

Sleeping

Accommodations are varied; from the storied heights – literally – at the Fairmont Banff Springs Hotel to the humble pleasures of a hostel, there is something for every taste and budget. The one caveat is that if you turn up on a summer weekend without something already arranged you may end up enjoying the recline function of your car's seats. In fact for a little street theater, drop by the VIC on a summer Friday evening to see the hordes groveling for anything they can get. If you're truly stuck this is the place to go as the staff track vacancies across the area.

The rates listed below are for the peak summer season. Travelers in spring and fall will find bargains (not crowds) everywhere. There are modest spikes in rates during the ski season coinciding with holidays.

MOTELS & HOTELS

About 20 places line Banff Ave north of Elk St; generally fairly large, they cater to tour groups and entice visitors with numerous perks like saunas and hot tubs. Many places are geared toward skiers and boarders, offering rooms with multiple beds and kitchens.

Fairmont Banff Springs Hotel (☎ 403-762-2211, 800-441-1414; www.fairmont.com; 405 Spray Ave; r $400-1000; P ✖ ☐ ☒) This is the hotel everyone wants to stay at and it's the place that helped put Banff on the map. The architecture itself is artful and the hotel's location overlooking the Bow Valley is stunning. This is not your anonymous Marriott either; rather as you wander the floors you get a sense of history and the feeling that you are actually someplace special as opposed to just expensive. Guests of the 770 rooms have access to a lavish spa, pools, a golf course and that rarely found resort amenity, a bowling alley. In winter there is an ice-skating rink. Restaurants, cafés and bars – as many as 18 depending on the season – span the gamut of tastes. Rooms come in all shapes and sizes; feel free to ask to see a few before you decide. Although the rack rates are high, frequent specials bring the cost under $300 per night with extras like meals and parking included.

Banff Traveller's Inn (☎ 403-762-4401, 800-661-0227; www.bannftravellersinn.com; 401 Banff Ave; r from $180; P ❄ 🖵) This is a very good motel right near the center of town. The rooms come with large balconies; other amenities include a large outdoor hot tub and heated underground parking.

Banff Ptarmigan Inn (☎ 403-762-2207, 800-661-8310; www.bestofbanff.com; 337 Banff Ave; r from $220; P ❄ 🖵) Post and beam construction sets off this otherwise modern and comfortable inn with large rooms, balconies, a hot tub and a popular restaurant (p274), Caramba!

Rimrock Resort Hotel (☎ 403-762-3356, 800-661-1587; www.rimrockresort.com; Mountain Rd; r from $280; P ❄ 🖵 🐾) If you tire of the indoor pool you can hop over to the adjacent Upper Hot Springs at this very attractive property 4km outside of town. This large resort offers a free shuttle to town, excellent mountain views and large, luxurious rooms with a long list of amenities including balconies.

Banff Voyager Inn (☎ 403-762-3301, 800-879-1991; www.banffvoyagerinn.com; 555 Banff Ave; r from $120; P ❄ 🐾) This basic motel shares its contact information and its amenities with the adjacent **Spruce Grove Motel** (545 Banff Ave; r from $150). At both you can enjoy the outdoor pool, indoor hot tub and prices that are pretty good for the location.

Irwin's Mountain Inn (☎ 403-762-4566, 800-661-1721; www.irwinsmountaininn.com; 429 Banff Ave; r from $125; P ❄ 🖵) Irwin offers covered parking and a hot tub, sauna and high-speed Internet. The location and amenities, such as a coin laundry are handy.

B&BS & TOURIST HOMES

The Banff/Lake Louise Tourism Bureau has an online guide (www.banfflakelouise .com) to over 60 of the area's B&Bs and tourist homes. Most B&Bs provide private rooms and full breakfasts, while tourist homes – basically B&Bs without the breakfast – offer rooms in houses or small separate cabins.

The prices for B&Bs and tourist homes depend on size, facilities, duration of stay and season, but they generally range from $55 to $100 for a single or double, though rates can creep higher in July and August. Call around before landing on a doorstep, because some places prefer to rent weekly and others will turn you away if you've, say, got a keg in tow.

For a good deal and a quiet time, try **Tan-Y-Bryn** (☎ 403-762-3696; www.tan-y-bryn.zip411.net; 118 Otter St; r $40-75; P), which has been housing tourists since 1926. The clean rooms lack TVs or bathrooms but you do get a continental breakfast in bed.

You'll find several tourist homes on Marten St. **Holiday Lodge** (☎ 403-762-3648; www .banffholidaylodge.com; 311 Marten St; r $65; P) is in a historic house. The antique-furnished rooms have bathrooms and TV/VCRs. **Mountain Country B&B** (☎ 403-762-3282; www.banff mountaincountry.com; 427 Marten St; r $100-130; P) is in a barn-like cedar building close to town. It has private decks for guests, spa tubs and TV/VCRs.

HOSTELS

HI Banff Alpine Centre (☎ 403-670-7580, 866-762-4122; www.hihostels.ca; 801 Coyote Dr; dm member/non-member $27.50/31.50, r $79/89; P 🖵) This large facility, off Tunnel Mountain Rd, consistently scores among the top HI hostels worldwide. There's a café, patios and decks, fireplaces and more. Numerous activity packages are available summer and winter.

Banff Y Mountain Lodge (☎ 403-762-3560; www.ymountainlodge.com; 102 Spray Ave; dm summer/winter $28/26, r $59/43) This lodge makes a great alternative to the hostel, especially given its central location. It accommodates both men and women in its 117 dorm beds and 45 private rooms. The facilities include a café and common cooking area.

HI Castle Mountain Hostel (dm member/non-member $19/23) On the Bow Valley Parkway, this rustic hostel holds up to 36 people and includes pit toilets and volleyball courts. For information, contact the HI Banff Alpine Centre.

CAMPING

Banff National Park contains 13 campgrounds, most of which lie right around

THE ROCKIES

the town or along the Bow Valley Parkway. Most are only open between May or June and September. They are all busy in July and August, and availability is on a first-come, first-served basis, so check in by noon or you may be turned away. Campgrounds with showers always fill up first.

Tunnel Mountain Campground (tent sites $22) On Tunnel Mountain Rd, this campground actually includes three separate campgrounds: two primarily cater to RVs needing electrical hookups and one, Village 1, accommodates only tents, with a whopping 618 tenting sites. Close to town, Tunnel Mountain has flush toilets and showers. Elk freely roam, and at night you may hear coyotes howling.

At Two Jack Lake there are two campgrounds. **Two Jack Lakeside Campground** (sites $22), 12km northeast of Banff on Lake Minnewanka Rd, offers 74 sites and showers; it's open from mid-May to mid-September. About 1km north, **Two Jack Main Campground** (sites $17) features 380 sites and flush toilets but no showers.

Johnston Canyon Campground (sites $22), about 26km along the Bow Valley Parkway west of Banff, is wooded and fairly secluded with flush toilets and showers. The **Castle Mountain Campground** (sites $17), 2km north of Castle Junction on the Bow Valley Parkway, is a smaller campground without showers.

Eating

Like any resort town, Banff has plenty of restaurants. However, there are those that cater only to tourists who aren't likely to return, and there are those sought out even by discriminating locals. We've listed the latter here.

RESTAURANTS

Bumper's Beef House (☎ 403-762-2622; 603 Banff Ave; meals $25-35; ☯ dinner) Though Bumper's is north of downtown, it remains a local institution. Prime rib in several sizes is the specialty, aged 21 days by the restaurant. Don't like beef? Well there is the lone fish on the menu, although everyone will enjoy the large salad bar.

Banffshire Club (☎ 403-762-6369; Fairmont Banff Springs Hotel, 405 Spray Ave; meals $70-150; ☯ dinner Tue-Sat) From the 600 different vintages on the wine list to the superb service, this is *the* fine-dining experience in Banff. Ever-changing menus from chef Daniel Buss focus on Canadian ingredients. The results are light, interesting and fresh dishes. Perhaps the best way to enjoy them is with the *degustation* menu. Whatever you enjoy, do it properly clothed; there is a dress code.

Grizzly House (☎ 403-762-4055; 207 Banff Ave; meals $15-30; ☯ 11:30am-late) The romantic atmosphere, with dark lighting and secluded booths, also feels a bit like the inside of a tree. The menu centers on fondue, and you and your partner can dip away to your heart's content. Adventurous eaters can cook up exotics like buffalo and caribou meat, although the bread is just fine. There's a good patio out front as well.

Coyote's Deli & Grill (☎ 403-762-3963; 206 Caribou St; meals $6-25; ☯ breakfast, lunch & dinner) The open kitchen here gives you a chance to see the chefs in action. For a front-row seat, hop up on a chair at the counter. The hip and lively setting is as refreshing as the Southwestern menu. The breakfasts are a cut above the average.

Caramba! (☎ 403-762-3667; 337 Banff Ave; meals $17-26; ☯ breakfast, lunch & dinner) Dinner is the main event here when the kitchen gets to flex its Mediterranean muscles. Enjoy the curry chicken and chorizo pasta out on the patio. Or you might have the penne with smoked duck. Or...

Melissa's Restaurant (☎ 403-762-5511; 217 Lynx St; meals $8-22) The 1928 log building looks like a wooden cabin inside and an English cottage outside, which is just one of the many reasons it's popular with kids (the kids' menu filled with faves is another reason). It offers breakfast, lunch and dinner and the menu (filled with adult faves as well) includes pizza, burgers, steaks and seafood. The huge breakfasts are popular; enjoy them on the patio. The bar has frequent specials.

Silver Dragon (☎ 403-762-3939; 3rd fl, 211 Banff Ave; meals $10-15; ☯ lunch & dinner) Another place that gets good reviews from local parents; kids and adults both like the food and between courses there's always the diversion of the killer views out the windows. Kids enjoy watching the crabs in the crab tank. You decide if they're old enough to know how they get to crab heaven.

CAFÉS
Evelyn's Coffee Bar (☎ 403-762-0352; 201 Banff Ave, Town Centre Mall; muffin $2; ☷ 7am-11pm) The best local coffee place, Evelyn's serves good sandwiches and excellent baked goods like healthy muffins made on the premises. It's a local gathering place.

Sunfood Cafe (☎ 403-760-3933; 2nd fl, 215 Banff Ave; meals $7-15; ☷ lunch & dinner) This is Banff's best choice for vegetarians who don't want to morosely ponder a menu with only one offering for them. The selection at this casual place in the Sundance Mall teams with interesting and tasty veggie offerings like the fine avocado and cheese sandwich.

QUICK BITES
Bruno's Café & Grill (☎ 403-762-8115; 304 Caribou St; meals $5-10; ☷ 8am-5pm) offers good salads, burgers and all-day breakfast. Enter on Beaver St. Next door in the same building, a mini-train chugs around the sushi counter at **Sushi House Banff** (☎ 403-762-4353; meals $6-12; ☷ lunch) and you take your pick from its cargo. You never know what you'll find in the caboose.

Aardvark Pizza & Sub (☎ 403-762-5500; 304A Caribou St; meals $4-12; ☷ 11am-4am) You'll find the best pizza and subs in town here. This is the place to go when the bars close and you've got the munchies.

Barpa Bill's (☎ 403-762-0377; 223 Bear St; meals $5; ☷ 11am-9pm) Tantalizing smells emanate from this small and simple purveyor of grilled souvlaki on pita.

SELF-CATERING
You can pick up some prepared deli foods and other picnic fixings at the biggest supermarket, **Safeway** (☎ 403-723-3929; 318 Marten St; ☷ 24hr), just off Banff Ave.

Entertainment
Banff is the social and cultural center of the Rockies. You can find current entertainment listings in the 'Summit Up' section of the weekly *Banff Crag & Canyon* newspaper.

PUBS
Nightlife in Banff easily goes past midnight in the peak seasons.

Wild Bill's Legendary Saloon (☎ 403-762-0333; 2nd fl, 201 Banff Ave) Dedicated to the memory of legendary Bill Peyto (see the boxed text, p266), Wild Bill's is, on any night, crammed with folks hoping to re-create some of its namesake's wilder exploits. Others just hoist a few from the patio and take in the view – or maybe they're looking for Peyto's ghost.

Rose & Crown (☎ 403-762-2121; 202 Banff Ave) A British-style pub with good burgers and such, the Rose & Crown is always popular. It has live rock, darts, pool and a great rooftop deck.

Pump & Tap (☎ 403-760-6610; lower level, 215 Banff Ave) When asked why it was his favorite pub, one young male hostel worker said: 'I get drunk and try to score.' His co-worker, a young woman, said: 'Oh really? I do the opposite.' The Pump & Tap is the slightly smelly pub of choice for young Banffites who like the cheap beer and overall vibe and can forget they're in the Sundance Mall.

CLUBS
Outabounds (☎ 403-762-8434; 205 Caribou St; cover $5-10) is a hot dance bar, while **Aurora Nightclub** (☎ 403-760-3343; lower level, 110 Banff Ave, Clock Tower Village Mall; cover $5-10) has the latest dance music as well as a long martini list.

Getting There & Away
It's really a crime that VIA Rail no longer serves Banff, as the tracks from Calgary to Vancouver go right through town. There is an ongoing effort to rectify this, especially as the best way to nearby Calgary is by train.

Brewster (☎ 403-762-6767; www.brewster.ca) Operates a daily express bus to/from Jasper (adult/child $57/28.50), Calgary (adult/child $42/21).

Greyhound buses (☎ 403-762-1092; 100 Gopher St) Buses operate from the spiffy Brewster terminal. Services east to Calgary and west to Vancouver.

Rocky Mountain Sky Shuttle (☎ 403-762-5200; adult/child $18/9) Runs several shuttles daily to/from Lake Louise; reserve in advance. Greyhound and Brewster also provide links.

Getting Around
TO/FROM THE AIRPORT
The **Banff Airporter** (☎ 403-762-3330, 888-449-2901; adult/child $40/20) offers frequent service to/from Calgary airport (two hours).

BUS
Banff Transit (adult/child $1/.50; ☷ 7am-midnight) offers two routes. One route follows Spray

and Banff Aves between the Fairmont Banff Springs Hotel and the RV parking lot north of town; the other goes from the Luxton Museum along Banff Ave, Wolf St, Otter St and Tunnel Mountain Rd to the HI Banff Alpine Centre and Tunnel Mountain Village Campgrounds. Service is good, every 30 minutes.

CAR
All of the major car rental companies have branches in Banff.

TAXI
Banff Taxi (☎ 403-762-4444)
Legion Taxi (☎ 403-762-3353)

LAKE LOUISE
The much-visited and stunning Lake Louise sits in a small glacial valley, surrounded by tree-covered, snow-capped mountains. Come here early in the morning, when it's less crowded, and your chances of seeing the classic reflection in the water increase. One of the Rockies' best-known and original hotels, the Fairmont Chateau Lake Louise, sits grandly at the northern end of the lake.

The lake, known as the jewel of the Rockies, lies about 57km northwest of Banff, at the conjunction of Hwys 1 and 93. Before you get to the lake, you'll reach the uninspiring village of Lake Louise, which is essentially nothing more than the Samson Mall shopping center and a service station. Though small, the convenient strip of shops can provide you with everything from postal services to groceries and liquor, from restaurant meals to hiking boots (in case you left yours at home). The town is essentially a tourist attraction; few permanent residents actually live here except for those who staff the hotels.

The lake, named for Queen Victoria's daughter Louise (neither of whom ever came to the lake), is 5km uphill from the village. If you're walking, it takes about 45 minutes on the footpath.

At 1731m above sea level, Lake Louise is high enough to escape the arctic air but still averages a chilly 4°C.

Information
Parks Canada and the Banff/Lake Louise Tourism Bureau offer information at the

Visitor Info Centre (☎ 403-522-3833; 🕐 8am-7pm summer, 9am-5pm winter) beside the Samson Mall in the village; the center also features a good exhibition on the geological and natural history of the Rocky Mountains.

Woodruff & Blum (☎ 403-522-3842; Samson Mall; 🕐 9am-10pm summer, 9am-8pm winter) carries general guides and maps to the Canadian Rockies; very helpful.

Sights
Obviously you need to go and see **Lake Louise**. The vast parking lot is a five-minute drive from Hwy 1. Easy walks are 2.5km along the north side of the lake or 1.1km along the southeast side. There are no trails circling the entire lake.

Overlooking the scene, the iconic Lake Louise Chalet opened in 1890 to alleviate some of the pressure on the Banff Springs Hotel. Renamed Chateau Lake Louise in 1925 (and Fairmont Chateau Lake Louise after the upscale chain gobbled it up), the hotel features 486 rooms on eight floors, six restaurants and three lounges. Though smaller and less fabled than its Banff counterpart, it enjoys a lakeside setting just as grand. You can join the other millions of tourists who wander through the hotel every summer on their own. At certain times, **tours** (☎ 403-522-3511) are offered; check for details.

Mt Whitehorn and the Lake Louise ski area lie east of the village, 4.5km along Lake Louise Dr. In summer a **gondola** (☎ 403-522-3555; adult/child $20/10; 🕐 8:30am-6pm mid-May–Sep) takes you to the top, where you can hike the trails and enjoy views of Lake Louise and Victoria Glacier. The ticket price includes an array of programs, including guided walks and hikes, and there is an interpretive center. If you're hungry, you can pay slightly more (breakfast/lunch $2/6) for a good buffet meal at the Lodge of the Ten Peaks at the top.

Though lesser known than Lake Louise, **Moraine Lake** may be more impressive, naturally speaking. Surrounded by peaks and a deep teal in color, it is nothing less than stunning. If you get your hands on an old $20 bill (first produced in 1969), take a look at the picture on the back and you'll recognize the view of the lake. Look for an attractive lodge, gift shop and numerous trails. The lake sits in the gorgeous Valley of the

Ten Peaks 15km (mostly uphill) from the village. To get there, take Lake Louise Dr toward the Chateau, turn left on Moraine Lake Rd and follow it to the end. If you're camping, you can also take the free shuttle from the campgrounds (see below).

Activities

Lake Louise boasts 75km of **hiking** trails, many of which lead to beautiful alpine meadows that fill up with colorful wildflowers in July and August. It is common to see pikas (plump furry animals also called conies) and the larger, more timid marmots along these trails. You often hear ice rumbling on the slopes too. Note that trails may be snowbound beyond the 'normal' winter season – often there are avalanche warnings well into July. The Parks Canada booth at the Visitor Info Centre gives out excellent trail information.

Many of the hiking trails become cross-country ski trails in winter. For downhill types, Lake Louise boasts the largest **skiing** area in Canada. The resort operates in conjunction with Ski Banff at Mt Norquay and Sunshine Village. See p271 for details on all three areas.

Rock climbing on the Back of the Lake, a backwater crag, is popular, partly because it's easy to access. There are lots of different routes with interesting names like 'Wicked Gravity' and 'Chocolate Bunnies from Hell'. Other places to climb, of varying degrees of difficulty, include Fairview Mountain, Mt Bell and Eiffel Peak. But no one, not even very experienced climbers, should venture out to any of these spots without getting the full avalanche and trail conditions report from Parks Canada. For contact information, see p266.

Wilson Mountain Sports (☎ 403-522-3636; lakelouisewilsons.com; Samson Mall; ski packages $31, mountain bikes $35 per day; ☺ 9am-10pm summer, 9am-8pm winter) rents out a full range of winter sports gear as well as fairer weather gear like mountain bikes, camping equipment and climbing gear.

Sleeping

Fairmont Chateau Lake Louise (☎ 403-522-3511, 800-441-1414; www.fairmont.com; 111 Lake Louise Dr; r $400-800; [P] ⊠ 🖵 🏊) On the tip of the famous lake, this hotel features a more scenic location and a quieter, less touristy

atmosphere than its sister hotel in Banff, especially at night after the tour buses have gone. The wide assortment of rooms range from the small and comfy to the grand and very comfy; a slew of restaurants and bars beckon. Specials and off-season packages can bring the room rate way down.

Paradise Lodge & Bungalows (☎ 403-522-3595; www.paradiselodge.com; 105 Lake Louise Dr; cabins from $195; [P]) Cute cabins and a lodge with renovated and comfortable interiors make this a good choice. Kids will love the large playground.

HI Canadian Alpine Centre at Lake Louise (☎ 403-522-2200, 866-762-4122; www.hihostels.ca; dm members/non-members $23.50/27.50, r $75/85; [P] 🖵) On Village Rd north of Samson Mall, this excellent giant lodge has all the charm of a mountain chalet without requiring the big expenditure. The hostel arranges hiking trips and offers interpretive programs on summer evenings. Reserve well in advance for peak periods.

Lake Louise Campgrounds (☎ 403-522-3980; tent site $22) Parks Canada operates these two campgrounds, both on the Trans-Canada Hwy. The tenting campground, off Moraine Lake Rd, contains 220 summer-only sites while the RV campground, at the south end of Fairview Rd off Lake Louise Drive, offers 189 sites ($25) year-round. Both have flush toilets and showers.

Eating

You'll find several places to eat at all price levels in the **Fairmont Chateau Lake Louise** (see above). Options range from the formal Fairview Dining Room to the casual Poppy Brasserie to the take-out Chateau Deli.

Lake Louise Station (☎ 403-522-2386; meals $6-18; ☺ lunch & dinner) One kilometer from the Samson Mall on Sentinel Rd, here you get the chance to eat in a historic 1884 train station or on its patio. The menu is broad; the soup and sandwiches get compliments from locals.

Trailhead Fresh Foods (☎ 403-522-2006; Samson Mall; sandwiches $7; ☺ 9am-6pm) Trailhead Fresh Foods has salads, sandwiches and baked goods that are just that: fresh.

Getting There & Around

See p275 in the Banff section for transport to/from Banff, Jasper, Calgary and beyond.

The **bus terminal** (☎ 403-522-3870) is at Samson Mall; Greyhound and Brewster stop here.

ICEFIELDS PARKWAY

Opened in 1940, this 230km road (Hwy 93) that links Lake Louise with Jasper remains one of the most spectacular stretches of asphalt in Canada. The highway follows a lake-lined valley between two chains of the Eastern Main Ranges, which make up the Continental Divide. From here watershed rivers flow either eastward toward the Atlantic Ocean or westward toward the Pacific. The mountains here are the highest, craggiest and maybe the most scenic in all the Rockies. If you're on the bus, you'll see the best scenery if you sit on the left-hand side going from Lake Louise to Jasper.

The highway is in good condition, but it's slow going nonetheless. In addition to the gawking tourists (you'll be one of them), animals including goats, bighorn sheep and elk often linger beside the road or even on it. Anthropomorphizers will swear they are posing for pictures.

You can drive the route in a couple of hours, but stopping at the many viewpoints, picnic spots and sights, or hiking on one of the many trails, can require a full day or longer. You can take your time and camp along the way or stay at one of the many rustic hostels. Cycling the Icefields Parkway is so popular that often you'll see more bikes than cars on the road. Because of the terrain, it's easier to bike from Lake Louise to Jasper than vice versa.

Parks Canada publishes a worthwhile brochure, the *Icefields Parkway*, which includes a map and describes the sights along the way. Note the pictures of animals posing.

As is so often the case, the best time to see **Peyto Lake**, one of the world's most beautiful glacial lakes, is early in the morning. Further north, around **Waterfowl Lake**, moose are plentiful. Other points of interest include **Sunwapta Falls** and **Athabasca Falls**, 55km and 32km from Jasper. Both falls are worth a stop, though you may be appalled by the bonehead decision to put an ugly utility road bridge over the most scenic part of Athabasca Falls.

Athabasca Glacier

About halfway between Lake Louise and Jasper is the Athabasca Glacier, a fat tongue of the vast Columbia Icefield (see the boxed text, below), itself a big frozen river whose meltwaters feed many rivers, creeks and lakes.

The **Icefield Centre** (☎ 780-852-6288; ⌚ 9am-5pm May–mid-Sept, 9am-6pm Jun-Aug), across the highway from the glacier, contains numerous well-designed displays that explain glaciers. One of the best is a time-lapse film showing a glacier in action as it alters the ground beneath it. The Parks Canada desk offers trail details, ecology information and backcountry trek planning. In addition to the obligatory gift shop, the center has several restaurants that fully enjoy their monopoly status.

You can walk to the toe of the glacier from the visitor center, or you can save yourself from slogging across the moonscape of gravel by driving the short distance.

VANCOUVER ON ICE

The Columbia Icefield contains about 30 glaciers and reaches the epic volume of 350m thick in places. This remnant of the last Ice Age covers 325 sq km – about the size of Vancouver – on the plateau between Mt Columbia (3747m) and Mt Athabasca (3491m) off the parkway connecting Lake Louise to Jasper. This mother of rivers straddling the Continental Divide is the largest icefield in the Rockies and feeds the North Saskatchewan, Columbia, Athabasca, Mackenzie and Fraser River systems with its meltwaters. They flow to three oceans: the Pacific, the Atlantic and the Arctic.

The mountainous sides of this vast bowl of ice rise to some of the highest heights in the Rocky Mountains, with nine peaks over 3000m. One of the icefield's largest glaciers, the Athabasca, runs close to the road, although global warming means that it has been in retreat for some years. The **Icefield Centre** (☎ 780-852-6288; ⌚ 9am-5pm May–mid-Sep, 9am-6pm Jun-Aug) is the place to go for all things on ice. Although rides on the Snocoaches are popular, there's a certain purity to walking up to the huge thing and experiencing its force on your own.

WATCHING WILDLIFE

Nowhere else on earth can you observe the collection of critters found in the Canadian Rockies. Like most people, you're probably looking out for the big guys – black and grizzly bears, moose, bighorn sheep and elk – but keep your eyes and ears open and your senses in tune to the murmurings of nature. There's wildlife moving all around you, whether you can see it or not. Small animals such as pikas, martens, marmots and squirrels skitter by, while 277 species of birds nest, hunt, mate, sing and squawk in the Canadian Rockies. Frogs, snakes and salamanders slither under rocks. Give yourself a couple of hours one day and just sit and wait to see what pops out and tickles your senses. But while you're at it, keep an eye out for those big bears too. The Parks Canada info centers in Banff, Lake Louise and Jasper all sell excellent publications that will help you identify this myriad wildlife.

For an engrossing look, **Athabasca Glacier Icewalks** (☎ 800-565-7547; ☯ Jun-Sep), with a desk in the visitor center, offers a three- to four-hour **'Ice Cubed' trip** ($45; ☯ 11am, Mon-Wed, Fri & Sat) up the glacier and a five- to six-hour **'Icewalk Deluxe' trip** ($50; ☯ 11am, Thu & Sun) to various destinations in the snowfields. Bring warm clothes. Gear is provided.

You'll find it impossible to miss the hype and hard-sell for Brewster's **Snocoach ice tours** (☎ 403-762-6735, 877-423-7433; www.brewster.ca; adult/child $30/15; ☯ 9am-5pm Apr-Sep, 10am-4pm Oct). On busy days, up to 5000 people take a tour. The 90-minute trip takes you out on the ice and to vast areas of the glacier that can't be seen from the road.

Sleeping

You will find a few Parks Canada campgrounds along the way, all with pit toilets and no showers. **Columbia Icefield Campground** (sites $13; ☯ mid-May until the first snow), close to the Icefield Centre, has 33 tents-only sites with picnic tables and firewood. Also nearby is **Wilcox Creek Campground** (sites $10; ☯ Jun-Sep), with similar amenities and 46 sites. Remember, you're in glacier territory and it gets downright cold at night.

The Parkway is also lined with a good batch of rustic **HI hostels** (☎ 403-670-7580, 866-762-4122; www.hihostels.ca; dm members/non-members $19/23; ☯ Apr-Oct, other times confirm). Most lie quite close to the highway in scenic locations. Though these small spots lack showers, there's usually a 'refreshing' stream nearby. Choices include the excellent **HI Mosquito Creek Hostel**, on the Icefields Parkway about 27km north of Lake Louise; it has a fireplace, sauna and 32 beds in four cabins. Ice and rock climbers should head to the **HI Rampart Creek Hostel**, 11km north of the Saskatchewan River Crossing, with its sauna and 24 beds. The **HI Hilda Creek Hostel** has reopened after a fire in 2002.

Closer to Jasper along the Icefields Parkway are **HI Beauty Creek Hostel**, 87km south of Jasper, and **HI Athabasca Falls Hostel**, 32km south of Jasper. Both are managed by the **HI Jasper International Hostel** (☎ 780-852-3215, 877-852-0781; www.hihostels.ca; dm members/non-members $13/18; ☯ Apr-Oct, other times confirm).

The Icefield Centre contains the Brewster-run **Icefields Chalet** (☎ 780-852-6550, 877-423-7433; www.brewster.ca; r $110-200; Ⓟ), which has 32 rooms.

JASPER NATIONAL PARK

At 10,878 sq km, Jasper National Park is larger, wilder and less explored than Banff National Park but, like Banff, offers excellent hiking trails. Established later, in 1907, Jasper attracts fewer tourists than Banff, making it a quieter, more peaceful destination. Must-see sights like the **Maligne Canyon** justifiably attract crowds, but there is also the vast, little-explored land of alpine lakes, glaciers and stunning peaks north of Jasper for the more adventurous.

Unfortunately, fires in 2003 charred many areas visible from Hwy 16 east of Jasper. Parks Canada plans numerous programs to document and explain nature's recovery.

JASPER
pop 4000

Jasper, 369km southwest of Edmonton and 376km east of Prince George, is Banff townsite's northern counterpart and, in many ways, a more pleasant place. The town is smaller, with fewer things to see and do,

THE ROCKIES

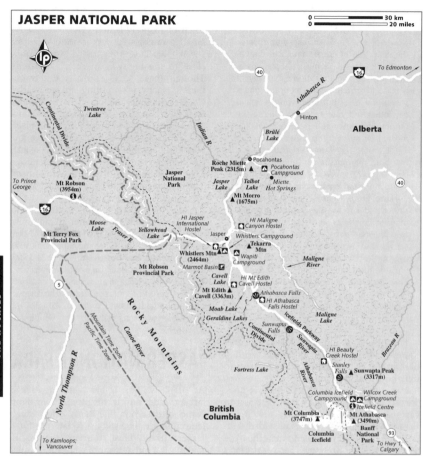

JASPER NATIONAL PARK

0 — 30 km
0 — 20 miles

To Edmonton

Hinton

Alberta

Twintree Lake

Continental Divide

Indian R.

Athabasca R.

Brûlé Lake

Roche Miette Peak (2315m) ▲

Pocahontas

Pocahontas Campground

Jasper National Park

Jasper Lake

Talbot Lake

Miette Hot Springs

To Prince George

Mt Robson (3954m)

Mt Morro (1675m) ▲

HI Jasper International Hostel

HI Maligne Canyon Hostel

Moose Lake

Yellowhead Lake

Jasper

Whistlers Campground

Fraser R.

Mt Terry Fox Provincial Park

Whistlers Mtn (2464m)

Tekarra Mtn

Wapiti Campground

Maligne River

Mt Robson Provincial Park

Marmot Basin

Cavell Lake

HI Mt Edith Cavell Hostel

Mt Edith Cavell (3363m) ▲

Athabasca Falls

HI Athabasca Falls Hostel

Maligne Lake

Moab Lake

Geraldine Lakes

Rocky Mountains

Canoe River

Mountain Time Zone

Pacific Time Zone

Sunwapta Falls

Continental Divide

Icefields Parkway

Sunwapta River

Brazeau R.

North Thompson R.

HI Beauty Creek Hostel

Fortress Lake

Stanley Falls

Athabasca River

Sunwapta Peak (3317m) ▲

Columbia Icefield Campground

Wilcox Creek Campground

British Columbia

Mt Columbia (3747m) ▲

Icefield Centre

Mt Athabasca (3490m) ▲

Columbia Icefield

Banff National Park

To Kamloops; Vancouver

To Hwy 1; Calgary

THE ROCKIES

but the quieter, less tourist-oriented streets offer a respite from the frenzy of Banff.

It's also a good connecting point. The Yellowhead Hwy (Hwy 16) and the VIA Rail line run east to Edmonton and west to Mt Robson and onto Prince George. The Icefields Parkway travels south to Lake Louise. And the town is not so small that it doesn't have its own nightlife and ample opportunities to shop and gather supplies.

Wildlife is incredibly abundant throughout Jasper National Park; you'll often see elk and black bears munching on the side of the road. In town the most visible members of the animal population are the elk, which like to hang out downtown during the autumn rutting and spring calving sea-

sons. Besides leaving millions of nut-size pellets of poop on almost every surface, they occasionally charge tourists and emit a haunting cry like that of a child in agony. Keep your distance.

History

Archeological evidence shows that First Nations people lived here as early as 12,000 years ago. It is believed that the Native Indians came here seasonally, arriving with the snowmelt to gather food, then leaving again once everything iced over. Many groups used the area, including Shuswap, Sekani and Beaver from the west, Iroquois and Stoney from the east and Cree from throughout the area.

In the early 1800s David Thompson and the North West Company established a fur-trading route into the Kootenays over Athabasca Pass. Fur traders soon intermarried with Iroquois and Cree, creating a Métis 'mixed-blood' group whose descendants shaped Jasper's history. Though the fur trade slowly died out, the steady flow of scientists and explorers did not. People were curious about the great glaciers, and soon adventurers and mountaineers were exploring the majestic peaks. In 1930 the National Parks Act was passed, fully protecting Jasper as a national park.

Orientation

The main street, Connaught Drive, has everything, including the train and bus station, banks, restaurants and souvenir shops. Outside the train station, a 21m **totem pole** carved by a Haida artist from the Queen Charlotte Islands was erected in 1920. Nearby is an old CN steam engine. Patricia St, parallel to Connaught Drive, is also parallel in terms of the services it offers. And no, it's not just you – the street numbers throughout town, when posted at all, are difficult to follow.

Off the main street, the town consists of small wooden houses, many with flower gardens befitting this alpine setting.

Information

The weekly community newspaper, the *Booster*, fully lives up to its name.

BOOKSTORES

Many of the gift stores have a few books and maps but the town really needs a good bookshop. Interested?

INTERNET ACCESS

More Than Mail (☎ 780-852-3151, 888-440-3151; 620 Connaught Sq Mall; $1 per 15min; ⊙ 9am-10pm summer, 9am-6pm winter) Also stores luggage and offers business services.

LAUNDRY

Coin-Op Laundry (☎ 780-852-3852; 607 Patricia St; ⊙ 8am-11pm) Has showers.

LIBRARY

Jasper Municipal Library (☎ 780-852-3652; 500 Robson St; ⊙ 11am-9pm Mon-Thu, 11am-5pm Fri & Sat) Small and friendly, limited Internet access.

MEDICAL SERVICES

Seton General Hospital (☎ 780-852-3344; 518 Robson St; ⊙ 24hr)

POST

Post office (☎ 780-852-3041; 502 Patricia St; ⊙ 9am-5pm Mon-Fri)

TOURIST INFORMATION

Right in the heart of town is the Parks Canada **Jasper Information Centre** (☎ 780-852-6176; www.parkscanada.ca; 500 Connaught Dr; ⊙ 9am-7pm summer, 9am-4pm winter), easily one of Canada's most eye-pleasing tourist offices. Built in 1913 as the park office and superintendent's residence, the stone building is surrounded by flowers and plants. The large lawn is a popular meeting place that's often strewn with travelers. **Jasper Tourism & Commerce** (☎ 780-852-3858; www.discoverjasper.com) operates from the same building. In addition, **Friends of Jasper National Park** (☎ 780-852-4767) have a store in the building selling a good selection of books and maps, and offering information on their various programs.

Sights & Activities

Jasper-Yellowhead Museum & Archives (☎ 780-852-3013; 400 Pyramid Lake Rd; adult/child $4/3; ⊙ 10am-9pm summer, 10am-5pm spring & fall, Thu-Sun winter) This small but classy institution provides a context to the Canadian Rockies that's missing from other exhibits. Stories of the area are presented in an engaging manner; the development of tourism shows how rich tourists 100 years ago swanned around the Rockies on the backs of laborers earning $3.50 per day. Other good exhibits cover early explorers and the story of how not one but two railroads were built through the area by investors with more cash than sense (can anyone say 'Internet bubble'?).

The busy **Jasper Tramway** (☎ 780-852-3093; adult/child $20/10; ⊙ 9am-dusk) goes up Whistlers Mountain – named for the whistling marmots that live up top – in seven minutes and offers panoramic views 75km south to the Columbia Icefield and 100km west to Mt Robson in BC. Board the tramway gondolas at the lower terminal, about 7km south of town along Whistlers Mountain Rd off the Icefields Parkway. The upper terminal sits at the lofty height of 2277m. You'll find a restaurant and hiking trails up there. From the upper terminal, it's a

JASPER TOWNSITE

0 ————— 200 m
0 ————— 0.1 miles

INFORMATION
Coin-Op Laundry......................... 1 D5
Friends of Jasper National Park..(see 2)
Jasper Information Centre........... 2 C3
Jasper Municipal Library............. 3 B3
Jasper Tourism & Commerce.....(see 2)
More Than Mail.......................... 4 D5
Police Station............................. 5 B3
Post Office................................. 6 C3
Seton General Hospital............... 7 B4

SIGHTS & ACTIVITIES   (pp281-3)
Freewheel Cycle......................... 8 C6
Gravity Gear.............................. 9 C6
Jasper Adventure Centre.........(see 29)
Jasper-Yellowhead Museum &
   Archives.............................. 10 B3
Maligne Rafting Adventures.... 11 C3
Maligne Tours.......................... 12 C6
Walks & Talks Jasper............... 13 D5

SLEEPING   (pp283-4)
Amethyst Lodge........................ 14 C2
Astoria Hotel............................ 15 C3
Athabasca Hotel....................... 16 D5
Chateau Jasper......................... 17 C1
Park Place Inn........................... 18 D6
Tonquin Inn.............................. 19 C1

EATING & DRINKING   (pp284-5)
Atha-B Pub...............................(see 16)
Bear's Paw Bakery.................... 20 C3
Caledonia Grill.......................... 21 D5
D'ed Dog Bar & Grill.............(see 15)
Fiddle River Seafood Co........... 22 D5
Jasper Pizza Place..................... 23 C3
Miss Italia Ristorante................ 24 D5
Robinson's IGA......................... 25 C3
Soft Rock Café.......................... 26 D6
Spooners Coffee Bar................. 27 D6
Villa Caruso.............................. 28 C4

ENTERTAINMENT
Chaba Theatre......................... 29 D5

TRANSPORT   (p285)
Bus Depot................................ 30 D6

To Patricia (7km) &
Pyramid Lakes (7km)

To HI Maligne Canyon Hostel
(11km); HI Pocahontas Campground;
Miette Hot Springs (61km);
Lake Annette; Lake Edith;
Fairmont Jasper Park Lodge

Pyramid Lake Rd

Juniper St

Patricia Cir

Athabasca River

Aspen Ave

Balsam Ave

Cedar Ave

Bonhomme St

Colin Cres

Pyramid Ave

Elm Ave

Turret St

Pyramid Lake Rd
Maligne Ave

Miette Ave

Patricia St

Hazel Ave

Tonquin St
Pine Ave
Turret St
Geikie St
Willow Ave
Spruce Ave

Patricia St

Connaught Dve

VIA Rail

Yellowhead Hwy

Icefields Pkwy

See Inset

THE ROCKIES

To Whistlers (3km); Wapiti
Campgrounds (5km); HI Jasper International
Hostel (6km); Jasper Tramway (7km)

Inset
Robson St
Miette Ave
Patricia St
Connaught Dve

VIA Rail
Station

Miette River

To HI-Mt Edith Gavell Hostel;
Marmot Basin (19km)

0 ————— 100 m
0 ————— 0.1 miles

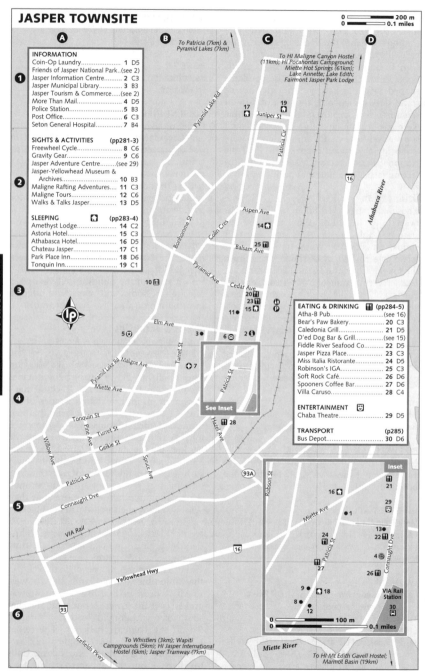

45-minute walk to the summit over the tree line, where it can be very chilly.

Lakes Annette and **Edith**, 3km northeast of town along Lodge Rd (off the Yellowhead Hwy), sit at an altitude of about 1000m and can be warm enough for a quick swim. In the wooded parks around the lakes, you'll find beaches, hiking and bike trails, picnic areas and boat rentals.

The small and relatively quiet **Patricia** and **Pyramid Lakes**, about 7km northwest of town along Pyramid Lake Rd, offer picnic sites, hiking and horse-riding trails, fishing and beaches; you can rent canoes, kayaks and windsurfers. In winter you can go cross-country skiing or ice skating. It's not uncommon to see deer, coyotes or bears nearby.

Tours

Historic walking tours of Jasper are offered by **Friends of Jasper National Park** (☎ 780-852-4767; Jasper Information Centre; $2; 7:30pm mid-May–mid-Sep). The group offers a range of other excellent tours and walks as well.

Walks & Talks Jasper (☎ 780-852-4994, 888-242-3343; booking office 614 Connaught Dr) leads small groups of people on personalized tours that include **wildlife tours** ($45; 7am Jun-Oct) and Mount Edith Cavell Meadows **picnics** ($65; 9:30am Jun-Oct).

Jasper Adventure Centre (☎ 780-852-5595; 604 Connaught Dr in the Chaba Theatre in summer, 306 Connaught Dr in winter) offers numerous walks and activities. **Nature walks** (adult/child $35/15; 7am & 6:30pm summer) offer the promise of beaver and other iconic critters.

Brewster (☎ 780-852-3332; www.brewster.ca) runs a four-hour **Discover Jasper trip** (adult/child $41/20.50; May-Oct) to some of the local sights, including Jasper Tramway, Pyramid and Patricia Lakes, and Maligne Canyon. Longer trips are also available; book at the Jasper Adventure Centre.

Sleeping

Like everything else, prices are more relaxed here than in Banff. Rates below are for the peak summer season.

MOTELS & HOTELS

Fairmont Jasper Park Lodge (☎ 780-852-3301, 800-441-1414; www.fairmont.com; r $450-750; P) Close to town except that the intervening Lac Beauvert and the Athabasca River mean it's a 5km drive northeast. The lodge has a massive stone and log cabin-style main building, and nine restaurants and bars. The resort features every possible amenity, including horseback riding and a world-class golf course. In winter you can skate on the lake or enjoy a sleigh-ride. The public lounge – open to one and all – is the best place in Jasper to relax and write a postcard.

Amethyst Lodge (☎ 780-852-3394, 888-852-7737; www.mtn-park-lodges.com; 200 Connaught Dr; r from $200; P) This is one of those places you want to be on the inside looking out. But it's what's inside that counts and here the rooms are large and clean and have balconies. There are frequent specials, even in summer.

Astoria Hotel (☎ 780-852-3351, 800-661-7343; www.astoriahotel.com; 404 Connaught Dr; r from $150; P) In a lively location, the Astoria has a fun bar. The basic rooms are very clean and have fridges.

Park Place Inn (☎ 780-852-9770, 866-852-9770; www.parkplaceinn.com; 623 Patricia St; r $180-250) Even though it's in a newer building, Park Place has rooms decorated with a classic 1930s theme. Each is different but some have claw-foot bathtubs; all have fridges and/or wet bars.

Athabasca Hotel (☎ 780-852-3386, 877-542-8422; www.athabascahotel.com; 510 Patricia St; r $100-150; P) This hotel is in a historic building and has a range of nicely decorated rooms. Some share baths, others have full facilities.

On the north side of town, about a 10-minute walk from the center are a number of serene and comfortable lodges. The **Tonquin Inn** (☎ 780-852-4987, 800-661-1315; www.tonquininnrockies.com; 100 Juniper St; r $180-220; P) includes an indoor pool, two outdoor hot tubs, a sauna and more. **Chateau Jasper** (☎ 780-852-5644, 800-661-9323; www.decorehotels.com; 96 Geikie St; r from $300; P) is a quiet and refined motel with large rooms and an indoor pool, hot tub, pub and restaurant.

TOURIST HOMES & B&BS

There are over 100 tourist homes in Jasper – private homes that offer rooms to travelers. Many have separate entrances, full facilities, amenities such as fireplaces and high-speed Internet and more. They can be both comfortable and good value. There are only a few B&Bs in Jasper, mostly because anyone

THE ROCKIES

serving food needs to jump through several bureaucratic hoops of approval. Some places may sneak you a muffin with a cup of tea.

Contact the **Jasper Home Accommodations Association** (PO Box 758, Jasper, Alberta T0E 1E0; www.stayinjasper.com) to receive its useful list of rooms or you can pick up a copy at the Jasper Information Centre, or look on the Internet. Rates average $55 to $70 and drop considerably in the off-season.

HOSTELS

HI Jasper International Hostel (☎ 780-852-3215, 877-852-0781; www.hihostels.ca; dm member/non-member $18/23; P 🖳) On Whistlers Rd toward the Jasper Tramway, 6.3km south of Jasper, the hostel runs a shuttle bus into town.

Also south of Jasper are two hostels that can be booked through the Jasper hostel. **HI Mt Edith Cavell Hostel** (dm member/non-member $13/18; summer; P), on Mt Edith Cavell Rd 13km from the junction with Hwy 93A, sits below the Angel Glacier. The hostel offers excellent access to hiking trails, including the gorgeous Tonquin Valley. The rustic accommodations include outhouses and creek water only. Also rustic and close to good hiking, the **HI Maligne Canyon Hostel** (dm member/non-member $13/18; closed Wed winter), 11.5km east of town on Maligne Canyon Rd, contains 24 beds in two cabins.

CAMPING

Jasper National Park contains 10 campgrounds operated by **Parks Canada** (☎ 780-852-6176; www.parkscanada.ca). They are generally open from May to September, although a few stay open until the first snowfall (which may not be that much later). Closest to town is **Whistlers Campground** (tent site $22), about 3km south of town on Whistlers Rd (off the Icefields Parkway). The good set-up here – which includes electricity, showers and flush toilets – means that it can get crowded, despite having 781 sites. In summer films and talks are presented nightly.

About 2km further south on the Icefields Parkway, **Wapiti Campground** (tent site $22, winter $14), beside the Athabasca River, is the only campground in the park that stays open during winter. Facilities include flush toilets and showers. **Pocahontas Campground** (site $17), at the turnoff to the Miette Hot Springs, has 140 sites and flush toilets but no showers.

Eating & Drinking

Jasper Pizza Place (☎ 780-852-3225; 402 Connaught Dr; pizza $12; 11am-late) Locals love this place, where the thin and cracker-crisp pizza is excellent. You can eat on the rooftop patio or at the sidewalk tables. This is a good place for kids.

Villa Caruso (☎ 780-852-3920; 2nd fl, 640 Connaught Dr; meals $20-35; lunch & dinner) Bright, open and bustling, Villa Caruso has good lunches, which show a slight Greek bent owing to the owners. Dinners center on fresh fish and excellent steaks. Changing pasta dishes use local ingredients. The service is excellent. There are tables outside in season.

Fiddle River Seafood Co (☎ 780-852-3032; 2nd fl, 620 Connaught Dr; meals $25-40; dinner) For the best seafood in town, this is the place. The menu boasts a long and changing list of fresh fish, most prepared in interesting and inventive ways. The staff, wine list and views are top notch.

Caledonia Grill (☎ 780-852-4070; 105 Miette Ave; meals $8-26) The light and open dining space hints at the good fresh food here. Banana bread or French toast for breakfast, great tall sandwiches for lunch and the changing dinner menu anchored by steaks and seafood set the tone.

Miss Italia Ristorante (☎ 780-852-4002; 2nd fl, 610 Patricia St; meals $10-20; lunch & dinner) Follow the scent of garlic to get here. The pasta is made fresh daily and the owners and staff are both charming and friendly.

CAFÉS

Bear's Paw Bakery (☎ 780-852-3233; 4 Cedar Ave; 7am-4pm Tue-Sun) Here you'll find a variety of fresh-baked goods, juices and coffee.

Spooners Coffee Bar (☎ 780-852-4046; 2nd fl, 610 Patricia St; coffee $2; breakfast & lunch) Spooners serves good coffee and gigantic homemade cinnamon buns. Lunch salads are good as are the fresh juices. Enjoy them from the large deck.

Soft Rock Café (☎ 780-852-5850; 632 Connaught Dr; meal $6; 7am-10pm) Serving breakfast all day, it also has a good sidewalk patio for relaxing. The name is a misnomer however; many times it could be called the Jazz Café or the Blues Café.

THE ROCKIES

PUBS

Except for the cries of rutting elk, Jasper can get quiet pretty early. Make your own noises at the places described below, which can be lively quite late.

Atha-B Pub (☎ 403-852-3386; 510 Patricia St) In the Athabasca Hotel, this pub regularly features live rock bands and dancing. It's a longtime institution with lots of regular characters.

De'd Dog Bar & Grill (☎ 780-852-3351; 404 Connaught Dr; burgers $9; ☺ noon-late) Here you can overhear your adventure guides gossiping about your shortcomings. Gets a fun local crowd who enjoy the good beer on tap and the burgers. Look for the photo showing the source of morning breath.

SELF-CATERING

The best supermarket is **Robinson's IGA** (☎ 780-852-3195; 218 Connaught Dr; ☺ 8am-6pm).

Getting There & Away

BUS

Brewster (☎ 780-852-3332; www.brewster.ca; 607 Connaught Dr) In the bus depot in the VIA Rail station. Express bus to Lake Louise, Banff and Calgary.

Greyhound (☎ 780-852-3926; 607 Connaught Dr) In the bus depot in the VIA Rail station. Services to Edmonton, Prince George, Kamloops and Vancouver. Luggage-storage service.

TRAIN

VIA Rail (☎ 780-852-4102; 607 Connaught Dr) has a mini-hub in Jasper. The *Canadian* stops at Jasper three times a week en route between Vancouver and Toronto. In addition, VIA's *Skeena* runs three times a week to Prince George, where the train continues to Prince Rupert after an overnight stay.

Getting Around

TO/FROM THE AIRPORT

Brewster (☎ 780-852-3332; www.brewster.ca; adult/child $80/40) has a daily bus to Calgary International airport.

BUS

Hostel Shuttle (☎ 780-852-4056; ☺ summer) links the area's hostels; there is a frequent service from the Totem Pole to the HI Jasper International Hostel ($3).

TAXI

Jasper Taxi (☎ 780-852-3600)

AROUND JASPER

About 12km east of Jasper on the way to Maligne (ma-*leen*) Lake on Maligne Lake Rd, you'll pass **Maligne Canyon**, a limestone gorge about 50m deep, with waterfalls and interesting rock formations. You can walk from the teahouse along the floor of the canyon. Continue 21km further up the road to **Medicine Lake**, the level of which rises and falls due to the underground drainage system; sometimes the lake disappears completely.

The largest glacier-fed lake in the Rockies and the second-largest in the world, **Maligne Lake** lies 48km southeast of Jasper at the end of Maligne Lake Rd. The lake is promoted as one of the most scenic of mountain lakes, but this will be difficult to understand if you only stay near the parking lots and chalet. A little effort, however, will be rewarded. A stroll down the **east side lake trail** takes under an hour and leaves 90% of the crowds behind.

Maligne Tours (☎ 780-852-3370; Jasper Tour Center, 627 Patricia St) has a lock on local activities. The Chalet offers a range of decent food. Nearby you can rent a canoe ($15 per hour) – recommended – at the historic Curly Philips Boathouse. **Boat cruises to Spirit Island** (adult/child $35/17.50; ☺ frequent boats, Jun-Aug) are necessary if you want the iconic shot of the lake, island and soaring peaks beyond. And don't forget to stop off a few times on your drive to and from the lake – there are a number of almost untouched trails alongside the rushing **Maligne River**.

If you don't have a car to get to the lake, Maligne Tours runs a **shuttle service** (one-way $14; ☺ mid-May–Oct) from Jasper.

To rest your weary bones, stop at **Miette Hot Springs** (☎ 780-866-3939; adult/child $6.25/5.25; ☺ May–mid-Oct), 61km northeast of Jasper off the Yellowhead Hwy (Hwy 16) near the park boundary. Miette has the warmest mineral waters in the Canadian Rockies. Left alone, the springs produce a scalding 53.9°C, but the water is cooled to a more reasonable 39°C. The modern spa includes three pools (hot, warm and freezing) and incredible surrounding scenery.

Activities

HIKING

Fewer hikers tramp through Jasper than Banff but more wildlife scampers through the woods, which means that you stand a good chance of spotting some. In addition to the hikes around the lakes (see p285), many other paths meander through the terrain. The Parks Canada leaflet *Day Hikers' Guide to Jasper National Park* offers good descriptions of hikes that last anywhere from a couple of hours to all day. If the weather has been wet, you may want to avoid the lower horse trails, which can become mud baths. Topographic maps are available for all routes; buy them at the Visitor Info Centre.

If you're hiking overnight, definitely pick up copies of Parks Canada *Backcountry Visitors' Guide* and the *Summer Trails Jasper National Park*, which offers overnight trail descriptions along with a map. If you're camping in the backcountry, you have to obtain a backcountry permit from Parks Canada.

CYCLING
As in Banff National Park, you can cycle on the highways and on most of the trails in the park. For more information, pick up a copy of *Trail Bicycling Guide, Jasper National Park* at the Visitor Info Centre. At **Freewheel Cycle** (☎ 780-852-3898; www.freewheeljasper.com; 618 Patricia St; 8am-8pm) you can ask the staff about good rides and pick up the free *Mountain Biking Trail Guide*. You also might want to ask which trails the horses are using, so you can be sure you don't go there. Freewheel rents out bikes from $30 per day.

ROCK CLIMBING
With all the rock around, it's no wonder climbers are in harness heaven in Jasper. Experienced climbers like to head to the popular Mt Morro, Messner Ridge, Mt Athabasca, Mt Andromeda and Mt Edith Cavell. In winter you can ice-climb on the frozen waterfalls. Stop by **Gravity Gear** (☎ 780-852-3155, 888-852-3155; 618 Patricia St; 9am-8pm) where you can get good advice and rent equipment.

Climbing classes and guided climbs are available from Paul Valiulis at **ICPeaks** (☎ 780-852-1945; www.icpeaks.com).

WHITEWATER RAFTING
Calm to turbulent rafting can be found on the **Sunwapta River** and the **Athabasca River**

near Athabasca Falls. Rafting (or any boat usage) is prohibited on the **Maligne River** to protect the habitat for threatened Harlequin ducks.

Numerous companies offer trips of varying lengths. **Maligne Rafting Adventures** (☎ 780-852-3370, 866-625-4463; 627 Patricia St; adult/child from $44/22) runs trips on the Athabasca and the Sunwapta. **Jasper Adventure Centre** (☎ 780-852-5595; 604 Connaught Dr in the Chaba Theatre in summer, 306 Connaught Dr in winter) offers numerous trips from $45.

SKIING
Jasper National Park's only ski area is **Marmot Basin** (☎ 780-852-3816, 800-473-8135; www.skimarmot.com; one-day lift pass adult/child $58/20), which lies 19km southwest of town off Hwy 93A. It features 84 good trails for both beginners and experts, plenty of scenic cross-country trails, eight lifts and a chalet. The drop is 914m.

Near Maligne Lake, the **Moose Lake Loop** (8km) and the trail in the **Bald Hills** (11km) are easy introductions to the 200km of cross-country skiing in the park. The skiing season runs from December to May.

MT ROBSON PROVINCIAL PARK
The highest peak in the Canadian Rockies is not in one of the great national parks but sits majestically in its own BC provincial park to the west of Jasper National Park. The Yellowhead Hwy (Hwy 16) and the railway link the park to Jasper. While you're on the Yellowhead, watch for roadside markers detailing the work of the interned Japanese laborers who built this stretch of road during WWII.

Ambitious climbers have been tackling Mt Robson since 1907, but the sharp-edged ice castle wasn't successfully summitted until 1913. Mountaineers from all over the world come every summer to try to repeat this feat on Robson, considered one of the world's most challenging climbs.

At the base of the mountain, the **Mt Robson Visitor Info Centre** (☎ 250-566-4325; 9am-6pm summer) offers information on the park and runs interpretive programs during summer. One of the highlights of the park is the popular trip to **Berg Lake**, a two-day hike to the base of Mt Robson. Along the way, you'll pass numerous glaciers, including the Berg Glacier, which clings to Robson's northwest face. Periodically, bits of glacier fall into the lake, filling it with icebergs. You need to register and pay at the park **visitor centre** (☎ 800-689-9025; www.discovercamping.ca; backcountry fee $5) at Mt Robson before venturing onto the Berg Lake Trail.

The Fraser River begins its long and sometimes tumultuous journey through British Columbia at its headwaters in the southwest corner of the park. (The Fraser spills into the Pacific Ocean near Vancouver after traveling some 1280km.) In August and September you can see salmon spawning in the river at Rearguard Falls. You also stand an excellent chance of seeing moose in the park.

Adjoining the park's western end is the tiny **Mt Terry Fox Provincial Park**, named after the runner who lost a leg to cancer, then attempted to run what he called the 'Marathon of Hope' across Canada, aiming to raise $1 from every Canadian for cancer research. Fox averaged a remarkable 37km a day until a recurrence of cancer forced him to end his run after 144 days and 5376km.

SLEEPING

Accommodations include three park-run campgrounds and two private spots. Close to the Visitor Info Centre, both **Robson Meadows Campground** and **Robson River Campground** offer showers, flush toilets and firewood (site $17). **Lucerne Campground** (site $14) is 10km west of the Alberta border on the southern shore of Yellowhead Lake. The facilities include only pit toilets and pump water.

Mount Robson Lodge (☎ 250-566-4821, 888-566-4821; www.mountrobsonlodge.com; r $70-125) has cabins and rooms with fine views of the mountain and the Fraser River.

THE ROCKIES

Cariboo-
Chilcotin

Fewer than 100,000 people live in the vast Cariboo and Chilcotin areas, which sit like a wide cummerbund around the waist of BC. The Cariboo takes its name from the *cariboeuf*, later known as caribou, which populated the area during the gold rush. East of the Fraser River and west of the Cariboo Mountains, the Cariboo region follows the 1858 Cariboo Wagon Road (now known as the Gold Rush Trail), which starts at 'Mile 0' in Lillooet and heads north to the historic town of Barkerville. Towns named for their distance from Lillooet sprouted up along the route, which explains unlikely monikers such as 100 Mile House, 108 Mile House and 150 Mile House.

West of the Fraser River and sprawling all the way over the Coast Mountains, the entire Chilcotin region has only one paved road – and even parts of it are gravel. From Williams Lake, Hwy 20 heads west, passing large stretches of open ranges and grasslands, with access points to some very remote provincial parks. The road winds through Tweedsmuir Provincial Park and finally reaches Bella Coola, a remote fishing village on BC's southwest coast, 456km later. This is a minor outpost in the great untrammeled reaches of British Columbia – the Kitimat Ranges and the Coast Mountains.

This area is also home to the waterfall-filled Wells Gray Provincial Park, in the far east of the region, and Bowron Lake Provincial Park, near historic Barkerville, where you'll find one of the best canoe circuits in the world.

HIGHLIGHTS

- Reliving the gold rush days in **Barkerville** (p294)
- Paddling the **Bowron Lake** (p295) canoe circuit
- Hooting and hollering at the **Williams Lake Stampede** (p292)
- Following Hwy 20 over 'The Hill' to **Bella Coola** (p297) and the rain forest
- Tracing Alexander Mackenzie's route from **Quesnel** (p293) to the coast on Highway 20

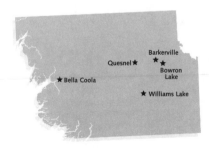

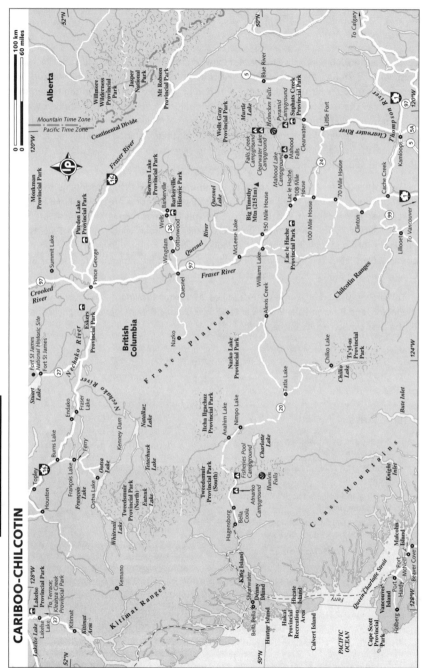

CARIBOO-CHILCOTIN

WELLS GRAY PROVINCIAL PARK

In the Cariboo Mountains about halfway between Kamloops and Jasper, off the Yellowhead Hwy (Hwy 5), lies this enormous 541,000-hectare wilderness park, a seldom-visited jewel filled with incredible waterfalls.

It is the fourth-largest park in BC, after Tatshenshini-Alsek, Tweedsmuir and the Spatsizi Wilderness Plateau. The drainages of the Clearwater River and its tributaries define the park's boundaries and give visitors five major lakes, two large river systems and plenty of waterfalls to explore.

Though First Nations people have long lived in the area, it was a group of Overlanders who named the river for its crystal-clear waters in 1862. Wells Gray almost became a rail route when the Canadian Pacific Railway (CPR) was looking for a route over the Rockies, but it was bypassed when the CPR chose the more southern, yet controversial Kicking Horse Pass. The area remained vast wilderness until various settlers started moving in. Fur-trapper John Ray was the first White man to settle in the area and one of the last to leave. Remnants of his homestead, the **Ray Farm**, are now a park attraction. When giant waterfalls were discovered in 1913, people began making appeals to the government to protect the area as parkland. It finally happened in 1939, and the park took its name from a parks official, Arthur Wellesley Gray.

Most people enter the park through the town of **Clearwater** on Hwy 5, but you can also reach it from 100 Mile House on Hwy 97 or from Blue River on Hwy 5 (see Getting There & Away, below). Many sights, including the absolutely incredible **Helmcken Falls**, where the Murtle River plunges 137m into a misty abyss, are accessible by a short road branching off the Wells Gray Corridor, which travels the 68km length of the park.

In Clearwater the **Visitor Info Centre** (☎ 250-674-2646; www.ntvalley.com/clearwaterchamber; 425 E Yellowhead Hwy at Clearwater Valley Rd; 9am-5pm Jul & Aug, Mon-Fri Apr-Jun & Sep-Dec) distributes lots of useful information and maps of the park.

Activities

You'll find opportunities for **hiking**, **cross-country skiing** or **horseback riding** along more than 20 trails of varying lengths. Another great way to explore the park is by **canoeing** on Clearwater, Azure, Murtle and Mahood Lakes. Clearwater Lake lies at the north end of the Wells Gray Corridor. A narrow navigation channel from the north end of Clearwater Lake connects to the west end of Azure Lake; the two lakes form an upside-down 'L'. You can only reach the 6900-hectare Murtle Lake from the Blue River park entrance. You can reach Mahood Lake, on the southwest side of Wells Gray, from 100 Mile House. Rustic backcountry campgrounds dot the area around all four lakes. To rent canoes, contact **Clearwater Lake Tours** (☎ 250-674-2121; www.clearwaterlaketours.com; canoes from $35 per day).

The **Clearwater River** makes for some excellent, adrenaline-pumping white-water rafting. **Interior Whitewater Expeditions** (☎ 250-674-3727, 800-661-7238; www.interiorwhitewater.bc.ca; 3hr-trip adult/child $82/59) runs the river with a variety of trips.

Sleeping

There are no commercial operations in the park, but just outside of the south gate you'll find a couple of excellent accommodations options along Clearwater Valley Rd.

Helmcken Falls Lodge (☎ 250-674-3657; www.helmckenfalls.com; 4373 Clearwater Valley Rd; r $120-150) A rustic delight – guests can stay in cozy log cabins, with delicious meals featuring home-baked breads served in the main lodge. The lodge rents canoes and offers horseback-riding trips. Cross-country skiers like to congregate here in winter.

Wells Gray Guest Ranch (☎ 250-674-2792, 866-467-4346; www.wellsgrayranch.com; r $125) This ranch has no end of activities for guests, including hiking, riding and canoeing. You can camp in a tepee for $15 or in your own tent for $14.

There are four rustic **campgrounds** (☎ 250-587-6250; tent site $5) in the park, all with pit toilets but no showers. One of the most bucolic, the 50-site **Pyramid Campground** is just 5km from the park's south entrance on the road from Clearwater.

Getting There & Away

There are three access points to the park. The most popular entrance is the south gate, 36km north of Clearwater on Clearwater Valley Rd. You can also reach the park from 100 Mile House via an 86km gravel road that leads to Mahood Falls and

CARIBOO-CHILCOTIN

SADDLE SORES AND THE GREAT OUTDOORS

When was the last time you sat on a horse? That long, eh? Well, here in cowboy country, that just ain't good enough. So don yer chaps and cowboy hats and shuffle on up to the saddle – it's time to ride. With all the ranching going on in the Cariboo, it's no surprise to find out that hopping on a horse or rounding up some cattle is as simple as, well, hopping on a horse. Dozens of guest ranches in the Cariboo offer everything from old-fashioned trail-riding and hayrides to overnight cattle drives and sing-alongs by the campfire. Whether you're looking to learn to ride or you've always wanted to wrangle cattle, there's probably a guest ranch for you. From rustic cabin accommodations to luxurious spas, most guest ranches serve up excellent food and down-home hospitality. Find out more by contacting **BC Guest Ranchers Association** (☎ 250-374-6836; www.bcguestranches.com).

---

the west end of Mahood Lake. From Blue River, north of Clearwater, a 24km gravel road and 2.5km track lead to Murtle Lake in the southeast part of the park.

GOLD RUSH TRAIL/CARIBOO HIGHWAY

Following the Gold Rush Trail (Hwy 97) north of Lillooet, you'll find **Clinton**, the self-proclaimed 'Guest Ranch Capital of BC'. Its downtown streets feature western decor and some roaming dudes in cowboy boots. The service center for the southern Cariboo region, **100 Mile House** offers some excellent cross-country skiing.

With boundless open ranges and rolling grassy hills, the southern interior makes excellent territory for cattle raising. Working ranches are tucked into many folds of the Cariboo-Chilcotin landscape. The Cariboo alone boasts 500 cattle ranches, which produce 20% of the beef for the province.

Williams Lake
pop 11,500

Williams Lake is a major cross-roads: you can follow Hwy 20 west 456km to the coastal town of Bella Coola; or you can follow the Cariboo Hwy (Hwy 97) north to McLeese Lake, a small lakeside resort with log cabins, then on to Quesnel and Prince George. To the south is Kamloops and Vancouver.

Williams Lake makes no attempt to hide that it's in the tree-cutting business. Lumber yards, piles of logs and other evidence of the town's five mills surround the downtown area. About 65% of the population works in forestry. As such, the town is a rather charmless supply hub known

mostly for a huge cowboy party that's BC's answer to the Calgary Stampede.

In 1919 the Pacific Great Eastern Railway (now BC Rail) pushed its way into Williams Lake. People partied so much they decided to reenact the whole shebang again the following year. This marked the birth of the **Williams Lake Stampede** (☎ 250-398-8388, 800-717-6336; williamslakestampede.com), an annual four-day party that happens on the Stampede Grounds in early July, when the town is suddenly overrun with spur-clicking cowboys and leather-clad cowgirls. It's serious business for the cowboys who come here from all over to compete in activities such as roping, cattle penning and the always exciting bull-riding. Fringe events include the popular Stampede Queen Coronation and loggers' sports. Hotels fill up while the stampede takes over town, and the event keeps getting bigger. One-day tickets to the festival cost around $10 to $15.

The **Visitor Info Centre** (☎ 250-392-5025; www.bcadventure.com/wlcc/; 1148 Broadway S off Hwy 97; 🕑 9am-4pm, 9am-5pm summer) is the usual good source of regional knowledge. As an added bonus, you may have a chance to stroke the ego of Williams Lake Willie, the town mascot.

The excellent **Museum of the Cariboo Chilcotin** (☎ 250-392-7404; 113 4th Ave N; adult/child $2/free; 🕑 10am-4pm Mon-Sat summer, 11am-4pm Tue-Sat winter) features a very interesting exhibit on the history and paraphernalia of the Stampede, including photos of each 'Queen' from the annual pageant, dating back to 1933. It's interesting that prior to 1964 there was both a First Nations and a White queen. The museum also explores the history of ranching and logging in the area and includes the **BC Cowboy Hall of Fame**.

SLEEPING & EATING

Being a crossroads, Williams Lake has several chain motels. Outside of Stampede season (short as it is), you should be able to find a room.

Drummond Lodge Motel (☎ 250-392-5334, 800-667-4555; www.drummondlodge.com; 1405 Hwy 97 S; r $69-85; ❇ 🖳) This is the nicest place to stay in Williams Lake. The large rooms – some with balconies – have high-speed Internet access. There's a continental breakfast and lovely gardens to enjoy.

Wildwood Campsite (☎ 250-989-4711; www.wlbc .net/~letscamp; tent site $15) This friendly place, with decent shade, is the best choice for camping. During the Stampede, you can camp on the Stampede Grounds for $10.

There are a few small places to eat downtown and lots of fast-food places along the highways. But the best choice is the excellent **Laughing Loon Pub** (☎ 250-398-5666; 1730 Broadway S; meals $8-20; ❇ 11am-late). Built out of materials recovered from demolished historical buildings, this pub boasts an elegance – and a great patio – you don't usually find in these parts. It has good food that goes well beyond just burgers, with steaks and salmon from renowned regional suppliers.

GETTING THERE & AROUND

Buses run north to Prince George and south to Vancouver from the **Greyhound bus depot** (☎ 250-398-7733; 215 Donald Rd, just off Hwy 97).

Quesnel

pop 11,000

Neither Quesnel's picturesque setting at the confluence of the Fraser and Quesnel Rivers nor the carefully cultivated flowers along the riverfront trails can disguise the fact that this is first and foremost a logging town, similar to Williams Lake, 120km to the south. An **observation tower** at the north end of town overlooks Two-Mile Flat, a large industrial area devoted to wood products. The town's welcome sign reads 'The Gold Pan City', but the resource they're extracting is different now – perhaps a more fitting name would be 'The Fallen-Tree City', for the massive, overwhelming piles of logs that sit around waiting to be processed.

From Quesnel, Hwy 26 leads east to the area's main attractions, **Barkerville Historic Park** and **Bowron Lake Provincial Park**.

The **Visitor Info Centre** (☎ 250-992-8716; www.northcariboo.com; 703 Carson Ave; ❇ 8am-6pm daily summer, 9am-4pm Mon-Fri winter) offers free Internet access.

The nice little **Quesnel Museum** (adult/child $3/1.50; ❇ 8:30am-6pm summer, 8:30am-4:30pm Mon-Fri winter), in the same building as the Visitor Info Centre, features a quirky array of antiques from the gold-rush days, a cool coin collection and other interesting displays.

Feel like a walk in the woods? One of the great ones is northwest of Quesnel; the refurbished **Alexander Mackenzie Heritage Trail** follows ancient trails from the Fraser River west to Bella Coola, on the Pacific Ocean. In 1793 Alexander Mackenzie made the first recorded crossing of continental North America in his search for a supply route to the Pacific Ocean. His carved graffiti can still be seen in a rock near Bella Coola. This 420km trail winds its way through forest and mountains and makes for a tough 16-day walk. At least one food drop is required. You can do some of the more accessible segments for a few days – for example, the section through the southern end of Tweedsmuir Provincial Park. You can also take day hikes from Quesnel. To get to the trailhead, follow the Blackwater Rd west from Quesnel. For detailed trail guides, including the excellent 200-page guide *Steps of Alexander Mackenzie*, contact the **Alexander Mackenzie Trail Association** (☎ 250-762-3002; PO Box 425, Station A, Kelowna, BC V1Y 7P1). For more information, contact the **Quesnel Forest Office** (☎ 250-992-4400).

SLEEPING & EATING

Econolodge (☎ 250-992-2187, 800-663-1585; www .econolodge.com; 530 Carson Ave; s/d from $48/52; ❇ 🖳) A good choice downtown with an indoor pool and large rooms, and it's right across the street from the ice arena if you decide to score a hat trick.

Murphy's Pub (☎ 250-747-3400; 2330 Hydraulic Rd at Hwy 97; burgers $8; ❇ noon-late) Murphy's serves good burgers ($8) and has a lively atmosphere; lots of mill workers come here for an after-work pint.

GETTING THERE & AWAY

Greyhound (☎ 250-992-2231; 365 Kinchant St) buses run south to Kamloops, Kelowna and Vancouver, and north to Prince George. **Quesnel airport** (YQZ) is just north of town at

CARIBOO-CHILCOTIN

the junction of Hwys 97 and 26. Air Canada Jazz flies to/from Vancouver.

Barkerville

Between 1858 and 1861, when the Cariboo Wagon Rd (now Hwy 97) edged north from Kamloops to Quesnel, ramshackle towns hastily built by gold prospectors from around the world sprang up along the road. In 1862 one member of this new international population hit the jackpot, making $1000 in the first two days of his claim. Despite his luck, Cornishman Billy Barker probably had no clue that more than 100,000 salivating miners would leap into his footsteps, crossing rivers, creeks and lakes to storm the Cariboo Wagon Rd in search of gold. Soon Barkerville sprang up to become, for a brief time, the largest city west of Chicago and north of San Francisco. In its heyday, some 10,000 people resided in the muddy town, hoping to hit jackpots of their own.

If Billy was clueless about the gold rush, then he most certainly never predicted that people would still be flocking here to see Barkerville as it was, albeit with more fudge for sale than when the miners were here.

AUTHOR'S CHOICE

On the way to or from Barkerville, and 26km from Quesnel on Hwy 26, watch for **Cottonwood House Historic Site** (☎ 250-992-2071 summer, 250-983-6911 winter; www.cottonwoodhouse.ca; adult/child $4.50/free; ☻ 10am-5pm May & Jun, 9am-6:30pm Jul & Aug). This is something of an undiscovered gem, a classic roadhouse from the 1860s that has been restored so that it's now a fascinating attraction. Routes throughout the north were lined with these types of places, each about a day's travel apart. This project, completed in conjunction with the local schools, is very well done. Aside from the roadhouse itself, there are trails that lead to other restored buildings, including a general store and barns. There's a café that sells homemade ice-cream and some interesting demonstration gardens. With the trees rustling in the breeze, you can imagine what a welcome sight this roadhouse was for weary travelers.

Happily there is the odd bit of horse poop here and there to lend some authenticity.

This restored gold-rush town, now called **Barkerville Historic Park** (☎ 250-994-3332; www .heritage.gov.bc.ca; adult/child $9/5.25; ☻ 8am-8pm May-Sep), is 89km east of Quesnel at the end of Hwy 26. More than 125 buildings have been restored to their former glory, including a hotel, various stores and a saloon. In summer people dressed in period garb roam through town, and if you can tune out the crowds the effect is quite neat. (In the Theatre Royal, dancing shows are staged in a family-friendly manner the rough-and-tumble miners would have hooted at.) The free historic walking tours relate the history of the gold rush, the experience of the Chinese workers who built the Cariboo Hwy and the finer details of the art of panning for gold.

Outside of summer, the park is open but most of the attractions are closed, which may actually make for a more atmospheric visit. The quiet streets echo from the winds and you just might be able to take yourself back in time – until you step in horse poop.

Nearby **Wells**, 8km west of Barkerville, is also a historic town with accommodations, restaurants and a general store. It's well worth a ramble. The Wells **Visitor Info Centre** (☎ 250-994-2323, 877-451-9355; www .wellsbc.com; ☻ 9am-6pm summer) runs an information center just off the highway in a small old general store. The town exists in two closely related parts: the older area up on the hill and the string of shops along the highway.

SLEEPING & EATING

St George Hotel (☎ 250-994-0008, 888-246-7690; www.stgeorgehotel.bc.ca; r $130-190) Inside the historic park, this hotel dates from the 1890s. The rooms are all filled with antiques. A stay here – it must be very quiet, even spooky, after the last day-trippers have left – includes a large breakfast. You can also try the town's other B&B for a simpler experience: **Kelly House** (☎ 250-994-3328, 800-994-3312; r $80-90).

Wells Hotel (☎ 250-994-3427, 800-860-2299; 2341 Pooley St; r $60-130) Popular since 1933 and home to a good restaurant, pub and patio, Wells Hotel is pretty much the hub of the town. The cheaper rooms have shared baths. Rates include a continental breakfast.

Cottonwood House (☎ 250-992-2071 summer, 800-983-6911 winter; www.cottonwoodhouse.ca; tent site $10, cabin for up to six $25) Here you get both the fascinating setting and a good deal on basic accommodations that share a toilet and shower building. You can relive the days when weary travelers gave their dogs well-earned rest at the end of a hard day.

BC Parks (☎ 250-398-4414) runs three campgrounds in tiny Barkerville. Closest to the townsite and mostly used by campers with tents (not RVs) is **Government Hill Campground** (tent site $14). Facilities include pit toilets but no showers.

Bear's Paw Cafe (☎ 250-994-2346; meals $5-8; ☿ lunch) This café is a real find, right on Hwy 26 in Wells. The food is fresh and there's a bakery. Beer and wine are served; enjoy your drink on the nice patio.

BOWRON LAKE PROVINCIAL PARK

Surrounded by snowy peaks, this 149,207-hectare park boasts one of the best **canoe trips** in the world. The 116km circular canoe route passes through 10 lakes: Bowron, Kibbee, Indianpoint, Isaac, McLeary, Lanezi, Sandy, Babcock, Skoi and Swan – and over sections of the Isaac, Cariboo and Bowron Rivers. In between are eight portages, with the longest 2km over well-defined trails that can accommodate wheeled canoe carriers. The trip takes seven to 10 days. You'll find backcountry campgrounds along the way; to make sure there are sites for everyone, the park service only allows 27 canoes to start the circuit each day. You must bring your own food (or catch your own fish).

The Mowdish Range runs right through the middle of the loop, while the Cariboo Range surrounds the perimeter of the park, affording spectacular views in every direction. With all these mountains around, it's no wonder the park is often cool and wet. Wildlife abounds. You might see moose, black and grizzly bears, caribou and mountain goats. In late summer you stand a good chance of spotting bears on the upper Bowron River, where they feed on spawning sockeye salmon.

You can paddle the circuit any time from mid-May to October. Most people do it in July and August, but September is also an excellent choice, since that's when the tree leaves change color. Mosquitoes, which thrive in the wet, relatively windless environment, are at their worst in the spring.

Before planning your trip, visit the BC Parks website (wlapwww.gov.bc.ca/bcparks/explore/parkpgs/bowron.htm) to download the essential Bowron Lake Canoe Circuit Pre-Trip Information document. You will then need to make reservations with **BC Parks** (☎ 800-435-5622, ☎ 250-387-1642 outside North America) to reserve your circuit, which can be done around January 2. The fee is $60 per person plus an $18 reservation fee. Once you get to the park, you must go to the Registration Centre, at a time given to you when you make your reservation, to check in and undergo an orientation.

You can also leave the multi-day paddle to the hard-core types and just do day trips on Bowron Lake, which require no advance registration or fee.

CANOE RENTALS & GUIDES

Whitegold Adventures (☎ 250-994-2345, 866-994-2345; www.whitegold.ca; Hwy 26, Wells) offers guided paddles of Bowron Lake that start at $45 for a day trip on the lake. A full eight-day circuit with guides and food costs $1200 per person.

Bowron Lake Lodge (see below) offers 10-day canoe rentals from $125. **Becker's Lodge** (see below) offers similar services.

SLEEPING

Bowron Lake Lodge (☎ 250-992-2733, 800-519-3399; www.bowronlakelodge.com; r $60-125) Open from May until November, this friendly lodge on the lake at the end of Bowron Lake Rd offers different types of accommodations including cabins. You can also camp right on the lake for $20 (for two people).

Becker's Lodge (☎ 250-992-8864, 800-808-4761; www.beckers.bc.ca; s/d $69-200) Just up the road, the attractive Becker's features a cozy restaurant and nice log chalets and cabins. Tent sites cost $20, including firewood and use of the facilities.

Bowron Lake Provincial Park Campground (tent site $14) Near the Registration Centre, this campground has 25 non-reservable tent sites and pit toilets.

Getting There & Away

By car turn off Hwy 26 just before Barkerville and follow the 28km-long gravel Bowron Lake Rd.

CARIBOO-CHILCOTIN

BOWRON LAKE PROVINCIAL PARK

HIGHWAY 20

Just west of Williams Lake, Hwy 20 crosses over the Fraser River, which marks the boundary between the Cariboo and the Chilcotin. This vast, scarcely inhabited land of grassland plateaus, lakes and ranches sprawls west to the Coast Mountains. Over the mountains, the landscape makes a dramatic shift to craggy bluffs and rushing rivers before dropping down into the wet, lush central coast.

The distance between Williams Lake and Bella Coola, on the coast, is a long 456km. Bella Coola is only accessible by car on Hwy 20 or by ferry. No buses travel this route, so if you don't have a car your best bet is to hire one (hitchhiking would take forever).

From Hwy 20 you can take numerous side roads – most of which are gravel – to some of the province's most remote provincial parks that are still accessible by car. Excellent canoeing on the lake chain in **Nazko Lake Provincial Park** draws adventurers to this park, 167km northwest of Williams Lake along the Alexis Lakes Rd, off Hwy 20. You can get to the north end of 233,240-hectare **Ts'yl-os Provincial Park** (*sigh*-loss) by turning south at the town of Tatla Lake, 220km west of Williams Lake. After the turn, follow the road for 63km to the rustic campground on the north tip of Chilko Lake. Wildlife thrives here, and Chilko Lake is chock-full of fish.

Hwy 20 meanders up into the mountains, passing by small towns whose services are

---

GREASE TRAILS

Oolichan, spelled a bunch of different ways – eulachon, oulachen, even hooligan – is a small, black-and-silver smelt-fish known to many coastal First Nations groups as 'salvation' fish, since the oolichan were the first to show up in the river after the long, cold winter. Oolichan run in two- to four-year cycles. Schools are huge, and First Nations groups could net millions of the tiny, oily fish with little effort. They prized the oolichan for its butter-like oily fat; at the end of winter, consuming the fish must have felt like eating a hunk of chocolate after a lengthy stint adhering to an unrewarding diet.

The First Nations people placed the fish in pits and applied weight to squeeze out the oil, which was then scooped off and placed in wooden boxes, where it could be stored for up to two years. Oolichan oil made an excellent dipping sauce for dried berries or salmon.

Inland native groups would travel overland to the coast to vie for this delicious indulgence. They would leave a trail of oolichan drippings, and their routes effectively became 'grease trails'.

---

limited. West of Anahim Lake, the road becomes gravel. It soon begins its descent into the Bella Coola Valley via the legendary 'Hill', a winding narrow road over Heckman Pass. The road includes a stretch of steep, 18%-grade downhill that keeps you clenching the wheel the whole way down. At the bottom of the Hill is the 'freedom road', built by Bella Coola residents so they could access the interior. Prior to 1955 the only way out of Bella Coola was by boat.

Tweedsmuir Provincial Park (South)

You are already in this gigantic, roughly arrowhead-shaped park when you drive the Hill. At 981,000 hectares, **Tweedsmuir** (☎ 250-398-4414) is the second-largest provincial park in BC (next to Tatshenshini-Alsek in the northwest corner of BC). The Dean River, roughly halfway up the park, divides Tweedsmuir into north and south. Hwy 20 is the only road through this mostly wilderness park, and it skirts the park's southern tip.

Alexander Mackenzie traveled through this area on his way to becoming the first white person to make it to the northwest coast. Long before that, Bella Coola and Chilcotin Indians thrived along the rivers full of salmon.

The park's features include the **Rainbow Range**, north of Hwy 20. The colorful dome of eroded rock and lava mountains appears, at certain lights, orange, red, yellow and purple. Most of the hiking in the park requires serious planning ahead of time. Popular treks include the 16km route to **Hunlen Falls**, which plummet 260m into the Atnarko River at the north end of Turner Lake, and some

portions of the **Alexander Mackenzie Heritage Trail** (p293). You'll find two campgrounds (sites $12) along Hwy 20.

BELLA COOLA & AROUND
pop 820

The remote village of Bella Coola sits at the mouth of the Bella Coola River where it spills into the Bentinck Arm of the Pacific Ocean. Rainfall is high and the village is surrounded by the sharp, spectacular Coast Mountains. More than one-third of the population is made up of First Nations people, descendants of the Nuxalk-Carriers who first blazed the trails later used by Alexander Mackenzie. The Native Indians were probably shocked to see Mackenzie come down the Bella Coola River in 1793. The Nuxalk (*new*-hawk) are well known for their carvings, paintings and their trademark use of cobalt blue, which you'll see in artwork throughout the town.

Superb hiking trails radiate from Bella Coola, including a trail to 17th-century **petroglyphs**, carved deep into the rock. You can only explore these with a tour; ask around town for one of the many locals who are happy to provide this service. Sadly, long-time 'good-will ambassador' Darren Edgar died in 2002. The **Bella Coola Museum** (☎ 250-799-5657; 10am-5pm, closed Sat summer), on Hwy 20 just west of Mackenzie St, merits a visit if you find it open. It sometimes makes 'unplanned' closures.

Just 16km east of Bella Coola on Hwy 20 is **Hagensborg**, settled in 1895 by a hardy group of Norwegians whose hand-hewn homes were built with crude saws and axes.

Attracted to the area because it resembled their homeland, the Norwegians stayed and entrenched themselves in northern BC. Today the Scandinavian influence is still evident, and many residents still speak Norwegian. West of Bella Coola is the small coastal village of **Bella Bella**, accessible only by boat or plane.

GREAT BEAR RAINFOREST

Morning mist gently rises off BC's quiet central coast, revealing an emerald labyrinth of tiny islands and inlets that nudge up against the foreboding shore of the mainland. If you could soar like an eagle over this wet coastal wilderness, you'd follow the long green fingers of the pristine fjords, coast high above secluded waterfalls or float along the ridges overlooking deep river valleys. On the lonely shores you'd see timber wolves and grizzly bears, even the white Kermode bear, often referred to as the 'spirit bear'. Offshore you'd see spawning salmon searching for river mouths, sea lions playing in the lapping waves and, further out, whales and porpoises feeding in the rich waters. You'd hear birdsong and squawks, and it might be days before you'd see a human being.

This is the Great Bear Rainforest, a vast 3-million-hectare area containing the largest contiguous tract of coastal temperate rainforest left on earth. This endangered forest type is distinguished by its proximity to oceans, the presence of mountains and heavy rainfall. Accessible only by boat or floatplane, the Great Bear Rainforest, dubbed such for its large grizzly bear population, follows the Inside Passage from the top edge of Vancouver Island to the Alaska border, 400km north. Short, rugged brush forests with muskeg lowlands cover its outer fringes, but along the Passage huge granite buttresses line the deepwater fjords. These almost secret passages lead to rich valleys adorned with ancient Sitka spruce, Pacific silver fir, yellow cedar and western red cedar, many growing 100m tall and living more than 1500 years.

The forest industry's voracious appetite for such timber jewels – previously untouched because of their difficult access – has put the Great Bear Rainforest and all of its inhabitants seriously at risk. Forest companies try to keep up with high consumption levels and demand for BC softwoods in the USA, Europe and Japan. Meanwhile, wildlife habitat suffers the consequences. Thousands of genetically distinct races of wild Pacific salmon swim and spawn in the area's waters. They provide food to bears, birds and even vegetation, with their decomposing bodies adding nutrients to the soil. Massive clear-cutting has already devastated many of the Great Bear Rainforest's productive watersheds, and the reverberation continues to wreak havoc up and down the food chain.

Coastal temperate rainforests are rare; they originally covered only 0.2% of the world's land base. Today almost 60% of that 0.2% has disappeared, and not because of natural disturbances – forest fires don't occur often in the wet coastal forests. Logging and development alone have wiped out much of the forest. North America's ancient rainforest once stretched from Alaska to Northern California. Today no single undeveloped, unlogged coastal watershed larger than 5000 hectares exists south of the BC border. Only small pockets survive elsewhere in the world and they are all at risk of disappearing forever.

Though some protectionist measures have preserved chunks of the Great Bear Rainforest as parkland, environmentalists say it's just not enough. Meanwhile, forestry companies are bidding top dollar to cut trees as fast as they can. Established in 1990 to combat the destruction, the **Raincoast Conservation Society** (☎ 250-957-2480; www.raincoast.org), a nonprofit organization based in Victoria and Bella Bella, works to protect the area by documenting bear and salmon behavior and educating the public on the area's tenuous future. The organization achieved a significant victory in 2001 when the BC government announced that 20 unlogged river valleys comprising 600,000 hectares in Great Bear would be protected; however, another 65 eligible valleys remain without protection. Agreements to preserve additional areas are proving difficult and some 37 areas of untouched rainforest are being given annual reprieves from logging while negotiations continue.

For a glimpse of this unique area, take a ride on the BC Ferries' Discovery Coast or Inside Passage ferries. Expect to see the rainforest's beauty and its tragedy.

For information on the area, contact **Bella Coola Valley Tourism** (☎ 250-982-2212; www .bellacoola.ca).

SLEEPING & EATING
Bella Coola Motel (☎ 250-799-5323; motel@bellacoola valley.com; r $60-80) On Burke Ave at Clayton St, this motel includes the only campground right in town. Motel rooms are in separate cabins complete with kitchens. You can rent scooters, bikes and canoes here.

Bella Coola Valley Inn (☎ 250-799-5316, 888-799-5316; www.bellacoolavalleyinn.com; r $65-95) This place, at the corner of Dean St and Hwy 20, has large rooms; the inn contains a restaurant and the Salty Dog Pub – Artie would love it.

Gnome's Home (☎ 250-982-2504; www.gnomes home.ca; site $15-18) On Hwy 20 in Hagensborg, Gnome's Home offers shady sites. Amenities include flush toilets, showers and a covered cooking area. Kill time pondering the meaning of the little gnome logo.

Moore's Organic Market (☎ 250-799-5975; South Grant Rd, 5km east of Bella Coola) Here you'll find a good selection of fresh, baked and preserved items. Much of the produce is grown locally. It certainly rains enough.

GETTING THERE & AWAY
BC Ferries (☎ 888-223-3779; www.bcferries.com) runs the Discovery Coast ferry, which links Bella Coola and Port Hardy, three times a week in summer only.

The North

Northern BC is a vast, sparsely populated region dominated by the Rockies and Coast Mountains and decorated with swift rivers, fish-filled lakes and lush forests. If you're starting the Alaska Highway from Dawson Creek, it may seem like things are starting off slow, but just wait. When you turn west and then north from Fort Nelson, you're heading into a remarkable landscape that will have you exclaiming, 'That's the most wonderful thing I've ever seen!' each time you go around a bend. Until, that is, you go around another bend and have to say it again. On the coast, Prince Rupert is an underrated town that is also a gateway to the remarkable Queen Charlotte Islands – a beguiling and mysterious place that matches all of its hype.

Should you be fortunate enough to take the ferry south from Prince Rupert or north to Alaska and the Yukon, you'll be in for the trip of a lifetime. The summer waters abound with whales, dolphins, otters and more. Soon you'll be saying 'Oh look, another eagle'.

If you find yourself missing haute cuisine, remember what you're coming here for: the scenery, the wildlife and the sheer beauty. You're here to meet the locals, who are eager to welcome you into their relaxed and friendly lives. Join them in some outdoor sports: this is a great area to raft, hike, kayak or ski. Learn about First Nations people, too: here more than anywhere else in BC you can access this aspect of the area's culture and history.

HIGHLIGHTS

- Riding the ferry through the **Inside Passage** (p323) en route to Alaska and the Yukon
- Following the scenic **Alaska Highway** (p308) from Fort Nelson to the Yukon
- Beachcombing on the wild, windswept shores of the **Queen Charlotte Islands** (p324)
- Dining on fresh halibut and salmon in **Prince Rupert** (p322)
- Following the totem pole trail through the **Hazeltons** (p316)

★ Alaska Hwy

★ The Hazeltons

Prince Rupert ★

Queen Charlotte Islands ★

★ Inside Passage

THE NORTH

58°N

142°W   140°W   138°W   136°W   134°W   132°W

Yukon Territory

Alaska Hwy

Alaska (USA)

St Elias Mountains

Tatshenshini-Alsek Provincial Wilderness Park

Skagway

7

Atlin

Atlin Provincial Park & Recreation Area

British Columbia

Continental Divide

Cassiar

Good Hope Lake

58°N

Coast Mountains

Pacific Time Zone

Alaska Time Zone

Juneau

Tuya River

Dease Lake

Dease Lake

Grand Canyon of the Stikine

Stikine River Recreation Area

Telegraph Creek

Mt Edziza Provincial Park

Iskut

Kinaskan Lake Provincial Park

0   50 km
0   30 miles

Kispiox

Babine Range

Alaska (USA)

Nisga'a Memorial Lava Bed Provincial Park

37

Gitanyow

South Hazelton

Hazelton

New Hazelton

Kitwanga

Kitwanga Fort National Historic Site

Babine Mountains Recreation Area

Meziadin Lake Provincial Park

Meziadin Junction

37

Portland Inlet

Khutzeymateen Grizzly Bear Sanctuary

Seven Sisters Peaks (2755m)

Smithers

Ski Smithers

Driftwood Canyon Provincial Park

Granisle

Topley Landing

Stewart Hyder

Cambria Icefields

Terrace

16

Lakelse Lake Provincial Park

Topley

56°N

Prince Rupert

Port Edward

Port Essington

Skeena River

Lakelse Lake

Houston

Burns Lake

Meziadin Lake Provincial Park

Kitimat

British Columbia

François Lake

Portland Inlet

Kitimat Ranges

Skeena R

Chatham Channel

54°N

Dixon Entrance

Masset

Naikoon Provincial Park

Graham Island

Banks Island

Douglas Channel

16

Queen Charlotte City

Skidegate

Sandspit

PACIFIC OCEAN

Moresby Island

Queen Charlotte Islands

Hecate Strait

Aristazabal Island

52°N

Gwaii Haanas National Park Reserve

138°W   136°W   134°W   132°W   130°W

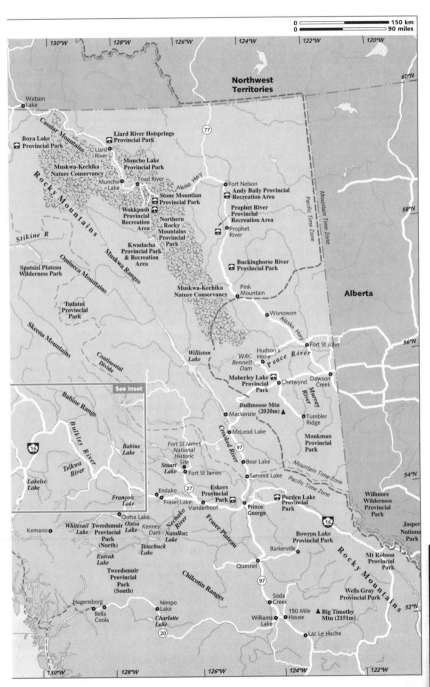

PRINCE GEORGE
pop 74,000

In 1807 Simon Fraser's men cut the first spruce trees down to build Fort George for the North West Company. Since then, vast cutting and milling of the tree earned Prince George the title of 'spruce capital of the world', though most of the town's spruces sit in piles instead of forests. Prince George, dominated by pulp mills, is a sprawling and not very interesting or attractive town, but it serves as a useful crossroads and gateway to the north.

Because it's so close to the center of BC, many tree-planters, truckers, loggers and travelers end up killing time in Prince George, which means that bustling bars, motels and hotels have sprung up to cater to visitors' needs. There's also a couple of worthwhile museums that help add context to your visit to the north.

The University of Northern British Columbia, which opened in 1994, has grown quickly and helped diversify the town's culture away from the purely industrial. And note that the town mascot, the cleverly named 'Mr PG Mascot' may be the least likely mascot ever to be sold as an endearing plush toy.

Orientation

Hwy 97 from Cache Creek becomes a commercial strip cutting through the center of town before heading north on its way to Dawson Creek (406km) and Mile 0 of the Alaska Hwy. The Yellowhead Hwy (Hwy 16) becomes Victoria St as it runs through town. At 1st Ave, Victoria St comes to an abrupt end. The Yellowhead continues on 1st Ave and crosses over the Yellowhead Bridge on its way eastward, headed for Jasper (376km) and Edmonton. On the south end of town, Hwy 16 veers westward to become the long, scenic route to Prince Rupert (724km). The downtown area is small, with little character.

Information

BOOKSTORES

Stock up now as the selection does not get better as you head further north.

Books & Company (☎ 250-563-6637; 1685 3rd Ave; ☿ 8am-6pm Mon, Wed & Sat, 8am-9pm Thu, 8am-10pm Fri, 10am-5pm Sun) In a beautiful building downtown.

Mosquito Books (☎ 250-563-6495; 1600 15th Ave; ☿ 9am-8pm) In the Parkwood Centre.

LAUNDRY
Coin Laundry (231 George St; ☿ 7am-7pm)

LIBRARY
Prince George Library (Bob Harkins Branch; ☎ 250-563-9251; 887 Dominion St, Civic Centre; ☿ 10am-9pm Mon-Thu, 10am-5:30pm Fri & Sat, 1-5pm Sun Sep-May) Free Internet access.

MEDICAL SERVICES
Prince George Regional Hospital (☎ 250-565-2000; 2000 15th Ave; ☿ 24hr)

MONEY
Banks and ATMs abound in Prince George and wherever you are you usually will be very close to one, especially the latter.

POST
Main post office (☎ 250-561-2568; 1323 5th Ave; ☿ 8:30-5pm Mon-Fri)

TOURIST INFORMATION
Note that Prince George's VICs may consolidate in a new location in the VIA Rail station; even Mr PG Mascot may make the move.

Visitor Info Centre (☎ 250-562-3700, 800-668-7646; www.tourismpg.bc.ca; 1198 Victoria St; ☿ 8:30am-5pm

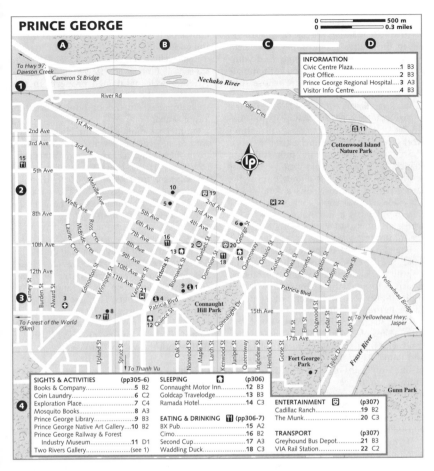

PRINCE GEORGE

Mon-Sat, closed Sat winter) Second location (☎ 250-563-5493; Hwy 97 and Hwy 16; ☼ 9am-7pm summer)

Sights & Activities

Exploration Place (☎ 250-562-1612; Fort George Park; adult/child $10.95/8.95; ☼ 10am-5pm summer, 10am-5pm Wed-Sun winter), southeast of the downtown area on the corner of 20th Ave and Queensway, was once prosaically known as the Fraser–Fort George Regional Museum. But extensive renovations brought big changes including a SimEx ride simulator (where you get shaken up like a can of paint at the hardware store), a public atrium and 12,000 sq feet of exhibition space devoted to nature and history. Once you get past the gloss designed to attract people afraid

of the word 'museum' the centre is a very good stop. There's lots of good historical stuff – especially on the Carrier, Cree and Kwakiutl peoples – and it's fun to check out the Nature Exchange, where kids can trade rocks and other items they've found.

Prince George Railway & Forest Industry Museum (☎ 250-563-7351; 850 River Rd; adult/child $6/5; ☼ 9am-5pm May 15-Oct 15) is situated beside Cottonwood Island Nature Park and features a large and growing collection of train memorabilia, including many old cars and cabooses, a unique 1903 wooden snow plow and a 1913 steam-powered crane. On the forestry side of things, there's an antique chainsaw display and a logging arch truck, used to push around logs.

The **Prince George Native Art Gallery** (☎ 250-614-7726; 1600 3rd Ave; ☺ 9am-5pm Tue-Fri, 10am-4pm Sat) in the Native Friendship Centre, sells works by local artists. You may find yourself just standing in awe as you contemplate the art produced by a culture whose spiritual life is so closely tied to nature.

Two Rivers Gallery (☎ 250-614-7800; 725 Civic Centre Plaza; adult/child $5.50/2, admission free Thu; ☺ 10am-5pm Tue-Sat, until 9pm Thu, noon-5pm Sun) features works by local and regional artists.

Six companies operate pulp mills in Prince George. To find out – literally – what all the stink is about, one of the largest firms, Canfor, runs a **forestry tour** (☎ 250-561-5700; admission free; ☺ 2pm Mon-Tue & Thu-Fri). This is a fascinating way to see where all our wood comes from. Note that the minimum age is 12.

The 33-hectare **Cottonwood Island Nature Park**, north of downtown between the railway tracks and the river, is a protected riparian forest with a good network of trails. Many birds, beavers and moose thrive in the wet cottonwood forest.

The 130-hectare **Forests of the World** features 15km of easily navigable interpretive trails with plaques that tell about local flora and fauna. The forest lies at the north end of the University of Northern British Columbia campus west of town. To get there, follow 15th Ave west and turn right on Foothills Blvd. Then turn left on Cranbrook Hill Rd and left again on Kueng Rd, which you follow to the forest.

If you've ever wanted to stroke a llama, you'll have your chance at **Strider Adventures** (☎ 250-963-9542, 800-665-7752; www.pgweb.com/strider). The company offers nature hikes that last from four hours to seven days at prices from $30 per person. It's a great deal, you hike and enjoy the scenery and the environmentally sensitive Peruvian icon carries your stuff.

Sleeping
MOTELS & HOTELS
Ramada Hotel (☎ 250-563-0055, 800-830-8833; www.ramadaprincegeorge.com; 444 George St; r $110-180; P ☒ ☐ ☒) A good choice for business travelers, if a tad bland. Nice indoor pool, large rooms and a well-equipped and free business center are the primary allures.

Goldcap Travelodge (☎ 250-563-0666, 800-663-8239; www.goldcapinn.com; 1458 7th Ave; r $63-76;

P ☒) An old standby that remains a good choice by being well maintained and offering good value.

Connaught Motor Inn (☎ 250-562-4441, 800-663-6620; 1550 Victoria St; r $65-90; P ☒ ☐ ☒) Another well-maintained property in the center, this tidy motel offers three good ways to relax: an indoor pool, a hot tub and a sauna.

Numerous motels line the Hwy 97 strip west of the center of town. You should have no problems finding a room here. **Esther's Inn** (☎ 250-562-4131, 800-663-6844; www.esthersinn.com; 1151 Commercial Cres; r $60-100; P ☒ ☒) Even if it's pissing down outside, it's Tiki paradise inside at Esther's which has Polynesian gardens under its cavernous roof.

B&BS
An association of B&B owners operates the **Bed & Breakfast Hotline** (☎ 250-562-2222, 877-562-2626; www.princegeorgebnb.com), a free booking service that will help you arrange a B&B in your price range. The association also provides transportation from the train or bus station. For more information, visit the website (above). You can also get a listing of B&Bs from the Visitor Info Centre.

CAMPING
Beware that most campgrounds around Prince George cater to RVs, meaning that the tenting sites are generally not ideal.

Bee Lazee Campground (☎ 250-963-7263, 866-679-6699; 15910 Hwy 97S; tent site $14), 10km south of town, features full facilities, including free hot showers, a pool and laundry. As the name suggests, the place also includes a honey farm. You get to be lazy while the bees are busy.

Eating & Drinking
Look for locally brewed Pacific Coast Brewing beers; the Canterbury and Ironhorse are excellent. Call ☎ 250-562-2424 for tour information.

Cimo (☎ 250-564-7975; 601 Victoria St; meals $10-25; ☺ lunch Mon-Fri, dinner Mon-Sat) The stylish and casual décor is spare, which lets you concentrate on the food. Owned by two Italians, the menu features fresh pasta and other Mediterranean treats.

Thanh Vu (☎ 250-564-2255; 1604 20th Ave at Spruce St; meals $8-12; ☺ lunch Mon-Fri, dinner) is popular with locals who like its fresh Vietnamese cuisine. The chili garlic ginger pork and the shrimp salad are treats.

Waddling Duck (☎ 250-561-5550; 1157 5th Ave; meals $6-20; ☼ dinner Mon-Sat) is a dinner house cum British pub. The menu doesn't hold surprises (burgers, pasta, steaks etc) but the food makes up for it by being surprisingly good. Enjoy it and the many beers at a sidewalk table.

BX Pub (☎ 250-561-2900; 433 Carnie St & 5th Ave; meals $6-10; ☼ 11am-late) is a large and friendly neighborhood joint near the center. The pub menu is good as are the many outdoor tables where you can usually find a good crowd from the university.

Second Cup (☎ 250-562-1930; 1600 15th Ave; Parkwood Centre; coffee $2; ☼ 7am-8pm) has great coffee and muffins. It's a local hang-out.

Entertainment
For dancing, polish off your cowboy boots and swagger on over to the bustling **Cadillac Ranch** (☎ 250-563-7720; 1380 2nd Ave; cover varies; ☼ 3pm-2am), where the band or the DJ plays only country music and you can two-step to your heart's content. The club gets many touring live acts like Ken McCoy.

The Munk (☎ 250-564-3773; 1192 5th Ave; cover $5; ☼ late Wed-Sun) has a gothic theme and many varying theme nights, from Top 40 to punk.

Getting There & Away
AIR
Prince George airport (YXS; ☎ 250-963-2400) is on Airport Rd off Hwy 97. Air Canada Jazz serves Vancouver; low-fare Westjet serves Calgary, Vancouver and Victoria.

BUS
Greyhound (☎ 250-564-5454; 1566 12th Ave) Greyhound offer a service to Dawson Creek, Kamloops, Prince Rupert, Vancouver and Whitehorse.

TRAIN
VIA Rail station (1300 1st Ave) VIA's *Skeena* heads west three times a week to Prince Rupert and east three times a week to Jasper and Edmonton.

Getting Around
To get to downtown hotels and motels from the airport, take the **Airporter bus** (☎ 250-563-2220; $10).

Prince George Transit (☎ 250-563-0011) operates local buses.

Major car rental agencies have offices at the airport. For a cab, try **Prince George Taxi** (☎ 250-564-4444).

PRINCE GEORGE TO DAWSON CREEK
As you travel north from Prince George, the mountains and forests give way to gentle rolling hills and farmland as Hwy 97 follows the spectacular 1923km-long Peace River. Beginning in the mid-1700s, the Cree and Beaver First Nations lived along the river and called it the 'river of beavers' for its huge populations of these thick-furred rodents. The two tribes warred periodically over the boundaries of the river, finally coming to an agreement about 200 years ago. They renamed the river the 'Peace'. The east-flowing Peace River carves the only sizeable opening through the Rockies to Alberta, making the climate in this region more similar to the prairie climate in Alberta. The climate also affects the political and social slant of the northeast communities; people read Alberta newspapers, know more about Alberta politics and tend to get their city fix in Grand Prairie instead of, say, Prince George or Vancouver.

If you are making this drive, you are probably heading north to bigger and better things. Although there are a few diversions along the way to the start of the Alaska Highway should you need them, there's really no reason to dawdle on your way to Dawson Creek.

For the first 150km north of Prince George, Hwy 97 passes Summit, Bear and MacLeod Lakes, with provincial parks and camping along the way. North of MacLeod Lake, Hwy 39 heads west for 29km to **Mackenzie** (pop 6000), which sits on the southern shores of the 200km-long **Williston Lake**, the largest artificial reservoir in North America and the largest lake in BC. Mackenzie's claim to tourism fame is the 'world's largest tree crusher', a mammoth piece of machinery that sits, ironically, beside a wooded area along the town's main street. The big yellow crusher was used to clear the floodplain under what is now Williston Lake.

The next stop off Hwy 97, **Chetwynd** (pop 3280), 300km north of Prince George, is little more than a strip of services along the highway. This industrial town contains two sawmills, a pulp mill and a gas plant; it's no surprise that such a gritty place has become known for its chainsaw art. More than 15 carvings of varying sizes are spread around town, including the bears under the 'Welcome to Chetwynd' sign.

From Chetwynd you can head north through Hudson's Hope along Hwy 29 and avoid Dawson Creek and Fort St John on your way north.

Hudson's Hope (pop 1100), 66km north of Chetwynd on Hwy 29, overlooks the Peace River. The town's economy revolves around livestock ranching, grain and forage crops. Wildlife in the area is abundant (10 of North America's big game species are found here), but the biggest spectacle is the **WAC Bennett Dam** (☎ 250-783-5048; admission free; ⏱ 9:30am-4:30pm mid-May–mid-Oct). One of the world's largest earth-filled structures, the hydro-electric dam is 24km west of Hudson's Hope. Tours take you 150m down inside the dam where you can learn about the wonders of electricity. Watch out for leaks.

From Chetwynd you can take Hwy 29 94km south to **Tumbler Ridge** (pop 2500). From here you can continue another 45km along the dirt Murray River Rd to **Kinuseo Falls**. Located inside **Monkman Provincial Park**, the spectacular falls are 60m higher than Niagara Falls. You can walk along a five-minute trail to the upper lookout or carry on 20 minutes further to the Murray River and look up at the falls. The **Kinuseo Falls Campground** offers 42 wooded campsites ($14) close to the river and falls.

As for Tumbler Ridge, it was born in the early 1980s to service the enormous Quintette Mine, the world's largest open-pit coalmine. But coal giveth and coal taketh away and the local coalmines mostly closed between 2000 and 2003. Modern, clean and quiet Tumbler Ridge is a town in search of a future.

ALASKA HIGHWAY

DAWSON CREEK
pop 11,500

Dawson Creek, 412km north of Prince George on Hwy 97, is notable as the starting point – **Mile 0** – for the Alaska or Alcan

---

WHAT TIME IS IT ANYWAY?

Most of the northwestern communities share the same time zone as Alberta – Mountain Standard Time (MST) – while much of the rest of the province is on Pacific Standard Time (PST). However, the timeline does an odd little boogie through the region. Like Prince George, Mackenzie is on PST, as is Fort Nelson and all points west of it. Chetwynd, Hudson's Hope, Tumbler Ridge, Dawson Creek and Fort St John are on MST and do not observe Daylight Saving Time. This means that in winter those towns are one hour ahead of the rest of BC; in summer, everybody's on the same time since Pacific Daylight Saving Time is the same as Mountain Standard Time.

(short for Alaska–Canada) Hwy. Beginning at Dawson Creek, the Alaska Hwy goes through Watson Lake and Whitehorse in the Yukon all the way to Fairbanks in Alaska, some 2237km (although progress in the form of road improvements keeps nibbling away at that total).

Known only as the 'Beaver Plains', the immediate area saw no White settlement until the turn of the 20th century. In 1879, the town's namesake, Dr George Mercer Dawson, led a survey team through here in search of a route to bring the railway over the Alberta Rockies. Though the railway didn't happen until later, Dawson's studies aided settlement and prompted later exploration for oil and natural gas. Unlike many other explorers, Dawson studied Native communities and languages, which, along with his geological and botanical studies across Canada, earned him the title 'Father of Canadian Anthropology'.

When the Northern Alberta Railway (NAR) finally chugged into town in 1931, the city quickly became a thriving agricultural center.

The Dawson Creek **Visitor Info Centre** (☎ 250-782-9595, 866-645-3022; ⏱ 8am-7pm summer, 9am-5pm Mon-Sat spring & fall, Tue-Sat winter) is in the NAR Park along the highway, which becomes Alaska Ave as it runs through town. The visitor info centre located in the nicely restored old train station, also has a fun little museum, good for a few moments of diversion.

Sadly for Dawson Creek boosters, there is virtually no link to the popular TV show *Dawson's Creek* which ran for six seasons and followed the lives of four teens (who certainly looked well into their 20s by the show's end) in a town near Boston. So sadly the closest you'll get to Dawson, Jen, Joey and the rest is with the boxed DVD collection for sale at the Wal-Mart at the edge of town.

A signpost in the middle of the intersection of 102nd Ave and 10th St has become a highly photographed post that celebrates the start of the Alaska Hwy. The real **Mile 0** is actually at the east end of NAR Park – a signpost used to stand there, but the cars slowing down to look hindered traffic and now the sign is gone. Given that the biggest reason to come to Dawson Creek is to head north on the Alaska Hwy, now's the time to put the pedal to the metal and get out of town.

Sleeping & Eating

If you're not clearing out of town in a hurry, there are many places to stay – some belonging to chains that will come to seem like old friends as you journey north.

The lovable **Alaska Hotel** (☎ 250-782-7998; www.alaskahotel.com; 10209 10th St; r $30-45; P 💻) is Dawson Creek's oldest hotel. The management's philosophy is 'deluxe evolutionary' which means 'always changing for the better'. The small rooms have furnishings that were new when the Alaska Hwy opened. And we're not making this up, a patron in the very fun **bar** said: 'The beds squeak. If you get lucky, you can play the bedspring symphony'. It'll be up to you to decide if you're going for A sharp or B flat. Bathrooms are shared. Even if you don't make music here, you can listen to live music in the bar. The **Alaska Café** (☎ 250-782-7040; meals $8-15; ⓧ lunch & dinner) in the hotel is an excellent restaurant, the best in town. Creative touches on the menu of pasta, steaks and seafood shows there's a savvy chef in the kitchen.

Those non-musically inclined will enjoy the **George Dawson Inn** (☎ 250-782-9151, 800-663-2745; www.georgedawsoninn.bc.ca; 11705 8th St; r $72-84; P ⓧ), with a restaurant and pub, and big, comfy rooms, with oodles of TV channels and fridges for cold stuff.

The **Mile 0 RV Park & Campground** (☎ 250-782-2590; www.citydirect.ca/mile0; site $12) should

---

ENGINEERING MARVEL

Northeastern British Columbia was once just a massive tract of wilderness, with a geography of squishy muskeg ground and vast prairies, so different from the rest of the province that no one really knew what to do with it. With harsh winters and short, hot summers, the massive land attracted few residents, which meant that people tapped into only a speck of its rich natural resources. While the rest of the province was settled and growing, the Peace region was 'that snowy place up there somewhere'. Finally, though, events totally unrelated to this big chunk of forest put the Peace on the proverbial map.

It was wartime and the US feared for its unprotected Alaska coast. There was nothing except wind and snow to prevent a Japanese attack on the long, segmented arm of Alaska's Aleutian Islands. The only way up there was by plane or by boat along the long, stormy coast. Americans needed a land route through Canada to move troops in to protect Alaska.

The engineering feat that ensued was truly incredible. With no time to waste, survey crews stormed through the vast forests, followed soon after by more than 11,000 troops, 16,000 civilian workers and 7000 pieces of equipment. From the air, it looked like a massive razor had come along and shaved a thick strip of the forest's heavy beard. More than 8000 culverts and 133 bridges closed the river gaps. A mere nine months and six days after work started, the 2453km-long route from Dawson Creek to Fairbanks, Alaska, officially opened on November 20, 1942. The cost? A then-astonishing and today still-remarkable $135 million.

Though no one ever attacked Alaska, the highway was an integral part of settlement in the Peace and in the entire northern region of BC. The highway is a vital link between the USA and Canada – and the scenery isn't bad either. For a good idea of what the road was like in its early days, check out the historic segment north of Fort St John (p310).

For more on the Alaska Highway, see p345.

actually be called the Kilometer 2.5 RV Park & Campground as that's where it is on the Alaska Hwy. It offers hot showers, laundry and basic tent sites for $10.

There's a good **Farmer's Market** (⊗ 8am-noon Sat May-Oct) by the VIC. It's a good way to get some tasty locally produced items for the journey ahead.

Getting There & Away

At the **Greyhound** (☎ 250-782-3131; 1201 Alaska Ave) terminal you'll find buses north to the Yukon, and southwest to Prince George.

DAWSON CREEK TO FORT NELSON

As the Alaska Hwy heads northwest from Dawson Creek and crosses the Peace River on its way into the foothills of the Rocky Mountains, the landscape again changes, with the prairies soon left behind.

About 28km north of Dawson Creek, look for signs and a road to the east that is a 10km remnant of the original Alaska Hwy. The highlight of this pretty little drive is the **Kiskatinaw Bridge**, a 163m curved wooden structure that you drive across. The north end of the road is 41km south from Fort St John.

Fort St John, 75km north of Dawson Creek on Hwy 97, mainly functions as a service center for the oil and gas industries and the surrounding farms. Don't let it serve as a service center for you, even if a local tourism official in noting the town's many trained mechanics says 'It's a great place to break down!'. 'There's not much here', another local said, regarding recent events in Fort St John, 'Wal-Mart opened and the bookstore closed'.

But should you need a break, the **Fort St John–North Peace Museum** (☎ 250-787-0430; 9323 100th St; adult/child $3/2; ⊗ 9am-5pm Mon-Sat) is well done. Check out the giant stuffed polar bear, a vial filled with the first drops of oil, and the story of Jack Baker, who went from airline manager to brain surgeon in one day.

As you continue up the Alaska Hwy, you will have plenty of time to marvel at the scenery as the road gradually leaves the foothills and begins a gentle climb into the Rocky Mountains. Most towns on the highway have only one or two service stations. **Wonowon** (One-o-One), is named for its place at Mile 101 on the highway.

During highway construction, soldiers were stationed here to staff the Blueberry Checkpoint, where anyone traveling the road would have to stop. The soldiers would search your car and send you back if you didn't have enough provisions (and spare auto parts) to make it through the vast wilderness that lay ahead.

Next, you will pass **Pink Mountain**, so named for the incredible pink hue the mountain takes on at sunrise. Before hitting Fort Nelson, you'll pass by a few provincial parks, all of which are nice spots to camp, with water and pit toilets. First, at Km 278, is the **Buckinghorse River Provincial Park**, where you might see moose grazing alongside the river if you get up early. The 34 sites cost $12.

Prophet River Provincial Recreation Area, at Km 350, offers 12 sites ($14) and access to a section of the original Alaska Hwy.

At Km 430, you'll see signs to **Andy Bailey Provincial Recreation Area**, 11km off the highway on a gravel road. The park enjoys access to quiet Jackfish Lake. The entry fee is by donation only. The scenery over this entire stretch is pleasant enough but ultimately rather dull. And there's a dearth of rest stops.

Fort Nelson

pop 4700

The last sizeable town in BC, Fort Nelson boasts the northernmost traffic light and the northernmost golf course. Like Fort St John, Fort Nelson started as a fur-trading post, but the town didn't flourish until the Alaska Hwy came through. But 'flourish' is perhaps too grand a word. Up here in the northeastern portion of the province, bears outnumber people 16 to 1. Barely a dozen cops work in the entire area, and if there's a storm, it'll be a long while until anyone gets there to help. First Nations people – mostly Dene – make up about 15% of the population.

Fort Nelson, 483km north of Dawson Creek, mainly functions as a service center and industrial town, home to Canada's largest gas processing plant and BC's largest wood products plant (which is bigger than 13 football fields). Though the winters are long, dark and cold, that's when most of the logging takes place – when the muskeg freezes over and trucks can

RYAN'S WILD DAY

It was the end of a long day driving. I was heading east to Fort Nelson on a late summer day when it still seemed absurdly light out, given the hour. Heading down the hill from Stone Provincial Park, I saw a variety of lumps moving along the roadside. They were porcupines. Big porcupines. Really big and healthy porcupines out for what I guessed was their evening stroll. It was my first time seeing these guys and it was fascinating, all those quills. All that auto glass between me and them.

I had become used to seeing lots of deer at almost all hours while driving. In the Yukon I'd seen moose (a personal triumph as I'd always had a soft spot for the huge beasts). But I hadn't seen what I found around a curve a few kilometers further along: a herd of elk. In the road, just standing there with not a thought of giving way for a guidebook writer on a schedule. I sat. They stood. There were no other cars. I took a few photos. Very up close, very personal. Eventually I made my way through the herd. I did a lot of yelling, 'Hey elk, go eat some grass.'

A few more klicks up the road and there it was, a large black bear hanging out by the roadside, definitely not hitch-hiking, in fact not really doing anything. I stopped a good distance away and just watched its sleek pelt ripple as it slowly ambled along. Eventually I got to Fort Nelson. I reminded myself, this is why you come to the north.

get into places not accessible in summer. Almost anyone driving the Alaska Hwy stops here, mostly because it's a long way to anywhere else. To serve this traffic, motels continue to spring up along the highway. Also, exploration by energy companies has poured money into the area, so there's a slight boomtown feel.

The **Visitor Info Centre** (☎ 250-774-2541; www.northernrockies.org; 5500 50th Ave N; ⏰ 8am-8pm summer) has local information.

The **Fort Nelson Heritage Museum** (☎ 250-774-3536; adult/child $3/2; ⏰ 8:30am-7:30pm summer), also at the west end of town, shows a movie about the highway's construction. You can check out a trapper's cabin or get a close-up look at a big stuffed moose.

SLEEPING & EATING

Super 8 Fort Nelson (☎ 250-233-5025, 888-482-8884; www.super8.com; 4503 50th Ave; r $80-120; P �併 🖫 🖭) A nice new hotel with an indoor pool and a good free breakfast. The top-notch rooms have high-speed Internet access as well as fridges and microwaves.

The bustling **Blue Bell Inn** (☎ 250-774-6961, 800-663-5267; bluebell@pris.bc.ca; s/d $69/79; P) contains a restaurant, 24-hour convenience store, coin laundry and good rooms with kitchenettes.

If you want to camp close to town, go to the **Westend Campground & RV Park** (☎ 250-774-2340; site $17; 🖫), two blocks west of town. The full facilities include laundry, pay showers and a wildlife display.

The most popular spot in town for a meal is the lively and fun **Dan's Neighbourhood Pub** (☎ 250-774-3929; 4204 50th Ave N; meal $7-15). The usual steaks, pasta and burger menu also has salads and everything is quite good.

FORT NELSON TO WATSON LAKE

Now the fun begins. The drive west and then north from Fort Nelson passes through awesome terrain. Be prepared for vistas, peaks, lakes and a heck of a lot of animals. Muncho Lake is an azure jewel among the Rockies.

At Km 393, past Fort Nelson, the Liard Hwy (Hwy 77) heads north to the North-west Territories, Fort Simpson and the remote Nahanni National Park.

At Km 600, 140km west of Fort Nelson, the highway passes through the north end of beautiful **Stone Mountain Provincial Park**, in the eastern Muskwa Ranges of the Rockies; the 'stone mountain' in question is Mt St Paul (2127m). The incredible vistas at the 1267m Summit Pass will leave you breathless. The park's 28-site campground ($14), open May to October, offers access to hiking trails and backcountry camping. Look for the dramatic hoodoos – eroded stone pillars – at **Wokkpash Creek.**

At the tiny town of **Toad River**, a former hunting lodge, **Toad River Lodge** (☎ 250-232-5401; www.toadriverlodge.com; r $50), that was opened by two brothers who worked as surveyors for the Alaska Hwy project, still rents out rooms. The lodge's restaurant ceiling is lined with hundreds of baseball caps from around the world.

Muncho Lake Provincial Park

Spruce forests, vast rolling mountains and some truly breathtaking scenery surround Muncho Lake Provincial Park, located at Km 650. This 88,412-hectare park lies along the emerald-green Muncho Lake, and the highway curves along the lake's west shore. 'Muncho' means 'big lake' in the Tagish language, and at 12km long, it's one of the largest natural lakes in the Rockies. For the highway construction crews, cutting the rocky bluff along the lakeside was the most difficult and costly part of the construction. Today, it's an unforgettable piece of road. Stone sheep often gather alongside the highway to lick the artificial accumulations of salt from the stones. The mountains are part of the Terminal Range, which mark the northernmost section of the Rocky Mountains, ending at Liard River (60km northwest). The mountains extending northward into the Yukon and Alaska are the Mackenzies, which are geologically different. Of Muncho Lake's two campgrounds, **Strawberry Flats Campground** (site $14) is especially stunning. It's on a point overlooking the lake's turquoise waters.

There are a few lodges scattered along the highway through the park. **Northern Rockies Lodge** (☎ 250-776-3481, 800-663-5269; www.northern-rockies-lodge.com; site $20, r $60-80) is a newer and more comfortable place on the water with a campground, nice rooms and a restaurant.

Liard River Hotsprings Provincial Park

This park's mineral springs have been used for centuries by Natives, trappers and explorers, and could very well be the best natural hot springs you'll ever dip into. The underground bubbling springs create a lush boreal marsh and tropical vegetation that seems very out of place this far north. An incredible 250 species of plants, including 14 different varieties of orchids, grow in this unique ecosystem.

Just 500m along a boardwalk from the parking lot leads to the large **Alpha pool**, where you can sit and soak for hours. If you get tired of that, walk around and check out some of the strikingly green ferns or colorful wildflowers that thrive in the heat and humidity. From the Alpha pool, stroll five minutes further up the boardwalk to the deeper, slightly cooler **Beta pool**. Fewer people come here, so take the opportunity to jump in and swim over to the sides where it's shallower; be sure to let the warm bottom mud ooze through your toes.

The park's **campground** (☎ 800-689-9025; www.discovercamping.ca; site $17) has 52 sites. Rangers run interpretive programs throughout the summer. Visiting the pools is free, but beware that the pools can get really busy in July and August. If you can't come in the spring or fall, try coming later at night, when the families have gone to bed. The park gate closes from 10pm to 6am; outside of these hours you can still go in the springs, but if you're not camping in the park, you need to leave your car outside the gate and walk in.

From here it is 220km to Watson lake and the Yukon. Look for **scenic overlooks** of the Liard River.

YELLOWHEAD HIGHWAY

The 3185km Yellowhead Hwy (Hwy 16) actually starts on the Canadian prairies at Winnipeg, Manitoba, climbing west through the provinces of Saskatchewan, Alberta and BC. In the North, it is the only road that connects the east and west sides of the province. VIA Rail's Skeena line follows the Yellowhead from Jasper to Prince Rupert.

From Prince George, the highway meanders along into the heart of the Lakes District at Burns Lake, through the alpine outdoor adventure town of Smithers to the Hazeltons, an area rich in First Nations history. From there, it cuts southwest to Terrace, a service town that leads into the rich Nass Valley. The 147km drive from Terrace to Prince Rupert is consistently rated one of the most scenic in the province; the Skeena River flows alongside it as it meanders through verdant mountains rich in wildlife. From Prince Rupert, ferries cruise in every direction: north to Alaska, south to Vancouver Island or west to the Queen Charlotte Islands, where the Yellowhead Hwy begins again, the only paved road on the islands.

VANDERHOOF

pop 4600

The first settlement of any size west of Prince George (97km away), Vanderhoof is mainly a service center most noted for its annual **air show** held the fourth weekend in July, when hundreds of small plane owners fly their planes in, camp nearby and generally have a good time. Tucked in the fertile Nechako River Valley, this town occupies the geographical center of the province. Prime grazing lands – cattle, buffalo and dairy farming – along with forestry, provide the main sources of income here. Vanderhoof is Dutch for 'of the farm', which is appropriate as it was the first permanent agricultural settlement in the province.

FORT ST JAMES NATIONAL HISTORIC SITE

Simon Fraser, searching for a navigable route to the Pacific Ocean, founded this outpost as a place to trade furs with area trappers, mostly Carrier people, who were a branch of the Dene First Nations. The Carriers got their name from the mourning ritual of widows, who carried the ashes of deceased husbands in pouches on their backs until a memorial potlatch could be held. Early French-speaking traders referred to them as 'Porteurs' (porters), which the English-speaking traders later changed to 'Carriers'.

Fraser's post became a commercial center and headquarters of the district of New Caledonia. In 1821 the fort became a Hudson's Bay Company outpost and operated until the early 20th century. Though the relationship between the fur traders and Carriers was an amicable one, it altered some of the hunter-gatherer instincts of the Carrier people and introduced a new kind of greed and materialism, all of which changed the Carriers forever.

In 1971, the **Fort St James National Historic Site** (☎ 250-996-7191; adult/child $5.95/3; ☼ May-Sep) underwent a major restoration to return it to its 1896 glory. After the excellent restoration job, the site today gives visitors an interesting look into recent yet pivotal history. Docents in each of the six major buildings give background on the structure's function and the people who lived there. Among the nuggets of info you'll learn is that people had to trap a whole lot of beavers just to trade for one blanket. There is a nice little café with views of the serene lake. This is a must-see detour.

It is 66km on Hwy 27 to the fort from the Hwy 16 turnoff, 7km past Vanderhoof.

BURNS LAKE

pop 2530

Burns Lake, 229km west of Prince George, serves as the center of the Lakes District and northern gateway to Tweedsmuir Provincial Park. It also hosts the popular **Burns Lake Bluegrass Festival**, which takes place in mid-July. Out in the middle of the lake is **Deadman's Island Provincial Park**, the province's smallest provincial park, named after an accident that killed two men working on the Grand Trunk Railway.

The carved trout sign that welcomes you to Burns Lake is a testimony to the serious anglers who descend upon the area's many lakes in spring and in summer to catch rainbow and cutthroat trout, char, kokanee, ling cod and salmon, among other fish.

Like other towns along the Yellowhead, Burns Lake experienced its population boom during the construction of the Grand Trunk Railway. Today, it is primarily a lumber town and a worthwhile place to stock up on groceries or to sleep for a night. Like most people, you'll probably want to head to the wilderness.

One of the best spots for canoeing, kayaking and fishing is 177km-long **Babine Lake**, 34km north of Burns Lake on the Babine Lake Rd. The stunning lake is well worth the detour. You can also access the lake from Topley on Hwy 16.

For information on the best fishing holes, area fishing lodges or boat rentals, see the **Burns Lake Visitor Info Centre** (☎ 250-692-3773; bldcoc@mailcity.com; 540 Hwy 16; ☼ 9am-5pm summer, Tue-Fri winter).

Sleeping & Eating

You cannot go wrong at the **Burns Lake Municipal Campground**, beside the lake, and the **Len Radley Memorial Park Campground**. The sites are – get this – free. Yes, free, though you can only stay for 72 hours. Turn south (left if you're coming from the east) at the carved trout sign.

Right in the heart of town is the **Lakeland Inn** (☎ 250-692-7771, 888-441-2999; www.hwy16.com /Lakeland/; 329 Hwy 16; r from $50; P ✕ ⛭ ⛲), with a good restaurant, bar and small but clean rooms.

New Leaf Caffe (☎ 250-692-3434; 425 Hwy 16; snack $4; ☺ lunch & dinner Mon-Sat) is a health food store that also serves coffees, baked goods and sandwiches.

TWEEDSMUIR PROVINCIAL PARK (NORTH)

Encompassing more than 981,000 hectares, Tweedsmuir is the province's second-largest provincial park. On the north and northwest, the park is bordered by the Ootsa–Whitesail Lakes Reservoir, on the west and southwest by the Coast Mountains and on the east by the Interior Plateau. The park is divided into North Tweedsmuir and South Tweedsmuir by the Dean River. The only road in the park, Hwy 20, runs through the southern section near Bella Coola on the central coast (see p296). Otherwise, you need to boat in from the Ootsa–Whitesail Lakes Reservoir, or access the park by floatplane.

Unlike many parks named for British dignitaries, Tweedsmuir took its moniker from someone who actually saw the park. In fact, John Buchan, Baron Tweedsmuir of Elsfield and also Canada's 15th governor general, traveled extensively through the park on horseback and by floatplane before it was ever named for him.

Wildlife abounds in this remote area and includes woodland caribou, goats, moose, black and grizzly bears and wolves. Up in the air, look for willow ptarmigans, gray-crowned rosy finches and golden-crowned sparrows. In the Nechako Reservoir, look for the fish-hunting ospreys in the fallen logs.

From Burns Lake, you can access North Tweedsmuir by following Hwy 35 south and catching the free ferry across Francois Lake (every 50 minutes from 5:30am to 10pm). Follow signs to the boat launch and park ranger station at Chikamin Bay (staffed May through October).

Most people will spend time on **Eutsuk Lake**, which forms a system of joining waterways with **Ootsa**, **Whitesail** and **Tetachuck Lakes**. Except Eutsuk, most lakes were dramatically raised in 1952 with the building of the Kenney Dam and the creation of the Nechako Reservoir. The raised waters were deemed necessary to generate enough power to serve the giant Alcan aluminum smelter in Kitimat.

Anyone venturing into wild Tweedsmuir should plan carefully and be ready to experience full wilderness camping and boating. You will need to be totally self-sufficient and prepared for any conditions.

SMITHERS
pop 5800

In the heart of the pretty Bulkley Valley, surrounded by the stunning Hudson Bay, Bulkley and Babine Mountains, Smithers prides itself on being 'the town for all seasons', and has turned itself into a hotbed of outdoor adventure and activity.

Smithers was chosen as the divisional headquarters of the Grand Trunk Railway and was the first village to be incorporated in BC (1921). It became a town in 1967 and today is a government and administrative center with a casual alpine feel that's epitomized by Alpine Al, a wooden statue standing at the head of Main St. Al, along with his 10-foot-long alpenhorn, is the town's distinctive mascot.

The people of Smithers absolutely love their town, and try hard to balance the allure of tourist money with the downside of growth.

Smithers has the area's best restaurants and accommodations. This is an excellent choice for a stop on the Yellowhead.

Information

The weekly *Interior News* is a wonderful community newspaper that has stories about such things as the local woman who grew a 1kg radish.

There are a couple good bookstores here. **Mountain Eagle Books & Bistro** (☎ 250-847-5245; 3775 3rd St; ☺ 9am-6pm Mon-Sat) has a good range of books and is an excellent spot for community information.

Besides books, lots of magazines and newspapers, **Van's News** (☎ 250-847-3848; 1126 Main St; ☺ 8am-9pm) has paid Internet access ($1 per 15 minutes).

The name says it all: at **Wash the Works** (☎ 250-847-4177; 4148 Hwy 16; ☺ 8am-8pm) you get coin-operated cleaning for your clothes, your car and your body.

Across the parking lot from the Buckley Valley Museum, the **Visitor Info Centre** (☎ 250-847-5072, 800-542-6673; www.tourismsmithers.com; 1411

Court St; 9am-6pm summer, 9am-5pm Mon-Fri winter) has free Internet access.

Sights

Smithers' **Main St** is a delightful place to go for a stroll, with a full range of shops and services. There are enjoyable walks along the **Bulkley River** in town at **Riverside Park**.

In the 1925 courthouse now called the Central Park Building, at the junction of Main St and Hwy 16, you'll find the **Bulkley Valley Museum** (250-847-5322; admission free; 10am-5pm, closed Sun winter), which features exhibits on Smithers' pioneer days. In the same building, the **Smithers Art Gallery** (250-847-3898; admission free; 11am-5pm Mon-Sat summer, 11am-4pm Tue-Sat winter) displays works by local and regional artists.

The 1810m **Kathlyn Glacier**, left over from the Ice Age, carved a mile-wide gulch into Hudson Bay Mountain and recedes a little bit every year. Gushing waterfalls cascade off its back, providing spectacular views in summer and world-class ice climbing in winter. From the parking lot, a short, easy trail leads to a viewing platform at the base of the glacier's **Twin Falls**. More adventurous types can do the steep three-hour climb to the toe of the glacier. The less adventurous can view the glacier from the highway, a little further west of town. To get there, drive 4km west of Smithers, then take Kathlyn Glacier Rd and follow the signs for 6.1km.

Driftwood Canyon Provincial Park (250-847-7320), 11km northeast of Smithers, was created in 1976 to protect the rich fossil beds that were discovered around 1900 along the Driftwood Creek. Formations found in the shale indicate that plants, insects and animals lived in the area some 50 million years ago. Over time, the running creek eroded through the sedimentation, finally exposing the fossil beds.

Today, you can walk to a viewing platform on the east bank of the creek, where interpretive panels describe the area's geological significance. To get to the park, follow Hwy 16 for 3km east of Smithers, then turn onto Babine Lake Rd. Next turn left on Telkwa High Rd, then right onto Driftwood Rd.

Five kilometers past Driftwood Canyon, you'll reach the parking lot and access point to the west end of the **Babine Mountains**

Provincial Park (250-847-7329), a 32,400-hectare park deep in the glorious backcountry wilderness of the Babine Range of the Skeena Mountains. Trails to glacier-fed lakes and subalpine meadows provide accessible hiking and mountain biking in summer. In winter, the trails make excellent routes for snowshoeing and cross-country skiing. Look for healthy populations of moose, marmots and mountain goats. You can backcountry camp here.

Activities

Fat-tire riding is popular throughout the Bulkley Valley, and if you're interested in mountain biking, you'll find some excellent maintained trails for all levels of rider. Stop by **McBike & Sport** (250-847-5009; 1191 Main St; 9am-6pm Mon-Sat) for trail information. The shop rents bikes for $20/30 per half day/full day and leads guided tours.

For an injection of pure adrenaline, join a whitewater rafting trip on the Babine River to Hazelton in the Bulkley River Canyon. **Suskwa Adventure Outfitters** (250-847-2885, 888-546-7238; www.suskwa.com; from $100) offers one-day trips as well as longer, more complex, itineraries.

Whitewater kayaking is also popular on the Bulkley River. Rent kayaks and gear at **Aquabatics** (250-847-3678, 800-748-2333; 1960 Hudson Bay Mountain Rd; from $30 per day; 9am-6pm summer). One of the best places to go is Tatlow Falls, especially for the Whitewater Rodeo (below).

For skiing, try **Ski Smithers** (250-847-2058; www.skismithers.com; one-day lift pass adult/child $35/18), a low-key ski resort on Hudson Bay Mountain, with 35 mostly intermediate runs. The vertical drop is 533m. Anyone interested in learning more about ice or rock climbing should contact **Bear Mountaineering** (250-847-2854; www.bearmountaineering.ca). A two-day basic rock- or ice-climbing course costs $200.

Festivals & Events

If you're around in late June, do not miss the annual **Midsummer Festival** (250-847-1971; www.bvfms.org; adult/child $40/30), which features live music and good community fun.

The annual **Whitewater Rodeo** takes place in late July or August, depending on water levels. Crowds gather along the riverbank to watch expert paddlers perform tricks.

Sleeping

Camping is available at the **Riverside Municipal Park** (☎ 250-847-1600; site $8). The sites have a pretty location right on the river and there are lockers. You can drive or make the 10-minute walk up Queen St from the center.

Camp in a beautiful setting at **Tyee Lake Provincial Park** (☎ 800-689-9025; www.discovercamping.ca; site $20) in nearby Telkwa, 8km east of Smithers on Hwy 16. The park contains flush toilets, showers, lake access and 59 wooded sites.

Many motels line Hwy 16 offering pretty similar – and decent – rooms.

Stork Nest Inn (☎ 250-847-3831; www.storknestinn.com; 1485 Main St; r $59-72; P X 🖳) has an enviable location right at the intersection with Hwy 16. The comfortable rooms come with a full breakfast and high-speed Internet access.

Fireweed Motor Inn (☎ 250-847-2208; fireweedmotorinn@hotmail.com; 1515 Main St N; s/d $53/58; P X 🖳 🐾), just north of the highway beside the fire hall, offers basic but clean and comfortable rooms.

For a rural treat, stay at the **Logpile Lodge** (☎ 250-847-5152; logpile@bulkley.net), a beautifully hand-constructed Swiss-style chalet overlooking the scenic mountains and valley. The private rooms, which come with balconies, range from $80 to $120, including breakfast. Call for directions.

Eating

Schimmer's Bakery & Coffee Shop (☎ 250-847-3455; 3763 4th Ave; meals $5-7; ⏱ 5am-5pm Tue-Sat) is a classic and simple place with lovely pastries and other baked goods.

The **Alpenhorn Pub & Bistro** (☎ 250-847-5366; 1261 Main St; meals $7-12; ⏱ 11am-late) has the best onion rings you will ever taste. The rest of the pub menu is also good. The fireplace in the middle of the pub makes it cozy, and the James Douglas beer is tasty.

Getting There & Away

Four km west of town off Hwy 16 is **Smithers Airport** (YYD; ☎ 250-847-3664). Air Canada Jazz serves Vancouver. Locally owned Hawk Air (☎ 800-487-1216; www.hawkair.net) also serves Vancouver.

Greyhound (☎ 250-847-2204) is based at 4011 Hwy 16.

The **VIA Rail** Skeena stops in Smithers; the station is at the south end of Main St.

MORICETOWN

pop 670

Going 20km west of Smithers, the small burg of Moricetown is built near the **Bulkley River Gorge**. Here there is a centuries-old Salmon Trap used by local First Nations people to net salmon each summer. The view and the spectacle of the huge silvery fish leaping through the water makes this an excellent stop.

NEW HAZELTON & AROUND

Named after the hazelnut bushes growing along the river terraces, the distinct towns of New Hazelton, Hazelton and South Hazelton (area pop 6500) sit within the walls of the rugged Rocher de Boule (Mountain of Rolling Rock), near the confluence of the Skeena and Bulkley Rivers. The area abounds in First Nations villages; this is the place to see **totem poles**.

The Skeena River (River of Mist) has long been an integral part of the area. The Gitksan and Wet'suwet-en people, who have lived here for more than 7000 years, first navigated cedar canoes along the treacherous Skeena all the way out to the coast. Fur trappers arrived in the area around 1866.

The town became an active and boisterous commercial center in the early 1900s. Soon, the influx of people spread, scattering inland to find riches in the mines, to stake land claims and build farms. When the Grand Trunk Railway construction crews rolled through in 1914, they brought more people, more rowdiness and some general confusion about which Hazelton was which.

Here's the deal: Hazelton (also called the Old Town) was the first settlement, established long before the train showed up. Once it did, Hazelton was slated to become a ghost town with the founding of the 'South' and 'New' Hazeltons. The new communities vied for the position of commercial center and remained in a bitter and ridiculous battle while the train went bankrupt. Today, **New Hazelton** is the commercial center; South Hazelton is essentially tacked onto it. The original Hazelton is a pioneer town with shops and the 'Ksan Historical Village. Between Hazelton and New Hazelton is **Two Mile**, exactly two miles from either town. Its strategic spot made it a busy brothel town, populated mostly by European women – though today the town is barely discernable.

The area's **Visitor Info Centre** (☎ 250-842-6071; junction of Hwys 16 & 62; ☼ 8am-8pm Jul & Aug, 9am-5pm May, Jun & Sep) is an essential stop for sorting through the various local sights. The photocopied 'Hazeltons Explorers Journey' is vital, but also spend $2 for the photocopied 'Tour of the Totems'. There are motels, campgrounds and restaurants in each of the Hazeltons.

You can easily spend a half day or more exploring the Hazeltons and the totem poles in **Kispiox** (below) and **Gitanyow** (p333).

Hazelton

About 2km into your 7km drive to Hazelton from the VIC, you cross the fascinating one-lane suspension **Hagwilget Bridge** 100m over the Skeena River. You can stop and walk across for some vertigo-inspiring views. In Hazelton take a stroll the banks of the Skeena River and explore the historic buildings. Placards along the river detail local history.

'Ksan Historical Village & Museum (☎ 250-842-5544; www.ksan.org; $2; ☼ 8am-7pm mid-April–Sep) is a replicated Gitksan Native village. It makes for easy one-stop shopping in the culture but for the complete experience take one of the **guided tours** (adult/child $10/8.50; every 30min) which provide much-needed context. Tours take you through the Frog House of the Distant Past, the Wolf House of Feasts and the Fireweed House of Masks and Robes. Along the way, you'll learn about Gitksan arts, culture and beliefs. Note that the village is very popular and can get mobbed in summer.

Kispiox

This small First Nations village (population 800) is unremarkable except for the line of 16 remarkable **totem poles**. That many are fairly new shows the continuing resurgence of First Nations culture and art. Kispiox is reached by a 13km paved road of the same name which begins near Hazelton. Watch for a wonderful **organic fruit farm** on the left as you near Kispiox. If your timing is right, you can get a bucket of the best raspberries you've ever had for $3.

NEW HAZELTON TO PRINCE RUPERT

The turnoff for the Stewart-Cassiar Hwy, Hwy 37, to the totem-pole-filled village of **Gitanyow** is 25km west of New Hazelton. See p333 for the section covering this route to the Yukon.

Terrace (pop 12,100) is a logging, government, service and transportation center astride the Skeena River. Although a good-sized town, there is no reason to linger here on your way west (or east).

However, **Nisga'a Memorial Lava Bed Provincial Park** (☎ 250-798-2277, tour information ☎ 250-633-2991) is an interesting detour. Jointly managed by the Nisga'a Nation and the government, this 18,000-hectare park in the beautiful Nass Basin, 100km north of Terrace along the Nisga'a Hwy, is one of the most unique parks in the province. About 250 years ago, a massive volcanic eruption spilled hot, heavy lava onto the Nass floodplain. The thick molten lava spread 10km long and 3km wide, destroying entire villages, suffocating vegetation and killing more than 2000 Nisga'a ancestors. The lava rerouted the Nass River to the north edge of the valley, where it still flows today.

The lava created various formations (depending on the speed at which it flowed), including lava tubes, chunks and rope-like Paahoehoe lava. The pale gray rocks look almost furry with the hardened ash; the effect is reminiscent of a lunar landscape. Most of the trails in the park are short and accessible from the highway. The only way to see the volcanic cone is on a three-hour guided tour ($14) given by a member of the Nisga'a Nation.

About 20km past the park boundary, you'll find the **Visitor Interpretation Centre** (☎ 250-638-9589; ☼ 9am-5pm summer) in a traditional Nisga'a longhouse. Here you can get information on the history of the Nisga'a and pick up the *Self-Guided Auto Tour* brochure ($1), which offers good descriptions of park highlights. There's a 16-site **campground** (site $14) beside the visitor center – the only accommodation in the park.

Nestled in the pit of the Douglas Channel's Kitimat Arm 58km south of Terrace (at the southernmost point of Hwy 37), **Kitimat** (pop 10,100) has so much natural potential – towering mountains, a deep protected port, fresh- and salt-water fishing – that it could've been a wilderness paradise. But it's not; Kitimat is a purely industrial town.

THE NORTH

WATCHING WILDLIFE

Though wildlife viewing is good at any time of the year, there are certain high seasons along the northern BC coast when you're likely to see more of a particular animal.

Animal	Best viewing time
grizzly & black bear	mid-Apr–Jun; Aug–Sep
kermode bear	Sep–mid-Oct
humpback whale	Aug–Oct
killer whale	May–mid-Jul
gray whale	mid-Aug–Oct
bald eagle	year-round (especially mid-Mar–mid-Apr
seal & sea lion	year-round
porpoise	year-round

The 146km drive between Terrace and Prince Rupert is one of the most scenic in BC. Hwy 16 runs right alongside the ever-widening Skeena River. At time there is barely enough room for the road and the parallel train tracks between the river and the sheer rock walls of the hillside.

PRINCE RUPERT
pop 15,200

After Vancouver, 'Rupert', as it's known, is the largest city on the mainland BC coast. Had fate not intervened, there was the chance that Prince Rupert would have become the largest city on the coast.

The town was the brainchild of Charles Hays, the general manager of the Grand Trunk Railway who, in 1906, saw in the vast harbor setting the potential to build a town that would rival Vancouver. Serious financial problems plagued the railway when Hays, who was off gallivanting, unwisely booked passage on the *Titanic*. He died. To make matters worse, WWI came along, stripping the region of young men, and the railway eventually suffered the indignity of having its assets frozen by the courts. The Grand Trunk Railway ultimately became part of the Canadian National Railway system.

The town never developed into the vast metropolis Hays envisioned but instead became a fishing center for the Pacific

Northwest. Its port – the world's deepest natural ice-free port – handles timber, mineral and grain shipments to Asia. The collapse of fishing in recent years and the Asian economic crisis have dealt Rupert further blows from which the town is still trying to recover. Many fishing folk who have lived and breathed by the sea for generations have had to scramble to earn a living.

Once known as the world's halibut capital, Prince Rupert has adopted a new title, the 'City of Rainbows', which is one way of saying that it rains a lot. In fact, it rains 220 days a year, giving the city one of the highest precipitation rates in all of Canada. Despite this, the town's setting is magnificent, especially when it's not raining, misty, foggy or particularly cloudy. Surrounded by mountains and situated at the mouth of the Skeena River, the area displays a rugged beauty. Wind- and rain-swept houses stand high on the cliffs looking out at the fjord-like coastline, ready to accept whatever this harsh climate delivers.

Prince Rupert is an ideal starting point for trips to Alaska and the Queen Charlotte Islands. It's a town with culture, good restaurants, fun places to stay and as noted above, is very beautiful. Ferries converge here from the south and Vancouver Island, and from Alaska to the north. It's also the gateway to the splendid Queen Charlotte Islands.

First Nations History

Various clans of northwest coast First Nations have inhabited the area, following oolichan and salmon runs, for almost 10,000 years. Though more than 20 distinct Native cultures lived here throughout history, the majority were (and still are) Tsimshian (pronounced sim-*she*-an), as evidenced by the remains of 55 villages dotted around the harbor. Prior to the arrival of Europeans, this was one of the most populated areas in North America; archaeological digs have uncovered evidence of human habitation dating back thousands of years.

When the Europeans arrived in 1834, nearby Port Simpson (then called 'Fort' Simpson) became a Hudson's Bay Company trading post that eventually lured the Tsimshians away from their seclusion

GRIZZLIES GALORE

One of the most unique pockets in BC's purse full of parks, the 45,000-hectare **Khutzeymateen Grizzly Bear Sanctuary** is one of the few remaining grizzly habitats in the world. Located 45km northeast of Prince Rupert, the park sits in the remote Khutzeymateen River Valley, the traditional territory of the Gitsees people, who used the valley for fishing, hunting, trapping and growing food such as berries, crab apples and potatoes.

When Europeans arrived in North America, an estimated 200,000 grizzlies lived on the continent. Today, that estimate hovers at only 25,000, 50 of which live in the Khutzeymateen.

The Khutzeymateen (pronounced kootsa-ma-teen) was permanently protected as parkland in 1992. In 1994, the area became officially designated as a 'grizzly bear sanctuary' to be jointly managed by the provincial government and the Tsimshian First Nations.

Because grizzlies are reclusive by nature and do better when left alone, the human presence in the park is heavily restricted, though you can join a boat tour or take a floatplane in for a peek.

There are currently only two tour guides licensed to lead groups into the sanctuary.

Tom Ellison, Ocean Light II Adventures (☎ 604-328-5339; www.oceanlight2.bc.ca; 363-1917 West 4th Ave, Vancouver, V6J 1M7)

Dan Wakeman, Sun Chaser Charters (☎ 250-624-5472; www.citytel.net/sunchaser/; Box 1096, Prince Rupert, BC, V8J 4H6)

---

in Prince Rupert. The usual slew of disease weakened the First Nations populations, and in 1884 the government banned the Natives from holding potlatches, one of the highest forms of celebration in First Nations culture. The failing population and cultural oppression hit hard, and decades of struggle to retain land and cultural freedom ensued.

Today, the Tsimshian population in Prince Rupert is thriving. Like the Haida on the Queen Charlotte Islands, the Tsimshians have a strong oral history and incredible artistic ability, both of which have allowed them to recapture and build upon their cultural past.

Orientation

Prince Rupert is on Kaien Island and is connected to the mainland by a bridge. The Yellowhead Hwy passes right through the downtown area. Cow Bay, named for a dairy farm that used to be located here, has become a historic waterfront area full of shops and restaurants situated just north of downtown.

Information

Unfortunately, there's no bookstore in Prince Rupert.

INTERNET ACCESS

Java Dot Cup (☎ 250-622-2822; 516 3rd Ave W; ☺ 7am-9pm) Has numerous terminals plus a decent café.

LAUNDRY

Maytag Laundry (☎ 250-624-6811; 2276 7th St; ☺ 8am-8pm)

LIBRARY

Prince Rupert Library (☎ 250-627-1345; 101 6th Ave W; ☺ 10am-5pm Mon- Fri, 1-5pm Sat & Sun)

MEDICAL SERVICES

Prince Rupert Regional Hospital (☎ 250-624-2171; 1305 Summit Ave; 24hr) In Roosevelt Park.

CATCHING FISH

All five species of salmon – chinook, coho, chum, pink and sockeye – live in the waters of the northwest, especially at the mouth of the Skeena River and at the head of Chatham Sound. Halibut, lingcod and rockfish also show up in high numbers.

Fish	Best catching time
chinook salmon	May–Jul
coho & chum salmon	July–Sep
pink salmon	Jul–mid-Sep
sockeye salmon	Jun–Aug
halibut	May–Sep
lingcod	year-round
rockfish	year-round

THE NORTH

PRINCE RUPERT

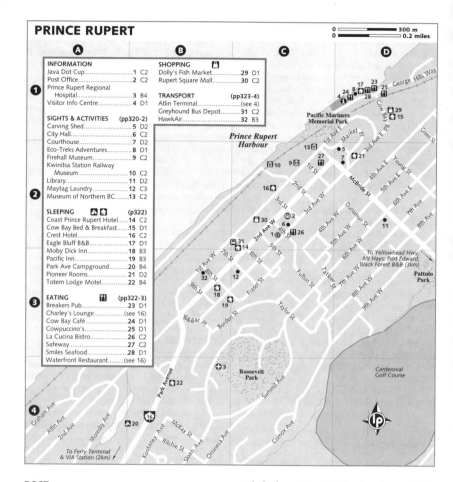

INFORMATION
Java Dot Cup...........................1 C2
Post Office..............................2 C2
Prince Rupert Regional
  Hospital...............................3 B4
Visitor Info Centre...................4 D1

SIGHTS & ACTIVITIES (pp320-2)
Carving Shed..........................5 D2
City Hall.................................6 C2
Courthouse.............................7 D2
Eco-Treks Adventures.............8 D1
Firehall Museum......................9 C2
Kwinitsa Station Railway
  Museum..............................10 C2
Library...................................11 D2
Maytag Laundry......................12 C3
Museum of Northern BC.........13 C2

SLEEPING (p322)
Coast Prince Rupert Hotel......14 C2
Cow Bay Bed & Breakfast.......15 D1
Crest Hotel............................16 C2
Eagle Bluff B&B......................17 D1
Moby Dick Inn........................18 B3
Pacific Inn..............................19 B3
Park Ave Campground.............20 B4
Pioneer Rooms.......................21 D2
Totem Lodge Motel.................22 B4

EATING (pp322-3)
Breakers Pub.........................23 D1
Charley's Lounge................(see 16)
Cow Bay Café.........................24 D1
Cowpuccino's.........................25 C2
La Cucina Bistro.....................26 C2
Safeway.................................27 C2
Smiles Seafood......................28 D1
Waterfront Restaurant........(see 16)

SHOPPING
Dolly's Fish Market.................29 D1
Rupert Square Mall.................30 C2

TRANSPORT (pp323-4)
Atlin Terminal.....................(see 4)
Greyhound Bus Depot..........31 C2
HawkAir.................................32 B3

POST

Post office (☎ 250-627-3085; Rupert Square Mall; 8:30am-5pm Mon-Fri)

TOURIST INFORMATION

Visitor Info Centre (☎ 250-624-5637, 800-667-1994; www.tourismprincerupert.com; 100 1st Ave W; 8am-9pm summer, 9am-5pm winter) In an impressive Cow Bay Atlin Terminal which also serves as a dock for the increasing numbers of visiting cruise ships.

Sights & Activities

The **Museum of Northern British Columbia** (☎ 250-624-3207; 100 1st Ave W; adult/child $5/1; 8am-8pm Mon-Sat, until 5pm Sun summer, 9am-5pm winter) resides inside a post-and-beam building styled after a First Nation longhouse. This is something not to be missed. Through excellent exhibits and superb documentation, the museum shows how local civilizations enjoyed sustainable cultures that lasted for thousands of years. Using technologies based on steam, the people were able to make items as diverse as soup ladles (from goat horns) to canoes (from huge spruce logs). The displays include a wealth of excellent Haida, Gitksan and Tsimshian art. Special tours are well worth the time. You'll learn fascinating details such as who succeeded a Tsimshian chief (hint: it wasn't the son). The **Winter Feast tour** ($5) includes a taste of soapberry pudding, which is surprisingly tasty given the berries' name.

THE NORTH

DETOUR

About 20km south of Prince Rupert, the **North Pacific Cannery Village Museum** (☎ 250-628-3538; 1889 Skeena Dr; adult/child $12/10; ☼ 9am-6pm mid-May–Sep), in the town of Port Edward, explores the history of fishing and canning along the Skeena River. The fascinating complex, built over the town, was used from 1889 to 1968. Today, exhibits document the miserable conditions of the workers, along with the workings of this industry that helped build the region. The museum should be high on your list of sights and can easily occupy half a day. Guides provide insight into working conditions; watch the recently restored canning line in action and think about what was required of the average worker to fill 14 trays of cans in four minutes. The complex includes a café with excellent breakfasts, homemade chowder and salmon dinners ($12 and up) and **B&B accommodation** (☎ 250-628-3538; r from $75) inside an old bunkhouse. If you're really intrigued, the booklet *Everlasting Memory* is a good purchase ($17). Prince Rupert Transit (p324) offers bus service to the site.

Included with the museum admission, the **Kwinitsa Station Railway Museum** (☼ 9am-5pm summer), down the hill on Bill Murray Drive, is housed in an old train station. It documents the drama surrounding the building of the railway to Rupert.

You'll see **totems** all around town; two flank the statue of Charlie Hays beside City Hall on 3rd Ave. Many totems are replicas of very well-known traditional works. In summer, the Museum of Northern British Columbia (p320) offers guided **heritage and totem walking tours** around town (free with admission). Call for tour times. To witness totem-building in action, stop by the **Carving Shed**, next door to the courthouse. Often you'll see local artists there working on jewelry or cedar carvings.

A 10-minute walk from the center, **Cow Bay** is a delightful place for a stroll. The eponymous spotted décor is everywhere but somehow avoids grating. There are shops, cafés and a good view of the waterfront where you can see fishing boats unloading their catch.

The **Prince Rupert City & Regional Archives** (☎ 250-624-3326; 100 1st Ave E; ☼ 10am-3pm) contains a huge collection of photographs, nautical charts and books.

Fire engine buffs – and confused rock fans – should check out the rebuilt 1925 REO Speedwagon fire engine at the small **Firehall Museum** (☎ 250-627-4475; 200 1st Ave W; donation; ☼ 10am-4pm summer), beside the real fire hall.

You can picnic, swim, fish, hike or take out a canoe at **Diana Lake Provincial Park** and **Prudhomme Lake Provincial Park**, about 16km east of town on Hwy 16.

More than 70 charter-boat operators run **fishing** trips out of Prince Rupert, some with great success; in 1997, a few happy tourists landed a 106kg (234lb) halibut. The VIC has a comprehensive list or you can wander Cow Bay and chat with the skippers.

If you're interested in kayaking, **Eco-Treks Adventures** (☎ 250-624-8311; www.citytel.net/eco treks; 203 Cow Bay Rd) offers a variety of guided trips, including a 90-minute introductory course for $40. It also rents kayaks from $25 for two hours. Prince Rupert has a huge tide range, with tides rising or falling up to four feet an hour. Be sure to get the low-down on the tides before venturing out on the water.

Of the many **hiking** trails in and around town, one path goes up 732m **Mt Hays** from the Butze Rapids parking lot, east of town on Hwy 16. On a clear day, you can see local islands, the Queen Charlotte Islands and even Alaska.

Beginning at a parking lot on the Yellowhead Hwy, 3km south of town just past the industrial park, trails lead to Mt Oldfield, Tall Trees (you'll see some old cedars) and **Butze Rapids**. The rapids walk is a flat, 4km loop to Grassy Bay with interpretive signs; the others are more demanding. The VIC offers details on these and others.

Tours

Pike Island is a small island past Digby Island outside of the harbor. Thriving villages were based there as long as 2000 years ago, and remnants and evidence can be seen today. **Seashore Charters** (☎ 250-624-5645, 800-667-4393; www.pikeisland.ca; Atlin Terminal; adult/child $45/35) runs half-day trips to Laxspa'aws, as the island is known, that include a 40-minute boat ride each way and the services of a First Nation guide. Call for schedules.

Seashore Charters also offers various harbor tours from $35 per person.

Festivals & Events

JUNE
Seafest (☎ 250-624-9118) celebrates Rupert's seaside location with parties and events.

AUGUST
Udderfest (☎ 250-624-3626) presents five days of fringe theater performed by local groups and national performers.

Sleeping

Rupert has a range of accommodations, but when all three ferries have pulled in (a sort of tourism 'triple witching night'), beds inspire competition. Book ahead.

MOTELS & HOTELS
Crest Hotel (☎ 250-624-6771, 800-663-8150; www.crest hotel.bc.ca; 222 1st Ave W; r $110-165; P ⚆ 💻) has some of the best views on the entire coast. The deluxe rooms are large and comfortable and there's a hot tub with the view. But more importantly the Crest is very popular locally for its excellent restaurant (p323) and bar.

Coast Prince Rupert Hotel (☎ 250-624-6711, 800-663-1144; www.coasthotels.com; 118 6th St; s/d from $105/117; P ⚆ 💻) features good views from many of the large rooms and various business services.

Pacific Inn (☎ 250-627-1711, 888-663-1999; www .tkp-biz.com/pacificinn; 909 3rd Ave W; r $59-80; P) features a restaurant and large rooms with understated décor.

Totem Lodge Motel (☎ 250-624-6761; 1335 Park Ave; s/d from $59/79; P) is a good choice, but because it's close to the ferry terminal it fills up fast. The converse is that it's a hike from the center. Decent rooms come with continental breakfast. There's a laundry so you can get on the boat smelling your best.

Moby Dick Inn (☎ 250-624-6961, 800-663-0822; 935 2nd Ave W; r $69-89; P) boasts very nice rooms, TVs with dozens of channels and a guest laundry. There's no discount for those yelling 'Thar she blows!' Although you could do it in the whirlpool.

Pioneer Rooms (☎ 250-624-2334, 888-794-9998; www.citytel.net/pioneer; 167 3rd Ave E; dm $16 s/d $35/43; P 💻) The closet thing to a hostel. Greatly improved over recent years – the flowers out front and new paint aren't just window-dressing – the small rooms and bathrooms are spotless. There's a small kitchen and barbecue facilities out back.

B&BS
You'll find more than a dozen B&Bs in Prince Rupert.

Eagle Bluff B&B (☎ 250-627-4955; www.citytel.net/ eaglebluff/; 201 Cow Bay Rd; r $45-90) anchors Cow Bay. It's in a heritage building that has had a colorful restoration. There's a variety of rooms with and without bathrooms.

Nearby, the **Cow Bay Bed & Breakfast** (☎ 250-627-1804; 20 Cow Bay Rd; r from $75) perhaps milks the local schtick once too often by declaring itself 'the cream of B&Bs'. Rooms feature cozy duvets spread on every bed in its northwest-coast theme rooms.

Rupert's B&Bs help pick up the slack when the ferries converge. Typical is the **Black Forest B&B** (☎ 250-624-4601; www.blackforestbb.ca; 260 Prince Rupert Blvd; r $70-100). It has large and comfortable rooms in a quiet neighborhood that make it a good choice for families.

For something completely different, see the **North Pacific Cannery Village Museum**, see the boxed text, 321.

CAMPING
The municipal **Park Ave Campground** (☎ 250-624-6861, 800-667-1994; 1750 Park Ave; site $12), near the ferry terminal, contains 87 sites, hot showers, laundry and flush toilets. Tent sites are on wooden platforms so your tent doesn't get soaked when (not if) it rains. In summer, on nights when the ferry arrives, it's best to book ahead.

Eating & Drinking

RESTAURANTS
With fishing a major local industry, it's not surprising to find seafood on just about every menu. Salmon and halibut are headliners.

Cow Bay Café (☎ 250-627-1212; 205 Cow Bay Rd; meals $10-15; ☽ lunch & dinner, closed Sun) The friendly chef serves up something great every night. The creative menu changes daily but there are always a half dozen mains and amazing desserts to choose from. Enjoy one of the deck tables overlooking the harbor or bide your time perusing the library of cookbooks (they could write their own).

Smiles Seafood (☎ 250-624-3072; 113 Cow Bay Rd; meals $8-20; ☺ lunch & dinner) Top billing goes to this storied joint on the waterfront at Cow Bay. Since 1934 it's served fresh ocean fare, as well as steaks and sandwiches – try the 'House of Fish sandwich'. There's a patio. Flip over the placemat for a look at the menu from 1945, when a sardine sandwich on toast cost 25¢.

Waterfront Restaurant (☎ 250-624-6771; 222 1st Ave; meals $15-30; ☺ breakfast, lunch & dinner) Fortunately, the staff here are more creative in the kitchen than in the naming department. Restaurant of the Crest Hotel, the Waterfront has a complex meat and seafood menu, with halibut and salmon putting in star performances.

CAFÉS
Cowpuccino's (☎ 250-627-1395; 25 Cow Bay Rd; coffee $1.50; ☺ 7am-8pm) is a mellow coffeehouse with good baked goods.

In the center, **La Cucina Bistro** (☎ 250-624-4444; 427 3rd Ave W; sandwiches $9; ☺ lunch Mon-Sat) is an authentic Italian deli that smells fantastic and has food to match.

PUBS
Breakers Pub (☎ 250-624-5990; 117 George Hills Way; snacks $6; ☺ 11am-late) is a good place for a drink, a snack or a meal. This busy place features an outdoor patio and a thick menu with tasty fresh fish specials.

SELF-CATERING
If you're on a tight budget, stock up on food for the ferry at the **Safeway** supermarket (☎ 250-624-5125; 200 2nd Ave W; ☺ 7am-10pm).

Dolly's Fish Market (☎ 250-624-6099; 7 Cow Bay Rd; ☺ 10am-7pm) is the sparkling purveyor of locally caught fish in many forms, including smoked and in soup. The giant cookies are great.

Getting There & Away
There's no shortage of modes of transit in Rupert.

AIR
Prince Rupert airport (YPR; ☎ 250-622-2222; www .ypr.ca) is on Digby Island, across the harbor

from town. The entire process of getting to/from town to the airport is an adventure involving a bus and a ferry (adult/child $11/8). The airport website actually has a cute animation that helps it all make sense. But given the complexities, you must check in for your flight at your airline's downtown terminal two hours before flight time, as this is where you ultimately arrive and depart. Be sure to confirm all the details with your airline or the airport. The airport has a café.

Air Canada Jazz (Atlin Terminal) Serves Vancouver.
Harbour Air (☎ 800-689-4234) Service to/from Sandspit, Queen Charlotte Islands.
HawkAir (☎ 866-429-5247; www.hawkair.ca; Howard Johnson Highliner Plaza Hotel, 815 1st Ave W) Serves Vancouver.

TRAIN
The western terminus **VIA Rail station** (BC Ferries Terminal) operates the tri-weekly Skeena from Jasper and Prince George.

BUS
Greyhound (☎ 250-624-5090; 112 6th St) buses depart to Prince George.

FERRY
Ferries share the same general harbor area, although the Alaska Marine Highway terminal is behind large fences as it is considered a US border crossing. All the boats listed below have cafeterias and will let you pitch a tent on deck.

BC Ferries (☎ 250-386-3431) Inside Passage to Port Hardy; adult/child $102.50/51.25, car from $241.50, cabin from $60; 15 to 25 hours; three per week summer, one per week winter; Queen Charlotte Islands, Skidegate; adult/child $23.50/11.75, car from $86.50, cabin from $40; eight hours; six per week summer, three per week winter.
Alaska Maritime Highway (☎ 250-627-1744, 800-642-0066; www.Alaska.gov/ferry) To Ketchikan, Wrangell,

Petersburg, Juneau, and Yukon – connecting towns of Haines (33 hours) and Skagway (35 hours); adult/child to Skagway $152/76, car from $380, cabin from $100; book vehicles and cabins well in advance; three per week summer, two per week winter.

Getting Around

Prince Rupert Transit (☎ 250-624-3343; www.bus online.ca; adult/child $1.25/1) Service in the central area; infrequent service to the ferry port and North Pacific Historic Fishing Village ($2.50 for two). The main downtown bus stop is at the Rupert Square Mall on 2nd Ave.

Most major car rental companies are represented in Rupert.

A one-way trip to the ferry with **Skeena Taxi** (☎ 250-624-5318) is about $9.

QUEEN CHARLOTTE ISLANDS

pop 6000

The Queen Charlotte Islands, sometimes known as the Canadian Galapagos, are a dagger-shaped archipelago of some 154 islands lying 80km west of the BC coast and about 50km from the southern tip of Alaska. This sparsely populated, wild, rainy and almost magical place swarms (literally) with bald eagles.

Believed to be the only part of Canada that escaped the last Ice Age, the islands abound with flora and fauna that are markedly different from those of the mainland. Essentially still a wilderness area, the Queen Charlottes are warmed by an ocean current that rolls in from Japan, which means the islands get hit with 127cm of rain annually. All these factors combine to create a landscape filled with thousand-year-old spruce and cedar rainforests and waters teeming with marine life.

The islands have been inhabited continuously for 10,000 years and are the traditional homeland – Haida Gwaii – of the Haida nation, generally acknowledged as the prime culture in the country at the time the Europeans arrived. Though they were fearsome warriors who dominated BC's West Coast, they had few defenses against the diseases – primarily smallpox and tuberculosis – that were introduced by European explorers. In 1835, the Haida population was estimated at 6000 people; in 1915, that number had shrunk to only 588.

Today, the Haida are proud, politically active and defiant people who make up one-third of the Charlottes' population. In the 1980s, they led an internationally publicized fight to preserve the islands from further logging. A bitter debate raged, but finally the federal government decided to save South Moresby and create South Moresby Gwaii Haanas National Park. (Logging still goes on in other parts of the Queen Charlottes.) More recently they have successfully negotiated with institutions like the Field Museum in Chicago to have the remains of ancestors, once dug up by anthropologists, returned – 160 have returned from Chicago alone.

The arts of the Haida people – notably their totem poles and carvings in argillite (a dark, glass-like slate found only in southeast Alaska and on these islands) – are world renowned. You'll see evidence of the Haida's artistry throughout the islands.

A visit to the Charlottes will not be especially rewarding for those who treat it like a lark or another tick on the checklist of sights. Rather, the islands reward those who invest time to get caught up in their allure, their culture and their people. The more time you put in, the more you will get back. Certainly you have to put the time in for a place like the Gwaii Haanas National Park Reserve Haida Heritage Site, as a visit requires significant preparations. But those who fall into the rhythms of the Charlottes may not escape their spell. Many come back year after year, others never leave.

FLORA & FAUNA

The Queen Charlotte Islands – widely assumed to have escaped the last Ice Age – boast a unique ecosystem. Poor drainage systems near the north end of Graham Island result in the growth of sphagnum moss and gentian, surrounded by lodgepole pine and yellow cedar. Elsewhere, mighty stands of western hemlock, Sitka spruce and western red cedar cover the landscape. Four unique species of moss, one liverwort and six species of flowering plants grow here. *Senecio newcombi*, a yellow flowering daisy, grows here and nowhere else.

The islands also have their own unique versions of pine marten, deer mouse, black bear and short-tailed weasel. The Dawson caribou (a subspecies of the caribou) once lived here but was hunted to extinction. Unfortunately, introduced species have come in and caused trouble. Though you aren't likely to see any, rats have become a big problem since their arrival (probably on the first trading ships in the mid-1700s). Raccoons and beavers, introduced for the fur trade, have also turned into a nuisance; like the rats and red squirrels, they prey on nesting shorebirds. Beavers clog up drainages, flooding lakes and streams. Sitka blacktail deer were introduced at least five times between 1880 and 1925 as an alternate food source. Lacking natural predators, the deer became so prolific that residents are now allowed to hunt 10 deer per person per season to help control the population.

Home to 15% of all nesting seabirds in BC, the Queen Charlottes contain the only confirmed nesting site of horned puffins in Canada. A whopping 30% of the world's ancient murrelets nest here, as do most of the province's Peales peregrine falcons. There are no snakes on the islands.

From late April through late June, it's common to see gray whales traveling by on their 16,000km annual migration route along the West Coast. Starting in Mexico's Baja, the whales pass by California, Oregon and Washington in the US, then BC, before arriving in Alaska, their final destination before turning around and heading back down. They travel further than any other migrating animal. The islands also include the largest sea lion rookery in BC.

ORIENTATION
Mainland ferries dock at Skidegate on Graham Island, the main island for population (80%) and commerce. The principal town is Queen Charlotte City (QCC), 7km west of Skidegate. The main road on Graham Island is Hwy 16, which is fully paved. It links Skidegate in the south with Masset 101km north, passing the small towns of Tlell and Port Clements. Tow Hill in Naikoon Provincial Park is 26km along the coast east of Masset.

Graham Island is linked to the Moresby Island to the south by a small and frequent ferry from Skidegate. The airport is in Sandspit on Moresby Island, 22km east of the ferry landing at Aliford Bay. The only way to get to Gwaii Haanas National Park which covers the south part of Moresby Island is by boat or plane.

INFORMATION
The islands' relative remoteness, coupled with the lure of the land and Haida culture, has put the Charlottes on the traveler's map. While there are a number of hostels and services that meet the needs of the intrepid, it's still all but mandatory to make arrangements for accommodations in advance. It's also important to remember that the Queen Charlotte Islands are rural and remote.

If you plan to visit the Gwaii Haanas National Park Reserve Haida Heritage Site – and that's the number one reason for coming to the islands – then you should understand that a visit takes several days (see the separate heading about Gwaii Haanas, p000). Don't be one of the dullards who hop off the ferry expecting to see everything in a few hours and then depart. You won't. That said, don't be discouraged if you don't have time or money to do a long boat or kayaking trip; you can always arrange a one-day paddle or boat trip and you can actually see a lot by car or bike. Regardless, take some time to go beachcombing along the white sandy beaches, watch the sunset or chat with the locals, whose ideas and lifestyles are shaped by the salty fresh air and solitude.

Pick up a copy of the weekly *Queen Charlotte Islands Observer* (www.qciobserver .com; $1.50) which includes the *Islands This Week* supplement that covers just that.

Bookstores
Northwest Coast Books (☎ 250-559-4681; 720 Hwy 33, QCC; ◐ 8:30am-4pm Mon-Fri) Huge specialty selection.

Emergency
Ambulance (☎ 800-461-9911)
RCMP (☎ 559-4421, Masset 626-3991; QCC)

Internet Access
Chubbie Bucks Coffee Bar (☎ 250-559-8420; 3201 3rd Ave, QCC; $3 per 15min; ◐ 9am-6pm) Upstairs from Rainbows Spirit Gallery, which seems to sell everything that ever washed up on a beach.

THE NORTH

QUEEN CHARLOTTE ISLANDS

Langara Island
Lepas Bay
Frederick Island
Graham Island
Hippa Island
Rennell Sound
Cone Head
Rennell Sound Campground
Yakoun Lake
Hayden Turner Campground
Skidegate Channel
Chaatl Island
Hibben Island
Moresby Camp
Moresby Island
Tasu Sound
Gwaii Haanas National Park Reserve
Gowgaia Bay
Upper Victoria Lake
Lower Victoria Lake
Flamingo Inlet
Cape Freedom
Louscoone Inlet
Anthony Island
Ninstints/SGaang Gwaii
Kunghit Island

Dixon Entrance
Tow Hill/Blowhole
McIntyre Bay
Old Masset
Masset
Rose Point
Rose Spit
Agate Beach Campground
Fife Point
Naikoon Provincial Park
East Beach
Cape Ball
Port Clements
Masset Inlet
Tlell
Misty Meadows Campground
Halibut Bight
Queen Charlotte City
Skidegate
Joys Campground
Sandspit
Alliford Bay
Copper Bay
Gray Point
Gray Bay Campground
Cumshewa Inlet
Skedans
Louise Island
Selwyn Inlet
Talunkwan Island
Tanu Island
Tanu
Dodge Point
Windy Bay
Lyell Island
Hotspring Island
Ramsay Island
De la Beche Inlet
Juan Perez Sound
Scudder Point
Burnaby Island
Skincuttle Inlet
Ikeda Cove
Carpenter Bay
Benjamin Point
Houston Stewart Channel
Rose Harbour
Luxana Bay
Cape St James
Kerouard Island

Chatham Sound
Ferry
Hecate Strait

Louise Narrows
Darwin Sound
Burnaby Narrows

PACIFIC OCEAN

THE NORTH

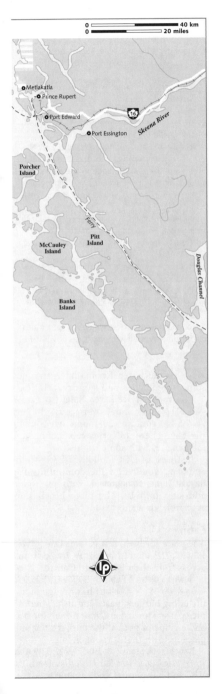

Laundry
Coin laundry (117 3rd Ave, City Centre Store complex, QCC; ⏱ 8am-6pm)

Medical Services
Queen Charlotte Islands General Hospital (☎ 250-559-4506, emergency ☎ 250-559-4300 ; 3209 3rd Ave, QCC; ⏱ 24hr) There is a small satellite facility in Masset (☎ 250-626-4711 emergency). For major emergencies, patients are generally sent to Prince Rupert by air ambulance.

Money
ATMs are easily found in QCC, Masset and Sandspit. Occasionally communication is lost to the mainland so bring a few extra days' cash.

Post
QCC post office (☎ 250-559-8349; 117 3rd Ave; ⏱ 9am-5pm Mon-Fri, noon-4pm Sat) In the same shopping complex as the City Centre Store.

Telephone
Cell phones don't won't work on QCI. Darn. The area code is still 250.

Tourist Information
In Queen Charlotte City the **Visitor Info Centre** (☎ 250-559-8316; www.qcinfo.com; 3220 Wharf St, QCC; ⏱ 8am-noon May 1-15, 10am-7pm May 16-Sep 7, 10am-2pm Sep 8-Sep 30) occupies a nice building on the water on Wharf St. The center offers a wealth of knowledge about the islands and some good natural history displays. A second Visitor Info Centre opens at the airport in Sandspit following roughly the same hours as above. Both carry marine and topographical charts.

In Masset, the **Visitor Info Centre** (☎ 250-626-3982; 1450 Christie St; ⏱ 10am-4pm summer) is near the entrance to town from the south.

At the VICs, ask about **Haida community feasts**. These frequent events welcome visitors, who for a modest fee can enjoy the many delectable dishes made from the plethora of local foods like crabs, salmon, mushrooms and berries.

QUEEN CHARLOTTE CITY
pop 1050
This small fishing village serves as the commercial center of the islands – the spot where you'll find the most restaurants and accommodations, plus the headquarters for most of the adventure outfitters on

THE NORTH

HISTORICAL PRESERVATION ON A SIMPLE CEDAR LOG

Whether you're driving around the Hazelton area, sipping coffee in Prince Rupert or walking the windswept beaches on the Queen Charlotte Islands, you'll definitely be awed by the art around you.

Though most First Nations groups on the northwest coast lack formal written history as we know it, centuries of traditions manage to live on. Instead of communicating their rich pasts through words on a page or historical documents, the native tribes have told stories through the masterful art of carving, drawing and painting. Art has long been a method of expression, intimately linked with historical and cultural preservation, religion and social ceremony.

The artistry of northwest coast native groups – Tsimshian, Haida, Tlingit, Kwakiutl and Nuxalk – is as intricate as it is simple. One of the most spectacular examples of this is the totem pole. Carved from a single cedar trunk, totems identify a household's lineage in the same way a family crest might identify a group or clan in England, although the totem pole is more of a historical pictograph depicting the entire ancestry. Like a family crest, totem poles carry a sense of prestige and prosperity.

Despite the expression 'low man on the totem pole', the most important figures are usually at eye level; figures at the bottom usually serve an integral, grounding function that supports the rest of the pole. Totem figures can represent individuals, spirits, births, deaths, catastrophes or legends.

Unless you're an expert, it's not so easy to identify what's what on a totem. Here are a few rules of thumb: birds are always identified by their beaks: ravens have a straight, midsize beak; eagles feature a short, sharp, downturned beak; while hawks have a short, downturned beak that curls inward. Bears usually show large, square teeth, while beavers feature sharp incisors and a cross-stitched tail.

A few animals appear as if viewed from overhead. For example, the killer whale's fin protrudes outward from the pole as if its head faces downward. The long-snouted wolf also faces downward,

the islands. The community of permanent residents takes the massive summer influx of tourists in stride. People are friendly and eager to share tips about the islands' secret spots. Once they get the socializing out of their systems, they'll hunker down and watch the storms roll over the island throughout fall, winter and spring.

Sleeping

One of the best places to stay on the islands, **Premier Creek Lodging** (☎ 250-559-8415, 888-322-3388; www.qcislands.net/premier, 3101 3rd Ave; dm $19, r $30-75) offers accommodations that range from hostel-type dorms to lodge-style rooms complete with balconies and ocean views. Hostel beds include the use of a communal kitchen and barbecue. The lodge rooms are in a refurbished 1910 heritage building and range from small singles with shared bath to suites with kitchens and fabulous views of Bearskin Bay.

Gracie's Place (☎ 250-559-4262, 888-244-4262; 3113 3rd Ave; www.graciesplace.ca; r $100-150) is filled with both character and characters. This is a nice older house in the middle of town with

views to the water. Rooms have antiques, some have kitchen and laundry facilities.

The modern **Sea Raven Motel** (☎ 250-559-4423, 800-665-9606; www.searaven.com; 3301 3rd Ave; r $45-95; 🛜) contains 29 rooms overlooking the bay. There are private balconies and kitchenettes with some rooms.

Just west of QCC, follow 3rd Ave to the end, and you'll find the community-run **Hayden Turner Campground**, with pit toilets and sites for $10. The three beach sites, accessible via a short trail, cost $5.

Eating

The place for breakfast is **Lam's Café** (☎ 250-559-4202; 3223 Wharf St; meal $7; 🕙 7am-3pm), just across from the Visitor Info Centre.

Howler's Bistro & Pub (☎ 250-559-8602; 2600 3rd Ave; meals $7-15; 🕙 noon-late) has a huge menu, including burgers, pasta and fish. There's a nice patio. Downstairs, join others for beer and a game of pool at the pub; it's the only place in town that stays open late.

Isabel Creek Store (☎ 250-559-8623; 3219 Wharf St; 🕙 10am-5:30pm Mon-Sat) is across from the VIC and has natural and organic foods.

as does the frog. The pointy-headed shark (or dogfish), with a grimacing mouth full of sharp teeth, faces upward, as does the humpback whale.

Though totem symbols are usually interconnected and complex, animals possess certain undeniable characteristics:

black bear – serves as a protector, guardian and spiritual link between humans and animals.
beaver – symbolizes industriousness, wisdom and determined independence.
eagle – signifies intelligence and power.
frog – represents adaptability, the ability to live in both natural and supernatural worlds.
hummingbird – embodies love, beauty and unity with nature.
killer whale – symbolizes dignity and strength (often depicted as a reincarnated spirit of a great chief).
raven – signifies mischievousness and cunning.
salmon – typifies dependable sustenance, longevity and perseverance.
shark – exemplifies an ominous and fierce solitude.
thunderbird – represents the wisdom of proud ancestors.

The carving of totem poles was largely squashed after the Canadian government outlawed the potlatch ceremony in 1884. Most totems only last 60 to 80 years, though some on the Queen Charlotte Islands are more than 100 years old. When a totem falls, tradition says that it should be left there until another is erected in its place.

Today, totem carving is experiencing a revival, though the poles are often constructed for nontraditional uses, such as public art. Modern totems commissioned for college campuses, museums and public buildings no longer recount the lineage of any one household but instead stand to honor the First Nations and their outstanding artistry. Besides the active work on the mainland around the Hazeltons (p316) and Gitanyow (p333), you can see new totem poles at the carving shed in Skidegate (below).

SKIDEGATE

pop 740

Skidegate (pronounced 'skid-a-git'), a Haida community on the shores of Rooney Bay, is a growing community dedicated to the revival of Haida culture and art. The community has big plans to build a heritage center that are slowly progressing. Meanwhile, the excellent **Haida Gwaii Museum at Qay'llnagaay** (☎ 250-559-4643; adult/child $3/1.50; ☺ 10am-5pm summer, closed Sun May & Sep, closed Sun & Mon other times) sits on Sealion Point, an ancient basalt outcropping that juts into Skidegate Inlet. Inside the museum, you'll find an excellent collection of Haida art, including button blankets, Brentwood boxes, silver and gold jewelry and argillite totems. Here you can learn about Bill Reid, one of the most renowned and prolific Haida artists. The good displays on the area's natural history include an extensive bird collection.

Adjoining the museum is Andy Wilson's **carving shed** where you can learn the remarkable story about how islanders rediscovered ancient technologies to build a huge cedar

canoe for the Vancouver World's Fair in 1986. There's always something going on here; six new totems have been erected since 2001. During the summer of 2003 visitors were invited to create boxes to hold the remains of Haida ancestors that were expected to be returned from various international museums; a both moving and culturally bonding experience.

TLELL

pop 370

The small artsy community of Tlell, 40km north of Skidegate, is the southern gateway to **Naikoon Provincial Park** and home to the park headquarters (☎ 250-557-4390; ☺ 9am-4pm summer). Here you can obtain information on the tides and check out the interpretive displays. Ask to watch the video describing the flora and fauna in the park.

The beautiful 72,640-hectare park on the northeast tip of Graham Island is comprised mostly of sand dunes and low sphagnum bogs surrounded by stunted and gnarled lodgepole pine and red and yellow cedar. The word 'naikoon' is a

THE NORTH

corruption of 'nai-kun', meaning 'long nose' – the name for the 5km-long Rose Spit that separates the stormy Hecate Strait and Dixon Entrance. The park is loosely divided into North (at Masset) and South (at Tlell). You'll find campgrounds and interesting hikes at either end.

From Tlell, take the worthwhile **Pesuta Trail** to the wreck of the *Pesuta*, a timber-hauling ship that ran aground in 1928. The trail begins at the Tlell River Picnic Area, just off Hwy 16 past the park headquarters, and follows the river to East Beach. You then follow the high tide line out to the wreck. Allow about seven hours to make the 10km roundtrip.

See North Coast later for details on the north end of the Naikoon Provincial Park.

Just off Hwy 16, **Crystal Cabin Gallery** (☎ 250-557-4383; 778 Richardson Rd; ⌚ 9am-5pm) is a shop filled with works by local artists. There's a great selection. Outside is a fascinating sculpture/installation, the **Tlell Stone Circle**.

Sleeping & Eating

Stay in a gorgeous beechwood beachhouse surrounded by dunes at **Cacilia's B&B** (☎ 250-557-4664; www.qcislands.net/ceebysea; r $30-60), just off Hwy 16. It's a lovely and restful spot and Cacilia can fill you in on all the local intrigue.

The **Dress for Les** (☎ 250-557-2023; ⌚ 10am-5pm) consignment store and café is the de facto community center for the area. It's usually full of people. Stop by to sip a cappuccino or find out about local events.

Naikoon Provincial Park (☎ 250-557-4390) contains two excellent campgrounds. **Misty Meadows Campground** (site $14), just off Hwy 16 at the south end of the park, features nice, wooded sites, some of which have wooden platforms so your tent doesn't get soaked. A short trail leads to the beach. See Tow Beach, p000, for information on Agate Beach Campground, the other campground.

PORT CLEMENTS

pop 558

Locally referred to as 'Port', this logging and harbor town lies 21km north of Tlell on Hwy 16. For years it was known for the Golden Spruce, a huge genetically unique spruce that had a low chloroform count and

thus a golden color. In 1997 a deranged surveyor cut it down to protest 'the hypocrisy of logging'. The act didn't just kill the tree, it traumatized the community as well. (The convicted cutter supposedly drowned while trying to return to the islands by kayak across the open ocean for his sentencing.) Today, a seedling sprouted from a golden spruce pinecone grows gamely behind a huge fence near the museum. The jury is out as to whether it has inherited its parents' golden genes.

There are two good walks near Tlell. About 1km south on Juskatla Rd is **Sunset Park**, which has a 2km boardwalk into the marshes and a tall watchtower from where you can see oodles of birds, otters and other critters. The **Golden Spruce Walk**, 5km further south, may now only feature the stump of its namesake but this actually lets you focus more on the amazing and verdant coast rainforest along the 3km trail. Just after the start, bear to the right and you'll see a huge cedar growing on the side of a yet larger spruce.

The **Port Clements Museum** (☎ 250-557-4285; ⌚ 9am-1pm Mon-Fri summer) on Bayview Drive focuses on the local logging industry.

Golden Spruce Motel (☎ 250-557-4325, 877-801-4653; www.qcislands.net/golden; 2 Grouse St; r $42-62) is a good place for an active holiday. Owner Rolf Bettner can set you up for just about anything you want to do. The breakfasts are good as well.

One of the best restaurants on the island, **Hummingbird Café** (☎ 250-557-8583; 9 Cedar Ave; meals $10-20; ⌚ dinner Tue-Sat) serves wonderful fresh fish dishes. Come hungry.

MASSET & OLD MASSET

pop 1620

Though small and quiet, Masset is home to many businesses. Old Masset, 4km down the road from Masset, is a Haida community. You'll see the remains of a Cold War military base in these parts, although long gone, its legacy is affordable albeit bland ex-military housing that has attracted people to the area. There are a few artists with studios here – ask at the VIC – otherwise you won't need to linger long on your way to the north coast.

Sleeping & Eating

Shops, cafés and a grocery store line Main St. Local celebrity and chef extraordinaire

David Phillips runs the **Copper Beech House** (☎ 250-626-5441; www.copperbeechhouse.com; 1590 Delkatla Rd, Masset; r $50-80). This rambling old house backs onto the Masset Harbour and features rooms that come complete with a teddy bear on every bed. Get Phillips to cook for you and you might never leave. Ask about hostel accommodation in return for chores (like gardening or washing dishes).

The pleasant **Harbourview Lodging** (☎ 250-626-5109, 800-661-3314; 1618 Delkatla St; r $50-90) is on the marina. It offers clean, comfortable rooms and free juice and muffins in the morning. The nicest rooms have their own deck and barbecue.

The **Village of Masset Campground** (☎ 250-626-3968; site $10), 1km from Masset on Tow Hill Rd (just beyond the bridge going out to Naikoon), offers flush toilets, a coin laundry and hot showers.

The **Sandpiper Restaurant** (☎ 250-626-3672; 2062 Collison Ave; meals $8-15; ☯ lunch & dinner Mon-Sat) is the place to go for steaks and fresh seafood.

NORTH COAST

To enjoy some good bird-watching, head to the **Delkatla Wildlife Sanctuary**, off Tow Hill Rd north of Masset. The 26km of road alone after that will make you glad you came out to the islands. The road parallels some of the wildest beaches you'll see then runs for stretches under a canopy of moss-draped trees arching over the road. It's mystic, beautiful and a bit primordial.

Near the end of the road lies **Tow Hill**, a columnar basalt outcropping an hour's hike from a parking lot. At the top, you'll enjoy incredible views of the north end of Naikoon Provincial Park as well as north to Alaska. Also worth checking out is the **Blowhole**, which spurts out ocean water on incoming tides.

For real adventure, hit the **Cape Fife Loop Trail**, a 21km loop that takes you over the Argonaut Plain to Fife Point and Rose Spit. At the very end of the road is the **Tlie-lang Campground** (☎ 250-626-5115, site $10), a Haida-run placed that is truly rustic. You can park on the packed sand and see the beach stretching seemingly forever east into the mists. People staying here typically wade out into the surf, catch a few Dungeness crabs and then boil them up

for dinner. A visitor center was set to open in 2004.

A few kilometers back down the road, **Agate Beach Campground** (☎ 250-557-4390) sits right on the sand. On clear days, you can see straight through to Alaska. Named for the pretty glass-like stones found along the beaches, Agate Beach can get windy and downright cold after dark. The facilities include a shelter (if you need to get out of the wind and rain), pit toilets and sites that cost from $12.

If you're looking to stay dry, the **Alaska View Lodge B&B** (☎ 250-626-3333, 800-661-0019; www.alaskaviewlodge.com; r $70-90) is on the beach 10.5km from Masset. The warm and cozy rooms are the perfect counterpoint to the pounding surf.

Rapid Richies Rustic Rentals (☎ 250-626-5472; www.beachcabins.com; cabins $40-70), 10km from Masset, is the perfect place to get away and perfect your alliteration. Cabins come with views that are almost senselessly scenic.

SANDSPIT
pop 460

Sandspit is just that – a long sandy spit jutting out into Hecate Strait. The only community on Moresby Island, Sandspit is home to the airport and a couple of stores. It's also the major gateway into Gwaii Haanas, though if you're heading to the park from QCC, you will get off the ferry at Alliford Bay and bypass the town.

GWAII HAANAS NATIONAL PARK RESERVE

Protected since 1988, this huge, wild park encompasses Moresby and 137 smaller islands at the south end of the Queen Charlottes. This 640km-long stretch of rugged coastline is true wilderness at its best. If you take out a kayak, you can paddle for days without seeing another human being (though you'll see lots of wildlife). Recent archaeological finds have documented more than 500 ancient Haida sites, including villages and burial caves dotted throughout the islands. The most famous (and photographed) village is **Ninstints – SGaang Gwaii** (Anthony Island), where rows of totem poles stare eerily out to sea. This ancient village was declared a Unesco World Heritage site in 1981. (On the Charlottes, you'll notice that Ninstints is now more commonly referred to as SGaang

Gwaii (pronounced skung gwhy, which is the more traditional name.) Other major sights include **Skedans** on Louise Island and **Hotspring Island**, where you can soak away the bone-chilling cold in natural springs. The ancient sites are protected by the Haida Gwaii Watchmen, who live on the islands during summer.

Information

Access to the park is by boat or plane only. A visit demands a decent amount of advance planning and usually requires several days. If you want to travel independently, you need to reserve in advance, as only a limited number of people can be in the park at any given time (see below). Once on the Charlottes you must attend an orientation session before you enter the park.

Anyone who has not visited the park during the previous three years must attend a free 90-minute orientation session. These are both informative and entertaining as you not only learn about the many do's and don'ts but also about the park, its culture and wildlife. Confirm the schedule, but the sessions are generally held daily at 8am at the QCC VIC and coincide with Vancouver flights at the Sandspit VIC at the airport. Some tour companies arrange their own orientations.

Contact Parks Canada's **Gwaii Haanas office** (☎ 250-559-8818; parkscan.harbour.com/Gwaii; Box 37, QCC, BC, V0T 1S0) with questions and to obtain the essential annual information pack.

RESERVATIONS & FEES

Beginning each February 1, you can reserve a space to enter the park (☎ 800-435-5622, ☎ 250-387-1642 outside of North America) for the period May 1 to September 30. The reservation fee is $15 per person. In addition there are user fees of $10 per person per night for the first five nights with a flat rate of $60 for anything up to 14 days. Longer than that is $80. Each day from May 1-Sep 30, six standby spaces are made available at the QCC VIC at 8am. Demand for these can be fierce. From Oct-Apr there is no need for reservations or to pay fees.

Tours

The easiest way to get into the park is with a tour company. The Visitor Info Centre in QCC can provide you with lists of operators, many of whom are located in Vancouver and Victoria.

On the islands, **Queen Charlotte Adventures** (☎ 250-559-8990, 800-668-4288; queencharlotteadventures.com) offers one- to 10-day trips using power boats, kayaks or sailboats. Prices start at $140 for a one-day trip to Skedans. The owners take an active role in protecting the ecology of the preserve.

Another excellent company is **Moresby Explorers** (☎ 250-637-2215, 800-806-7633; www.moresbyexplorers.com), which operates a summer base camp so you get to the good sites faster. A 10-day kayaking trip to the totem poles of the southern park islands is $1585.

Both of the above companies rent kayaks and other gear to independent travelers.

Getting There & Away

AIR

Sandspit airport (YZP; ☎ 250-559-0052) Air Canada Jazz flies daily to/from Vancouver. **Canadian Western** (☎ 866-835-9292; www.cwair .com) flies several times a week to/from Vancouver. **Harbour Air** (☎ 800-689-4234) runs a service to/from Prince Rupert.

FERRY

BC Ferries (☎ 250-386-3431) has a service between Prince Rupert and Skidegate (adult/child $23.50/11.75, car from $86.50, cabin from $40; eight hours; six per week in summer, three per week in winter).

Ferries also run between Skidegate Landing and Alliford Bay (adult/child $5/2.50, cars from $12.50; 20 minutes hourly from Alliford Bay 7am to 10pm, Skidegate 7:30am to 10:30pm).

Getting Around

Off Hwy 16, most of the roads are gravel or worse. Many are logging roads and you have to contend with the very real hazard of encountering a speeding logging truck. If you plan to go on these roads contact **Weyerhauser** (☎ 250-557-6810; ⏲ 6:30am-5:30pm Mon-Fri) to check conditions.

If you want a car, you'll have to weigh the high cost of local car rental against the cost of bringing a vehicle on the ferry. Two rental companies are **Budget** (☎ 250-637-5688) and **Rustic Car Rentals** (☎ 250-559-4641, 877-559-4641; citires@qcislands.net).

Eagle Cabs (☎ 877-747-4461) meets flights and ferries.

STEWART-CASSIAR HIGHWAY

The remote Stewart-Cassiar Hwy (Hwy 37) is Canada's most westerly road system linking BC to the Yukon and Alaska. West of here, you need to take ferries to go north; east of here, it's just thick wilderness until you get to the Alaska Hwy. This raggedy route rivals the Alaska Hwy for scenery. The highway meets Hwy 16 at Kitwanga, 714km from the Yukon. Officially the highway becomes the Stewart-Cassiar Hwy at Meziadin Junction.

If you've come this far, don't miss the chance to take the 134km side trip west to the rough-and-tumble twin border towns of Stewart, BC, and Hyder, Alaska, which sit on the coast at the head of the Portland Canal. You'll pass by glaciers, waterfalls and breathtaking scenery.

The Stewart-Cassiar is not the place for paranoid drivers. About 15% of the highway is still covered in gravel, making the ride often slow and bumpy. RVs and large trucks can be a menace, but so too are madcap drivers. The best thing to do is to drive slowly and enjoy the ride and the views. For road conditions call ☎ 250-771-4511, 250-847-9692, www.th.gov.bc.ca/roadreports.htm. The service stations in the table below are not open long hours.

KITWANGA

The turn north to Kitwanga on Hwy 37 is 240km from Prince Rupert. Kitwanga, along with nearby Gitwangak, Gitanyow and Kispiox, is the traditional home of the Gitksan First Nations people, who traded along this section of the Skeena River for centuries. The area includes spectacular totems, as well as the **Kitwanga Fort National Historic Site**. A path with interpretive signs follows a route up Battle Hill, where Canada's only Indian fort commanded the valley in pre-colonial days.

GITANYOW

Otherwise known as Kitwancool, this small First Nation town is home to more than a dozen stunning **totem poles** dating from more than 100 years ago to the present. Behind the array is a community center that is sometimes open and that has displays of local cultural items. The town is 21km north of Hwy 16 and well worth the detour even if you are not going further on Hwy 37.

MEZIADIN JUNCTION

Meziadin Lake Provincial Park (☎ 250-638-8490), about 155km north of Kitwanga, has become a popular fishing spot and campground with pit toilets, a boat launch and 60 sites, some of which are on the lake. Don't get gas here; instead, go a little further to Meziadin Junction, where the gas is cheaper and there are more services. From here, you can continue north to the Yukon or go west on Hwy 37A for 67km to Stewart. En route, watch for the stunning **Bear Glacier**, the largest ice tongue of the Cambria Icefields; it practically leaps onto the highway and glows a bright blue, even at night.

STEWART & HYDER

The long Portland Canal, a steep ocean fjord that extends from the coast 90km into the mountains, finally stops at Stewart,

HIGHWAY 37

Gas stations	Supplies & services	Distance from Hwy 16 junction
Meziadin Junction	gas, repairs restaurant & groceries	156km
Bell II	gas, repairs, restaurant	250km
Tatogga	gas, restaurant (summer)	390km
Iskut	gas, groceries	405km
Dease Lake	gas, repairs, groceries	488km
Good Hope Lake	gas, groceries	626km
Jct Hwy 37 & Alaska Hwy	gas, repairs, restaurant	727km

THE NORTH

Canada's most northerly ice-free port. The fjord cuts a natural border between Canada and the USA, which is why Hyder, Stewart's closest US neighbor, is only 3km away and is only connected to other parts of Alaska by water.

Stewart (pop 600) was once a bustling mining town where prospectors flocked after hearing about the discovery of gold. The boom, however, was short-lived, and when the riches ran dry, so did the population. Today, Stewart's port shuffles logs to southerly ports and **Hyder** (pop 95, give or take a couple of dogs) ekes out an existence as the 'friendliest ghost town in Alaska'. Some 40,000 tourists come through every summer, and most of them get 'Hyderized' by slamming back a shot of '190-proof' at the **Glacier Inn** (☎ 250-636-9248), whose walls are covered in signed dollar bills. For a good look at the isolated beauty of the area, watch *Insomnia*, a 2001 thriller with Robin Williams and Al Pacino.

The towns collectively greet visitors to the area, and you wouldn't know they're in separate countries if it weren't for the small customs booth. Although more wary than in years past, the border checks still watch mostly for guns and un-taxed liquor (that could potentially be brought in to Hyder by boat). They say the postal code (V0T 1W0) sums it up: Very Old Town, One Way Out. You can use Canadian currency in both towns, and you can mail letters via the US Postal Service in Hyder or Canada Post in Stewart.

From Hyder, take the Salmon Glacier Rd to **Fish Creek**, about 3km past Hyder, where you can see the salmon swimming upstream to spawn and watch bears hungrily feeding on them. The best time to do this is between late July and September. The gravel road, which runs parallel to Alaska's Tongass National Forest on the other side of the Salmon River, ultimately heads up to the spectacular Salmon Glacier. Before attempting this beautiful but bumpy drive, pick up a copy of the *Salmon Glacier Self Guided Auto Tour* from the **Visitor Info Centre** (☎ 250-636-9224, 888-366-5999; 222 5th Ave; ⏰ 9am-7pm summer, limited winter hours) in Stewart.

Sleeping

Over in Hyder, the **Grand View Inn** (☎ 250-636-9174; www.grandviewinn.net; r $60) has modern rooms, some with kitchenettes. There are good views of the bears wandering the streets.

In Stewart, the bifurcated **King Edward Motel/Hotel** (☎ 250-636-2244, 800-663-3126; www.kingedwardhotel.com; r $60-100; P ✂) is downtown on 5th Ave.

The **Rainey Creek Municipal Campground** (☎ 250-636-2537; 8th Ave; site $12) in Stewart, has showers and flush toilets. Expect similar conditions at the **Bear River Trailer Court & RV Park** (☎ 250-636-9205; www.stewartbc.com/rvpark; tent site $12), just off Hwy 37A as you come into Stewart.

NORTH OF MEZIADIN JUNCTION

At the Tahltan town of **Iskut**, the gateway to Spatsizi Plateau Wilderness Park (below), you'll find a grocery store, gas pump and places to stay.

South of Iskut, the **Red Goat Lodge** (☎ 250-234-3261, 888-733-4628; redgoatlodge@aol.com; site/dm/r $13/20/55-95), on the shores of Eddontenajon Lake, is a haven for travelers, with a coin laundry and communal kitchen facilities. You can camp alongside the lake or stay in one of the cabins. The lodge rents canoes and organizes trips into the parks.

North of Iskut, the **Bear Paw Resort** (☎ 250-234-3005; www.room42.com/wilderness; r from $75) features an alpine hotel and theme-room cabins starting at $55. The resort offers horseback riding, and boating and canoeing on the river, as well as hiking trips. There's also a restaurant, saloon, hot tub and sauna.

Parks

On the Stewart-Cassiar Hwy, you'll come across pretty **Kinaskan Lake Provincial Park**. This park, excellent for trout fishing, offers lakeside campsites ($12) with pit toilets (but no showers) and free wood.

Spatsizi Plateau Wilderness Provincial Park is a vast and wild place that is mostly inaccessible. The park entrance is 136km east of Hwy 37 at Tatogga along primitive roads, which pretty much end when you get to the park. The park's trails are often little more than vague notions across the untouched landscape.

Stikine River Recreation Area, a narrow park west of Dease Lake (p335), connects the Spatsizi Plateau Wilderness Park with the Mt Edziza Provincial Park and serves as the pull-out for canoe trips starting in Spatsizi. Past the bridge, the river thrusts through the spectacular **Grand Canyon of the Stikine**, an 80km stretch through a steep-walled canyon that is completely unnavigable by boat.

The 230,000-hectare **Mt Edziza Provincial Park** protects a volcanic landscape featuring lava flows, basalt plateaus and cinder cones surrounding an extinct shield volcano. Though it's inaccessible by car, you can hike, horseback ride or fly into the park by making arrangements in Telegraph Creek or Dease Lake.

The stunning little **Boya Lake Provincial Park**, about 100km north of Dease Lake, surrounds the shockingly turquoise Boya Lake. Dotted with small tree-covered islets, this warm lake looks like something out of the tropics. You can camp right on the shore. The campground includes pit toilets, a boat launch and 45 sites ($12).

Dease Lake

Although the area was once an important supply point for construction of the Alaska Highway to the north, Dease Lake today is a small stop on the highway, a halfway point between Hwy 16 and Whitehorse. The couple of hotels in town include the **Northway Motor Inn** (☎ 250-771-5341; r $68-80) which has a restaurant and basic rooms. Newer accommodations can be found on the east side of the highway at the **Arctic Divide Inn** (☎ 250-771-3119; s/d $65/70), where rooms in a lovely log cabin include a continental breakfast.

West from Dease Lake is **Telegraph Creek**, a wilderness town 113km along Telegraph Creek Rd. The drive is rugged but scenic.

ATLIN

pop 480

Surrounded by the huge ice fields and glaciers of the northern Coast Mountains, this remote town in the northwestern-most corner of BC sits alongside the 145km-long land-locked fjord known as Atlin Lake. Born in 1898 on the back of the Klondike Gold Rush, Atlin had gold of its own in nearby Pine Creek, which brought in a fast rush of prospectors. In town, colorful houses face the lake, with boats or float-planes parked in front. Atlin served as the location for the film *Never Cry Wolf*, based on the book by Farley Mowat.

At the southwest corner of the lake is the imposing **Llewellyn Glacier**, whose meltwater carries glacial sediment to the lake, making it a fantastic hue of aquamarine. The glacier lies in the **Atlin Provincial Park & Recreation Area** – 271,134 hectares of ice fields and glaciers, all of it only accessible by float-plane or boat. For any ventures into the wilderness, be it by kayak or skis, contact **Backcountry Sports** (☎ 250-651-2424).

The small **Atlin Museum** (☎ 250-651-7522; www.atlin.net; 10am-4pm summer), housed in a 1902 schoolhouse, offers area information; it's open mid-May to early September.

To get to Atlin, drive all the way to the end of the Stewart-Cassiar Hwy, just west of Watson Lake in the Yukon, and turn west onto the Alaska Hwy (Hwy 1). Turn south off Hwy 1 at Jake's Corner and follow Hwy 7; from there, it's 98km along a partial gravel road to the town.

TATSHENSHINI-ALSEK PROVINCIAL WILDERNESS PARK

Jointly managed by BC Parks and the Champagne and Aishihik First Nations, this park on the northwest tip of BC is part of the Unesco World Heritage site that includes Kluane National Park and Reserve in the Yukon, and Glacier Bay and Wrangell-St Elias National Parks in Alaska. It is only accessible through the Yukon or Alaska. At nearly a million hectares, the park superseded Tweedsmuir Provincial Park (981,000 hectares) as the largest park in the province. The place evokes intense historical sentiment for the Champagne and Aishihik people, who are trying to reclaim the land from the government. In 1999 the remains of a man, thought to be about 500 years old, were found in one of the melting glaciers. Named 'Kwaday Dan Sinchi' (meaning 'not long ago person found'), the corpse was studied intensively before ultimately being cremated and returned to the ground near where he was found.

Yukon Territory

Every year more and more visitors discover the Yukon's rugged charm and beauty during the short summer season, or arrive later to strap on skis or snowshoes and experience the extreme winter landscape.

Whitehorse, the capital, has a thriving cultural life. Dawson City is simply a fun place to be during the summer. With good road access, transportation and services, costs in the Yukon are reasonable compared to other remote areas of Canada. It's also a great place for kids.

And then there's the land. What land! From the Unesco-recognized Kluane National Park and Reserve in the south to the Ivvavik National Park in the Arctic, the Yukon landscape is wild and offers endless opportunities to explore. Stand on a bluff overlooking the surging, silver Yukon River and you see a vista unchanged in eons.

The Yukon offers an abundance of outdoor opportunities – world-class hiking and mountaineering, cycling, canoeing, rafting, kayaking, camping and fishing – amid a scenic splendor of mountains, forests, fast-flowing rivers and tundra. Mountain ranges, including some that stretch from the Rockies, almost entirely cover the territory, which is 80% wilderness. There are large populations of moose, caribou, bears, sheep, beavers, porcupines, coyotes and wolves, which far outnumber the humans. A trip to the Yukon is an adventure of a lifetime – unless you do like so many and return often.

HIGHLIGHTS

- Paddling the fast-flowing **Yukon River** (p339) or its tributaries
- Hiking the greenbelt of **Kluane National Park** (p350) or flying over its icy heart
- Following the gold-seekers on the **Gold Rush trail** (p353)
- Ambling down the gold-rush era streets of **Dawson City** (p357)
- Experiencing the 747km **Dempster Highway** (p363), the last great adventure road, for wide-open tundra and a chance to cross the Arctic Circle

★ Eagle Plains
★ Dempster Highway
★ Dawson City
★ Yukon River
★ Kluane National Park

YUKON TERRITORY

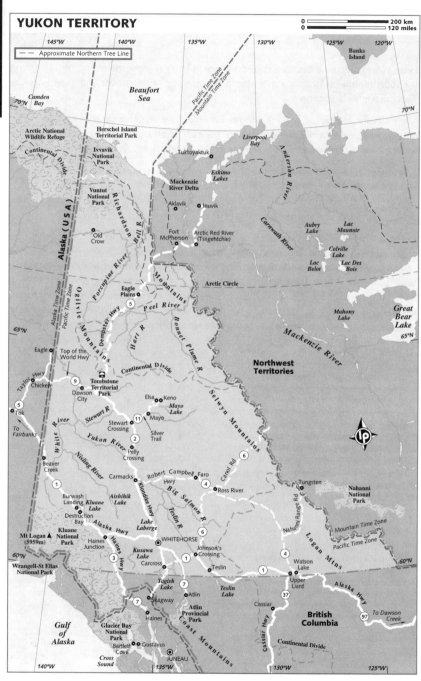

YUKON TERRITORY

0 ———————— 200 km
0 ———————— 120 miles

– – – Approximate Northern Tree Line

145°W 140°W 135°W 130°W 125°W 120°W

Banks
Island

*Beaufort
Sea*

Pacific Time Zone
Mountain Time Zone

*Camden
Bay*

70°N

70°N

Arctic National
Wildlife Refuge

Herschel Island
Territorial Park

Ivvavik
National
Park

*Liverpool
Bay*

Tuktoyaktuk

Continental Divide

Anderson River

Vuntut
National
Park

Mackenzie
River Delta

*Eskimo
Lakes*

Aklavik Inuvik

Cornwath River

*Aubry
Lake*

*Lac
Maunoir*

Old
Crow

Fort
McPherson

Arctic Red River
(Tsiigehtchie)

*Colville
Lake*

*Lac
Belot*

*Lac Des
Bois*

Richardson

Bell R

Mountains

Eagle
Plains

Arctic Circle

*Mahony
Lake*

*Great
Bear
Lake*

5

Peel River

Porcupine River

Ogilvie

Mountains

65°N

65°N

Hart R

Bonnet Plume R

Mackenzie River

Eagle

Top of the
World Hwy

Continental Divide

Northwest
Territories

Taylor Hwy

Chicken

9

Tombstone
Territorial
Park

Dawson
City

Elsa Keno

*Mayo
Lake*

Selwyn Mountains

5

Tok

To
Fairbanks

White River

Stewart R

11

Stewart
Crossing

Mayo

Silver
Trail

2

Yukon River

Pelly
Crossing

Nisutlin River

Beaver
Creek

Canol Rd

6

1

Carmacks

Robert Campbell

Faro

Tungsten

Nahanni
National
Park

Burwash
Landing

*Aishihik
Lake*

Hwy

4

Big Salmon R

Ross River

*Kluane
Lake*

Destruction
Bay

Alaska Hwy

Klondike Hwy

Nahanni Range Rd

Mt Logan ▲
(5959m)

Kluane
National
Park

Haines Hwy

*Lake
Laberge*

Teslin R

6

Mountain Time Zone

Pacific Time Zone

Logan Mtns

Wrangell-St Elias
National
Park

Haines
Junction

WHITEHORSE

Johnson's
Crossing

3

*Kusawa
Lake*

1

4

Watson
Lake

60°N

60°N

Carcross

Teslin

1

*Tagish
Lake*

7

Upper
Liard

37

*Gulf
of
Alaska*

7

Skagway

Atlin

*Teslin
Lake*

Cassiar

British
Columbia

97

To Dawson
Creek

Haines

Atlin
Provincial
Park

Cassiar Hwy

Alaska Hwy

Glacier Bay
National
Park

Coast Mountains

Continental Divide

*Cross
Sound*

Bartlett
Cove

Gustavus

JUNEAU

140°W 135°W 130°W 125°W

ORIENTATION

The Yukon is between the Northwest Territories and Alaska, with British Columbia to the south and the Beaufort Sea to the north. It's a sub-Arctic region about one-third the size of Alaska.

The Alaska Hwy is the main route through the Yukon, and there are a number of other scenic and demanding drives, including the Dempster Hwy, the only north-south road to cross the Arctic Circle.

INFORMATION

The Yukon has six **Visitor Reception Centres** (VRCs; ☉ 8am-8pm mid-May–mid-Sep), which are known as Visitor Info Centres (VICs) in BC. They are in Beaver Creek, Carcross, Dawson City, Haines Junction, Watson Lake and Whitehorse. **Tourism Yukon** (☎ 867-667-5340; www.touryukon.com) will send free information, including the annual *Yukon* magazine with specifics on regional activities, events and accommodations. It also distributes an excellent highway map. A number of other tourism publications are highly useful, including *Art Adventures on Yukon Time, Into the Yukon Wilderness, Places to Go on Yukon Time* and more.

It's also worth noting the extremes in daylight hours and temperatures. Whitehorse may experience long, 19-hour sunny days in July but come January it's light for a mere six hours (actually, 'light' is the wrong term, think 'less dark') and the average temperature is −18.7°C. For all but the hardiest, the Yukon is truly a summer destination.

ACTIVITIES

The Yukon VRCs can supply you with information and answer questions on hiking, canoeing, rafting, cycling, gold prospecting, skiing, fishing and various adventure trips. There are outfitters and tour companies to handle arrangements, but you really don't need an organized trip and you don't need to be wealthy to fully enjoy the Yukon.

Hiking

The best known route is the Chilkoot Trail, which begins in Alaska, but Kluane National Park in the territory's southwest corner also has excellent hikes, from short and easy to long and demanding. The Tombstone

---

ONLY IN THE YUKON

Certain details about the Yukon are different from British Columbia. Important ones are:
Police ☎ 867-667-5555
Medical emergencies ☎ 867-667-3333, ☎ 911 in Whitehorse.
Telephone area code ☎ 867, Alaska ☎ 907
Road condition information ☎ 867-456-7623
Territory campgrounds cannot be reserved. The fee at all campgrounds is $12 per night.

Mountain area north of Dawson is also good, with the North Fork Pass considered the classic hike of the region. For Northern Alpine terrain, try MacMillan Pass at the Northwest Territories border, accessible by Canol Rd north from Ross River.

Canoeing

Canoeists have many choices, from easy float trips down the waters of the Yukon River and its tributaries to challenging whitewater adventures.

Gentle trips down the Yukon from Whitehorse range from a few hours to 16 days all the way to Dawson, and are popular. Many people start or end at Carmacks, the halfway point, making an eight-day trip. Boat rental and return charges for an eight-day, one-way trip are about $200 and transport can be arranged.

Kayaking & Whitewater Rafting

The Alsek and Tatshenshini rivers are ranked among the best and wildest in North America. They're found in British Columbia, south of Kluane, and are accessible from Haines Junction. Other major areas are the Lapie (near Ross River) and Takhini (north of Whitehorse) rivers.

Fishing

For anglers, www.yukonfishing.com provides regulations and a list of what's where as well as the best time and means to catch your prize salmon, trout or grayling.

Wildlife-Watching

Yukon Tourism publishes an excellent *Wildlife Viewing Guide* that details the critters you can expect to see in the territory, many right along the highways.

For an unforgettable introduction into the world of Yukon hunting, pick up the government publication *Hunting Regulations Summary*. Besides telling you how to bag a moose it has a section on determining the sex of caribou that will stay with you long after other memories of your trip fade.

FESTIVALS & EVENTS

The Yukon has a number of events that are big deals throughout the territory. When you have a total population of 31,000, it's easy to get everyone's attention.

The Yukon Quest (February) 1600km dog-sled race goes from Whitehorse to Fairbanks, Alaska.

Kluane Chilkat International Bike Relay (June) Bikers ride 237.8km from Haines Junction to Haines, Alaska.

International Storytelling Festival (June) Whitehorse festival features First Nation participants.

Discovery Day (3rd Monday of August) Many, many folks head to Dawson (p357) to celebrate the discovery of gold or just to have a good time. Most of the territory shuts down.

Klondike Trail '98 Road Relay (September) Some 100 running teams of 10 each complete the overnight course from Skagway to Whitehorse.

WHITEHORSE

pop 23,000

The Yukon's capital is a pleasant place that makes a good base to start a Yukon trip. If you have traveled by land from the south, it's a good place to stop and gather your wits. There are good restaurants, an active artistic community and a few things to do. Escaping artists and writers mix well with government workers and grizzled old timers. If you're planning a wilderness adventure, this is where you can get fully outfitted.

Spread along the banks of the Yukon River, Whitehorse is the largest town in the territory. The official city limits cover 421 sq km, making it one of the largest urban-designated areas in Canada. Despite this, the central core is quite small and it's easy to walk around. Downtown is designed on a grid system and the main traffic routes are 2nd and 4th Aves.

The town sits just off the Alaska Hwy between Dawson Creek in British Columbia (1430km to the east), where the highway starts, and Fairbanks in Alaska (970km west). Despite its growth, Whitehorse still has something of a frontier feel even if it is home to two-thirds of the Yukon's population. The downtown is compact – although the arrival of Wal-Mart on the edge could cause unpalatable sprawl.

Information

BOOKSTORES

Mac's Fireweed Books (☎ 867-668-2434; www.yukonbooks.com; 203 Main St; 🕙 8am-midnight summer) has a superb selection of history, geography and wildlife titles plus a section on First Nations culture. It also carries topographical maps, road maps, magazines and newspapers.

Well-Read Books (☎ 867-393-2987; wellreadbooks.yk.net; 4194 4th Ave; 🕙 9am-6pm Mon-Sat, 10am-5pm Sun) has a large and varied selection of used books. Here's a chance to buy that trashy novel guilt-free.

EMERGENCY

☎ 911

INTERNET ACCESS

Wired Cabin (☎ 867-393-3597; 107 Jarvis St; $2 per 15min; 🕙 9am-midnight)

LAUNDRY

Norgetown (☎ 867-667-6113; 4213 4th Ave; 🕙 8am-9:30pm)

LIBRARY

Whitehorse Library (☎ 867-667-5239; 2071 2nd Ave; 🕙 9am-9pm Mon-Fri, 10am-6pm Sat & 1-9pm Sun) Free Internet access for 15 minutes.

MEDICAL SERVICES

Whitehorse General Hospital (☎ 867-393-8700; 5 Hospital Rd; 🕙 24hr)

POST

Post office (☎ 867-667-2485; 211 Main St; 🕙 9am-6pm Mon-Fri, 11am-4pm Sat) In the basement of Shoppers Drug Mart.

TOURIST INFORMATION

VRC (☎ 867-667-3084; 100 Hanson St; 🕙 8am-8pm mid-May–mid-Sep, 9am-4:30pm Mon-Fri winter)

Sights

MUSEUMS

Yukon Beringia Interpretive Centre (☎ 867-667-8855; www.beringia.com; Km1473 Alaska Hwy; adult/child $6/4; 🕙 8:30am-7pm mid-May–mid-Sep) focuses on Beringia, an area that, during the last Ice Age, encompassed the Yukon, Alaska and eastern Siberia yet was untouched by

WHITEHORSE

0 ——————— 500 m
0 ——————— 0.3 miles

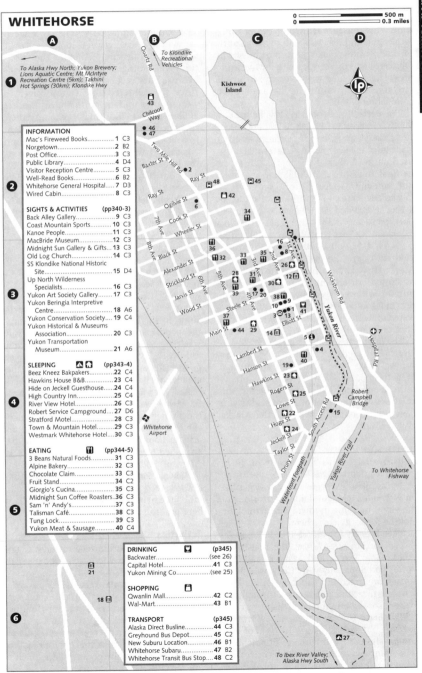

To Alaska Hwy North; Yukon Brewery;
Lions Aquatic Centre; Mt. McIntyre
Recreation Centre (5km); Takhini
Hot Springs (30km); Klondike Hwy

INFORMATION
Mac's Fireweed Books.............. 1 C3
Norgetown................................ 2 B2
Post Office............................... 3 C3
Public Library........................... 4 D4
Visitor Reception Centre............ 5 C3
Well-Read Books....................... 6 B2
Whitehorse General Hospital..... 7 D3
Wired Cabin............................. 8 C3

SIGHTS & ACTIVITIES (pp340-3)
Back Alley Gallery..................... 9 C3
Coast Mountain Sports............ 10 C3
Kanoe People.......................... 11 C3
MacBride Museum.................... 12 C3
Midnight Sun Gallery & Gifts.... 13 C3
Old Log Church....................... 14 C3
SS Klondike National Historic
  Site..................................... 15 D4
Up North Wilderness
  Specialists........................... 16 C3
Yukon Art Society Gallery........ 17 C3
Yukon Beringia Interpretive
  Centre................................. 18 A6
Yukon Conservation Society..... 19 C4
Yukon Historical & Museums
  Association.......................... 20 C3
Yukon Transportation
  Museum............................... 21 A6

SLEEPING (pp343-4)
Beez Kneez Bakpakers............. 22 C4
Hawkins House B&B................ 23 C4
Hide on Jeckell Guesthouse..... 24 C4
High Country Inn..................... 25 C3
River View Hotel..................... 26 C3
Robert Service Campground..... 27 D6
Stratford Motel....................... 28 C3
Town & Mountain Hotel.......... 29 C3
Westmark Whitehorse Hotel.... 30 C3

EATING (pp344-5)
3 Beans Natural Foods............ 31 C3
Alpine Bakery......................... 32 C3
Chocolate Claim...................... 33 C3
Fruit Stand............................. 34 C2
Giorgio's Cucina..................... 35 C3
Midnight Sun Coffee Roasters.. 36 C3
Sam 'n' Andy's........................ 37 C3
Talisman Café......................... 38 C3
Tung Lock.............................. 39 C3
Yukon Meat & Sausage........... 40 C4

DRINKING (p345)
Backwater............................(see 26)
Capital Hotel.......................... 41 C3
Yukon Mining Co..................(see 25)

SHOPPING
Qwanlin Mall.......................... 42 C2
Wal-Mart............................... 43 B1

TRANSPORT (p345)
Alaska Direct Busline.............. 44 C3
Greyhound Bus Depot............. 45 C2
New Suburu Location.............. 46 B1
Whitehorse Subaru.................. 47 B2
Whitehorse Transit Bus Stop.... 48 C2

glaciers. Interactive displays re-create the time. This museum is the most interesting local sight, and it's just south of the airport. From downtown, take the airport bus from Ogilvie St and then walk south for five minutes. This is a good way to occupy yourself if you're stuck waiting at the airport for connecting flights.

The perfectly restored **SS Klondike** (☎ 867-667-4511; South Access Rd & 2nd Ave; adult/child a guided tour $5/3; ☼ 9am-5:30pm mid-May–mid-Sep) was one of the last and largest sternwheelers used on the Yukon. Built in 1937, it made its final run upriver in 1955 and is now a museum and national historic site.

MacBride Museum (☎ 867-667-2709; cnr 1st Ave & Wood St; adult/child $5/3.50; ☼ 10am-9pm Mon-Fri, 10am-7pm Sat & Sun mid-May–Sep) looks like a log cabin with a turf roof. It has a collection from First Nation cultures, the fur trade, gold-rush days and the construction of the Alaska Hwy. There's the requisite collection of stuffed critters and a mixed bag of old mining equipment. At the entrance, check out the good shot of the old Whitehorse waterfront. In summer there are lectures at 7pm on the collections.

The **Yukon Transportation Museum** (☎ 867-668-4792; 30 Electra Circle; adult/child $6/4; ☼ 10am-6pm May-Aug) covers the perils and adventures of getting around the Yukon by plane, train, truck and dog sled. Check out the crashes in the bush pilot room and if you have a mud fetish, you'll love the Alaska Hwy exhibit.

OTHER SIGHTS

Built by the town's first priest in 1900, the **old log church** (☎ 867-668-2555; 303 Elliott St; adult/child $2.50/1; ☼ 10am-6pm mid-May–Aug) is the only wooden cathedral in the world and the oldest building in town. Try to imagine looking for forgiveness here.

Yukon Brewery (☎ 867-668-4183; 102 Copper Rd; ☼ 11am-6pm, tours 11am & 4pm), the makers of Yukon Gold, Arctic Red, Winter Lead Dog Porter and Sourdough Ale (the owner's favorite), are based in Whitehouse. You'll be drinking these fine products all through the Yukon, so you might as well visit.

Whitehorse Fishway (☎ 867-633-5965; admission free; ☼ 8am-8pm summer) is one of the coolest sights in Whitehorse. The fishway is a 366m wooden fish ladder (world's longest!) that gives fish a road past the

hydro-electric plant just south of town. The real attraction here is the large viewing window that lets you look eye to eye with returning salmon before they continue swimming. If they look pooped it's because they've been swimming 2792km since they entered the Yukon River in west Alaska and they still have another 208km to go before finally reaching their spawning grounds. There's an excellent free booklet available. The fishway is on Nisultin Drive off 2nd Ave after it crosses the Robert Campbell Bridge.

About 10km off the Klondike Hwy (Hwy 2) north of town in a quiet wooded area are the **Takhini Hot Springs** (☎ 867-633-2706; Km10 Takhini Hot Springs Rd; adult/child $7/5.50; ☼ 8am-10pm summer). The pools aren't huge but it's a good place to avoid hypothermia, even in the summer.

Art Galleries

Yukon Art Society Gallery (☎ 867-667-4080; 305 Wood St; ☼ 11am-5pm Mon-Sat) Here you can get an answer to 'Why have all the hippie artists come to the Yukon?' Answer: 'It's cheap, the people are laid-back and the air and water are clean'. This small space shows and sells works by local artists. You can also get good leads on the dozens of artists in the area whose galleries you can visit.

Back Alley Gallery (☎ 867-667-2002; 204A Main St; ☼ noon-5pm Tue-Sat) is located just where the name implies; it's a sleek space that exhibits and sells works by noted Yukon artists. Look for works by mixed media artist Scott Price, the willow works of Bob Atkinson and more.

Midnight Sun Gallery & Gifts (☎ 867-668-4350; 205C Main St; ☼ 9am-9pm summer) Don't be put off by the hype for fudge (!), there's real art here past the schtick.

Activities

Whitehorse has no shortage of ways to get your feet wet (even literally) in the myriad of Yukon activities.

Coast Mountain Sports (☎ 867-667-4074; 208 Main St; ☼ 9:30am-6pm Mon-Sat, until 9pm Thu & Fri, noon-4pm Sun) has a large selection of outdoor clothing and equipment, including stove fuel.

Ride history on a restored **trolley** (adult/child $1/free; ☼ 10am-5pm summer) that runs along the river. It doesn't really go anywhere but it's fun for kids.

WALKING & HIKING

You can walk a scenic 15km loop around Whitehorse's waters that includes a stop at the fishway. From the SS *Klondike* head south on the **waterfront footpath** until you reach the footbridge across the Miles Canyon and the Yukon River. Then head north along the east side of the water that includes **Schwatka Lake**. The **Yukon River Trail** will take you past the fishway. Cross the Robert Campbell Bridge and you are back in the town center. You may see coyotes, beavers and mule deer.

Around Whitehorse you can go hiking and biking, particularly at **Mt McIntyre Recreation Center**, up Two Mile Hill Rd, and at **Grey Mountain**, east of town. All along the **Ibex River Valley** west of Whitehorse is good for biking. The hiking trails there become cross-country ski trails in winter.

SWIMMING

Whitehorse Lions Aquatic Centre (☎ 867-668-7665; 200 Hamilton Blvd; adult/child $5.25/2.50) is a huge new palace of a swim centre that only needs to serve mai-tais to give Hawaii some stiff competition. Call for daily lap and children's swim times year-round.

CANOEING & KAYAKING

Whitehorse is the starting place for popular canoe and kayak trips to Carmacks or on to Dawson City. It's an average of eight days to the former and 16 days to the latter.

Kanoe People (☎ 867-668-4899; www.kanoepeople.com; cnr 1st Ave & Strickland St), at the river's edge, can arrange any type of trip (canoe/kayak to Carmacks $195/255; to Dawson City $325/450). These prices for unguided trips include an orientation session and drop-off. Bicycle rentals are also available. The store has a great view of the river. Vast amounts of gear, maps and guides are for sale. In addition you can book trips to the increasingly popular Big Salmon River. The staff are patient, helpful and just plain friendly.

Up North Wilderness Specialists (☎ 867-667-7035; www.upnorth.yk.ca; 103 Strickland St) offers similar services and competitive prices. Its staff speak German.

Tours

The **Yukon Historical & Museums Association** (☎ 867-667-4704; 3126 3rd Ave; $2; ☺ 10am-4pm Mon-Sat summer) offers downtown walking tours four times daily. Meet at their office in the 1904 Donneworth House.

The **Yukon Conservation Society** (☎ 867-668-5678; www.yukonconservation.org; 302 Hawkins St; ☺ 10am-2pm Mon-Fri Jul & Aug) arranges free nature hikes in the area, including fun children's programs. Most leave at 10am, although a few go at 1pm.

Gold Rush Float Tours (☎ 867-668-4836; cnr 1st Ave & Wood St; adult/child $58/32; ☺ summer) offers something more adventurous – 2½-hour trips on re-created gold-rush rafts down the Yukon River.

Sleeping

MOTELS & HOTELS

High Country Inn (☎ 867-667-4471, 800-554-4471; www.highcountryinn.yk.ca; 4051 4th Ave; r $89-209; P ✗ 🖵) The High Country Inn is modern, friendly and the best high-end place. Rooms – some with large Jacuzzis – have free high-speed Internet access.

Westmark Whitehorse Hotel (☎ 867-668-9700, 800-544-0970; www.westmarkhotels.com; 201 Wood St; r $129-209; P ✗ 🖵) Rooms here are nice but unexceptional, although the service is good. Here's your chance to find out what's going on with the bus tour set.

Town & Mountain Hotel (☎ 867-668-7644, 800-661-0522; www.townmountain.com; 401 Main St; r $79-99; P ✗) This is a good mid-range choice and the newer rooms are comfortable.

Stratford Motel (☎ 867-667-4243; 401 Jarvis St; s/d $69/79; P ✗) The central Stratford is good; some of the 49 rooms have kitchenettes.

River View Hotel (☎ 867-667-7801; www.riverview.ca; 102 Wood St; r $109-139; P 🖵) The big rooms here are much brighter and nicer than the dreary hallways would suggest.

B&BS

There are scores of B&Bs around Whitehorse; many are mere rooms in houses. The VRC has a list.

Hawkins House B&B (☎ 867-668-7638; www.hawkinshouse.yk.ca; 303 Hawkins St; r $96-163; P 🖵) This lovely Victorian-style establishment has four distinct rooms, each with private bath and balcony. The second B comes at a price: $7.

HOSTELS

There are two good budget options in Whitehorse, both in a quiet residential area close to the center.

Beez Kneez Bakpakers (☎ 867-456-2333; hostel@ klondiker.com; 408 Hoge St; dm/r $20/50; **P** 🖳) This hostel offers a kitchen and free use of bicycles.

Hide on Jeckell Guesthouse (☎ 867-633-4933; www.hide-on-jeckell.com; 410 Jeckell St; dm $20; **P** 🖳) Rates include kitchen facilities, a fireplace and strong morning coffee. There's a 10% discount for those arriving by bicycle (tandem 20%).

An International Whitehorse Hostel across from the VRC has been in the planning stage for years. Like the Motherlode, its opening date is elusive.

CAMPING

As if Wal-Mart didn't pose a big enough threat to local shop-owners, its policy of allowing RVs to park in its dusty and barren parking lot overnight for free (so they can wake up and go buy something they don't need?) has severely hurt local campgrounds. Scores of people in $150,000 RVs prefer the charms of Wal-Mart to the pretty spots listed below.

Robert Service Campground (☎ 867-668-3721; sercamp@hotmail.com; Robert Service Way; sites $14) This popular tents-only campground along the river is just 1km south of town along the South Access Rd, with showers, firepits and a small store.

Hi Country RV Park (☎ 867-667-7445; hicountryrv@ polarcom.com; 91374 Alaska Hwy; tent sites $14; 🖳) At the top of Robert Service Way, this campground in a wooded setting offers hookups, showers, laundry and modem access.

Takhini Hot Springs (☎ 867-633-2706; www.tak hinihotsprings.yk.ca; Km 10 Takhini Hot Springs Rd; tent sites $17; 🦫) You may camp at these hot springs about 30km northwest of town off the Klondike Hwy.

Yukon Government Campgrounds (☎ 867-667-5648) South of Whitehorse on the Alaska Hwy are two campgrounds: Wolf Creek (16km from town), set in a wooded area, and Marsh Lake (50km) with nearby beach access. Sites include firewood.

Eating

CAFÉS

Midnight Sun Coffee Roasters (☎ 867-633-4563; 4168 4th Ave; coffee $2; 🕑 7am-10pm) Tables inside and outside are always hopping (is it the caffeine?). The coffee roasting happens right by the door. The baked goods like paninis and muffins are also good.

Alpine Bakery (☎ 867-668-6871; 411 Alexander St; meals $4-10; 🕑 8am-6pm Mon-Sat) This bakery in a log building has great bread, rolls and pizza from organic ingredients. The preserves made with Yukon berries are a treat, as is the patio.

Chocolate Claim (☎ 867-667-2202; 305 Strickland St; light meals $4-8; 🕑 7am-6pm Mon-Sat, 10am-3pm Sun) This inviting place has its own bakery with pastries, soups and sandwiches and, as the name implies, fine chocolates. There's a rotating collection of local art on the walls.

Talisman Café (☎ 867-667-2736; 2112 2nd Ave; meals $5-12; 🕑 9am-8pm Mon-Sat, 9am-3pm Sun) The popular Talisman is tasty for any meal, with good breakfasts, huge salads, burgers, burritos and vegetarian dishes.

Yukon Meat & Sausage (☎ 867-667-6077; 203 Hanson St; sandwiches $5; 🕑 9am-5:30pm Mon-Sat) A classic deli that makes yummy sandwiches to eat in or take out. The grocery section has lots of unusual items.

RESTAURANTS

Giorgio's Cucina (☎ 867-668-4050; 206 Jarvis St; meals $15-30; 🕑 dinner) Popular with discerning locals, Giorgio's has an open kitchen where you can see the excellent steaks, seafood and fresh pasta being put through their paces.

Sam 'n' Andy's (☎ 867-668-6994; 506 Main St; meals $10-15; 🕑 11am-11pm) Busy Sam 'n' Andy's specializes in Mexican food and big portions. Although the food loses some authenticity crossing two national borders, it's a fun place. You can have a beer or margarita with your meal in the garden out front.

Tung Lock (☎ 867-668-3298; 404 Wood St; meals $7-20; 🕑 11am-11pm) Of several Chinese restaurants, this one is recommended. Seafood is emphasized, but there is a wide selection of Chinese and a few Western dishes. All the usual standards make an appearance on the popular $9 lunch buffet.

SELF-CATERING

Fruit Stand (☎ 867-393-3994; 208 Black St; 🕑 10am-7pm summer) A cross between a stand and a store that sells fresh foods, many organic and many from the Yukon. Buy some berries and try the fireweed honey. Yum.

Extra Food (☎ 867-667-6251; 303 Ogilvie St; 🕑 8:30am-7pm Mon Wed & Sat, 8:30am-9pm Thu & Fri,

10am-6pm Sun) For backcountry and paddling provisions, Extra Food in the Qwanlin Mall is the largest supermarket and has a huge bulk-foods section.

3 Beans Natural Foods (☎ 867-668-4908; 308 Wood St; ☼ 10am-6pm Mon-Sat) For good organic and bulk food, vitamins and juice, try 3 Beans.

Drinking & Entertainment

There are a lot of local bands playing in Whitehorse – maybe because it's too far for others to get there. To find out who's playing where, check out the fliers that appear on trash cans all over town.

Capital Hotel (☎ 867-667-2565; 103 Main St; ☼ 3pm-late) This place has a lively bar scene and live music almost every night. It draws a large, mostly young crowd who appreciate the many drink specials.

Backwater (☎ 867-667-7801; 102 Wood St; ☼ 4pm-late) The secluded booths are good for tête-à-têtes; whispered entreaties are muffled by the live jazz and other music. In the River View Hotel, the bar has happy hour from 4pm to 7pm.

Yukon Mining Co (☎ 867-667-6457; 4051 4th Ave; meals $7-15; ☼ 11am-midnight summer) A lively pub located in the High Country Inn, it has a huge outdoor deck, good barbecued fresh fish and lots of TVs for watching games. There's an excellent selection of beers.

Getting There & Away

AIR

Air North (Canada ☎ 800-661-0407, US ☎ 800-764-0407; www.flyairnorth.com) serves Dawson City, Old Crow and Inuvik in the Yukon, Juneau and Fairbanks in Alaska, and Vancouver, Edmonton, Calgary.

Condor (☎ 800-524-6975; www.condoramericas.com) Germany (☎ 01803 400 290; www.thomascook.de) operates weekly service to Frankfurt in summer with Thomas Cook Travel.

Whitehorse airport (YXY) is five minutes west of downtown off the Alaska Hwy.

Zip (☎ 866-432-1947; www.4321zip.com), Air Canada's low-cost carrier, serves Vancouver.

BUS

Alaska Direct Busline (☎ 867-668-4833, 800-770-6652; 509 Main St) Service to Anchorage (US$165, 18 hours) and Fairbanks (US$140, 14 hours) and points en route such as Haines Junction (US$40, three hours) and Beaver Creek ($70, seven hours); three per week in summer. Skagway four per week (US$50, three hours).

Dawson City Courier (☎ 867-393-3334) Whitehorse to Dawson City ($90, eight hours) Sunday to Friday. Call to arrange pick-up.

Greyhound (☎ 867-667-2223; 2191 2nd Ave) Northern end-of-the-line. Service south along the Alaska Hwy to Dawson Creek and beyond including Vancouver (41 hours).

Getting Around

BUS

Whitehorse Transit System (☎ 867-668-7433) Main stop at Qwanlin Mall. Route 2 serves airport, center & Robert Service Campground ($2, every 70 minutes, Monday to Saturday).

CAR & RV

Hertz, **Budget** and **National** can be found at the airport. Check your rate very carefully as it is common for a mileage charge to be added after the first 100km, which will get you barely anywhere in the Yukon. Also understand fully your insurance coverage and who pays for a cracked windshield and other damage that can easily occur on gravel roads.

Klondike Recreational Vehicles (☎ 867-668-2200; www.klondike-rv.com; 107 Copper Rd) Rents all shapes and sizes of RV from $165 to 200 per day, and you can get them equipped with canoes. Offers one-way rentals to/from Kamloops, British Columbia.

Whitehorse Subaru (☎ 867-393-6550; raman@yt .simpatico.ca; 2289 2nd Ave; new location (17 Chilkoot Way) Usually can beat the large firms on price.

TAXI

Yellow Cab (☎ 867-668-4811) Airport $14.

ALASKA HIGHWAY – BC TO WHITEHORSE

The Alaska Hwy, the main road in the Yukon, is 2451km long and starts in Dawson Creek, British Columbia (p308). It enters the Yukon in the southeast and passes through Watson Lake, Whitehorse, Haines Junction and Beaver Creek en route to Fairbanks, Alaska. The road is Hwy 97 in British Columbia, Hwy 1 in the Yukon and Hwy 2 in Alaska.

A joint project between the USA and Canada, the highway was built in 1942 as part of the war effort and originally called the Alaska-Canada Military Hwy. The highway is now paved and much tamer than the original, except for a few stretches where road construction is taking place. In fact wherever you live you'll probably wish the roads were as good as this.

THE ALASKA HIGHWAY

The construction in 1942 of the Alaska Hwy is considered one of the major engineering feats of the 20th century. Canada and the USA had originally agreed to build an all-weather highway to Fairbanks from the south as early as 1930, but nothing serious was done until WWII. Japan's attack on Pearl Harbor, then its bombing of Dutch Harbor in the Aleutians and occupation of the Aleutian islands of Attu and Kiska, increased Alaska's strategic importance. The US army was told to prepare for the highway's construction a month before Canada's prime minister, WL Mackenzie King, signed the agreement granting the USA permission to do so.

The route chosen for the highway followed a series of existing airfields – Fort St John, Fort Nelson, Watson Lake and Whitehorse – known as the Northwest Staging Route.

Thousands of US soldiers and Canadian civilians, including First Nations people, built the 2450km gravel highway between Dawson Creek in British Columbia and Fairbanks in Alaska. They began work on March 9, 1942 and completed it before falling temperatures (in what was to be one of the worst winters in recorded history) could halt the work. Conditions were harsh: sheets of ice rammed the timber pilings; floods during the spring thaw tore down bridges; and bogs swallowed trucks, tractors and other heavy machinery. In the cold months the road crews suffered frostbite, while in the summer they were preyed on by mosquitoes, black flies and other biting insects.

The original road had many curves and slopes because, with the bulldozers right behind them, the surveyors didn't have time to pick the best route. In April 1946 the Canadian part of the road (1965km) was officially handed over to Canada. In the meantime, private contractors were busy widening, graveling and straightening the highway; leveling its steep grades; and replacing temporary bridges with permanent steel ones. In 1949 the Alaska Hwy was opened to full-time civilian traffic and for the first time year-round overland travel to Alaska from the south was possible.

The completion of the highway opened the northwest to exploitation of its natural resources, changed settlement patterns and altered the First Nations' way of life forever.

The name of the highway has gone through several incarnations. It has been called the Alaskan International Hwy, the Alaska Military Hwy and the Alcan (short for Alaska-Canada) Hwy. More irreverently, in the early days it was also known as the Oil Can Hwy and the Road to Tokyo. Officially, it is now called the Alaska Hwy but many people still affectionately refer to it simply as the Alcan.

The Alaska Hwy begins at 'Mile 0' in Dawson Creek in northeastern British Columbia and goes to Fairbanks, Alaska, although the official end is at Delta Junction (Mile 1422) about 155km southeast of Fairbanks (Mile 1523).

Milepost signs were set up in the 1940s to help drivers calculate how far they had traveled along the road. Since then improvements, including the straightening of the road, mean that its length has been shortened and the mileposts can't be used literally. On the Canadian side the distance markers are in kilometers. Mileposts are still much in evidence in Alaska, and communities on both sides of the border still use the original mileposts for postal addresses and as reference points.

Until the mid-1970s conditions along the highway were difficult. The highway is now completely paved except for stretches where road crews are doing summer maintenance work on potholes and frost heaves (raised sections of pavement caused by water freezing below). Millions of dollars are spent annually on maintaining and upgrading the road.

As vital an artery as the Alaska Highway is today, it's easy to forget how it changed the Yukon and actually – despite being an American project – served to more fully integrate the Yukon into Canada. Prior to the road's construction people had to go through American ports such as Skagway and Haines on sea voyages down the coast to British Columbia; the Yukon was effectively cut off by land from the rest of Canada. Now drives to Vancouver and Calgary are relatively easy, putting the Territory within reach for any Canadian with a car.

You can get a sense of what building the road entailed (and why everybody took boats before 1942) at the VRC in Watson Lake (p347) and the Yukon Transportation Museum in Whitehorse (p342).

Each summer the Alaska Hwy is busy with visitors driving RVs. At times there are 10 of these homes-on-wheels for every car or truck. Services for gasoline, food and lodging occur at regular intervals.

Along with the mythic lure of the Alaska Hwy is the tangible sense of adventure that comes from actually going on a real trip. The Yukon will really make you feel advententurous, as if you're going somewhere different. It has no choice – sometimes towns are separated by hundreds of kilometers. The scenery is dramatic and you can't help but be charmed by the idiosyncrasies of the people in some of the more remote towns along the way. Then, between the RVs, are the cars piled with household goods. College students off to school? Pioneers in search of a new life? Refugees from an old life? As the miles roll past you can make up your own answers.

Watson Lake
pop 1500

Originally named after Frank Watson, a British trapper, Watson Lake is the first town in the Yukon as you head northwest on the Alaska Hwy from British Columbia. It's a big rest stop but otherwise skippable.

The **VRC** (☎ 867-536-7469; Km1021 Alaska Hwy; ☼ 8am-8pm summer), at the junction of the Alaska and Robert Campbell Hwys, has a fun little museum on the history of the territory and the Alaska Hwy. The town has campgrounds, motels, gas, ATMs and a Greyhound station. The **Watson Lake Library** (☎ 867-536-7517; ☼ 10am-8pm Tue-Fri, noon-6pm Sat) has free Internet access.

The town is famous for its **Signpost Forest** just outside the VRC. The first signpost was 'Danville, Illinois' nailed up in 1942 by Carl Lindlay, a homesick US soldier working on the Alaska Hwy. Others added their own signs and now there are over 50,000. You can have your own sign made on the spot or find a way to bring one from home...

Twenty-six kilometers west of Watson Lake is the junction with the Cassiar Hwy (Hwy 37), which heads south into British Columbia.

Teslin
pop 450

Teslin, on the Nisutlin River 272km west of Watson Lake, began as a trading post

in 1903 to serve the Tlingits (pronounced lin-kits). The Alaska Hwy brought both prosperity and rapid change for this First Nation population. The good **George Johnston Museum** (☎ 867-390-2550; Km 1294 Alaska Hwy; adult/child $5/3; ☼ 9am-5pm mid-May–early Sep) has photographs, displays and artifacts on the Tlingits and the gold-rush days. There's canoeing and camping at nearby Teslin Lake.

Just west of Teslin, the new **Tlingit Heritage Centre** (☎ 867-390-2526; ☼ 9am-5pm) has a pleasant lakeside spot with dramatic carved masks setting off the light building. Displays introduce you to First Nation culture.

Johnson's Crossing & Canol Rd

About 53km north of Teslin is Johnson's Crossing at the junction of the Alaska Hwy and Canol Rd. During WWII, the US army built the Canol pipeline at tremendous human and financial expense to pump oil from Norman Wells in the Northwest Territories to Whitehorse. The only services on Canol Rd (Hwy 6) are in Ross River at the Robert Campbell Hwy (Hwy 4) junction. Canol Rd ends near the Northwest Territories' border; to go any farther you have to hike the demanding **Canol Heritage Trail**.

ROBERT CAMPBELL HIGHWAY

From Watson Lake, this 588km gravel road (Hwy 4) is an alternative route north to Dawson City; it meets the Klondike Hwy near Carmacks. Named after Robert Campbell, a 19th century explorer and trader with the Hudson's Bay Company, it's a scenic and less traveled route that parallels several major rivers and has few services.

Ross River, 373km from Watson Lake at the junction with the Canol Rd (Hwy 6), is home to the Kaska First Nation and a supply center for the local mining industry. There's a campground and motels in town, and a government campground at **Lapie Canyon**.

Faro, 10km off the Robert Campbell Hwy on the Pelly River, was created in 1968 to support the huge copper, lead and zinc mine in the Anvil Mountains. Downtown, the **Campbell Region Interpretive Centre** offers advice on viewing the abundant wildlife, particularly Fannin sheep, which live only in the Yukon. Staff can direct you to trails, including ones that lead to a waterfall or Mount Mye. There are motels, a campground nearby and some trails around town.

GLACIER BAY NATIONAL PARK (ALASKA)

Sixteen tidewater glaciers spill out from the mountains to the sea, making this unusual icy preserve one of the most renowned in the world. The glaciers here are in retreat, revealing plants and animals that fascinate naturalists. The humpback whales are by far the most impressive residents, but there are also harbor seals, porpoises, orcas and sea otters. Above the waterline are brown and black bears, wolves, moose and 200 species of birds. Most people prefer to kayak the small inlets and bays, particularly Muir, where cruise ships are not allowed. There are few trails except around the **park headquarters** (☎ 907-697-2627; www.nps.gov/glba) in Bartlett Cove. Ranger-led **rainforest walks** (☒ 2:30pm) are highly recommended.

There are a number of inns and cabins in **Gustavus**, the small village adjacent to the park, or you can stay in the free campground near park headquarters.

Gustavus Inn (☎ 907-697-2254; 800-649-5220; www.gustavusinn.com; r adult/child US$160/80 includes meals) This charming family homestead lodge is well known for its gourmet dinners, which feature homegrown vegetables and fresh local seafood served family-style. Guests have free use of bicycles, and there's courtesy transportation to/from Bartlett Cove. Reserve well in advance.

The only boat connections to Glacier Bay are from Juneau, Alaska, but it's a quick flight to Gustavus. **Skagway Air** (Skagway ☎ 907-983-2218, Haines ☎ 907-766-3233; www.skagwayair.com) flies daily from Haines and Skagway. A 90-minute scenic flight over Glacier Bay costs US$130/90 for adult/child.

HAINES (ALASKA)

pop 2400

This pretty harbor town sits on the Lynn Canal at the end of Hwy 3 from Haines Junction in the Yukon. Surrounded by mountains and with the salty smell of the sea, Haines is a wonderfully quiet compared to other southeastern Alaska towns such as Skagway, as few cruise ships dock here in the summer (although you can watch them elephant walk their way to Skagway across the water). There are three state parks and good hiking. Haines is also the departure point for longer raft trips on the Tatshenshini or Alsek

in British Columbia, flights to Alaska's Glacier Bay National Park and the Inland Passage on the Alaska Marine Hwy.

Prices for Haines are in US$. Alaska time is one hour earlier than Yukon time. For more coverage of Haines and Skagway, see Lonely Planet's *Alaska*.

Information

Emergency ☎ 911
Haines Visitor Bureau (☎ 907-766-2234, 800-458-3579; www.haines.ak.us; 122 2nd Ave; ☒ 8am-7pm Mon-Fri, 9am-6pm Sat & Sun) Trail maps available.
Public library (☎ 907-766-2545; 111 3rd Ave; ☒ 10am-9pm Mon-Thu; 10am-4:30pm Fri, 12:30-4:30pm Sat & Sun) Gorgeous new building with free Internet access.
Quick Stop Laundry (☎ 907-66-2330; Mile 0 Haines Hwy; ☒ 7am-midnight) Coin showers, next to post office.
US post office (☎ 907-766-2930; Mile 0 Haines Hwy; ☒ 9am-5:30pm Mon-Fri, 10am-4pm Sat)

Sights & Activities

American Bald Eagle Foundation (☎ 907-766-3094; Haines Hwy & 2nd Ave; adult/child US$3/1; ☒ 9am-5pm) This center features an impressive display of more than 100 species of eagles and a video of the massive annual gathering of bald eagles at Chilkat River. Better yet is the live video of an eagle's nest (in season).

If you need more American icons, say a few thousand, the **Alaska Chilkat Bald Eagle Preserve**, from Mile 9 to Mile 32 along the Haines Hwy, has a local population of eagles that congregate by the thousands in November for the late salmon run.

Sheldon Museum (☎ 907-766-2366; 11 Main St; admission US$3; ☒ 10am-5pm Mon-Fri, 7-9:30pm Wed & Thu, 1-5pm Sat & Sun) houses a collection of indigenous artifacts and relics from Haines' pioneer and gold-rush days, including the sawn-off shotgun Jack Dalton used to convince travelers to pay his toll.

Fort Seward, the first and for a time the only army post in Alaska, was established in the early 1900s and designated a national historical site in 1972. The **Alaska Indian Arts Center** (☎ 907-766-2160; 13 Fort Seward Dr; ☒ 9am-5pm Mon-Fri), in the former post hospital, features resident artists working in the Tlingit manner. A small gallery sells their work. Commissioned totem poles are usually in progress. Near the fort's parade ground is **totem village**, where you can see two tribal houses, and **Sea Wolf Art Studio** (☎ 907-766-2558), which features the work of Tresham Gregg, one of the area's best known artists.

South of town on the **Chilkat Peninsula** is the lovely 11km **Seduction Point** coastal trail and the steep 4.5km climb to **Mt Riley**. North of Haines is the demanding all-day route to **Mt Ripinsky** summit (1095m). Stop at the visitor bureau for the detailed *Haines is for Hikers* pamphlet before setting out.

Sockeye Cycle Company (☎ 907-766-2869; www .cyclealaska.com; 24 Portage St, Fort Seward; US$20 per half-day; ☼ 9am-6pm) offers mountain bike rentals and advice on routes and guided tours, including the popular Chilkat Pass in Tatshenshini-Alsek Park.

Chilkat Guides (☎ 907-766-2491; www.raftalaska .com) offers unforgettable wilderness raft trips down the Tatshenshini and Alsek Rivers to the coast of Glacier Bay. In Haines, there's a four-hour daily raft trip (adult/ child US$79/52) through the Bald Eagle Preserve that's appropriate for children.

Sleeping & Eating

Keep your eyes peeled and your gullet open for anything by Haines Brewing. And if you have some of their wonderful Spruce Bud Ale (made with just that) you might just start checking real estate prices.

Captain's Choice Motel (☎ 907-766-3111, 800-478-2345; www.capchoice.com; 108 2nd Ave N; r US$75-100; ℗ 🐾) The cap'n offers the town's nicest lodging, especially rooms with private balconies. The motel's big flower-ringed sundeck overlooking Lynn Canal is a nice place to while away the day watching boats and whales plying the waters.

Summer Inn B&B (☎ 907-766-2970; www.sum merinn.wytbear.com; 247 2nd Ave; r US$70-100; ℗) A relaxing place with a sourdough pancake breakfast. This B&B is right in town and has good views.

Chilkat State Park (Mud Bay Rd; sites US$6) On the scenic Chilkat Peninsula 11km southeast of Haines, this park with water, privies and firepits has good views of Lynn Canal and of the Davidson and Rainbow Glaciers.

Fireweed (☎ 907-766-3838; Bldg 37 Blacksmith Rd; meals US$4-16; ☼ 11am-10pm) In Fort Seward, Fireweed has a great deck, where you can happily munch away on pizzas, seafood, salads, lovely desserts and more, much of it organic. Sip fresh juices or quaff Haines Brewing beers.

Mountain Market & Café (☎ 907-766-3340; 151 3rd Ave; meals US$4-10; ☼ 7am-7pm Mon-Fri, 7am-5pm Sat & Sun) This busy market has a café with bagels, big sandwiches and Sunday brunch.

Getting There & Away

Haines is linked to Haines Junction in the Yukon by, you guessed it, the scenic Haines Hwy.

Alaska Direct Busline (☎ 800-770-6652) Service to Haines Junction, Tok and beyond. Reserve.

Alaska Maritime Highway (☎ 800-642-0066; www.Alaska.gov/ferry) To Prince Rupert, BC (adult/child US$143/71.50, car from US$359, cabin from US$100; 32 hours; two/three per week winter/summer), Ketchikan, Wrangell, Petersburg, Juneau and Haines. Book vehicles and cabins well in advance.

Haines–Skagway Fast Ferry (☎ 907-766-2100, 888-766-2103; www.chilkatcruises.com) Adult/child US$24/12, 35 minutes, three daily. Reserve.

HAINES HIGHWAY

In a mere 259km you get to visit Alaska, BC and the Yukon as well as going from sea level to wind-blown passes high above the treeline where June snow is common. All this and more is between Haines, Alaska and Haines Junction on the Alaska Hwy in the Yukon. The route is popular with cyclists, many of whom compete here in the annual Kluane Chilkat International Bike Relay.

There are myriad places to pull over and admire the beauty. One not to miss near the Yukon border is **Million Dollar Falls**. Thundering through a narrow chasm, the surging water is just super.

ALASKA HIGHWAY – WHITEHORSE TO ALASKA
Haines Junction
pop 800

Small on the map but large in appeal, Haines Junction makes an excellent base for exploring Kluane National Park or to launch a serious mountaineering, backcountry or river trip. Edged by the Kluane Range and surrounding green belt, the views are dramatic and access is easy via the Alaska Hwy from Whitehorse (158km) or Tok, Alaska (498km); also via the Haines Hwy (Hwy 3) from Haines, Alaska (237.8km).

You'll know you've reached Haines Junction when you see a huge **sculpture** that looks like a nightmare cupcake at the intersection of the Alaska and Haines Hwys. In a blow to unattractive public art everywhere, critics have taken literal pot shots at the critters depicted on the flanks of the work.

The **VRC** (☎ 867-634-2345; Logan St; ☼ 8am-8pm Yukon Tourism, 9am-5pm Parks Canada) is in the Kluane National Park headquarters building. There are good displays.

The post office, bank, and ATM are inside **Madley's Store** (☎ 867-634-2200; Hwy 3; ☼ 8am-9pm), which carries everything from fresh berries and never-fresh donuts to spark plugs and fishing tackle.

All shops, lodging and services, including a **Shell station** (☎ 867-634-2246), are clustered around the Alaska and Haines Hwys junction.

Alaska Direct Busline (☎ 800-770-6652) runs a service to Haines, Whitehorse and west to Alaska. It is necessary for you to reserve a seat.

ACTIVITIES

The ridges looming over Haines Junction don't begin to hint at the beauty of Kluane National Park (below). Although the park should be your focus, there are some good activities in and around Haines Junction.

For a good way to stretch your legs after hours of driving, there's a pretty 5.5km **nature walk** along Dezadeash River where Hwy 3 crosses it at the south end of town. At Pine Lake campground, 6km east of town on the Alaska Hwy, there's good **swimming**, picnic tables and a sandy beach with firepits.

Paddlewheel Adventures (☎ 867-634-2683; www .paddlewheeladventures.com; Logan St), opposite the VRC, arranges Tatshenshini rafting trips ($100 per person, includes lunch), Kluane helicopter hikes and other tours and fishing trips at a range of prices. It rents mountain bikes or canoes ($25 per day) and provides local transportation.

On a sunny day, consider an inspiring 40- to 120-minute flight over the icy heart of Kluane National Park with **Kluane Glacier Tours** (☎ 867-634-2916; Km 1632 Alaska Hwy), which charges $115 to $325 per person with three passengers. Call for schedules.

SLEEPING & EATING

There's a little thicket of motels in Haines Junction.

Alcan Motor Inn (☎ 867-634-2371, 888-265-1018; www.yukonweb.com/tourism/alcan; s/d $85-115; P ✖ ▣) Alcan has large, modern rooms with great views of Kluane. There's dozens of channels on the large TVs, continental breakfast and a coin laundry.

Paddlewheel Cabins (☎ 867-634-2683; Auriol St; cabin $50) Opposite the Village Bakery, Paddlewheel Adventures has two well-equipped cabins with wood stoves, small kitchens and a shared bath.

Raven Motel (☎ 867-634-2500; www.yukonweb .com/tourism/raven; 181 Alaska Hwy; s/d $110/125; ☼ meals $35-50 dinner; P ✖) The Raven has deluxe motel rooms and a well-known restaurant. It's the latter that has brought the Raven acclaim. The menu has French and Italian inspirations but the ingredients are Canadian, many organic. Wonderfully composed salads and house-made desserts are recommended. Each course is flawlessly served and the accompanying wines are first-rate.

On the Alaska Hwy, 6km from town, **Pine Lake Campground** is a good choice, with wooded sites and a day-use area. In town, **Kluane RV Campground** (☎ 867-634-2709, 866-634-6789; Km 1635 Alaska Hwy; sites from $14) has wooded grounds, public showers and a laundromat.

Village Bakery & Deli (☎ 867-634-2867; Logan St; sandwiches $6; ☼ 7am-9pm; ▣) Opposite the VRC, this laid-back place with an outdoor deck has delicious pizza, soup and sandwiches. Don't miss the salmon barbecue ($14.95) with live music at 7pm on summer Fridays. There's also free Internet access.

Kluane National Park & Reserve

This rugged and magnificent wilderness covers 22,015 sq km in the southwest corner of the Yukon. With British Columbia's Tatshenshini-Alsek Provincial Park to the south and Alaska's Wrangell-St Elias National Park to the west, this is one of the largest protected wilderness areas in the world. Kluane (kloo-wah-neee), which is a Unesco World Heritage site, gets its name from the Southern Tutchone word for 'lake with many fish'.

There are two information centers operated by Parks Canada. In **Haines Junction** (☎ 867-634-7250; www.parkscanada.gc.ca /Kluane; ☼ 9am-5pm) the facility is also shared with Tourism Yukon (p339). A second

FOREST HOLOCAUST

Just as much of Kluane National Park is covered in ice, so too is much of the park covered in dead trees, millions upon millions of them. You'll see it as you drive - entire swathes of yellowing and brown spruce. It's the result of an infestation of spruce beetles unlike any in recorded memory, and the destruction extends south and west through the Kenai Peninsula in Alaska. The cause is easy to identify: the little spruce beetle. But why have these naturally co-existing creatures suddenly destroyed the entire forest, rather than claiming a relatively few older trees each year, as normally happens? Why are the beetles boring into healthy trees as well? The answers are many but one thing is clear, the destruction of the trees in Kluane and elsewhere has happened shockingly quickly.

The first signs were noted in 1994, and by 2000 it was clear that much of the spruce forest would be gone. Some theories point to a drought in 1992 that weakened trees and produced the warm conditions that allow beetles to thrive. Others suggest that this is part of a natural cycle that sees the spruce die off every 250 years or so, although evidence of this is sketchy at best. Certainly the die-off has been good for other, healthy trees such as birch and alder, which are favored by moose and other critters; these are managing nicely. But nothing is likely to thrive if the prophesized inferno occurs. The hundreds of thousands of acres of dead trees are fuel waiting for what will be the mother of all forest fires.

That huge fire will create a huge amount of smoke, and that smoke will add to global warming, and at the end of the day most people – scientists included – point to the effects of global warming as the cause of the death of the Kluane forest. The drought and the warm days are part of a bigger trend to warmer winters in the north. It's thought that in recent years conditions have been mild enough that the annual mass beetle-freeze that kept things in check has not occurred. Instead, the little buggers can go right on munching and reproducing and killing spruce trees. We talked to a helicopter pilot who has been flying around Kluane for 20 years. Describing his politics as 'to the right of Attila the Hun,' he said he'd never given much credence to global warming, figuring it was more chatter from liberals. 'But,' he admitted, 'every year the glaciers get smaller, the winters are warmer and now the forest is gone.

'I'm a believer now.'

Just 18km past Haines Junction on the Alaska Hwy, Parks Canada has a **Spruce Beetle Walk.** This 1.7km loop trail into the dead and dying forest has good explanatory signs on the phenomenon. For instance, seemingly healthy trees that have sap running down their bark are probably already doomed, as this is the trees' last-ditch effort at self-protection from the beetles. It's a worthwhile, if sobering, stop.

center at **Tachal Dhal** (Sheep Mountain; Km 1706.8 Alaska Hwy; 9am-5pm) covers visitors arriving from the west and is the starting point for hikes at the north end. Get a copy of the *Recreation Guide* which shows the scope of the park (and how little is actually easily accessible). The map also shows hiking opportunities, which range from 10 minutes to 11 days.

The park consists primarily of the still-growing **St Elias Mountains** and the world's largest non-polar **ice fields**. Two-thirds of the park is glacier and interspersed are valleys, glacial lakes, alpine forest, meadows and tundra. The Kluane Ranges (averaging 2500m) are seen along the western edge of the Alaska Hwy. A green belt wraps around the base where most of the animals and vegetation live. Turquoise **Kluane Lake** is the Yukon's largest. Hidden are the immense ice fields and the towering peaks, including **Mt Logan** (5959m), Canada's highest mountain, and **Mt St Elias** (5488m), the second highest. Partial glimpses of the interior peaks can be found at the Km 1622 viewpoint on the Alaska Hwy from Whitehorse and around the Donjek River Bridge, but the best views are definitely from the air. When you climb over the ridge and see that Kluane is literally a sea of glaciers stretching over the horizon you'll understand what all the Unesco fuss is about.

Parks Canada runs a range of **interpretive programs** through the summer from both visitors centers. Guided walks (free, one to two hours) and the more ambitious guided hikes ($20; four to six hours) are recommended.

The green-belt area of the park is a great place for **hiking**, either along marked trails or less-defined routes. There are about a dozen in each category, some following old mining roads, others traditional First Nation paths. The Parks Canada hiking leaflet has a map and lists the trails with distances and starting points, including limited possibilities for **mountain biking**. Detailed trail guides and topographical maps are available at the information centers. Talk to the rangers before setting out. They will help select a hike and provide updates on areas that may be closed due to bear activity. **Overnight hikes** require backcountry permits ($8 per person per night) and you must have a bear-proof food canister ($5 per day, $150 deposit).

The Tachal Dhal information center is the starting point for **Slims West**, a popular 60km roundtrip trek to **Kaskawulsh Glacier** – one of the few that can be reached on foot. This is a difficult and world-class route that takes from three to five days to complete. An easy overnight trip is the 5.8km (each way) **Bullion Creek** trail. **Sheep Creek** is a moderate 10km day hike. The **Auriol** trail starts 7km south of the town and is a 15km loop above the tree line providing some good views. From Kathleen Lake, **King's Throne** is a 5km one-way route with a steep 1220m elevation gain. Great views of the Alsek Valley are waiting at the top.

Fishing is good and wildlife abounds. Most noteworthy are the thousands of Dall sheep that can be seen on **Sheep Mountain** in April, May and September. There's a large and diverse population of grizzly bears, as well as black bears, moose, caribou, goats and 150 varieties of birds, among them eagles and the rare peregrine falcon.

Famous among mountaineers, the internationally renowned **Icefield Ranges** provide excellent climbing on Mt Logan, Mt Kennedy and Mt Hubbard. April, May and June are considered the best months and climbers should contact the park well in advance for information and permits.

The only campground technically within the park is at **Kathleen Lake** (site $10), 24km south of Haines Junction off the Haines Hwy.

Winters are long and can be harsh, though some venture out on skis or snowshoes starting in February. Summers are short and generally temperatures are comfortable from mid-June to mid-September, which is the best time to visit. Note that freezing temperatures can occur at any time, especially in the high country, so bring appropriate clothing and rain gear.

Destruction Bay
pop 50

This small village on the shore of Kluane Lake is 107km north of Haines Junction. Like Haines Junction and Beaver Creek, it started off as a camp and supply depot during the construction of the Alaska Hwy. It was given its present name after a storm tore through the area. There's boating and fishing on Kluane Lake and the village has a gas station and government campground at **Congdon Creek** (Km 1723 Alaska Hwy). Note any bear warnings as the area's abundant in ripe berries, a principal food source for bears.

Burwash Landing
pop 65

Burwash Landing, 19km north of Destruction Bay, predates the Alaska Hwy with a brief gold strike on nearby 4th of July Creek. It's also home of the Kluane First Nation and noted for the excellent **Kluane Museum** (☎ 867-841-5561; Km1759 Alaska Hwy; adult/ child $4/2; ☼ 9am-9pm mid-May–early Sep). The museum features intriguing animal exhibits (note the stunning moose) and displays on natural and First Nation history. The little town has a gas station.

Beaver Creek
pop 110

Tiny Beaver Creek, Canada's westernmost town, is on the Alaska Hwy 457km northwest of Whitehorse and close to the Alaska border. The **VRC** (☎ 867-862-7321; Km 1202 Alaska Hwy; ☼ 8am-8pm) has a wildflower exhibit and information on the Yukon and Alaska. Just past the VRC is a goofy life-sized **sculpture park** where you can get friendly with a Mountie or up-close to a beaver.

The Canadian customs checkpoint is just north of town; the US customs checkpoint is 27km farther west. The border is open 24 hours.

Of the four motels in town, the **Westmark Inn Beaver Creek** (☎ 867-862-7501, 800-544-0920; www.westmarkhotels.com; 1202 Alaska Hwy; dm $20, r $79-99; P) is notable for having hostel rooms. It also has an evening show that features staff pressed into service. Helping drive show attendance is the fact that the spartan rooms lack TVs. However the pub is nice, the food in the restaurant is tasty and there are good beers in both.

Alaska

You'll soon note that the incredible scenery of the Alaska Hwy dims a bit once you cross into its namesake state. The Alaska Hwy department seems to have a 'bulldoze it and leave' philosophy so the route is much more torn up and despoiled than the pristine conditions in the Yukon.

From the US border, it's 63km (39 miles) to **Tetlin National Wildlife Refuge** on the Alaska Hwy; it makes an interesting stop before you reach the border. The **visitor center** (☎ 867-883-5321; ☺ 9am-4pm) has good displays on the refuge and its myriad species. The views are good as well.

The turn for the Taylor Highway (Hwy 5) which connects with the Top of the World Hwy and Dawson City is 117km (73 miles) past Tetlin. Another 19km (12 miles) past the junction is **Tok** (pop 1400), which has a slew of motels, restaurants and services.

KLONDIKE HIGHWAY

The 716km Klondike Hwy, from Skagway in Alaska through the northwestern corner of British Columbia to Whitehorse and Dawson City, more or less follows the **Gold Rush Trail**, the route some 40,000 gold seekers took in 1898. The highway, open year-round, is paved most of the way but there are some long stretches of gravel where construction is taking place. Smoke and forest fires (or scorched remains) may be seen through the summer but the road is rarely closed. The stretch from Skagway to Carcross is a scenic marvel of lakes and mountains.

Skagway (Alaska)

pop 800

Skagway is a little town that most travelers either love or hate. Although it's in the USA, it can only be reached by car using the Klondike Hwy from the Yukon through British Columbia. It's the starting point for the famed Chilkoot Trail and the White Pass & Yukon Railway (a narrow gauge railroad). Alaska Marine Hwy ferries link the town with Haines, Alaska, and points south as far as Prince Rupert, British Columbia, and Bellingham, Washington. It's also the most popular stop for Alaska cruise lines. John Muir described Skagway during the gold-rush era as 'an anthill stirred with a stick'. You'll recall this quote on summer afternoons when cruise ships disembark as many as 7500 day-tripping passengers on the narrow streets.

From the ferry terminal, the foot and vehicle traffic spills onto Broadway and the center of town. There's a post office, banks, campgrounds, hotels, restaurants and shops, some selling furs and diamonds. Most of the buildings have been restored. The Klondike Hwy runs into the center from the opposite end. If you are coming by ferry, you may wish to head into the Yukon via much more mellow Haines (p348).

INFORMATION

Skagway is on Alaska time, which is one hour earlier than the Yukon.

Emergency ☎ 911

Skagway News Depot & Books (☎ 907-983-3354; 264 Broadway; ☺ 8:30am-8:30pm Mon-Fri, 8:30am-7:30pm Sat & Sun) Good selection of regional titles and topographical maps.

Skagway Visitor Bureau (☎ 907-983-2854, 888-762-1898; www.skagway.org; 245 Broadway; ☺ 8am-5pm) Complete area details.

Trail Centre (☎ 907-983-3655, 800-661-0486; www.nps.gov/klgo; cnr Broadway & 2nd; ☺ 8am-5pm summer) Run by Parks Canada and the US National Park Service; provides advice, permits, maps and a list of transportation options to/from the Chilkoot Trail.

US National Park Service (☎ 907-983-2921; cnr Broadway & 2nd St; ☺ 8am-8pm Jun-Aug, 8am-6pm May-Sep) Offers free daily walking tours and the *Skagway Trail Map* for area hikes.

SIGHTS

Skagway is a delightful place to arrive by ferry; you step off the ferry right into a bustling town.

A seven-block corridor along Broadway, part of the historic district, is home to the restored buildings, false fronts and wooden sidewalks of Skagway's golden era. The **Arctic Brotherhood Hall**, which houses the Skagway Convention & Visitors Bureau, is hard to miss, as there are 20,000 pieces of driftwood tacked to its front.

Near the corner of 3rd Ave and Broadway is **Mascot Saloon Museum** (admission free; 9am-5pm early May-late Sep), a renovation project of the NPS. Built in 1898, the Mascot was one of 70 saloons during Skagway's heyday as 'the roughest place in the world.'

Moore's Cabin (5th Ave at Spring St) is Skagway's oldest building. Captain William Moore and his son, Bernard, built the cabin in 1887, when they staked out their homestead as the founders of the town. Moore had to move his home to its present location when gold-rush stampeders overran his homestead.

At the southeastern end of 7th Ave is a 1900 granite building housing **Skagway Museum** (907-983-2420; 7th Ave at Spring St; adult/student US$2/1; 9am-5pm). The museum has sections devoted to various aspects of local history, including Native heritage, the Klondike gold rush, and the railroad and maritime industries.

SLEEPING & EATING
Reservations are strongly recommended during July and August.

Gold Rush Lodge (907-983-2831, 877-983-3509; www.goldrushlodge.com; 611 Alaska St; r US$105-120; P) A short walk from town, this place manages to avoid most of the hubbub. An older motel with a mountain-lodge motif, the Gold Rush has comfortable rooms with TV/VCRs and friendly service.

Sergeant Preston's Lodge (907-983-2521; sgt-prestons@usa.net; 370 6th Ave; r US$75-95; P) This tidy motel offers 30 rooms right in the center of things. The good Sergeant – well, actually a surrogate – will pick you up at the ferry.

There's free camping, but no water at **Dyea Campground**, 14km from town on Dyea Rd at the start of the Chilkoot Trail. Near the ferry, try **Pullen Creek RV Park** (907-983-2768, 800-936-3731; 501 Congress St; sites from US$18).

Haven Café (907-983-3553; cnr 9th Ave & State St; light meals US$4-8; 6am-10pm) A great place for breakfast (panini, granola, yogurt) or a light lunch or dinner. The aptly named coffeehouse is removed from the heart of the fray and makes a great place to kick back while you plan your next move.

Bonanza Bar & Grill (907-983-6214; Broadway between 3rd & 4th Aves; sandwiches US$7-11; 10am-midnight) A spacious restaurant/sports pub with a number of good microbrew beers on tap.

GETTING THERE & AWAY
From Skagway to Whitehorse on the Klondike Hwy (Hwy 2) is 177km. The road is modern and paved, and customs at the border usually moves fairly quickly.

White Pass & Yukon Railway (WP&YR; 907-983-2217, 800-343-7373; www.wpyr.com; cnr 2nd Ave & Spring St; mid-May–mid-Sep) offers a rail and bus connection to/from Whitehorse (adult/child US$95/47.50). Primarily a tourist train, the White Pass & Yukon offers roundtrip daily sightseeing tours of this truly gorgeous route into Canada that parallels the original White Pass trail. The trains were once the only link to Whitehorse, but now they mostly terminate in Fraser, British Columbia, just over the Canadian border.

Alaska Direct Busline (800-770-6652) Service to Whitehorse.

Alaska Maritime Highway (800-642-0066; www.Alaska.gov/ferry) To Prince Rupert, BC (adult/child US$152/76, car from US$380, cabin from US$100; 35 hours; two/three weekly winter/summer), Ketchikan, Wrangell, Petersburg, Juneau and Haines. Book well in advance.

Haines–Skagway Fast Ferry (907-766-2100, 888-766-2103; www.chilkatcruises.com) Adult/child US$24/12, 35 minutes, three per day. Reservations necessary.

Chilkoot Trail
Skagway was the landing point for many in the gold-rush days of the late 1890s. From there began the long, slow, arduous and often deadly haul inland to the Klondike goldfields near Dawson City. One of the main routes from Skagway, the Chilkoot Trail over the Chilkoot Pass is now extremely popular with hikers.

The well-marked 53km trail begins near Dyea, 14km northwest of Skagway, then heads northeast following the Taiya River to Lake Bennett in British Columbia, and takes three to five days to hike. It's considered a difficult route with good weather and can be treacherous in bad. You must be in good physical condition and come fully equipped. Layers of warm clothes and rain gear are essential. Solo hikers will not have a problem finding company.

THE TOUGHEST PEOPLE YOU'D EVER MEET

Some 40,000 dreamers traveled from Skagway to Dawson City in 1897–98 in search of gold. Most didn't strike it rich and in fact most left the Yukon poorer than when they arrived – a consequence of overly optimistic claims, bad luck and the highly efficient apparatus in place to fleece even those few who did strike it rich.

It started when ships docked in Seattle and San Francisco in the summer of 1897 crammed with gold from the Yukon. Word that there was lots more spread quickly, and the fact that Canada would allow non-Canadians to stake claims and that the gold around Dawson City was placer gold – fairly easily mined without special tools – fueled the fire. Boats poured into Skagway that fall, turning it into the boomtown recalled today. That winter – could there have been a worse time for this? – thousands made their way up the Chilkoot Trail to the Canadian border. Only those with at least a thousand pounds of supplies were allowed into Canada; the country had enough problems without a bunch of starving miners dying all over the place. Consider this: the average miner had to walk, in the snow, the equivalent of 1800 miles to pack their supplies (few could afford animals or help to cover the 30 miles between Dyea and Bennett). And that was always going uphill, loaded.

Once in Bennett, the prospective prospectors built boats out of whatever they could find. When the ice broke at the end of May, one of the motliest flotillas ever assembled set sail for Dawson on the Yukon. Of course, few of these people knew what to expect or had any experience with whitewater rafting. Although the number is not known, it is guessed that far more people drowned during the summer of 1898 on the Yukon River and its tributaries than perished on the Chilkoot Trail. Those that made Dawson faced lawlessness, claim-jumpers, deprivation and a myriad of other hardships. Those that survived – whether they struck it rich or not – are the toughest people you'd ever meet.

The Klondike Hwy generally follows the Gold Rush Trail (as Parks Canada calls it) past Whitehorse as far north as Minto. If you want to stay on the route of the prospectors to Dawson City, you'll need a canoe from one of the outfitters in Whitehorse and you'll need several days to navigate the Yukon River.

Along the trail you'll see hardware, tools and supplies dumped by the gold seekers. At several places there are wooden shacks where you can put up for the night, but these are usually full so a tent and sleeping bag are required. There are 10 designated campgrounds along the route, each with bear caches. The most strenuous part of the trail is over the Chilkoot Pass. The elevation gain on the trail is 1110m.

At the Canadian end you can either take the WP&YR train from Bennett back to Skagway or further up the line to Fraser, where you can connect with a bus for Whitehorse.

The Chilkoot Trail is a primary feature of the **Klondike Gold Rush International Historic Park**, a series of sites managed by both Parks Canada and the US National Park Service that stretches from Seattle, Washington to Dawson City. See the Skagway section (p353) for details on contacting both services, which issue a preparation guide for the trail and an all-but-mandatory trail map (US$2).

Each hiker must obtain one of the 50 permits available each day. It's vital to reserve in advance. Parks Canada/US National Park Service (☎ 867-667-3910, in Skagway ☎ 800-661-0486) charges $50 for a permit plus $10 for a reservation. The permits must be picked up from the Trail Centre in Skagway (p353). Each day eight of the 50 available permits are issued on a first-come, first-served basis.

Carcross
pop 427

Carcross, 74km southeast of Whitehorse, is the first settlement you reach in the Yukon from Skagway on the Klondike Hwy. The site was once a major seasonal hunting camp of the Tagish people, who called the area *Todezzane* (literally 'blowing all the time'). The present town name is an abbreviation of Caribou Crossing and refers to the local woodland caribou herds. The **VRC** (☎ 867-821-4431; ☷ 8am-8pm) is in the old train station and provides a top-notch walking tour booklet of the area buildings, many removed from Bennett by boat when the White Pass & Yukon Railway extended north and that town was abandoned in 1900. The station also has good displays on the local history.

Two kilometers north of town, **Carcross Desert**, the world's smallest, is the exposed sandy bed of a glacial lake that retreated after the last Ice Age. Strong winds allow little vegetation to grow.

With its old buildings, picturesque railroad bridge over Lake Bennett and overall feel, Carcross is worth the extra 45km you'll drive detouring off the stretch of the Alaska Hwy between Whitehorse and Jakes Corner.

Whitehorse to Carmacks

North of Whitehorse, between the Takhini Hot Springs Rd and Carmacks, the land is dry and scrubby, although there are some farms with cattle and horses. The Klondike Hwy skirts several lakes where you can go swimming, boating and fishing. The largest is lovely **Lake Laberge** with a beach, 40km north of Whitehorse, followed by **Fx Lake**, 24km farther north, and **Twin Lakes**, 23km south of Carmacks. Each has a government campground with shelters and pump water. Near Carmacks the mountains become lower, more rounded hills and the land more forested. On the way to Dawson City, gas stations have taken to selling gargantuan cinnamon buns, which might be better called dough bombs.

Carmacks

pop 400

Perched on the banks of the Yukon River, Carmacks was once a fueling station for riverboats and a stopover on the overland trail from Whitehorse to Dawson City. Originally known as Tantalus, the town name was changed to Carmacks to honor George Washington Carmack who, along with Skookum Jim and Tagish Charley, discovered gold at Bonanza Creek in 1896 and sparked the Klondike gold rush. There are gas stations, a campground and motels here, as well as a junction for the Campbell Hwy (see the Robert Campbell Hwy section earlier). Otherwise there's little reason to linger.

North of town about 25km, the **Five Finger Recreation Site** has excellent views of the legendary treacherous stretch of the rapids which tested the wits of riverboat captains. There's a 1.5km steep walk down to the rapids.

Pelly Crossing

Look for **Penny's Place** (burgers $7; 9am-6pm) along the road. The shakes are real and the burgers are real good. The fun-filled washrooms have a collection of dog photos.

Stewart Crossing

pop 50

Once a supply center between Dawson City and Whitehorse, Stewart Crossing sits at the junction of the Klondike Hwy (Hwy 2) and the Silver Trail (Hwy 11), another route taken by prospectors in search of silver.

Canoeists can put in here for the very good five-day **float trip** down the Stewart River to the Yukon River and on to Dawson City. Though you travel through wilderness, and wildlife is commonly seen, it is a trip suitable for the inexperienced. Canoeists should organize and outfit in Whitehorse (p343) or Dawson City (see p360).

The tiny town has a café and gas station. At times there's a roadside visitor info hut that can supply useful information on the Silver Trail and its towns.

Silver Trail

The Silver Trail heads northeast to three old mining and fur-trading towns: **Mayo**, **Elsa** and **Keno**. The road is paved as far as Mayo (52km). **Mt Haldane** is 26km beyond Mayo with a 6km trail to the top and good views. The towns are almost ghost towns and are fascinating places to wander around. Yukon Tourism publishes excellent walking tours to all three which can be found at VRCs. At each of these towns, you'll really feel like you're at the end of the road. And if you want to be sure something will be open, call first.

In Keno City, 60km past Mayo and near Elsa, **Mooseberry Bakery** (867-995-2383; meals $6; lunch) is in a 1922 log cabin and has great homemade food. There's also a small **museum** (867-995-3103; 10am-6pm).

There are some outdoor possibilities in the area as well as campgrounds and other lodgings, although there are no services in Elsa. **Keno Hill** in Keno City, with its signposts and distances to cities all over the world, offers more views of the mountains and valleys. There are hiking trails in the vicinity, ranging from 2km to 20km long, providing access to old mining areas and alpine meadows.

Tintina Trench

The Tintina Trench can be seen from a lookout 60km south of Dawson City. The trench, which holds much of the Yukon's mineral wealth, is also its most important geological feature, with sides of the valley revealing evidence of plate tectonics.

DAWSON CITY

pop 1800

Dawson City, a compact town at the confluence of the Yukon and Klondike rivers just 240km south of the Arctic Circle, became the heart of the Klondike gold rush. Once known as 'the Paris of the North' with a population in the west second only to San Francisco, it had deluxe hotels and restaurants, plush river steamers and stores with luxury goods. Many attractions remain from its fleeting but vibrant fling with world fame and some of the original buildings are still standing. Parks Canada is involved in restoring or preserving those considered historically significant and regulations ensure that new buildings are built in sympathy with the old. With unpaved streets and board sidewalks, the town still has a gritty edge-of-the-world feel.

The town is built on permafrost, which begins just a few centimeters down. Buildings have foundations of planks resting on gravel and many show the seasonal effects of heaving. Outside of town are the eerie piles of tailings, which look like the work of mammoth gophers. These huge mounds are actually from gold dredges that sucked up the swampy earth at one end and left it behind sans gold at the other. Some 100 years after the original gold rush, dozens of enterprises are still mining for gold in the region around Dawson City.

Summer sees a large influx of tourists and seasonal workers. RVs roam the streets like caribou. But by September, 'flee sale' signs begin to appear all over town as seasonal residents head south. For those remaining, Dawson is a cold and quiet place.

For many travelers, a summer visit to Dawson will be the highlight of their

THE YUKON CRACKS UP

The river that gives the Yukon Territory its name begins in a web of tributaries near the Llewellyn Glacier in northwest British Columbia. Although the majority of its 3200km length and its delta are in Alaska, the stretch of the Yukon in the Yukon itself is fabled for its historic and natural wonder.

From the 1890s until after WWII, the river was both a vital and dangerous link from Whitehorse to Dawson City. Its turbulent waters are opaque with glacial silt and mud, which hide submerged hazards. Each April or May the break-up of the frozen waters produces earth-shaking floes that see truck-sized chunks of ice tossed about like toys. Dawson City celebrates this impossible-to-schedule event each year and there is a contest to guess when the first cracks will appear. The break-up is not all fun and games, however. In 1979 an ice jam at Dawson City backed up water and flooded the town.

Yukon trip. Plan on staying at least two or three days.

Orientation

The town is small enough to walk around in a few hours. The Klondike Hwy leads into Front St (also called 1st Ave) along the Yukon River. Just north of town, a free ferry crosses the Yukon River to the Top of the World Hwy and onward to Alaska. Dawson is 527km from Whitehorse.

Like a ray of sunshine in January, street numbers are a rarity in Dawson. Unless noted otherwise, opening hours and times given below cover the period mid-May to mid-September. For the rest of year, most sights, attractions and many businesses are closed.

Information

The weekly *Klondike Sun* has a good listing of special events and activities.

BOOKSTORES

Maximilian's (☎ 867-993-6537; Front St; ⏰ 8am-8pm) Excellent selection of regional books, magazines and out-of-town newspapers. Topographical and river maps. Goofy gifts like the fund-raising 'Women of Dawson' calendar ($20).

LAUNDRY

Wash House Laundromat (☎ 867-993-6555; cnr 2nd Ave & Queen St; ☉ 9am-8pm) Has showers.

LIBRARY

Dawson City Community Library (☎ 867-993-5571; cnr 5th Ave & Queen St; ☉ 10am-5pm Mon & Sat, until 8pm Tue-Fri) Has Internet access.

MEDICAL SERVICES

Dawson Medical Clinic (☎ 867-993-5744; Church St near 6th Ave) Doctors always on call.

POST

Post office (☎ 867-993-5342; 5th Ave & Princess St; ☉ 8:30am-5:30pm Mon-Fri, 9am-noon Sat)
Old post office (cnr King St & 3rd Ave) Mail drop and stamps for sale (noon-6pm) Beautiful restored building.

TOURIST INFORMATION

VRC (☎ 867-993-5566; cnr Front & King Sts; ☉ 8am-8pm) Also has a Parks Canada desk.
Western Arctic Information Centre (☎ 867-993-6167; Front St , opposite the VRC; ☉ 9am-8pm) Maps and information on the Northwest Territories, Inuvik and the Dempster Hwy including road updates (☎ 800-661-0750).

Sights

Dawson and its environs teem with places of historic interest. Parks Canada does an excellent job of providing information and tours. In addition to the individual sight fees listed below, there is a good-value **pass** (adult/child $28/14) valid for all the Parks Canada sites and tours. For information, go to the Parks Canada desk in the VRC.

ROBERT SERVICE CABIN

Called the 'Bard of the Yukon', Robert W Service lived in this typical gold-rush **cabin** (cnr 8th Ave & Hanson St; admission free; ☉ 10am-4pm) from 1909 to 1912. Don't miss the readings of Service's poems (adult/child $5/2.50; ☉ 10am & 3pm) by a Parks Canada employee. Long-time reader Tom Byrne has decamped to the Westmark Inn (see Robert Service Show, p360).

DAWSON CITY MUSEUM

This **museum** (☎ 867-993-5291; 5th Ave; adult/child $7/5; ☉ 10am-6pm) houses a collection of 25,000 gold-rush artifacts. Engaging exhibits walk you through the hard-scrabble lives of the miners. The museum is housed in the land-

mark 1901 Old Territorial Administration building. It was designed by noted architect Thomas W Fuller, who also designed the old post office and other buildings around town. Next door is the old locomotive barn with historic trains.

COMMISSIONER'S RESIDENCE

Built in 1901 to house the territorial commissioner, this proud building (adult/child $5/2.50; ☉ 10am-5pm, tour times vary) was designed to give potential civic investors confidence in the city. The building is also noted for being the long-time home of Martha Black, who came to the Yukon in 1898, owned a lumberyard and was elected to the Canadian Parliament at age 70.

SS KENO

The voyage from Whitehorse to Dawson was not an easy one. The season was short and there were perilous areas of whitewater to navigate on the way. The SS *Keno* (adult/child $5/2.50; ☉ 10am-6pm) worked the rivers for more than half a century. Moored along the river, the boat has many good displays about travel 100 years ago.

MINE SITES

There are two national historic sites outside of town that relate to the early gold-mining days. **Dredge No 4** (Bonanza Creek Rd; adult/child $5/2.50; ☉ 10am-4pm Fri-Wed, 10am-2pm Thu), off the Klondike Hwy 13km south of town, is a massive dredging machine that tore up the Klondike Valley and left the tailings, which remain as a blight on the landscape. One kilometer farther south on the highway is **Bear Creek Mining Camp** (adult/child $5/2.50; ☉ tours 1:30pm & 2:30pm), site of the large community and shop complex which sprang up around the Klondike gold dredges in 1905 and lasted for 60 years.

TR'ONDËK HWËCH'IN CULTURAL CENTRE

Inside this beautiful wood building on the riverfront (☎ 867-993-6768; www.trondek.com; Front St; $5; ☉ 10:30am-6pm) there's a slide show and interpretative talks on the Hän Hwëch'in (River People), who were the first to inhabit the area. The collection includes traditional artifacts and First Nation regalia. Locally made crafts are for sale. Check on the schedule of cultural tours. There are also frequent performances of authentic dances.

DAWSON CITY

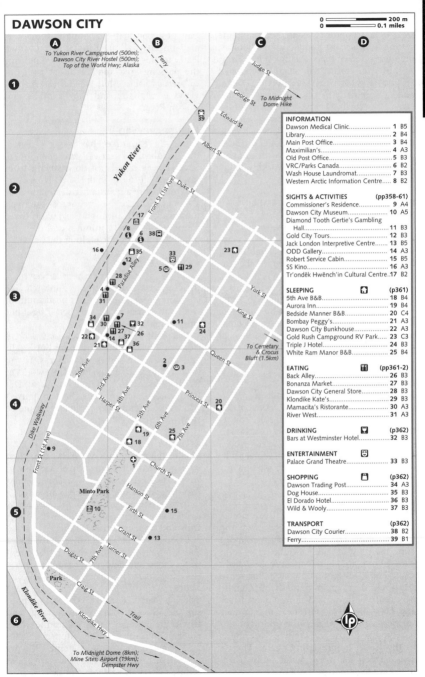

0 — 200 m
0 — 0.1 miles

A **B** **C** **D**

To Yukon River Campground (500m);
Dawson City River Hostel (500m);
Top of the World Hwy; Alaska

Ferry

Yukon River

Judge St

George St

To Midnight
Dome Hike

Edward St

Albert St

Front St (1st Ave)

Duke St

York St

King St

To Cemetary
& Crocus
Bluff (1.5km)

Queen St

Princess St

2nd Ave

3rd Ave

4th Ave

5th Ave

6th Ave

7th Ave

Harper St

Church St

Dike Walkway

Front St (1st Ave)

Minto Park

Hanson St

Firth St

Grant St

Turner St

Dugas St

7th Ave (1st Ave)

Park

Craig St

Klondike Hwy

Klondike River

Trail

To Midnight Dome (8km);
Mine Sites; Airport (19km);
Dempster Hwy

INFORMATION	
Dawson Medical Clinic	1 B5
Library	2 B4
Main Post Office	3 B4
Maximilian's	4 A3
Old Post Office	5 B3
VRC/Parks Canada	6 B2
Wash House Laundromat	7 B3
Western Arctic Information Centre	8 B2

SIGHTS & ACTIVITIES	(pp358-61)
Commissioner's Residence	9 A4
Dawson City Museum	10 A5
Diamond Tooth Gertie's Gambling Hall	11 B3
Gold City Tours	12 B3
Jack London Interpretive Centre	13 B5
ODD Gallery	14 A3
Robert Service Cabin	15 B5
SS Kino	16 A3
Tr'ondëk Hwëch'in Cultural Centre	17 B2

SLEEPING	(p361)
5th Ave B&B	18 B4
Aurora Inn	19 B4
Bedside Manner B&B	20 C4
Bombay Peggy's	21 A3
Dawson City Bunkhouse	22 A3
Gold Rush Campground RV Park	23 C3
Triple J Hotel	24 B5
White Ram Manor B&B	25 B4

EATING	(pp361-2)
Back Alley	26 B3
Bonanza Market	27 B3
Dawson City General Store	28 B3
Klondike Kate's	29 B3
Mamacita's Ristorante	30 A3
River West	31 A3

DRINKING	(p362)
Bars at Westminster Hotel	32 B3

ENTERTAINMENT	
Palace Grand Theatre	33 B3

SHOPPING	(p362)
Dawson Trading Post	34 A3
Dog House	35 B3
El Dorado Hotel	36 B3
Wild & Wooly	37 B3

TRANSPORT	(p362)
Dawson City Courier	38 B2
Ferry	39 B1

1
2
3
4
5
6

JACK LONDON INTERPRETIVE CENTRE

In 1898 Jack London lived in the Yukon, the setting for his most popular animal stories, including *Call of the Wild* and *White Fang*. At the writer's **cabin** (8th Ave at Grant St; admission $2; ☺ 10am-1pm & 2-6pm) there are talks at 11:30am and 2:15pm daily. A labor of love by historian Dick North, Dawne Mitchell and others, this place is a treasure trove. Read the stories about 'Jack', a local dog, which Jack, the noted author, used as a model for Buck in *Call of the Wild*, and how North was able to locate a photo of London working in the Klondike.

DIAMOND TOOTH GERTIE'S GAMBLING HALL

This re-creation of an 1898 **saloon** (☎ 867-993-5575; cnr Queen St & 4th Ave; $7; ☺ 7pm-2am) is complete with small-time gambling, a honky-tonk piano and dancing girls. The casino's winnings go toward town restoration, so go ahead, lose a bundle. On weekends it can get packed as locals jostle with tourists to support preservation. The enjoyable floor shows are a model for the town's often used, or it could be said over-used, logo of a dancehall girl.

ROBERT SERVICE SHOW

Longtime Robert Service re-enactor Tom Byrne gives his captivating **readings** (☎ 867-993-5543; Westmark Inn, 5th Ave; $10; ☺ 3pm) of the works of Robert Service. The fun, educational readings are in an atrium, although you sorta wish he and Parks Canada would sort things out so he can return to the cabin (p358). This is definitely worth the time for those in the thrall of his poetry.

MIDNIGHT DOME

The quarried face of this hill overlooks the town to the north, but to reach the top you must travel south of town about 1km, turn left off the Klondike Hwy onto New Dome Rd, and continue for about 7km. The Midnight Dome, at 880m above sea level, offers great views of the Ogilvie Mountains, Klondike Valley, Yukon River and Dawson City. From here on summer solstice, you can witness the midnight sun barely sink below the Ogilvie Mountains to the north before rising again. There's also a steep **trail** from Judge St in town; maps are available at the VRC.

CEMETERY & CROCUS BLUFF

Less of a slog than marching to the dome, a 15-minute walk up King St behind town leads to the historic cemeteries. Look for the parking area and the short path out to pretty Crocus Bluff which has excellent views of Dawson and the Klondike and Yukon Rivers.

SHIP GRAVEYARD

When the Klondike Hwy was completed, the paddlewheel ferries were abandoned. Several were sailed just downstream from town and left to rot on the bank. Now overgrown, they're a fascinating destination for a short hike. Take the ferry across the river, then walk north through the Yukon River Campground for 10 minutes and then another 10 minutes north along the beach.

ART GALLERIES

Dawson is another northern city with a thriving arts community – although like so many others, most artists head south in winter in search of not just better light but simply light.

ODD Gallery (☎ 867-993-5005; cnr 2nd Ave & Princess St; ☺ 10am-8pm) This small but bright and open space shows local works. If you have a chance to see the incredible works of Shelley Hakonson, you're in for a treat. Defying categorizations, this Dawson native's whimsical assemblages could and should be shown in major galleries.

Activities

One of the main do-it-yourself canoe float trips goes from Dawson three days downstream to Eagle City, Alaska. This popular trip is good for inexperienced canoeists.

Dawson Trading Post (☎ 867-993-5316; Front St; canoe $30 per day) rents out canoes, with longer trips and transportation arranged.

Dawson City River Hostel (☎ 867-993-6823; www .yukonhostels.com), across the river, can also rent you a canoe and help make arrangements.

Tours

Gold City Tours (☎ 867-993-5175; Front St), opposite the SS *Keno*, has a daily city tour and trip to the Bonanza Creek gold mine where you can do some panning (adult/child $40/20). Vans go to Midnight Dome ($12 per person) at 11pm daily. The office also books airline tickets and airport shuttles.

Parks Canada docents, often in period garb, lead excellent **walking tours** (adult/child $5/2.50; ☽ 9:30am, some days extra tours) of Dawson. This is a great way to learn about individual buildings and learn about Paradise Alley, now humdrum, but in its time home to over 400 prostitutes who worked out of tiny dwellings – some of which survive. You can also take an **audio-tape tour** (adult/child $5/2.50; ☽ 9:30am-4:30pm) where you guide yourself.

Festivals & Events
Dawson City Music Festival (☎ 867-993-5384; www .dcmf.com). Features well-known Canadian musicians. It's very popular – tickets sell out two months in advance and the city fills up – so reservations are a good idea (late July).

Discovery Day The premier annual event in Dawson City celebrates you-know-what of 1896. On the third Monday in August there are parades and picnics. Events begin days before, including a very good art show.

Sleeping
Most places are open from May to September and fill up in July and August. The VRC will tirelessly search for vacant rooms on busy weekends if you arrive without a reservation. Many places will pick you up at the airport, a not inconsiderable distance. Ask in advance.

MOTELS, HOTELS & INNS
Bombay Peggy's (☎ 867-993-6969; www.bombay peggys.com; cnr 2nd Ave & Princess St; r $79-169; ☽ year-round; P ⬚) In a renovated old brothel, Peggy's is the most stylish place to stay in town. Rooms range from 'snugs' with shared bath to suites. There's a great pub downstairs.

Aurora Inn (☎ 867-993-6860; www.aurorainn.ca; 5th Ave; r $90-180; ☽ year-round; P ⬚) The Aurora has bright, large and nicely decorated rooms with friendly service. Breakfast ($10) is fresh and good; there's an excellent restaurant as well (see below).

Triple J Hotel (☎ 867-993-5323, 800-764-3555; www.triplejhotel.com; cnr Queen St & 5th Ave; r $109-129; P) Triple J occupies the whole block with nice cabins for two with kitchenettes and porches, and basic motel rooms. Go with the cabins.

Dawson City Bunkhouse (☎ 867-993-6164; www .bunkhouse.ca; r $49-109; P) This is a good frontier-style place with clean, basic rooms, some sharing a bathroom. Note that the

solid wood construction means it can get noisy as guests liquored up at nearby saloons go clomping about.

El Dorado Hotel (☎ 867-993-5451, 800-661-0518; www.eldoradohotel.ca; cnr 3rd Ave & Princess St; s/d $122/132; ☽ year-round; P ☒) The El Dorado has good, large, modern rooms. The hotel offers good services for business travelers – there are some in Dawson.

B&BS
White Ram Manor B&B (☎ 867-993-5772; pbarthol@ yknet.yk.ca; cnr 7th Ave & Harper St; r $35-99; ☽ year-round; P ⬚) This roomy pink house with a decent view has nice common spaces, a laundry, BBQ and hot tub.

Bedside Manner B&B (☎ 867-993-6948; cnr 8th Ave & Princess St; s/d $79/89; ☽ year-round; P ⬚) This small place is comfortable and the owner can give lots of good advice on local events and activities.

5th Ave B&B (☎ 867-993-5941; www.5thavebandb .com; 702 5th Ave; r $85-135; ☽ year-round; P ⬚) This is another homey place in a neighborhood of historic homes near the museum.

HOSTELS
Dawson City River Hostel (☎ 867-993-6823 summer; www.yukonhostels.com; dm member/non-member $15/19, r $39; P) This fun hostel is across the river from town and five minutes up the hill from the ferry landing. It's a rustic and funky spot with good views, cabins, a wooded area for tents, cooking shelter and communal bathhouse. There's no electricity and lockers are recommended for your gear. Owner Dieter Reinmuth is a character and a charmer.

CAMPING
Yukon River Campground is on the western side of the river about 250m up the road to the right after you get off the ferry. It's the pleasant destination of smart campers.

Gold Rush Campground RV Park (☎ 867-993-5247; goldrush@yukon.net; cnr 5th Ave & York St; RV sites $16, $26.50 with full hook-ups) is literally one big parking lot downtown for RVs.

Eating
Klondike Kate's (☎ 867-993-6527; cnr King St & 3rd Ave; meals $6-20) Everybody likes Kate's and with good reason: the locally smoked King salmon is killer, and there's a long list of

other dishes and great desserts. Locally a favorite, it's a fun spot out on the covered patio and it's open for breakfast, lunch and dinner.

Mamacita's Ristorante (☎ 867-993-2370; 2nd Ave; meals $8-22; 🕑 lunch & dinner) Portions of the excellent pasta dishes are insanely large. The pizzas are popular as are the sandwiches. Good service.

Aurora Inn Restaurant (☎ 867-993-6860; 5th Ave; meals $9-25; 🕑 lunch & dinner) Excellent hearty meals are served in a bright and cheery space. The menu leans towards German but there is food for all tastes. The steaks at dinner, replete with fresh mushrooms, are tops.

Back Alley (☎ 867-993-5800; 2nd Ave; meals $7-14; 🕑 lunch & dinner) Behind the Westminster Hotel, this place serves great souvlaki sandwiches and pizza and is a top choice. There are outside tables or you can get free delivery in town.

River West (☎ 867-993-6339; cnr Front & Queen Sts; snacks $2-5; 🕑 7am-7pm) The best of several places along Front St, this café has excellent coffee, bagels, soup and sandwiches on delicious bread. The tables outside are a local meeting spot.

Bonanza Market (☎ 867-993-6567; 2nd Ave; sandwiches $5; 🕑 8am-6pm) A good market with interesting and organic fresh foods. The deli makes scrumptious sandwiches.

Dawson City General Store (☎ 867-993-5475; cnr Front & Queen Sts; 🕑 8am-8pm) This is one of the largest supermarkets north of Whitehorse, with fresh produce and baked goods.

Drinking

Bombay Peggy's (☎ 867-993-6969; cnr 2nd Ave & Princess St; 🕑 11am-11pm) Peggy's is a delightful place for a drink with good beers on tap and a fine wine selection. There are some nice quiet tables out back.

Bars at Westminster Hotel (3rd Ave; 🕑 noon-late) These two bars are variously known as the 'Snakepit' or 'Armpit' or simply 'Pit.' The one to your left as you face the pink building has a great old tin roof which matches the age of some of the timeless characters hanging out by the bar. The bar to the right has more of a '70s motif as well as live music many nights. Both get lively.

Shopping

Dawson Trading Post (☎ 867-993-5316; Front St; 🕑 9am-7pm) sells interesting old mining

gadgets, antiques, books and stones and old mammoth tusks so you can take up carving.

Dog House (☎ 867-993-5405; Front St; 🕑 10am-7pm) is the local center for dog-sledding. Summer exhibits explain how to 'mush!'

Wild & Wooly (☎ 867-993-5170; cnr 3rd Ave & Princess St; 🕑 10am-7pm) has all sorts of lovely locally made jewelry along with quite fashionable men's and women's clothes. Look for the items made from mammoth tusk ivory.

Getting There & Away

Dawson City airport (YDA) is 19km east of town off the Klondike Hwy.

Air North (☎ 800-661-0407 in Canada, ☎ 800-764-0407 in the US; www.flyairnorth.com) Serves Whitehorse, Old Crow and Inuvik in the Yukon and Juneau in Alaska.

Dawson City Courier (☎ 867-993-6688; pick-up cnr 2nd Ave & York St) Whitehorse ($90, eight hours, Sunday to Friday); Inuvik ($262, minimum six people). Reserve.

Alaska Trails & Tours (☎ 888-600-6001) Van service from Anchorage, Fairbanks and Tok ($95, eight hours; three per week).

TOP OF THE WORLD HIGHWAY

At the northern end of Dawson City's Front St the ferry crosses the Yukon River to the scenic Top of the World Hwy (Hwy 9). Open only in summer, the road is mostly paved in Canada for the 106km to the US Border along ridge tops.

You'll really feel on top of the world as you complete the border crossing: it's treeless and alpine. Note the border crossing has very strict **hours** (🕑 9am-9pm Pacific (Yukon) Time, 8am-8pm Alaska Time May 15-Sep 15); don't be one minute late or you'll have to turn back and try the next day.

On the US side the road becomes all gravel. After 19km (12 miles) you reach the Taylor Hwy (Hwy 5). The old gold mining town of **Eagle** on the Yukon River is 104km (65 miles) north.

South 46km (29 miles), you encounter **Chicken**, a small idiosyncratic community of 37 which has a couple of shops and a bar that even at 11am is filled with a good percentage of the local population commenting on the 'goddamn government'.

Another 124km (77 miles) south and you reach the Alaska Hwy and **Tok**. From here you can return to the Yukon. Tok is a town with a range of services and motels.

VUNTUT NATIONAL PARK

Vuntut, a Gwich'in word meaning 'among the lakes,' was declared a national park in 1993. It's north of the village of **Old Crow**, the most northerly settlement in the Yukon. Each spring a porcupine caribou herd of 160,000 follows a migration route north across the plain to calving grounds near the Beaufort Sea. In Canada these calving grounds are protected within Ivvavik National Park and extend into Alaska where they are part of the Arctic National Wildlife Refuge.

With its many lakes and ponds, Vuntut National Park is visited by around 500,000 **waterbirds** each autumn. Archaeological sites contain fossils of ancient animals such as the mammoth, plus evidence of early humans. The only access to the 4345 sq km park is by chartered plane from Old Crow, which itself is reachable only by air. The park has no services or facilities.

It's probably worth quoting the official Parks Canada website regarding Vuntut: 'There are no facilities or services of any kind in the park. Travelers must be entirely self-sufficient and able to handle any medical or wildlife-related emergency on their own.'

So there you are.

IVVAVIK NATIONAL PARK

Ivvavik, meaning 'a place for giving birth to and raising the young,' is situated along the Beaufort Sea and adjoining Alaska and covers 10,170 sq km. The park is dominated by the British Mountains and its vegetation is mainly tundra. It's on the migration route of the porcupine caribou and is also a major waterfowl habitat. There are no facilities or services.

The park holds one of the world's great whitewater rivers, the **Frith River**, which can be navigated for 130km from Margaret Lake near the Alaskan border north to the Alaska Sea. When the river meets Joe Creek, the valley narrows to a canyon and there are numerous areas of whitewater rated Class 2 and Class 3 plus.

Access is by charter plane from either Old Crow or Inuvik.

HERSCHEL ISLAND TERRITORIAL PARK

Off the coast of Ivvavik is Herschel Island in the Beaufort Sea, below the Arctic Ocean and about 90km south of the packed ice. Rich in plant, bird and marine life, particularly ringed seals and bowhead whales, it was an important area for the Thule. They called it *Qikiqtaruk* (literally 'it is an island'). There have been several waves of people through the area, but the Thule, expert whale hunters, were thought to be the first to make a permanent settlement here about 1000 years ago.

Pauline Cove is deep enough for ocean vessels and protected from the northerly winds and drifting pack ice. As a haven for ships, it became a key port during the last days of the whaling industry when the whales were hunted first for lamp oil and then for baleen. Bowhead whales had the longest bones and were the most desirable for women's corsets. Fashion nearly drove them to extinction. Following the whalers and their families, who numbered about 1500, was an Anglican missionary in 1897, whose members tried to win converts among the Thule. The whaling station was abandoned around 1907, though the Canadian police continued to use the island as a post until 1964.

The flight across the MacKenzie Delta to reach the island is spectacular. At Pauline Cove, park rangers provide a tour of the historical buildings and lead a hike above the harbor to a hill carpeted with tiny wildflowers in July. The rangers are wonderful hosts and some have family connections to the island. Primitive camping during the short summer season (from late June to August) is possible. There are fire rings, wind shelters, pit toilets and limited water. Access is by chartered plane, usually from Inuvik (p364), 250km southeast. Most visitors spend half a day.

DEMPSTER HIGHWAY

The Dempster Hwy (Hwy 5 in the Yukon, Hwy 8 in the Northwest Territories) starts 40km southeast of Dawson City off the Klondike Hwy. It heads north over the Ogilvie and Richardson Mountains beyond the Arctic Circle and on to Inuvik in the Northwest Territories, near the shores of the Beaufort Sea.

The highway, which celebrated its 25th anniversary in 2004, makes road travel along the full length of North America possible. While Inuvik is a long way from

Dawson City – 747km of gravel road – the scenery is remarkable: mountains, valleys, rivers and vast open tundra. The highway is open most of the year but the best time to travel is between June and early September when the ferries over the Peel and Mackenzie rivers operate. In the winter, ice forms a natural bridge over the rivers, which become ice roads.

The Dempster is closed during the spring thaw and the winter freeze-up; these vary by the year and can occur from mid-April to June and mid-October to December respectively.

Accommodations and vehicle services along the route are scarce. There is a gas station at the southern start of the highway at **Klondike River Lodge** (☎ 867-993-6892). The lodge will rent jerry cans of gas you can take north and return on the way back. Then it's 370km to Eagle Plains and the next services.

The **Eagle Plains Hotel** (☎ 867-993-2453; eagleplains@yknet.yk.ca; r $112-124) is open year-round and offers 26 rooms. The next service station is 180km farther at **Fort McPherson** in the Northwest Territories. From there it's 216km to Inuvik.

The Yukon government has three campgrounds – at **Tombstone Mountain** (73km from the start of the highway), **Engineer Creek** (194km) and **Rock River** (447km). There's also a Northwest Territories government campground at **Nitainlaii Territorial Park**, 9km south of Fort McPherson. For maps and information on the road ask at the Western Arctic Information Centre in Dawson City (p358).

The road is a test for drivers and cars. Travel with extra gas and tires, and expect to use them. Call ☎ 800-661-0750 for road and ferry reports.

Tombstone Territorial Park

The Yukon's newest territorial park, Tombstone is 73km up the Dempster Hwy, with the good **Dempster Highway Interpretive Centre** (⏱ 9am-5pm summer) and an adjoining campground with expansive views. The pointed shape of the prominent peak was a distinctive landmark on First Nation routes and is now an aerial guide for pilots. There are several good **day hikes** leading from the center, as well as longer, more rigorous backcountry trips

for experienced wilderness hikers. With no established trails, these require skilled map-reading. Note that weather can change quickly, so bring appropriate gear even for day hikes. In mid-June there's hiking with some snow pack; July is best for wildflowers, balancing the annoyance of bug season.

It's possible to visit Tombstone as a day trip from Dawson City or to spend the night at the campground (pit toilets, river water, firewood) to experience a bit of the Dempster and see the headwaters of the Klondike River. All hikers should check in at the center for updates.

Inuvik (NWT)
pop 3400

If you're driving the Dempster Hwy you're probably coming to Inuvik. Although it's in the Northwest Territories, its main access is from the Yukon. It is also the staging point for trips to Vuntut and Ivvavik National Parks and Herschel Island Territorial Park in the far north of the Yukon.

Inuvik lies on the East Channel of the Mackenzie River 97km south of the Arctic Coast. It was built in 1955 as an administrative post for the government. It has nearly two months of permanent daylight in the summer and a month of darkness in the winter. Although looking rough around the edges like many towns in the far north, it is an interesting place to visit – even if you are just passing through to the parks.

The **Western Arctic Visitors Centre** (☎ 867-777-4727, in winter ☎ 867-777-7237; www.town.inuvik.nt.ca; 284 Mackenzie Rd; ⏱ 9am-8pm summer) is a good place to start gathering information.

Boreal Books (☎ 867-777-3748; 181 Mackenzie Rd; ⏱ 9am-6pm summer) is a good source for northern books and maps, including topographical and marine charts.

ACTIVITIES
Several local companies specialize in tours of varying duration to the Yukon parks. Other services include logistical work for independent travelers as well as gear rental.

Arctic Nature Tours (☎ 867-777-3300; www.arcticnaturetours.com) offers a range of trips. An overnight trip to Herschel Island by floatplane costs $600.

Western Arctic Adventures & Equipment (☎ 867-777-2594; www.inuvik.net/canoenwt/) is run by an Arctic biologist who specializes in logistics and planning for independent travelers.

SLEEPING

In Inuvik, like much of the north, smaller is better when it comes to accommodation.

Arctic Chalet B&B Inn (☎ 867-777-3535; www .arcticchalet.com; 25 Carn St; r $100-130) has a range of comfortable rooms and cabins. The welcoming hosts will give you rides and otherwise facilitate your stay in Inuvik.

GETTING THERE & AWAY

Most people drive the Dempster to Inuvik, but flying can save you two days' travelling time and about four tires. Dawson City is 747km south.

Mike Zubko Airport (YEV) 14km south of town.

Air North (☎ 800-661-0407, USA ☎ 800-764-0407; flyairnorth.com) has services to Whitehorse and Dawson City, some flights via Old Crow.

Directory

CONTENTS

PRACTICALITIES

- The electric current is 110 volts, 60 cycles; plugs have two flat parallel pins with an optional round grounding pin, the same as the US.

- For all emergencies ☎ 911 in BC; see the boxed text, p339 for emergency numbers in the Yukon Territory

- Most towns have a daily or weekly newspaper, the *Vancouver Sun* provides good regional coverage.

- For radio listeners, signs at the entrances to towns provide local tuning information for the CBC Radio One network.

- Buy or watch videos on the NTSC system.

- Use the metric system, although popular references to the imperial system as still used in the US survive.

ACCOMMODATIONS

Most areas of British Columbia have abundant accommodations, available for a wide range of prices. The North and the Yukon are the only exceptions; this far-flung region has almost nothing in the way of hostels, and its relatively few and generally spartan motel rooms are priced higher than comparable establishments elsewhere.

The annual directory published by Tourism BC (☎ 800-435-5622, 250-387-1642 outside North America), *British Columbia Approved Accommodation Guide,* is a detailed guide to what's available in all classes of lodgings. The guide is free; it's available at Visitor Info Centres or from Tourism BC.

In this book we have listed in order of preference: motels and hotels first, and followed by B&Bs, hostels and campgrounds. The exception is Vancouver city where accommodations are listed by price range: budget, mid-range and top end. In Vancouver you can stay in a budget room for less than $100, or a top-end room for $200 or more; mid-range is generally everything in between.

Seasonal Rates

The prices given in this book are for the peak summer season. In very few instances a town's peak season is the winter and these cases are noted. Expect discounts of up to 50% from the high-season rates we have listed outside of summer in most of British Columbia and the Yukon. Exceptions to this occur if there is a special event on, or at winter sports areas during holidays.

Vancouver has rates that ebb and flow depending on conventions, events and other factors. Often good weekend deals are available for mid-range accommodations on weekends, when business travelers have left town. Note also that rates listed do not include the various taxes, see p374.

Reservations

It's common now for places to have websites that let you view and book rooms, see specials and other details. We've listed them in this book. A good strategy is to check out a place's website first and then cross-reference it with one of the large internet booking services such as Travelocity (www.Travelocity.com) and Expedia (www .expedia.com). The problem with the internet services, however, is that they often do not list interesting independent places. Certainly it is always worthwhile to call a place you are interested in staying at and ask about any special deals. We saved 50% and got a slew of normally costly extras free at one well-known resort just by asking: 'Do you have any specials?'

It's always good to reserve in advance, especially for places where you really want to stay. This is vital during the peak season and on busy weekends around holidays. Conversely, it's usually not necessary to reserve in a town like Fort Nelson in the north, which has a string of largely similar motels aimed at people bedding down for the night along the Alaska Highway.

Motels & Hotels

Rates vary tremendously around the province. Urban and resort locations have the highest prices; plan to spend close to $100 for a basic double room with a private bath during high season in Vancouver and Victoria. (In small, non-resort towns you can usually find a motel room for half that amount.) Prices change seasonally, too; they're highest in summer for most of the province, except ski resort areas like Whistler, where they're highest in winter. Expect higher rates for holidays and special events.

Children can often stay free in the same room as their parents, but the age limits for free stays vary. Many motels (and an increasing number of suite-style hotels) offer kitchenettes. As a happy compromise, quite a few mid-range motels now include a small refrigerator and microwave in their standard-room price.

The quality of hotels and motels varies greatly. A lovely roadside motel bedecked in flowers and perfect for a break will often be next to a dingier establishment replete with a dodgy dog wandering about the parking lot. Generally however the typical motel room in the BC and the Yukon includes private facilities, one or two large beds, a tea and coffeemaker, and a TV with dozens of channels. Truly luxurious places can be found in Vancouver, Victoria and the Rockies.

B&Bs

With an estimated 3200 B&Bs in British Columbia and the Yukon, the choices are almost overwhelming. North American B&Bs are typically more upscale than the casual, family-style pensions found in Europe. Many (especially those catering to honeymooners and other romantic escapists) require reservations and have fairly strict policies on children, pets, smoking and so on. But there's a wide range of places, and with a bit of investigation you can find somewhere that fits your needs and price range. Prices span the gamut, although basic places are in the $50 to $75 range.

With busy towns like Kelowna having over 60 B&Bs, it is a good idea to check with the local VIC, which usually has complete listings along with photos and descriptions. In the Rockies, B&Bs are prevalent and can provide good basic and private lodging. Other B&Bs may be in a wilderness setting with a range of activities. Often a B&B can be a good place in an area like the Queen Charlotte Islands, where it's useful to get a variety of local information on activities.

Hostels

Hostels are common in touristed areas of BC. Most have beds for about $15 to $22 per person per night. These are usually in dorm-style rooms with four to six beds, although many hostels offer private rooms for additional money. Expect shared baths, kitchen facilities and common areas where you can meet fellow travelers. Amenities might include a variety of activity discounts, laundry facilities, Internet access, game rooms, bike or other sporting gear rentals and group outings to area pubs and attractions.

We've listed hostels throughout the books. The main group is affiliated with Hostelling International (HI; www.hihostels.ca). SameSun (www.samesun.com) operates budget lodges and hostels in many ski areas. There are also many independent hostels in popular locations such as Vancouver.

Camping

Camping is among the most popular activities enjoyed by residents and visitors. There are many available places to camp, from primitive forest sites to deluxe campgrounds with resort-style amenities. Reservations are a good idea during the summer, and they're essential in the most popular places for holiday long weekends.

The annual BC Tourism booklet *Super Camping Guide* (www.camping.bc.ca) is a good resource for finding private, RV-oriented campgrounds, although it also lists BC Parks sites. Look for the guide at visitor centers, or online at www.camping.bc.ca. Private campground sites cost about $20 to $35 a night for two people, depending on the services (electricity, water, cable TV) your rig requires. Tent sites usually cost about $17 to $23, but most tent campers will be happier in a less-expensive, more outdoorsy BC Parks or BC Forest Service campground.

British Columbia Parks manages hundreds of campgrounds, with fees ranging from $12 per party for basic sites to $24 per party for the most highly developed campgrounds. About 70 popular parks offer reserved sites. For these places we have included the reservation contact information; phone ☎ 800-689-9025 or check out www.discovercamping.ca. Most BC Parks' campgrounds, however, are not reservable. Instructions at the entrance will tell you where to check in or otherwise register and pay your fee. At popular ones, arrive early to avoid disappointment.

There are over a thousand Ministry of Forests campgrounds, but in a bid to save money, the ministry has deemed over 700 to be 'user-managed' which basically means you stay there for free and take care of everything yourself. At campgrounds the ministry still takes an active interest where there is a fee of $10 a night with no reservations taken.

The Yukon has scores of government campgrounds in scenic locations. None accept reservations and all charge $12 per night. *Places to Go on Yukon Time* is a good annual government publication that lists the territory's campgrounds. It's free from Visitor Resource Centres.

Parks Canada campgrounds are not reservable and charge $12 to $24 a night.

BUSINESS HOURS

Stores in downtown retail areas open around 9am or 10am and close around 5pm or 6pm. Suburban shopping centers, discount stores and grocery stores typically stay open until 9pm; some groceries and pharmacies are open 24 hours. On Sunday, businesses have more limited hours, with department stores and some shopping centers not opening until noon and closing at 5 pm. In small towns most businesses will be closed on Sundays.

At eating establishments, breakfast hours are typically 6am to 10am, lunch 11am to 2pm and dinner 5pm to 9pm, although in smaller cities and towns restaurants may be closed by 8:30pm. Pubs usually open from 11am until after midnight and often serve food until 10pm or 11pm.

CHILDREN

British Columbia and the Yukon are an excellent destination for children. The parks and museums often have programs geared for youngsters, all but the most extreme activities are suitable for children and quite simply, the little ones are welcome everywhere. Vancouver for children in the Vancouver chapter (p72) for ideas on where to take the youngsters.

Lonely Planet's *Travel With Children* is a good resource for taking along the family.

Practicalities

Car rental firms offer child seats, most public restrooms have diaper-changing facilities and better motels and hotels can suggest child-minding facilities. At ski resorts, there is usually a range of programs that can occupy children for hours if not days. Bars and pubs often have family rooms, since kids cannot be in drinking establishments. The one caveat relates to accommodation at rural and wilderness places – some do not cater to children. However other rural establishments have a full range of child-specific activities. When in doubt ask.

CLIMATE

British Columbia has a varied climate, influenced by latitude, mountainous terrain and distance from the moderating effects of the Pacific Ocean. On the coast it is mild, with warm, mostly dry summers (June through September) and cool, very wet winters (December through March). The interior is much drier, particularly in the south along the Okanagan Valley, which gets less than 347mm of rain each year (compared to 6550mm at Henderson Lake on Vancouver Island's Barkley Sound); summers are hot and winters are cold. In the mountains, summers are short, with warm days and cool nights. Winter snowfalls are heavy.

The Yukon has short mild summers which can be a true delight. But those other eight to 10 months a year can be cold with winter temperatures well below freezing and quite dark.

See p9 in the When to Go section for additional details.

CUSTOMS

Along with your personal possessions, you are allowed to bring into Canada a duty-free allowance of 1.14L (40oz) of liquor, 1.5L or two 750mL bottles of wine, or 8.5L of beer or ale, as well as up to 200 cigarettes, 50 cigars or 400g of tobacco. Only those at least 19 years old, the age of adulthood in BC, can bring in alcohol and tobacco products. You are allowed to bring in gifts up to a total value of $60. Gifts with a value higher than $60 are subject to duty and taxes on the over-limit value.

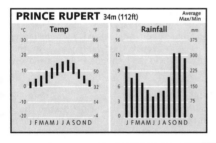

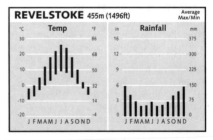

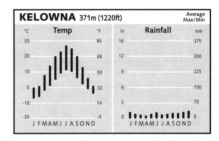

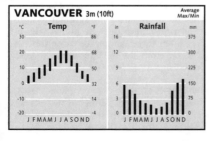

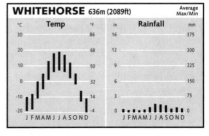

Sporting goods, including cameras, film and two days' worth of food can be brought into the country. It's probably worthwhile to register excessive or expensive sporting goods and cameras with customs, as this will save you time and trouble when leaving, especially if you plan on crossing the Canadian-US border a number of times.

If you are bringing a dog or cat into the country you will need proof that it has had a rabies shot in the past 36 months. For US citizens this is usually easy enough, but for residents of other countries there may well be more involved procedures. To avoid problems check with the Canadian Food Inspection Agency (www.inspection.gc.ca), which also handles plant and animal health, before leaving home.

Pleasure boats may enter Canada either on the trailer or in the water and can stay up to one year. An entry permit is required and is obtainable from the customs office at or near the point of entry. All boats powered by motors over 10hp must be licensed.

Pistols, fully automatic weapons, any firearms less than 66cm (26 inches) in length and self-defense sprays (like pepper or mace) are not permitted into the country.

DANGERS & ANNOYANCES

British Columbia and the Yukon are generally very safe places. Violent crime is unusual, but theft can occur.

Urban Problems

Vancouver is plagued with car break-ins, car theft and bicycle theft. Always lock your car and take anything of value with you or secure it in the trunk. Rent a car locally, if possible, because vehicles with out-of-province plates are most vulnerable to break-ins. Parking is a major hassle in Vancouver, too; it's best not to bring a car at all, if possible. Always lock your bicycle with a sturdy U-shaped lock. No matter where you travel, always be aware of your surroundings and never leave personal belongings such as shoulder bags or backpacks in a location where you can't lock them up or watch them at all times.

Beggars work the streets of Vancouver and, to a lesser extent, Victoria. Drug abuse is a problem in the city, which means many panhandlers are only after enough money to pay for their next fix.

Outdoor Hazards

BEARS

Bear attacks, though rare, are a very real threat in BC and the Yukon. See the boxed text, p31 for tips on protecting yourself.

BLACKFLIES & MOSQUITOES

In spring and summer, blackflies and mosquitoes can be murder in the interior and northern reaches of BC and the Yukon. There are tales of lost hikers going insane from the bugs. This is no joke – they can make you miserable. Most people will know that the effect of a bite (or sting, technically, by the mosquito) is a small itchy bump inflicting just a minor, passing pain and an unsightly welt and ensuing itch. The potential trouble is mainly psychological; the cumulative effects of scores of bites can keep you up at night, itchy, grumpy and paranoid that you're being eaten alive.

Building a fire will help, and camping in a tent with a zippered screen is a necessity. In clearings, along shorelines or anywhere there's a breeze you'll be safe, which is why Vancouver and the coast are relatively bug-free.

Perfume evidently attracts the wrong kind of attention. Wherever you go, bring liquid or spray repellents. DEET, an ingredient often used in repellents, is very effective, but is harmful to the environment and should not be used on young children.

FIRE

Campfires should be confined to fire rings at designated campgrounds, or fire pans in the backcountry. Before going to bed or leaving an area, make sure fires (including cigarettes) are completely out. Special care must be taken during the summer months, when fire danger is at its highest. Forest fires often force temporary campfire bans even far from the burning areas, so obey posted signs.

SWIMMERS ITCH

A tiny parasite in some of BC's lakes can generate this pesky rash. However, warnings are usually posted at places where it's a problem. To prevent itching, apply baby oil before you enter the water and dry off completely with a towel after getting out.

TICKS
Wood ticks hop onto warm-blooded hosts from tall grasses and low shrubs throughout the region. They're most troublesome March through June. Protect your legs by wearing gaiters, or pants tucked into socks. Give yourself, your children and pets a good going over after outdoor activities. According to BC Parks literature, if you find a tick burrowing into your skin, it's most easily removed by grasping and pulling it, gently, straight up and out with a small pair of tweezers. Disinfect the bite site with rubbing alcohol. Save the tick in a small plastic or glass container if possible. That way, a doctor can inspect it if a fever develops or the area around the bite appears to be infected. See p386 in the Health chapter for information on lyme disease.

WATER
Tap water in BC is safe to drink, but in the backcountry you'll need to purify environmental water before drinking it. The simplest way of purifying water is to boil it – vigorous boiling for five minutes should be satisfactory even at high altitude. (Remember that water takes longer to come to a boil at high altitudes, so be patient.)

Simple filtering will not remove all dangerous organisms, so if you cannot boil water it should be treated chemically. Chlorine tablets (Puritabs, Steritabs or other brandnames) will kill many pathogens, but not giardia or amoebic cysts. Iodine is very effective in purifying water and is available in tablet form (such as Potable Aqua), but follow the directions carefully and remember, too much iodine can be harmful.

DISABLED TRAVELERS
British Columbia is generally an easy place for disabled travelers to get around. Vancouver provides a scheduled bus service for people with disabilities, and BC Transit runs lift-equipped buses on many of its local systems throughout the province. Contact the local transit systems listed throughout this book for more information. **Greyhound Canada** (☎ 800-661-8747; www.greyhound.ca) offers various services to passengers with special needs, and the major airlines all offer special services to physically challenged passengers.

Vancouver Taxi (☎ 604-255-5111) runs wheelchair-accessible cabs in BC's largest city, and many other companies throughout the province have similar services. Public and private parking lots have designated spaces for disabled drivers. Many motels and other accommodations have rooms designed for people with mobility problems.

BC Coalition of People with Disabilities (☎ 604-875-0188, TTY 604-875-8835 ; www.bccpd.bc.ca) Has an advocacy service and can answer questions on disability issues in the province.

BC Disability Sports (☎ 604-737-3039; www .disabilitysport.org) Information on activities.

DISCOUNT CARDS
Seniors (generally those over 65) and students (those with a valid International Student Identity Card) will qualify for discounts on admissions to museums, parks and other attractions listed in this book. The cost is usually somewhere between the low price given for children and the high price given for adults.

DOCUMENTS
Visitors to Canada need a valid passport. The exception are those from the USA who need a driver's license and one other proof of identification such as a valid birth certificate. It's important for visitors from the USA to note this change as it used to be possible to enter Canada with just a driver's license. Some Canadian border workers may let you in with just a driver's license but then you may have problems when you encounter the US border crossing on your return.

EMBASSIES & CONSULATES
Canadian Embassies, High Commissions & Consulates
The following are the embassies and consulates recommended for visa, immigration and travel matters in each country by Citizenship and Immigration Canada (www.cic.gc.ca).

Australia Visa Immigration Office (☎ 02-9364 3050; www.dfait-maeci.gc.ca/Australia; 111 Harrington St, Level 5, Quay West, Sydney, NSW 2000)
France Embassy (☎ 01-44 43 29 00; www.dfait-maeci .gc.ca/canadaeuropa/france; 37 Ave Montaigne, 75008 Paris)
Germany Embassy (☎ 030 20 31 20; www.dfait-maeci .gc.ca/canadaeuropa/germany/; 12th Fl, Friedrichstrasse 95, 10117 Berlin)
Ireland See the UK.
Japan Embassy (☎ 81-3 5412 6200; www.canada net.or.jp; 3-38, Akasaka 7-chome, Minato-ku, Tokyo 07-8503)
Netherlands See Germany.
New Zealand See Australia.
UK High Commission (☎ 020-7258 6600; www .Canada.org.uk; MacDonald House, Immigration Section, 38 Grosvenor St, London W1K 4AA)
US Embassy: (☎ 202-682 1740; www.can-am.gc.ca /washington, 501 Pennsylvania Ave NW, Washington, DC 20001); Seattle consulate (☎ 206-443 1777; www.dfait-maeci.gc.ca/seattle; Plaza 600 Building, 5th Fl, Sixth & Stewart, Seattle, 98101)

Consulates in British Columbia
In Vancouver there are several dozen consulates (but no embassies), which are located in Ottawa, Ontario, the capital of Canada. For consulates not listed here, check the Yellow Pages under 'Consulates & Other Foreign Government Representatives'. Key consulates include the following:
Australia (☎ 604-684-1177; Ste 1225, 888 Dunsmuir St)
France (☎ 604-681-4345; Ste 1201, 736 Granville St)
Germany (☎ 604-684-8377; Ste 704, 999 Canada Place)
Ireland (☎ 604-683-9233; Ste 401, 1385 W 8th St)
Japan (☎ 604-684-5868; Ste 900, 1177 W Hastings St)
Netherlands (☎ 604-684-6448; Ste 821, 475 Howe St)
New Zealand (☎ 604-684-7388; Ste 1200, 888 Dunsmuir St)
UK (☎ 604-683-4421; Ste 800, 1111 Melville St)
USA (☎ 604-685-4311; 1095 W Pender St)

FESTIVALS & EVENTS
There are scores of regional and local festivals and events in BC. See the Getting Started chapter (p10) for a list of our favorites, and the regional listings for details. BC Day (first Monday in August) is a cause for widespread celebration and parades.

The Yukon virtually shuts down and parties for Discovery Day, the third Monday of August which celebrates the discovery of gold near Dawson City in 1896.

FOOD
For a full discussion of what to eat, how and when to eat it, see the Food & Drink chapter, p45.

GAY & LESBIAN TRAVELERS
In BC there is a vast gulf between the urban attitude toward gays and lesbians and the sensibilities you'll encounter in the hinterlands. In Vancouver and the Lower Mainland, gay and lesbian couples are numerous and welcome, and few people look askance at public displays of affection. In places like Victoria, Nanaimo, the Okanagan and Nelson, gay life is a bit more underground, but still visible to anyone who's interested. But in further-flung towns and the Yukon, any gay or lesbian communities that exist are hard to find, and people are advised to keep their orientation to themselves to avoid harassment or, at the minimum, discomforting stares.

The gay rights movement in Canada began in Vancouver when, in 1964, a group of feminists and academics started the Association for Social Knowledge, the first gay and lesbian discussion group in the country. In 2003 it became the second province after Ontario to allow gay marriage.

The Vancouver Gay and Lesbian Business Directory (www.glba.org) is a good source of regional information and contacts.

HOLIDAYS
National public holidays are celebrated throughout Canada. Banks, schools and government offices (including post offices) are closed and transportation, museums and other services are on a Sunday schedule. Holidays falling on a weekend are usually observed the following Monday, and these long weekends (Victoria Day, Canada Day, BC Day and Labour Day) are among the busiest on BC's roads and waterways. Either plan your visit for a different time or secure accommodations far ahead for any of these long-weekends. The following is a list of the main public holidays:

JANUARY
New Year's Day (January 1)

MARCH/APRIL
Easter (Good Friday, Easter Monday)

MAY
Victoria Day (Monday preceding May 24)

JULY
Canada Day (July 1)

AUGUST
BC Day (first Monday of the month; BC only)
Discovery Day (third Monday of August; Yukon only)

SEPTEMBER
Labour Day (first Monday of the month)

OCTOBER
Thanksgiving (second Monday of the month)

NOVEMBER
Remembrance Day (November 11 – banks and government offices closed)

DECEMBER
Christmas Day (December 25)
Boxing Day (December 26; many retailers open, other businesses closed)

INSURANCE

Residents of British Columbia are covered by the provincial health-care system. Visitors to the province, however, are not, so it's smart to take out travel insurance before leaving home. Not only does it cover you for medical expenses (p385) and luggage theft or loss, but also for cancellations or delays in your travel arrangements under certain circumstances, such as becoming seriously ill the day before your scheduled departure.

Before obtaining special travel insurance, check what's already covered by your other insurance policies or credit card; you might find that you won't need to take out a separate policy. The critical questions to ask your current insurers and those offering coverage are: 'Who pays if I get sick in BC?' 'Who pays if my trip is canceled or delayed (assuming you would have a liability)?' And 'Who pays if my belongings are stolen?'

INTERNET ACCESS

Telephone jacks for dialing into the Internet are common in mid-range and more expensive motels and hotels. You will have to supply your own cord as well as having an access number to call. Few services offer access numbers outside of the major cities.

The Legal Age for

- Drinking: 19
- Voting: 18
- Heterosexual and lesbian sex: 14
- Gay sex: 18
- Driving: 16

However, the high-speed access trend is sweeping BC, and many places offer free high-speed Internet access in your room. You'll need your own Ethernet cable but otherwise you and your laptop will be good to go. This is a great way for downloading and sharing digital photos of your trip as they occur. Aunt Lois will be thrilled to get email with your photo of a moose.

If you don't carry a laptop (it is, hopefully, a vacation you're on), Internet access is common in most BC and Yukon libraries. At most libraries it is free although there may be time restrictions. Some VICs also offer free Internet access. In large towns some cafés have Internet access but this is not as common as in the past, rates can reach $3 for 15 minutes or more.

LEGAL MATTERS

If you are arrested, you are allowed to remain silent. There is no legal reason to speak to a police officer; however, never walk away from an officer until given permission. If arrested you must be formally told of the charges and you are allowed to make one phone call. You also have the right to an interpreter if English is not your first language. If you don't have a lawyer or someone who can help you, call your consulate. The police will give you the number on request.

If you want legal advice or referral to a lawyer, contact the **Legal Services Society** (Lower Mainland ☎ 604-408-2172, rest of BC ☎ 1-866-577-2525; www.lss.bc.ca).

MAPS

Free local and regional maps also are available from Visitor Info Centres in BC and Visitor Resource Centres in the Yukon.

Members of the Canadian Automobile Association or American Automobile Association (CAA/AAA) or affiliated clubs can get free maps before leaving home or from offices in BC. Bookstores, gas stations and convenience stores usually sell a wide variety of maps, ranging from regional overviews to detailed street atlases. Lonely Planet's *City Map to Vancouver* has both, and is rain-proof.

If you plan to do much hiking or other land-based backcountry activities, you'll want to invest in good topographical maps. Gem Trek Publishing (www.gemtrek.com) offers some of the best Rocky Mountain maps in scales from 1:35,000 to 1:100,000. These can be widely purchased through the Rockies. Other topographical maps as well as marine charts are available at bookstores and sporting-goods shops. Good sources are noted in the information listings in the individual chapters.

MONEY

The Canadian dollar ($) is divided into 100 cents (¢). Coins are 1¢ (penny), 5¢ (nickel), 10¢ (dime), 25¢ (quarter), $1 (loonie) and $2 (toonie) pieces. The 50¢ coin is seldom seen. Notes come in $5, $10, $20, $50 and $100 denominations. Bills in larger denominations are produced but rarely used, and even the $50 and $100 bills can prove difficult to cash. Canadian bills are all the same size but vary in their colors and images. Some denominations have two styles as older versions in good condition continue to circulate.

See p9 for information on costs.

ATMs

Major banks and ATMs are common throughout BC and the larger towns of the Yukon. Using an ATM card to withdraw Canadian currency from your account is handy and usually a fiscally wise choice. Service fees are generally lower at bank ATMs than at machines found in restaurants, bars and stores.

Exchanging Money

Although some businesses in British Columbia, especially along the US border, accept a variety of currencies, it's best to exchange your money soon after arriving in the province. There are several 24-hour currency exchange machines placed throughout Vancouver International Airport, as well as several full-service Royal Bank branches within the terminals. Currency exchange offices are abundant in Vancouver and Victoria, as well as other larger towns throughout the province. Note, however, that most charge a commission fee and give less favorable exchange rates. If you are coming from the USA (or elsewhere for that matter), the best thing to do is use your ATM card to withdraw cash once you cross the border.

Taxes & Refunds

The Goods & Services Tax (GST) adds 7% to just about every product, service and transaction, with groceries being one of the few exceptions. BC's provincial sales tax (PST) adds another 7% to the bill and is applied to most items except groceries, books and magazines. Always remember to add 14% to prices so you won't be surprised when you are handed the bill.

Some guesthouses and B&Bs don't charge GST for rooms, and foreign visitors can try asking for an exemption from the GST on their hotel bill when making payment. If paid, however, the GST added to all accommodations is refundable. The provincial sales tax is nonrefundable; however, items shipped out of BC directly by the seller are exempt.

In addition to a refund on accommodations GST, foreign visitors also get a GST refund on nonconsumable goods bought for use outside Canada, provided the goods are removed from the country within 60 days. Tax paid on services or transportation is not refundable nor is the tax paid on consumable items such as restaurant meals, gas and tobacco. The value of the goods and accommodations taxed must be at least $200 (and each individual receipt for goods must total at least $50 before taxes) and you must have original receipts; credit-card slips and photocopies are not accepted as proof of purchase. Receipts for goods must either be validated at the border if you leave by private vehicle, or accompanied by your boarding pass or tickets as proof of when you left the country by plane, bus, train or boat. Receipts for accommodations do not need to be validated, but they must be originals.

Get a copy of the *Tax Refund for Visitors to Canada* brochure, which explains all the regulations and includes a rebate form. There is a welter of rules in order to obtain a refund. Brochures are widely available in BC, or through the **Visitor Rebate Program** (within Canada ☎ 800-668-4748, outside Canada ☎ 902-432-5608; www.ccra.gc.ca/visitors).

After you leave Canada you mail the form to the address shown and assuming you have jumped through all the hoops, you should expect a check (in US dollars for US citizens, Canadian dollars for eveyone else) within 60 days. Be wary of refund services described in brochures distributed by private companies, which charge a fee that you need not pay if you go direct through Revenue Canada. Your receipts will not be returned.

Travelers driving to the USA can claim an immediate cash rebate on Canadian goods and/or accommodations at duty-free shops on the border at Abbotsford, Aldergrove, Kingsgate, Osoyoos and Surrey. Be sure to have the original receipts and proof of residence (picture identification such as a passport or driver's license).

Tipping

Tipping is expected by restaurant and bar servers, as well as by taxi drivers, hairdressers, barbers and baggage carriers. In restaurants, bars and clubs the staff are paid a minimum wage and rely on tips to make a reasonable living. Never tip less than 10% of the pre-tax bill; leave 15% if the service was fine, up to 20% if it was exceptional. Some restaurants impose a service charge on the bill, in which case no tip should be given. You needn't tip in fast-food, take-out or buffet-style restaurants where you serve yourself.

Taxi drivers, hairdressers, barbers and tour guides get 15% if their service is satisfactory. Baggage carriers (in airports or hotels) receive $1 for the first bag and 50¢ for each additional bag. Don't forget to leave a few dollars for the motel or hotel housekeeping staff if you stay more than one night.

Travelers Checks

Travelers checks are accepted at places used to seeing tourists but their usage is becoming less frequent as travelers use ATMs for their cash needs.

POST

Canada Post (www.canadapost.ca) is reliable and easy to use. Postal service counters have been installed in convenience stores, groceries and even flower shops. Postal rates for postcards/letters to the US are 65¢/90¢, to the rest of the world $1.25/1.75.

SHOPPING

The best souvenirs and gifts from BC and the Yukon are items made by local artisans. We give numerous tips about where to find local treats and creations throughout the book. If in doubt, a bottle of Okanagan Valley wine always goes down well.

SOLO TRAVELERS

BC and the Yukon can be good places for solo travelers. The people are generally friendly, so striking up conversations is easy. In addition, the many activities and other attractions often lend themselves to meeting others should you desire this. However, this is also the place to enjoy perfect solitude if this is what you're looking for. The one caveat is if you're going out into the backcountry where traveling alone can leave you more exposed to bear attack or accident.

TELEPHONE

Pay phones are common in cities and towns, however you'll need coins to work them. The exception is if you buy a long-distance service phone card that can be used for domestic and international calls. These come in a myriad of flavors from a myriad of companies and are sold in a myriad of places (convenience stores, gas stations etc). It's worth comparing prices if you are going to buy one. Once bought, you use a phone to call an access number, enter your account number and the number you wish to call.

If you are calling another number in Canada, you will usually need to start with a 1. Conversely, in many towns in this book, you only need to use the last seven digits of the phone number if you are calling within that town. You drop the first three which are the area code (250, 604, 867 etc).

TIME

Most of BC and the Yukon is on Pacific Standard Time, which is eight hours behind Greenwich Mean Time; four hours behind Atlantic Standard Time (encompassing the Maritime Provinces apart from

---

NUMBERS TO KNOW:

- **Emergencies** ☎ 911 in BC; see the boxed text, p339 for emergency numbers in the Yukon Territory

- **Information/Directory Services**: ☎ 411

- **Country Code** for calling Canada from abroad: ☎ 1

- **Toll-free** telephone numbers begin with: ☎ 888, 877, 866, 800

Newfoundland which is 4½ hours behind); three hours behind Eastern Standard Time (including Montreal, Ottawa and Toronto); two hours behind Central Standard Time (including Winnipeg and Regina); and one hour behind Mountain Standard Time (including Edmonton and Calgary). But the eastern part of the province (including Cranbrook, Fernie, Golden, Dawson Creek and Fort St John) observes Mountain Time.

The province generally observes Daylight Saving Time; clocks go forward one hour on the first Sunday in April and are turned back one hour on the last Sunday in October. For exceptions to this, see the boxed text 'What Time Is It Anyway?' on p308.

TOURIST INFORMATION

With tourism being such a major part of the economy for both BC and the Yukon, it's no surprise that the tourism infrastructure is well-funded and easy to use.

Tourism BC (☎ 800-435-5622, outside North America ☎ 250-387-1642; www.tourismbc.com) has over a hundred Visitor Info Centres (VICs) in towns and cities around the province. These are excellent local resources for ideas, planning, reservations, maps, activities information and much more. They are usually along major roads and are well-marked with blue, green and yellow signs. Hours vary, but larger offices are typically open at least 8am to 6pm daily in summer and 9am to 5pm on weekdays the rest of the year. The listings in this book give details.

The Yukon maintains six **Visitor Resource Centres** (VRCs; ☎ 867-667-5340; www.touryukon.com) at major entry points to the territory. The range of information is invaluable; hours generally reflect those of BC.

Besides excellent free literature that may satisfy your reading needs for the trip, the BC and Yukon tourist offices can be good places to buy specialist guidebooks and maps.

VISAS

Residents of Australia, France, Germany, Ireland, the Netherlands, New Zealand, the United Kingdom and the USA do not need visas to visit Canada. But residents of 130 other nations do. Check with Citizenship & Immigration Canada (www.cic.gc.ca/english/visit/visas.html) to see if you need a Temporary Resident Visa. If so, contact the Canadian embassy, high commission or consulate charged with handling visa affairs for your country (www.cic.gc.ca/english/offices/missions.html). Fees can run to $75 or more and the application process may take a while. A separate visa is required for visitors intending to work or go to school in Canada.

If you decide to stay in Canada beyond your visa, check on the current rules, regulations and procedures for applying to do so (www.cic.gc.ca/english/applications/visitor.html).

WOMEN TRAVELERS

British Columbia is generally a safe place for women traveling alone, although the usual precautions apply. In Vancouver, the Main and Hastings Sts area is best avoided, and it's probably not a good idea to go for a walk in Stanley Park on your own after dark. In more remote parts of the province, particularly the North, women traveling alone will find themselves a distinct minority.

But it's worth noting that the more populated and frequently visited parts of BC are great for women travelers. Hostels usually have formal or informal group outings to pubs and local attractions, and many outfitters, ski areas and the like offer trips and classes geared to women. With these opportunities, BC is an excellent place to experiment with new recreational activities and meet many like-minded women and men who enjoy adventure and active travel.

Transport

GETTING THERE & AWAY

British Columbia is easily reached from major international points as well as from the USA. Getting to the Yukon usually requires a simple plane connection, although getting there by car and boat can be half the fun.

AIR

Though many BC-bound travelers will fly into Vancouver, people who are most interested in the Rockies may want to travel instead to Calgary, Alberta, just a short distance from Banff, Yoho and Jasper National Parks and other mountain attractions.

> **THINGS CHANGE...**
>
> The information in this chapter is particularly vulnerable to change. Check directly with the airline or a travel agent to make sure you understand how a fare (and ticket you may buy) works, and be aware of the security requirements for international travel. Shop carefully. The details given in this chapter should be regarded as pointers and are not a substitute for your own careful, up-to-date research.

> **YVR AIRPORT IMPROVEMENT FEE**
>
> All passengers departing Vancouver International Airport (YVR) are required to buy an Airport Improvement Fee ticket. The cost is $5 for those traveling to a destination within BC or the Yukon; $10 for passengers traveling to other North American destinations including Hawaii and Mexico; and $15 for people traveling to destinations outside North America. Children under age two and passengers with same-day connecting flights through YVR are exempt.
>
> Be aware that there is yet another line in the Vancouver airport for this; you will have to line up after going through your initial check-in, and cash is best, but ticket machines (still another line!) will take credit cards. The abundance of very long queues in this airport makes us wonder why no one has thought to add the fee to the tickets, sparing travelers the bother.

Airports

Vancouver International airport (YVR; ☎ 604-207-7077; www.yvr.ca) is 13km south of downtown Vancouver near the suburb of Richmond. It's Canada's second-busiest airport, handling nearly 16 million passengers a year, and likely to be your port of entry to BC if you fly. It has good connections throughout Western Canada, and there is international service to the USA, Europe and Asia.

The main airport has two terminals, international and domestic. The smaller south airport terminal, off Inglis Drive, handles small regional airlines and seaplanes. There is a shuttle bus between the two terminals.

For Rockies-bound travelers, **Calgary International airport** (YYC; www.calgaryairport.com) has service from the USA and Europe. **Edmonton airport** (YEG; www.edmontonairports.com) has service from the USA.

Kelowna Airport (YLW) has service to/from Seattle with Alaska Airlines subsidiary Horizon Air, which makes the Okanagan

Valley an easy connection for travel from the USA.

Whitehorse airport (YXY) in the Yukon has service to Alaska and summer flights to/from Germany.

Airlines

Airlines with international service to Vancouver include:

Air Canada (☎ 888-247-2262; www.aircanada.ca)
Air China (☎ 604-685-0921)
Alaska Airlines/Horizon Air (☎ 800-252-7522; www.alaskaair.com)
America West (☎ 800-235-9292; www.americawest.com)
American Airlines (☎ 800-433-7300; www.aa.com)
British Airways (☎ 800-247-9297; www.british-airways.com)
Cathay Pacific Airways (☎ 604-214-1180; www.cathaypacific.com)
China Airlines (☎ 604-682-6777; www.china-airlines.com)
Continental Airlines (☎ 800-231-0856; www.flycontinental.com)
Delta Air Lines (☎ 800-221-1212; www.delta.com)
Japan Airlines (☎ 800-525-3663; www.japanair.com)
KLM (☎ 800-447-4747; www.klm.nl)
Korean Air (☎ 800-438-5000; www.koreanair.com)
Lufthansa Airlines (☎ 800-563-5954; www.lufthansa-ca.com)
Northwest Airlines (☎ 800-225-2525; www.nwa.com)
Singapore Airlines (☎ 604-689-1223; www.singaporeair.com)
United Airlines (☎ 800-241-6522; www.ual.com)

Airlines with international service to Whitehorse in the Yukon include:

Air North (Canada ☎ 800-661-0407, USA ☎ 800-764-0407; www.flyairnorth.com) From Alaska.
Condor (☎ 800-524-6975; www.condoramericas.com); Germany (☎ 01803 400 290; www.thomascook.de) In conjunction with Thomas Cook Travel operates weekly summer service to Frankfurt.

Tickets

With so many international airlines flying there, Vancouver is a competitive place for airfares. To get a good idea of what's being charged, check websites like Expedia (www.expedia.com), Orbitz (www.orbitz.com) and Travelocity (www.travelocity.com). Individual airline websites often have specials that apply only on that airline, so it's a good idea to check those flying from your part of the world

as well. Note also that connections on to various BC cities can add little to the airfare. The regional chapters list important airports, so it doesn't hurt to check fares to those as well, if you want to get close to your final destination by air.

From Asia

STA Travel proliferates in Asia, with branches in Bangkok (☎ 02-236 0262; www.statravel.co.th), Singapore (☎ 6737 7188; www.statravel.com.sg), Hong Kong (☎ 2736 1618; www.statravel.com.hk) and Japan (☎ 03 5391 2922; www.statravel.co.jp). Another resource in Japan is **No 1 Travel** (☎ 03 3205 6073; www.no1-travel.com); in Hong Kong try **Four Seas Tours** (☎ 2200 7760; www.fourseastravel.com/english).

From Australia

For the location of **STA Travel** branches call ☎ 1300 733 035 or visit www.statravel.com.au. **Flight Centre** (☎ 133 133; www.flightcentre.com.au) has offices throughout Australia. For online bookings, try www.travel.com.au.

From France

Recommended agencies include:
Anyway (☎ 0892 893 892; www.anyway.fr)
Lastminute (☎ 0892 705 000; www.lastminute.fr)
Nouvelles Frontières (☎ 0825 000 747; www.nouvelles-frontieres.fr)
OTU Voyages (www.otu.fr) This agency specializes in student and youth travelers.
Voyageurs du Monde (☎ 01 40 15 11 15; www.vdm.com)

From Germany

Recommended agencies include:
Expedia (www.expedia.de)
Just Travel (☎ 089 747 3330; www.justtravel.de)
Lastminute (☎ 01805 284 366; www.lastminute.de)
STA Travel (☎ 01805 456 422; www.statravel.de) For travelers under the age of 26.

From The Netherlands

One recommended agency is **Airfair** (☎ 020 620 5121; www.airfair.nl).

From New Zealand

Both **Flight Centre** (☎ 0800 243 544; www.flightcentre.co.nz) and **STA Travel** (☎ 0508 782 872; www.statravel.co.nz) have branches throughout the country. The site www.travel.co.nz is recommended for online bookings.

From the UK & Ireland

Discount air travel is big business in London. Advertisements for many travel agencies appear in the travel pages of the weekend broadsheet newspapers and *Time Out*.

Recommended travel agencies include the following:

Bridge the World (☎ 0870 444 7474; www.b-t-w.co.uk)
Flightbookers (☎ 0870 010 7000; www.ebookers.com)
Flight Centre (☎ 0870 890 8099; www.flightcentre.co.uk)
North-South Travel (☎ 01245 608 291; www.north southtravel.co.uk) North-South Travel donates part of its profit to projects in the developing world.
Quest Travel (☎ 0870 442 3542; www.questtravel.com)
STA Travel (☎ 0870 160 0599; www.statravel.co.uk) For travelers under the age of 26.
Trailfinders (www.trailfinders.co.uk)
Travel Bag (☎ 0870 890 1456; www.travelbag.co.uk)

From the USA

Use the online booking agencies mentioned above as well as the airlines' own websites.

LAND
Border Crossings

Points of entry on the US–Canada border are open 24 hours except as noted.

Along the southern BC border, Friday and Sunday are especially busy at the major border crossings. Delays can be especially bad on the holiday weekends in summer, particularly at the Blaine, Washington (WA)–Douglas crossing south of Vancouver, where you may have to wait several hours. Either avoid crossing at these times, or drive to one of the other Lower Mainland crossings such as Aldergrove or Huntingdon.

From west to east along the southern BC border, crossings, with the US Hwy/Canada Hwy, include:

Point Roberts, WA–Boundary Bay
Blaine, WA–Douglas SR543/BC15
Blaine, WA–Surrey I-5/BC99
Lynden, WA–Aldergrove (☼ 8am-midnight) SR539/BC13
Sumas, WA–Huntingdon SR9/BC11
Oroville, WA–Osoyoos US97/BC97
Ferry, WA–Midway (☼ 9am-5pm)
Laurier, WA–Cascade (☼ 8am-midnight) US395/BC395
Boundary, WA–Waneta (☼ 9am-5pm)
Metaline Falls, WA–Nelway (☼ 8am-midnight) SR31/BC6
Porthill, ID-Rykerts (☼ 7am-11pm Apr-Oct, 8am-midnight Nov-Mar) SR1/BC21
Eastport, ID-Kingsgate US95/BC95
Roosville, MT-Roosville US93/BC93

In the North, crossings are as follows:

Hyder, AK–Stewart (☼ 8:30am-4:30pm)
Skagway, AK–Fraser, BC (☼ 8am-midnight) SR98/BC2
Dalton Cache, AK–Pleasant Camp, BC (☼ 8am-mid night) SR7/BC4
Alcan, AK–Beaver Creek SR2/YT1
Boundary, AK on the Top of the World Hwy (☼ 9am-9pm Pacific (Yukon) Time, 8am-8pm Alaska time, May 15-Sep 15)

From the USA
BUS

You can travel to many places in BC from the USA via **Greyhound** (☎ 800-661-8747; www.greyhound.com). Most of the routings require you to travel between Seattle and Vancouver and then transfer. **Bigfoot Adventure Tours** (☎ 888-244-6673; www .bigfoottours.com; $32) runs a daily shuttle linking Vancouver and Seattle hostels during the summer.

For service from Alaska to the Yukon, see p345.

CAR

The US highway system connects directly with Canadian highways at many points along the BC border (above). Gas is generally cheaper in the USA.

TRAIN

Amtrak (☎ 800-872-7245; www.amtrak.com) connects Vancouver to Bellingham and Seattle with one train and two buses daily that take four hours. From Seattle, Amtrak trains go south to Portland, San Francisco and Los Angeles, and east to Minneapolis and Chicago.

From Canada
BUS

Greyhound Canada (800-661-8747; www.greyhound.ca) has routes into BC from Edmonton through Dawson Creek, as well as Jasper and in the south near the US border from Winnepeg.

TRAIN

VIA Rail (☎ 888-842-7245; www.viarail.ca) runs the *Canadian* between Vancouver and Toronto. Stops include Kamloops, Jasper, Edmonton, Saskatoon and Winnipeg. It's a scenic trip, but it only runs three times a week.

SEA
Alaska Cruises

The BC and Alaska coast is one of the world's most popular – and profitable –

cruise destinations. In total, more than 35 vessels from over a dozen cruise lines make hundreds of sailings between Vancouver and Alaska every year from May to October. **CruiseMates** (www.cruisemates.com/articles/ports/alaska/) has a useful roundup of the many lines and boats now sailing the Inside Passage. Many include Vancouver in their itineraries. Some boats are now doing the run from US ports such as Seattle and San Francisco, making it possible to create a package where you can sail one-way to/from BC or even the Yukon via Skagway in Alaska and travel by ground or air the other way. However a complex itinerary such as this would require the services of a travel agent.

From the USA

The **Alaska Marine Highway** (AMH; ☎ 800-642-0066; www.alaska.gov/ferry) sails from Bellingham, Washington along the stunning inside passage to Haines and Skagway in Alaska, which are prime access points to the Yukon. These trips take almost four days, and fares to Skagway are adult/child $296/148, car from $756 and cabin from $227. The ferries run twice a week in summer and once a week in winter. It is one of the most spectacular voyages anywhere – note the number of cruise ships that do it – and the advantage of the ferry is that you can bring your car to Alaska with you.

The AMH ships are comfortable with decent cabins, good, fresh-cooked food and usually a park ranger offering commentary on the many sights that include scads of wildlife such as whales. Many people pitch tents on the deck. Reservations for this route are a must.

Another AMH option is to take the boat from Prince Rupert in BC to Haines or Skagway and then on to the Yukon (p323). This route is nearly the equal in terms of scenery with the Bellingham run and it takes half as long.

You can get to Victoria by ferry from Seattle, Port Angeles and Anacortes, Washington (p139).

GETTING AROUND

AIR

Canada's airline industry is shaping up to be a battle of two airlines: Air Canada

and its subsidiaries versus upstart Westjet. The winner is bound to be the traveler. Westjet, based in Calgary, is a no-frills airline with tight seating that is driving down prices in the markets it serves. It links Vancouver, Victoria, Prince George, Kelowna and cities east, with more destinations being added monthly. Air Canada has responded with Zip, its own low-fare, no-frills carrier.

Air Canada Jazz, the big airline's regional carrier, links numerous small towns in BC with Vancouver, and a few with Calgary. Other small airlines fill in the gaps making it possible to get from Vancouver to some of the smallest towns in the province.

See p345 for details of Yukon air links.

Airlines

Larger airlines providing regional service in BC and the Yukon are as follows:
Air Canada/Air Canada Jazz (☎ 888-247-2262; www.aircanda.ca)
Air North (☎ 800-661-0407; www.flyairnorth.com)
Hawkair (☎ 866-429-5247; www.hawkair.net)
Pacific Coastal Airlines (☎ 604-273-8666; www.pacific-coastal.com)
Westjet (☎ 800-538-5696; www.westjet.ca)
Zip (☎ 866-432-1947; www.4321zip.com)

BICYCLE

British Columbia Cycling Coalition (www.bccc.bc.ca) is the best source of information on bicycling as transportation in BC. Bike rentals are widely available, and in the various regional chapters of this book you will find bicycle-rental listings for many towns. You can take your bike on most forms of public transportation. Call ahead to the air, ferry, bus and train companies listed to see what their rates and requirements are.

BOAT

The blue-and-white BC Ferries are a symbol of coastal British Columbia as well as a mode of transportation. You'll find extensive details on BC Ferries service in the Vancouver & Around, the Vancouver Island and the Whistler & the Sunshine Coast chapters.

What follows is an overview of services, plus details on the long-distance Inside Passage and Discovery Coast Passage routes.
BC Ferries Corporation (☎ 888-223-3779, outside BC ☎ 250-386-3431; www.bcferries.com) operates a

fleet of 40 ferries on BC's coastal waters. Formerly a government-run operation, it has been privatized and there is much speculation about its future direction, although by law it has to maintain present services for the immediate future. The biggest change you may notice is that the food service has been improved.

The newly privatized BC Ferries is also starting to offer various specials which can combine a number of ferry rides at one low price. Check to see what's on offer for when you want to travel. One popular package is SailPass, which gives you either four consecutive days of ferry travel for $119 or seven consecutive days for $149. The pass includes unlimited travel on the Southern Gulf Islands, Northern Gulf Islands and Brentwood Bay–Mill Bay routes, along with one round trip on each of the Mainland–Vancouver Island and Sunshine Coast crossings.

Another good package is CirclePac, a four-route travel package that gives you up to 15% off regular, one-way fares on each of the following routes: Horseshoe Bay–Langdale, Earls Cove–Saltery Bay, Powell River–Comox, and Vancouver Island–Mainland (your choice of Nanaimo-Horseshoe Bay, Nanaimo–Tsawwassen, or Swartz Bay–Tsawwassen). This is a good deal for exploring Vancouver Island and the Sunshine Coast on the Circle Tour (p13).

Vancouver area service

The two busiest routes are from Tsawwassen (about an hour's drive south of downtown Vancouver) to Swartz Bay (a half-hour drive north of Victoria), and from Horseshoe Bay (a half-hour drive north of downtown Vancouver) to Departure Bay near Nanaimo on Vancouver Island. From Tsawwassen, ferries also go to Duke Point near Nanaimo, and to the Southern Gulf Islands (Salt Spring, Galiano, Mayne, Saturna and the Pender Islands). From Horseshoe Bay, ferries also go to Bowen Island and the Sunshine Coast.

Other BC Ferries routes cover Gabriola Island, Thetis Island, Kuper Island, Texada Island and the Northern Gulf Islands (namely Denman, Hornby, Quadra, Cortes, Malcolm and Cormorant).

Generally, it's much cheaper to travel on BC Ferries without a motorized vehicle. You can take bicycles, canoes or kayaks onboard. See the website www.bcferries.com for complete information.

Vehicle reservations known as **Reserved Boarding** (☎ 888-724-5223, outside BC ☎ 604-444-2890; www.bcferries.com) are recommended for weekends on the Tsawwassen–Swartz Bay, Horseshoe Bay–Departure Bay and Tsawwassen–Duke Point routes.

Inside Passage

The Inside Passage route between Port Hardy and Prince Rupert is among the most scenic boat trips in the world. Generally the *Queen of the North* sails northbound from Port Hardy at 7:30am every other day in summer, arriving in Prince Rupert at 10:30pm. The southbound sailings have a similar schedule. There are sailings October through May, too. You must reserve space on Inside Passage sailings.

Fares to/from Prince Rupert are adult/child $102.50/51.25, car from $241.50, cabin from $60.

Discovery Coast Passage

This route covers the stretch between Port Hardy on Vancouver Island and Bella Coola on the central BC coast. It's shorter than the Inside Passage route, but just as scenic. Ships run only from mid-June through mid-September. Reservations are necessary. Fares are adult/child $106.25/53.25, cars from $212.50.

Boats run on various schedules, with possible stops including Namu, McLoughlin Bay, Klemtu and Shearwater.

There are no cabins on the *Queen of Chilliwack*, which sails the Discovery Coast Passage, but there are reclining lounge seats where you can sleep. Some passengers even set up their tents on deck and sleep there.

Queen Charlotte Islands

For details on the Queen Charlotte Islands services from Prince Rupert, see p323.

BUS

Greyhound Canada (800-661-8747; www.greyhound.ca) covers most of BC and has service into the Yukon along the Alaska Highway as far as Whitehorse.

TRANSPORT

Backbackers Bus

There's a backpackers' bus service run by **Moose Travel Network** (☎ 888-388-4881, outside of North America ☎ 604-777-9905; www.moosenetwork .com; $399; ☯ daily Jun-Sep, less often May & Oct), running small buses on a circle route that includes Vancouver, Kamloops, Jasper, Banff, Revelstoke and Kelowna. For one fare you can get on and off between segments. The buses stop at major (and minor) scenic highlights along the way and there are all sorts of group activities. The buses can be a lot of fun and each day's run ends at a hostel.

CAR & MOTORCYCLE

British Columbia and the Yukon is a big place, and if you want to see a lot of it on your own timetable, a car or motorcycle is usually the way to go. In many ways, driving is the best way to travel in the region. You can go where and when you want, use secondary highways and roads, and get off the beaten track. You can use ferries to cover some segments and create interesting circular routes.

Automobile Association

With 24 offices throughout the province, the **British Columbia Automobile Association** (BCAA; ☎ 877-325-8888; www.bcaa.com) provides its members, and the members of other auto clubs (such as AAA in the USA), with travel information, maps, travel insurance and hotel reservations. It also provides service in the Yukon. Many people join for the **emergency roadside assistance** (☎ 604-293-2222, Lower Mainland ☎ 800-222-4357).

Fuel & Spare Parts

At the time of writing, gasoline (petrol, usually just called gas in BC) costs from 65¢ in the competitive Vancouver area to 90¢ per liter in the uncompetitive north.

Places to purchase fuel are common in southern BC. In the north along roads such as the Alaska Hwy, service stations are spaced at regular intervals. But on some side roads and out-of-the-way places don't expect to find a gas station. A good rule is to fill up your tank when your level is about half empty (or half full if you're feeling optimistic).

Auto parts and mechanics who have seen it all also exist at regular intervals on major roads in the north. But it is still a good idea to carry at least one full-service spare tire – especially if you will be driving on one of the gravel highways. If you break down, someone is bound to come along who can at least take you to a town with a mechanic. But if you drive an uncommon car, be prepared to settle in while parts are shipped north.

Rental/Hire

Major car-rental firms have offices at airports in BC and Whitehorse, as well as some city centers. In smaller towns there are often independent firms; these are listed through the book. It's again worth noting that you should clarify your insurance coverage for things like gravel damage if you will be driving off major paved roads.

By shopping around you can find some pretty good deals. Just watch out for deals that don't offer unlimited kilometers for driving. And never buy the rental car company's gas if offered when you pick up your car, it's a bad deal. Buy your own and return it full. If you are considering a one-way rental, look out for high fees.

CAR RENTAL FIRMS

Alamo (☎ 800-462-5266; www.alamo.com)
Avis (☎ 800-272-5871; www.avis.com)
Budget (☎ 800-268-8900; www.budget.com)
Hertz (☎ 800-263-0600; www.hertz.com)
National (☎ 800-227-7368; www.nationalcar.com)

RECREATIONAL VEHICLES

Recreational vehicles (RVs) are hugely popular in BC and the Yukon, and RV rentals must be booked well before the summer travel season. In high season, mid- to large-size vehicles cost $200 or more a day, including 100km per day. One-way rentals, say from BC to the Yukon, are possible but you'll pay a surcharge. Also budget plenty for fuel, because RVs typically get very poor gas mileage. In the Vancouver area RV rental companies include:
Alldrive Canada (☎ 403-245-2935, 888-736-8787; www.alldrive.com)
West Coast Mountain Campers (☎ 604-279-0550; www.wcmcampers.com)

Whitehorse in the Yukon is a popular place for picking up RVs. **Klondike Recreational Vehicles** (☎ 867-668-2200; www.klondike -rv.com; 107 Copper Rd) rents all shapes and sizes of RVs from $165 to $200 per day, and you can get them equipped with canoes. They also offer one-way rentals to/from Kamloops, British Columbia.

Road Hazards
It's best to avoid driving in areas with heavy snow, but if you do, be sure your vehicle has snow tires or tire chains. Many Canadian cars have four-season radial tires. If you get stuck, don't stay in the car with the engine going; every year people die of carbon monoxide suffocation by doing this during big storms. A single candle burning in the car will keep it reasonably warm.

Service stations are few and far between in many parts of BC, so keep an eye on the gas gauge and try not to dip below half a tank. Make sure the vehicle you're driving is in good condition and take along some tools, spare parts, water and food.

Some additional precautions apply for off-the-beaten-track travel. Gravel logging roads tend to be particularly dangerous. Logging trucks have the right of way in every instance, and they'll often zoom past you, kicking up gravel and dust. It's best not to drive on logging roads at all during weekday working hours.

Gravel roads of all kinds – such as the many gravel highways in the Yukon – can take a toll on windshields, so if you're renting, sort out breakage coverage in advance. (Some rental companies prohibit customers from taking cars on gravel roads.) Keep a good distance from the vehicle in front of you, and when you see an oncoming vehicle (or a vehicle overtaking you), slow down and keep well to the right. Carry a spare tire.

Wild animals on the road are another potential hazard. Most run-ins with deer, moose and other critters occur at night when wildlife is active and visibility is poor. Many areas have roadside signs alerting drivers to possible animal crossings. Keep scanning both sides of the road and be prepared to stop or swerve. A vehicle's headlights often mesmerize an animal, leaving it frozen in the middle of the road. Try flashing the lights, as well as using the horn.

Road Rules
North Americans drive on the right side of the road. Speed limits, which are posted in kilometers, are generally 50km/h in built-up areas and 90km/h on highways. A right turn is permitted at a red light after you have come to a complete stop, as is a left turn from one one-way street onto another one-way street; U-turns are not allowed. Traffic in both directions must stop when stationary school buses have their red lights flashing – this means children are getting off and on. In cities with pedestrian crosswalks, cars must stop to allow pedestrians to cross.

The use of seat belts is compulsory throughout Canada. Children under age five must be in a restraining seat. British Columbia law requires motorcyclists to drive with the lights on and for cyclists and passengers to wear helmets. The blood-alcohol limit when driving is 0.08%, about two drinks.

You may notice that the vast majority of drivers keep their headlights on throughout the day; this is not mandatory but is recommended.

HITCHHIKING
Hitchhiking is fairly common in BC and the Yukon, especially in rural areas, near ski resorts and on the Gulf Islands. Nevertheless, hitchhiking is never entirely safe in any country in the world, and is not recommended. Travelers who decide to hitchhike (or pick up hitchhikers) should understand that they are taking a risk. If you do choose to hitchhike, do it only in pairs. Hitching on the Trans-Canada Hwy is illegal until 40km past the Vancouver city limits.

LOCAL TRANSPORTATION
British Columbia has excellent, widespread local public transportation in the area around Vancouver and Victoria. Outside of these areas service can be sparse, erratic or infrequent. Look in the regional chapters for details on each town's offerings, or see the province-wide website www.transitbc.com, which features links to the local bus systems. Most places have taxi companies.

In the Yukon, public transit in Whitehorse will suffice if you just need to get from the airport to town and hook up with a tour operator or gear rental place. But keep in mind what one veteran Yukon guide told us: 'Please tell people to rent a car. People turn up in the strangest places expecting there to be a bus or something. They don't exist.'

TRAIN

Railroad service is limited in BC. The national carrier, **VIA Rail** (☎ 888-842-7245; www.viarail.ca) has only one route from Vancouver. The *Canadian* departs a paltry three times a week and makes few stops in BC, including outside of Kamloops before reaching Jasper. VIA Rail also runs the *Skeena* between Prince Rupert and Jasper thrice weekly. It's a daytime-only trip with an overnight stay in Prince George and stops in Terrace, New Hazelton, Smithers, Houston and Burns Lake. Passengers on the *Skeena* have a choice of service class and fare, and you book your own lodgings in Prince George.

One-way fares from Vancouver to Jasper are $130 to $150; Prince Rupert to Jasper $120 to $170. Like the airlines, VIA Rail offers various discounts for round trips and other seasonal offerings.

On Vancouver Island, VIA Rail runs the *Esquimalt & Nanaimo Railiner*, also known as the *E&N Railiner* or the *Malahat*, a short, scenic trip from Victoria to Courtenay up the coast of Vancouver Island, with one train daily in each direction (p139) which is often threatened with a permanent shut-down.

The province's own railroad, BC Rail, ended its delightful service from Vancouver to Prince George as part of the government's cost-cutting measures.

Health by Dr David Goldberg

There's a high level of hygiene found in this region, so most common infectious diseases will not be a significant concern for travelers. Also, superb medical care is widely available.

BEFORE YOU GO

INSURANCE

The Canadian health-care system is one of the finest in the world. Excellent care is widely available. Benefits are generous for Canadian citizens, but foreigners aren't covered. Make sure you have travel-health insurance if your regular policy doesn't apply when you're abroad. (Check the Subwwway section of the Lonely Planet website at www.lonelyplanet.com/subwwway for more information.) Find out in advance if your insurance plan will make payments directly to providers or reimburse you later for overseas health expenditures.

ONLINE RESOURCES

There is a wealth of travel-health advice on the Internet. The World Health Organization publishes a superb book, called *International Travel and Health*, which is revised annually and is available online at no cost at www.who.int/ith/. Another website of general interest is MD Travel Health at www.mdtravelhealth.com, which provides complete travel-health recommendations for every country, is updated daily and is available at no cost.

MEDICAL CHECKLIST

- Acetaminophen/paracetamol (Tylenol) or aspirin
- Anti-inflammatory drugs (eg ibuprofen)
- Antihistamines (for hay fever and allergic reactions)
- Antibacterial ointment (eg Neosporin or Bactroban) for cuts and abrasions
- Steroid cream or cortisone (for poison ivy and other allergic rashes)
- Bandages, gauze, gauze rolls
- Adhesive or paper tape
- Scissors, safety pins, tweezers
- Thermometer
- Pocket knife
- DEET-containing insect repellent for the skin
- Permethrin-containing insect spray for clothing, tents, and bed nets

Bring medications in their original containers, clearly labeled. A signed, dated letter from your physician describing all medical conditions and medications, including generic names is also a good idea. If carrying syringes or needles be sure to have a physician's letter documenting their medical necessity.

It's usually a good idea to consult your government's travel-health website, if one is available, before departure:

Australia (www.dfat.gov.au/travel/)
United Kingdom (www.doh.gov.uk/traveladvice/index.htm)
United States (www.cdc.gov/travel/)

IN CANADA

AVAILABILITY & COST OF HEALTH CARE

For immediate medical assistance anywhere in BC, call ☎ 911; in the Yukon, call ☎ 867-667-3333. In general, if you

RECOMMENDED VACCINATIONS

No special vaccines are required or recommended for travel to Canada. All travelers should be up-to-date on routine immunizations, listed below.

Vaccine	Recommended for	Dosage	Side effects
tetanus-diphtheria	all travelers who haven't had booster within 10 yrs	one dose lasts 10 years	soreness at injection site
measles	travelers born after 1956 who've had only one measles vaccination	one dose	fever; rash; joint pains; allergic reactions
chickenpox	travelers who've never had chickenpox	two doses one month apart	fever; mild case of chickenpox
influenza	all travelers during flu season (Nov–Mar)	one dose	soreness at the injection site; fever

have a medical emergency, the best bet is to find the nearest hospital and go to its emergency room.

If you have a choice, a university hospital can be preferable to a community hospital, though you can often find superb medical care in small local hospitals and the waiting time is usually shorter. If the problem isn't urgent, you can call a nearby hospital and ask for a referral to a local physician, which is usually less expensive than a trip to the emergency room.

Pharmacies are abundantly supplied, but you may find that some medications which are available over-the-counter in your home country require a prescription in Canada.

INFECTIOUS DISEASES

There are several infectious diseases that are unknown or uncommon outside North America. Most are acquired by mosquito bites, tick bites or environmental exposure.

West Nile Virus

Infections were unknown in Canada until recently, but West Nile virus has now been observed in many provinces, including Saskatchewan, Alberta, Ontario, Quebec, and Manitoba. The virus is transmitted by Culex mosquitoes, which are active in late summer and early fall, and generally bite after dusk. Most infections are mild or asymptomatic, but the virus may infect the central nervous system, leading to fever, headache, confusion, lethargy, coma, and sometimes death. There is no treatment for West Nile virus.

At the time of writing there was no evidence of the virus in British Columbia or the Yukon. For the latest update on the areas affected by West Nile, go to the Health Canada website at www.hc-sc.gc.ca /english/westnile/index.html. See Mosquito Bites (p387).

Lyme Disease

This has been reported from the southern parts of the country. The infection is transmitted by deer ticks, which are only 1mm to 2mm long. Most cases occur in late spring and summer. The first symptom is usually an expanding red rash that is often pale in the center, known as a bull's eye rash. However, in many cases, no rash is observed. Flu-like symptoms are common, including fever, headache, joint pains, body aches and malaise. When the infection is treated promptly with an appropriate antibiotic, usually doxycycline or amoxicillin, the cure rate is high. For prevention tips, see Tick Bites (p387).

Giardiasis

This parasitic infection of the small intestine occurs throughout North America and the world. Known colloquially in BC as 'Beaver fever', Giardiasis has symptoms that may include nausea, bloating, cramps, and diarrhea, and may last for weeks. Avoid drinking directly from lakes, ponds, streams and rivers, which may be contaminated by animal or human feces.

Rabies

Rabies is a viral infection of the brain and spinal cord that is almost always fatal. In Canada most cases of human rabies relate to exposure to bats. Rabies may also be contracted from raccoons, skunks, foxes, and unvaccinated cats and dogs. All animal bites and scratches must be promptly and thoroughly cleansed with large amounts of soap and water, and local health authorities contacted to determine if there is a risk of rabies. If there is any possibility, however small, that you have been exposed to rabies, you should seek preventative treatment, which consists of rabies-immune globulin and rabies vaccine, and is quite safe. In particular, any contact with a bat should be discussed with health authorities, as bats have small teeth and may not leave obvious bite marks.

HIV/AIDS

This infectious disease occurs throughout Canada.

ENVIRONMENTAL HAZARDS
Cold Exposure

Cold exposure may be a significant problem, especially in the northern parts of the country. To prevent hypothermia, keep all body surfaces covered, including the head and neck. Synthetic materials such as Gore-Tex and Thinsulate provide excellent insulation. Since the body loses heat faster when wet, stay dry at all times. Change inner garments promptly when they become moist. Keep active, but get enough rest. Consume plenty of food and water. Be especially sure not to have any alcohol. Caffeine and tobacco should also be avoided.

Watch out for the 'Umbles': stumbles, mumbles, fumbles and grumbles, important signs of impending hypothermia. If someone appears to be developing hypothermia, you should insulate them from the ground, protect them from the wind, remove wet clothing or cover with a vapor barrier such as a plastic bag, and transport immediately to a warm environment and a medical facility. Warm fluids (not coffee or tea) may be given if the person is alert enough to swallow.

Mosquito Bites

When traveling in areas where West Nile or other mosquito-borne illnesses have been reported, keep yourself covered (wear long sleeves, long pants, hats and shoes rather than sandals). Apply a good insect repellent, preferably one containing DEET, to exposed skin and clothing. Avoid contact with eyes, mouth, cuts, wounds or irritated skin. Products containing lower concentrations of DEET are as effective, but for shorter periods of time. In general, adults and children over 12 should use preparations containing 25% to 35% DEET, which lasts about six hours. Children aged between two and 12 years should use preparations containing no more than 10% DEET, applied sparingly, which will last about three hours. Neurologic toxicity has been reported from DEET, especially in children, but appears to be extremely uncommon and generally related to overuse. DEET-containing compounds should not be used on children under age two. Insect repellents containing certain botanical products, including oil of eucalyptus and soybean oil, are effective but last only 1½ to two hours. Products based on citronella are not effective.

For additional protection, you can apply permethrin to clothing, shoes, tents, and bed nets. Permethrin treatments are safe and remain effective for at least two weeks, even when items are laundered. Permethrin should not be applied directly to skin.

Tick Bites

To protect yourself from tick bites, follow the same precautions as for mosquitoes, except that boots are preferable to shoes, and pants tucked in. Be sure to perform a thorough tick check at the end of each day, with the aid of a friend or mirror. Ticks should be removed with tweezers, grasping them firmly by the head. Insect repellents based on botanical products cannot be recommended to prevent tick bites.

Mammal Bites

Most animal injuries are directly related to a person's attempt to touch or feed the animal. Any bite or scratch by a mammal, including bats, should be promptly and thoroughly cleansed with large amounts of soap and water, followed by application of an antiseptic such as iodine or alcohol. The local health authorities should be contacted immediately for possible post-exposure rabies treatment.

HEALTH

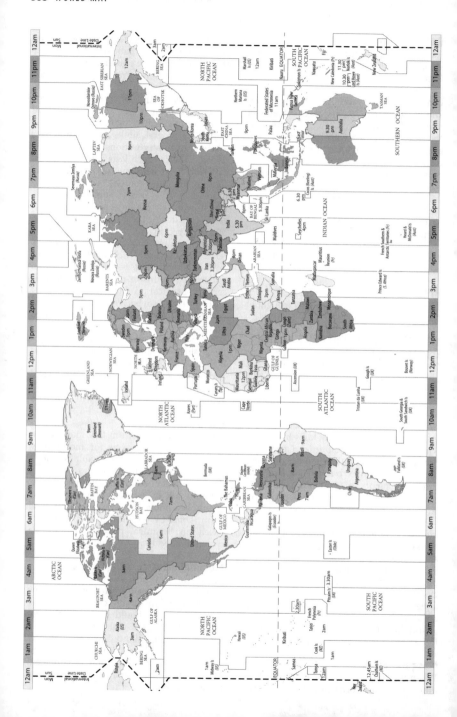

Glossary

A

aurora borealis – charged particles from the sun that are trapped in the earth's magnetic field and appear as other-worldly, colored, waving beams; also called the northern lights

B

beaver fever (giardiasis) – disease affecting the digestive tract, caused by bacteria found in many freshwater streams and lakes; can be avoided by boiling drinking water

boreal – refers to the Canadian north and its character, as in the boreal forest or the boreal wind

C

Canadian Shield – a plateau of rock formed 2.5 billion years ago that covers much of the northern region of Canada; also known as the Precambrian or Laurentian Shield

clear-cut – an area where loggers have cut every tree, large and small, leaving nothing but stumps

coulees – gulches, usually dry

Cowichan – a Native Indian people originally from the Lake Cowichan area on Vancouver Island; also the name given to the hand-knitted, 100% wool sweaters they produce

CPR – in BC, usually an acronym for the Canadian Pacific Railway

F

First Nations – denotes Canada's aboriginal peoples; often used instead of Native Indians or Native people

G

gasoline – petrol, known as gasoline, fuel, or simply gas; mostly sold unleaded in Canada

GST – the 7% goods and services tax levied on most purchases throughout Canada

H

hoodoo – distinctive vertical pillar shape carved into a rock face by rainfall and glacial erosion

I

icefield – a large, level expanse of floating ice

Inside Passage – sea route from the Alaskan Panhandle to Washington state that runs between the coast of mainland BC and the chain of islands off the coast

inukshuk – stone figures built by the Inuit next to lakes to lure animals into the water, where they could be hunted from kayaks

L

loon – aquatic bird, known as a diver in British English

loonie – Canada's one-dollar coin, which depicts a loon on one side

Lower Mainland – common term for the southwestern part of BC, including metropolitan Vancouver

M

Métis – Canadians of mixed French and Native Indian ancestry

Mounties – Royal Canadian Mounted Police (RCMP)

muskeg – undrained boggy land found in northern BC

N

névé – compacted snow that forms the surface of the upper part of a glacier

no-see-um – any of various tiny biting insects that are difficult to see and can annoy travelers in the woods or along beaches; can be kept out of tents with no-see-um netting, a very fine mesh screen

O

Ogopogo – monster similar to the Loch Ness monster, thought to reside in Okanagan Lake; has never been photographed

P

The Peace – Short for the Peace River Region of BC, in the northeast

portage – process of transporting boats and supplies overland between navigable waterways; can also refer to the overland route used

petroglyphs – ancient paintings or carvings on rock

potlatch – competitive ceremonial activity among some BC Native people (usually coastal), traditionally involving the giving of lavish gifts in order to emphasize the wealth and status of a chief or clan; now often just refers to a wild party or revel

PST – Provincial Sales Tax, currently 7% in BC; when coupled with the GST, it can bring the tax on many purchases to 14%

Q

Quay – pronounced 'key'; a city's waterfront docks area, as in North Vancouver's Lonsdale Quay or Port Alberni's Harbour Quay

GLOSSARY

R

RCMP – Royal Canadian Mounted Police, the main law-enforcement agency throughout Canada

RV – recreational vehicle (commonly a motor home), used for traveling or camping; 'caravan' in British English

S

sourdough – a person who has completed one year's residency in northern Canada

spelunking – exploration and study of caves

T

taiga – coniferous forests extending across much of subarctic North America and Eurasia

toonie – slang name for a Canadian two-dollar coin

trailer – in Canada and the USA, a caravan or a mobile home

U

Up Island – on Vancouver Island, anywhere north of Victoria

Behind the Scenes

THIS BOOK

This second edition of *British Columbia* was written by Ryan Ver Berkmoes and Graham Neale. Ryan wrote most of the front chapters, except the Culture chapter, and all regional chapters, except Vancouver & Around, Whistler & the Sunshine Coast, Vancouver Island and the Southern Gulf Islands, which Graham wrote. The first edition of this guide was written by Julie Fanselow and Debra Miller; the Yukon chapter was based on Susan Rimerman's chapter for LP's *Canada* 8. Dr David Goldberg wrote the Health Chapter.

THANKS from the Authors

Ryan Ver Berkmoes First I have to thank the gods (which depending on my mood some days might be devils) who gave me the unexpected chance to work on this book. I love BC and the Yukon and am happy for any chance to return. One problem is thanking all the people up north who helped me with my research. Kindness and generosity are the norm of Canadians, so it's hard to highlight any one person – although I'll always buy a bottle of Becks for Jim Kemshead in the Yukon.

At Lonely Planet thanks need to flow to this book's commissioning editor Erin Corrigan, who was both inspiring and giving in ways she may not even comprehend. I also must thank Virginia Maxwell, Robert Reid, Maria Donohoe and Susan Rimerman for helping me with the myriad of challenges that came our way before research on this book began. Finally I have to thank Toyota for my little Echo, which quintupled its mileage in BC and the Yukon and handled every treacherous logging road with an aplomb that the gas-guzzling SUVs could only dream about.

Graham Neale I had a speech prepared in case I won, but I've lost my notes so I'll just wing it.

Emily inspired and made me believe I could do this before I ever thought I could; she was there on the turn-around, most of the time, and I thank her. Brad The Raider came up huge by moving my stuff twice, dealing with drama and taking my most important plants. Ed The Steeler selfishly got married in the middle of this project, but he and his wonderful wife Ale made amends by opening their doors and dinner table to my homeless self. Amy, Kirk and Oami made the home stretch possible, without their help this book would be unfinished.

My Mom and Doug, my Dad and Ann, Don and Jan, Paul and Lorna; they gave advice, leads, sleeping places and home-cooked meals; it gets no better than that. My Grandma turned 90, and then made me gingersnaps – wow. MacLeod, Hoffmann, Austin: thanks dudes. Thanks to the tourism officials I met for information and libations.

Thanks to Erin, who gave me this chance in the first place. Thanks and apologies to Vert, the fish who died, solving the dilemma of what to do with him. The game of soccer is a glorious thing and deserves a huge thanks for always being there and always raising the intensity. Pinky the Ballcap gets mad props for being my ever-faithful companion and ever-present thinking-cap muse.

Last but not least: I thank you, yes you; without you to read this book there is no reason to write it.

THE LONELY PLANET STORY

The story begins with a classic travel adventure: Tony and Maureen Wheeler's 1972 journey across Europe and Asia to Australia. There was no useful information about the overland trail then, so Tony and Maureen published the first Lonely Planet guidebook to meet a growing need.

From a kitchen table, Lonely Planet has grown to become the largest independent travel publisher in the world, with offices in Melbourne (Australia), Oakland (USA), London (UK) and Paris (France).

Today Lonely Planet guidebooks cover the globe. There is an ever-growing list of books and information in a variety of media. Some things haven't changed. The main aim is still to make it possible for adventurous travellers to get out there – to explore and better understand the world.

At Lonely Planet we believe travellers can make a positive contribution to the countries they visit – if they respect their host communities and spend their money wisely.

BEHIND THE SCENES

CREDITS

This guide was commissioned and developed in Lonely Planet's Oakland, CA, office by Erin Corrigan. Erin would like to thank Publishing Manager Maria Donohoe for all her guidance. Overseeing production were Bridget Blair (Project Manager) and Kyla Gillzan (Editorial House Style Coordinator). Cartography for this guide was developed by Alison Lyall. Cartography was coordinated by Valentina Kremenchutskaya and Herman So, with assistance from Csanad Csutoros, Jack Gavran, Kusnandar, Kim McDonald, Amanda Sierp and Chris Tsismetzis. Editing was coordinated by EdInk. Thanks to the editors and proofreaders who helped EdInk including Miriam Cannell, Kate Church, Paul Harding, Alexandra Payne and Sally Steward, and to Max McMaster for the index. Brendan Dempsey designed and prepared the cover. Thanks to PAGE people, Jenni Quinn and Peter Dyson, who laid the book out and made everything fit on the page.

Series Publishing Manager Susan Rimerman oversaw the redevelopment of the regional guides series with the help of Virginia Maxwell and Regional Publishing Manager Maria Donohoe, who also steered the development of this title. The series was designed by James Hardy, with series mapping development by Paul Piaia. The series development team included Shahara Ahmed, Jenny Blake, Anna Bolger, Erin Corrigan, Nadine Fogale, Dave McClymont, Leonie Mugavin, Rachel Peart, Lynne Preston, Howard Ralley, Valerie Sinzdak and Bart Wright.

THANKS from Lonely Planet

Many thanks to the travellers who used the last edition and wrote to us with helpful hints, useful advice and interesting anecdotes:

A Christy Allen, Amy Almquist, Riley Anderson, S Arnold, Terry Aspinall, John Atkin **B** Adam Becalski, Phil Beicken, Brian Benson, Michael Brasier, Crystal Briggeman, Tracy Broadbent, Leigh Burbidge, Dwight Burditt, Ron Burdo **C** Mary Ann Camann, Paul Cammaert, Colleen Carroll, Matt Catalano, Julian Chen, Chungwah Chow, Pierre Chum, Charles Citroen, Matthew Clark, Mike Clyne, Sarah Coleopy, David Coleopy, Victoria Conlin, Leanne Cormack, Tim Costley-White, Callum Couston, Krystyna Cynar **D** Chuck Davis, Richard Dawson, Karen DeRosa, Mike DeRosa, Yves Desrichard, Julia Dickinson, Jean Dragushan, Shannon Draper, Bob Dronight **E** Tom Elvin, Chris Enting, Emily Evans **F** Vincent Fodera, Marian Fortner, Timothy Fowkes, Kevin Freer **G** Eric Gagnon, Christina Gamouras, Richard Gavey, Ferdinando Emilio Giammichele, Mr & Mrs Goertz, Robin Goldsbury, Dayna Gorman, Jules Grant, Ken Guappone, I Guest, Lisa Guiton, Patrick Guiton, Jon Guy, Lise Guyot **H** Gill Hamson, Deborah Hardoon, Chris Hartt, Paula Harvey, Richard Head, Mario Heinzig, Martin Helmantel, Saskia Helmantel, Jennifer Hildebrand, Katherine

Hobbs, James Holgate, Simon Huang, Winona Hubbard, Graham Hunt, Martin Hunt **I** Jeroen Immerzeel **J** Catriona Johnson, Sally Johnston, Jane Jones, Sarah Dan Jones **K** Steven Kabanuk, Graham Kenyon, Brian King, Tyler Kirsh, Tom Korecki, Daniel Kruse **L** Stuart Lamble, Hans Laue, Sylvie Laurenty, Ellen Lewers, Corey Lewis, Damien Liu, J G Lloyd, Andreas Lober, Karl Lorenz, Collombet Lucile, Kim Lyons **M** Ray MacKenzie, Laura MacKenzie, Dave Macmeekin, Maurice Maher, Mary Jane Mahony, Carol Maier, Leslie Maldonado, Alex Marbach, Ian Matthews, Riccardo Mazzoni, Pat McDonald, Paul McFarlane, Gerard McNamee, Bronwyn McNaughton, Simon Miller, Jeanette Mills, Karen Mistilis, Stephanie Monaghan, Renate Moser, Peter Murray **N** Don Nelson, Luca Nonato, Kate Norris, Ken Nutini **O** Dean Ogle, Brendan P O'Rourke **P** Dick Parsons, Anthony Pasko, Lori Pasko, Jayde Patching, Paula Patterson, Jo Payne, Mary Peachin, Andrew Pilliar, Andrew Pinch, Sonia Pinkney, Vanessa Pocock, Bill Pollard, Mike Preece, Sheila Preece, Meredith Preston **R** Anita Rafidi, Roger Randall, Shirley Randall, Mike Reams, Alex Rooke, Marco Roos, Petra Rossback, John Rouhiainen **S** Gwyn Sarkar, Robin Sarkar, Jeanne Schmidt, Verena Sellmer, Richard Semple, Maureen Shipton, Heidi Smith, Peter Smith, Robert Smith, Melia Sorenson, Kaz Stafford, Michael Stanley, Joe Stead, Ester Strijbos, Joe Stryvoke, John Sturley, Arden Sutherland **T** Calvin Tam, David Taylor, Cyrus Teng, Paul Terbasket, Marcelle Thibodeau, John Turecek **U** Dennis Urbonas **V** Annerieke van Hoek, Monique van Leest, Madelon van Luijk, Isabelle Vassot, Angele Vautour, Vincent Verdult, Anna Vickery, Veronica Villa, Geert Voets, Paul Vuksanovich **W** Vicki Walker, Debbie Weijers, Zita Wenzel, Amanda Williams, Alison Wilson, Karin Winkelmann, Peter Winter, Bob Wood, Wendy Worley, Douglas Wright **Y** Coran York **Z** Natacha Zana

SEND US YOUR FEEDBACK

We love to hear from travellers – your comments keep us on our toes and help make our books better. Our well-travelled team reads every word on what you loved or loathed about this book. Although we cannot reply individually to postal submissions, we always guarantee that your feedback goes straight to the appropriate authors, in time for the next edition. Each person who sends us information is thanked in the next edition – and the most useful submissions are rewarded with a free book.

To send us your updates – and find out about LP events, newsletters and travel news – visit our award-winning website: **www.lonelyplanet.com**.

Note: We may edit, reproduce and incorporate your comments in Lonely Planet products such as guidebooks, websites and digital products, so let us know if you don't want your comments reproduced or your name acknowledged. For a copy of our privacy policy visit www.lonelyplanet.com/privacy.

BEHIND THE SCENES

Index

000 Map pages
000 Location of colour photographs

000 Map pages
000 Location of colour photographs

000 Map pages
000 Location of colour photographs

MAP LEGEND

ROUTES

Tollway	Track
Freeway	One-Way Street
Primary Road	Unsealed Road
Secondary Road	Street Mall/Steps
Tertiary Road	Tunnel
Lane	Walking Trail
Under Construction	Walking Path

TRANSPORT

Ferry	Rail
Metro	Rail (Underground)
Monorail	Tram
Bus Route	Cable Car, Funicular

HYDROGRAPHY

River, Creek	Glacier
Intermittent River	Canal
Swamp	Water
Reef	Lake (Dry)

BOUNDARIES

International	Regional, Suburb
State, Provincial	Ancient Wall
Marine Park	Cliff

AREA FEATURES

Airport	Forest
Area of Interest	Land
Beach, Desert	Park
Building	Reservation
Campus	Sports
Cemetery, Christian	Urban

POPULATION

CAPITAL (NATIONAL)	CAPITAL (STATE)
Large City	Medium City
Small City	Town, Village

SYMBOLS

Sights/Activities
- Beach
- Buddhist
- Canoeing, Kayaking
- Christian
- Diving, Snorkeling
- Monument
- Museum, Gallery
- Picnic Area
- Point of Interest
- Pool
- Ruin
- Shinto
- Skiing
- Winery, Vineyard
- Zoo, Bird Sanctuary

Eating
- Eating

Drinking
- Drinking
- Café

Entertainment
- Entertainment

Shopping
- Shopping

Sleeping
- Sleeping
- Camping

Transport
- Airport, Airfield
- Border Crossing
- Bus Station
- Cycling, Bicycle Path
- General Transport
- Taxi Rank
- Trail Head

Information
- Bank, ATM
- Embassy/Consulate
- Hospital, Medical
- Information
- Internet Facilities
- Parking Area
- Petrol Station
- Police Station
- Post Office, GPO
- Telephone
- Toilets

Geographic
- Lighthouse
- Lookout
- Mountain, Volcano
- National Park
- Pass, Canyon
- Shelter, Hut
- Waterfall

LONELY PLANET OFFICES

Australia
Head Office
Locked Bag 1, Footscray, Victoria 3011
☎ 03 8379 8000, fax 03 8379 8111
talk2us@lonelyplanet.com.au

USA
150 Linden St, Oakland, CA 94607
☎ 510 893 8555, toll free 800 275 8555
fax 510 893 8572, info@lonelyplanet.com

UK
72–82 Rosebery Ave,
Clerkenwell, London EC1R 4RW
☎ 020 7841 9000, fax 020 7841 9001
go@lonelyplanet.co.uk

France
1 rue du Dahomey, 75011 Paris
☎ 01 55 25 33 00, fax 01 55 25 33 01
bip@lonelyplanet.fr, www.lonelyplanet.fr

Published by Lonely Planet Publications Pty Ltd
ABN 36 005 607 983

© Lonely Planet 2004

© photographers as indicated 2004

Cover photograph: Reflection of the northern Selkirks in a pool on Abbott Ridge; Donald C & Priscilla Alexander Eastman/Lonely Planet Images (front); Statue of Harry Winston Jerome in Stanley Park, Vancouver; Richard Cummins/Lonely Planet Images (back). Many of the images in this guide are available for licensing from Lonely Planet Images: www.lonelyplanetimages.com.